British Literary Manuscripts

Series II
from 1800 to 1914

Catalogue by
VERLYN KLINKENBORG

Checklist by
HERBERT CAHOON

Introduction by
CHARLES RYSKAMP

THE PIERPONT MORGAN LIBRARY
in association with
DOVER PUBLICATIONS, INC.
NEW YORK

The preparation of this work was made possible through a grant from the Research Resources Program in the Division of Research Programs of the National Endowment for the Humanities, a Federal agency.

Published in Canada by General Publishing Company, Ltd. 30 Lesmill Road, Don Mills, Toronto, Ontario.
Published in the United Kingdom by Constable and Company, Ltd., 10 Orange Street, London WC2H 7EG.

British Literary Manuscripts/Series II: From 1800 to 1914 is a new work, first published by Dover Publications, Inc., in 1981 in association with The Pierpont Morgan Library.

International Standard Book Number: 0-486-24125-4
Library of Congress Catalog Card Number: 80-71101

Manufactured in the United States of America
Dover Publications, Inc.
180 Varick Street
New York, N.Y. 10014

Introduction

This second volume of *British Literary Manuscripts* illustrates the course of English literature from 1800 to World War I through a series of reproductions of autograph manuscripts and letters. [The first volume begins just before the year 800 with a manuscript fragment of the monumental work by the Venerable Bede, *Historia Ecclesiastica*, and ends about 1800 with autographs of Blake and Burns.]

A companion volume, *American Literary Autographs from Washington Irving to Henry James*, was published by The Pierpont Morgan Library in association with Dover Publications in 1977. A checklist, similar to the one in that book, is located at the end of this second volume of the present publication, in this case showing all of the British literary manuscript holdings, from the sixteenth century to the present, in the Morgan Library, including acquisitions through 1980. This will afford scholars and other libraries a ready reference to one of the three or four most important collections of British literary autographs in the world.

Our aim is to present a popular guide to this subject. Most surveys of historical or literary autographs are expensive books, often in several volumes. This guide, however, should be within the reach of any school or college library, young students and beginning collectors. The two volumes cover a wider range of time and of genres, and a larger number of authors, than such distinguished books on the subject as W. W. Gregg (editor), *English Literary Autographs 1550–1650* (Oxford, 1925, 1928, 1932); P. J. Croft, *Autograph Poetry in the English Language: Facsimiles of Original Manuscripts from the Fourteenth to the Twentieth Century* (London, 1973); and Anthony G. Petti, *English Literary Hands from Chaucer to Dryden* (London, 1977). Unlike those volumes, these two have more to do with literary values and the author's reputation than with technical aspects of manuscripts. We have not tried to present a palaeographical survey, nor have we analyzed any of the handwritings. We have not provided principles of textual study, nor methods of identifying hands and editing manuscripts.

Each entry in the present volumes briefly describes the manuscript from which the illustration is taken and relevant aspects of the life and work of the author. There are comments on the particular leaf or leaves chosen and the importance of the work or the letter from which it came. We have also attempted to list the major manuscript resources for many of the authors so that those who wish to pursue their studies further will be able to do so easily, and the reproductions given may help in identifying holograph material of the leading British writers.

Before 1700, British literary holographs are indeed rare, but after 1800 there are so many to choose from that this second volume covers only a little more than one hundred years. The most important collections we could draw on in the Library are those of Sir Walter Scott (the finest group of his manuscripts, including those of the novels *The Antiquary*, *Guy Mannering*, *Ivanhoe* and *Old Mortality*, many of his poems—among them *The Lady of the Lake* and *Rokeby*, historical and critical prose, journals, and more than 400 of his letters), the largest collection of Coleridge letters in existence, many of them with poems, and the largest collection of Jane Austen's manuscripts and letters; among the manuscripts of Byron are those of *Beppo*, *The Corsair*, a number of cantos of *Don Juan*, *Manfred*, *Marino Faliero*, *Mazeppa*, *The Prophecy of Dante* and *Werner*, a number of shorter poems, as well as letters by him and most of his family. For Keats there are such celebrated works as *Endymion*, "Ode to Psyche," "On First Looking into Chapman's Homer" and a few of his best letters; Lamb's "Dissertation upon Roast Pig" and a distinguished group of poems and letters; Shelley's "Indian Serenade" (in Mary Shelley's hand) and "Stanzas, Written in Dejection, Near Naples." For Thackeray: *The Rose and the Ring*, *Vanity Fair*, *The Virginians*, other novels, prose works, poems and nearly 200 letters. There are about 1,400 letters from Dickens, and among his manuscripts are those of *A Christmas Carol*, *The Cricket on the Hearth* and *Our Mutual Friend;* the manuscripts of Wilkie Collins' *The Moonstone* and *The Woman in White*, several other works, and 270 letters; Trollope's *He Knew He Was Right* and *The Way We Live Now;* Meredith's *Diana of the Crossways;* Charlotte Brontë's *The Professor* (and poems by Emily and Anne). There are John Stuart Mill's *Principles of Political Economy;* Ruskin's *Modern Painters*, *The Stones of Venice* and about 1,900 letters. The Brownings can be represented by *Dramatis Personae* and *Sonnets from the Portuguese*. The riches are almost overwhelming: it is therefore no wonder that we could not extend the entries for this volume further into the twentieth century. Also, the problems of copyright become increasingly difficult, so that it might, in some cases, be nearly impossible to represent some authors with autograph manuscripts and letters.

The second volume has 130 entries for 113 authors and all of these were selected from the collections of the Morgan Library except seventeen which were chosen from private libraries in the United States. We are deeply grateful to all of the donors to the Library over many years and to those who permitted their manuscripts to be used. We are especially indebted to Mr. Gordon N. Ray, a Trustee of the Library, for allowing us to show twelve manuscripts from his collection and for his keen interest in the preparation of this volume.

It is generally recognized that of the great American collectors who were active at the end of the nineteenth century and the first part of this, J. Pierpont Morgan (1837–1913) "was the most catholic in his tastes." We think of his collecting above all in relation to many kinds of art from many thousands of years. The same is true of the written records which he gathered together, from the earliest tablets and papyri to books and manuscripts of his own contemporaries. He began by collecting autographs, specimens of the handwriting of the principal figures of his day. When still a schoolboy, before he was fifteen, he had acquired the autograph of President Millard Fillmore and, in response to Morgan's request, six letters from bishops of the Protestant Episcopal Church. The collection of autographs is, therefore, the cornerstone of all of the Morgan collections: at The Pierpont Morgan Library, The Metropolitan Museum of Art and throughout the United States and the world.

By 1883, Morgan had a library with only a few fine books, but many more excellent autographs: letters of Robert Burns, Alexander Hamilton and George Washington, and one of the finest collections of autographs of the signers of the Declaration of Independence. Morgan's passion for collecting literary and historical manuscripts never abated, and it was very strong also in his son, J. P. Morgan (1867–1943). In the course of time, owing to the dazzling collections of medieval and Renaissance manuscripts, early printed books and drawings, and the wealth of European materials in The Pierpont Morgan Library, the importance of the English and American collections of manuscripts, both literary and historical, has been diminished in the public eye. Yet in both fields, the collections of autograph manuscripts are among the finest in the world.

The foundation of the Morgan collection of British literary manuscripts was the purchase a century ago, in 1881, by Junius Spencer Morgan, father of Pierpont, of the original manuscript of Sir Walter Scott's *Guy Mannering*. Junius later gave it to his son. But not until after his father's death in 1890 did Pierpont begin to buy on a large scale, which he continued to do for nearly a quarter century, to the time of his death in 1913. He was aided and stimulated by his nephew, Junius S. Morgan, by his brilliant young librarian, Miss Belle da Costa Greene, and by many dealers, of whom the firm of J. Pearson & Co. in London was the most important. Those were the years during which the notable manuscripts of Burns, Byron, Dickens, Keats, Ruskin and Scott came to the Library. The manuscript of Book I of Milton's *Paradise Lost* was acquired by Mr. Morgan after it had been offered for sale at an auction devoted only to this manuscript held at Sotheby's in London, 25 January 1904, but had been bought in by the owner.

After Pierpont Morgan's death, his son, J. P. Morgan, added many fine British literary manuscripts to the collection, including Thackeray's *The Rose and the Ring* and letters and manuscripts of John Locke, Jane Austen and the Brownings, among others. The collection has continued to grow since the death of J. P. Morgan in 1943 through purchases, gifts from the Fellows of the Library, and individual donations. Sir Philip Sidney, Sir Francis Bacon, Coleridge, Wordsworth, the Brontës, Ruskin and Gilbert & Sullivan are among the many authors now represented by letters and manuscripts of the first rank.

Since this guide and the checklist at the end of the volume may call the attention of scholars to manuscripts in the Morgan Library which they may wish to see, inquire about or have copied photographically, it should be noted that applications for cards of admission to the Reading Room are made on forms provided for the purpose; cards are readily issued to qualified and accredited scholars. Graduate students and scholars having no institutional affiliation are expected to present with their applications suitable references concerning their fitness to handle rare manuscript materials. Prior notification of visits by those from out of town is advisable in order to insure the availability of the manuscripts desired, but it is not insisted upon. The Reading Room is open from Monday through Friday, 9:30–4:45, except holidays.

In the past three years we have recatalogued all of the English literary manuscripts in The Pierpont Morgan Library. This project was made possible by a generous grant from the National Endowment for the Humanities. The work was carried out by Mr. Verlyn Klinkenborg under the supervision of Mr. Herbert Cahoon, Curator of Autograph Manuscripts in the Library. These two volumes of British literary manuscripts are also chiefly due to their work, and in particular to the efforts of Mr. Klinkenborg, who deserves great credit for his diligent research and for his lively and graceful skill in preparing all of the entries. The photographs were prepared by Mr. Charles V. Passela, assisted by Mr. C. Mitchell Carl. We also owe thanks to Mr. Reginald Allen, Mrs. Ronnie Boriskin, Miss Deborah Evetts, Mrs. Sara Feldman Guérin, Dr. Paul Needham, Mrs. Patricia Reyes and Mr. Rigbie Turner of the staff of the Library, as well as to Mr. Arthur A. Houghton, Jr., Mr. H. Bradley Martin, Mr. Gordon N. Ray and the anonymous owner of manuscripts not in the Morgan Library which were used in this publication. The Firestone Library of Princeton University was invaluable in providing many reference and research materials. At Dover Publications Mr. Hayward Cirker and Mr. Stanley Appelbaum were of special help in preparing this volume.

CHARLES RYSKAMP
Director
The Pierpont Morgan Library

Contents

The dates are those of the particular autographs being reproduced.

1. Jeremy Bentham: letter to Lord Holland, 1811
2. William Cobbett: letter to Chadwick and Ireland, 1832
3. Samuel Rogers: letter to Mrs. Mitchell, 1791
4. Thomas Robert Malthus: letter to William Otter, 1830
5. Maria Edgeworth: draft of "The Miner," ca. 1798–9
6. James Hogg: *Familiar Anecdotes of Sir Walter Scott*, 1833
7. William Wordsworth: "Description of a Beggar," 1797
8. William Wordsworth: letter to Lady Beaumont, 1807
9. Sir Walter Scott: *The Lady of the Lake*, 1809–10
10. Sir Walter Scott: *Old Mortality*, 1816
11. Sydney Smith: letter to Admiral Sir Sidney Smith, 1826
12. Samuel Taylor Coleridge: letter to Robert Southey, ca. 1797
13. Samuel Taylor Coleridge: letter to Sir George and Lady Beaumont, 1803
14. Samuel Taylor Coleridge: "S. T. Coleridge's Confession of Belief," ca. 1816–7
15. Robert Southey: *The Life of Cowper*, 1835
16. Jane Austen: *Lady Susan*, ca. 1805
17. Jane Austen: letter to Cassandra Austen, 1801
18. Charles Lamb: "A Dissertation upon Roast Pig," ca. 1822
19. Walter Savage Landor: letter to Eliza Lynn Linton, 1860
20. Thomas Campbell: "Lochiel's Warning," 1802
21. William Hazlitt: "The Fight," 1821
22. John Galt: letter to Richard Bentley, 1836
23. Thomas Moore: *Lalla Rookh* (second version), ca. 1815
24. Charles Robert Maturin: letter to William Conyngham Plunket, 1801
25. Leigh Hunt: *The Palfrey*, 1842
26. Thomas De Quincey: "Lake Reminiscences," ca. 1839
27. Thomas Love Peacock: corrections in a copy of *The Genius of the Thames* (1810)
28. Mary Russell Mitford: "Country Excursions" from *Belford Regis*, ca. 1833–4
29. George Gordon Noel Byron: *The Corsair*, 1813
30. George Gordon Noel Byron: *Manfred*, ca. 1816–7
31. George Gordon Noel Byron: *Don Juan*, Canto I, 1818
32. Richard Harris Barham: "The Jackdaw of Rheims," ca. 1836–7
33. Percy Bysshe Shelley: "Stanzas, Written in Dejection, Near Naples," 1818
34. Percy Bysshe Shelley: letter to Joseph Severn, 1821
35. Captain Frederick Marryat: *Mr. Midshipman Easy*, ca. 1835
36. John Clare: "Rural Evenings" from *Village Scenes and Subjects on rural Occupations*, 1820
37. William Carleton: "National Literature and Mr. Lever," 1843
38. John Keats: "On First Looking into Chapman's Homer," 1816, and "The day is gone and all its sweets are gone," 1819
39. John Keats: *Endymion*, 1818
40. John Keats: "Ode to Psyche," 1819
41. Thomas Carlyle: *Wotton Reinfred*, 1827
42. Mary Wollstonecraft Shelley: additions in a copy of *Frankenstein*, 1823
43. Thomas Hood: "The Assistant Drapers' Petition," 1838
44. Thomas Babington Macaulay: *The History of England*, Volume V, 1856–9
45. John Henry Newman: letter to Rev. George Townsend, 1837
46. Harriet Martineau: *Society in America*, Volume I, ca. 1836–7
47. Edward George Earle Lytton Bulwer-Lytton: *The Last Days of Pompeii*, Chapter IV (Book 5), 1833–4
48. George Borrow: "Legend. Isle of Moy"
49. Benjamin Disraeli: *The Voyage of Captain Popanilla*, ca. 1827

50. WILLIAM HARRISON AINSWORTH: "Ket's Rebellion," 1877
51. ELIZABETH BARRETT BROWNING: *Sonnets from the Portuguese,* ca. 1846
52. JOHN STUART MILL: letter to Thomas Carlyle, 1837
53. CHARLES DARWIN: letter to John Stevens Henslow, 1839
54. EDWARD FITZGERALD: letter to Anna Biddell, 1875
55. ALFRED TENNYSON: "The Brook," ca. 1854
56. ALFRED TENNYSON: "Achilles Over the Trench," ca. 1863–4
57. ELIZABETH CLEGHORN GASKELL: letter to Charles Dickens, 1850
58. ARTHUR HENRY HALLAM: letter to William Henry Brookfield, 1832
59. WILLIAM MAKEPEACE THACKERAY: *Vanity Fair,* 1847
60. WILLIAM MAKEPEACE THACKERAY: letter to Mrs. William Henry Brookfield, 1850
61. CHARLES DICKENS: *A Christmas Carol,* 1843
62. CHARLES DICKENS: letter to Wilkie Collins, 1858
63. CHARLES DICKENS: *Our Mutual Friend,* 1865
64. CHARLES READE: *Hard Cash,* 1862–3
65. ROBERT BROWNING: *Dramatis Personae,* 1864
66. ROBERT BROWNING: letter to George Moulton-Barrett, 1882
67. ANTHONY TROLLOPE: *The Way We Live Now,* 1873
68. CHARLOTTE BRONTË: *The Professor,* 1846
69. EMILY BRONTË: "The night of storms has past," 1837/ ANNE BRONTË: "To Cowper," 1842
70. ARTHUR HUGH CLOUGH: "Mari Magno," ca. 1852–3
71. CHARLES KINGSLEY: letter to Philip Gosse, 1853
72. GEORGE ELIOT (MARIAN EVANS): *Scenes of Clerical Life,* 1856–7
73. JOHN RUSKIN: *The Stones of Venice,* 1851–2
74. JOHN RUSKIN: *Modern Painters,* 1860
75. SIR RICHARD FRANCIS BURTON: letter, 1864
76. MATTHEW ARNOLD: letter to Thomas Arnold, 1857
77. COVENTRY PATMORE: additions to *The Angel in the House,* 1856
78. WILKIE COLLINS: *The Woman in White,* 1859–60
79. THOMAS HENRY HUXLEY: letter to Edith Trench, 1863
80. RICHARD DODDRIDGE BLACKMORE: letter to Edward Marston, 1899
81. DANTE GABRIEL ROSSETTI: "The Blessed Damsel," dated 1847
82. GEORGE MEREDITH: *Diana of the Crossways,* ca. 1883–4
83. GEORGE MEREDITH: "The Main Regret," 1901
84. CHRISTINA GEORGINA ROSSETTI: "Song," 1848
85. CHARLES LUTWIDGE DODGSON ("LEWIS CARROLL"): "Double Acrostic"
86. SIR LESLIE STEPHEN: *The History of English Thought in the Eighteenth Century,* ca. 1875–6
87. JAMES THOMSON ("BYSSHE VANOLIS"): *The City of Dreadful Night,* 1870–3
88. WILLIAM MORRIS: letter to Thomas James Cobden-Sanderson, 1885
89. GEORGE DU MAURIER: *Peter Ibbetson,* ca. 1889–90
90. SAMUEL BUTLER: "A lecture on the genesis of feeling," 1887
91. SIR WILLIAM SCHWENCK GILBERT: *The Pirates of Penzance,* 1879
92. ALGERNON CHARLES SWINBURNE: "At Eleusis," ca. 1864–5
93. WALTER PATER: "Dante Gabriel Rossetti," 1883
94. LOUISE DE LA RAMÉE ("OUIDA"): "The Child of Urbino," ca. 1882
95. THOMAS HARDY: "The Romantic Adventures of a Milkmaid," 1882–3
96. THOMAS HARDY: "The Abbey Mason," 1911
97. WILLIAM HENRY HUDSON: *Far Away and Long Ago,* 1917
98. GERARD MANLEY HOPKINS: letter to Edward William Urquhart, 1867
99. ROBERT BRIDGES: letter to Alfred Miles, 1891
100. WILLIAM ERNEST HENLEY: "Night-Sketch" & "Ennui," ca. 1875
101. ROBERT LOUIS STEVENSON: *Weir of Hermiston,* 1892–3
102. MARY AUGUSTA (MRS. HUMPHRY) WARD: *Robert Elsmere,* 1887
103. GEORGE MOORE: *Memories of My Dead Life,* ca. 1905–6
104. SIR ARTHUR WING PINERO: letter to Sir Arthur Sullivan, 1889
105. OSCAR WILDE: *The Picture of Dorian Gray,* 1890
106. GEORGE BERNARD SHAW: "Dramatists Self-Revealed," 1925
107. GEORGE GISSING: postal card to Arthur Henry Bullen, 1897
108. JOHN DAVIDSON: *Ballads and Songs,* ca. 1894
109. JOSEPH CONRAD: letter to W. E. Henley, 1924
110. FRANCIS THOMPSON: letter to Wilfrid Meynell, 1895
111. SIR ARTHUR CONAN DOYLE: *Sir Nigel,* 1905
112. ALFRED EDWARD HOUSMAN: letter to Grant Richards, 1923
113. SIR JAMES MATTHEW BARRIE: *The Admirable Crichton,* 1902
114. RUDYARD KIPLING: *Captains Courageous,* 1896
115. WILLIAM BUTLER YEATS: "Aodh to Dectora," ca. 1898

116. HERBERT GEORGE WELLS: letter to W. E. Henley, 1900
117. ERNEST CHRISTOPHER DOWSON: "Non sum qualis eram . . . ," 1891
118. ARNOLD BENNETT: *Clayhanger*, 1910
119. JOHN GALSWORTHY: *The Pagan*, ca. 1901
120. GEORGE WILLIAM RUSSELL ("AE"): letter to William Hard, 1921
121. HILAIRE BELLOC: "John Vavassour," ca. 1930
122. JOHN MILLINGTON SYNGE: letter to John Masefield, 1903
123. MAX BEERBOHM: "The Golden Drugget," 1918
124. FORD MADOX FORD: "Galsworthy," ca. 1936
125. GILBERT KEITH CHESTERTON: "Open Letter: On the Collapse of the Cosmopolitan Club," ca. 1912–3
126. EDWARD THOMAS: letter to C. F. Cazenove, 1914
127. EDWARD MORGAN FORSTER: "Art for Art's Sake," 1949
128. JAMES JOYCE: *Chamber Music*, ca. 1903–4
129. DAVID HERBERT LAWRENCE: "Eloi, Eloi, lama sabachthani?," ca. 1914–5
130. RUPERT BROOKE: "Sonnet," 1914

COMPLETE CHECKLIST OF BRITISH LITERARY MANUSCRIPTS AND AUTOGRAPHS IN THE PIERPONT MORGAN LIBRARY, *page 263*

Alphabetical List of Authors

The numbers are those of the 130 specimens reproduced.

AE: 120
Ainsworth, William Harrison: 50
Arnold, Matthew: 76
Austen, Jane: 16, 17

Barham, Richard Harris: 32
Barrie, Sir James Matthew: 113
Beerbohm, Max: 123
Belloc, Hilaire: 121
Bennett, Arnold: 118
Bentham, Jeremy: 1
Blackmore, Richard Doddridge: 80
Borrow, George: 48
Bridges, Robert: 99
Brontë, Anne: 69
Brontë, Charlotte: 68
Brontë, Emily: 69
Brooke, Rupert: 130
Browning, Elizabeth Barrett: 51
Browning, Robert: 65, 66
Bulwer-Lytton, Edward George: 47
Burton, Sir Richard Francis: 75
Butler, Samuel: 90
Byron, George Gordon Noel: 29–31

Campbell, Thomas: 20
Carleton, William: 37
Carlyle, Thomas: 41
Carroll, Lewis: 85
Chesterton, Gilbert Keith: 125
Clare, John: 36
Clough, Arthur Hugh: 70
Cobbett, William: 2
Coleridge, Samuel Taylor: 12–14
Collins, Wilkie: 78
Conrad, Joseph: 109

Darwin, Charles: 53
Davidson, John: 108
de la Ramée, Louise: 94
De Quincey, Thomas: 26
Dickens, Charles: 61–63
Disraeli, Benjamin: 49
Dodgson, Charles Lutwidge: 85
Dowson, Ernest Christopher: 117
Doyle, Sir Arthur Conan: 111
du Maurier, George: 89

Edgeworth, Maria: 5
Eliot, George: 72

FitzGerald, Edward: 54
Ford, Ford Madox: 124
Forster, Edward Morgan: 127

Galsworthy, John: 119
Galt, John: 22
Gaskell, Elizabeth Cleghorn: 57
Gilbert, Sir William Schwenck: 91
Gissing, George: 107

Hallam, Arthur Henry: 58
Hardy, Thomas: 95, 96
Hazlitt, William: 21
Henley, William Ernest: 100
Hogg, James: 6
Hood, Thomas: 43
Hopkins, Gerard Manley: 98
Housman, Alfred Edward: 112
Hudson, William Henry: 97
Hunt, Leigh: 25
Huxley, Thomas Henry: 79

Joyce, James: 128

Keats, John: 38–40
Kingsley, Charles: 71
Kipling, Rudyard: 114

Lamb, Charles: 18
Landor, Walter Savage: 19
Lawrence, David Herbert: 129
Lytton: *see* Bulwer-Lytton

Macaulay, Thomas Babington: 44
Malthus, Thomas Robert: 4
Marryat, Captain Frederick: 35
Martineau, Harriet: 46
Maturin, Charles Robert: 24
Meredith, George: 82, 83
Mill, John Stuart: 52
Mitford, Mary Russell: 28
Moore, George: 103
Moore, Thomas: 23
Morris, William: 88

Newman, John Henry: 45

Ouida: 94

Pater, Walter: 93
Patmore, Coventry: 77
Peacock, Thomas Love: 27
Pinero, Sir Arthur Wing: 104

Reade, Charles: 64
Rogers, Samuel: 3
Rossetti, Christina Georgina: 84
Rossetti, Dante Gabriel: 81
Ruskin, John: 73, 74
Russell, George William: 120

Scott, Sir Walter: 9, 10
Shaw, George Bernard: 106
Shelley, Mary Wollstonecraft: 42
Shelley, Percy Bysshe: 33, 34
Smith, Sydney: 11
Southey, Robert: 15
Stephen, Sir Leslie: 86
Stevenson, Robert Louis: 101
Swinburne, Algernon Charles: 92
Synge, John Millington: 122

Tennyson, Alfred: 55, 56
Thackeray, William Makepeace: 59, 60
Thomas, Edward: 126
Thompson, Francis: 110
Thomson, James: 87
Trollope, Anthony: 67

Ward, Mary Augusta (Mrs. Humphry): 102
Wells, Herbert George: 116
Wilde, Oscar: 105
Wordsworth, William: 7, 8

Yeats, William Butler: 115

1

Jeremy Bentham
1748–1832

Autograph letter signed, dated Barrow Green House, 8 September 1811, to Lord Holland. 3 pp. 248 x 199 mm. From the Collection of Mr. Gordon N. Ray.

When Bentham entered the nineteenth century at the age of fifty-two—a highly esteemed author on the subject of jurisprudence—his prose style had more than reached the midpoint of its degeneration from clarity and simplicity into a convoluted language that "darkens knowledge," as Hazlitt commented. It is not, therefore, principally as a writer that he enters this catalogue, but as a philosophical starting point for a half-century of reform. His was the Linnaean activity of classification; what he codified (to use his own coinage) was the law, a body of texts and practices that, in England at least, is self-accreting. This characteristic of the law led Bentham to seek, in John Stuart Mill's words, "the *why* of everything," to demand an accounting of its utility. But as Mill also pointed out, Bentham's distinct strength as a philosopher, his method of exhaustive analysis, is related to his greatest weakness as a man; his knowledge of human nature "is wholly empirical; and the empiricism of one who has had little experience." Bentham's great acquaintance with the laws of England, the design of his own vision of society, and his little acquaintance with the imaginative, irrational workings of men caused many to question his presumption to judge of utility according to the principles of pleasure and pain. He was, as both Hazlitt and Mill recognized, "a boy to the last," preserved by the limitations and narrowness of his own manner of living.

This letter to Lord Holland provides an amusing, if somewhat wooden, example of Bentham's deficiencies as a prose stylist, certainly as a personal correspondent. It concerns the misdirection of "two masses of paper" which has caused Bentham "two opposite apprehensions," the second of which is "that, having reached Your Lordship's hands, they have, for and by means of a load of lumber, the value of which may have been found to be—not simply = 0 but negative, subjected you to an imposition. . . ."

Bentham's manuscripts are preserved in the Library of University College, London, and in the British Library.

By a concurrence of circumstances, not worth troubling Your Lordship with, I feel myself haunted by two opposite apprehensions. One is—that the aforesaid masses *have not, either of them, reached Your Lordship's hands. The other is—that, having reached Your Lordship's hands, they have, for and by means of a load of lumber, the value of which may have been found to be—not simply = 0 but negative, subjected you to an imposition, from which I had taken such precautions, as I flattered myself would prove effectual, to save you harmless. In the latter case, if Your Lordship will be pleased to give directions to Your Solicitor, to prosecute me, by a civil* action on this case—*(for, being free from malice, one indictment, (I humbly submit to his better judgment) will not lie for it—) I am ready, with all contrition, to let judgment go by default, payings costs and damages. . . .*

By a concurrence of circumstances, not worth troubling Your Lordship with, I feel myself haunted by two opposite apprehensions. One is — that the aforesaid _masses_ have not, either of them, reached Your Lordship's hands. The other is — that, having reached Your Lordship's hands, they have, for and by means of a load of lumber, the value of which may have been found to be — not simply = 0 but negative, subjected You to an imposition, from which I had taken such precautions, as I flattered myself would form a shield, to save You harmless. In the latter case, if Your Lordship will be pleased to give directions to Your Solicitor, to prosecute me, by a civil _action on the case_ — (for, being free from malice, an indictment, (I humbly submit to his better judgment) will not lie for it —) I am ready, with all contrition, to let judgment go by default, paying costs and damages.

In

In the mean time, if, by your own, — or rather, to save in one case unnecessary addition to already excessive trouble, by any _other_, hand — You would have the charity to favour me with such few words as may be necessary, simply to let me know, whether the nuisance in question has or has not reached Your hands, you will much oblige

My Lord,

Your Lordship's very respectful
however troublesome humble Servant

Jeremy Bentham.

2

William Cobbett
1762–1835

Autograph letter signed, dated Morpeth, 29 September 1832, to Messrs. Chadwick and Ireland. 1 p. 237 x 195 mm.

One of the most engaging and controversial men to enter public life during the period of turmoil between the American Revolution and the Reform Bill of 1832 was William Cobbett, a ceaseless talker with a basket of facts and epithets by his side, a relentlessly practical moralist and a rural rider, wandering the back roads and farm lanes of England in order to ascertain the country's condition and the rate at which his agricultural ideas—published in works like *Cottage Economy* (1821–2)—were being disseminated. But most of all one recognizes in Cobbett the conservatism (expressed as desire for reform) that comes from an intensely happy childhood—the repository of his values—the world of which (in Cobbett's case) was threatened by "Pitt's false money, Peel's flimsy dresses, Wilberforce's potatoe diet, Castlereagh and Mackintosh's oratory, Walter Scott's poems . . . with all the bad taste and baseness and hypocrisy which they spread over this country . . . ." (The simplest expression of his reforming code might be: what is good for boys is good for the country.) In a broad flood of publications—ranging from his American writings as "Peter Porcupine" to his "Rural Rides," published in his long-lived periodical, the *Political Register*—Cobbett urged a return through reform to an economic climate unsophisticated by "tax-eaters" and "borough-mongers," where bread was baked with milk and beer was brewed at home. The political changes he advocated are well represented in the letter shown here, in which Cobbett orders handbills for a series of four lectures to take place in Edinburgh. Because this letter was written after the Reform Bill had been passed, it includes his call for the "new electors" to understand the pledges that they should insist upon "before they give their votes . . . including, amongst those measures, a total abolition of tithes, lay as well as clerical, in all parts of the kingdom."[2]

Cobbett's manuscripts are widely distributed, but an important group is gathered in the Library of Nuffield College, Oxford.

---

1. On the necessity of a great change in the management of the affairs of the nation; on the numerous grievances, inflicted on the country, by the Boroughmonger parliaments; and, on the duty of electors to pledge candidates to measures which shall remove those grievances.

2. On the nature of the pledges which electors ought to insist upon before they give their votes; and, on the justice and necessity of the measures to which they would be bound by those pledges, including, amongst those measures, a total abolition of tithes, lay as well as clerical, in all parts of the kingdom.

3. On the injustice of taxing the people to pay interest to those who are called fundholders; and on the resources, possessed by the nation, for making, from motives of indulgence and compassion, such provision for a part of the fundholders as may be found necessary to preserve them from utter ruin.

4. On the mischief ~~of paper~~ and iniquity of paper-money generally; and on the necessity of putting a stop, as speedily as possible, to all paper-money of every description. . . .

Morpeth, 29. Sepr. 1832.

Gentlemen,

Please to have printed a number of handbills (what you consider sufficient, and distributed as soon as you can. The following to be printed word for word.

1. On the necessity of a great change in the management of the affairs of the nation; on the numerous grievances, inflicted on the country, by the Boroughmonger parliaments; and, on the duty of electors to pledge candidates to measures which shall remove those grievances.

2. On the nature of the pledges which electors ought to insist upon before they give their votes; and, on the justice and necessity of the measures to which they would be bound by those pledges, including, amongst those measures, a total abolition of tithes, lay as well as clerical, in all parts of the kingdom.

3. On the injustice of taxing the people to pay interest to those who are called fundholders; and on the resources, possessed by the nation, for making, from motives of indulgence and compassion, such provision for a part of the fund-holders as may be found necessary to preserve them from utter ruin.

4. On the mischiefs ~~of paper~~ and iniquity of paper-money generally; and on the necessity of putting a stop, as speedily as possible, to all paper-money of every description.

You will see by the above that there must be *four* lectures. You may give notice for the 9th, 10th, 11th and 12th. If you can get the Theatre it will, I think, be the most suitable place, for the reasons which I have, in my letter of yesterday stated.

I am,
Gentlemen,
your most obedient servant.
Wm Cobbett.

P.S. I shall go to some *inn* on the evening of the eighth, and then I will send to you.

3

Samuel Rogers
1763–1855

Autograph letter signed, dated Paris, 29 January 1791, to Mrs. Mitchell. 4 pp. 230 x 182 mm. Sharp-Viljoen Collection.

One of the functions of lyric verse in the latter half of the eighteenth century was to explore the aesthetic potential of individual emotions and mental activities. Philosophers had distinguished discrete psychological categories, but it fell to the poets to adorn them with images and consider the sensory effects they produced. Odes on virtually every mental power appeared, and a poetical cottage industry was soon thriving, manufacturing poems on the pleasures of melancholy, imagination, piety, hope, fear and, in 1792, memory. *The Pleasures of Memory* was written by Samuel Rogers, and like Thomas Campbell's *Pleasures of Hope* it enjoyed a tremendous popularity. Opinion among his peers was divided, however. Coleridge called Rogers a "drivelling Booby" and Shelley taunted Byron by asking him how he could possibly defend "The Pleasures of *Mummery*." But Byron placed Rogers just below Scott in his pyramid of living poets and in *English Bards and Scotch Reviewers*, his radically foreshortened survey of contemporary poetry, called upon "melodious Rogers" to "Restore Apollo to his vacant throne." Rogers was more likely to accomplish this feat by securing a loan or a pension for the deposed god than by advancing Apollo's claims in verse. With a fortune from his family's bank, he set himself up as a man of taste and became London's premier literary host, capable of performing such interesting feats as introducing Sir Walter Scott to Fanny Burney. Around his abundant breakfast table, virtually every person of literary consequence gathered at one time or another to hear Rogers indulge in the pleasures of memory in what Scott called "his dry quiet sarcastic manner."

The letter shown here records some of the events that took place during a trip to Paris in early 1791. Rogers' account of the effects of the French Revolution is highly optimistic, for he saw in Paris a people "beating as it were with one pulse in the cause of liberty & their country . . . ."

[Starting midway down left-hand side:] Paris is in some parts very grand, but in general, not equal to London. Coaches & buggies of all shapes rumble along without springs the Ladies walk without hats, & the men with immense muffs, cockades & copper buckles. The very beggars & the servants behind Carriages wear muffs. These things are amusing to an Englishman, but are instantly forgot, when he observes so many thousands beating as it were with one pulse in the cause of liberty & their country & just now beginning to live. The same spirit exists [illegible deletion] every where. At St Denis, one of our horses was restive. "So, so, said a boy, you wont be quiet, Mr. L'Abbé Maury." We were yesterday introduced to M. de la Fayette. He was dining with 40 or 50 officers & rose very politely to receive us. He is a tall handsome man about 35. & speaks English well. . . .

that could not be resisted. & when I saw the innocent gaiety of the ~~p~~ villagers of Clermont, my heart bled to think of the oppressions which so amiable & generous a people have so long endured. The country thro' which we passed was open & uneven, & in many parts well-wooded. Beyond Chantilly, that superb monument of bad taste, the Prince of Condé's palace where I paid my respects to the armour of Henry IV & the grande Condé, the road winds thro' woods & vineyards that are still pleasant ~~[illegible]~~ amidst the dreariness of winter. We arrived here last monday evening. Paris is in some parts very grand, but in general, not equal to London. Coaches & buggies of all shapes rumble along without springs the Ladies walk without hats, & the men with immense muffs, cockades & copper-buckles. The very beggars & the servants behind Carriages wear muffs. These things are amusing to an Englishman, but are instantly forgot, when he observes so many thousands beating as it were with one pulse in the cause of liberty & their country & just now beginning to live. The same spirit exists ~~[illegible]~~ every where. At St Denis, one of our horses was restive, "So, so, said a boy, you wont be quiet, Mr L'Abbé Maury." We were yesterday introduced to M. de la Fayette. He was dining with 40 or 50 officers & rose very politely to receive

us. He is a tall handsome man, about 35. & speaks English well. In the evening Mr Keay called & we dine with him tomorrow. He intends to be in England next month, to stay a year there & to settle, if he can find a house near Reading. To day we dine with the Marquis de la Fayette & sup with his Aid de Camp M. Chatelet, a very genteel sensible man. Tomorrow morning Mr Mirabeau takes us to the National Assembly. On tuesday we dine with the Duke de la Rochefaucault & thursday with the Duke de Liancourt. So our time is well taken up. There ~~[illegible]~~ was a little tumult here last thursday, but we heard nothing of it till next day; & Paris is, I believe, as tranquil as [...] One strong proof of this is that the Aristocrats [...] their sentiments without reserve. The national g[...] form an excellent police, & are posted every where over the City. We have seen two theatres that are far more elegant than our London Houses & formed on a better principle, being ~~[illegible]~~ semicircular. The Comte d'Artois & the other Refugees are not expected back, as the time allowed is expired. The business of the ~~Clergy~~ Assembly proceeds but slowly at present on account of the immense number of Clergy that flock to take the oath. But the dignitaries still hold out, & they are now thinking to proceed to the election of new Bishops which measure will effectually break all opposition — When I know any thing of the

THOMAS ROBERT MALTHUS
1766–1834

Autograph letter signed, dated 22 June 1830, to William Otter. 4 pp. 225 x 183 mm. From the Collection of Mr. Gordon N. Ray.

When Malthus died, Sydney Smith lamented: "Poor Malthus! everybody regrets him;—in science and in conduct equally a philosopher, one of the most practically wise men I ever met, shamefully mistaken and unjustly calumniated . . . a virtuous martyr to truth." Calumniation of Malthus began in 1798 when his most influential work, *An Essay on the Principle of Population*, was published. From then on, in the minds of most persons (whatever their political alliances) Malthus was "identified with a principle" which was summarized thus by Hazlitt: "the population cannot go on perpetually increasing without pressing on the limits of the means of subsistence, and . . . a check of some kind or other must, sooner or later, be opposed to it." William Cobbett, gifted in the invective of name-calling, dubbed Malthus the "check-population parson" and even the good Sydney Smith, "one of his friends, the Edinburgh Reviewers" (Cobbett's phrase), could not pass up a jest on the topic of Malthus' *Essay:* writing to Lady Holland in 1831, he remarked that "if there are no appearances of approaching fertility [Malthus] is civil to every lady." To all these forms of opprobrium and humor, Malthus was immune, secure in his reputation as a renowned political economist and unusually content among his friends and his family. The letter shown here was written to one of Malthus' best friends, William Otter, with whom he traveled through Norway, Sweden, Finland and Russia in 1799. It is primarily a casual letter, recounting a trip with his wife and daughter to visit his wife's family, the Eckersalls. His sole venture into professional topics is in praise of "a Treatise on Ethics by [Sir James] Mackintosh": "It shews prodigious reading and a great mastery of the subject; and I think will establish his fame as a metaphisician, and theoretical moralist."

Manuscripts by Malthus are extremely rare.

[Starting line 14, left-hand side:] Emily, most happily for us, continues quite well: She had a slight cold in her head at Malvern, and I began to be really alarmed, thinking she was going to follow the bad examples of her parents, but it went off without any such alarming consequence. The medical men have assured us that there is nothing contagious in our coughs, but M^{rs} M^s has so much resembled mine, and is characterised by so much of a similar obstinacy, that we could not help feeling some anxiety on the subject. We arrived here last tuesday and found all the Eckersalls well. We shall probably stay till the end of our vacation. Every body is complaining of the weather, and people are much puzzled as to what they had best do about this grass. Not much has been cut in our valley; but Mr Eckersall means I believe to begin at a[ll] events tomorrow. The crops are not so good as one should have expected.

I have been reading a Treatise on Ethics by Mackintosh intended for one of the introductory essays in the new Edition of the Encyclopædia Britannica which is coming out. A few copies have been printed seperately, and he was so good as to send me one. I admire it very much indeed, and agree with him almost always. . . .

it was not likely she should recover very rapidly. Her cough indeed has been worse than mine, and has continued longer in the first stage, that of irritation, which has by no means yet subsided. We are told however that when that goes, there will not probably remain the same kind of defluxion that I have, and which even this second change of air to a very different situation from that of Haileybury, has not very essentially abated. I think however it is diminished, some days decidedly so, but on others it seems to encrease again. We shall not probably get quite well till the regular warm weather comes, and that seems to be put off sine die. Emily, most happily for us, continues quite well. She had a slight cold in her head at Malvern, and I began to be really alarmed, thinking she was going to follow the bad examples of her parents, but it went off without any such alarming consequence. The medical men have assured us that there is nothing contagious in our coughs, but Mrs M's has so much resembled mine and is characterised by so much of a similar obstinacy that we could not help feeling some anxiety on the subject. We arrived here last Tuesday and found all the Eckersalls well. We shall probably stay till the end of our vacation. Every body is complaining of the weather, and people are much puzzled as to what they had best do about their grass. Not much has yet been cut in our valley; but Mr Eckersall means I believe to begin at all events tomorrow. The crops are not so good as one should have expected.

I have been reading a Treatise on Ethics by Mackintosh intended for one of the introductory essays in the new Edition of the Encyclopaedia Britannica which is coming out. A few copies have been printed separately, and he was so good as to send me one. I admire it very much indeed, and agree with him almost always. It shews prodigious reading

5

MARIA EDGEWORTH
1767–1849

Autograph manuscript draft of "The Miner" ["Lame Jervas"], unsigned and undated, but written ca. 1798–9. 45 pp. 92 x 195 mm. MA 893.

As a little girl, Maria Edgeworth narrowly escaped becoming the victim of experimental education. Her father, Richard Lovell Edgeworth, had unsuccessfully attempted to raise her elder brother according to the romantic principles of Rousseau's *Emile*, but Maria, as the eldest daughter, was taught and learned to teach in the midst of an ever-growing family, where practical, if thoughtful, education was the only expedient. Many of her earliest stories were written for children, a kind of writing in which the temptation to be fanciful is great, but the temptation to inject a strong moral note is even greater. In some of her books for adults—including *Popular Tales* (1804), where "Lame Jervas" appeared—the tincture of utility prevails. "Lame Jervas" is the story of a boy, once employed as a horse tender in the Cornish tin mines, who acquires wealth and distinction by honoring a few home truths. Maria Edgeworth extends the available usefulness of her tale by interweaving fiction with fact, some of it even documented in footnotes. In the course of his adventures Lame Jervas is assisted by several patrons modeled on actual men. The owner of the mines is based on William Reynolds, who, like Edgeworth's father, was an inventor; while in India Jervas encounters Dr. Andrew Bell, who developed the "Madras" system of education and whose work on that subject is duly cited in a note. And when Prince Abdul Calie compliments Jervas on his ability to explain the uses of various mathematical instruments, we are informed that Jervas, in gratitude for the quality of his own education, "alludes to a book entitled, 'A Description of Pocket and Magazine Cases of Drawing Instruments . . .'" by John Barrow, a "private teacher of mathematics."

This manuscript draft of "Lame Jervas" records an extremely early version of the tale; many of the episodes are merely sketched in broad outlines and one page lists several questions to be asked of Dr. Davies Giddy (later Gilbert, President of the Royal Society): "*Gin*—do miners drink it." This manuscript also contains drafts for a prose work called "The Union" and notes for dramatic scenes.

~~*From*~~ *From the time I was five or six years old till I was thirteen I was employed in the mine we were in together yesterday——describes all he suffered from the tyranny of his elders when he was* trap-door-boy *(v reports of Socy. for bettering poor) & the habits of deceit which he learned in order to evade the tyranny of those who imposed upon him an undue share of work.—how he in his turn became a* foal—a leader ~~of~~ of a tram, *or sledge for drawing coals—one day a load of coals overturned fell upon his leg and lamed him—*~~*Mr. xxx.*~~ *the proprietor of the mine (Mr. William Reynolds, hearing of the accident sent a surgeon to him & was very kind to him during his illness—came to see him—. . .*

told them his story nearly in the following manner.

~~From~~ From the time I was five or six years old till I was thirteen I was employed in the mine we were in together yesterday — describes all he suffered from the tyranny of his elders when he was trap=door=boy (v reports of Soc.y for bettering poor) & the habits of deceit which he learned in order to evade the tyranny of those who imposed upon

him an undue share of work — how he in his turn became a foal — a leader ~~of~~ of a tram, or sledge for drawing coals — one day a load of coals overturned fell upon his leg and lamed him — Mr ~~***~~ (Mr. William Reynolds) the proprietor of the mine hearing of the accident sent a surgeon to him & was very kind to him during his illness — came to see him — refused to let his overseer turn

6

James Hogg
1770–1835

Autograph manuscript of "Familiar Anecdotes of Sir Walter Scott," undated but written in 1833. 14 pp. 420 x 262 mm. MA 192.

A bit of rude Scots pastoral come to life, James Hogg was possessed by a bluff, hardy egotism, proof against the endearments of friends who called him, among other things, "Boar of the forest" and "the honest grunter." How could an autobiography begin more directly than his does? "I like to write about myself;" he declared, "in fact, there are few things which I like better." Hogg's self-esteem assisted him greatly in his rise from entertaining his "associate quadrupeds" in the stable with an old violin to meeting Wordsworth arm in arm with De Quincey under the Aurora Borealis at Rydal Mount. The impediments to Hogg's ascent in the world could hardly have been greater than they were. His scanty reading was picked up under the eyes of the flocks he tended, and his earnest desire for fame was sparked by a "half daft man" who recited "Tam o'Shanter" for him in the summer of 1797. With sublime assurance, Hogg concluded that he would be a second Burns, for reasons that sound suspiciously like the professional contempt of a herdsman for a member of a rival farm craft: "I have much more time to read and compose than any ploughman could have, and can sing more old songs than ever ploughman could in the world." The ploughman, however, had the advantage of being able to write, which Hogg could not do at the time.

But once he learned, his reputation as a successor to Burns was quick in coming. He published volumes of verse, articles, a manual he fondly called "Hogg on sheep," and a succession of prose tales. Today he is best remembered for a sensational novel about demonic possession, *Confessions of a Justified Sinner* (1824), not much noticed in its day, for his *Memoirs* and for his *Familiar Anecdotes of Sir Walter Scott*. *Familiar Anecdotes* creates an odd impression of Hogg's reverence for Scott; sometimes the herdsman bows to the golden calf, and sometimes the calf is made to kneel to the herdsman. This passage (beginning about three-fourths down the page) is an account of Scott's conversation and his first meeting with Hogg.

Hogg's manuscripts are distributed rather widely, the largest groups being found at the National Library of Scotland, Edinburgh, and at Yale University.

I first met with Sir Walter at my own cottage in the wilds of Ettrick Forest as above narrated and I then spent two days and two nights in his company. When we parted he shook my hand most heartily and invited me to his cottage on the banks of the North Esk above Lasswade. "By all means come and see me" said he "and I will there introduce you to my wife. She is a foreigner. As dark as a blackberry and does not speak the broad Scots so well as you and me. Of course I don't expect you to admire her much but I shall insure you of a hearty welcome.

I went and visited him the first time I had occasion to be in Edinr expecting to see Mrs Scott a kind of half blackamore whom our Sherrif had married for a great deal of money. I knew nothing about her and had never heard of her save from his own description but the words "as dark as a blackberry" had fixed her colour indelibly on my mind. Judge of my astonishment when I was introduced to one of the most beautiful and handsome creatures as Mrs Scott whom I had ever seen in my life. A brunnette certainly with raven hair and large black eyes but in my estimation a perfect beauty. . . .

- poise to that but ye ken weel it was written lang afore the other was heard of +
yes I know that a part of it was in MS. last year but I suspect it has been greatly
exaggerated since + As I am an honest man sir there has not been a line altered or added
that I remember of. The original copy was printed. Mr Blackwood was the only man
beside yourself who saw it. He read it painfully which I now know you did not and
I appeal to him + Well well. As to its running counter to Old Mortality I have nothing
to say. Nothing in the world. I only tell you that with the exception of Old Nanny
the crop-eared Covenanter who is by far the best character you ever drew in your life
I dislike the tale exceedingly and assure you it is a distorted a prejudiced and untrue
picture of the Royal party + It is a devilish deal truer than yours though; and on that
ground I make my appeal to my country" And with that I rose and was going off
in a great huff + No no! stop" cried he "You are not to go and leave me again in bad
humour. You ought not to be offended at me for telling you my mind freely + Why to be
sure it is the greatest folly in the world for me to be sae. But ane's beuks are like his
bairns he disna like to hear them spoken ill o' especially when he is conscious that
they dinna deserve it + Sir Walter then after his customary short good humoured laugh
repeated a proverb about the Gordons, which was exceedingly *apropos* to my feelings at the
time but all that I can do I cannot remember it though I generally remembered every
that he said of any import. He then added "I wish you to take your dinner with me to
day. There will be no body with us but James Ballantyne who will read you some
-thing new and I wanted to ask you particularly about something which has escaped me
at this moment. Ay it was this. Pray had you any tradition on which you founded
that ridiculous story about the Hunt of Eildon + "Yes I had" said I "as far as the two white
hounds are concerned and of the one putting the poisoned cup twice out of the Kings hand
when it was at his lips + That is very extraordinary" said he "for the very first time
I read it it struck me I had heard something of the same nature before but how or where
I cannot comprehend. I think it must have been when I was on the nurse's knee or
lying in the cradle yet I was sure I had heard it. It is a very ridiculous story that Mr Hogg
The most ridiculous of any modern story I ever read. What a pity it is that you are
not master of your own capabilities for that tale might have been made a good one"
+ It was always the same on the publication of any of my prose works. When the
Three perils of Man appeared he read me a long lecture on my extravagance in
demonology and assured me I had ruined one of the best tales in the world. It is
manifest however that the tale had made no ordinary impression on him as he
subsequently copied the whole of the main plot into his tale of Castle Dangerous.
+ Sir Walter's conversation was always amusing always interesting. There was a conciseness
a candour and judiciousness in it which never was equalled. His anecdotes were
without end and I am almost certain they were all made off hand for I never heard one
of them either before or after. His were no Joe Miller jokes. The only time ever his conversation
was to me perfectly uninteresting was with Mr John Murray of Albemarle street London
Their whole conversation was about noblemen parliamenters and literary men of all
grades none of which I had ever heard of or cared about; but every one of which Mr
Murray seemed to know with all their characters variety and propensities. This information
Sir Walter seemed to drink in with as much zest as I did his whisky toddy and this con-
-versation was carried on for two days and two nights with the exception of a few
sleeping hours and there I sat beside them all the while like a perfect stump; a thing
who never got in a word not even a blest. I wish I had the same opportunity again +
I first met with Sir Walter at my own cottage in the wilds of Ettrick forest as above narrated
and I then spent two days and two nights in his company. When we parted he shook my hand
most heartily and invited me to his cottage on the banks of the North Esk above Lasswade
"By all means come and see me" said he "and I will there introduce you to my wife. She
is a foreigner. As dark as a blackberry and does not speak the broad Scots so well as you and me
Of course, I don't expect you to admire her much but I shall insure you of a hearty welcome
+ I went and visited him the first time I had occasion to be in Edinr expecting to Mrs Scott
a kind of half blackamore whom our sherrif had married for a great deal of money. I
knew nothing about her and had never heard of her save from his own description
but the words "as dark as a blackberry" had fixed her colour indelibly on my mind.
Judge of my astonishment when I was introduced to one of the most beautiful and
handsome creatures as Mrs Scott whom I had ever seen in my life. A brunette certainly
with raven hair and large black eyes but in my estimation a perfect beauty. I found her
quite affable and she spoke English very well save that she put always the d for the ~~th~~ th and left
the aspiration of the h out altogether. She called me all her life Mr Og. I understood perfectly
well what she said but for many years I could not make her understand what I said
She had frequently to ask an explanation from her husband And I must say this of Lady Scott
though it was well known how jealous she was of the rank of Sir Walter's visitors yet I was
all my life received with the same kindness as if I had been a relation or one of the family although
one of the most homely of his daily associates. But there were many others both poets and
play-actors whom she received with no very pleasant countenance. Jeffery and his
satellites she could not endure and there was none whom she disliked more than Brougham

7

William Wordsworth
1770–1850

Autograph manuscript of "Description of a Beggar" ["The Old Cumberland Beggar"], unsigned and undated but written in 1797. 1 p. 386 x 240 mm.

When his sister wrote to Sara Hutchinson in early 1801, Wordsworth included—"for Coleridges entertainment"—a parallel column of contradictory reactions to the poems in the second edition of *Lyrical Ballads* (1800), including "The Old Cumberland Beggar." While the poet's brother could report that "Indeed every body seems delighted with the Cumberland beggar," Charles Lamb had remarked in a letter (paraphrased by Wordsworth) that "The instructions [are] too direct You seem to presume your readers are stupid." In fact, Lamb's letter had been more delicately phrased than that, for he had implied that Wordsworth was far less guilty than "many many novelists & modern poets" of violating the "unwritten compact between Author and reader; I will tell you a story, and I suppose you will understand it." By openly expressing his preference for "beautiful bare narratives," Lamb had unwittingly offended Wordsworth, who, like Tennyson, his successor as poet Laureate, was extremely sensitive to criticism. Almost immediately after sending his comments to Wordsworth, Lamb received "a long letter of four sweating pages" which conveyed the "'wish that [Lamb's] range of *Sensibility* was more extended. . . .'" Understandably, he was amused at Wordsworth's presumption: "after one has been reading Shaksp. twenty of the best years of one's life, to have a fellow start up, and prate about some unknown quality, which Shakspere possess'd in a degree inferior to Milton and somebody else!"

In this critical instance, Lamb was correct, for "The Old Cumberland Beggar" begins well but soon ventures off into explicit moralizing and a polemic of sorts against the poor laws and the "HOUSE, misnamed of INDUSTRY," i.e., the workhouse. This manuscript supports some of Lamb's criticism; it preserves only the descriptive passages, heavily revised and overscored, that were praised by Lamb, and a passage (published in the first edition of *Lyrical Ballads* [1798] as "Old Man Travelling") which gently and appropriately draws conclusions about the spiritual state of "one by nature led/ To peace. . . ." The more intrusive moral elements to which Lamb objected were added after the "Description of a Beggar" had been divided. Other manuscripts of "The Old Cumberland Beggar" survive in the Wordsworth Museum at Grasmere.

He travels on a solitary man/ His age has no companion. On the ground/ His eyes are turned and as he moves along/ They move along the ground: and evermore/ In stead of Nature's fair variety/ Her ample scope of hill and dale, of clouds/ And the blue sky the same short ~~of length~~ span of earth/ Is all his prospect. When the little birds/ Flit over him ~~and~~ if their quick shadows strike/ Across his path he does not lift his head/ Like one whose thoughts have been unsettled. So/ Bow-bent, his eyes for ever on the ground/ He plies his weary journey, seeing still/ And never knowing that he sees some straw/ Some scattered leaf or marks which in one track/ ~~Of Cart or Chariot wheel the nailes have left/ The nails of cart or chariot whell have left impressed on the/ Impress'd Impressed on the white road in the same line/~~ In the same never ending line impressd/ ~~One never ending Line on the nails, at distance still the same/ Of cart or chariot wheel have left impress'd/ On the white road at distance still the same/~~ The nails of cart or chariot wheel have left/ Impress'd on the white road, in the same line/ At distance still the same. Poor Traveller! . . .

Description of a Beggar.

He travels on a solitary man
His age has no companion. On the ground
His eyes are turned and as he moves along
They move along the ground: and evermore
Instead of Nature's fair variety
Her ample scope of hill and dale, of clouds
And the blue sky the same short ~~length~~ span of earth
Is all his prospect. When the little birds
Flit over him ~~and~~ if their quick shadows strike
Across his path he does not lift his head
Like one whose thoughts have been unsettled. So
Bow-bent, his eyes for ever on the ground
He plies his weary journey, seeing still
And never knowing that he sees some straw
Some scattered leaf or marks which in one track
~~Or cart or chariot wheel the wains have left~~
~~[illegible]~~
~~In the same never ending line in perfect~~
~~[illegible]~~
~~Of cart or chariot wheel have left [illegible]~~
~~On the white road — at distance still the same~~
The nails of cart or chariot wheel have left
Impressed on the white road, in the same line
At distance still the same. ~~Poor Traveller~~
~~[illegible]~~
~~Disturb the summer dust. Him boys and girls~~
~~The vacant and the busy maids and youths~~
~~And urchins newly breech'd all pass him by~~
~~insensibly [illegible]~~
~~Him even the slow-paced waggon leaves behind~~
~~One never ending line [illegible]~~
~~Or chariot wheel have left on the white road~~
~~Impressed at distance still the same~~ Poor Traveller!
His staff trails with him, his slow footsteps scarce
Disturb the summer dust. He is so still
In look and motion that the miller's dog
Is tired of barking at him. Boys and girls
The vacant and the busy, maids and youths
And urchins newly-breech'd all pass him by
Him even the slow-paced waggon leaves behind.
His bending figure and his face in every limb his look
Have expression of a man by whom
All effort seems forgotten one to whom
Long patience hath such mild composure given
That patience now doth seem a thing of which
He hath no need.

35.

resigned to quietness
a man altogether

WILLIAM WORDSWORTH

Autograph letter signed, dated 21 May 1807, to Lady Beaumont.
5 pp. 400 x 252 mm. MA 1581.

Near the end of this extraordinary letter to Lady Beaumont (whose husband, Sir George, was one of Wordsworth's most gracious patrons) Wordsworth recalls a remark made to her by Coleridge that defines the intention of most critical writing in the Romantic period and certainly explains the purport of this letter: "every great and original writer, in proportion as he is great or original, must himself create the taste by which he is to be relished; he must teach the art by which he is to be seen. . . ." Wordsworth might well have thought this task at least partially achieved after the publication of the "Preface" to the second edition of *Lyrical Ballads* (1800). In 1807, however, the appearance of *Poems in Two Volumes*, which contains most of his finest short poems, provoked an unappreciative "immediate effect . . . upon what is called the Public," an effect that led Lady Beaumont to write to the poet in moral and critical support. In his turn, Wordsworth sent her an epistle that conveys in unequivocal terms his opinion of the reading public and, more importantly, his profound faith in his poetic mission. "Trouble not yourself," he writes, "upon [the poems'] present reception; of what moment is that compared with what I trust is their destiny, to console the afflicted, to add sunshine to daylight by making the happy happier, to teach the young & the gracious of every age, to see to think & feel, and there fore to become more actively & securely virtuous. . . ." While Wordsworth believed in the destiny of his poems, he also felt safe in scorning his contemporary audience, for "their imagination has slept; and the voice which is the Voice of my Poetry without Imagination cannot be heard."

The Morgan Library owns a remarkable collection of letters, primarily addressed to Sir George and Lady Beaumont, called the Coleorton Papers, after Coleorton, their home in Leicestershire, where Wordsworth was staying when he wrote the letter shown here. Some of the items in this collection are fifty letters by William and Dorothy Wordsworth, twenty-four letters by Coleridge, and numerous other letters by such men as Sir Uvedale Price, William Gilpin, Sir David Wilkie, Sir Humphry Davy and Joseph Farington.

Trouble not yourself upon their present reception, of what moment is that compared with what I trust is their destiny, to console the afflicted, to add sunshine to daylight by making the happy happier, to teach the young & the gracious of every age, to see to think & feel, and there fore to become more actively & securely virtuous; this is their office which I trust they will faithfully perform long after we, [illegible deletion] (that is, all that is mortal of us) are mouldered [illegible deletion] in our graves. I am well aware how far it would seem to many I overrate my own exertions when I speak in this way in direct connection with the Volumes I have just made public. I am now however afraid of such censure insignificant as probably the majority of those poems would appear to [illegible deletion] very respectable persons; I do not mean London Wits & Witlings for these have too many bad passions about them to be respectable even if they had more intellect than the benign laws of providence will allow to such a heartless existence as theirs is; . . .

upon this I shall insist elsewhere; at present let me confine myself to my object which is to make you my dear Friend as easy-hearted as myself with respect to these Poems. Trouble not yourself upon their present reception; of what moment is that compared with what I trust is their destiny, to console the afflicted, to add sunshine to daylight by making the happy happier, to teach the young & the gracious of every age, to see to think & feel, and therefore to become more actively & securely virtuous; this is their office which I trust they will faithfully perform long after we, (that is, all that is mortal of us) are mouldered in our graves. I am well aware how far it would seem to many I overrate my own exertions when I speak in this way in direct connection with the Volume I have just made public. I am not however afraid of such censure insignificant as probably the majority of those poems would appear to very respectable persons; I do not mean London Wits & Witlings for these have too many bad passions about them to be respectable even if they had more intellect than the benign laws of providence will allow to such a heartless existence as theirs is; but grave, kindly natured worthy persons who would be pleased if they could. I hope that these Volumes are not without some recommendations even for Readers of this class, but their imagination has slept; and the voice which is the Voice of my Poetry without Imagination cannot be heard. — Leaving these I was going to say a word to such Readers as Mr Rogers. Such! how would he be offended if he knew I considered him only as a representative of a class, and not an unique! Pity says Mr R. that so many trifling things should be admitted to obstruct the view of those that have merit. Now let this candid judge take by way of example the sonnets which probably with the exception of two or three other Poems for which I will not contend appear to him the most trifling, as they are the shortest, I would say to him, omitting things of higher consideration there is one thing which must strike you at once if you will only read these poems, that those to Liberty at least have a connection with, or a bearing upon each other, and therefore, if individually they want weight, perhaps, as a Body, they may not be so deficient, at least this ought to induce you to suspend your judgement and qualify it so far as to allow that the writer aims at least at comprehensiveness. But dropping this, I would boldly say at once, that these Sonnets while they each fix the attention upon some important sentiment separately considered, do at the same time collectively make

a Poem on the subject of civil liberty and national independence which either for simplicity of style or grandeur of moral sentiment is alas! likely to have few parallels in the Poetry of the present day. Again, turn to the "Moods of my own Mind" there is scarcely a Poem here of above thirty lines, and very trifling these poems will appear to many but, omitting to speak of them individually, do they not, taken collectively, fix the attention upon a subject eminently poetical, viz. the interest which objects in nature derive from the predominance of certain affections more or less permanent more or less capable of salutary renewal in the mind of the being contemplating these objects? — This is poetic, & essentially poetic, & why? because it is creative. But I am wasting words for it is nothing more than you know and if said to those for whom it is intended it would not be understood. — — I see by your last letter that Mrs Fermor has entered into the spirit of these "Moods of my own Mind". Your transcript from her letter gave me the greatest pleasure, but I must say that even she has something yet to receive from me. I say this with confidence from her thinking that I have fallen below myself in the Sonnet beginning, "With Ships the sea was sprinkled far & nigh." As to the other which she objects to I will only observe that there is a misprint in the last line but two "And though" this wilderness, for "And through the wilderness" that makes it unintelligible. This sonnet for many reasons though I do not abandon it I will not now speak of; but upon the other I could say something important in conversation & will attempt now to illustrate it by a comment which I feel will be very inadequate to convey my meaning. There is scarcely one of my Poems which does not aim to direct the attention to some moral sentiment or to some general principle, or law of thought, or of our intellectual constitution. For instance in the present case, who is there that has not felt that the mind can have no rest among a multitude of objects of which it either cannot make one whole, or from which it cannot single out one individual whereupon may be concentrated the attention divided among or distracted by a multitude. After a certain time we must either select one image or object which must put out of view the rest wholly, or must subordinate them to itself while it stands forth as a Head.

"Now glowed the firmament
With living sapphires; Hesperus that led
The starry Host rode brightest; till the Moon
Rising in clouded majesty at length
Apparent Queen unveiled her peerless light
And o'er the dark her silver mantle threw."

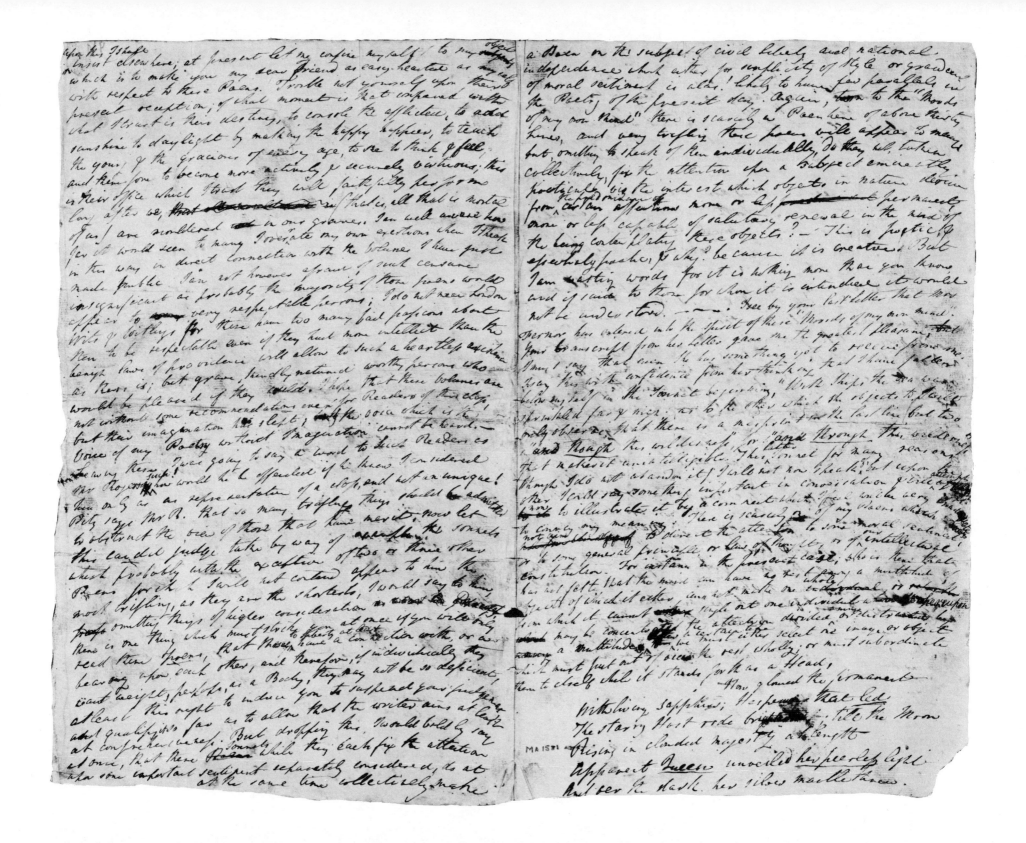

9

Sir Walter Scott
1771–1832

Autograph manuscript of "The Lady of the Lake," unsigned and undated, but written 1809–10. 255 leaves. 269 x 200 mm. MA 443.

Wordsworth, Coleridge and their partisans found Walter Scott to be a chafing, if philosophically negligible, reminder of their own limited financial success, as those who discriminate between higher and lower literary pleasures are apt to do when they find that the public prefers the lower in droves. De Quincey seems to have had this feeling at heart when he called "a hornet's nest" down upon himself at a dinner party in 1810 by denigrating Scott's fame in the following manner (as copied from his letter by Dorothy Wordsworth): "whereas, heretofore, if one *would* read novels, one must do it under the penalty thereunto annexed of being accredited for feeble-mindedness, and *missiness;* now (by favour of W.S.) one might read a Novel, and have the credit of reading a poem." This explanation was meant to discredit Scott's immensely popular poetical romances, including his best, the recently published *Lady of the Lake;* instead, it most adequately explains why they are so engaging. The same scenes, the same historical themes and texture, the same vivid grasp of incident and action that characterize Scott's novels also fill his verse romances. Scott himself occasionally maligned these works; he tired of the meter of *The Lady of the Lake*, felt that it had been written too quickly, and called it (somewhat pejoratively) "a grand romance ambling on all four like the palfry of Queen Guenever." This, however, is the unjust modesty of the author, for these poems, especially *The Lady of the Lake*, offer the finest of historical romance ("our marvelling boy-hood legends") and the purest of narratives.

The passage shown here is the opening of the Third Canto, a section that makes plain Scott's deep historical sense—"Time rolls his ceaseless course"—and his reliance upon the traditional lore of the Highlands:

> Yet live there still who can remember well,
>   How, when a mountain Chief his bugle blew,
> Both field and forest, dingle, cliff, and dell,
>   And solitary heath, the signal knew.

The Morgan Library also owns the complete manuscript of *Rokeby* and portions of *The Bridal of Triermain* and *The Lay of the Last Minstrel*, as well as several shorter poems.

Time rolls his ceaseless course. — The race of yore/ Who danced our infancy upon their knee,/ And told our marvelling boy-hood legends store,/ Of their strange ventures pass'd by land or sea,/ How are they blotted from the things that be!/ How few, all weak and ~~wearied~~ withered of their force,/ Wait on the verge of dark eternity,/ Like stranded wrecks, the tide returning hoarse,/ To sweep them from our sight! — Time rolls his ceaseless course.

Yet live there still who can remember well,/ How, when a mountain Chief his bugle blew,/ Both field and forest, dingle, cliff, and dell,/ And solitary heath, the signal knew;/ And fast the faithful clan around him drew,/ What time the warning note was keenly wound,/ What time aloft the kindred banner flew,/ While clamorous war-pipes yell'd the gathering sound,/ And while the Fiery Cross glanced, like a meteor, round.

1)

The Lady of the Lake
Canto Third

Time rolls his ceaseless course. # The race of yore
Who danced our infancy upon their knee,
And told our marvelling boy-hood legends store,
Of their strange ventures happ'd by land or sea,
Now are they blotted from the things that be!
Now few, all weak and ~~[illegible]~~ withered of their force,
Wait on the verge of dark eternity,
Like stranded wrecks, the tide returning hoarse,
To sweep them from our sight! # Time rolls his ceaseless course. §

Yet live there still who can remember well,
Now, when a mountain Chief his bugle blew,
Both field and forest, dingle, cliff and dell,
And solitary heath, the signal knew;
And fast the faithful clan around him drew,
What time the warning note was keenly wound,
What time aloft the kindred banner flew,
While clamorous war-pipes yell'd the gathering sound, §
And while the Fiery Cross glanced, like a meteor, round.

10

SIR WALTER SCOTT

Autograph manuscript of "Old Mortality," signed Jedediah Cleishbotham and dated Gandercleugh, 15 November 1816. 304 leaves. 242 x 188 mm.MA 445.

Scotland is a country that can be described as a balance of landscapes, highland and lowland, fertile river valleys and barren moors, the opposing prospects visible from the turret of Tillietudlem: "the one richly cultivated and highly adorned, the other exhibiting the monotonous and dreary character of a wild and inhospitable moorland." The topographical position of Tillietudlem, the home of Lady Margaret and Edith Bellenden in Scott's *Old Mortality*, offers two useful metaphors. It provides an image of balance, reflecting the dilemma faced by Henry Morton, who in his search for political moderation is caught between two forces: the King's Life-Guards, represented by Claverhouse and Bothwell—men "cultivated and highly adorned" but savagely implacable—and the Covenanters, the "western whigs," led by John Balfour and Ephraim Macbriar—"wild and inhospitable," driven to rebellion in 1679 by the systematic religious persecution of Scotland's Privy Council. Although Hazlitt saw in Scott an unreasoning veneration for the past, *Old Mortality*, perhaps the greatest of his novels, defies that judgement; it is an historical fiction not only because it concerns events that took place in the late seventeenth century but also because it explores the way in which a person of conscience from any period can be crushed by historical problems that are, in themselves, timeless.

Tillietudlem is also a pass, controlling access to the moor from the valley of the Clyde beneath. In this sense, it offers an apt image of Scott himself, the man chiefly responsible for the transmission of Scottish history and tradition—the relics of a ruder and less cultured era—to refined readers of the early nineteenth century, especially those in the south. Scott's service to his native country in this respect is immeasurable; and his function at times resembles that of Old Mortality, the aged Covenanter who wandered through Scotland cleaning and refurbishing the graves of his fellow partisans and who is one of several narrative personae through which the story of *Old Mortality* is filtered.

The Morgan Library preserves an unrivaled number of manuscripts of Scott's novels, among them *The Antiquary*, *Guy Mannering*, *Ivanhoe*, *Peveril of the Peak*, *St. Ronan's Well* and *Woodstock*.

[Starting midway:] All heads were now bent from the battlements of the turret which commanded a distant prospect down the vale of the river. The Tower of Tillietudlem stood or perhaps yet stands upon the angle of a very precipitous bank formd by the juncture of a considerable brook with the Clyde. There was a ~~br~~ narrow bridge of one steep arch over the brook near its mouth ~~at~~ over which & along the foot of the high and broken banks ~~beneath which~~ wended the public road ~~which~~ & the fortalice thus command~~ed~~ing both bridge and pass ~~and~~ had been in times of war a fort of considerable importance ~~tending to secu~~ the possession of which was necessary to secure the the communication of the upper and wilder districts of the country with those ~~which~~ beneath where the valley expands & is more capable of cultivation. . . .

^ One to three is as great odds as ever fought and won & I never knew any body that cared to take it except old Corporal Raddlebanes: But these d—d books put all pretty men's actions out of countenance. I dare say you would think very little of Raddlebanes along side of Artamenes—

^ formed by the junction of a considerable brook with the Clyde. There was a narrow bridge of one steep arch over the brook near its mouth over which & along the foot of the high and broken bank

^ but the level ground and gentle slopes near the river form cul: tivated fields of an irregular form

^ for the ware.

wounded — But I know the reason — you will persist in reading these nonsen: sical romances day and night and whimpering for distresses that never existed — Why how the devil can you believe that that Artamenes or what d'ye call him fought single handed with a whole battalion^x I would hear the fellows that write such nonsense brought to the picquet for leasing-making" — Lady Margaret herself something attached to the perusal of romances took up the cudgels "Monsr Scuderi" she said "is a sol: =dier brother and as I have heard a ~~b~~ complete one & so is the Sieur D'Urfé" — "More shame for them — they should have known better what they were writing about. For my part I have not read a book these twenty years ex: cept my bible, the Whole Duty of Man, and of late days Turner's Pallas armata on the ordering of the pike exercize and I dont like his discipline much neither. He wants to draw up the cavalry in front of a stand of pikes instead of being upon the wings. Sure am I if we had done so at Kilsythe instead of having our handful of horse on the flanks the first discharge would have sent them back among our highlanders — But I hear the kettle-drums —

All heads were now bent from the battlements of the turret which commanded a distant prospect down the vale of the river. The Tower of Tillietudlem stood or perhaps yet stands upon the angle of a very precipitous bank^ ~~beneath which~~ winded the public road ~~which~~ & the fortalice thus commanding both bridge and pass ~~and~~ had been in times of war a ^post of considerable importance ~~tending to~~ ~~to~~ the possession of which was necessary to secure the the communication of the upper and wilder districts of the country with those ~~which~~ beneath where the valley expands & is more capable of cultivation. The view down the river is of a grand woodland character^ interspersed with hedge row trees and copses ~~[illegible]~~ the inclosures seeming ~~[illegible]~~ as it were to have been cleared out of the forest ^which surrounds them and occupies in unbroken masses the steeper decli: vities and more distant banks. The noble stream in colour a clear and sparkling brown like the hue of the Cairn Gorm pebbles rushes ~~[illegible]~~ through this romantic region in bold sweeps and curves partly visible and partly concealed by the trees which clothe its ~~ban~~ banks. With a providence unknown in other parts of Scotland the peasants have in most cases planted orchards around their cottages and the general blossom of the apple trees at this season of the year gave all the lower part of the view the appearance of a flower garden Looking up the river the character of the scene was varied considerably. ^A hilly ~~[illegible]~~ waste and uncultivated country approached close to the banks of the river; the trees were few and limited to the neighbour hood of the stream and the rude moorlands swelled at a little distance into shapeless and heavy hills which were again surmoun ted in their turn by a range of lofty mountains dimly seen on the

Sydney Smith
1771–1845

Autograph letter signed, undated but written between 18 and 21 April 1826, to Admiral Sir Sidney Smith. 1 p. 228 x 187 mm.

In an article (the manuscript of which is in the Morgan Library) on *The Opinions of Lord Holland* (1841), Macaulay stated that of Holland House men "will remember that constant flow of conversation, so natural, so animated, so various, so rich with observation and anecdotes; that wit which never gave a wound. . . ." These words encompass the reputations of many men, but chief among them must be Sydney Smith—one of the founders of the *Edinburgh Review*, a Whig, wit and clergyman of penetrating good sense—whom Macaulay called the "Smith of Smiths" and Thomas Moore (another intimate of Holland House) referred to as "the incomparable Sydney," "Prince of Wits." Reputed wits often die literary deaths of attrition, as once-fresh phrases grow stale with the years, but Smith's wit—gently humorous, shored up by unrelenting logic, and broadly humane—remains as vivid as ever, particularly in his letters.

Unfortunately, Smith's ascent in the Church of England was inhibited by the very qualities that made him such a great (and amusing) man. He attacked the bigotry of bishops wherever it appeared, argued for Catholic emancipation in his most famous work, *The Letters of Peter Plymley* (1807–8), and exercised a wit of such renown that he seemed unsuited for the higher ranks of the church. But such a rejection of Smith was a minority opinion. In praising the virtues of "good temper" to Richard Monckton Milnes (later Lord Houghton), he recounted an anecdote that explains the fondness he engendered in so many people and illuminates Macaulay's comment about "wit which never gave a wound": "Lord Dudley, when I took leave of him, said to me, 'You have been laughing at me for the last seven years, and you never said anything I wished unsaid.' This pleased me."

This letter was written to Sir Sidney Smith, with whom Smith was often confused, during Smith's visit to Paris in 1826. He proposed that they "accept invitations in common— You shall go as the Clergyman when it suits your convenience, and I will go as the Hero. The Physiognomists and Craniologists will discover in you a Love of Tithes—and of conformity to articles—and in me a contempt of death and a Love of Glory."

Hotel Virginie Rue St. Honore Dear Sir: I am much oblig'd by your kind offer of taking me to the Museum of Denon but I am unfortunately engag'd to some Ladies—to see other Sights.— I think you and I should set up a Partnership—and accept invitations in common— You shall go as the Clergyman when it suits your convenience, and I will go as the Hero. The Physiognomists and Craniologists will discover in you a Love of Tithes—and of conformity to articles—and in me a contempt of death and a Love of Glory. We shall destroy these imposters by our plan—many thanks for your politeness. I will take an early opportunity of paying my respects to you. I am dr Sr yr [3 illegible words] Sydney Smith To Admiral Sir Sidney Smith

299

Hotel Virginie
Rue St Honoré

Dear Sir,

I am much obliged by your kind offer of
taking me to the Museum of Denon
I am unfortunately engaged to some Ladies
to see other sights. – I think you and I
should set up a Partnership – and accept
invitations in common — You shall go as
the Clergyman when it suits your convenience,
and I will go as the Hero. The Physiognomists
and Craniologists will discover in you a
Love of Tithes – and of conformity to articles – and
in me a contempt of death and a Love of Glory
We shall destroy these impostors by our plan –
many thanks for your politeness – I will take
an early opportunity of paying my respects to you
and I am yr Obt Sert

Sydney Smith

12

Samuel Taylor Coleridge
1772–1834

Autograph letter signed, undated, but written ca. 17 July 1797, to Robert Southey. 4 pp. 340 x 210 mm. MA 1848.

Explaining the failure of his "Monody on the Death of Chatterton" in this letter to Southey, Coleridge remarked, "A young man by strong feelings is impelled to write on a particular subject—and this is all his feelings do for him. They set him upon the business & then they leave him." A more succinct analysis of Coleridge's main difficulty as a poet could not be found. Like an evangelical dependent upon deep emotional assurance of God's providence, Coleridge and Wordsworth (who was staying with Coleridge at Stowey at the time this letter was written) relied upon "strong feelings" as an essential moving force in what Coleridge called the "shaping spirit of Imagination." When these feelings died, the link to the divinity that infused nature died too. In the letter shown here, Coleridge sent to Southey a draft of one of his finest poems, "This Lime-Tree Bower My Prison." While Charles Lamb, Wordsworth and the latter's sister Dorothy were out walking one evening, Coleridge ("lam'd by the scathe" of hot milk which Sara Hutchinson had accidentally spilled on his foot) remained behind in a somewhat self-pitying state, seated in a lime-tree bower where he composed these lines. The poem is an imaginative attempt to envision the landscape over which his friends are passing, but it also becomes a test of his feelings for nature—of his ability to evoke in himself the "deep joy" brought on by the setting sun—and a measure of his own uncertainty whether "Nature ne'er deserts the wise and pure. . . ."

The Morgan Library is the repository of one of the largest collections of Coleridge letters in the world. Fully one-fifth of the letters published by Earl Leslie Griggs now reside here, including Coleridge's letters to Southey (92), to Godwin (41) and to Sir George and Lady Beaumont (24).

[On recto page:] Charles Lamb has been with me for a week—he left me Friday morning./ The second day after Wordsworth came to me, [illegible deletion] dear Sara accidently emptied a skillet of boiling milk on my foot, which confined me during the whole time of C. Lamb's ~~residence~~ stay & still prevents me from all walks *longer than a furlong. While Wordsworth, his Sister, & C. Lamb were out one evening;/ sitting in the arbour of T. Poole's Garden, which communicates with mine, I wrote these lines, with which I am pleased——*

Well—they are gone: and here must I remain,/ Lam'd by the scathe of fire, lonely & faint,/ This lime-tree bower my prison. They, meantime,/ My Friends, whom I may never meet again,/ On springy heath, along the hill-top edge,/ *elastic, I mean./ Wander delighted, and look down, perchance,/ ~~Wand'ring well pleas'd, look down on grange or dell/~~ On that same rifted Dell, where many an Ash &c/ Or that ~~deep gloomy deep fantastic Rift,~~ where many an Ash/ Twists it's wild limbs beside ~~the some~~ the ferny rock,/ The ferns, that grow in moist places, grow five or six together & form a complete "Prince of Wale's Feathers"—i.e. plumy.—/ Whose plumy ferns for ever nod and drip/ Spray'd by the waterfall. But chiefly Thou,/ My gentle-hearted Charles! thou, who hast pin'd/ And hunger'd after Nature many a year/ In the great City pent, winning thy way,/ With sad yet bowed soul, thro' evil & pain/ And strange calamity.— . . .*

makes ~~one~~ one's blood circulate, like ipecacuanha.— But so it is. A young man by strong feelings is impelled to write on a particular subject—and this is all, his feelings do for him. They set him upon the business & then they leave him.— He has such a high idea of what Poetry ought to be, that he cannot conceive that such things as his natural emotions may be allowed ~~ought~~ to find a place in it—his learning therefore, his fancy, or rather conceit, and all his powers of buckramm are put on the stretch—. It appears to me, that strong feeling is not so requisite to an author's being profoundly pathetic, as taste & good sense.

Poor old Wag!—his mother died of a dish of a clotted Cream, which my mother sent her as a present.—

I rejoice that your poems are all sold.— In the ballad of Mary, the Maid of the Inn, you have properly enough made the diction colloquial—but "engages the eye", applied to a Gibbet strikes me as slipslop[p]ish—from the imperfect meaning of the word "engaging".— Your praise of my Dedication gave me great pleasure.— From the 9th to the 14th the five lines are flat & prosaic—& the versification ever & anon has too much of the rhyme or couplet cadence—& the metaphor on the diverse sorts of friendship is hunted down—but the poem is dear to me, and in point of taste I place it next to "Low was our pretty cot" which I think the best of my poems.—

I am as much a Pangloss as ever—only less contemptuous, than I used to be, when I argue how unwise it is to feel contempt for any thing— I had been on a visit to Wordsworth's at Racedown near Crewkerne—and I brought him & his sister back with me & here I have settled them—. By a combination of curious circumstances a gentleman's seat, with a park & woods, elegantly & completely furnished—with 9 lodging rooms, three parlours & a Hall—in a most beautiful & romantic situation by the sea side—4 miles from Stowey—this we have got for Wordsworth at the rent of 23 £ a year, taxes included!!— The park and woods are his for all purposes he wants them—i.e. he may walk, ride, & keep a horse in them—& the large gardens are altogether & entirely his.— Wordsworth is a very great man—the only man, to whom at all times & in all modes of excellence I feel myself inferior—the only one, I mean, ~~whom~~ I have yet met with—for the London Literati appear to me to be very much like little Potatoes—i.e. no great Things!—a compost of Nullity & Dullity.

Charles Lamb has been with me for a week—he left me Friday morning.— The second day after Wordsworth came to me, ~~my~~ dear Sara accidentally emptied a skillet of boiling milk on my foot, which confined me during the whole time of C. Lamb's stay ~~continuance~~ & still prevents me from all walks longer than a furlong.— While Wordsworth, his Sister, & C. Lamb were out one evening; sitting in the arbour of T. Poole's garden, which communicates with mine, I wrote these lines, with which I am pleased—

Well—they are gone: and here must I remain,
Lam'd by the scathe of fire, lonely & faint,
This lime-tree bower my prison. They, meantime,
My Friends, whom I may never meet again,
On springy† heath, along the hill-top edge,
~~[illegible]~~ Wander delighted, and look down, perchance,
~~Or deep [illegible] gloomy Rift~~ On that same rifted Dell, where many an Ash
Twists it's wild limbs beside the ferny rock,
Whose plumy ferns for ever nod and drip
Spray'd by the waterfall. But chiefly Thou,
My gentle-hearted Charles! thou, who hast pin'd
And hunger'd after Nature many a year
In the great City pent, winning thy way,
With sad yet bowed soul, thro' evil & pain
And strange calamity.— Ah slowly sink
Behind the western ridge; thou glorious Sun!
Shine in the slant beams of the sinking orb,
Ye purple Heath-flowers! Richlier burn, ye Clouds!
Live in the yellow light, ye distant Groves!
And kindle, thou blue Ocean! So my friend
Struck with joy's deepest calm, and gazing round
On the wide view, may gaze till all doth seem
Less gross than bodily, a living Thing
That acts upon the mind, and with such hues
As cloathe the Almighty Spirit, when he makes
Spirits perceive his presence!

A Delight
Comes sudden on my heart, and I am glad
As I myself were there! Nor in this bower

I heard from C. Lamb of Favell & Le Grice. Poor Allen! I knew nothing of it.— As to Rough, he is a wonderful fellow! and [illegible] returned from the army, cut me for a month, till he saw that other people were as much attached to me as before.

† elastic, I mean.

The ferns, that grow in moist places, grow five or six together & form a complete "Prince of Wales's Feathers"—i.e. plumy.—

You remember, I am a Berkleian!

13

SAMUEL TAYLOR COLERIDGE

Autograph letter signed, undated but written 31 August 1803, to Sir George and Lady Beaumont. 4 pp. 404 x 280 mm. MA 1581.

Some of Coleridge's finest verse was inspired by a potential seam in his friendship with Wordsworth: the disparity between their poetical talents. From the first, he yielded the palm to his friend: "Wordsworth is a very great man—the only man, to whom *at all times* & in *all modes of excellence* I feel myself inferior. . . ." Often the two men read and criticized each other's poetry, and twice that practice drew from Coleridge a kind of despairing emulation in verse, a downcast celebration of poetic genius that overshadowed his own: once on a night in January 1807 when Wordsworth had finished reading *The Prelude* (this resulted in "To William Wordsworth") and once in early April 1802 after Coleridge had heard the first four stanzas of "Ode: Intimations of Immortality." The first draft of the poem that resulted from the latter reading, "Dejection: An Ode," betrays profound emotional confusion in Coleridge; it is a complex lament for the failings of imagination and the failure of his marriage and an unrestrained statement of his love for Sara Hutchinson, to whom it was sent as a verse epistle. During the next six months, Coleridge gradually reworked the poem, deleting the more personal references, changing the person apostrophized (from Sara and Edmund in earlier versions, to William in the manuscript shown here, and finally to an unspecified lady), and giving it a more coherent shape. In this letter to Sir George and Lady Beaumont, the poem lacks its final two and a half stanzas, for even sixteen months after it was begun, Coleridge still found "Dejection" too "doleful" to copy out in its entirety.

This letter to the Beaumonts is the more remarkable because it also includes a transcript in Dorothy Wordsworth's hand of her brother's poem "Resolution and Independence." It has been argued that this poem was written in response to "Dejection: An Ode."

Dejection, an Ode.—(Imperfect) April 4 1802/ *"Late, late yestreen I saw the new Moon/ "With the old Moon in her Arm,/ "And I fear, I fear, my dear Mastér,/ "We shall have a deadly Storm.* The Ballad of Sir Pat. Spence.

Well! if the Bard was weatherwise, who made/ The grand old Ballad of Sir Patrick Spence,/ This Night, so tranquil now, will not go hence/ Unrous'd by winds that ply a busier Trade/ Than that which moulds yon Clouds in lazy Flakes,/ Or the dull sobbing Draft, that drones and rakes/ Amid the Strings of this Eolian Lute,/ Which better far were mute! For lo! the new moon, winter-bright!/ And overspread with phantom Light,/ With swimming phantom Light o'erspread/ But rimm'd and circled with a silver Thread,/ I see the Old Moon in her Lap foretelling/ The coming on of Rain and squally Blast!/ And O! that even now the Gust were swelling,/ And the Slant Night-shower driving loud & fast!/ Those Sounds which oft have [illegible deletion] rais'd me while they aw'd/ And sent my Soul abroad,/ Might now perhaps their wonted Influence give,/ Might startle this dull Pain, and make it move and live. . . .

As if he had been reading in a book;
And now such freedom as I could I took
And, drawing to his side, to him did say,
"This morning gives us promise of a glorious day."

A gentle answer did the Old Man make
In courteous speech which forth he slowly drew;
And him with further words I thus bespake,
"What kind of work is that which you pursue?
"This is a lonesome place for one like you."
He answer'd me with pleasure & surprize,
And there was while he spake a fire about his eyes.

His words came feebly from a feeble chest,
Yet each in solemn order follow'd each
With something of a pompous utterance drest,
Choice word & measur'd phrase, beyond the reach
Of ordinary men, a stately speech,
Such as grave livers do in Scotland use,
Religious Men who give to God & Man their dues.

He told me that he to the Pond had come
To gather Leeches, being old and poor,
That 'twas his calling, better far than some,
Though he had many hardships to endure:
From Pond to Pond he roam'd, from Moor to Moor,
Housing with God's good help by choice or chance
And in this way he gain'd an honest Maintenance

The Old Man still stood talking by my side
But soon his voice to me was like a Stream
Scarce heard, nor word from word could I divide
And the whole body of the Man did seem
Like one whom I had met with in a Dream,
Or like a Man from some far region sent
To give me human strength, & strong admonishment.

My former thoughts return'd, the fear that kills,
The hope that is unwilling to be fed,
Cold, pain, and labour, & all fleshly ills,
And mighty Poets in their misery dead,
And now, not knowing what the Old Man had said,
My question eagerly did I renew,
"How is it that you live, & what is it you do?"

He with a smile did then his words repeat
And said, that wheresoe'er they might be spied
He gather'd Leeches, stirring at his feet
The waters in the Ponds where they abide

Once he could meet with them on every side;
But fewer they became from day to day,
And so his means of life before him died away.

While he was talking thus the lonely place,
The Old Man's shape & speech all troubl'd me.
In my mind's eye I seem'd to see him pace
About the weary Moors continually,
Wandering about alone and silently,
While I these thoughts within myself pursu'd,
He, having made a pause, the same discourse renew'd.

And now with this he other matter blended
Which he deliver'd with demeanor kind
Yet stately in the main; & when he ended
I could have laugh'd myself to scorn to find
In that decrepit Man so firm a mind;
"God," said I, "be my help & stay secure!
"I'll think of the Leech-gatherer on the lonely Moor"

Dejection, an Ode — (Imperfect) April 4th 1802.

"Late, late yestreen I saw the new moon
"With the old moon in her Arm,
"And I fear, I fear, my dear Master,
"We shall have a deadly Storm.

The Ballad of Sir Patk. Spence.

Well! if the Bard was weatherwise, who made
The grand old Ballad of Sir Patrick Spence,
This Night, so tranquil now, will not go hence
Unrous'd by winds that ply a busier trade
Than that which moulds yon Clouds in lazy Flakes,
Or the dull sobbing Draft, that drones and rakes
Upon the Strings of this Eolian Lute,
Which better far were mute!

For lo! the New moon, winter-bright!
And overspread with phantom Light,
With swimming phantom Light o'erspread
But rimm'd and circled with a silver Thread;
I see the Old Moon in her Lap, foretelling
The coming on of Rain and squally Blast!
And O! that even now the Gust were swelling,
And the slant Night-shower driving loud & fast!
Those Sounds which oft have rais'd me while they aw'd
And sent my Soul abroad,
Might now perhaps their wonted Influence give,
Might startle this dull Pain, and make it move and live.

A Grief without a Pang, void, dark, and drear,
A stifled, drowsy, unimpassion'd Grief,
That finds no natural Outlet, no Relief
In word, or Sigh, or Tear —
O dearest William! in this heartless Mood,
To other thoughts by yonder Throstle woo'd,
All this long Eve, so balmy and serene,
Have I been gazing on the western sky
And its' celestial Tint of yellow Green —
And still I gaze! and with how blank an eye!
And those thin Clouds, above, in flakes and bars,
That give away their motion to the Stars;
Those Stars, that glide behind them or between,
Now sparkling, now bedimm'd, but always seen;
Yon crescent moon, as fix'd as if it grew
In its' own starless cloudless Lake of Blue;
I see them all so excellently fair —
I see, not feel, how beautiful they are!

My genial Spirits fail,
And what can these avail
To lift the smoth'ring weight from off my Breast?
It were a vain Endeavour
Tho' I should gaze for ever
On that green Light, which lingers in the West:
I may not hope from outward forms to win
The Passion and the Life, whose Fountains are within!

O William! we receive but what we give:
And in our Life alone does Nature live.
Ours' is her Wedding-garment, ours' her Shroud!
And would we aught behold of higher worth
Than that inanimate cold World allow'd
To the poor loveless ever-anxious Crowd —
Ah! from the Soul itself must issue forth
A Light, a Glory, a fair luminous Cloud
Enveloping the Earth!
And from the Soul itself must there be sent
A sweet and potent Voice, of its' own Birth,
Of all sweet Sounds the Life and Element!
O pure of Heart! thou need'st not ask of me
What this strong Music in the Soul may be,
What, and wherein doth it exist,

This Light, this Glory, this fair luminous Mist
This beautiful, and beauty-making Power!
Joy, dearest Bard! but such as ne'er was given
Save to the Pure, and in their purest Hour,
Joy, effluent Countenance, is the Power
Which wedding Nature to us gives in Dower
A new Earth and new Heaven
Undreamt of by the Sensual and the Proud!
This is the sweet Voice, This the luminous Cloud,
Our hidden selves rejoice!
And thence flows all that charms or Ear or Sight,
All Melodies the echoes of that Voice,
All Colours a Suffusion from that Light!

Yes, dearest William! Yes!
There was a Time, when tho' my Path was rough,
This Joy within me dallied with Distress;
And all Misfortunes were but as the Stuff
Whence Fancy made me Dreams of Happiness:
For Hope grew round me, like the climbing Vine
And Fruits and Foliage, not my own, seem'd mine.
But now Afflictions bow me down to Earth —
Nor care I, that they rob me of my Mirth —
But O! each Visitation
Suspends what Nature gave me at my Birth,
My shaping Spirit of Imagination!

+ + + + + + + + + + × × ×!

I am so weary of this doleful Poem that I must leave off / of the other Poems I will transcribe in a Sheet by themselves. — I have been very ill — & it is well for those about me, that in these visitations of the Stomach my Disgusts combine with myself & my own Compositions — not with others & the works of others. — I received the Apple-Thwaite Writings from the Lawyer, made over to W. Wordsworth in due form, with much parchment Parade. — I have consulted Mr Edmondson — as to the safety & propriety of my going into Scotland in an open

14

SAMUEL TAYLOR COLERIDGE

Autograph manuscript of "S. T. Coleridge's Confession of Belief with respect to the true grounds of Christian morality," unsigned and undated but written ca. 1816–7. 4 pp. 228 x 185 mm. MA 1422. Purchased as the gift of Mr. De Coursey Fales.

"Does the Past live with me alone?" Coleridge entered this question in his notebook at Highgate on Christmas 1816; it suggests the isolation of a man of conservative integrity in years of "expedient" radicalism and governmental "wickedness." Writers like Hazlitt (by this time a bitter enemy) accused Coleridge of merely echoing the "'dark and rearward abyss' of thought" without recognizing that for him the past was the richest and most consequential of puzzles; in John Stuart Mill's words, "the very fact that any doctrine had been believed by thoughtful men, and received by whole nations or generations of mankind, was part of the problem to be solved. . . ." Christianity was the doctrine of most concern to Coleridge throughout his life, and in December 1816 he renewed the task of "supporting our Religion" with *The Statesman's Manual; or the Bible the Best Guide to Political Skill and Foresight*, the first of two "Lay Sermons." The intellectual center of Coleridge's conservatism—the meaning of his question about the past—is revealed in his attack in this work on the complacency of enlightenment, the intellectual pride of modernism. The Christian truths, he contends, "are considered as so true as to lose all the powers of truth, and lie bed-ridden in the dormitory of the soul, side by side, with the most despised and exploded errors." His argument suggests that in an *eruditulorum natio* ("'a nation of trivially learned people'") the old wisdom is as good as no wisdom at all. His recommendation applies to all ages: reject "this frivolous craving for novelty" and seek a "union of old and new . . . this characterizes the minds that feel the riddle of the world and may help to unravel it!"

The manuscript shown here contains Coleridge's explicit statement concerning the "true grounds of Christian morality," which he believes lie not in "feelings" but in the conviction "that all . . . intentional acts have consequences in a future state." This confession is dated 1817 in another hand but it may possibly date from late 1816, for section four, reproduced here, closely resembles a passage in *The Stateman's Manual.*

---

4. All men, the good as well as the bad, and the bad as well as the good, act with motives. But what is a motive to one person, is no motive at all to another— The pomps and vanities of the World supply mighty *motives to an ambitious man; but are so far from being a* motive *to a ~~regenerate person~~ humble Christian, that he rather wonders, ~~what~~ how they can be even a temptation to any man in his senses who believes himself to have an immortal soul. Therefore that a Title, or the power of gratifying sensual Luxury, is the motive with which A acts, and no motive at all to B. must* arise from *the different state of the moral Being in A and in B: consequently,* Motives too, *as well as* Feelings, *are* effects; *and they become causes only in a secondary or derivative sense.*

5. Among the motives of a ~~true~~ probationary Christian the practical conviction, that all ~~our~~ his intentional acts have consequences in a future state;. . .

Tho' under proper discipline they are fitted to be both aids and ornaments of Virtue. They are to Virtue what Beauty is to Health.—

4. All men, the good as well as the bad, and the bad as well as the good, act with motives. But what is a motive to one person, is no motive at all to another. The pomps and vanities of the world supply mighty motives to an ambitious man; but are so far from being a motive for a humble Christian, that he rather wonders, how they can be, even a temptation to any man in his senses who believes himself to have an immortal soul. Therefore that a Title, or the power of gratifying sensual luxury, is the motive with which A acts, and no motive at all to B. must arise from the different state of the moral Being in A and in B: consequently, motives too, as well as Feelings, are effects; and they become causes only in a secondary or derivative sense.

5. Among the motives of a probationary Christian the practical conviction, that all his intentional acts have consequences in a future state, that as he sows here, he must reap hereafter; in plain words, that according as he does or does not avail himself of the Lights and Helps given by God thro' Christ he must go either to Heaven or

Hell; is the most impressive— were it only from pity to his own soul, as an everlasting sentient Being.

6. But that this is a motive, and the most impressive of motives, to any given person, arises from and supposes, a commencing state of Regeneration in that person, of mind and heart. That, therefore, which constitutes a regenerate state, or with a view to which, is the true Principle, on which, all our Actions, Feelings, and Motives ought to be grounded.

7. The different operations of this radical Principle, (which Principle is called in Scripture sometimes Faith, and in other places Love) I have been accustomed to call good Impulses: because they are the powers, that impel us to do what we ought to do.—

8. The Impulses of a full-grown Christian are 1. Love of God — 2. Love of our Neighbor for the Love of God. 3. An undefiled Conscience, which prizes above all comprehensible advantages that Peace of God, which passeth all understanding.

15

Robert Southey
1774–1843

Autograph manuscript of "The Life of Cowper," unsigned, dated Keswick, 6 October 1835. 276 leaves. 190 x 150 mm. MA 412.

When Rest Fenner, the publisher, complained in 1816 about Coleridge's slow progress in completing the first of his promised "Lay Sermons," Coleridge responded by explaining his method of composition and concluded emphatically: "*I am not Southey.*" Without undervaluing Southey's "wider immediate utility"—a phrase that could never have been applied to himself—Coleridge was merely emphasizing the distinction (which he would not have thought of in these terms) between one of the greatest minds of all time and a remarkably competent man of letters. When contemporary critics (e.g., Byron) were not condemning Southey's bigotry or his contradictory politics, they turned upon his facility: "He had written much blank verse, and blanker prose,/ And more of both than anybody knows." But this charge against Southey's prodigious output and the implication that because it was prodigious it was also worthless is unjust; Southey was not a hack, merely a writer absorbed totally in the world of letters whose chief talent was his ability to bring his energies to bear on a wide range of subjects in a very short time. Though his verse acquired a modest reputation, his prose works, especially *The Life of Nelson* (1813, the year he accepted the poet laureateship) and *The Life of Wesley* (1820), became very popular. While working on a history of Portugal in 1802, he described to a friend the pleasure he took in research, a description that accounts for his easy productivity and Coleridge's rejection of his method: "The fact is that in compiling history much of the work is mere idleness for one who loves reading—a book and a pencil to mark your way. The mass of volumes which it is necessary to examine is enormous, but that is all easy sauntering pastime."

The Life of Cowper, the manuscript of which is shown here, was completed by Southey in October 1835 and it served as the biographical introduction for *The Works of William Cowper*, which appeared in fifteen volumes between 1835 and 1837. This edition belies Southey's underestimation of his own labors, for it was prepared with diligence and with a structure "discursive enough to comprehend much of the literary history of [Cowper's] age." The Morgan Library also owns the manuscripts of Southey's *Life of Bunyan* and *Thalaba the Destroyer.*

On the same day that he had written the Cast-away Mr Johnson laid his old favourite Vincent Bourne before him; & from time to ~~called~~ time invited in like manner his attention to many ~~a~~ Greek & Latin pieces of the minor poets. [illegible deletion] From employment of this kind he seems never to have shrunk again till utterly incapacitated by bodily weakness. [In December they removed to a much more commodious house in the same town, ~~& Cowper had not passed many weeks in this his last earthly habitation, before his feet & ancles became dropsied~~ Hayley was at the time printing his Essay on Sculptures, & in composing a note upon the work of Dædalus ~~dance~~ representing the dance of Ariadne, as described in the Iliad he ~~observed~~ perceived by ~~the remarks of a~~ a remark of D'Hancarville in his Antiquités Etrusques, Grecs et Romaines, *that both Pope & Cowper had injured the passage by mistaking the meaning of the word. He wrote therefore to Mr Johnson, hoping that Cowper would correct the error, because he quoted the lines in his book. It was immediately altered; & the improved line written by Cowper 'in a firm & delicate hand'. . . .*

On the same day that he had written the Cast-away, Mr Johnson laid his old favourite Vincent Bourne before him; ~~&~~ from letter to ~~[illegible]~~ time, invited in like manner, he attended to many a Greek & Latin piece of the minor poets. ~~[illegible]~~ From employ-ment of this kind he seems never to have shrunk again till utterly incapacitated by bodily weakness. [In December they removed to a much more commodious house in the same town, ~~[illegible]~~ ~~[illegible]~~ Hayley was at this time printing his Essay on Sculpture, & in composing a note upon the work of Daedalus ~~[illegible]~~ representing the dance of Ariadne as described in the Iliad, he ~~[illegible]~~ perceived by ~~[illegible]~~ a remark of Dr Hancarville in his Antiquités Etrusques, Grecs et Romaines, that both Pope & Cowper had injured the passage by mistaking the meaning of one word. He wrote therefore to Mr Johnson, hoping that Cowper would correct this error, because he quoted the lines in his book. It was immediately altered; & the improved lines written by Cowper 'in a firm & delicate hand' — (no doubt the same letter-by-letter writing that he after-

23 wards noticed) were enclosed to ~~[illegible]~~ Felpham by Mr Johnson. 'Words are not strong enough,' said Hayley in his reply, 'to express my delight in your kind letter, & the

Feb 1. 1800 friendly Homeric favours from our dear reviving bard. What an enchanting vignette calutes! — I wrote to the dear bard himself, because I think he must be well enough to receive a letter of genuine gratitude with some degree of pleasure. But I enclose my letter to you, that you may deliver it at the most favourable moment of the day.'

The letter, if it were delivered to Cowper ~~[illegible]~~ was not likely to raise the sick spirit. for it spoke of the long & severe sufferings, & also but utterly hopeless condition of Thomas Hayley, to whom he had been so much attached, — & who in fact died only a week after him. But it enclosed a sonnet, inscribed

To our most kind & most dear Cowper.

(Hayley's Memoirs 2. 102. the poem.)

It was happy for Hayley that he could always cheer himself with hope, even in the most hopeless circumstances. The lines which Cowper sent him ~~[illegible]~~ in this form last altered were the last he ever wrote. On the day that ~~[illegible]~~ they arrived at Felpham decided appearances of dropsy were perceived in his ancles & feet. A physician was called, & he with difficulty was induced to follow his prescriptions, & by the last week in February his weakness ~~[illegible]~~ was such that he could no longer bear the motion of a carriage; he now ceased to come down stairs; but was still able after breakfasting in bed to ~~[illegible]~~ remove into another room & remain there till evening. Before the end of March he was con-fined altogether to his chamber; but except at breakfast he sat up to his meal. Nothing could be plainer than his state of mind. Dr Lubbock, of Norwich, happening to visit a patient in an adjoining village, was requested to see him; & upon his asking him how he felt, — 'Feel!' said Cowper, 'I feel unutterable despair!'

JANE AUSTEN
1775–1817

Autograph manuscript of "Lady Susan," unsigned and undated but written ca. 1793–4 and transcribed in fair copy ca. 1805. 158 pp. 191 x 157 mm. MA 1226.

Jane Austen's juvenile productions (if such a phrase could ever do justice to her delightful early writings) gradually recede from parody and burlesque until we are left with the formal perfection and sober social comedy of her great novels. In *Volume the First*, *Volume the Second* and *Volume the Third* (her anthologies of juvenilia) she learned the art of concealment; for the satire and open hilarity of stories like "Love and Freindship" do not disappear in the later works: they are hidden under more animated, lifelike masks. *Lady Susan*, the manuscript of which is shown here, marks an extremely important stage in Austen's progressive adaptation of characters who move in a broader (and less ingenuous) world than those in the stories created primarily for the entertainment of her family. Her first such creation, Lady Susan Vernon, is a cold one by design. As Reginald De Courcy, eventually one of Lady Susan's dupes, writes before meeting her, she "possesses a degree of captivating Deceit which must be pleasing to witness & detect." As he to his folly and we to our pleasure learn, Lady Susan proudly disguises her deceit with facile language. "If I am vain of anything," she says in the passage reproduced here, "it is of my eloquence. Consideration & Esteem as surely follow command of Language, as Admiration waits on Beauty." By the end of the story, her hollowness of language has been found out, her plans fouled and the brittle structure of her eloquence replaced by a terse conclusion, which humorously suggests Jane Austen's increasing dissatisfaction with the epistolary format: "This Correspondence, by a meeting between some of the Parties & a separation between the others, could not, to the great detriment of the Post office Revenue, be continued longer."

The Morgan Library also owns the first six leaves of *The Watsons*, memoranda concerning the dates of composition of her novels and their profits, and the satirical "Plan of a Novel."

But she shall *be punished, she* shall *have him. I have sent Charles to Town to make matters up if he can, for I do not by any means want her here. If Miss Summers will not keep her, you must find me out another school, unless we can get her married immediately.—Miss S. writes word that she could not get the young Lady to assign any cause for her extraordinary conduct, which confirms me in my own private explanation of it.—*

Frederica is too shy I think, & too much in awe of me, to tell tales; but if the mildness of her Uncle should *get anything from her, I am not afraid. I trust I shall be able to make my story as good as her's.—If I am vain of anything, it is of my eloquence. Consideration & Esteem as surely follow command of Language, as Admiration waits on Beauty. And here I have opportunity enough for the exercise of my Talent, as the cheif of my time is spent in Conversation. . . .*

But she shall be punished, she shall have him.
I have sent Charles to Town to make matters up if
he can, for I do not by any means want her here.
If Miss Summers will not keep her, you must find
me out another School, unless we can get her married
immediately. — Miss S. writes word that she could
not get the young Lady to assign any cause for her
extraordinary conduct, which confirms me in my own
private explanation of it. —

Frederica is too shy I think, & too much in
awe of me, to tell tales; but if the mildness of her
Uncle should get anything from her, I am not a:
:fraid. I trust I shall be able to make my story
as good as her's. — If I am vain of anything, it is of
my eloquence. Consideration & Esteem as surely follow
command of Language, as Admiration waits on Beauty.
And here I have opportunity enough for the exercise
of my Talent, as the chief of my time is spent in

Conversation. Reginald is never easy unless we are
by ourselves, & when the weather is tolerable we pace
the shrubbery for hours together. — I like him on the
whole very well, he is clever & has a good deal to say,
but he is sometimes impertinent & troublesome. —
There is a sort of ridiculous delicacy about him which
requires the fullest explanation of whatever he may
have heard to my disadvantage, & is never satisfied
till he thinks he has ascertained the beginning & end
of everything.

This is one sort of Love — but I confess
it does not particularly recommend itself to me.
I infinitely prefer the tender & liberal Spirit of
Manwaring, which impressed with the deepest con:
viction of my merit, is satisfied that whatever I
do must be right; & look with a degree of Con:
:tempt on the inquisitive & doubting Fancies of that
Heart which seems always debating on the reason:
:ableness

17

Jane Austen

Autograph letter signed with initials, dated 21 May [1801] to her sister Cassandra. 4 pp. 232 x 188 mm. MA 977.

One who turns to the letters of Jane Austen expecting to find a familiar authorial voice and the same extended analyses of character that one finds in her novels will be disappointed. Her correspondence is almost as difficult to read through as Coleridge's, but where his unceasing allusions draw from a recondite universe of learning, hers seem to encompass an entire island populated by neighbors, friends, cousins, immediate family and persons of whom she has only heard report. The letters that have survived (about one hundred and fifty) are, like the one shown here, primarily addressed to her sister Cassandra Austen. They provide a text for which Cassandra provided a context, and we in turn are left with familial shorthand where we might have preferred the greater amplitude of a letter writer like William Cowper or Edward FitzGerald. Still, amid the briefly sketched details of dress, weather, comings goings and conversations—details engrossing in themselves—the quick humor and perspicacious eye of Jane Austen are everywhere evident. In many cases her own novels provide us with a backdrop, otherwise missing, for the letters to Cassandra. For example, the epistle shown here was written in May 1801, after the Austen family had left its home at Steventon and moved to Bath, which she portrayed in *Northanger Abbey* and *Persuasion*. It records some of her reactions to the incessant social activity in Bath ("I hate tiny parties—they force one into constant exertion") and to a walk with a Mrs. Chamberlayne, who, it seems, was a capital walker and climber of hills. "I could with difficulty keep pace with her," she writes, "yet would not flinch for the world.—On plain ground I was quite her equal—and so we posted away under a fine hot sun, *She* without any parasol or any shade to her hat, stopping for nothing, & crossing the Church Yard at Weston with as much expedition as if we were afraid of being buried alive.—After seeing what she is equal to, I cannot help feeling a regard for her."

The Morgan Library owns the largest collection of Jane Austen letters, including forty-five to Cassandra.

[Starting midway down right-hand page:] We are to have a tiny party here tonight; I hate tiny parties—they force one into constant exertion.—Miss Edwards & her father, Mrs. Busby & her nephew Mr. Maitland, & Mrs. Lillingstone are to be the whole;—and I am prevented from setting my black cap at Mr. Maitland by his having a wife & ten Children.—My Aunt has a very bad cough; do not forget to have heard about that *when you come, & I think she is deafer than ever. My Mother's cold disordered her for some days, but she seems now very well;—her resolution as to remaining here, begins to give way a little; she will not like being left behind, & will be glad to compound Matters with her enraged family.—You will be sorry to hear that Marianne Mapleton's disorder has ended fatally; she was believed out of danger on Sunday, but a sudden relapse carried her off the next day.—So affectionate a family must suffer severely: . . .*

which I believe he means to accept. — Our party at Ly Fust's
was made up of the same set of people that you have al-
-ready heard of; the Winstones, Mrs Chamberlayne, Mrs Busby,
Mrs Franklyn & Mrs Maria Somerville; yet I think it was not
quite so stupid as the two preceding parties here. — The friend-
-ship between Mrs Chamberlayne & me which you predicted
has already taken place, for we shake hands whenever
we meet. Our grand walk to Weston was again fixed for
Yesterday, & was accomplished in a very striking manner;
Every one of the party declined it under some pretence or
other except our two selves, & we had therefore a tete a tete;
but that we should equally have had after the first two
yards, had half the Inhabitants of Bath set off with us. — It
would have amused you to see our progress; — we went up
by Sion Hill, & returned across the fields; — in climbing a hill
Mrs Chamberlayne is very capital; I could with difficulty keep
pace with her — yet would not flinch for the World. — on plain
ground I was quite her equal — and so we posted away
under a fine hot sun, She without any parasol or any
shade to her hat, stopping for nothing, & crossing the Church
Yard at Weston with as much expedition as if we were
afraid of being buried alive. — After seeing what she is
equal to, I cannot help feeling a regard for her. — As to a-
-greeableness, she is much like other people. — Yesterday Even-
-ing we had a short call from two of the Miss Arnolds,
who came from Chippenham on Business; they are very civil,
and not too genteel, and upon hearing that we wanted a
House recommended one at Chippenham. This morning
we have been visitted again by Mrs & Miss Holder; they wanted
us to fix an evening for drinking tea with them, but my
Mother's still remaining cold allows her to decline every thing
of the kind. — As I had a

separate invitation however, I believe I shall go some after-
-noon. It is the fashion to think them both very detestable,
but they are so civil, & their gowns look so white & so nice
(which by the bye my Aunt thinks an absurd pretension in
this place) that I cannot utterly abhor them, especially
as Miss Holder owns that she has no taste for Music.
After they left us, I went with my Mother to help look at some
houses in New King Street, towards which she felt some kind
of inclination — but their size has now satisfied her; — they
were smaller than I expected to find them. One in particular
out of the two, was quite monstrously little; — the best of the
sittingrooms not so large as the little parlour at Steventon,
and the second room in every floor about capacious enough
to admit a very small single bed. — We are to have a
tiny party here tonight; I hate tiny parties — they force
one into constant exertion. — Miss Edwards & her
father, Mrs Busby & her nephew Mr Maitland, &
Mrs Lillingstone are to be the whole; — and I a
prevented from setting my black cap at Mr Maitlan
by his having a wife & ten Children. — My aunt has
a very bad cough; do not forget to have heard about
that when you come, & I think she is deafer than ever.
My Mother's cold disordered her for some days, but she
seems now very well; — her resolutions as to remaining
here, begins to give way a little; she will not like being
left behind, & will be glad to compound Matters with her
enraged family. — You will be sorry to hear that Marianne
Mapleton's disorder has ended fatally; she was believed
out of danger on Sunday, but a sudden relapse carried
her off the next day. — So affectionate a family must
suffer severely; & many a girl on early death has been praised
into an Angel I believe, on slighter pretensions to Beauty, Sense &

CHARLES LAMB
1775–1834

Autograph manuscript, signed "Elia," of "A Dissertation upon Roast Pig," undated but written ca. 1822. 5 pp. 370 x 247 mm. MA 966.

"In every thing that relates to *science*," wrote Charles Lamb in "The Old and the New Schoolmaster," "I am a whole Encyclopædia behind the rest of the world." The essays published under the pseudonym Elia are predicated upon Lamb's affections rather than his reason, for he steered through life not with charts and tables but by way of sympathies and antipathies, the warm and cold currents that surrounded him. Consequently, his perceptions are aesthetic; and he saved his severest pity for those to whom nothing comes "not spoiled by the sophisticating medium of moral uses." One glorious phrase from "The Old and the New Schoolmaster" sums up the appreciative imprecision of Lamb's approach to life: "I guess at Venus only by her brightness." Whether "A Dissertation upon Roast Pig" is primarily a contribution to comic or culinary literature, it certainly displays the sensory bias in Lamb's character. With the skill of a medieval divine imparting distinctions, he dissects the pleasures of "crackling" and its "adhesive Oleaginous": "O call it not fat—but an indefinable sweetness growing up to it—the tender blossoming of fat—fat cropped in the bud—taken in the shoot—in the first innocence—the cream and quintessence of the child-pig's yet pure food. . . ."

However, the most amusing portion of "A Dissertation upon Roast Pig" is the false history with which it opens. Basing his tale on an ancient Chinese manuscript (actually an idea borrowed from his friend Thomas Manning), Lamb spins out the absurd tale of Bo-bo and his father Ho-ti who accidentally discover the pleasures of roast pig when their house burns down over their sow and her litter of piglets. The section of manuscript reproduced here describes the consequences of the rather dim logic they apply to the situation: "It was observed that Ho-ti's cottage was burnt down now more frequently than ever. Nothing but fires from this time forward. . . . As often as the sow farrowed, so sure was the house of Ho-ti to be in a blaze. . . ."

This is perhaps the finest of Lamb's literary manuscripts in existence. The largest collection of his papers is in the Huntington Library, San Marino, California.

Bo-bo was strictly enjoined not to let the secret escape, for the neighbours would certainly have stoned them for a couple of abominable wretches, who could think of improving upon the good meat which God had sent them. Nevertheless strange stories got about. It was observed that Ho-ti's cottage was burnt down now more frequently than ever. Nothing but fires from this time forward. Some would break out in broad day, others in the night-time. As often as the sow farrowed, so sure was the house of Ho-ti to be in a blaze; and Ho-ti himself, which was the more remarkable, instead of ~~being angry with~~ chastising his son, seemed to grow more indulgent to him than ever. At length they were watched, the terrible mystery discovered, and father and son summoned to take their trial at Pekin, then an inconsiderable assize town. Evidence was given, the obnoxious food itself produced in Court, and verdict about to be pronounced, when the Foreman of the Jury begged that some of the burnt pig, of which the culprits stood accused, might be handed into the box. . . .

"You graceless whelp, what have you got there devouring? is it not enough that you have burnt me down three houses with your dog's tricks, and be hanged to you, but you must be eating fire, and I know not what — what have you got there, I say"?

"O father, the pig, the pig, do come and taste how nice the burnt pig eats —"

The ears of Ho-ti tingled with horror. He cursed his son, and he cursed himself that ever he should beget a son that should eat burnt pig.

Bo-bo, whose scent was wonderfully sharpened since morning, soon raked out another pig, and fairly rending it asunder, thrust the lesser half by main force into the fists of Ho-ti, still shouting out "Eat, eat, eat the burnt pig, father, only taste — O Lord" — with such-like barbarous ejaculations, cramming all the while as if he would choke.

Ho-ti trembled every joint while he grasped the abominable thing, wavering whether he should not put his son to death for an unnatural young monster, when the crackling scorching his fingers, as it had done his son's, and applying the same remedy to them, he in his turn tasted some of its flavor, which, make what sour mouths he would for a pretence, proved not altogether displeasing to him. In conclusion (for the Manuscript here is a little tedious) both father and son fairly sate down to the mess, and never left off, till they had dispatched all that remained of the litter.

Bo-bo was strictly enjoined not to let the secret escape, for the neighbours would certainly have stoned them for a couple of abominable wretches, who could think of improving upon the good meat which God had sent them. Nevertheless strange stories got about. It was observed that Ho-ti's cottage was burnt down now more frequently than ever. Nothing but fires from this time forward. Some would break out in broad day, others in the night-time. As often as the sow farrowed, so sure was the house of Ho-ti to be in a blaze; and Ho-ti himself, which was the more remarkable, instead of chastising ~~being angry with~~ his son, seemed to grow more indulgent to him than ever. At length they were watched, the terrible mystery discovered, and father and son summoned to take their trial at Pekin, then an inconsiderable assize town. Evidence was given, the obnoxious food itself produced in Court, and verdict about to be pronounced, when the Foreman of the Jury begged that some of the burnt pig, of which the culprits stood accused, might be handed into the box. He handled it, and they all handled it, & burning their fingers, as Bo-bo & his father had done before them, and Nature prompting to each of them the same remedy, against the face of all the facts, and the clearest charge which Judge had ever given, ~~again~~ to the surprise of the whole Court, townsfolk, strangers, reporters, and all present, without leaving the box, or any manner of consultation whatever, brought in a simultaneous verdict of Not Guilty.

The Judge, who was a shrewd fellow, winked at the manifest iniquity of the decision; and, when the Court was dismissed, went privily, & bought up all the pigs that could be had for love or money. In a few days his Lordship's townhouse was observed to be on fire. The thing took wing, and now there was nothing to be seen but fires in every direction. Fuel & pigs grew enormously dear all over the district. The Insurance Offices one & all shut up shop. People built slighter and slighter every day, ~~[illegible]~~ until it was feared that the very science of Architecture would in no long time be lost to the world. Thus this

19

Walter Savage Landor
1775–1864

Autograph letter unsigned, dated 20 August [1860] to Eliza Lynn Linton. 4 pp. 209 x 134 mm. MA 769.

Few of us today have ever felt like Tibby Schlegel, a character in E. M. Forster's novel *Howard's End*, for whom "the only thing that made life worth living was the thought of Walter Savage Landor" and the prospect of having parts of *Imaginary Conversations* read to him during the day. But Landor's readers throughout his long life are well represented by the fervent, learned Tibby. In 1798 the anonymous appearance of Landor's *Gebir: A Poem in Seven Books* gave rise to a small, admiring crowd of what Coleridge was obliged to call "Gebirites"; and long after Landor had earned a second and more enduring popularity with *Imaginary Conversations of Literary Men and Statesmen* (1824–9), he was sustained in his difficult late years by Robert Browning, made the object of a pilgrimage by Swinburne and addressed as "Father" by a young novelist named Eliza Lynn Linton, to whom he wrote the letter reproduced here. Landor had begun life with the greatest worldly prospects, but the intemperate energy of "forty lions concentrated into one Poet" (Dickens' phrase) destroyed both his financial and familial security, eventually reducing him to impoverished exile in Florence, where he was glad of a surrogate daughter. In his letters to Mrs. Linton (who experienced her own share of marital problems) Landor could exchange literary news and favors and, more importantly, he could openly express the paternal feelings he no longer entertained for what he called the "ungrately" members of his own family.

In this letter to Mrs. Linton (one of forty-eight in the Morgan Library) Landor discusses the literary contributions of "women of genius," including a novel by Harriet Beecher Stowe entitled *The Minister's Wooing:* "no *man* alive has given the world a novel so excellent." Today, Landor is perhaps best known as the original of Boythorn in Dickens' *Bleak House*, a novel which, despite Landor's characteristically emphatic opinion, may be more excellent than *The Minister's Wooing*.

Besides Landor's letters to Mrs. Linton, the Morgan Library also owns eighteen letters from Swinburne to Mrs. Linton, which largely concern Landor.

[Starting with line 13:] You know my estimate of your writings, and not only for their purity of style, but for their vigour of intellect. What does the author think of Madame de Stael and Mrs Stowe? The last book I have been reading I have red a second time; it is the Minister's Wooing. *It should have left off at the marriage of the young lovers—but no* man *alive has given the world a novel so excellent.—It is generally thought that the ancients were less complimentary to women of genius than the moderns. The poetry of Sappho and some others, was extolled by them. The two Odes of the tawny Lesbian are quoted [by Longinus . . . .]*

The poet wide-awake/ Kisses in former times I've seen/ Which, I confess it, rais'd my spleen./ They were contrived by Love to mock/ The battledor and shuttlecock,/ Given, return'd; how strange a play/ Where neither loses, all the day,/ And both are, even when night sets in,/ Again as ready to begin.' I am not sure I have not play'd/ This very game with some gay maid:/ Perhaps it was a dream, but this/ I know was not; I know a kiss/ Was given me in the sight of more/ Than ever saw me kist before./ Modest as winged angels are,/ And no less brave, and no less fair,/ She came across, nor greatly fear'd/ The horrid brake of wintery beard.

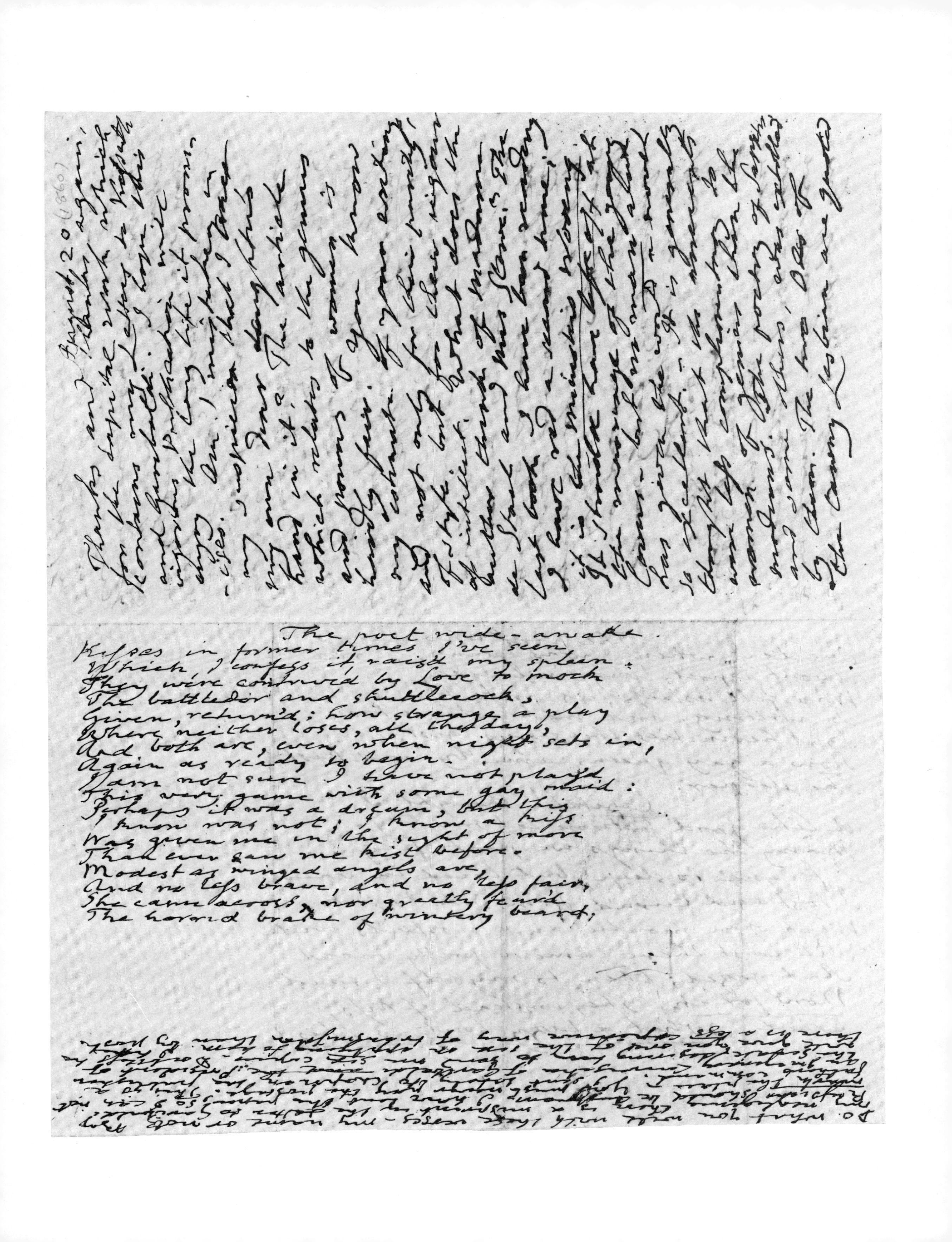

The poet wide-awake.

Kisses in former times I've seen
Which, I confess it, rais'd my spleen:
They were contrived by Love to mock
The battledor and shuttlecock.
Given, return'd; how strange a play
Where neither loses, all the day,
And both are, even when night sets in,
Again as ready to begin.
I am not sure I have not play'd
This very game with some gay maid:
Perhaps it was a dream, but this
I know was not; I know a kiss
Was given me in the sight of more
Than ever saw me kiss before.
Modest as winged angels are,
And no less brave, and no less fair,
She came across, nor greatly fear'd
The horrid brake of wintery beard;

20

Thomas Campbell
1777–1844

Autograph manuscript of "Lochiel's Warning," unsigned, dated 16 June 1802. 3 pp. 222 x 182 mm. MA 889.

From Campbell, much was expected, little received, though, as Hazlitt remarked, "after having produced two poems that have gone to the heart of a nation, and are gifts to a world, he may surely linger out the rest of his life in a dream of immortality." The two poems are *The Pleasures of Hope* (1799) and *Gertrude of Wyoming: A Pennsylvanian Tale* (1809), to which might be added another two that also went to the heart of Great Britain: "Hohenlinden" and the poem shown here, "Lochiel's Warning," both published in 1803. After the alarming burst of fame that accompanied Campbell's early years, he published little worth reading and seems to have subsided from a poet "whose youthful promise was great" (Scott's phrase) into a mere man of letters, whose time was absorbed by diverse projects, among them the founding of London University. This literary falling-off was generally attributed to what Leigh Hunt called "an extreme cautiousness in his writings," an opinion Scott confirmed when he observed in his journal that "somehow he wants audacity . . . ." Campbell, however, lacked this quality only on the written page. Writing to Francis Wrangham in 1818, Coleridge recounted the "best thing I ever heard of Campbell": at a dinner given by Longman, the publisher, Campbell had proposed a toast to Napoleon; when the rest of the guests demurred, he reiterated his toast, "BUONAPARTE—*for having shot a bookseller!*" Macaulay, who had a trenchant way of putting things, attributed this social brazenness to "morning draughts of gin and water": "For the argument, 'it is but the third hour of the day,' however forcible when used by St Peter, was by no means decisive to Tom Campbell's sobriety."

"Lochiel's Warning" concerns a fictional meeting between a wizard and Donald Cameron, known as "Gentle Lochiel," chief of the Cameron clan, who supported the young Pretender, Charles Stuart, during the Rebellion of 1745. Specifically, the wizard predicts disaster at Culloden, where the Highland forces were defeated, and the downfall of the "crested Lochiel."

The Morgan Library also owns a manuscript of "Hohenlinden" that was transcribed "at the desire of the eldest son of Campbell's dearly esteemed Allan Cunningham," and the manuscripts of his *Life of Mrs. Siddons* and his translation of *Medea*.

Down soothless insulter I trust not the tale;/ For never shall Albin a destiny meet/ So black with dishonour, so foul with retreat./ Tho her perishing ranks should be strew'd in their gore,/ Like Ocean weeds heapd on the surf-beaten shore,/ Lochiel, untainted by flight, or by chains,/ While a fragment of life in his dagger remains,/ Shall victor exult, or in death be laid low,/ With his back to the field, & his feet to the foe;/ And leaving in battle no blot on his name,/ Look proudly to Heavn from the deathbed of Fame.

Wizard

Ha laugh'st thou Lochiel my vision to scorn?
Proud bird of the mountain thy plume shall be torn!
Yon eyrie, from whence the bold eagle came forth,
With its red desolation shall beacon the north.
Heav'ns fire is around thee to blast & to burn:
Return to thy dwelling, all lonely return!
For the blackness of ashes shall mark where it stood,
And a wild mother scream o'er her famishing brood.

Lochiel.

False Wizard avaunt! I have marshall'd my clan,
Whose swords are a thousand, whose bosoms are one:
They are true to the last of their blood & their breath;
And like reapers descend to the harvest of death,
All plaided & plumed in their tartan array;
And their pipe shall the cock-crow of victory play.
Then Wizard go blind thy old wavering sight,
And darkness will cover the phantoms of fright.

Wizard.

Lochiel Lochiel! my sight I may seal;
But man cannot cover what God would reveal:
Tis the sunset of life gives me mystical lore,
And coming events cast their shadows before.
I tell thee those banners of boasted array
Desolation shall sweep with her besom away;

But where is the iron bound prisoner where?
For the red eye of battle is shut in despair.
The captive is strangled! Oh mercy dispell
Yon sight that it freezes my spirit to tell!
Life flutters convuls'd in his wavering limbs,
And his blood-streaming nostril in agony swims.
Accurs'd be the faggots that blaze at his feet,
Where his heart shall be thrown ere it ceases to beat,
With the smoke of its ashes to poison the gale—

Lochiel

Down soothless insulter I trust not the tale;
For never shall Albin a destiny meet
So black with dishonour, so foul with retreat.
Tho her perishing ranks should be strew'd in their gore,
Like Ocean weeds heap'd on the surf-beaten shore.
Lochiel, untainted by flight, or by chains,
While a fragment of life in his dagger remains,
Shall victor exult, or in death be laid low,
With his back to the field, & his feet to the foe;
And leaving in battle no blot on his name,
Look proudly to Heaven from the death bed of Fame.

June 16 – 1802 –

21

William Hazlitt
1778–1830

Autograph manuscript of "The Fight," undated but written in late December 1821. 35 pp. 335 x 209 mm. MA 190.

This manuscript begins with the words "in the instant I lose the future." In the instant, Hazlitt could also lose the past. Somewhat more than a month after the trip to Hungerford that resulted in "The Fight," Hazlitt departed for Edinburgh ("'Stony-hearted' Edinburgh!") to obtain a divorce from his wife; her tolerance of his eccentricities had begun to fade in August 1820 when Hazlitt became hopelessly infatuated with Sarah Walker ("Infelice"), his landlord's daughter. Hazlitt's excursion to the countryside in December 1821 to see the contest between the Gas-man and Bill Neate was also a flight from London and Infelice, and an attempt to participate in an instant that was compelling enough to absorb his thoughts completely. That he left London in despair is evident from this manuscript, which contains passages that were deleted before publication. The page shown here records a moment of anguished self-recognition in which Hazlitt pivots between past and present until "the clattering of a Brentford-stage" ends his reverie. Hazlitt in search of distraction proved to be Hazlitt at his journalistic best. The frenetic, self-absorbed style of the opening of "The Fight" gradually gives way to a more objective description of the event itself, in which Neate defeats the favored Gas-man. And by the time Hazlitt finds himself in London again, he is a different man: "I got out, resigned my coat and green silk handkerchief to Pigott (loth to part with these ornaments of life), and walked home in high spirits."

Hazlitt manuscripts are not common, and this is perhaps the finest example of a literary manuscript in his hand. "The Fight" was published in the *New Monthly Magazine* in 1822 under the name "Phantastes."

---

should I return to her, after what had happened? Where go to live & die far from her? Oh! thou dumb heart, lonely, sad, shut up in the prison house of this rude form, that hast never found a fellow but for an hour & in very mockery of thy misery, speak, find bleeding words to express thy thoughts, break thy dungeon-gloom, or die ~~& wither of pure scorn~~ pronouncing the name of thy ~~Infelice~~ Clarissa! I thought of the time when I was a little happy ~~thoughtless~~ careless child, of my father's house, of my early lessons, of my brother's picture of me when a boy, of all that had since happened to me & of the waste of years to come—I stopped, faultered, & was going to turn back once more to make a longer truce with wretched~~ness & patch up a hollow league with love—when~~ suddenly I heard the clattering of a Brentford-stage ~~reminded me where I was,~~ & the fight rushed full upon my ~~shifting~~ fancy. ~~I felt~~ argued (not unwisely) that even a Brentford coach-man was better company

should I return to her, after what had happened?
Where go to live & die far from her? Oh! thou
dumb heart, lonely, sad, shut up in the prison
house of this rude form, that hast never found
a fellow but for an hour & in very mockery
of thy misery, speak, find bleeding words to
express thy thoughts, break thy dungeon-gloom,
or die pronouncing the name of thy Clarissa ~~& writer of pure [illegible]~~! I thought of the
time when I was a little happy careless ~~thoughtless~~ child,
of my father's house, of my early lessons, of my
brother's picture of me when a boy, of all that
had since happened to me & of the waste of years to
come — I stopped, faultered, & was going
to turn back once more to make a longer truce
with wretched~~ness & patch up a hollow league~~
~~with love — when~~ suddenly I heard the clattering of
a Brentford-stage ~~reminded me where I was~~,
& the sight rushed full upon my ~~shifting~~
fancy. I argued (not unwisely) that even
a Brentford coachman was better company

22

John Galt
1779–1839

Autograph letter signed, dated Greenock, 25 January 1836, to Richard Bentley. 2 pp. 261 x 207 mm.

The publication of literature expanded enormously in the first quarter of the nineteenth century, and if ever there were a publishing boom town, it was Edinburgh. The extraordinary conjunction of the *Edinburgh Review* and *Blackwood's Edinburgh Magazine* (familiarly known as "Maga"), as well as the activity of their owners in book publishing, created a local literary scene of almost unrivaled vigor. This unceasing production could be sustained only through the efforts of the human dynamos who propelled the Anglo-Scots literary machine, and among them John Galt. Today, his energy seems almost unbelievable. Between 1820, when he established his pace, and 1826, when he departed for Canada, twenty-one books by Galt appeared, ranging in significance from *All the Voyages Round the World* (by "Samuel Prior") to his masterpieces, the only serious challenges to Sir Walter Scott's dominance in the field of Scottish fiction, *The Ayrshire Legatees* (1821), *Annals of the Parish* (1821), *The Provost* (1822) and *The Entail* (1823). It was not uncommon for him to be immersed in three novels simultaneously while writing articles and sketches for Maga. But for Galt, literature was only of secondary importance; throughout his life he was also a devoted man of affairs for whom, unfortunately, venture after venture collapsed. From 1826 to 1829 he served as secretary of the Canada Company, organizing settlements in what was then "Upper Canada" and is now Ontario. In spite of his popularity with the Canadians, the Company dismissed him in 1829, and he returned to England impoverished.

Galt's immediate solution to this problem was to resume his feverish rate of publication, and he had soon added to his list *Lawrie Todd*, a potboiler based on his Canadian experiences, a life of Lord Byron, whom he had known in his younger days, two autobiographical works and two fine novels, among the first in Great Britain to deal with political themes, *The Member* (1832) and *The Radical* (1832). The letter shown here was written, characteristically, in the heat of negotiations with the publisher Bentley, for whom Galt had written some of his worst novels. Apparently, Bentley was a second choice, for Galt had offered his work on William Paterson to William Tait, who declined it, three weeks earlier. The paralysis Galt mentions afflicted him for the last five years of his life.

Most of Galt's surviving manuscripts and letters are in the National Library of Scotland, Edinburgh.

Greenock 25 Jan^y/36 Dear Sir My anomalous disease having again subsided with however the entire loss of the power of my feet, I have begun to look after literary matters and I wish to know how you are disposed as to the four novels you published. I think of an edition of each in one volume similar to yours of Lawrie Todd.

The separation of Cochrane Co sets me free as to my autobiography. I intend to suppress the appendix and to make the two vols into one as a companion to Byron, a second edition has long been wanted. . . .

Greenock 25 Jany/36

Dear Sir

My anomalous disease having again subsided with however the entire loss of the power of my foot, I have begun to look after literary matters and I wish to know how you are disposed as to the four novels you published. I think of an edition of each in one volume similar to yours of Lawrie Todd.

The separation of Cochrane & Co sets me free as to my autobiography. I intend to suppress the appendix and to make the two vols into one as a companion to Byron. A second edition has long been wanted.

I have recently arranged a small work under 200 pages which I undertook above a dozen of years ago for Constable & Co. It is "some account of William Paterson the founder of the banks of England & Scotland and the projector of the Darien colony" &c. It is very curious and a work of research. C: expected I would have found materials for two vols. &

ones

23

Thomas Moore
1779–1852

Autograph manuscript of "Lalla Rookh" (second version), unsigned and undated, but written ca. 1815. 187 leaves. 198 x 158 mm. MA 310.

Whether the East be Abyssinia, India or the Levant, the Orient has entranced the British for centuries. Its strangenesses are at once immense and intimate, and into them the Englishman enters as a man of imperial destiny—like Burton, Kipling and Lawrence—or seeks in their image a reservoir of fantasy at home—like Coleridge, FitzGerald and, one must add, Thomas Moore in *Lalla Rookh.* Because he was an Irishman, the East was England for Moore at birth, and with the proverbial Irish gift of song he quickly opened the doors of England's finest society, including those of Donington Hall (the seat of Lord Moira) and Holland House. The success of *Irish Melodies* (published in a series of parts beginning in 1808) and *Intercepted Letters; or, The Two-Penny Post Bag* (1813) was such that by 1815 he had become the accepted Whig rival to Scott and Byron. Based on a subject proposed by Samuel Rogers, *Lalla Rookh* was intended "to be the length of Rokeby, measured out upon the counter in Paternoster Row" and to compete in Oriental setting with *The Giaour* and *The Bride of Abydos.* In almost every way, *Lalla Rookh* succeeded, except in retaining the interest of posterity. Moore was a good judge of the relative merits of his works; quite rightly, he felt that in a race for the future "those little ponies, the 'Melodies,' will beat the mare, Lalla, hollow." *Lalla Rookh* remains one of those poems, as its eponymous heroine says of poets like Moore, "whose sweetness of the moment we ought gratefully to inhale, without calling upon them for a brightness and a durability beyond their nature."

Like so many Oriental tales, *Lalla Rookh* consists of a series of stories told within a larger framework of action, in this case the royal progress of Lalla Rookh, accompanied by the pedantic Fadladeen, and a young poet of Cashmere, who turns out to be the Prince to whom she is betrothed. The Morgan Library owns three manuscript versions of *Lalla Rookh;* shown here from the intermediate version is the beginning of the tale, "The Fire-Worshippers," which the poet Feramorz calls "a melancholy story, connected with the events of one of those brave struggles of the Fire-worshippers of Persia against their Arab masters . . . ."

The Morgan Library also houses the corrected proof sheets for *Lalla Rookh,* Moore's commonplace book and a group of juvenile poems written by Moore in a notebook he kept during the early 1790s.

The Fire-worshipper./ Tis moonlight ~~upon~~ over Oman's sky,/ Her isles of pearl look lovelily./ Tis moonlight ~~on~~ in Harmozia's† walls,/ And thro her Emir's porphyry halls—*/ ~~But no~~ All hush'd—there's not a breath in motion—/ The shore is silent as the ocean./ If zephyrs come, so light they come,/ Nor leaf is stirr'd, nor wave is driven,/ The wind-tower on the Emir's dome/ Stands breathless in ~~the clear a~~ the dark blue heaven!/ Can hardly win a breeze from heaven.*

Even he, that ~~haughty~~ tyrant Arab, sleeps,/ ~~Untroubled on his silken princely bed/~~ . . .*

'Tis moonlight over Oman's sea,
Her banks of pearl & palmy isles
Bask in the night-beam beauteously
[illegible]
And her blue waters sleep in smiles.

* The Persian gulf, sometimes so called.

† The present Gombaroon

* Where, some hours since, was heard the swell
Of martial trump & clash of bell
Bidding the beauteous sun farewell—
The peaceful sun, whom better suits
The music of the bulbul's nest,
Or the light touch of lovers' lutes
To sing him to his golden rest!

"At Gombaroon and other places in Persia they have towers for the purpose of catching the wind & cooling the houses." Le Bruyn — These wind-towers, he says, are very ornamental to the City.

"Many of the houses at Bushire have a bad-geer (literally a wind-catcher) or spire, of a square form, open at each side, which, acting as a funnel, cools the interior of the house, and admits the wind from whatever quarter it may blow." Kinneir's Memoir of the Persian Empire.

* "Iran is the true general name for the Empire of Persia."
Asiat. Research. Disc. 5.

Even he — that tyrant Arab — sleeps
Calm, while a nation round him weeps.
~~Calm, while the curse of [illegible]~~
That writhe beneath his fierce control
[illegible] like [illegible] his breath
And lightnings from unnumbered skies
Are waiting to avenge the shame

The Fire-worshipper.

—

'Tis moonlight over Oman's sea*
Her isles of pearl look lovelily.
'Tis moonlight in Harmozia's† walls,
And thro' her Emir's porphyry halls—
All hushed — there's not a breath in motion—
The shore is silent as the ocean.
If zephyrs come, so light they come,
Nor leaf is stirr'd, nor wave is driven;
The wind-tower on the Emir's dome
Can hardly win a breeze from heaven.
Stands breathless in the [illegible] blue heaven!

Even he, that tyrant Arab, sleeps, *
~~Untroubled, on his silken bed~~
Calm while a nation round him weeps
Calm mid the tears that Iran* weeps,
Calm mid the curses that she heaps
Each hour upon his ruthless head.

And wherefore not? Heaven send no worse
To [illegible] than a Guebre's curse,
And music has no [illegible] tone
Delights him like a Guebre's groan!

CHARLES ROBERT MATURIN
1780–1824

Autograph letter signed, dated 15 July 1801, to William Conyngham Plunket. 2 pp. 225 x 183 mm. MA 2640.

In his first letter to Walter Scott, written in 1812, Maturin described himself as "an obscure Irishman." This is exactly what he remains today, in spite of the natural, if limited, interest that attaches to the author of *Melmoth the Wanderer* (1820): an eccentric Dublin clergyman whose first (and only successful) play, *Bertram, or The Castle of St. Aldobrand* (1816), was sponsored by Scott and Byron and attacked by Coleridge in the twenty-third chapter of *Biographia Literaria*. Maturin's character seems to have embodied some of the qualities of the Gothic novel, of which *Melmoth* is an example, at least so far as the principles of literary composition were concerned. When he first saw the printed acting text of *Bertram*, which had enjoyed a remarkable twenty-two-night run at Drury Lane, he informed Scott that it had been "*un-Maturined*," and then attacked "whatever tends to Efface the radical distinctions of intellectual character, and reduce all the wild and wayward shoots of Mind, stubbed, unsightly and grotesque as they may be, to one smooth-shaven Level, by the ponderous operation of the Critical Roller." Unfortunately, "the wild and wayward shoots of Mind" in Maturin were not restrained by any innate artistic sensibility, and his writings represent the defeat of form by fancy, leading Byron to remark, "he has talent—but not much taste. . . ." Maturin himself realized that he was limited to a single literary effect, not much indebted for its success to taste: "I wish they would let me do what I am good for, sit down by my magic Cauldron, mix my dark ingredients, see the bubbles work, and the spirits rise. . . ."

This letter to the Irish politician William Conyngham Plunket, later lord-chancellor of Ireland and first Baron Plunket, was written just after Maturin had received his B.A. from Trinity College, Dublin. In it he apparently declines the task of canvassing political support for Plunket among his friends. The admiration he expresses for Plunket, one of the most important Irish champions of Catholic emancipation, provides an early indication of Maturin's strong interest in the political fate of Ireland. He also clearly states his dedication "to the sacred profession."

Maturin's letters to Scott are in the Library of the University of Texas, Austin, and the manuscript of *Bertram*, which Maturin presented to Scott, is in the library at Abbotsford, Scott's home.

It is wholly discrepant from my profession and pursuits, to assume the tumultuous Activity of one who wishes to render his services important or beneficial to a political friend. On me, Sir, your statement has powerfully operated, it has placed the Advantages of your Cause in a stronger light, it has obviated some Objections that had been suggested against it; and I avow, with pleasure, my Decision, in favor of one of those valued few, whose great, but unsuccessful efforts I have ever beheld with Applause and veneration. I regret, Sir, that my habits and pursuits prevent me from rendering more important services, or a more valuable attestation to your merit, than the offer of a Solitary Suffrage I am Sir &c C Maturin

It is wholly discrepant from my profession and pursuits, to assume the tumultuous Activity of one who wishes to render his services important or beneficial to a political friend – on me, Sir, your statement has powerfully operated, it has placed the Advantages of your Cause in a stronger light, it has obviated some Objections that had been suggested against it; and I avow, with pleasure, my Decision, in favor of one of those valued few, whose great, but unsuccessful efforts I have ever beheld with Applause and veneration – I regret, Sir, that my habits and pursuits prevent me from rendering more important services, or a more valuable attestation to your merits, than the offer of a Solitary Suffrage

I am, Sir &c

G Stuart

25

Leigh Hunt
1784–1859

Autograph manuscript of "The Palfrey," signed and dated Kensington, 6 April 1842. 47 pp. 228 x 178 mm. MA 198.

There have been greater critics than Leigh Hunt, men more scholarly in their love of literature, but few were ever steeped in poetry to the extent that he was. For all his saturation in verse, there is nothing musty about Hunt: he recognized with almost unerring taste the best and most durable of contemporary poets and he rescued his favorites from the past without falling into mere antiquarianism. Literature was the element in which Hunt lived: "I read incessantly when I am not writing, or when I have no companion. I read at breakfast, I read in my walks, I read at dinner, after dinner, after tea, after supper. I stick my book up against the loaf, or a salad-bowl, by my plate." In an essay called "Men and Books," published in 1833, Hunt remarked that below the greatest poets and novelists, he liked "those who are poets only because the others were—or at all events, principally so—poets by the grace of books." Hunt himself was a poet by the grace of books, and typically *The Palfrey* is at once a poem and an act of criticism.

In his preface Hunt recommends *The Palfrey* to readers as a sample of the "first spring blossoms of French and British genius, called *Lais* and *Fabliaux*." His enthusiasm for this ancient "light narrative poetry" depends partly on the effect he feels a wider acquaintance with it might have on English poetry: it might boost the "animal spirits" of English verse. *The Palfrey* abounds in animal spirits, and Hunt's carefree lines are the perfect, if undistinguished, conveyance for the delight he takes in his tale. The passage shown here reveals Hunt "running riot upon a rhyme of my own for several verses together," impugning the ardor of old men for young women.

The largest single group of Hunt manuscripts is in the Brewer Collection at the State University of Iowa, Iowa City.

Ah! pray let him think there are old girls too,/ Whose hearts would give his quite enough to do;/ Though in sooth grey-beards have *been, like Jove's of old,/ That have met a young lip, nor been thought too bold./ In Norfolk a wondrous old lord may be seen,/ Who at eighty was not more than forty, I ween;/ And I myself know a hale elderly man,/ In face & in frolic a very god Pan./ But marvels like these are full rare, I wis;/ And when elders in general young ladies would kiss,/ I exhort the dear souls to fight & to flee,/ Unless they by chance should run against me. . . .*

Ah! pray let him think there are old girls too,
Whose hearts would give his quite enough to do;
Though in sooth greybeards have been, like Jove's of old,
That have met a young lip, nor been thought too bold.
In Norfolk a wondrous old lord may be seen,
Who at eighty was not more than forty, I ween;
And I myself know a hale elderly man,
In face & in frolic a very god Pan.
But marvels like these are full rare, I wis;
And when elders in general young ladies would kiss,
I exhort the dear souls to fight & to flee,
Unless they by chance should run against me.

Alas! I delay as long as I can,
For who may find words for thy grief, sweet Anne?
'Tis hard when young heart, singing songs of tomorrow,
Is suddenly met by the old hag Sorrow.

THOMAS DE QUINCEY
1785–1859

Autograph manuscript of a portion of "Lake Reminiscences," undated but probably written in 1839. 2 pp. 227 x 181 mm. MA 903.

Among the few who initially understood the premises of his verse, Wordsworth inspired a devotion that was usually curbed only by meeting him in the flesh. Thomas De Quincey claimed to be one of the first to venerate the Lake poet, and, during the year of desolation in Wales and London that followed his flight from Manchester Grammar School in 1802, the thought of Wordsworth residing in the north of England was like a polestar. In a diary kept by De Quincey in the spring and early summer of 1803 he remarked that his leading mental trait was "*Facility of impression*. My hopes and fears are alternately raised and quelled by the minutest—the most trivial circumstances—by the slightest words." His consternation over the prospect of meeting the great Wordsworth may be imagined. Though he wrote to him, received kind letters in return, and twice walked to within a few miles of Grasmere, it was not until 1807, when Mrs. Coleridge and her children needed an escort to the Lake country, that the two men finally met. The rather unattractive manuscript shown here, the opening section of De Quincey's article on Wordsworth and Southey in *Tait's Magazine* for July 1839, records his anxiety upon being introduced to "this ideal creature."

De Quincey became an intimate of the Wordsworth family, was particularly beloved of Dorothy, and was crushed by the death of three-year-old Catherine Wordsworth. But his indiscreet relations with Margaret Parker, whom he married in 1817, and his increasingly evident dependence on opium severely strained a relationship which had for its foundation De Quincey's idealistic admiration of Wordsworth and Wordsworth's sublime condescension to be so admired. When, in 1839, De Quincey began to write his "Lake Reminiscences," he grievously offended the poet and his admirers by portraying Wordsworth in postures unbecoming to the absurd gravity of a national institution. This was not done in malice, so much as in tactless fascination with all that concerned Wordsworth. Only De Quincey could depict the skater of *The Prelude*, "the poet of the 'Excursion' sprawled upon the ice like a cow dancing a cotillon."

This part which follows below ~~and which~~ I will call Otho *to distinguish it from a certain other part already sent which I shall call ~~Galbo~~* Galba, *and a certain other part (also sent) which I shall call* Vitellius. — *Now the case is this: that whole part which contains the biography of Wordsworth is* Vitellius; *and it follows, from the known order of succession G.O.V. that it is to come in at a point to be hereafter indicated: and this present part Otho ought to follow in immediate succession to* Galba *which is the part describing my first arrival in company with M^r. Coleridge at W's cottage in 1807 the reason for this change of arrangement will appear afterwards. Otho p. 1 30 lines . . .*

This part which follows below I will call <u>Otho</u> to distinguish it from a certain other part already sent which I shall call <u>Galba</u>, and a certain other part (also sent) which I shall call <u>Vitellius</u>. — — Now the case is this: that whole part which contains the biography of Wordsworth, is <u>Vitellius</u>, and it follows, from the known order of succession G. O. V. that it is to come in at a point to be hereafter indicated: and this present part Otho ought to follow in immediate succession to Galba which is the part describing my first arrival in company with Mrs. Coleridge at W's cottage in 1807. The reason for this change of arrangement will appear afterwards.

<u>Otho p. 1</u>

30 lines

That night, the first of my personal intercourse with Wordsworth — the first in which I saw him face to face, was — it is little indeed to say — memorable: it was marked by a change even in the physical condition of my nervous system. Long disappointment, hope for ... baffled [and why should it be less painful because <u>self</u>-baffled?], vexation and self-blame, almost self-contempt, at my own want of courage to face the man whom of all since the Flood I most yearned to behold, — these feelings had impressed upon my nervous sensibilities a character of irritation — agitation — restlessness — eternal self-dissatisfaction which was gradually gathering into a distinct well-defined type that would, but for youth — almighty youth and the spirit of youth, have shaped itself into some nervous complaint wearing symptoms <u>sui generis</u> [for most nervous complaints in minds that are at all eccentric will be <u>sui generis</u>], and perhaps finally have been immortalised in some medical journal as the anomalous malady of an interesting young gentleman aged 22 who was supposed to have studied too severely and to have perplexed his brain with German metaphysics. To this result things tended — but in one hour all passed away. It was gone — never to return: the spiritual being whom I had anticipated, for whom I believed

"My fancy form'd him of th' angelic kind
Some emanation of th' all beauteous mind"

this ideal creature had "at length been seen; seen "in the flesh"; seen with fleshly eyes; and now, though he did not cease for years to wear something of the glory and the <u>aureola</u> which in Popish legends invests the head of superhuman beings, yet it was not longer as a being to be feared — it was as Raphael, the "affable" angel who conversed on the terms of man with man, that I now regarded him.

It was 4 o'clock perhaps when we arrived: at that hour the day-light soon declined; and in an hour and a half we were all collected about the tea-table. This with the Wordsworths, under the simple rustic system of habits which they cherished then and for twenty years after was the most delightful meal in the day; just as dinner is in great cities; and for the same reason; because it was prolonged into a meal of leisure and conversation. The reason why any meal favors and encourages conversation is pretty much the same as that which accounts for the breaking down of so many lawyers and generally their ill-success in the House of Commons. In the courts of law, when a man is haranguing upon general and abstract topics, if at any moment he feels getting beyond his depth, if he finds his anchor driving, he can always bring up and drop his anchor anew upon the <u>terra firma</u> of his case; the facts of this, as furnished by his brief, always assure him of a retreat as soon as he finds his more general thoughts failing him: and the consciousness of this retreat by inspiring confidence, makes it much less probable that they <u>should</u> fail. But in Parliament, where the advantage of a case with its facts and circumstances or the details of a statistical report does not offer itself once in a dozen times

27

Thomas Love Peacock
1785–1866

Autograph corrections and additions in an interleaved copy of "The Genius of the Thames" (London: Thomas and Edward Hookham, 1810). PML 16430.

Before he discovered his true genius as a satirical novelist in *Headlong Hall* (1816), *Nightmare Abbey* (1818) and *Crotchet Castle* (1831), Peacock made "slow approaches" to the "Temple of Fame" via rather indifferent verse that reflected the manner of a previous generation. His poems, though not generally admired, found at least one enthusiastic reader, Percy Bysshe Shelley, who, at the age of twenty, thought *The Genius of the Thames* "to be far beyond mediocrity in genius & versification, & the conclusion of 'Palmyra' the finest piece of poetry I ever read." (*Palmyra* originally appeared in 1806 and was reprinted in a revised edition with *The Genius of the Thames*, also revised, in 1812, the year in which Shelley met the author of these poems.) This grossly inflated estimate did not survive Shelley's acquaintance with Peacock, whom he liked as a man (and as a novelist) but who represented all that was conventional as a poet; in 1819, he contemptuously observed that Peacock was a "nursling of the exact & superficial school in poetry," a characterization worthy of Peacock's sarcastic tongue. In fact, the satirist was always uppermost in Peacock; the only kind of seriousness he could make successful was the kind associated with satire, and the only poems he could sell were the brilliant lyrics and parodies in his novels. Even the soberest themes afforded material for his satiric turn of mind, as he discovered without any apparent sense of contradiction in 1809. While still exploring the course of the river he celebrates in the poem shown here, he wrote to his friend and publisher, Edward Hookham, and concluded that "the Thames is as good a subject for satire as for panegyric."

But *The Genius of the Thames* is panegyric, after all, in a mode that owes more to Goldsmith and Cowper than to anyone still living in 1810. The passage shown here is part of what Peacock called his "Eulogium of the Thames," which includes, in true eighteenth-century fashion, a vision of ships from every country gathered "Beneath Britannia's milder sky,/ Where roves, oh Thames! the patriot's eye/ O'er thy refulgent tide."

The cot with woodbine wreathed around/ ~~The bank with reeds and flag flowers wave crowned/~~ The fields with waving corn embrowned/ ~~The lonely oak, that braves the northern breeze/ The spire, half veiled in tufted tree/ The busy town the cultured hill/ The sheltered cot, the restless mill/~~ The lonely oak's expansive pride/ The ~~tower~~ spire through ~~many~~ ancient trees descried/ ~~The sculptured and~~ [illegible deletion] ~~tide/~~ The fall that turns the frequent ~~hills~~ mill/ The seat that crowns the woodland hill/ The fisher's willow-mantled home/ The ~~gliding sail,~~ sculptured and the regal dome/ The classic temple flower-entwined/ ~~That church that ancient trees embower/ The fisher's hat the regal tower~~

The oak, in lonely grandeur free,
~~Lord of the forest and the sea;~~
~~The spreading plain~~ The village-spire, the cultured hill,
The ~~tranquil~~ shaded cot, the restless mill,
~~The lonely hamlet, calm and still;~~ Sheltered
~~The village-spire, the busy town,~~
~~The shelving bank, the rising down,~~
The fisher's boat, the peasant's home,
The woodland seat, the regal dome,
In quick succession ~~rise, to~~ charm the mind
The mind ~~with virtuous feelings warm~~,
Till, where thy widening current glides
To mingle with the turbid tides,
Thy spacious breast displays unfurled
The ensigns of the assembled world,

The cot with woodbine wreathed around
The ~~bank with weeds and flag-flowers wave~~ crowned
The fields with waving corn embrowned

~~The oak, that braves the northern breeze~~ lonely
~~The spire, half veiled in tufted trees~~
~~The busy town, the cultured hill~~
~~The sheltered cot, the restless mill~~
The lonely oak's expansive pride
The ~~tower~~ spire through ~~many~~ ancient trees descried
~~[illegible]~~
The fall that turns the frequent ~~hills~~ mills
The seat that crowns the woodland hill
The fisher's willow-mantled home
The ~~[illegible]~~ sculptured arch, the regal dome
The classic temple flower-entwined
~~That church that ancient trees embower~~
~~The fisher's hut the regal tower~~

28

Mary Russell Mitford
1787–1855

Autograph manuscript of "Country Excursions" from "Belford Regis," undated but written ca. 1833–4. 16 pp. 243 x 199 mm. MA 2346.

Somewhere between the Bath of Jane Austen and the Cranford of Mrs. Gaskell lies Mary Russell Mitford's Belford Regis (based on the town of Reading): "an honest English borough, fifty good miles from 'the deep, deep sea,' and happily free from the slightest suspicion of any spa, chalybeate or saline." Small towns have a quality all their own, for their very smallness makes the intensity of human ambitions and emotions seem that much greater. By nature, Mary Mitford was perfectly suited to gauge the life of villages and market towns, as she did in *Our Village* and *Belford Regis*. She took a keen interest in all forms and levels of society and all the possible strivings of men and women; she also preferred to know Reading intimately rather than London casually. Moreover, she was a "bold talker." All her friends (and they included such strange companions as B. R. Haydon, Elizabeth Barrett Browning and Ruskin) praised her conversation, and the serene virtues and acerbic pleasures of *Belford Regis* come directly from her conversational style. Like *Our Village*, *Belford Regis* is a series of stories linked mainly by locale and the winning personality of Mary Mitford. The tales often commence with the egotistical preliminaries natural to a born storyteller, and the segue into the story proper is usually as adroit as it is witty. In the passage shown here (from the tale called "Country Excursions"), Miss Mitford diverges from her account of the planning of a country excursion into a description of her own love of water parties. This wandering from the point leads, in fact, to the moral of her story: "Nobody not very sure of being picked up, should ever put herself in danger of falling overboard."

The Morgan Library owns all that appears to have survived of the manuscript of *Belford Regis*. A large collection of Mary Mitford's letters is in the Huntington Library; Elizabeth Barrett Browning's letters to her are in the library of Wellesley College.

[On recto page:] Par^{h} And perhaps the ~~damsels~~ ladies of B. were the wiser of the two. Far be it from me to depreciate ~~water~~ the water! [illegible deletion] writing as I am at ~~two~~ four oclock P. M. on the twenty sixth of this hot sunny drowthy August 1833, in my own little garden which has already emptied two ponds & is likely to empty the brook, my garden the working of which takes up ~~all~~ half the time of three people, & which although watered twice a day does yet poor thing look thirsty, & for my garden prematurely shabby & old, & who dearly as I love ~~my~~ that Paradise of flowers, have yet under the influence of the drought ~~been longing all day~~ & the heat & the glare of the sunshine, been longing all day to be lying under the great oak by the pool, at our own old place, looking through the green green leaves at the blue blue sky, & listening to the cattle as they plashed in the water; or better still to be in M^{r}. Dowsons little boat, that boat which is the very model of shape & make, rowed by that boatman of boatmen & companion of companions, & friend of friends, up his own Loddon river from [illegible deletion] the Fishing House at Arborfield, his own beautiful [illegible deletion] Arborfield ~~through~~ under the turfy terraces & majestic Avenues of the Park, & through the world of of still peaceful secluded water meadows where even the shy kingfisher who retires before cultivation & population with the instinct of the red Indian is not afraid to make her nest, untill we approach as nearly as in [illegible deletion] rowing we can approach to the main spring head...*

even the equally pitiable official personages of the old dramatist, they were not literally caged birds, & this was not London, on the contrary most of them had little slips of garden ground dusty & smoky where currants & gooseberries came to nothing & china roses would not blow; & many of them lived on the outskirts of the town & might have walked country-ward if they would; but they were bound by the minute & strong chains of habit & could turn no other way than to the street, the dull dark town [illegible]. Their feet had been so used to the pavement that they had lost all relish for the elastic tread of the greensward. Over the roadside paths were too soft for them, [illegible] flagstones for them, & turf although smooth & fine & thick & springy as a Persian carpet, although fragrant & aromatic as a bed of thyme — turf for those who liked it!

Two or three times in the year however even these street loving ladies were visited with a desire to taste a fresh air & become damsels & damsels errant for the day. The great river that glided so magnificently under the ridge of the C. hills within a mile of the town seemed to offer irresistible temptations to a water party; the more so as some of very fine parts of river scenery were within reach, & the whole course of the stream, whether sweeping grandly along its own rich meadows, or shut in by steep woody banks, was marked with great & varied beauty. But somehow or other a water party was too much for them. The river was navigable & in that strange & almost startling process of being raised or shaken in the locks there was a real or an apparent danger that would have discomposed their nerves & their dignity. — Ladies of a certain age should not squeal if they can help it, & the spinsters of [illegible] had an instinctive perception of the truth of this axiom, & although Mr. Singleton who liked the diversion of gudgeon fishing (the only fishing as far as I can perceive which requires neither trouble nor patience nor skill, & in which if you put the line in

you are pretty sure within a few minutes to pull a fish out) although Mr. Singleton who liked this quiet sport often tried to tempt his female friends into a sober water frolic he never could succeed. Water parties were reserved for the families of the neighbourhood.

And perhaps the ladies of [illegible] were the wiser of the two. For be it from me to depreciate the water! Far be it from me writing at four o'clock A. M. on the twenty sixth of this hot August drought August 1833, in my own little garden which has already emptied two ponds & is likely to empty the brook, my garden the watering of which takes up the time of three people, & which although watered twice a day does yet look thirsty, & for my garden prematurely shabby & old* & who dearly as I love that paradise of flowers, have yet under the influence of the drought & the heat & the glare of the sunshine been longing all day to be lying under the great oak by the pool, at our own old place looking through the green green leaves at the blue blue sky & listening to the cattle as they plashed in the water; or better still to be in Mr. Dowson's little boat, that boat which is the very model of shape & make, rowed by that boatman of boatmen & companion of companions, & friend of friends, up his own Loddon river from [illegible] the Fisher House at Arborfield, his own beautiful Arborfield under the tufty bowers & majestic avenues of the Park & through the wild of the secluded water meadows where even the shy kingfisher who retires before cultivation & population with the instinct of the red Indian is not afraid to make her nest, while we approach as nearly as we can in our rowing to the main spring head (for like the Nile the Loddon has many sources) of that dark clear & brimming river;

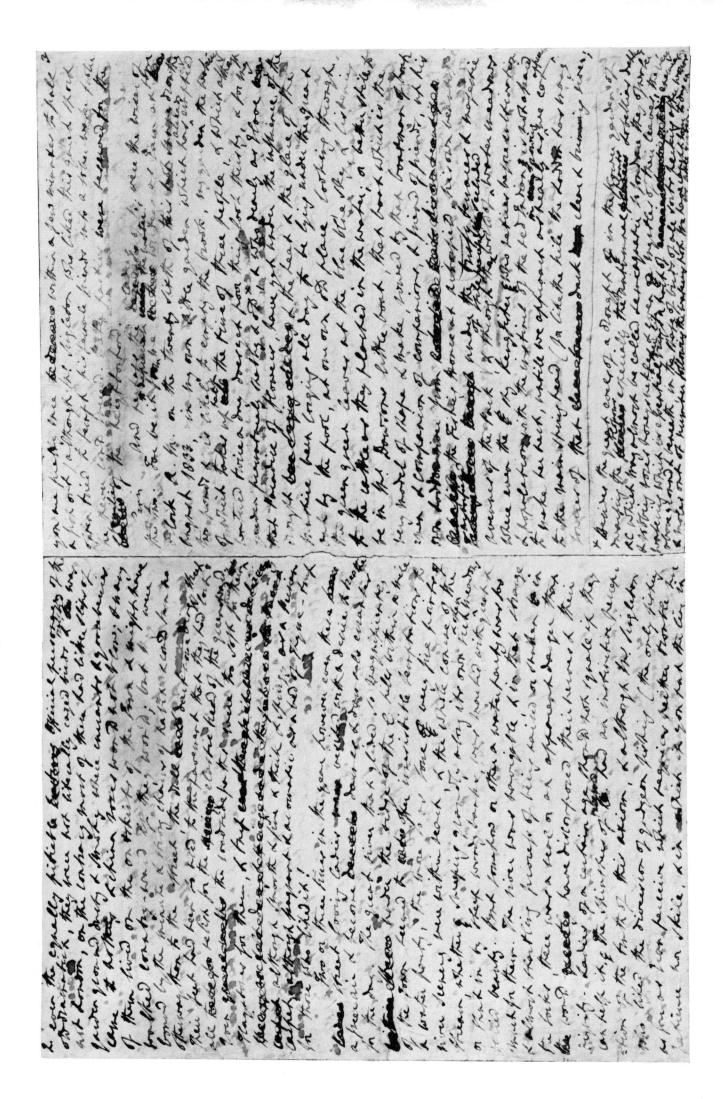

* Besides the great evils of a drought in the flower garden of dwarfing the blossoms especially the autumnal plants Lobelias dahlias &c which may almost be called semi-aquatic in fondness, they spoil [illegible] & robbing roses honeysuckles & even [illegible] the greenness of their leaves, the watering which is essential brings a host of [illegible] enemies above ground & beneath in the shape of birds of all sorts pecking after worms & moles out of number following the watering pot. We have caught [illegible] in our little garden.

George Gordon Noel Byron, Sixth Baron Byron
1788–1824

Autograph manuscript of "The Corsair," unsigned, dated 18 December 1813. 94 pp. 253 x 200 mm. MA 65.

Byron's claims for *The Corsair* were mainly numerical in nature: ten days to write it and ten thousand copies sold on the day of publication. He considered the meaning of numbers like these to be "a most humiliating confession, as it proves my own want of judgement in publishing, and the public's in reading things, which cannot have stamina for permanent attention." It was sufficient, he told Shelley, that *The Corsair* (like its predecessors *The Giaour* and *The Bride of Abydos* [both 1813]) had enough stamina to "shine, and in *boudoirs*." What has prevented *The Corsair* from remaining a work exclusively of the Regency boudoir, from surviving only in a comment like Jane Austen's—"I have read the Corsair, mended my petticoat, & have nothing else to do"—is the fact that Byron, writing quickly, "*con amore*, and much from *existence*," managed to strike off an arresting combination of an adventure tale about pirates—tinged with the novelty of Byronic alienation—a tragic love story and, like *Childe Harold's Pilgrimage*, a descriptive poem rich with his love of the Mediterranean and Aegean seas:

> Who that beheld that Sun upon thee set,
> Fair Athens! could thine evening face forget?
> Not he—whose heart nor time nor distance frees,
> Spell-bound within the clustering Cyclades!

Shown here is a passage from Canto I of *The Corsair*, section IX and part of section X. As is apparent from the directions at the top of the page on which it was written, section X was sent to the publisher, John Murray, after the rest of the poem. Quite clearly, this section was intended to add a third dimension to the character of Conrad, the Corsair, enabling the reader to interpret the subtle betrayals of deep emotion that pass over the countenance and figure of one who was "Warp'd by the world in Disappointment's school. . . ."

Send immediately Insert after (in Canto 1st) line "And where his frown of hatred darkly fell/ "Hope withering fled—& Mercy sighed farewell!

Section X/ Slight are the outward signs of evil thought,/ Within—within—'twas there the Spirit wrought!—/ Love hath all changes—Hate—Ambition—Guile—/ Betray no further than the bitter smile;/ The lip's least ~~curl~~ curl—the lightest paleness thrown/ Along the governed aspect speak alone/ Of deeper Passions—and to judge their mien/ He, who would see—must be himself unseen.—/ Then—when the hurried step—the upward eye—/ The clenched hand—the pause of Agony/ That listens startling lest the step too near/ Approach intrusive on that mood of fear—/ Then—when each feature working from the heart/ With feelings loosed to strengthen—not depart—/ . . .

His features' deepening lines and varying hue
At times attracted, yet perplexed the view—
As if within that murkiness of mind
Worked feelings fearful & yet undefined—
Such might it be—that none could truly tell
Too close enquiry his stern glance would quell
There breathe but few whose aspect could defy
The full encounter of his searching eye—
He had the skill when prying souls would seek
To watch his words & trace his passing cheek—
At once the observer's purpose to espy
And on himself roll back his scrutiny
Lest he to Conrad rather should betray
Some secret thought — than drag that chief's to day,
There was a laughing Devil in his sneer
That raised emotions both of rage & fear
And where his frown of hatred darkly fell
Hope withering fled—& Mercy sighed farewell!—

Send immediately

Insert after (in Canto 1st) line

"And where his frown of hatred darkly fell
"Hope withering fled—& Mercy sighed farewell!

Section X

Slight are the outward signs of evil thought,
Within—within—'twas there the Spirit wrought!—
Love hath all changes—Hate—Ambition—Guile—
Betray no further than the bitter smile;
The lip's least curl—the lightest paleness thrown
Along the governed aspect speak alone
Of deeper passions—and to judge their mien
He, who would see—must be himself unseen.—
Then—when the hurried step—the upward eye—
The clenched hand—the pause of Agony
That listens startling lest the step too near
Approach intrusive on that mood of fear—
Then—when each feature working from the heart
With feelings loosed to strengthen—not depart—

George Gordon Noel Byron

Autograph manuscript of "Manfred," unsigned and undated but written ca. September 1816–May 1817. 106 pp. 235 x 188 mm. MA 59.

Manfred is not a tragedy, but the afterstrains of one, the long-delayed postlude to an ambiguous act that destroyed Manfred's "sole companion": "her, whom of all earthly things/ That lived, the only thing he seem'd to love. . . ." Count Manfred is also the finest and most extreme portrayal of the Byronic hero, as Byron himself recognized; "he is one of the best of my misbegotten," he wrote to John Murray in July 1817, "say what you will." Byron began *Manfred* in the Alps and completed it at Rome; both places left a strong imprint upon the poem. To the Alps belong the original impulse and setting for the work, but to Rome belongs the credit for the beautiful passage shown here, from Scene iv of Act III. Like a similar section in Canto IV of *Childe Harold's Pilgrimage*, for which Byron had begun collecting materials while he was rewriting the last act of *Manfred*, this description of a Roman night conveys, in a way that the Alpine setting does not, the extent of Manfred's tragic fall, for the Alps, majestic and sublime, retain a purity that is almost solace to him. In the memory of a night "within the Colosseum's wall," when "The watchdog bay'd beyond the Tiber—and/ More near from out the Cæsar's palace came/ The Owl's long cry," he discovers a truer image of himself: "A noble wreck in ruinous perfection." (This passage also represents a softening of Manfred's contempt for "the creatures of clay that girded me.") And like the moon over the "chief relics of almighty Rome," the beauty of Byron's blank verse casts "a wide & tender light,/ Which softened down the hoar austerity/ Of rugged desolation" within Manfred's soul. In the few lines that remain of *Manfred* after this soliloquy, Manfred is claimed by evil spirits, grasps the Abbot's hand in a final gesture, and discovers, after all, that "'tis not so difficult to die."

[Recto page:] More near from out the Cæsar's palace came/ The Owl's long cry;—and interruptedly/ Of distant Sentinels the fitful song/ Began & ~~dying on~~ died upon the gentle wind—/ Some cypresses beyond the time-worn breach/ ~~Sk~~ Appeared to skirt the horizon—~~& but~~ yet they stood/ Within a bowshot—where the Cæsars dwelt—/ And dwell the tuneless birds of night amidst/ A Grove that ~~grows from broken~~ springs through levelled battlements—/ And twines its roots ~~in the dust tombs of conquerors~~ around the imperial hearths./ ~~Where~~ Ivy [illegible deletion] ~~usurps~~ usurps the Laurel's place of growth—/ ~~And~~ But the Gladiator's bloody circus stands/ ~~In ruinous perfection~~ A noble wreck in ruinous perfection—/ While Cæsar's chambers & the Augustan Halls/ Grovel on earth—~~in~~ in indistinct decay—/ And thou didst shine thou rolling Moon! upon/ All this & cast a wide & ~~gentle~~ tender light/ ~~That~~ Which softened down the hoar austerity/ Of rugged desolation—& filled up/ [As twere new the gaps of centuries . . . .]

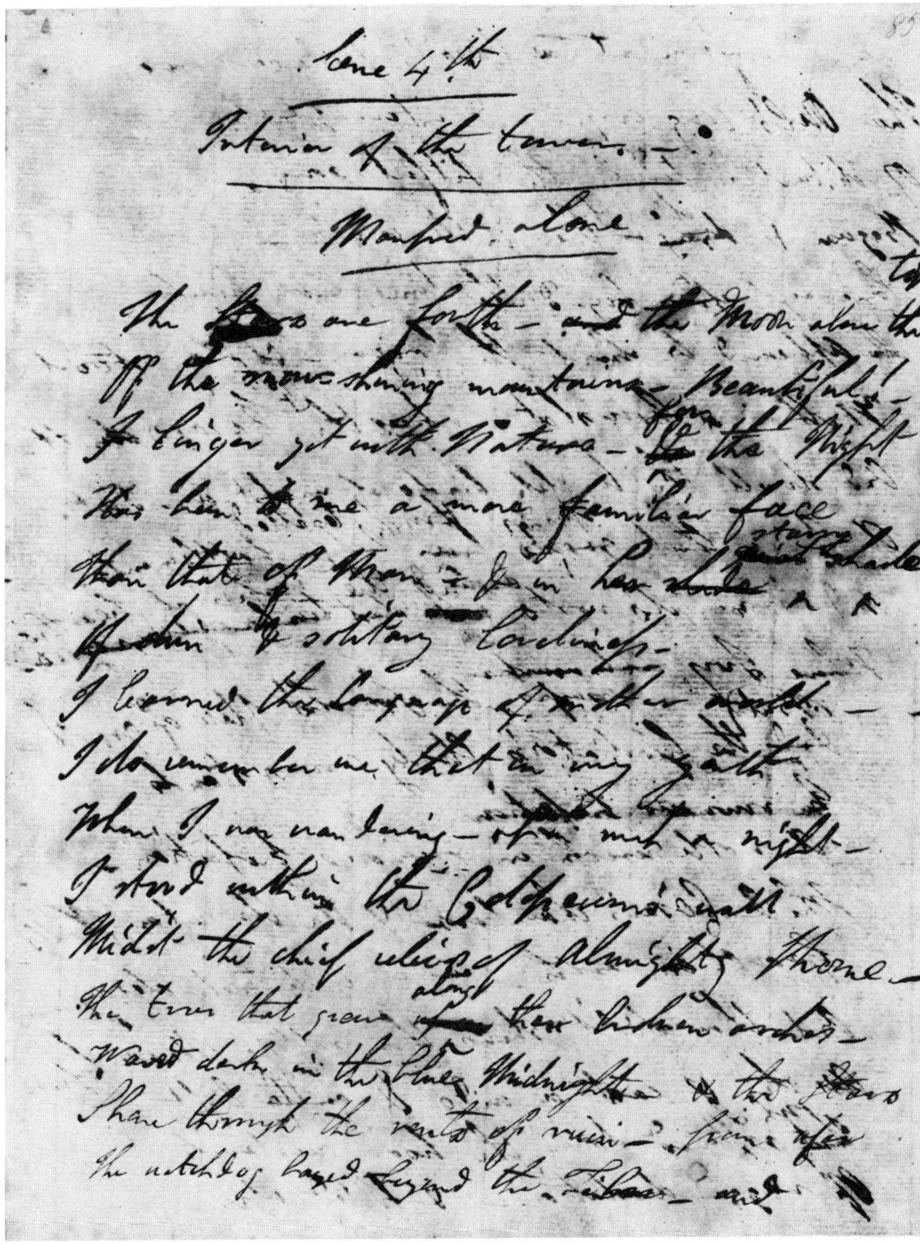
Scene 4th
Interior of the tower.—
Manfred alone—
The stars are forth—and the Moon above the tops
Of the snow-shining mountains.—Beautiful!
I linger yet with Nature—for the Night
Has been to me a more familiar face
Than that of Man—& in her starry shade
Of dim & solitary loveliness—
I learned the language of another world—
I do remember me, that in my youth
When I was wandering—upon such a night—
I stood within the Colosseum's wall
Midst the chief relics of almighty Rome—
The trees that grew along the broken arches—
Waved dark in the blue Midnight—& the stars
Shone through the rents of ruin—from afar
The watchdog bayed beyond the Tiber—and

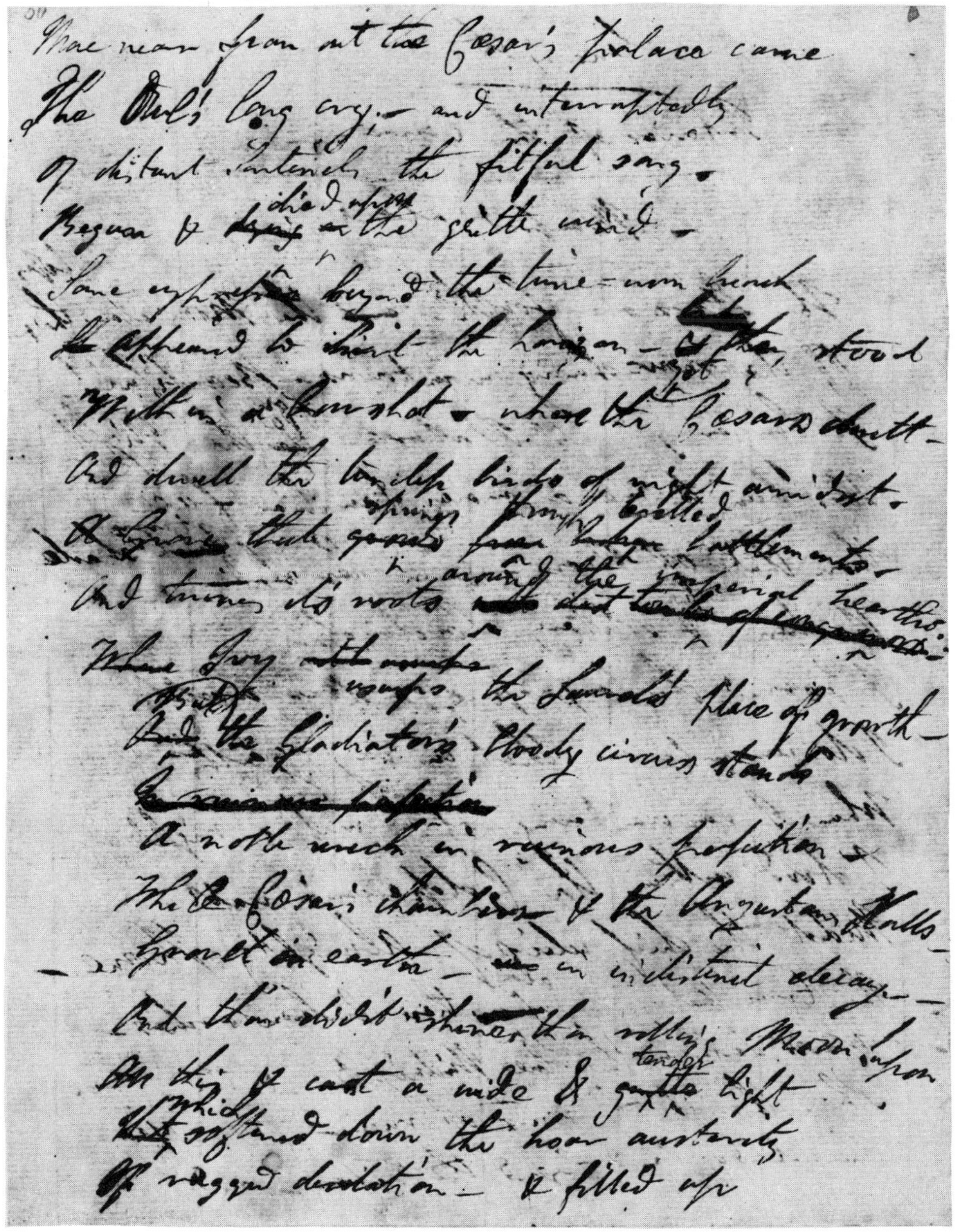
More near from out the Caesars' palace came
The Owl's long cry—and interruptedly
Of distant sentinels the fitful song
Begun & died upon the gentle wind—
Some cypresses beyond the time-worn breach
Appeared to skirt the horizon—yet they stood
Within a bowshot—where the Caesars dwelt—
And dwell the tuneless birds of night amidst
A grove which springs through levelled battlements—
And twines its roots around the imperial hearths—
Ivy usurps the laurel's place of growth—
But the Gladiator's bloody circus stands
A noble wreck in ruinous perfection—
While Caesar's chambers & the Augustan halls
Grovel on earth—in indistinct decay—
And thou didst shine thou rolling Moon upon
All this & cast a wide & tender light
Which softened down the hoar austerity
Of rugged desolation—& filled up

George Gordon Noel Byron

Autograph manuscript of "Don Juan," Canto I, unsigned, dated Venice, 3 July 1818. 89 pp. 278 x 193 mm. MA 56.

The Corsair was written in "the good old and now neglected heroic couplet," *Manfred* in blank verse, and *Don Juan* in ottava rima, adapted as a comic meter in England by John Hookham Frere (under the pseudonym of "Whistlecraft") but now irrevocably the property of Byron. In his hands ottava rima acquired a humorous elasticity it had never known, just as the story of the philogynous "Donny Johnny" inherited from him a previously unheard of topicality and license. Like Fielding's Tom Jones, Don Juan is an amorous innocent, and, like Fielding, Byron is a garrulous narrator, with personal and political interests that range far outside the proper limits of his tale. In *Beppo* (1818), where he first explored ottava rima, Byron had discovered the ease with which his chosen meter accommodated comic digression:

> This story slips for ever through my fingers,
> Because, just as the stanza likes to make it,
> It needs must be, and so it rather lingers.

And into the breach afforded by lingering meter and an episodic plot Byron soon slipped entire, at first rivaling then surpassing Don Juan as the main interest of the poem he had intended (in September 1818) to be "a little quietly facetious upon everything."

The pages reproduced here contain the final stanza of the Dedication and the opening stanzas of the first Canto. Although the Dedication to the poet laureate Southey had been an integral part of Byron's satiric strategy, the decision to publish the first two cantos anonymously led him to suppress it: "I won't attack the dog so fiercely without putting my name—" he wrote to Murray, "that is reviewer's work." The Dedication was first published in 1833. The opening stanzas (to which three more were added in the published version between stanzas II and III) describe Byron's choice of hero and his intention to "begin with the beginning" and to avoid "wandering as the worst of sinning."

The Morgan Library's collection of Byron manuscripts is one of the finest in existence. It includes the manuscripts of the first five and the thirteenth cantos of *Don Juan;* the entire manuscripts of *Beppo*, *Mazeppa*, *Marino Faliero*, "Morgante Maggiore," *The Prophecy of Dante* and *Werner;* as well as sixty-nine letters.

Meantime—Sir Laureat—I proceed to ~~dedid~~ dedicate—/ In honest simple verse this song to you—/ And if in flattering strains I ~~cannot~~ do not predicate—/ 'Tis that I still retain my "Buff & blue"/ My Politics as yet are all to educate—/ Apostasy's so fashionable too,/ ~~Thus far is well—but how I shall get go through—/ I know not yet but should be glad to learn—/ I give you joy of what/ Mean time inform me what y it is you earn?/~~ To keep one~~'s~~ creed's a task ~~that's~~ grown quite Herculean/ Is it not so my Tory Ultra-Julian?

1. I want a hero ~~—tis a curious~~ an uncommon want—/ When every Year or Month sends forth a new one/ Till after ~~certain weeks of fulsome~~ cloying the Gazettes with cant/ The Age discovers he is not the true one/ Of such as these I should not care to vaunt/ I'll therefore take our ancient friend Don Juan/ ~~You're doubtless~~ We all have seen him in the Pantomime/ Sent to the Devil—somewhat eer his time. . . .

2.) 10. Canto 1st.

Meantime — Sir Laureate — I proceed to dedicate —
In honest simple verse this song to you —
And if in flattering strains I do not predicate —
'Tis that I still retain my "Buff & blue"
My Politics as yet are all to educate —
Apostasy's so fashionable too,
To keep one's creed's a task grown quite Herculean
Is it not so my Tory Ultra-Julian?

1.

I want a hero — an uncommon want —
When every year & month sends forth a new one
Till after cloying the Gazettes with cant
The Age discovers he is not the true one
Of such as these I should not care to vaunt
I'll therefore take our ancient friend Don Juan
We all have seen him in the Pantomime
Sent to the Devil — somewhat ere his time.

2. VI

Most epic Poets plunge in "Medias res"
Horace commends it as the safest road —
And then your hero tells, whenever you please,
What went before by way of episode —
While seated after dinner at his ease
Beside his mistress in some soft abode —
Palace — or Garden, Paradise or Cavern —
Which serves the happy couple for a tavern.

3. VII

That is the usual method — but not mine —
My way is to begin with the beginning
The Regularity of my design
Forbids all wandering as the worst of sinning —
And therefore I shall open with a line
(Although it cost me half an hour in spinning)
Narrating somewhat of Don Juan's father —
And also of his mother if you'd rather. —

4. VIII

In Seville was he born — a pleasant City —
Famous for Oranges & women, he
Who has not seen it will be much to pity —
So says the proverb & I quite agree

Richard Harris Barham
1788–1845

Autograph manuscript of "The Jackdaw of Rheims," unsigned and undated but written ca. 1836–7. 8 pp. 104 x 79 mm. MA 3397.

While reminiscing in February 1878 about his first editor, John Ruskin sadly and affectionately recalled a few of "the lovely writers of old days, quaint creatures that they were," who, in the sweep of modern novels and metaphysics, had become "suddenly as unintelligible to us as the Etruscans." Among these authors were Mary Mitford, Thomas Hood, Sydney Smith and "steady-going old Barham, confessing nobody but the Jackdaw of Rheims, and fearless alike of Ritualism, Darwinism, or disestablishment. . . ." The shift in sentiment observed by Ruskin has carried these authors even farther away from our understanding and esteem; the great generation of verse humorists that includes Hood, Barham and Praed has particularly suffered from the increasing velocity of life. Like Sydney Smith (also a clergyman at St. Paul's—making it undoubtedly the best appointed parish for wit in England), Barham combined without discredit (indeed with applause) his religious profession and his secular literary avocations. He wrote theatrical reviews, two forgotten novels and an inimitable sequence of tales in verse and prose called *The Ingoldsby Legends, or Mirth and Marvels*, which initially appeared in 1837 in *Bentley's Monthly Miscellany*, edited by Dickens, and the *New Monthly Magazine*. In one of the Legends, Mrs. Botherby states that "the world . . . is divided into Europe, Asia, Africa, America, and Romney Marsh." It is in this last, appropriately designated "fifth quarter of the globe," that most of the Ingoldsby Legends, both mirthful and marvelous, are set. Though the brand of mild horror conveyed in the Legends has long since lost its ability to chill, Barham's humorous poems, especially the more topical and satirical ones, are still amusing. "The Jackdaw of Rheims," which Ruskin still knew by heart at the age of sixty-one, is his most famous Legend of all.

When the manuscript of "The Jackdaw of Rheims" was bound for a former owner, it was inserted out of order; hence the two leaves shown here are parts of two different stanzas, one before the Cardinal removes his turquoise ring, the other after the jackdaw has stolen it. The largest collection of Barham manuscripts is in the Berg Collection of the New York Public Library.

Carried Lavender water & eau de Cologne/ And a nice little boy ~~had~~ had a nice cake of soap/ Worthy of washing the hands of the Pope/ One nice little boy more/ A napkin bore/ Of the very best diaper fringed with pink/ And a Cardinal's Hat marked in permanent ink.

The Great Lord Cardinal turnd at the sight/ Of those nice little boys dress'd all in white/ From his finger he draws/ His costly turquoise/ And not thinking at all about little Jackdaws

. . .

The Friars are kneeling/ And searching and feeling/ The Carpet the ~~sides of the rom~~ floor & the walls & the ceiling/ The Cardinal drew/ Off ~~his~~ each plum coloured shoe/ Leaving both his red stockings exposd to the view/ They turnd up the dishes they turnd up the plates/ They took up the poker and raked out the grates/ They turn'd up the rugs/ They examined the mugs.

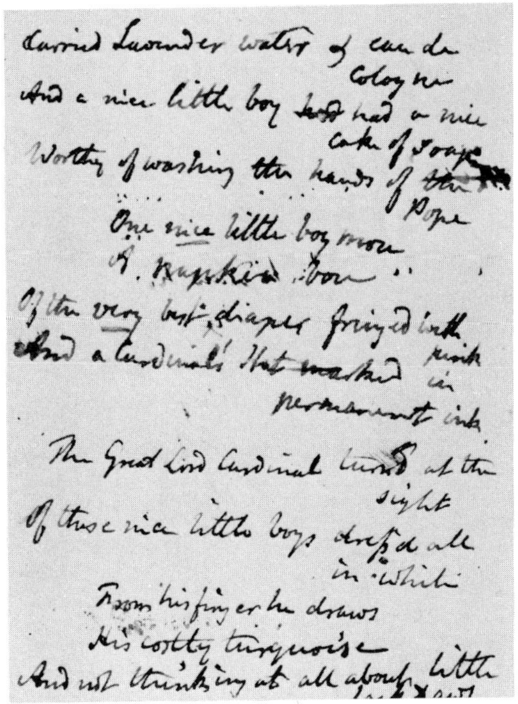
Carried lavender water & eau de Cologne
And a nice little boy had a nice cake of soap
Worthy of washing the hands of the Pope
One nice little boy more
A napkin bore
Of the very best diaper frized with pink
And a Cardinal's Hat marked in permanent ink.

The Great Lord Cardinal turns at the sight
Of these nice little boys dress'd all in white
From his finger he draws
His costly turquoise
And not thinking at all about little jack-daws

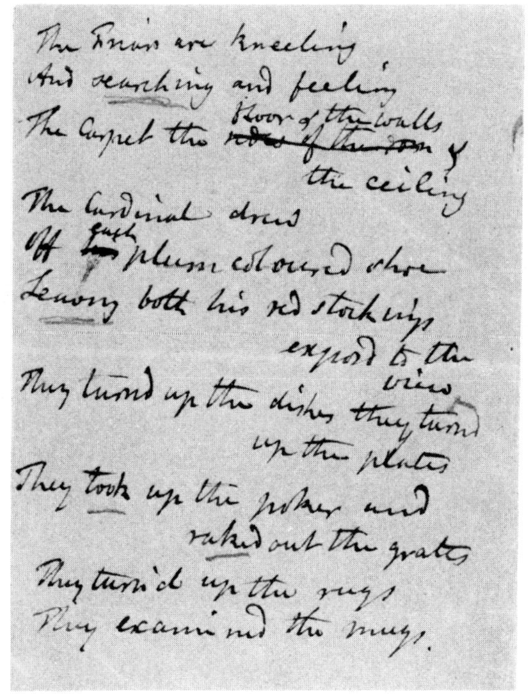
The Friars are kneeling
And searching and feeling
The carpet the floor of the walls & the ceiling
The Cardinal drew
Off each plum coloured shoe
Leaving both his red stockings exposed to the view
They turned up the dishes they turned up the plates
They took up the poker and raked out the grates
They turn'd up the rugs
They examined the mugs.

Percy Bysshe Shelley
1792–1822

Autograph manuscript of "Stanzas, Written in Dejection, Near Naples," unsigned, dated December 1818. 3 pp. 206 x 150 mm. MA 406.

Fearing for his health, Shelley "journeyed towards the spring" in Italy, in 1818, taking his unfortunate family with him; the end of December found them at Naples in "a lodging opposite the sea" and on the edge of collapse. The Shelleys' second child, Clara, had died at Venice in September, their servant Elise had just given birth to Shelley's illegitimate daughter, and there is reason to suspect that Claire Clairmont—Mary Shelley's step-sister—had just suffered a miscarriage of a pregnancy caused by the poet. Truly, it was a time—like so many others in their lives—when Shelley and these women might well have adopted the motto (from Jonson's *Every Man in His Humour*) that he had proposed in a letter to Peacock in July: "*Have you a stool there to be melancholy upon?*" As late as October 1818, in "Lines Written Among the Euganean Hills" (above Padua), Shelley had retained his faith that "in a sea of life and agony" a bark might still sail

> To some calm and blooming cove,
> Where for me, and those I love,
> May a windless bower be built,
> Far from passion, pain, and guilt.

But Shelley and his wife had discovered "care to be the thing that Horace describes it to be": a thing that cannot be fled. At Naples Shelley sat down in the "transparent might" of noon and, obeying the purest of lyric impulses, composed this poem, which in this manuscript bears the simple title, "Naples—December 1818," and a deleted subtitle: "Written during a fit of low spirits." Rather than search for a "frail bark," Shelley in this poem abandons himself to despair and longs for the moment when he might "hear the Sea/ Breathe o'er my dying brain its last monotony."

Another manuscript of this poem is in the Bodleian Library. This manuscript was once part of a notebook now preserved in the Library of Harvard University; like most of the rest of the poems in that notebook, it is a fair copy.

Alas, I have nor hope nor health/ Nor peace within, nor calm around/ Nor that content, surpassing wealth,/ The sage in meditation found/ And walked with inward glory crowned./ Nor fame nor power nor love nor leisure—/ Others I see whom these surround—/ Smiling they live & call life pleasure/ To me that cup has been dealt in another measure

Yet now despair itself is mild,/ Even as the winds & waters are;/ I could lie down like a tired child/ And weep away the life of care/ Which I have borne & yet must bear/ Till Death like Sleep might steal on me/ And I might feel in the warm air/ My cheek grow cold, & hear the Sea/ Breathe o'er my dying brain its last monotony

Some might lament that I were ~~dead~~ cold/ As I, when this sweet day is gone/ Which my lost heart, too soon grown old/ Insults with this untimely moan—/ They might lament—for I am one/ Whom men love not, & yet regret/ Unlike this day, which when the Sun/ Shall on it's cloudless glory set/ Will linger, though enjoyed, like joy in memory yet.

It flashing round me, & a tone
Arises from its measured motion
How sweet! did any heart now share in my emotion.

Alas, I have nor hope nor health
Nor peace within, nor calm around
Nor that content, surpassing wealth,
The sage in meditation found.
And walked with inward glory crowned—
Nor fame nor power nor love nor leisure—
Others I see whom these surround—
Smiling they live & call life pleasure
To me that cup has been dealt in another measure—

Yet now despair itself is mild,
Even as the winds & waters are;
I could lie down like a tired child
And weep away the life of care
Which I have borne & yet must bear
Till Death like Sleep might steal on me
And I might feel in the warm air
My cheek grow cold, & hear the Sea
Breathe o'er my dying brain its last monotony

Some might lament that I were ~~dead~~ cold
As I, when this sweet day is gone
Which my lost heart, too soon grown old
Insults with this untimely moan—
They might lament— for I am one
Whom men love not, & yet regret
Unlike this day, which when the Sun
Shall on its cloudless glory set
Will linger, though enjoyed, like joy in memory yet.

PERCY BYSSHE SHELLEY

Autograph letter signed, dated Pisa, 29 November 1821, to Joseph Severn. 3 pp. 246 x 181 mm. MA 790.

As Mary Shelley observed, one elegy, *Adonais*, served her husband and Keats alike, as did one graveyard in Rome. Keats and Shelley had first met at Leigh Hunt's cottage in Hampstead during the winter of 1816/7 and their initial approaches to each other had been somewhat tentative, particularly on Keats's part. But in 1820 they exchanged courteous, even friendly letters. To Keats, Shelley remarked that "consumption is a disease particularly fond of people who write such good verses as you have done . . . I do not think that young & amiable poets are at all bound to gratify its taste." Keats responded by suggesting that Shelley revise his poems more before publication, advice which he felt "must fall like cold chains upon you, who perhaps never sat with your wings furl'd for six Months together." Though Shelley had invited the younger poet to join him and Mary at Pisa, the two men did not see each other in Italy, and a final letter from Shelley arrived in Rome too late for Keats to read it. "For my part," wrote Shelley in this letter to Joseph Severn, who attended Keats in his last moments and sketched the sleeping poet on his deathbed, "I little expected when I last saw Keats at my friend Leigh Hunt's, that I should survive him." Little more than seven months after this letter was written, Shelley, his friend Edward Williams and their boat boy were drowned during a summer storm in the Gulf of Spezia. When Shelley's body washed ashore near Viareggio in August 1822, Hunt's copy of Keats's poems was found in his coat.

Shelley composed *Adonais*, his elegy on Keats, during the first two weeks of June 1822, while he and Mary, who was pregnant, lived at San Giuliano. He had intended to preface the poem with an extensive appreciation of *Hyperion*, but contented himself with attacking the reviewers who, he erroneously believed, had caused Keats's death by criticizing *Endymion* in the familiarly harsh manner of the day. (Keats's reaction to the review was "God help the Critic, whoever he be!") For Shelley, the death of a fellow poet of Keats's ability was too great an anticipation of his own fate: "my spirit's bark is driven,/ Far from the shore, far from the trembling throng/ Whose sails were never to the tempest given . . . ."

---

poet, & the total neglect & obscurity in which the astonishing remnants of his mind still lie, was hardly to be dissipated by a writer, who, however he may differ from Keats in more important qualities, at least resembles him in that accidental one, a want of popularity. I have little hope therefore that the Poem I send you will excite any attention nor do I feel assured that a critical notice of his writings would find a single reader. But for these considerations it had been my intention to have collected the remnants of his compositions & to have published ~~with~~ them with a life & criticism.— Has he left any poems or writings of whatever kind, & in whose possession are they? Perhaps you would oblige me by information on this point.—

Many thanks for the picture you promise me: I shall consider it among the most sacred relics of the past. For my part, I little expected when I last saw Keats at my friend Leigh Hunt's, that I should survive him.— . . .

poet, & the total neglect & obscurity in which the astonishing remnants of his mind still lie, was hardly to be dissipated by a writer, who, however he may differ from Keats in more important qualities, at least resembles him in that accidental one, a want of popularity.

I have little hope therefore that the Poem I send you will excite any attention nor do I feel assured that a critical notice of his writings would find a single reader. But for these considerations it had been my intention to have collected the remnants of his compositions & to have published ~~with~~ them with a life & criticism. — Has he left any poems or writings of whatever kind, & in whose possession are they? Perhaps you would oblige me by information on this point. —

Many thanks for the picture you promise me: I shall consider it among the most sacred relics of the past. For my part, I little expected when I last saw Keats at my friend Leigh Hunt's, that I should survive him. —

Should you ever pass through Pisa I hope to have the pleasure of seeing you, & of cultivating an acquaintance into something pleasant begun under such melancholy auspices. —

Accept my dear Sir the assurance of my sincere esteem, & believe me

Your most sincere & faithful Sert.

Percy B Shelley.

"Do you know Leigh Hunt? I expect him & his family here every day.

35

CAPTAIN FREDERICK MARRYAT
1792–1848

Autograph manuscript of "Mr. Midshipman Easy," undated but written ca. 1835. 292 pp. 325 x 190 mm. MA 261.

The finest nautical literature of the eighteenth century is largely fact—one thinks of Commodore Byron and Captain Cook—but the nautical classics of the nineteenth century are fiction. The British navy had moved from a period of exploration into a period of brilliant conquest, and for many men there was never a better reason to go to sea than the victorious death of Nelson, nor a better time than the first two decades of the 1800s. Less than a year after Trafalgar, Frederick Marryat shipped aboard the frigate *Imperieuse* as a First-Class Volunteer under the command of the dashing Lord Cochrane. Marryat remained twenty-four years in the service and distinguished himself in violent action all over the world—in the Mediterranean, off the shores of America and in Burma. His reputation for courage and practical ingenuity was somewhat undercut by his boatswain's temper, which, though an asset aboard ship, was a distinct liability when he retired from the navy in 1830 and began a second career as a man of letters. He worked his way into and out of several fortunes, for what his wit supplied, his temper and financial impetuosity destroyed.

Today, Marryat is remembered primarily for two children's books, *Masterman Ready* and *The Children of the New Forest*, and for his two finest novels, *Peter Simple* and *Mr. Midshipman Easy*, the latter shown here in manuscript. The virtues of Marryat's best works are simple but engaging: rapid pace, a fine eye for eccentric character, and copious adventure, told purely in the spirit of the humorist. His heroes are brazen but sensible young men, who command instinctively the respect of the noble, the enmity of the base and the adoration of the beautiful, and from whom the good things of life are withheld only long enough to make the plot tick. The passage shown here recounts Jack Easy's reunion with a Sicilian family whom he had rescued in the first volume.

The Morgan Library's manuscript of *Mr. Midshipman Easy* lacks the first five chapters; also in the Morgan Library are the manuscripts of *Percival Keene* and *Masterman Ready*.

[Starting with line 14:] Oblige me by showing me the palm of your hand. Agnes extended her little hand & Jack felt so very polite that he was nearly kissing it— However he restrained himself & examined the lines—

That you were educated in Spain, that you arrived here but 2 months ago, that you were captured & released by the English your mother has already told me. But to prove to you that I knew all that I must now be more particular. You were in a ship mounting 14 guns Was it not so. Donna Agnes nodded her head

I never told the Senor that, cried Donna Clara

She was taken by surprise in the night & there was no fighting The next morning, the English burst open the cabin door. Your Uncle and your cousin fired their pistols

Holy Virgin cried Agnes with surprise

The English Officer was a young man not very good looking—

There you are wrong Senor, he was very handsome

There is no accounting for taste Senora— You were frightened out of your wits & with your cousin you crouched down in the corner of the cabin. Let me examine that little line closer—you had, yes its no mistake—you had very little clothes on [illegible deletion] Agnes tore away her hand & covered her face—E vero—E vero—Holy Jesus. How could you know that! Of a sudden Agnes looked at our hero & after a minute appeared to recognize him. . . . .

ragged dress - but the cut of your coat have no respect for persons
We are under great obligations Jacko - and do not regard such trifles
You are all Kindness Senora replied Jacko - I little thought this
morning of my good fortune - I can tell the fortunes of others
but not my own -
You can tell fortunes, replied the old lady -
Yes Madam I am famous for it. Shall I tell your daughter's -
Donna Agnes looked at our hero & smiled incredulously -
I perceive that the young lady does not believe me - I must prove
my art by telling her of what has already happened to her -
"Will Senora then give me credit -
Certainly if you do that - replied Agnes -
Oblige me by showing me the palm of your hand - Agnes extended
her little hand & Jacko felt so very foolish that he was nearly
kissing it - However he restrained himself & examining the lines -
That you were educated in Spain that you arrived here but 2 months
ago, that you were robbed & abused by the English your mother
has already told me - but to prove to you that I know all that
I must now be more particular. You were in a ship mounting 14 guns
Was it not so - Donna Agnes nodded her head
I never told the Senor that, cried Donna Clara
She was taken by surprise in the night & there was no fighting
The next morning, the English burst open the cabin door - Your
Uncle & your cousin fired their pistols
Holy Virgin cried Agnes with Surprise
The English Officer was a young man not very good looking -
Then you are wrong - Senor, he was very handsome
There is no accounting for taste Senora - You were frightened out
of your wits & with your cousin you crouched down in the corner
of the cabin - Let me examine this little line close - you had - yes it's
no mistake - you had very little clothes on ~~[illegible]~~
Agnes threw away her hand & covered her face - E vero - E vero - Holy
Jesus. how could you know that! Of a sudden Agnes looked up
at our hero & after a moment attentively surveying him - Oh Mother

John Clare
1793–1864

Autograph manuscript of "Rural Evening" in a manuscript volume entitled "Village Scenes and Subjects on rural Occupations," dated Helpstone, 21 August 1820. 116 pp. 243 x 195 mm. MA 1320. Gift of Mrs. W. Murray Crane.

The vogue for country verse that swelled in the late eighteenth and early nineteenth centuries overtook John Clare in 1820. In that year Taylor and Hessey published *Poems Descriptive of Rural Life and Scenery*, three editions of which were sold out and a fourth begun before the year was over. The British reading public had always entertained a fondness for untutored writers of verse—among them the thresher-poet, the milk-woman of Bristol and, of course, Robert Burns—and to this group Clare was added, as the peasant-poet of Northamptonshire. The success of Clare's first volume raised him from utter poverty and allowed him to sample briefly the brilliant literary society associated with the *London Magazine*. But the charm of a peasant-poet depended, after all, on the condition that he remain a peasant, and Clare was doomed, partly by this simple fact of literary taste, to a life of intellectual isolation, the bitterness of a new tide of poverty and, eventually, madness.

Clare's poetical gift was genuine and long-lived, in spite of the galling frustrations inherent in being a "rhyming peasant." Poetry offered to him not a means of escape from the narrow ways of Helpstone but the possibility of lyrical communion with the natural world that so enriched and infused village life. "My heart had love for poesy/ A simple love a wild esteem/ As heart felt as the linnets dream/ That mutters in its sleep at night/ Some notes from extacys delight."

The notebook shown here contains sixteen poems, most of which were published, like "Rural Evening," in *The Village Minstrel* (1821), Clare's second volume of poetry. Most of Clare's numerous manuscripts are today housed in the Peterborough Natural Historical Society Museum and the Northampton City Library.

The sun now sinks behind the woodland green/ & twittering spangles glow the leaves between/ So bright & dazzling on the eye it plays/ As if noons heat had kindld to a blaze/ But soon it dims in red and heavier hues/ & shows wild fancy cheated in her views/ A mist like moister rises from the ground/ & deeper blueness stains the distant round/ The eye each moment as it gazes oer/ Still loosing objects which it markd before/ ~~For~~ The woods at distance changing like to clouds/ & spire points croodling under evenings shrouds/ Till forms of things & hues of leaf & flower/ In deeper shadows as by magic power/ With light & all in scarce percievd decay/ Puts on mild evenings sober garb of grey/ While in the sleepy gloom that blackens round/ Dies many a lulling hum of rural sound/ From cottage door farm yard & dusty lane . . .

Rural Evening

The sun now sinks behind the woodland green
& twittering spangles glow the leaves between
So bright & dazzling on the eye it plays
As if noons heats had kindled to a blaze
But soon it deepens red & heavier hues
& shows wild fancy cheated in her views
A mist like moisture rises from the ground
& deeper blackness dims the distant round
The eye each moment as it gazes oer
Still looses objects which it marked before
~~Fa~~ the woods at distance changing like to clouds
& spire points crowding under evenings shrouds
Till forms of things & hues of leaf & flower
In deeper shadows as by magic power
With light & all in scarce percieved decay
Puts on mild evenings sober garb of grey
While in the sleepy gloom that blackens round
Dies many a lulling hum of rural sound
From cottage door farm yard & dusty lane
Were home the cart horse tolters with the swain
& padded holm were ~~bawling~~ village boys resort
& ~~shout~~ bawl enraptured oer their evening sport
Till night awakens superstitious dread
& drives them prisoners to a restless bed
Thrice happy eve of days no more to me
Who ever thought sich change belongd to thee
When like to boys whom now thy gloom surrounds
I chasd the stag or ~~shouted~~ played at fox & hounds

37

William Carleton
1794–1869

Autograph manuscript of "National Literature and Mr. Lever," signed and undated, but written ca. September–October 1843. 17 pp. 318 x 185 mm. From the Collection of Mr. Gordon N. Ray.

"So, my young suckling of litherature, you're bound for Munster?—for that counthry where the swallows fly in conic sections—where the magpies and the turkeys confab in Latin, and the cows and bullocks will roar you Doric Greek. . . ." The intellectual attractions of such a region of learning, described in Carleton's "The Poor Scholar," lured many students from the "hedge schools" of Ireland to the south, where with luck and perseverance they might become priests. Carleton was one who set out on that road to the south, but he ended by taking a more secular course and becoming along the way one of the finest Irish novelists of the nineteenth century. Yeats remarked that Carleton had "the most Celtic eyes that ever gazed from under the brows of story-teller," and they gazed primarily on the peasantry of Ireland, the subject he was born to write about. His *Traits and Stories of the Irish Peasantry* (two series, 1830 and 1833) led many readers to declare him the Irish heir of Scott, though he has about him perhaps more of the forebear of Hardy. Unfortunately, *Traits and Stories* is one of the few bright spots in Carleton's career. At a time of fervent Irish nationalism, which sparked the Young Ireland movement, Carleton displayed an unfortunate tendency to waver over political matters as he had over religious ones. Owing to poverty, his later years were, as Yeats perhaps too strongly characterized them, "an Iliad of decadence."

The manuscript shown here represents the less attractive side of Carleton, for it is the manuscript of a vicious attack on Charles Lever, which was published in *The Nation* (Dublin) on 7 October 1843. This abuse of a fellow Irish novelist resulted from the fact that Lever had recently taken over the editorship of the *Dublin University Magazine*, and Carleton found himself excluded from its pages. Though the Young Ireland movement, which supported *The Nation*, was glad to have Carleton join them as a writer, it is doubtful whether this article could possibly have advanced their cause.

[Starting with line 13:] ~~The~~ One of the severest charges however which we have to bring against Mr. Lever is a ~~cunning~~ selfish and sordid devotion to his own interests ~~indulged in gratified~~ at the expence of our national Character—a feeling utterly incompatible with ~~the negligent grandeur and~~ the generous self-neglect which too often so frequently Characterizes ~~the principles of a man of genius~~ genius. We have been for a long time woefully misrepresented to our English neighbours and it is only of late that as Colonel Thompson says the force of Irish ~~genius~~ intellect has begun to ~~make~~ give them a truthful and wholesome impression of our country and her inhabitants. ~~to the English people~~. Mr. Lever however so far from drawing his representations of Irish life from our living people is forced from ignorance of their Character ~~their habits~~ and virtues to fall back upon the vile old travesties ~~of us~~ which are to be found in the dramatic malice of our enemies [illegible deletion] and in this spirit it is, which is of easy attainment that he panders to the English taste of the present day. . . .

with rather feeble expletives to dialogue 9
-ally Jones"—which he puts indiscriminately into the mouths of all
his characters from the Dukes of York and Wellington to
the most insipid subaltern in the army you will still find remaining nothing
but the stale flippant and frivolous profusion of chat equally such precisely as a smutty
butler might report only not so correctly given, for the butler's respect for his master would make him remember that he got a good many. If he possessed
any variety of style, if he could change the general nature of his
incidents—if he travelled only for a moment out of his own
eternal mannerism—if in fact he had any thing
about him that we could forgive we might feel satisfaction:
but there is nothing for he has scarcely ever written a page that is not a libel
upon his country or an insult upon her people.

One of the severest charges however which we have to bring against
Mr Lever is a selfish and sordid devotion to his own interests
at the expense of our national character—a feeling utterly
incompatible with the generous self-
neglect which so frequently characterizes genius.
We have been for a long time woefully misrepresented to our
English neighbours and it is only of late that as Colonel
Thompson says the force of Irish intellect has begun to
give them a truthful and wholesome impression of our country
and her inhabitants. Mr Lever however
so far from drawing his representations of Irish life from our
living people is forced from ignorance of their character
and virtues to fall back upon the vile and travesties
which are to be found in the dramatic malice of our
enemies and in this spirit it is, which is of easy attain
ment that he panders to the English taste of the present day
which has been formed upon those disgusting libels
that make us ridiculous to the world [illegible]
[illegible] does. Is it honest is it manly is it patrio
tic in him to write up to and beyond those farcical defa
mations of us which are enough to make any man who loves
his country no matter what is his creed feel the deepest indig
nation against these slavish instruments of national prejudice who
perpetrated them—And yet such is the fact. Mr Lever in truth
is literally selling us for pounds shillings and pence and not

JOHN KEATS
1795–1821

Autograph manuscripts of "On First Looking into Chapman's Homer" (undated but written in October 1816) and "The day is gone and all its sweets are gone" (undated but probably written on 10 October 1819). 2 pp. 182 x 168 mm. and 214 x 181 mm. MA 214.

In July 1819, John Keats wrote to Fanny Brawne from the Isle of Wight, "I cannot conceive any beginning of such love as I have for you but Beauty." All that was good in Keats's brief life began with beauty, whether it was to be found in Chapman's Homer or in Fanny Brawne. The two sonnets shown here—one a poem of awe, the other of agitation—both record his impressions of moments of great beauty; they were also written three years apart, a span of time that includes almost all his life of active writing. In October 1816 Keats had spent an entire night with Charles Cowden Clarke reading passages from George Chapman's seventeenth-century translation of Homer. Composed in a few hours after daybreak, "On First Looking into Chapman's Homer" was Keats's first major poem and a supreme expression of what one true poet finds in another. Three years later, again in October, Keats was reunited with Fanny Brawne, after he had spent most of the summer away from her at Shanklin on the Isle of Wight and at Winchester. Among the very last poems he wrote are several of deep passion to Fanny, including the sonnet shown here, "The day is gone and all its sweets are gone," probably written on the evening of their reunion.

Keats constantly experimented with verse forms, particularly with sonnets, adaptations of which provided the stanzaic elements for his odes. "On First Looking into Chapman's Homer" has a Petrarchan rhyme scheme (which Keats called "pouncing"), while "The day is gone and all its sweets are gone" follows the Shakespearean pattern ("too elegiac" because of its concluding couplet). In the summer of 1819 Keats's experiments in the sonnet form culminated in a "more interwoven" rhyme scheme, best used in "If by dull rhymes our English must be chained."

The manuscripts reproduced here are both early drafts; line seven of "On First Looking into Chapman's Homer" was changed when it was published in 1817 (a still earlier version of this poem is at Harvard), and the second and third quatrains of "The day is gone and all its sweets are gone" were reversed in later copies.

Much have I travell'd in the Realms of gold/ And many goodly States and Kingdoms seen/ Round many western islands have I been/ Which Bards in fealty to Apollo hold/ Oft of one wide expanse had I been told/ That deep brow'd Homer ruled as his Demesne/ Yet could I never judge what Men could mean/ Till I heard Chapman speak out loud and bold/ Then felt I like some Watcher of the Skies/ When a new Planet swims into his Ken/ Or like stout Cortez when with eagle eyes/ He star'd at the Pacific and all his Men/ Look at each other with a wild surmise/ Silent upon a Peak in Darien.

The day is gone and all its sweets are gone/ Sweet voice, sweet lips soft hand and softer breast/ Warm breath, tranc'd whisper, tender semitone/ Bright eyes, accomplish'd Shape, and langrous waist./ Vanish'd unseasonably at shut of eve/ When the dusk Holiday, or Holinight/ Of fragrant-curtain'd Love begins to weave/ The ~~texture thick of darkness~~ woof of darkness, thick, for hid delight/ Faded the flower ~~of beuty from my eyes gaze~~ and all its budded charms/ Faded the ~~voice~~ sight of ~~Love~~ Beauty from my ~~sad ears sad~~ eyes/ Faded the shape of Beauty from my ~~face~~ arms/ . . .

To Mariane Reynolds —

Much have I travell'd in the Realms of gold
And many goodly States and Kingdoms seen
Round many western islands have I been
Which Bards in fealty to Apollo hold
Oft of one wide expanse had I been told
That deep brow'd Homer ruled as his Demesne
Yet could I never judge what Men could mean
Till I heard Chapman speak out loud and bold.
Then felt I like some Watcher of the Skies
When a new Planet swims into his Ken
Or like stout Cortez when with eagle eyes
He star'd at the Pacific and all his Men
Look'd at each other with a wild surmise
Silent upon a Peak in Darien —

The day is gone and all its sweets are gone!
Sweet voice, sweet lips, soft hand and softer breast
Warm breath, tranc'd whisper, tender semitone
Bright eyes, accomplish'd shape, and languorous waist.
Vanish'd ~~unseasonably~~ at shut of eve
When the dusk Holiday, or Holinight
Of fragrant-curtain'd Love begins to weave
The ~~texture thick of darkness~~
woof of darkness, thick, for hid delight
Faded the flower ~~of beauty from my eyes~~ and all its budded charms
Faded the ~~voice~~ sight of ~~Love~~ Beauty from my ~~sad ears~~ sad eyes gaze
Faded the shape of Beauty from my arms
Faded the voice, ~~the whiteness~~ warmth, whiteness, ~~loveliness~~ paradise
But as I have read Love's Missal through to day
He'll let me sleep — seeing I fast and pray.

39

JOHN KEATS

Autograph manuscript of "Endymion," unsigned and undated, composed in 1817, transcribed in fair copy in early 1818. 184 leaves. 258 x 190 mm. MA 208.

Few poets have ever managed to write a preface as honest and humbly self-aware as that which Keats prefixed to *Endymion: A Poetic Romance*, an indifferent poem, as he knew, by a great poet, as he so earnestly desired to be. But the preface that was published in 1818—addressed "to men who are competent to look, and who do look with a zealous eye, to the honour of English literature"—replaced an earlier version, less satisfactory to Keats's friends and publishers because of its hostility to the public, "a thing I cannot help looking upon as an Enemy." Despite this difference, both prefaces express Keats's eagerness to thrust *Endymion* away from him and his keen awareness of its faults. When he began the poem in the spring of 1817, just after the publication of *Poems*, he was struggling with self-doubt: "I have asked myself so often," he wrote to Leigh Hunt, "why I should be a Poet more than other Men." From its inception, *Endymion* bore signs of being an exercise which Keats hoped would help him answer that question, for he described it to his brothers as "a test, a trial of my Powers of Imagination and chiefly of my invention which is a rare thing indeed. . . ." When the poem was completed, Keats knew it for what it was, "a feverish attempt, rather than a deed accomplished," but in spite of the drubbing it received in the press, he defended its composition in a letter to James Hessey, one of his publishers: "That which is creative must create itself—In Endymion, I leaped headlong into the Sea, and thereby have become better acquainted with the Soundings, the quicksands, & the rocks, than if I had stayed upon the green shore, and piped a silly pipe, and took tea & comfortable advice."

In the passage shown here, from Book II of *Endymion*, Keats laments the inadequacy of his own poetic powers to describe the erotic delights enjoyed by Endymion and Cynthia, goddess of the moon, and in so lamenting also expresses his fear that "the Count/ Of mighty Poets is made up. . . ." The Morgan Library owns the entire fair copy of *Endymion* and the manuscript of the suppressed preface. Besides numerous short poems, fragments and an important journal letter to George and Georgiana Keats (17–27 September 1819), the Morgan Library also houses a major collection of manuscripts by Richard Woodhouse and other members of the Keats circle.

At which soft ravishment, with doting cry/ They trembled to each other. Helicon!/ O fountain'd Hill! Old Homer's Helicon!/ That thou wouldst spout a little streamlet o'er/ These sorry pages; then the verse would soar/ And sing above this gentle pair like Lark/ Over his nested young: but all is dark/ Around thine aged top and thy clear fount/ Exhales in mist to Heaven. Aye, the Count/ Of mighty Poets is made up: the ~~Scroll~~ Scroll/ Is folded by the Muses: the bright roll/ Is in Apollo's hand: our dazed eyes/ Have seen a new tinge in the western skies:/ The World has done its duty. Yet, Oh yet/ Although the Sun of Poesy is set/ These Lovers did embrace and we must weep/ That there is no old Power left to steep/ A Quill immortal in their joyous tears./ . . .

At which soft ravishment, with doting cry
They trembled to each other. Helicon!
O fountain'd Hill! Old Homer's Helicon!
That thou wouldst spout a little streamlet o'er
These sorry pages; then the verse would soar
And sing above this gentle pair like lark
Over his nested young: but all is dark
Around thine aged top and thy clear fount
Exhales in mist to Heaven. Aye, the Count
Of mighty Poets is made up: the ~~Scroll~~ Scroll
Is folded by the Muses: the bright roll
Is in Apollo's hand: our dazed eyes
Have seen a new tinge in the western skies:
The World has done its duty. Yet, Oh yet
Although the Sun of Poesy is set
These Lovers did embrace and we must weep
That there is no old Power left to steep
A Quill immortal in their joyous tears.
Long time in Silence did their anxious fears
Question that thus it was; long time they lay
Fondling and Kissing every doubt away;
Long time ere soft camping sobs began
To mellow into Words, and then there ran
Two bubbling springs of talk from their sweet lips.

John Keats

Autograph manuscript of "Ode to Psyche," undated but written in the last week of April 1819. 3 pp. 223 x 185 mm. MA 210.

Through his "Ode to Psyche," John Keats passed from the annoying silence of two months' poetic frustration into the "wide Quietness" of May 1819, when he wrote three of the greatest poems in the English language: "Ode to a Nightingale," "Ode on a Grecian Urn" and "Ode to Melancholy." With this poem, invocation ended and Keats put deference aside: "Yes, I will be thy Priest and build a Fane/ In some untrodden Region of my mind." In the beginning of "Ode to Psyche," he still walks through the mythological landscape of *Endymion*, rich but conventional; by the end, he has begun to describe a country that is recognizably his own, where, for a brief time, a mortal priest may still minister to a goddess. "Ode to Psyche" is the prelude to the greater spring odes of 1819, a poem of imagined fulfillment leading to poems of inevitable transience and loss. Behind the promise of sexual union in the poem's last lines—"A bright torch, and a casement ope at night/ To let the warm love in"—there lies an allegory about the process Keats called "soul-making": the instruction of man's intelligence (Psyche) by love (Eros) and its painful pleasures. In his "Ode to Psyche," Keats anticipates the love of Psyche and Eros, the willing alliance of head and heart in "a World of Pains and troubles" where the poet must envy the ecstasy of the nightingale and the "melodist, unwearied,/ For ever piping songs for ever new." It always bears repeating that Keats wrote "Ode to Psyche" and its companion odes within the space of five weeks; but then, had he labored five years for such results, the miracle would not be less.

Two manuscripts of "Ode to Psyche" survive; this is the earlier and more important. The other is a copy of the poem included in a letter Keats wrote between 14 February and 3 May 1819 and sent to his brother George and his sister-in-law Georgiana in America. This letter also contains Keats's account of "soul-making" and is now in the Houghton Library, Harvard University.

[Starting with recto:] Yes, I will be thy Priest and build a Fane/ In some untrodden Region of my mind,/ Where branched thoughts, new grown with pleasant pain/ Instead of Pines shall murmur in the wind./ Far, far around shall those dark-cluster'd trees/ Fledge the wild ridged mountains steep by steep;/ And there by Zephyrs, streams, and birds and Bees/ The moss-lain Dryads shall be lull'd to sleep./ And in the midst of this wide Quietness/ A rosy sanctuary will I dress/ With the wreath'd trellis of a working brain,/ With buds and bells and Stars without a name,/ With all the gardener-Fancy e'er could feign,/ Who ~~plucking a thousand flower and never~~ breeding flowers will breed pluck~~s~~ the same/ ~~So bower'a Goddess will I worship thee~~/ And there shall be for thee all soft delight/ That shadowy thought can win—/ A bright torch, and a casement ope at night/ To let the warm Love ~~gide~~ in.

~~[illegible]~~

Fairer than these, though Temple thou hast none,
Nor Altar heap'd with flowers;
Nor Virgin Choir to make melodious moan
Upon the midnight hours;
Nor voice, nor lute, nor pipe, nor incense sweet
From chain-swung Censer teeming,
Nor Shrine, nor grove, nor Oracle, no heat
Of pale-mouth'd Prophet dreaming.

O Bloomiest! though too late for antique vows
Too, too late for the fond believing Lyre,
When holy were the haunted forest-boughs,
Holy the air, the Water, and the Fire:
Yet even in these days so far retir'd
From happy Pieties, thy lucent fans,
Fluttering ~~above~~ [among] the faint Olympians,
I see, and sing by my ~~clear~~ [own] eyes inspired.
O let me be thy Choir and make a moan
Upon the midnight hours;
Thy Voice, thy lute, thy Pipe, thy incense sweet
~~thy~~ [From] swinged Censer teeming;
Thy Shrine, thy Grove, thy oracle, thy heat
Of Pale mouth'd Prophet dreaming!

Yes. I will be thy Priest and build a Fane
In some untrodden Region of my mind,
Where branched thoughts, new grown with pleasant pain
Instead of Pines shall murmur in the wind.
Far, far around shall those dark-cluster'd trees
Fledge the wild-ridged mountains steep by steep;
And there by Zephyrs streams, and birds and Bees
The moss-lain Dryads shall be lull'd to sleep.
And in the midst of this wide Quietness
A rosy sanctuary will I dress
With the wreath'd trellis of a working brain,
With buds and bells and stars without a name,
With all the gardener-Fancy e'er could feign,
Who ~~plucking a thousand flowers and~~ [breeding flowers will] never [breed] plucks the same
~~So banish'd Goddess while I worship thee~~
And there shall be for thee all soft delight
That shadowy thought can win—
A bright torch, and a casement ope at night
To let [the] warm Love ~~glide~~ in.

41

Thomas Carlyle
1795–1881

Autograph manuscript of "Wotton Reinfred," unsigned and undated, but written in 1827. 51 pp. 258 x 191 mm. MA 70.

Almost every author hopes to "*write something of my own*," as Carlyle put it, to be something more than a man of letters, more than "but an Essayist." This manuscript represents Thomas Carlyle's first attempt at a book (a word with mysteries for him) that would come from contemplating the "wonderful Chaos within me, full of natural Supernaturalism, and all manner of Antideluvian fragments. . . ." Not surprisingly, this initial experiment was an autobiographical novel, entitled *Wotton Reinfred*, which Carlyle began in February 1827 and abandoned several months later. The passage shown here is essentially a bit of self-satire, a wiser Carlyle presenting his strongest case against a youthful Carlyle, alias Wotton Reinfred, the speculative young hero. "O Wotton Reinfred," the old doctor, Wotton's adversary in argument, exclaims, "thou art behind thyself, much learning doth make thee mad. . . . There hast thou sat poring over thy Geometries and Stereometries, thy Fluxions direct and inverse . . . till thy eyes are dazed with so many lamps, and for very light thou canst not see a glimpse." And yet, in the guise of this elder counsellor, Carlyle offers Wotton an escape from philosophical confusion: "I care not for thy Scepticism, Wotton: I tell thee, it will grow to be Belief, and all the sounder for thy once having doubted." The pattern of growth from scepticism to belief, from contemplation to action, became the central structure of *Sartor Resartus* (1833–4), the work that was Carlyle's all-important first book from himself. As for *Wotton Reinfred*, Carlyle concluded that "the metal is too unmalleable, often indeed quite cold, and the arm and the hammer have so little pith," a complaint that registers the difficulty he found in adapting the extraordinary vitality of his thought to the conventional form in which *Wotton Reinfred* is cast

The greatest collection of Carlyle letters and manuscripts is in the National Library of Scotland.

"Dropped? Aye, but ~~only at the end of the first act we have the the other four before us not the green one~~ not the green one, it is the painted curtain ~~and~~ that has dropped, and the first act truly is done, and we have other four to come to." Pity that our interlude of music were not gayer, but we must even put up with it, signs and groans tho' it be. O Wotton Reinfred thou art behind thyself, much learning doth make thee mad. I swear, it is even so," ~~continued he, rising into his usual rallying tone~~ lively tone. "There hast thou sat poring over thy Geometries and Stereometries, thy Fluxions direct and inverse, by the Newtonian and the Leibnitzian method, thy Universal History, thy Scotch Philosophy and French ~~Criticism~~ Poetics, till thy ~~very lamp of life is almost extinct within thee~~ eyes are ~~daz blasted dazzle~~ dazed with so many lamps, and for very light thou canst not see a glimpse, and so in thy head the world ~~within thee~~ is whirling ~~round thee~~ like a ~~toper's~~ sick man's dream, and for thee it has neither top nor bottom, ~~nor~~ beginning ~~nor~~ middle nor end! I care not for thy Scepticism, Wotton: I tell thee, it will grow to be Belief, and all the sounder for thy once having doubted. I say so because thy froward mind ~~tho' proud and~~ is honest withal, and thou lovest Truth ~~faithfully~~ sincerely. But Deuce take [it,] man! I would have had thee pleading in the ~~Chancery or Common Pleas like a brave youth, two months ago~~ Courts like a brave Advocate." . . .

have nothing more to do but undress; "but shuffle off this mortal coil."

"Dropped? Aye, but only at the end of the first act, longer than the other four before us; not the green one, it is the painted curtain that has dropped, and the first act truly is done, and we have other four to come to." Pity that our interlude of music were not gayer, but we must even put up with it, sighs and groans tho' it be. O Wotton Reinfred thou art beside thyself, much learning doth make thee mad. I swear, it is even so, lively tone! There hast thou sat poring over thy Geometries and Stereometries, thy Fluxions direct and inverse, by the Newtonian and the Leibnitzian method, thy Universal History, thy Scotch Philosophy and French Poetics, till thy eyes are dazed with so many lamps, and for very light thou canst not see a glimpse, and the world in thy head is whirling like a sick man's dream, and for thee it has neither top nor bottom, beginning middle nor end! I care not for thy Scepticism, Wotton: till then, it will grow to be Belief, and all the sounder for thy once having doubted. I say so because thy froward mind is honest withal, and thou lovest truth sincerely. But Deuce take the man! I would have had thee pleading in the Courts like a brave Advocate!"

"Illustrating the case of Stradling versus Stile!" cried Reinfred hastily, for the talk displeased him. "Rending my immortal spirit, in vain jangling, for a piece of bread? I have bread already."

"So much the better! But the honour, the use to others—"

"May be strongly doubted," cried the youth still more sharply.

"Well, I grant, it would not do," said the Doctor, hastening to quitting this rather thorny province. "Thou hadst a heart too, but we could not master it: six months of the Institute had no whit abated thy aversion, nay thy horror; and at last when I saw thee after a resolute night at the Justice of the Peace absolutely seized with a kind of tetanus or locked-jaw, I myself was obliged to vote that we should give it up."—"Heigh-ho!" ejaculated Wotton. "But now, in Heaven's name," continued the Doctor, "what is it that should so overcloud thee, nay bewilder thee, notwithstanding? Are we not here in thy own walled house, amid thy own freehold fields? Hast thou no talent that this world has use for? Young, healthy; a brother fellow of thy inches; learned too, tho' I say it, for thy years; and independent, if not rich! Pshaw! Is the game lost because the first trick has gone against thee? Patience, and shuffle the cards! Is the world all dead, because Edmund Walter is a scoundrel jackanapes, and —"

"Good God!" cried Wotton, starting from his seat, and pacing hurriedly over the floor, "can you not spare me? What have I to do with Edmund Walter? The tiger-ape!" cried he stamping on the ground: "with his bobs and shoulder-knots, his smirks and fleers! A gilt outside, and within, a very lazar-house! Gay meeches, a most frolick sunny thing; and in its heart the poison of asps! O the —But I will not curse him. No, poor devil! He but follows the current of his own vile nature, like the rest of us. God help him, —and me!" added he pausing with a deep sigh.

"Yet it is strange," said the other, "how this a puppy could master rhetoric [?] truly a thing. Strange that a bor cap and feather should have" Jane Montagu

"Doctor!" said Wotton ...

Mary Wollstonecraft Shelley
1797–1851

Autograph additions in a copy of "Frankenstein" (London: Lackington, et al., 1818) presented to Mrs. Thomas in 1823. PML 16799.

Mary Shelley's *Frankenstein; or, The Modern Prometheus* is probably the most famous literary production of the Romantic period, rivaled only by another work in the same vein, Coleridge's *Rime of the Ancient Mariner*. The idea for *Frankenstein* came to Mary Shelley during a wet summer at Montalègre, near Byron at Villa Diodati, under "the dark frowning Jura, behind whose range we every evening see the sun sink. . . ." After one long night during which she, Shelley and Byron had talked of galvanism and the experiments of Erasmus Darwin, Mrs. Shelley had a waking nightmare in which she saw a "pale student of unhallowed arts kneeling beside the thing he had put together. I saw the hideous phantasm of a man stretched out, and then, on the working of some powerful engine, show signs of life, and stir with an uneasy, half vital motion." Stunning as this image is, it would have been nothing without the ingenuity Mrs. Shelley brought to the construction of her narrative. In the preface to the 1831 edition of *Frankenstein*, she indicates that she had once intended to begin the story *in medias res*, with the words, spoken by Victor Frankenstein, "It was on a dreary night of November, that I beheld the accomplishment of my toils." Instead, urged by Shelley, she extended the narrative and began the story from the outside and the end, with Robert Walton's epistolary account of taking Frankenstein (who was in pursuit of his monster) on board his ship, which was on "a voyage of discovery towards the northern pole." Thus, by a man of heroic proportions who is himself receding daily from British reality, we are introduced to the man, Victor Frankenstein, who has a tale to tell beyond the bounds of all familiarity.

This copy of *Frankenstein* was given by the author to a Mrs. Thomas, a poetess who composed, in Shelley's words, "insufferable trash," but was kind to Mary Shelley in her own way in Geneva in 1823. Mrs. Thomas appears to have been a woman of strict propriety, for in an autograph note on a blank page of this book she writes: "I called on [Mrs. Shelley] in London in 1824 but as My friends disliked her Circle of Friends— and Mrs Shelley was then no longer in a Foreign Country helpless, Pennyless, and broken hearted;—I never returned Again. . . ." The additions made to this copy were not incorporated in any later edition published during her lifetime.

Nay if by moonlight I saw a human form, with a beating heart I squatted down amid the bushes fearful of discovery. And think you that it was with no bitterness of heart that I did this? It was in intercourse with man alone that I could hope for any pleasurable sensations and I was obliged to avoid it— Oh truly, I am grateful to thee my Creator for the gift of life, which was but pain, and to thy tender mercy which deserted me on life's threshold to suffer—all that man can inflict

the green banks interspersed with innumerable flowers, sweet to the scent and the eyes, stars of pale radiance among the moonlight woods; the sun became warmer, the nights clear and balmy; and my nocturnal rambles were an extreme pleasure to me, although they were considerably shortened by the late setting and early rising of the sun; for I never ventured abroad during daylight, fearful of meeting with the same treatment as I had formerly endured in the first village which I entered.

"My days were spent in close attention, that I might more speedily master the language; and I may boast that I improved more rapidly than the Arabian, who understood very little, and conversed in broken accents, whilst I comprehended and could imitate almost every word that was spoken.

While I improved in speech, I also

Nay if by moonlight I saw a human form, with a beating heart I squatted down amid the bushes fearful of discovery. And think you that it was with no bitterness of heart that I did this It was in intercourse with man alone that I could hope

learned the science of letters, as it was taught to the stranger; and this opened before me a wide field for wonder and delight.

"The book from which Felix instructed Safie was Volney's *Ruins of Empires*. I should not have understood the purport of this book, had not Felix, in reading it, given very minute explanations. He had chosen this work, he said, because the declamatory style was framed in imitation of the eastern authors. Through this work I obtained a cursory knowledge of history, and a view of the several empires at present existing in the world; it gave me an insight into the manners, governments, and religions of the different nations of the earth. I heard of the slothful Asiatics; of the stupendous genius and mental activity of the Grecians; of the wars and wonderful virtue of the early Romans—

for any pleasurable sensations and I was obliged to avoid it— Oh truly, I am grateful to thee my creator for the gift of life, which was but pain, and to the tender mercy which deserted me on life's threshold to suffer — all that man can inflict

THOMAS HOOD
1799–1845

Autograph manuscript of "The Assistant Drapers' Petition," undated but written in 1838. 2 pp. 350 x 165 mm. MA 195.

Like other literary forms and attitudes, satire has its seasons, too, which move in a complex relation to the evolutions of society. The sophisticated, virulent satire of Pope and Swift had ceased a century later to serve as a functional literary model, for the admonitory spirit of satire had been taken over by men whose work was predominantly comic rather than satiric. At the beginning of Queen Victoria's reign, Thomas Hood was one of the best of these writers, and his works plainly demonstrated the shift from the political vehemence of Swift's *Drapier's Letters* to the light social comedy of "The Assistant Drapers' Petition." Hood contributed to the *London Magazine* and the *New Monthly Magazine* but his most distinctive vehicle was his own *Comic Annual*, founded in 1829, when it supplanted his earlier annuals, *Whims and Oddities* and *The Gem*, and published regularly for the next ten years. In the pages of the *Comic Annual* Hood appeared not only as the author of comic poems and prose pieces but also as an illustrator and caricaturist. His rough and somewhat demented woodcuts have a comic rotundity about them that reflects the directness of his humor as well as the occasionally stark nature of his social commentary.

The world portrayed in Hood's poems and illustrations is without shade, broad in its outlines, and its comic nature tends more toward the grotesque than the sentimental. In this it resembles Hood's own life. His health was wretched, his relations with publishers were vexed by his own distrust of their motives, and, consequently, his finances were always in a state of disrepair. "The Assistant Drapers' Petition" was published in the *Comic Annual* of 1839 and was written while Hood and his family lived at Ostend during a period of self-exile from a host of financial miseries. Hood's manuscripts are scattered, but the Morgan Library houses a significant group of poems and prose sketches first published in the *Comic Annuals*. Today Hood is best remembered for "The Song of the Shirt" and "Miss Kilmansegg and Her Precious Leg."

The Drapers' Petition—/ Pity the sorrows of a class of men/ Who tho they bow to Fashion & frivolity/ No fancied claims or ~~wrongs~~ woes fictitious pen/ But wrongs ell wide and of a lasting quality.

Oppress'd and discontented with our lot/ Among the clamorous we take our station/ A host of Ribbon Men—yet is there not/ One piece of Irish in our agitation.

We do revere Her Majesty the Queen/ We venerate our glorious Constitution/ We joy King William's advent should have been—/ And only want a Counter Revolution.

'Tis not Lord Russel and his final measure/ 'Tis not Lord Melbourne's counsel to the throne/ 'Tis not this Bill or that gives us displeasure/ The measures we dislike are all our own.

The Cash law the "Great Western" loves to name—/ The tone our foreign policy pervading— /The Corn Laws—none of these we care to blame—/ Our evils we refer to over-trading.

The Assistant Draper's Petition.

"Now's the time and now's the hour"
Burns

"Seven's the main"
Crockford.

Of all the agitations of the time – and agitation is useful in disturbing the duckweed that is apt to gather on the surface of ~~still & deep waters~~ – human affairs – the ferment of the assistant shopmen in the Metropolis is perhaps the most beneficial. Many vital queries have lately disturbed the public mind – for instance ought the fleet of the Thames Yacht Club to be reinforced in the event of a war with Russia, or should the Little Pedlington Yeomanry be called out in case of a rupture with Prussia – but these are merely national questions, whereas the Draper's movement suggests an enquiry of paramount importance to Mankind in general – namely "When ought we to leave off?"

It is the standard complaint against Jokers, and Whistplayers, & Children, whether playing or crying – that they "never know when to leave off".

It is the common charge against English writers and flannel waistcoats – It is occasionally hinted of rich ~~old~~ & elderly relations – it is constantly said of snuff-takers, and gentlemen who enjoy a glass of good wine – that they "do not know when to leave off".

It is the fault oftenest found with certain preachers – sundry Poets & all prosers – scolds – parliamentary orators superannuated story tellers, the gossips – morning calls – and some leave-takers that they "do not know when to leave off". It is insinuated as to gowns and coats, of which waiting men & waiting women have the reversion.

It is the characteristic of a Change Alley Speculator, of a beaten boxer – of a builder's row with his own name to it – of Hollando-Belgic protocols – of German metaphysics, of works in numbers – of buyers & sellers on credit – of a theatrical cadence – of a stocking bad knit & of the Gentleman's Magazine that they "do not know when to leave off".

A Romp, – all Murphy's frosts, ~~rains~~ showers, storms ~~and~~ &c hurricanes – and the Wandering Jew are in the same predicament.

As regards the assistant Drapers, they appear to have arrived at a very general conclusion that their proper period for leaving off is at or about seven o'clock in the evening; and it seems by the following poetical address that they have rhyme as well as reason to offer in support of their resolution.

The Draper's Petition.

Pity the sorrows of a class of men
Who tho they bow to Fashion & frivolity
No fancied claims or ~~wrongs~~ woes fictitious pen
But wrongs ell wide and of a lasting quality.

Oppress'd and discontented with our lot
Amongst the clamorous we take our station
A host of Ribbon Men – yet is there not
One piece of Irish in our agitation.

We do revere Her Majesty the Queen
We venerate our glorious Constitution
We joy King William's advent should have been –
And only want a Counter Revolution.

'Tis not Lord Russel and his final measure
'Tis not Lord Melbourne's councils to the throne
'Tis not this Bill or that gives us displeasure
The measures we dislike are all our own.

The Cash law the "Great Western" loves to name –
The tone our foreign policy pervading –
The Corn Laws – none of these we care to blame –
Our evils we refer to over-trading.

THOMAS BABINGTON MACAULAY, FIRST BARON MACAULAY 1800–1859

Autograph manuscript of "The History of England," Volume V, undated but written 1856–9. 357 leaves. 322 x 202 mm. MA 253.

To Macaulay's mind, the writing of history in its ideal form ought to reconcile two contrasting means of representation. "The one," he wrote in the *Edinburgh Review* in 1828, "may be compared to a map, the other to a painted landscape." This analogy explains much of Macaulay's historical intention: for him, history offered a relative truth, based both on fact (the schematic topography of a map) and the impression created by fact (the topographical illusion of a landscape painting). Macaulay wished to render the past as a whole, to convey the romance of history along with its abstract proportions. Few men have been placed as well as he was to appreciate the contours of his chosen period, from the accession of James II "down to a time which is within the memory of men still living." Like all historians, Macaulay was obliged to absorb the factual background for his *History of England* in his study and in libraries across Europe. But in the House of Commons and in Calcutta, where he was a member of the Supreme Council of India, he also came to understand in a more immediate and political manner the directions in which Great Britain had developed since the Glorious Revolution; that is, he found himself in a position to assess and to celebrate "the history of physical, of moral, and of intellectual improvement" in the British Isles.

As his speeches in Parliament bore the marks of his essay writing, so his *History* bears the marks of his Parliamentary career. To begin with, it is unfinished. Public service stripped from Macaulay years that might have been given to the *History* but were instead wisely devoted to the Reform Bill and the recasting of India's penal code. As a result, the fifth volume was published posthumously in 1861, edited by his sister, Lady Trevelyan, and it extends chronologically only to the death of William III in 1702. Macaulay was at work on this volume until very near his death in December 1859; the handwriting deteriorates considerably and is rendered still more difficult to read by his lifelong habit of extensive abbreviation. The passage shown here recounts the last moments of William III.

The Morgan Library also owns a substantial portion of Macaulay's correspondence with his favorite sisters, Margaret and Hannah, as well as notebooks used in preparing the *History*.

[Deletions not recorded:] His f^{t} was ye more ad^{rble} bec: he was not w^{g} to die—He had very lly s^{d} to one of y^{s} whom he m^{t} l^{d}—"You know y^{t} I never fd death. There have been t^{s} when I sh^{d} have w^{d} it: but now y^{t} y^{s} g^{t} new p^{t} is opg before me I do wish to stay here a lle longer." Yet no w^{s} no q^{s} disg^{d} ye noble close of y^{t} noble career. To ye phy^{ns} ye K retd his thanks g^{ly} & gen^{ly}— . . .

[His fortitude was the more admirable because he was not willing to die. He had very lately said to one of those whom he most loved: "You know that I never feared death; there have been times when I should have wished it; but, now that this great new prospect is opening before me, I do wish to stay here a little longer." Yet no weakness, no querulousness, disgraced the noble close of that noble career. To the physicians the King returned his thanks graciously and gently. . .]

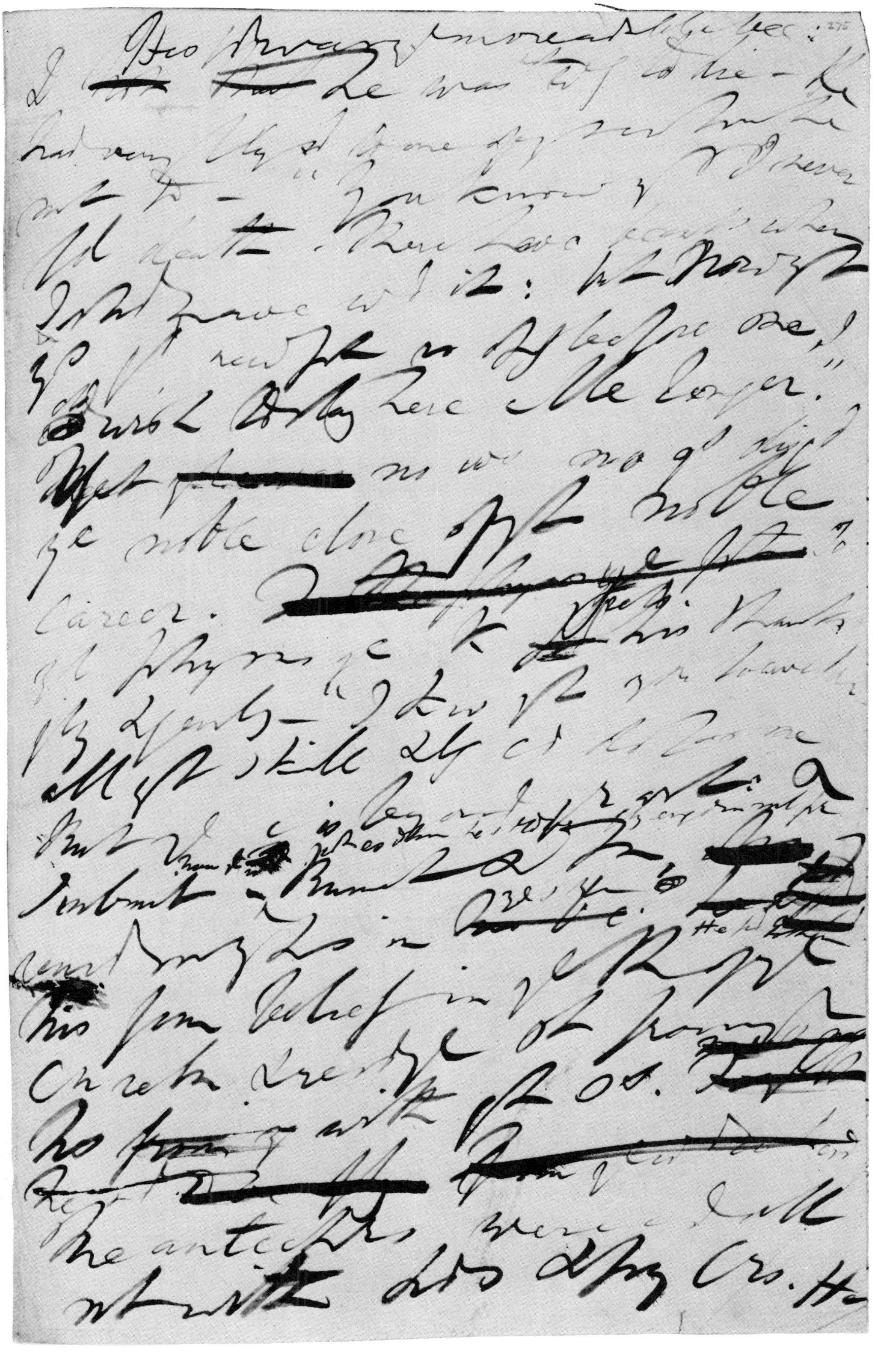

John Henry Newman
1801–1890

Autograph letter signed, dated 13 October 1837, to the Reverend George Townsend, with a letter by E. B. Pusey written on the same sheet. 4 pp. 228 x 186 mm.

As much as the Reform Bill of 1832 marked the triumph of reviving liberalism in England, it also marked the consolidation of conservative reaction. To a man like John Henry Newman, the threat posed by the Reform Bill seemed aimed directly at the clerical establishment. "Bishoprics," he wrote, "were already in course of suppression; Church property was in course of confiscation; Sees would soon be receiving unsuitable occupants." In *Apologia Pro Vita Sua* (1864) he observed quite bluntly that "the object of the [Oxford] Movement was to withstand the Liberalism of the day," which seemed to be eroding the formal, dogmatic structure of the Church of England. Though such a remark appears out of sympathy with the spirit of the times, Newman defended the Oxford Movement by appealing specifically to a common characteristic in contemporary literature. Scott's metrical romances, Wordsworth's philosophical poems, Southey's oriental fantasies and Coleridge's controversial writings, he argued, all seemed to express England's desire to reject "the dry and superficial character of the religious teaching and the literature of the last generation, or century," and to substitute in its place a deeper, more thoughtful approach to life. Through the Oxford Movement and *Tracts for the Times* (1833–41), Newman and his close associate Edward Bouverie Pusey sought to fulfill this desire within the precincts of the Anglican church.

For Newman and for many others (including Henry Edward Manning, later Cardinal Manning, who is mentioned in Pusey's section of the letter shown here) the Church of England eventually came to appear historically invalid and emotionally enervated, and they converted to Roman Catholicism, the most authentic expression of their conservatism. In this letter (written six years before Newman resigned his livings in the Anglican church and eight years before he became a Roman Catholic) Newman and Pusey respond to a petition, or "charge," sponsored by the Reverend George Townsend, prebendary of Durham, a writer against Catholic emancipation who voyaged to Italy in 1850 in a vain attempt to convert the Pope.

[Starting midway, verso:] Might not the difficulty be adjusted without compromising the feelings of either party, if you sent to the York or other Newspaper in the North such extracts from Dr Pusey's letter as directly bear upon the particular points animadverted on in your Charge, as from yourself, yet without expressing your opinion upon them? but I would gladly leave this matter to your better judgment, having stated the end *which is to be consulted.*

Let me thank you very warmly for your kind invitation of me to Durham, and beg in return to offer to you, should you come into the South, such hospitality as our Common Room can give, which at least shall not be behind Durham in heartiness.

I have talked with Dr Pusey on the Subject of your petition, in which I cordially concur, and wish it all the success which I trust sooner or later must attend it. I am, Revd Sir, Yours very faithfully John H. Newman.

-pulsion. Still, since it has taken place, it is plain it ought to be removed; and since we have had the disadvantage of your disapprobation, it is natural I should think it fair, as far as we have succeeded in removing it, to have the benefit of our success. It seems fair that in some way or other it should be signified that your Charge does not allude to myself or friends of mine, so far as it does not allude to us, & so far as its meaning has been modified by our explanations, even though you censure us the while, that such explanations were not sooner given.

Might not the difficulty be adjusted without compromising the feelings of either party, if you sent to the York or other Newspaper in the North such extracts from Dr Pusey's letter as directly bear upon the particular points animadverted on in your Charge, as from yourself, yet without expressing your opinion upon them? but I would gladly leave this matter to your better judgment, having stated the end which is to be consulted.

Let me thank you very warmly for your kind invitation of me to Durham, and beg in return to offer to you, should you come into the South, such hospitality as our Common Room can give, which at least shall not be behind Durham in heartiness.

I have talked with Dr Pusey on the subject of your petition, in which I cordially concur, and wish it all the success which I trust sooner or later must attend it.

I am, Revd Sir,

Yours very faithfully

John H Newman.

My dear Sir,

I am very sorry for the pain & trouble you have had, amid the anxiety resulting from so important a measure as that wh you have originated. I heartily agree in it, except with regard to the present meeting of Convocation, on wh. I have sent my thoughts, hastily expressed on [illegible] an emergency, but not conceived on a sudden, to the last British Mag. signed Canonicus.

With regard to our Oxford question, I agree with Mr Newman that the matter might best lay in your hands: your charge in its grammatical sense will be, & is, explained of us; we did not take it to ourselves: for this all for which you said, meaning other people will be construed of us. Leeds is S. of Durham, yet being in York Province, all we Southerns shall consider it as N. & so

Could you not then, without committing yourself, say that, understanding that all you had said in your Charge had been applied to people in Oxford to whom you did not altogether allude, and you thought it right to give the statements of one who lived on the spot what the real state of the case was? Of course, I do not wish you to extract such parts as blame yourself.

Your movement is a very important one; I send you in return a paper not yet published, & wh., in decency, must not be published, until it has been presented to ye A Bp, but wh. has some very important statements & principles. It is by a friend of ours Rev. H. S. Manning, Lavington Petworth, who has just been elected Proctor for the Archdeaconry of Chichester. I wish those who are turning their thoughts to our present perplexed state could consult & act together.

I hope, by ye bye, that if any investigation is made as to Chapter Leases &c, the Chapters will refuse to answer. (I think it wd be wrong to have any thing to do with a Committee, setting expressly for spoliation) & that they will forbid their Chapter Clerks so from doing so.

I thank you much for your renewed invitation to Durham, but I have really too much chalked out for me for some time to come. But in order to judge of us, & what [illegible]

Edward Bouverie Pusey, 1800-1882

HARRIET MARTINEAU
1802–1876

Autograph manuscript of "Society in America," Volume I, undated but written ca. 1836–7. 260 leaves. 253 x 205 mm. MA 873.

When Harriet Martineau visited the United States in 1834 she traveled, as she said, with "glimmerings of conviction" and a "pittance of knowledge." The first work to result from her journey was *Society in America* (1837), in which she attempted to reconcile conviction and knowledge by comparing "the existing state of society in America with the principles on which it is professedly founded. . . ." To her, as to many Europeans in the early nineteenth century, America presented the paradox of an ideologically radical nation bursting the seams of its chosen constitutional fabric. For the exuberance of Jacksonian democracy, typified more by boisterous fact than by adherence to first principles, Miss Martineau was indeed poorly prepared. In his own book about travels in America, Captain Marryat catalogued her deficiencies as an observer by calling her, with characteristic exaggeration, "that old, deaf English maiden lady." More justly, but with equal tactlessness, he also commented on her credulity, her inability to discern the peculiarly American habit of imposing fabrications upon strangers eager to be amazed. Where Marryat provides a rough sketch of a rude nation, Harriet Martineau, steeped in the intellectual tradition of the Unitarians, offers an abstract argument about the divergence of American society from its prescribed political forms.

Still, there are moments in *Society in America* when the analytical voice pauses to express wonder. In the passage shown here, the beginning of the chapter called "Economy," Miss Martineau describes her thoughts upon seeing Niagara Falls for the first time. In the millennial language so familiar in early accounts of America, she says, "I saw those quiet, studious hours of the future world when this cataract shall have become a tradition, and the spot on w$^{\underline{h}}$ I stood shall be the centre of a wide sea, a new region of life. This was seeing world-making." But the analytical voice soon returns, and it sums up her response to the power of Niagara and the fertility of the Mississippi: "Here was strong instigation to the exercise of analysis."

The Morgan Library houses not only all three manuscript volumes of *Society in America*, but also Captain Marryat's copy of that work.

While I stood in the wet whirlwind, with the crystal roof above me, the thundering floor beneath, & the foaming whirlpool & rush^{g} flood before me, I saw those quiet, studious hours of the future world when this cataract shall have become a tradition, & the spot on w$^{\underline{h}}$ I stood shall be the centre of a wide sea, ~~the habitation~~ a new region of life. This was seeing world-making. So it was on the Missis$^{\underline{i}}$, when a sort of scum on the waters betokened the birth place of a new land. All things help ~~to~~ in this creation. The cliffs of the upper Missouri detach their soil, & send it ~~down~~ thousands of miles down the stream. The river brings it, & deposits it, in continual increase, till a barrier is raised ag$^{\underline{st}}$ the rushing waters themselves. The air brings seeds, & drops them where they sprout, & strike downw$^{\underline{ds}}$, so that their roots bind the soft soil, & enable it to bear the weight of new accretions. The infant forest, floating, as it appeared, on the ~~bosom~~ surface of the turbid & rapid waters, may reveal no beauty to the painter; but to the eye of one who loves to watch the process of world-making, it is full of delight. These islands are seen in every stage of growth. . . .

& to wondering ears in studious hours, & believed in from the
sole evidence of its surviving grandeur & beauty. While
I stood in the wet whirlwind, with the crystal roof above me,
the thundering floor beneath, & the foaming whirlpool & rushing
flood before me, I saw those quiet, studious hours of the
future world when this cataract shall have become a
tradition, & the spot on wh I stood shall be the centre of
a wide sea, ~~the habitation~~ a new region of life. This was
seeing world-making. So it was on the Mississ^t, when a
sort of scum on the waters betokened the birth place of new
land. All things help ~~to~~ in this creation. The cliffs of the
upper Missouri detach their soil, & send it ~~some~~ thousands
of miles down the stream. The river brings it, & deposits it,
in continual increase, till a barrier is raised ag^st the
rushing waters themselves. The air brings seeds, & drops them
where they sprout, & strike downwds, so that their roots bind
the soft soil, & enable it to bear the weight of new accretions. The
infant forest, floating, as it appeared, on the ~~[illegible]~~ surface of
the turbid & rapid waters, may reveal no beauty to the
painter; but to the eye of one who loves to watch the
process of world-making, it is full of delight. These
islands are seen in every stage of growth. The cotton-wood
trees, from being like cresses in a pool, rise breast-high; then
they are like thickets, to whose shade the alligator may
retreat; then, like groves that bid the sun good-night ~~long~~
~~[illegible]~~ while he is still lighting up the forest;
then like the forest itself, with the wood-cutter's house
within its screen, ~~& wild~~ flowers spring up about its stems,
& the wild-vine climbing to meet the night breezes on
its lofty canopy. This was seeing world-making. Here was
strong instigation to the exercise of analysis. ^

~~[illegible]~~ I watched also the progress of ~~[illegible]~~ conventional life:
I saw it in every stage of advancement, ~~progress~~ from the clearing in the woods,

EDWARD GEORGE EARLE LYTTON BULWER-LYTTON 1803–1873

Autograph manuscript of Chapter IV (Book 5) of "The Last Days of Pompeii," unsigned and undated but written in the winter of 1833–4. 20 pp. 253 x 200 mm. MA 248.

On 14 November 1834 Sir William Gell, archaeologist and author of *Pompeiana* (1817–9 and a sequel in 1832), wrote to the abused and abusing Mrs. Edward Bulwer and asked her to convey his appreciation to her husband, whose latest novel, *The Last Days of Pompeii*, had been dedicated to him. Bulwer had generously complimented the man who had shown him "those disinterred remains of an ancient City," and Gell, in turn, told the novelist's wife, "It is impossible to say how much I feel flattered by Mr Bulwer's Kindness & honoured by his notice, & how much I am indebted to Him for praise which will really raise my price in the World." Whatever effect *The Last Days of Pompeii* might have had on Gell's price, it certainly increased Bulwer's, which had begun its rise with the publication of *Pelham: or the Adventures of a Gentleman*, his brilliant "fashionable" novel, in 1828. *The Last Days of Pompeii* is the perfect embodiment of a principle stated by Bulwer in its preface: "We understand any epoch of the world but ill, if we do not examine its romance;—there is as much truth in the poetry of life as in its prose." Such a claim could not please a man like John Stuart Mill, who would have pointed out "the gross blunders in scholarship & even in Latin grammar" had Bulwer not been a writer for his *London Review*, but for the more aesthetic and impressionable Ruskin too much could hardly be claimed for Bulwer (whom Carlyle called the "Mystagogue of the Dandiacal Body"): "His writings are full of an entangled richness of moving mind, glittering with innumerable drops of rosy and balmy and quivering dew. . . ." Fortunately, Bulwer (or Bulwer-Lytton, as he was known after taking his mother's surname) is infinitely better than Ruskin's praise of him, particularly in the very "fashionable" novels so roundly condemned by contemporary critics. There is nothing rosy or balmy in Bulwer's description, shown here, of the eruption of Vesuvius that led to the destruction of Pompeii.

The Morgan Library owns one of the finest collections of Bulwer-Lytton manuscripts in existence. Besides numerous chapters of *Pompeii* (the rest of this manuscript is still in the family), it also houses the manuscripts of *Alice*, *Ernest Maltravers*, *Harold* and *Zanoni*, and 159 letters, 108 of which are to W. C. Macready.

The ~~g~~ eyes of the crowd followed the gesture of the Ægyptian—and beheld with ineffable dismay—a vast vapour shooting from the summit of Vesuvius in the form of a gigantic pine tree—the branches ~~of this t~~ being of mingled blackness & fire—that shifted & wavered in their hues with every moment—now fiercely luminous—now of a dark & dying red—that again blazed terrifically forth with intolerable fire.—

There was a dead—heart-sunken silence thro' which there suddenly broke the roar of the Lyon—which from ~~with~~ beneath was echoed back—by the sharper & fiercer yells of its fellow beast—Dread seers were they of the burthen of the atmosphere & wild-prophets of the wrath to come!

of the avenging Orcus—burst forth against the false witness of my accusers.—"—

The eyes of the crowd followed the gesture of the Egyptian—and beheld with ineffable dismay—a vast vapour shooting from the summit of Vesuvius in the form of a gigantic pine tree—the branches being of mingled blackness & fire—that shifted & wavered in their hues with every moment—now fiercely luminous—now of a dull & dying red—that again blazed terrifically forth with intolerable fire.—

There was a dead—heart-sunken silence thro' which there suddenly broke the roar of the lion—which from within was echoed back—by the sharper & fiercer yells of its fellow beast.—Dread seers were they of the burthen of the atmosphere & wild—prophets of the wrath to come!

George Borrow
1803–1881

Autograph manuscript of "Legend. Isle of Moy," unsigned and undated. 4 pp. 205 x 166 mm. From the Collection of Mr. Gordon N. Ray.

George Borrow called himself Lavengro, which "in the language of the gorgios [non-gypsy races] meaneth Word Master." The temper of Borrow's word mastery was hardly academic; at its best it was not philology but linguistic exoticism, a belief in the talismanic power of words over man and beast. In *Lavengro* (1851) Borrow provides numerous examples of such a power, beginning with an episode that might have occurred when he was still an infant scribbling "holy letters" in "strange lines on the dust with my fingers," with an ape and dog for his companions. Given Borrow's faith in the mystery of words, there is nothing strange about his work as an agent in Russia and Spain for the British and Foreign Bible Society. His travels as a Bible salesman increased Borrow's gift of tongues; it was, in fact, his desire to learn Manchu that led the Society to employ him. His letters to the Society from abroad resulted in a famous book, called *The Bible in Spain: or the Journeys, Adventures and Imprisonments of an Englishman, in an Attempt to Circulate the Scriptures in the Peninsula* (1843), under which pious and Defoe-like title Borrow recounted tales of his life amidst a most ungodly set of vagabonds and villains. Despite the attractions of foreign peoples in foreign lands, Borrow's greatest love was for the Gypsies, whose manner of existence, language and appearance created a substratum of romance in England. To the Gypsies, Borrow was known not only as a word master, but also, equally to his delight, as a man of peculiar power over snakes and unusual skill with his fists.

Not surprisingly, Borrow was a prodigious translator and at his death left innumerable manuscripts of translations of songs, ballads and legends from many languages. Like most of these, the manuscript shown here is apparently unpublished; it concerns a battle which will continue until the day of judgment, because at night all the dead are awakened by witchcraft.

The largest collections of Borrow's manuscripts are in the Norwich Public Library and in the Romany Collection of the Brotherton Library at Leeds University.

[Starting line 11:] Thereupon Methin called to Mögni, entreating him to settle matters, offering him much gold by way of reparation. Thereupon Mogni answered. It is of no-use speaking of settlement for I have now drawn the sword Dainsleif which is made by the Dwarfs and is sure to kill whenever it is unsheathed, which never misses a blow or fails to wound whomsoever it smites. Methin answered: you have a sword it is true, but not victory: I call every sword good which is true to its master. Then they fought the battle which is called Madningarvig, and they fought all the day, and when it was evening the kings returned to their ships. And Mildr went at night to the field of battle, and waked up with her witchcraft all those who were dead. And the next day the kings went again to the field and fought, and so did all those who fell on the day before. . . .

visit to her father, and offered him men on
the part of Hethin who should settle the matter;
on the other hand assuring him that Hethin
was quite ready to fight and that Högni might
expect no quarter from him. Högni answered
his daughter very roughly, and when she
met Hethin she told him that Högni re
fused all composition, and bade him prepare
for battle. So they both went up upon the
island and put their forces in battle array.
Thereupon Hethin called to Högni, entreating
him to settle matters, offering him much
gold by way of reparation. Thereupon Högni
answered. It is of no-use speaking of settlement for I have now drawn the sword
Dainsleif which is made by the Dwarfs

and is sure to kill whenever it is unsheathed,
which never misses a blow or fails to wound
whomsoever it smites. Hethin answered:
you have a sword it is true, but not
victory. I call every sword good which is true
to its master. Then they fought the battle
which is called Hadningavig, and they fought
all the day, and when it was evening the
kings returned to their ships. And Hildr went
at night to the field of battle, and waked
up with her witchcraft all those who were
dead. And the next day the kings went again
to the field and fought, and so did all those
who fell on the day before. The battle went on
in this way day after day: all those who had
fallen and lay on the field of battle got
up and fought and their weapons which

Benjamin Disraeli, First Earl of Beaconsfield
1804–1881

Autograph manuscript of "The Voyage of Captain Popanilla," unsigned and undated but written ca. 1827. 222 pp. 260 x 200 mm. MA 13.

Of the many brilliant successes in the life of Benjamin Disraeli, perhaps the least unexpected was his success in literature. He had been raised in a thoroughly literary home, for his father was Isaac D'Israeli, a friend of Byron and Scott and the author of numerous belletristic and antiquarian works, among them *Curiosities of Literature* (1791–1834) and *Quarrels of Authors* (1814). His son's career as a writer began in a popular if acrimonious fashion with the publication of *Vivian Grey* (1826–7), a novel he spent much of his subsequent life trying to live down. Disraeli did not have that problem with his next book. Though *The Voyage of Captain Popanilla* did not, as the saying goes, fall stillborn from the press, it had time only to utter a "subacid pleasantry" on the state of things in general before it expired. Essentially, *Captain Popanilla* is omnibus satire, the product of a period of nervous collapse after Disraeli had completed the second part of *Vivian Grey*. Through the travels of Captain Popanilla, an untutored native from the Isle of Fantaisie who receives his education when a sea chest full of books washes ashore after a great storm, Disraeli satirizes the prevailing currents of thought in a manner that owes all too little to Swift. Because the books discovered by Popanilla bear a utilitarian, Benthamite cast, he soon finds himself asking questions like "What is the use of dancing?—what is the use of drinking wine?," questions that assault the foundations of society on Fantaisie. For his pains Popanilla is exiled and a remarkable course of adventures follows, primarily in the city of Hubbabub, a slenderly disguised London. All in all, *Captain Popanilla* is a political and philosophical *jeu d'esprit*, in which nothing, certainly not the author or his audience, is taken seriously. The passage shown here concerns the volition of the sea chest's lid and satirizes the linguistic works of James Hamilton.

~~Philosophers have often been struck by the little incidents upon which great things events depend~~

~~It would form the subject of~~ We sho[d] pursue an inquiry of great interest if we were here to ~~stop~~ pause and attempt to ascertain what wo[d] have been y probable conduct of Popanilla and the moral effects upon y social action of the isle of F. if the top of the sea chest had not ~~voluntarily~~ fallen off ~~of its own~~ by the agency of its own volition. ~~In the absence of all data upon the subject with nothing to guide us but our own acuteness~~ but as I am confidtly informed that this ~~is to be the next~~ will form y subject of discussion at the next meeting of the Union Debating Society it would be scarcely ~~be~~ fair ~~at present to proceed with it.~~ to anticipate their inferences. The top however did fall off and really revealed the ~~prettiest~~ neatest collection of little packages that ever pleased the eye of the admirer of spruce arrangement. Popanilla took up packets upon all possible subjects—smelt them—but they were not savory. He was sorely puzzled — At last he lighted on a slender volume bound in brown calf which with the confined but sensual ~~ideas~~ notions of a savage he mistook for gingerbread at least — It was "The Universal Linguist by M[r]. Hamilton or y art of ~~Smelling~~ Dreaming in Languages" ~~by~~—Illustrious Hamilton! had you been the clerk of the works during the blasphemy of Belus, Babel might have been built!...

~~Philosophers have often been struck by the little incidents upon which great things~~ events ~~depend~~

~~It would form the subject of~~ We shd. pursue an inquiry of great interest if we were here to ~~stop~~ pause and attempt to ascertain what wd. have been the probable conduct of Popanilla and the moral effects upon the social action of the isle of F. ~~voluntarily~~ if the top of the seachest had not fallen off ~~of its own~~ by a generosity of its own position. ~~In the absence of all data upon the subject with nothing to guide us but our own acuteness~~ but as I am convinced I am informed that this ~~is to be~~ will ~~the next~~ form the subject of discussion at the next meeting of the Union Debating Society it would be scarcely ~~be~~ fair ~~at present to proceed with it~~ to anticipate their inference. The top however did fall off and really revealed the ~~prettiest~~ neatest collection of little packages that ever pleased the eye of the admirer of spruce arrangement. Popanilla took up packets upon all possible subjects — smelt them — but they were not savory. He was sorely puzzled — At last he lighted on a slender volume bound in brown calf which with the confused but sensual ~~ideas~~ notions of a savage he mistook for gingerbread at least — It was "The Universal Linguist by Mr. Hamilton or the Art of ~~Smelling~~ Dreaming in Languages" &c — Illustrious Hamilton! had you been the clerk of the works during the blasphemy of Belus, Babel might have been built!!

No sooner had Popanilla passed that well formed nook which had been so often admired by the Lady whose lock of hair he had unfortunately lost ~~they~~ ~~[illegible]~~

William Harrison Ainsworth
1805–1882

Autograph manuscript of "Ket's Rebellion" ["The Fall of Somerset"], unsigned and undated but written in 1877. 558 pp. 228 x 180 mm. MA 5.

In 1881 the caption of a laudatory cartoon in *Punch* designated Ainsworth "the greatest axe-and-neck romancer of our time." Looking over his long list of novels, one might also proclaim him the greatest architectural romancer in English literature, for among his best works—written during the 1830s and '40s—are many bearing the names of buildings, real or fictional: *Rookwood* (1834), *The Tower of London* (1840), *Old St. Paul's* (1842–3), *Windsor Castle* (1843) and *Saint James's* (1844). On a lesser scale, Ainsworth was able to do with an edifice and its environs what Scott could do with the more tractable fabric of Scottish legend: translate the antiquarian spirit of the sixteenth and seventeenth centuries into a form palatable to the nineteenth-century reader. Ainsworth's research was painstaking and, with allowances for the course of his story, impeccable; it is hardly surprising that half the guest list for the dinner given in his honor at Manchester (his home city) in 1881 was composed of Fellows of the Society of Antiquaries. But Ainsworth was something more than a latter-day Dugdale searching among the records of Old St. Paul's; once the setting and the mood were established, he became an exceedingly brisk storyteller. Dick Turpin's ride to York (from *Rookwood*) is still famous, and the attractions of *Jack Sheppard* were such that in 1839 it outsold another tale of crime and criminals called *Oliver Twist*.

Ainsworth wrote almost ceaselessly, but after *The Flitch of Bacon* (1854) his day had past. The manuscript shown here, entitled "Ket's Rebellion," is a product of his later years, after he had left his home at Kensal Manor, where he regularly entertained the most brilliant members of London's literary society, and had moved to Brighton. The title "Ket's Rebellion" actually applies only to the opening section of this manuscript, in which Ainsworth uses the rebellion to set the scene in Norwich during the sixteenth century. In its revised form, this novel about the life and death of the Protector, the Duke of Somerset, was published in 1877 as *The Fall of Somerset*.

The youthful Edward the Sixth had scarcely been three years on the throne he ~~ha~~ was destined to occupy for so short a period, and his uncle, the Duke of Somerset, was still Protector, when insurrections broke out in divers parts of the Kingdom, most of which were easily quelled, with the exception of a formidable rising in the West, and another, still more formidable rising in the East. These alarming outbreaks arose from somewhat different causes. The Devonshire insurgents were opposed to the late religious innovations, and demanded a restoration of the ancient service, with its high mass, and other ceremonies; while the Norfolk ~~peasants~~ husbandmen bitterly complained that the Abbey lands, which before the Dissolution had been open to them for the pasture of their cattle, were now enclosed by the new proprietors. ~~and they the hinds themselves excluded~~ But this exclusion from the commons was not their only grievance. Wool then fetched a very high price, and it therefore suited the ~~new owners~~ new land-owners to breed sheep very extensively, and diminish the number of their cattle. Hence, they did not [illegible deletion] require so many neatherds and labourers as before, and thousands of poor men belonging to the ~~a~~ agricultural classes were thrown out of employment. . . .

(1)

Ket's Rebellion

Fair on Faint

(I. at Wymondham

[What happened Thomas's Day, 1549.

[The youthful Edward the Sixth had scarcely been three years
on the throne he was destined to occupy for so short a period, and
his uncle, the Duke of Somerset, was still Protector, when
insurrections broke out in divers parts of the Kingdom, most of
which were easily quelled, with the exception of a formidable
rising in the West, and another, still more formidable
rising in the East. [These alarming outbreaks arose from somewhat
different causes. The Devonshire insurgents were opposed to the
late religious innovations, and demanded a restoration of the
ancient service, with its high mass, and other ceremonies; while the
Norfolk husbandmen bitterly complained that the Abbey lands, which
before the Dissolution had been open to them for the pasture of their cattle,
were now enclosed by the new proprietors, and their exclusion from the commons
[But this was not their only grievance. Wool
then fetched a very high price, and it therefore suited the
new land-owners to breed sheep very extensively,
and diminish the number of their cattle. Hence, they did
not require so many neatherds and labourers as before,
and thousands of poor men belonging to the agricultural
classes were thrown out of employment. Moreover, owing to the
scarcity of oxen, meat had become excessively dear, so that
where plenty had reigned in the time of
the monks, sharp want had now to be endured
by the poor peasantry. But their complaints were unheeded by the
rich land-holders, and since redress could not be obtained
by quiet means, they determined to settle the matter in another
way. [Deep discontent, arising from similar causes,
prevailed throughout the sister county of Suffolk, so that in
all parts of East Anglia there was a strong tendency
to rebellion among the lower orders.

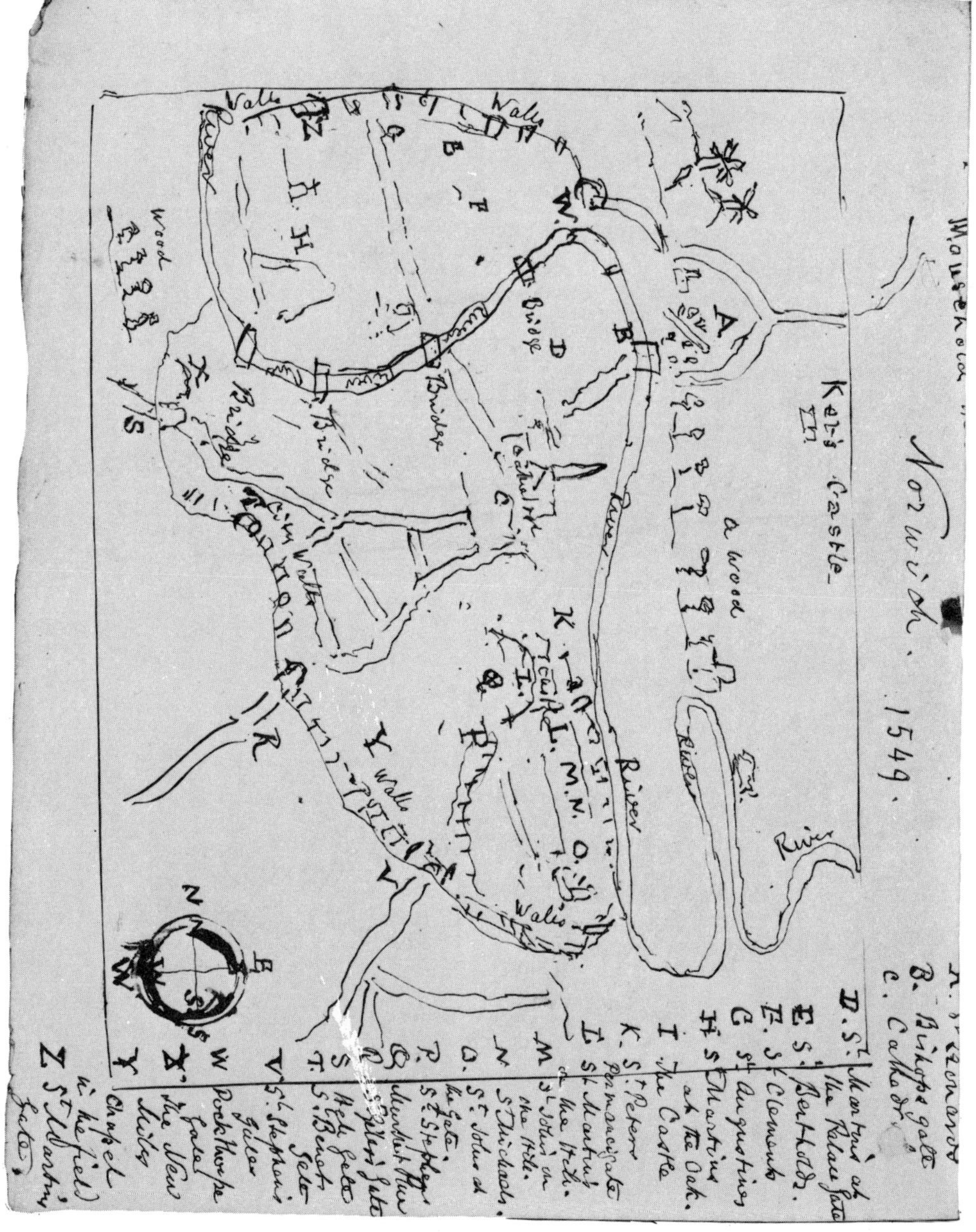

ELIZABETH BARRETT BROWNING
1806–1861

Autograph manuscript of "Sonnets from the Portuguese," unsigned and undated but written ca. 1846. 29 leaves. 159 x 101 mm. MA 933.

Everyone who reads or writes about the Brownings must at one time or another confront the story of their romantic love, a story of such mythic proportions that it has almost entirely entwined the two poets in the popular imagination. Between the unusual privacy and particularity of the Brownings' love letters, which break off in September 1846 just before they fled to Italy, and the broad, conventional outlines of the myth itself, which tells us little about the man and woman whom it concerns, there lies *Sonnets from the Portuguese*, neither too secret nor too diffuse, the only truly apt account of Elizabeth Barrett's feelings for Robert Browning. What these sonnets at times may lack in strength of imagery or emotional balance, they always make up in the confidence of their rhythms. The two shown here, Sonnets IV and XI, are among the best in this respect. The movement of these sonnets seems to offset a sense of inferiority, which Elizabeth Barrett is not shy of expressing; as they also make clear, it was always, among so many other things, the poet in each other that the Brownings loved:

> And dost thou lift this house's latch too poor
> In hand of thine? and canst thou think & bear
> To let thy music drop here unaware,
> In folds of golden fulness at my door?

Three manuscripts of *Sonnets from the Portuguese* survive, of which this is the earliest. That in the British Library contains all forty-four sonnets eventually published in *Poems* (1850), while the Morgan Library manuscript has only the first twenty-nine. The third manuscript is a fair copy prepared for the printer, and is still in private hands.

Thou hast thy calling to some palace-floor,/ Most gracious singer of high poems; where/ The dancers will break footing from the care/ Of watching up thy silent lips for more./ And dost thou lift this house's latch too poor/ In hand of thine? and canst thou think & bear/ To let thy music drop here unaware,/ In folds of golden fulness at my door?/ Look up and see the lattice broken in—/ The bats & owlets, builders in the roof./ My cricket chirps against thy mandolin!/ Hark! call no echo up in further proof/ Of desolation! there's a voice within,/ That weeps . . as thou must henceforth sing . . aloof!

And therefore if to love can be desert,/ I am not all unworthy. Cheeks as pale/ As those you see, . . and trembling knees that fail/ To bear the burden of a heavy heart,—/ This soul of a tired minstrel (better-girt/ To climb Aornus) that can scarce avail/ To pipe against the woodland nightingale,/ A melancholy music . . . . why advert/ To these things? O beloved, it is plain/ I am not of thy worth, nor for thy place:/ And yet because I love thee, I obtain/ From that same love, this vindicating grace,/ To love on still in truth and yet in vain,/ To bless thee, yet renounce thee, to thy face.

Sonnets . IV

Thou hast thy calling to some palace-floor,
Most gracious singer of high poems; where
The dancers will break footing from the care
Of watching up thy silent lips for more!—
And dost thou lift this house's latch too poor
For hand of thine? and canst thou think & bear
To let thy music drop here unaware,
In folds of golden fulness at my door?
Look up and see the lattice broken in—
The bats & owlets, builders in the roof!—
My cricket chirps against thy mandolin!
Hush! call no echo up in further proof
Of desolation! there's a voice within,
That weeps .. as thou must henceforth sing .. aloof!

Sonnets . XI

And therefore if to love can be desert,
I am not all unworthy. Cheeks as pale
As these you see,—and trembling knees that fail
To bear the burden of a heavy heart,—
This soul of a tired minstrel (better: girt
To climb Aornus) ~~[illegible]~~ can scarce avail
To pipe against the woodland nightingale,
A melancholy music . . . why advert
To these things? O beloved, it is plain
I am not of thy worth, nor for thy place!
And yet because I love thee, I obtain
From that same love, this vindicating grace,
To love on still in truth and yet in vain,—
To bless thee, yet renounce thee, to thy face.

52

John Stuart Mill
1806–1873

Autograph letter signed, dated 8 August 1837, to Thomas Carlyle.
3 pp. 228 x 183 mm.

As Mill portrays himself in the early chapters of his *Autobiography* (1873) he occasionally appears to be exactly the sort of person his friends sometimes thought him, a philosophical Frankenstein's monster, "a 'made' or manufactured man, having had a certain impress of opinion stamped on me which I could only reproduce. . . ." His peculiar education at the hands of his father (which included beginning Greek at the age of three) had given him, as he thought, "an advantage of a quarter of a century over my contemporaries," but while it opened up to him prospects that few men ever see, it also hid from him some of the ordinary sights seen by all. One of the persons most important to Mill's secondary education—the process by which he gradually freed himself from his father's influence—was Thomas Carlyle. Once Mill had accustomed himself to the poetical eccentricities of Carlyle's prose and Carlyle had recognized the fact that Mill was not about to become a "mystic," the two men overcame the chasm between them, a chasm that was an obstacle more in appearance than reality. Mill even went so far as to pass through a period of what he called stylistic "Carlylism," a "costume" which he felt "should be left to Carlyle whom alone it becomes & in whom it would soon become unpleasant if it were made common. . . ." On the subject of logic, about which Mill writes here, he believed that his differences from Carlyle's way of thinking were largely superficial. "Certainly," he writes, "we should at present, differ much in our language, but I question whether our opinions are so widely apart as they may seem."

At the time this letter was written, Mill was preoccupied with the composition of *A System of Logic*, which, he assured Carlyle, "I am getting on with, fast & satisfactorily." In fact, *A System of Logic* was not published until 1843; though Mill had been writing steadily for nearly twenty years (since the age of eighteen), it was his first original work to be published in book form.

The Morgan Library also owns Mill's manuscript of *Principles of Political Economy*, an early draft of *A System of Logic* in a scribal hand and his manuscript of a student essay, *Traité de Logique redigé d'après le cours de Philosophie de M. Gergonne. . . .*

Certainly we should at present, differ much in our language, but I question whether our opinions are so widely apart as they may seem. You call Logic the art of telling others what you believe. I call it, the art, not certainly of knowing ~~anyth~~ things, but of knowing whether you know them or not: not of finding out the truth, but of deciding whether it is the truth that you have found out. Of course I do not think that Logic suffices for this ~~inst~~ without anything else. I believe in spectacles but I think eyes necessary too. Neither do I mean by Logic, the Aristotelian way solely, or even mainly; nay, that *I do consider to be only a way of stating ~~the~~ a process of thought, not ~~a way of peculiar~~ itself a process ~~at all~~ of thought at all. I do not think that I can explain myself any farther in fewer words than my book will consist of. Thanks for your promise of reading it, which I did not more than half expect, & did not at all think myself entitled to claim. . . .*

on a subject so complicated & on which so many of the premisses have to be settled beforehand. Certainly we should at present, differ much in our language, but I question whether our opinions are so widely apart as they may seem. You call Logic the art of telling others what you believe. I call it, the art, not certainly of knowing ~~anything~~ things, but of knowing whether you know them or not: not of finding out the truth, but of deciding whether it is the truth that you have found out. Of course I do not think that Logic suffices for this ~~or~~ without any thing else. I believe in spectacles but I think eyes necessary too. Neither do I mean by Logic, the Aristotelian way solely, or even mainly; nay, that I do consider to be only a way of stating ~~the~~ a process of thought, not ~~a way of formula~~ itself a process ~~at all~~ of thought at all. I do not think that I can explain myself any farther in fewer words than my book will consist of. Thanks for your promise of reading it, which I did not more than half expect, & did not at all think myself entitled to claim.

I suppose you saw the three columns of the Times on your three volumes. Mr Sterling I suppose wrote it, & no doubt sent it to you – at least that is the belief I try to entertain whenever my conscience taunts me that I did not. In case you have not seen it, I can ~~write~~ give you in few words a summary of its contents: That the style is nearly the worst possible, everything else nearly the ~~worst~~ best possible. ~~Hist~~ The writer does not seem to be aware that this is something very like a contradiction in terms. But it is well meant, & cannot but give you many readers & Fraser some buyers who would not otherwise have been had. – However I fully sympathize in your wish to forget the book entirely. I promise you I shall forget mine soon enough after it is published: nay probably before.

I am very glad you are resting yourself by doing nothing. I am resting myself by doing something – something which is not mere everyday business, but allows me & requires one to exert my best (or some of my best) faculties. In truth I have not, for years before, had a mind free from occupation with pettinesses. That is the only true meaning of leisure – choice of work. It is not good for everybody, nor for anybody at all times: for me, just at present, it is good, & I am consequently happier than I have ever been since I had it last. I get a great deal into the country too, among trees & green fields, though with a very small share of rivulets ~~and~~ & altogether without the Solway tide waves you speak of. On the whole things go well with me, not the less so because I am as you say of yourself, "sadder" than I have ever been –

yours affectionately J. S. Mill

53

Charles Darwin
1809–1882

Autograph letter signed, dated 12 Upper Gower Street [November 1839] to John Stevens Henslow. 4 pp. 233 x 188 mm. The Dannie and Hettie Heineman Collection.

As an epigraph to his *On the Origin of Species* (1859), Darwin quoted Bacon's *Advancement of Learning:* "let no man out of a weak conceit of sobriety, or an ill-applied moderation, think or maintain, that a man can search too far or be too well studied in the book of God's word, or in the book of God's works. . . ." By adhering to the principle expressed in this quotation, Darwin effectively set the proponents of "God's word" and "God's works" at each other's throats; and the discrepancy between the biblical account of man's creation and the evolutionary account, as stated in Darwin's *The Descent of Man* (1871), remains, regrettably, a subject of heated disputation. Before Darwin was able to address the question of man's origin, however, he had first to unfold the theory presented in *On the Origin of Species*, to "stagger" the believers in the immutability of species, a virtually Platonic conception of the organization of the biological world. In doing so, Darwin presented his research confidently, but without arrogance. Writing to Henslow about Sir William Hooker (Henslow's botanical associate at Kew Gardens in the 1840s), Darwin could remark, in a manner altogether typical: "The Londoners say he is mad with envy because my book [*Origin of Species*] has been talked about: what a strange man to be envious of a naturalist like myself immeasurably his inferior!"

Henslow's effect on Darwin's career could hardly be overstated; not only was he a remarkably enthusiastic and sympathetic teacher, whom Darwin studied under at Cambridge, he was also responsible for placing his protégé on board *H.M.S. Beagle.* The correspondence between teacher and pupil, which began in 1831 during the preparations for Darwin's departure, lasted for nearly thirty years, until just before Henslow's death. The letter shown here was written after Darwin's marriage to Emma Wedgewood. Darwin encourages Henslow to prepare a work on "the very curious collection of plants from Galapagos" and a paper "on the general character of the Flora of T. del. Fuego. . . ." He also alludes to his own research: "I keep on steadily collecting every sort of fact which may throw light on the origin & variation of species."

The greatest collection of Darwin manuscripts is in the Cambridge University Library.

[Starting near bottom of verso:] I have been lately reading some remarks on the geograph. distrib. of plants & I am very curious to have a paper at some time from you on the general character of the Flora of T. del. Fuego, & especially of the Alpine Flora The one point of land which projects so far into temper [tear in manuscript] countries ought to be characterized by very peculiar forms in relation to the northern hemisphere.—Robert Brown has a very large & I believe perfect collection from Tierra del Fuego, which I daresay he would allow you to undertake, if you choose, as it has been in his possession about nine years.—. . .

me express at great length his views. I regret that Mr. Henslow has not been able to describe the species or even characterize the genera of the very curious collection of plants from Galapagos. — Do think once again of making one paper on the Flora of these islands like Roxburgh on St. Helena, or Endlicher on Norfolk Isd — I do not think ~~there~~ there will often occur opportunities of drawing up a monograph of more interest. — If your descriptions are scattered in different journals, the general character of the Flora never will be known & foreigners, at least, will not be able to refer to this & that journal for the several species — But you are the best judge. — I have been lately reading some remarks on the geograph. distrib. of plants, & I am very anxious to have a paper at some time from you on the general character of the Flora of T. del Fuego & especially of the Alpine Flora. The one point of land which projects so far into temperate countries ought to be characterized by very peculiar forms in relation to the northern hemisphere. — Robert Brown has a very large & I believe perfect collection from Tierra del Fuego, which I daresay he would allow you to undertake, if you chose, as it has been in his possession about nine years. — I do not believe anyone has published any general account of the Flora of Patagonia, — such as my collection is — it gives I am sure a very fair notion of the Flora & the climate being so peculiar, I cannot say anything more remarkable than the contrast of its ~~the~~ Flora with the of Tierra del Fuego, countries so near to each other. — Do think of these points. — I have written to Dr. Colclater — sent him my printed questions. — Don't forget to bear in mind, as you said you would for me, to notice any facts either hostile or corroboratory of my notion of the plants occasionally

Edward FitzGerald
1809–1883

Autograph letter signed with initials, dated Lowestoft, 18 January 1875, to Anna Biddell. 4 pp. 176 x 111 mm. MA 2180.

Like English gardens, the best English letters please by irregularity, a natural forgetfulness of form. Edward FitzGerald's correspondence provides one of the finest examples of this quality in the nineteenth century; for what he offers as an excuse for a wandering epistle—"I have written it off as it came into my Head"—usually serves as its highest recommendation. Where a man of FitzGerald's flexible sympathies is content to wander in prose, any reader must be content to follow. His letters combine the scenic virtues of London (which, as he aged, he came to dislike), of the countryside near Woodbridge in Suffolk, and of the sea at Lowestoft, as well as the intellectual rewards of his friendships with men like Thackeray, Carlyle, Tennyson and lesser-known, more intimate correspondents. But the chief entertainment of FitzGerald's letters is the image of FitzGerald himself in "an old room/ Beside a bright fire": "And there I sit/ Reading old things/ Of knights and ladies,/ While the wind sings:/ Oh! drearily sings!" To nearly all his friends, FitzGerald was unceasingly generous with his reading (indeed, with all his aesthetic pleasures). In the letter shown here, he writes to Anna Biddell, the sister of a nearby farmer, about one of Carlyle's last works, *Early Kings of Norway*, which appeared in serial form in *Fraser's Magazine* from January to March 1875. His comments reflect his affectionate memories of Carlyle and his pleasure in the sea: "I must write to T.C. to felicitate him on this truly 'Green Old Age'—Oh, it was good too to read it here, with that Old Sea (which also has not sunk into Decrepitude) rolling in from that North: and, as I looked up from the Book, there was a Norwegian Barque beating Southward, close to the Shore, & nearly all Sail set."

The Morgan Library also owns twenty-two of FitzGerald's letters to Horace Basham, and one from Tennyson to FitzGerald. The greatest collections of FitzGerald letters are in the Library of Trinity College, Cambridge and the Cambridge University Library.

Dear Miss Biddell— I am sending you a Treat. The old Athenæum told me there was a Paper by "Mr Carlyle" in this month's Magazine; & never did I lay out 2.6 better. And you shall have the Benefit of it, if you will. Why, Carlyle's wine, so far from weak evaporation, is only grown better by Age: losing some of it's former fierceness, and grown mellow without losing Strength. It seems to me that a Child *might read & write this Paper, while it w.^d puzzle any other Man to write such a one. I think I must write to T.C. to felicitate him on this truly "Green Old Age"—Oh, it was good too to read it here, with that Old Sea (which also has not sunk into decrepitude) rolling in from that North: and, as I looked up from the Book, there was a Norwegian Barque beating Southward, close to the Shore, & nearly all Sail set. . . .*

12. Marine Terrace: Lowestoft

Jan 18/74

Dear Miss Biddell—

I am sending you a Treat. The old Athenaeum told me there was a Paper by "Mr. Carlyle" in this month's Magazine; & never did I lay out 2.6 better. And you shall have the Benefit of it, if you will. Why, Carlyle's Wine, so far from weak evaporation, is only grown better by Age: losing some of its former fierceness, and grown mellow without losing strength. It seems to me that a Child might read & relish this Paper, while it would puzzle any other Man to write such a one. I think I must write to T.C. to felicitate him on this truly "Green Old Age"— Oh, it was good too to read it here, with that Old Sea (which also has not sunk into Decrepitude) rolling in from the North: and, as I looked up from the Book, there was a Norwegian Barque beating Southward, close to the Shore, & nearly all Sail set. Read—Read! You will, you must be pleased; & write to tell me so.

This Place suits me, I think: at this time of year: there is Life about me: & that Old Sea is always talking to one—telling its ancient Story.

Your Cousin Miss Airy wrote to ask me if I knew whose were two Lines which she quoted. She thought them to be either Burns' or Cowper's: so (I thought) they might have been, & of 500 People beside. But they touched on some peculiar Chord in herself, she said; & that made them seem more precious than to me they could seem.

My Niece Lucia goes hence some ten Days hence, upon a Visit to some old Friends hereabout. After all that, she will go to Boulge: & further I have not asked yet, nor she neither.

Yours always

E.FG.

55

Alfred Tennyson, first Baron Tennyson
1809–1892

Autograph manuscript of "The Brook," unsigned and undated but written ca. 1854. 8 pp. 211 x 136 mm. MA 465.

In 1848 Edward FitzGerald, who was no lover of Tennyson's later poetry and who had watched the "fiery Son of Gloom" wander about for nearly twenty years, told a friend that nothing "would now restore [Tennyson] to his native and abdicated powers, but such an event as the invasion of England!" As well as FitzGerald knew Tennyson, he failed to recognize that for "poets who deal in their own susceptibilities," as Tennyson did, not even the onset of war could propel them into heroic poetry. Though England was not invaded, her warships and troops did sail for the Crimea in early 1854, and in the fall of that year Tennyson began *Maud*, his first major work since the publication of *In Memoriam* and his acceptance of the poet-laureateship. *Maud* was hardly the poem FitzGerald might have expected from Tennyson in such circumstances; it is a study of madness, a monodrama in which the tumult of war resounds in the distance: "it was but a dream, yet it lightened my despair/ When I thought that a war would arise in defence of the right. . . ." And though *Maud, and Other Poems* (1855) was bitterly attacked upon publication, Tennyson believed its title poem to be one of his best. He read *Maud* to informal audiences again and again; Rossetti, Browning, Mrs. Browning and George Eliot are among the many who heard him. Eventually, even Tennyson must have realized that a two- or three-hour reading of such a trying poem as *Maud* might be an ordeal, for when he proposed to read it for William Allingham, he did so with the words, "'Allingham, would it disgust you if I read "Maud"? Would you expire?'"

"The Brook" was published in 1855 as one of the "other poems" in *Maud, and Other Poems;* its virtues were well characterized when George Eliot called it "rather a pretty idyl." Strangely, its popularity is indicated by the fact that it supplied James Thurber with the caption for one of his best cartoons: "I come from haunts of coot and hern."

I steal by lawns & grassy plots;/ I slide by hazel covers;/ I move the sweet forget-me-nots/ That grow for happy lovers.

I slip, I slide, I gloom, I glance/ Among my skimming swallows;/ I make the netted sunbeam dance/ Against my sandy shallows.

I murmur under moon & stars/ In brambly wildernesses;/ I linger by my shingly bar;/ I loiter round my cresses;

And out again I curve & flow/ To join the brimming river/ For men may come & men may go,/ But I go on for ever.

He found the bailiff riding by the farm
And talking from the point he drew him in
And there he mellow'd all his heart with ale,
Until they closed a bargain, hand in hand.

Then while I breathed in sight of haven, he,
Poor fellow, could he help it? recommenced,
And ran thro' all the coltish chronicle,
Wild Will, Black Bess, Tantivy, Tallyho,
Reform, White Rose, Bellerophon, the Jilt,
Arbaces, & Phenomenon & the rest,
Till, not to die a listener, I arose,
And with me Philip, talking still, & so
We turn'd our foreheads from the falling sun,
And following our own shadows thrice as long
As when they follow'd us from Philip's door,
Arrived, & found the Sun of sweet content
Re-risen in Katie's eyes, & all things well.

I steal by lawns & grassy plots,
I slide by hazel covers;
I move the sweet forget-me-nots
That grow for happy lovers.

I slip, I slide, I gloom, I glance
Among my skimming swallows;
I make the netted sunbeam dance
Against my sandy shallows.

I murmur under moon & stars
In brambly wildernesses;
I linger by my shingly bars;
I loiter round my cresses;

And out again I curve & flow
To join the brimming river
For men may come & men may go,
But I go on for ever.

Yes! men may come & go; & these are gone
All gone. My dearest brother, Edmund, sleeps,
Not by the well-known stream & rustic spire,
But unfamiliar Arno, & the dome
Of Brunelleschi, sleeps in peace: & he,
Poor Philip, of all his lavish waste of words
Remains the lean P. W. on his tomb:
I scraped the lichen from it: Katie walks
By the long wash of Australasian seas
Far off, & holds her head to other stars,
And breathes in converse seasons. All are gone.'

So Lawrence Aylmer, seated on a style
In the long hedge, & rolling in his mind
Old waifs of rhyme, & bowing over the brook
A tonsured head in middle age forlorn,
Mused, & was mute. On a sudden a low breath
Of tender air made tremble in the hedge
The fragile bindweed-bells & bryony rings;
And he look'd up. There stood a maiden near
Waiting to pass. In much amaze he stared
On eyes, a bashful azure, & on hair
In gloss & hue the chestnut when the shell
Divides threefold to show the fruit within:
Then, wondering, ask'd her 'Are you from the farm?'

ALFRED TENNYSON

Autograph manuscript of "Achilles Over the Trench," a translation of lines from "Iliad" xvii, unsigned and undated, but written ca. 1863–4. 2 pp. 229 x 162 mm. MA 464.

Besides their love for Arthur Hallam, whom one had known at Cambridge, the other at Eton, Tennyson and Gladstone were linked primarily by the fact that they commanded the constant attention of the British people. This fact helps explain their stiff courtesy toward each other at times when, had they been less conspicuous men, their differences might have been discussed with more animation and less punctilio. It was, for instance, Gladstone who, as Prime Minister, offered Tennyson a baronetcy, which was declined, and a peerage, which was accepted with the rather needless proviso, uttered in the House of Lords, that Tennyson was not therefore a Gladstone partisan. They fell out over literature, too, not only over such major poems as *Maud* and "Locksley Hall Sixty Years After," but also over fragmentary translations of Homer. At a dinner party in December 1865, Gladstone got hold of a manuscript book of Tennyson's translations from the *Iliad* which the poet hastily reclaimed, saying, "This isn't fair—no, this isn't fair. . . ." Tennyson was eventually persuaded to read from the manuscript, shown here, and Gladstone took his revenge for an evening of conversational affronts by interrupting the laureate with questions and corrections of his rendering of the Greek. In this, Gladstone exceeded the bounds of propriety, but not the bounds of his authority, for he spoke as the author of *Studies on Homer and the Homeric Age* (1858).

This manuscript includes two stages of Tennsyon's translation of *Iliad* xvii, lines 202 and following; it concerns the episode in which Achilles, standing aloof from the Achæans, "shouted, and Pallas far away/ Called; and a boundless panic shook the foe." Two other fragmentary translations from the *Iliad* also appear in this manuscript, as well as a few lines of Hebrew.

The principal collections of Tennyson manuscripts are at Trinity College, Cambridge, Harvard University and the Tennyson Research Centre at Lincoln.

So saying ~~lightfoot~~ the quick footed Iris ~~past away:~~ went:/ Then rose Achilles dear to Zeus; & round/ The warrior's mighty shoulders Pallas cast/ Her fringed Ægis, & around his head/ The glorious Goddess ~~crownd him with~~ wreathed a golden cloud,/ And from it kindled an ~~far~~ all-shining flame./ As when the smoke from a city goes to heaven/ Far off ~~upon~~ from out an island girt by foes;/ All day the men contend in grievous war/ From ~~out~~ their own city, & with the setting sun/ ~~Thick~~ The fires flame ~~the watchfires~~ thickly, & aloft the glare/ Goes streaming, that perchance the neighbours round ~~may see,~~/ ~~And~~ May see & sail ~~their ships &~~ to help them in their war:/ So from his head the splendour went to heaven:/ And o'er the dyke he stood, nor but with the Greeks/ ~~Mingled~~ He mixt not, as reverencing his mother's word;/ There standing cried; & Pallas over him/ Shouted. . . .

So saying ~~lightfoot~~ the quick-footed Iris ~~past away~~ went:
Then rose Achilles dear to Zeus; & round
The warrior's mighty shoulders Pallas cast
Her fringed Ægis, & around his head
The gorgeous Goddess ~~crowned him with~~ wreathed a golden cloud,
And from it kindled an ~~far~~ all-shining flame.
As when the smoke from a city goes to heaven
Far off ~~upon~~ from out an island girt by foes;
All day the men contend in grievous war
From ~~out~~ their own city, & with the setting sun
~~Thick~~ The fire flame ~~the watchfires~~ thickly, & aloft the glare
Goes streaming, that perchance the neighbours round ~~may see~~
~~And sail their ships~~ May see & to help them in their war:
So from his head the splendour went to heaven:
And o'er ~~the~~ the dyke he strode, but not with the Greeks
~~Mingled~~ He mixt not, ~~as~~ reverencing his mother's word;
There standing cried; & Pallas over him
Shouted; & ~~made a among rout below~~ one vast tumult shook the foe:
For like the ~~day~~ clear voice, when a trumpet shrills,
Blown by the fierce beleaguerers of a town,
So rang the ~~day~~ clear voice of Æakidês;

And when the ~~brazen voice~~ iron cry of Æakidês
Was heard among the Trojans, all their hearts
Were troubled, & the ~~beauteous~~ full-maned horses whirl'd
The chariots backward, knowing griefs at hand:
And ~~all~~ sheer-astounded were the charioteers
To see the dread unweariable fire
~~Which~~ That always o'er the great Peleion's head
Burnt, for the ~~grey~~ bright-eyed Goddess made it burn:
Thrice ~~from~~ the dyke he ~~gave~~ sent a mighty ~~cry~~ shout,
Thrice backward reel'd the Trojans & allies.
And there & then ~~Twelve of their best~~ noblest fell, ~~then & there, away~~
among their ~~Their~~ spears & chariots; but ~~the Greeks with joy~~ with joy the Achæans
~~Rejoicing~~ The Achæans drew ~~Drew out~~ Patroclus from ~~beneath the darts~~ the fight,
And ~~placed~~ laid him on ~~the~~ a litter, where his friends
~~Wept~~ Mourned round him, & with these Achilles ~~went~~ followed
~~Pouring~~ Weeping warm tears to see his best-beloved
~~Laid~~ Stretch'd on the bier, ~~by~~ gash'd ~~with cruel barbs~~ into gaping wounds,
Him, whom he ~~sent~~ sped with ~~horse~~ steeds & chariot ~~out~~ forth
To battle, nor ~~again beheld him come back~~ had welcomed his return.

Elizabeth Cleghorn Gaskell
1810–1865

Autograph letter signed, dated 8 January 1850, to Charles Dickens.
6 pp. 175 x 110 mm. MA 1352.

Mrs. Gaskell lived on the edge of Manchester, with the provincial home of her childhood—Knutsford, slipping out of its old ways—sixteen miles to the southwest and the miserable heart of the factory city always near at hand. Knutsford had clear ties to other country towns in literature (as Mrs. Gaskell illustrated in *Cranford*) but Manchester was like no place yet described. Her husband William, a Unitarian minister, found his mission among the poor industrial workers, and she shared with him a deeply sympathetic interest in the fate of that class. To her great credit, Mrs. Gaskell did not shrink from the squalor nor was she blind to the beauty of the scenes she discovered in the slums of Manchester. Though its low subject shocked many readers, her first novel, *Mary Barton* (1848), led to her rapid introduction to London's literary society. This in turn enabled her to extend her charitable activities. Less than ten months after meeting Dickens, she wrote to him bluntly in the letter shown here, presenting the case of a prostitute named Pasley whom she wished to rescue from prison and despair. "She looks quite a young child," Mrs. Gaskell wrote, "(she is but 16,) with a wild wistful look in her eyes, as if searching for the kindness she has never known.—and she pines to redeem herself." Through the knowledgeable assistance of Angela Burdett-Coutts (many of whose charitable interests Dickens administered) Pasley sailed for Australia on the fourth of March, and Mrs. Gaskell was provided with the central plot of *Ruth*, a somewhat strained novel about the redemption of a woman like Pasley.

Appropriately, most of Mrs. Gaskell's manuscripts and letters remain in the Midlands, at the Brotherton Library in Leeds and at the John Rylands University Library in Manchester.

---

miserable life! in the hopes, as she tells me, of killing herself, for "no one had ever cared for her in this world,"—she drank, "wishing it might be poison," pawned every article of clothing—and at last stole. I have been to see her in prison at Mr. Wright's request and she looks quite a young child (she is but 16,) with a wild wistful look in her eyes, as if searching for the kindness she has never known.—and she pines to redeem herself; her uncle (who won't see her, but confirms fully the account of the mother's cruel hardships,) says he has 30 £ of her father's money in his hands; and she agrees to emigrate to Australia, for which her expenses would be paid. But the account of common emigrant ships is so bad one would not like to expose her to such chances of corruption; and what I want you to tell me is, how Miss Coutts sends out her *protegees? under the charge of a matron? and might she be included among them? I want her to go out with as free and unbranded a character as she can; if possible, the very fact of her having been in prison &c to be unknown on her landing. I will try and procure her friends when she arrives; only how am I to manage about the voyage? and how soon will a* creditable *ship sail; for she comes out of prison on Wednesday, & there are two of the worst women in the town who have been in prison with her, intending to way-lay her, and I want to keep her out of all temptation, and even chance of recognition. Please, will you help me? . . .*

miserable life! in the hopes, as she
tells me, of killing herself, for "no one
had ever cared for her in this world,"—
she drank, "wishing it might be poison," pawned every article of clothing—
and at last stole. I have been to see
her in prison at Mr Wright's request,
and she looks quite a young child
(she is but 16,) with a wild wistful look
in her eyes, as if searching for the kindness she has never known,—and she
pines to redeem herself; her uncle (who
won't see her, but confirms fully the
account of the mother's cruel hardness,)
says, he has 30£ of her father's money
in his hands; and she agrees to emigrate
to Australia, for which her expenses
would be paid. But the account of
common emigrant ships is so bad
one would not like to expose her to
such chances of corruption; and what
I want you to tell me is, how Miss Coutts
sends out her protegees? under the
charge of a matron? and might she be
included among them? I want her to go
out with as free and unbranded a character as she can; if possible, the very
fact of her having been in prison &c to be

No 3 unknown on her landing. I
will try and procure her friends
when she arrives; only, how am I
to manage about the voyage? and
how soon will a *creditable* ship
sail; for she comes out of prison on
Wednesday, & there are *two* of the worst
women in the town who have been
in prison with her, intending to
way-lay her, and I want to keep
her out of all temptation, and even
chance of recognition. Please, will
you help me? I think you know
Miss Coutts. I can manage all except the voyage. She is a good reader
writer, and a beautiful needle-
woman; and we can pay all her
expenses &c.
Pray don't say you can't help me
for I don't know any one else to
ask, and you see the message you
sent about emigration some years
ago has been the mother of all this
mischief. Will you give my love to
Mrs Dickens & Miss Hogarth & believe me
Yours very truly E C Gaskell

Turn over

ARTHUR HENRY HALLAM
1811–1833

Autograph letter signed with initials, undated but written ca. August 1832, to William Henry Brookfield. 4 pp. 188 x 115 mm.

Every great age of verse has mourned a poet "too little and too lately known," whether his promise had begun to be fulfilled, like Sidney and Keats, or was still "early ripe," like Oldham and Hallam. Hallam is remembered differently from these other men both because his talents differed considerably from theirs and because Tennyson's elegy for him, *In Memoriam* (1850), is the protracted acknowledgment of a feeling far deeper than mere poetical regret. Though Edward FitzGerald, who saw an early version of the elegy in 1845, felt that "Lycidas is the utmost length an elegiac should reach," Hallam was clearly to be mourned according to a different standard than Edward King. In "Lycidas" and *In Memoriam* "the Poetic Soul walks itself out of darkness and Despair," but Tennyson's could not do so without calling into question the sublime assurances of God and Nature. "By the measure of my grief," Tennyson wrote, "I leave thy greatness to be guessed. . . ." *In Memoriam* was published seventeen years after Hallam's death, and beside the power and scope of Tennyson's poem the memory of what Hallam genuinely was seems very dim, though his praises abound. Gladstone, who knew him at Eton, firmly believed that Hallam's talents were eclipsed by the charms of his personality, and it is this fact that explains the love he engendered in Tennyson and Gladstone; "in this world there is one unfailing test of the highest excellence. It is that the man should be felt to be greater than his works. And, in the case of Arthur Hallam, all that knew him knew that the work was transcended by the man."

This letter to W. H. Brookfield (one of five in the Morgan Library) provides an idea of some of Hallam's personal qualities. The passage shown here describes his and Tennyson's return from a visit to the Rhine and his stay at Somersby, Tennyson's home. There, he was able to see the woman whom he loved, Tennyson's sister Emily: "I am a very unfortunate being; yet, when I look into Emily's eyes, I sometimes think there is happiness reserved for me." The fears and doubts he expresses here concern his father's objection to a possible marriage with Emily Tennyson.

The Morgan Library also owns the original typescript of Gladstone's "Personal Recollections of Arthur Henry Hallam."

I often vowed to Alfred I would write to you & as often he got into a pet, & jingled the bag of Naps, whose glad ringing sound began to come daily fainter on the ear, and their fair golden forms daily to occupy less space in the well stuffed portmanteau. We have now returned, & are at Somersby. I fear I cannot stay here long: but I snatch the gift of the hour, & am thankful. I have been very miserable since I saw you: my hopes grow fainter & fewer, yet I hope on, & will, until the last ray is gone, & then——. Emily, thank Heaven, is better than she has been, & I think rather more cheerful. Somersby looks glorious in full pride of leafy summer. I would I could fully enjoy it: but ghosts of the Past & wraiths of the Future are perpetually troubling me. I am a very unfortunate being; yet, when I look into Emily's eyes, I sometimes think there is happiness reserved for me. Certainly I am by nature sanguine & hopeful; I was not formed for despondency: if circumstances were as I wish them I hardly think I should moodily seek for new [illegible deletion] causes of disquiet. . . .

I often vowed to Alfred I would write to you
& as often he got into a pet, & jingled his
bag of Naps, whose glad ringing sound
began to come daily fainter on the ear,
and their fair golden forms daily to occupy
less space in the well stuffed portmanteau.
We have now returned, & are at Somersby.
I fear I cannot stay here long: but
I snatch the gift of the hour, & am
thankful. I have been very miserable
since I saw you: my hopes grow fainter
& fewer, yet I hope on, & will, until the
last ray is gone, & then —. Emily,
thank Heaven, is better than she has
been, & I think rather more cheerful.
Somersby looks glorious in full
pride of leafy summer. I would I
could fully enjoy it: but ghosts of the
Past & wraiths of the Future are
perpetually troubling me. I am a very
unfortunate being; yet, when I look
into Emily's eyes, I sometimes think
there is happiness reserved for me. Cert-
-ainly I am by nature sanguine &
hopeful; I was not framed for despondency.
If circumstances were as I wish them
I hardly think I should morbidly

seek for new causes of disquiet.
One thing I fear must be — even
if I succeed to the utmost of my hopes,
I think the affection of my own family
the faces of my home, the faces of my
fancy, will be lost to me. Already I
see it clearly diminishing: yet, what-
-ever guilt may weigh down my soul,
towards my father at least I feel I
have acted uprightly. I am certain I
have not deserved contempt or indiffer-
-ence: but pity rather, & tender counsel,
& perpetual love. I have been writing
you an unwarrantable letter: soon I will
write again, & more reasonably perhaps,
although I expect little else than misery
& slavery on my return home. I heard
the other day from Trench: he is
at Stradbally, mild & happy — bless
him! & thinking about the Church &
the Morning Watch still. Tennant is at
Cambridge, also Spedding — I saw them
passing through. Charley is a Revd!
& lives, poor fellow, at Tealby with
the old brute, who is bruter than ever.
Fred has had a new quarrel, & is prob-
-ably cut off with or without a shilling.
Alfred better in health & spirits than
I have seen him this long while.

59

William Makepeace Thackeray
1811–1863

Autograph manuscript of "Vanity Fair," unsigned and undated, but written in 1847. 112 leaves. 230 x 183 mm. MA 479.

Discussing Dickens' tendency to exaggerate, Thackeray in 1851 informed David Masson that "the Art of Novels *is* to represent Nature": "in a drawing-room drama a coat is a coat and a poker a poker; and must be nothing else according to my ethics. . . ." In *Vanity Fair* (1847–8) the quality of realism is not strained by mercy. Thackeray depicts coats and pokers, carriages and jewels, but they are all subordinated to his desire to portray another thing realistically: "*Vanitas Vanitatum!*" As Thackeray proves again and again in his greatest novel, vanity creates the most limited kind of dramatic irony (also the kind most useful to a humorist), for only the vain man is unaware of his vanity. From this fact, Thackeray intended to draw a "dark moral": "What I want," he told his mother, "is to make a set of people living without God in the world." Such a desire could easily have led him into egregious self-righteousness, but Thackeray defuses this possibility in several ways. His metaphor of being puppet master and his persistent inclusion within his narrative of imagined responses by readers tend to create an illusion of objectivity and lead one to conclude that, in one sense at least, *Vanity Fair* is a self-explaining novel. Finally, Thackeray does not slip into the vanity of excessive piety simply because his perception of the Becky Sharps and George Osbornes of the world is grounded in his own perception of himself: "Good God dont I see (in that may-be cracked and warped looking glass in which I am always looking) my own weakness wickednesses lusts follies shortcomings?"

The page of manuscript shown here is in Thackeray's vertical hand, and includes one of *Vanity Fair*'s reader reactions: "'We don't care a fig for her [Amelia Sedley]' writes some unknown correspondent. . . ." Visible at the center of the page is the figure of a head, which recalls the fact that *Vanity Fair* was illustrated by its author. Only Chapters 1–5, two versions of Chapter 6 and Chapters 8–13 survive in manuscript.

~~It becomes our duty now to quit And now, while these things are befalling in the country, we must travel back to London by the Sir Pitts coach, or that still more rapid conveyance the fancy, and have a little Chapter about~~ We *must now take leave of Arcadia, and those amiable people practising the rural virtues there, and travel back to London to enquire what has become of Miss Amelia.*

'We don't care a fig for her' writes some unknown correspondent with a pretty little hand-writing and a pink seal to her ~~little~~ note *'—she is* fade *and insipid'~~—&c &c &c I shan't~~ and adds some more kind remarks in this strain—wh. I should never have repeated at all, but that they are in truth prodigiously complimentary to the young lady whom they concern.*

Has the beloved reader in his experience of society never heard ~~that~~ similar remarks by good-natured female friends who always wonder what you can *see in Miss Smith that is so fascinating, or what* could *induce Major Jones to propose to that silly insignificant simpering Miss Thompson, who has nothing but her wax-doll face to recommend her?. What is there in a pair of pink cheeks and blue eyes forsooth?—these dear Moralists ask, and hint wisely that the gift of genius, the accomplishments of the mind, the mastery of Manquall's questions & a ladylike knowledge of botany & geology, the power of making poetry, the performance of rattling sonatas in the Herz manner, and so forth are ~~much~~ far more valuable endowments for a female than those fugitive charms wh. a few years will inevitably tarnish. It is quite ~~affecting~~ edifying to hear women speculate upon the worthlessness and the duration of beauty. . . .*

block Chap XII, Quite a Sentimental Chapter.

We must now take leave of ~~the innocent dwellers in~~ Arcadia, and those amiable people practising the rural virtues there, and travel back to London to ~~And now while these things are befalling in the country, we must travel back to London by the Sir Pitts Coach, or that still more rapid conveyance the fancy, and have a little chapter about~~ enquire what has become of Miss Amelia.

"We dont care a fig for her" writes some unknown correspondent with a pretty little hand-writing and a pink seal to her ~~little~~ note "she is fade and insipid" ~~&c~~ and adds some more kind remarks in this strain, wh. I should never have repeated at all, but that they are in truth prodigiously complimentary to the young lady whom they concern.

Has the beloved reader in his experience of society never heard ~~that~~ similar remarks by good-natured female friends; who always wonder what you can see in Miss Smith that is so fascinating; or what could induce Major Jones to propose for that silly insignificant simpering Miss Thompson, who has nothing but her wax-doll face to recommend her? What is there in a pair of pink cheeks and blue eyes forsooth? these dear Moralists ask, and hint wisely that the gifts of genius, the accomplishments of the mind, the mastery of Mangnall's questions & a ladylike knowledge of botany & geology, the power of making poetry, the performance of rattling sonatas in the Herz-manner, and so forth are ~~much~~ far more valuable endowments for a female, than those fugitive charms wh. a few years will inevitably tarnish. It is quite ~~affecting~~ edifying to hear women speculate upon the worthlessness and the duration of beauty.

But though virtue is a much finer thing, and those hapless creatures who suffer under the misfortune of good looks ~~are~~ ought to be ~~warned~~ continually put in mind of the fate wh. awaits them; and though very likely the Heroic female ~~such as~~ character wh. ladies admire is a more glorious and beautiful object than the kind fresh smiling artless tender little domestic goddess, whom men are inclined to worship — yet the latter and inferior sort of women must have this consolation — that the men do admire them after all: — that in spite of all our kind friends ~~warnings and~~ warnings & protests, we go on in our desperate error and folly, and shall to the end of the chapter. ~~And so~~ Indeed for my own part though I have been repeatedly ~~warned~~ told by persons for whom I have the greatest respect that Miss Brown is an insignificant chit ~~and Mrs Black has no brains~~ and Mrs. White has nothing but her petit minois chiffonné, and Mrs. ~~White~~ Black has not a word to say for herself, — yet I know ~~for~~ that I have had the most delightful conversations with Mrs. ~~B~~ ~~Black~~ White (of course, my dear Madam, they are inviolable) I see all the men in a cluster round Mrs. White's chair; — all the young fellows battling to dance with Miss Brown — and ~~in my heart I exclaim~~ so I am tempted to say to think that to be despised by her sex is a very great compliment

95

William Makepeace Thackeray

Autograph letter signed, undated but written 1–2 March 1850, to Mrs. William Henry Brookfield. 4 pp. 180 x 111 mm. MA 469.

In May 1843 Thackeray wrote one of his painfully affectionate and vivid letters to his wife, who was in an asylum in Paris; and amid news of Dickens in "geranium & ringlets," he also told her, jestingly, "I don't think I have fallen in love with any body of late, except pretty Mrs Brookfield." Thackeray's intimate friendship with Mrs. Brookfield was the result of two unhappy marriages: his own, and that of Jane Elton to the novelist's old Cambridge friend William Henry Brookfield. Thackeray's marriage had been destroyed by his wife's madness after the birth of their daughter Harriet, but the Brookfields had simply drifted apart on a pair of quite disparate expectations from life. By 1847, Thackeray was obliged to inform Brookfield that "you and God Almighty may know all my thoughts about your wife; I'm not ashamed of one of them." Mrs. Brookfield's and Thackeray's intimacy, though always innocent, continued to increase until the fall of 1851, when the strain of things led to hostile accusations on all sides and a virtual end of relations, epistolary and otherwise. After the break-up of his Brookfield friendships, Thackeray, upon hearing of a legacy left to them because they appeared to be a "model couple," commented to his mother: "O, no Satire is as satirical as the world is—no humbug in books like those out of 'em."

One conspicuous good to result from an otherwise disappointing relationship was Thackeray's letters to Mrs. Brookfield, among the best and most personal he ever wrote. This letter was written after the realization of the Brookfields' "nine years' dream," the birth of their daughter Magdalene, to whom Thackeray wrote on the day she was born. Thackeray teases Mrs. Brookfield about her doubts, asks her how much she would sell her baby for, and remarks of himself, "I feel like an old woman in thinking about you, and talk as such—you know it has been agreed that at one time of my existence I must have been a woman—darling duck, what a beauty I must have been!"

The Morgan Library owns one hundred and ten letters from Thackeray to Mr. or Mrs. Brookfield, as well as manuscripts of *Denis Duval*, *Lovel the Widower*, *The Rose and the Ring*, *The Virginians* and two of his lectures on *The Four Georges*, and numerous drawings.

I feel like an old woman in thinking about you, and talk as such—you know it has been agreed that at one time of my existence I must have been a woman—darling duck, what a beauty I must have been! We have been to the Zoological gardens this fine day, and amused ourselves in finding likeness to our friends in many of the animals. . . .

We had a dull dinner at Lady Ashburton's, a party of Baring's chiefly—and O such a pretty one—blue eyes gold hair alablaster shoulders and such a splendid display of them! Venables was there very shy and grand looking and awkward. How kind that man has always been to me. And a Mr Simeon of the Isle of Wight an Oxford man who won my heart by praising certain parts of Vanity Fair w^h people won't like. Carlyle glowered in in the evening: and a man who said a good thing speaking of a stupid place at the sea side Sandwich I think Somebody said Cant you have any fun there? O yes Corry said 'but you must take it with you'—a nice speech I think not only witty but indicating a gay cheerful heart. I intend to try after that: . . .

awful family. I feel like an old woman in thinking
about you, and talk as such - you know it has been agreed
that at one time of my existence I must have been a
woman - darling duck, what a beauty I must have been!
We have been to the Zoological gardens this fine day,
and amused ourselves in finding likenesses to our friends
in many of the animals. Thank Evns, both of the girls have
plenty of fun and humour, yours ought to have from both sides of
the house; and a deal of good besides farm If she do but pos:
:sess a mixture of Wm's disposition and your's. He will be
immensely tender over the child when nobody's by, I'm sure
of that: no father knows for a few months what it is, but
they learn afterwards — It strikes me I have made these
statements before.

We had a dull dinner at Lady Ashburton's, a party
of Barings chiefly - and o such a pretty one - blue eyes

gold hair alablaster shoulders and such a
splendid display of them! Venables was there very shy and
grand looking and awkward - How kind that man has al
ways been to me - And a Mr. Simeon of the Isle of Wight
an Oxford man who won my heart by praising certain
parts of Vanity Fair wh people won't like. Carlyle glowered
in in the evening: and a man who said a good thing
speaking of a stupid place at the sea side Sandwich I think
Somebody said Cant you have any fun there? O yes Corry
said 'but you must take it with you' - a nice speech I think
not only witty but indicating a gay cheerful heart. I in:
:tend to try after that: we intend to try after it: and by
action and so forth get out of that morbid dissatisfied
condition. Now I'm going to dress to dine with Lord
Holland - My servant comes in to tell me it's time. He's
a capital man an attentive alert silent plate-cleaning
intelligent fellow. I hope we shall go on well together

61

Charles Dickens
1812–1870

Autograph manuscript signed of "A Christmas Carol," dated December 1843. 68 leaves. 225 x 185 mm. MA 97

One of the liberties that come with the holiday season is a freer play of sentiment: what will do in December would never do in June. Annually for nearly a quarter of a century, Dickens acknowledged this fact, first in his Christmas books and then in the Christmas numbers of *Household Words* and *All the Year Round*. Nothing need be said about the fame of his first Christmas book, *A Christmas Carol*, the manuscript of which is shown here. In it, Dickens strips from Ebenezer Scrooge layer after layer of commercial flint until he exposes a vein of kindness and pure sentiment which, he believed, is common to all men and women, at some stratum of their character. Though this stratum lay very near the surface in Dickens, there is something Scrooge-like about him (and us) after all. *A Christmas Carol* draws its tremendous emotional power from the fact that it focuses so clearly on Scrooge, the outsider. The spirits of Christmases past, present and future exacerbate to an hysterical pitch the effect of Scrooge's isolation from a world in which decency and love prevail. In the end it was not the bad legs of Tiny Tim nor the plight of Bob Cratchit that drew tears from Dickens and his readers, past, present and future, but the reintegration of Scrooge into a world from which, it seemed, he had hopelessly banned himself.

Certainly, no one was more moved by *A Christmas Carol* than Dickens, in whom the tale brought forth memories of his own sad past. In a letter to C. C. Felton, dated 2 January 1844, he wrote (using the third person as if he were Scrooge in the story), "Over which Christmas Carol Charles Dickens wept, and laughed, and wept again, and excited himself in a most extraordinary manner, in the composition; and thinking whereof, he walked about the black streets of London, fifteen and twenty miles, many a night when all the sober folks had gone to bed. . . . Indeed it is the greatest success as I am told, that this Ruffian and Rascal has ever achieved."

Besides *A Christmas Carol*, the Morgan Library owns the manuscripts of two of Dickens' other Christmas books, *The Cricket on the Hearth* and *The Battle of Life*, as well as the manuscript of *No Thoroughfare*, which Dickens and Wilkie Collins wrote for the 1867 Christmas issue of *All the Year Round*.

At last the dinner was all done; ~~and~~ the ~~cloth table being~~ cloth was cleared ~~and~~ the hearth swept and the fire made up. The compound in the jug being tasted and ~~pronounced~~ considered perfect, apples and oranges were put upon the table, and a shovel full of chestnuts on the fire. Then all the Cratchit family drew round the ~~fire~~ hearth, in what Bob Cratchit called a circle—meaning half a one—and [illegible deletion] at Bob Cratchit's elbow, ~~sat~~ stood the family display of glass: two tumblers, and a custard cup without a handle.

~~They~~ [illegible deletion] They held the hot stuff from the jug, however, as well as Golden Goblets would have done; and Bob ~~serve~~ served it out with ~~a~~ beaming looks, while the chestnuts on the fire, spluttered and crackled ~~a cheerfully.~~ [illegible deletion] noisily. Then Bob proposed:

"A Merry Christmas to us all my dears. God bless us!" Which all the family re-echoed.

"God bless us every one!" said Tiny Tim, the last of all.

had had her doubts about the quantity of flour. Everybody had something to say about it, but nobody said or thought it was at all a small pudding for a large family. It would have been flat heresy to do so. Any Cratchit would have blushed to hint at such a thing.

At last the dinner was all done; the cloth was cleared, the hearth swept, and the fire made up. The compound in the jug being tasted and considered perfect, apples and oranges were put upon the table, and a shovel full of chestnuts on the fire. Then all the Cratchit family drew round the hearth, in what Bob Cratchit called a circle—meaning half a one. And at Bob Cratchit's elbow stood the family display of glass: two tumblers, and a custard cup without a handle.

They held the hot stuff from the jug, however, as well as golden goblets would have done. And Bob served it out with beaming looks, while the chestnuts on the fire sputtered and crackled noisily. Then Bob proposed:

"A merry Christmas to us all my dears. God bless us!"

Which all the family re-echoed.

"God bless us every one!" said Tiny Tim, the last of all.

He sat very close to his father's side upon his little stool. Bob held his withered little hand in his, as if he loved the child, and wished to keep him by his side, and dreaded that he might be taken from him.

"Spirit," said Scrooge, with an interest he had never felt before, "tell me if Tiny Tim will live."

"I see a vacant seat," replied the Ghost, "in the poor chimney corner, and a crutch without an owner, carefully preserved. The child will die."

"No no," said Scrooge. "Oh no, kind Spirit! Say he will be spared!"

"None other of my race," returned the Ghost, "will find him here. What then? If he be like to die, he had better do it, and decrease the surplus population."

Scrooge hung his head to hear his own words quoted by the Spirit, and was overcome with penitence and grief.

"Man!" said the Ghost, "if man you be in heart, not adamant, forbear that wicked cant until you have discovered What the surplus is, and Where it is. Will you decide what men shall live, what men shall die? It may be, that in the sight of Heaven, you are more worthless and less fit to live than millions like this poor man's child. Oh God! to hear the Insect on the leaf pronouncing on the too much life among his hungry brothers in the dust!"

Scrooge bent before the Ghost's rebuke, and trembling cast his eyes upon the ground. But he raised them speedily, on hearing his own name:

"Mr. Scrooge!" said Bob; "I'll give you Mr. Scrooge, the Founder of

Charles Dickens

Autograph letter signed, dated 11 August 1858, to Wilkie Collins.
4 pp. 178 x 112 mm. MA 93.

By 1857 Dickens had ceased to pretend that his marriage was anything but a failure. The contradictory needs that he had fused into an ideal of a wife—emotional refuge, intellectual partner, hostess, mother—had dissolved into separate roles filled by separate women, while Catherine Hogarth, the woman he married in 1836, had proved unsuited to him in every possible way. Barred from visions of marital concord, Dickens sought release from his frenetic labors through other means, none of them as rehabilitating as they should have been. This letter to Wilkie Collins alludes to two forms of escape, one—his friendship with Collins—largely confined to his middle years, the other—his public readings—beginning in 1858 and continuing until his farewell performances in the year of his death. Dickens and Collins met sometime in 1851 and as fellow novelists and devoted amateur actors they quickly formed a friendship characterized by a somewhat ribald bonhomie, as suggested by Dickens' mention in this letter of "that furtive and Don Giovanni purpose at which you hint." Nothing, however, transported Dickens so far into his own fantasies and away from his domestic problems as his series of public readings, first in London and then in the provinces. As he remarks here, the audiences were hesitant at first: "They dont quite understand beforehand what it is, I think, and expect a man to be sitting down in some corner, droning away like a mild bagpipe." His success was tremendous, and though he missed the quiet of his room and his desk, the pressure of his readings allowed him "to wear and toss my Storm away—or as much of it as will ever calm down while the water rolls—in this restless manner."

The Morgan Library has a collection of more than fourteen hundred letters by Dickens, one of the most prodigious letter writers of the nineteenth century, including most of his correspondence with Wilkie Collins, W. C. Macready and the Baroness Burdett-Coutts.

As to that furtive and Don Giovanni purpose at which you hint—that may be all very well for your *violent vigor, or that of the companions with whom you may have travelled continentally, or the Caliphs Haroon Alraschid with whom you have unbent metropolitanly; but Anchorites who read themselves red hot every night are chaste as Diana (I suppose* she *was by the bye, but I find I don't quite believe it when I write her name).*

We have done exceedingly well since we have been out—with this remarkable (and pleasant) incident; that wherever I read twice, the turn-away is invariably on the second occasion. They dont quite understand beforehand what it is, I think, and expect a man to be sitting down in some corner, droning away like a mild bagpipe. In that large room at Clifton, for instance, the people were perfectly taken off their legs by the Chimes—started—looked at each other—started again—looked at me—and then burst into a storm of applause. I think the best audience's I have yet had, were at Exeter and Plymouth. At Exeter, the best I have ever seen. At Plymouth, I read three times. Twice in one day. A better morning audience for Little Dombey, could not be. And the Boots at night, was a shout all through. . . .

not know aforehand the names of the best Hotels. As to what furtive and Don Giovanni purpose at which you hint, that may be all very well for your violent vigor, or that of the companions with whom you may have travelled continentally or the Caliphs Haroun Alraschid with whom you have undergone metropolitanly; but Anchorites who read themselves red hot every night are chaste as Diana (I suppose she was by the bye, but I find I don't quite believe it when I write her name).

We have done exceedingly well since we have been out — with this remarkable (and pleasant) incident; that wherever I read twice, the turn-away is invariably on the second occasion. They don't quite understand beforehand what it is, I think, and expect a man to be sitting down in some corner, droning away like a mild bagpipe. In that large room at Clifton, for instance, the people were perfectly taken off their legs by the chimes — started — looked at each other — started again — looked at me — and then burst into a storm of applause. I think the best audiences I have yet had, were at Exeter and Plymouth. At Exeter, the best I have ever seen. At Plymouth, I read three times. Twice in one day. A better morning audience for Little Dombey, could not be. And the Boots at night, was a shout all through.

I cannot deny that I shall be heartily glad when it is all over, and that I miss the thoughtfulness of my quiet room and desk. But perhaps it is best for me not to have it just now, and to wear and toss my storm away — or as

63

Charles Dickens

Autograph manuscript signed of "Our Mutual Friend," dated 2 September 1865. 449 leaves. 228 x 188 mm. MA 1202–1203.

Except the corpses, nothing in *Our Mutual Friend* remains still or content with its position in life for long. Everything—man, beast and object—dwells on the verge of some alarming mutation that threatens identity from within and without. The mystery at the novel's heart—who is our mutual friend?—is resolved to the reader's satisfaction before he reaches the middle of the book. But by that time, Dickens' metaphors of riotous animation have created a world in which creeping transformation overcomes almost everyone, and a dozen subordinate mysteries of identity have arisen, of the sort that troubles Twemlow: "the insoluble question whether he was Veneering's oldest friend, or newest friend." With the exception of a few humble but dignified characters, the cast of *Our Mutual Friend* is on the make, pushing upwards in society, abusing the means of its ascent and resurfacing itself with a polish that "smelt a little too much of the workshop and was a trifle stickey." No one rises more precipitously than Noddy Boffin, transformed from a hired slave into the Golden Dustman; and the mystery of his apparent corruption by wealth replaces the mystery of our mutual friend's identity. Following an impulse that degenerates into pernicious bibliomania, the first thing Noddy Boffin does upon coming into his fortune is to engage a literary man. In the passage shown here, he enters into delicate negotiations with Silas Wegg for the nightly reading of eight "wollumes" of the venerable classic, *Decline-and-Fall-Off-The-Rooshan-Empire*. Declining and falling off, Wegg introduces Boffin to the emperors Polly Beeious, Commodious and Vittle-us, eliciting from Boffin the remark, "I didn't think this morning there was half so many Scarers in Print. But I'm in for it now!"

Also shown here is a page from Dickens' part plans for *Our Mutual Friend*, which, like all of his novels, was published serially. In his part plans, he experimented with names, blocked out three or four chapters and recorded notes on character. For instance, on this sheet he rejects the names Solomon Wegg and Teddy Boffin and substitutes Chapter VII "In which Mr Wegg looks after himself" for "A Marriage Contract," which appeared as Chapter X.

This is the only manuscript of a major Dickens novel in the United States, and one of only two not in the Forster Collection of the Victoria and Albert Museum (*Great Expectations* is in the Wisbech and Fenland Museum, Cambridgeshire).

[Starting line 7 of page numbered 48:] "Could you begin tonight, Wegg?" he then demanded.

"Yes, Sir," said Mr Wegg, [illegible deletion] careful to [illegible deletion] leave all the eagerness to [illegible deletion] him. "I see no difficulty if you wish it. You are provided ~~with a~~ with the needful implement—a book Sir?"

"Bought him at a sale," said Mr Boffin. "Eight wollumes. ~~Wegg Mr. Wegg~~ Red and gold. Purple ribbon in every wollume, to keep the place. ~~Do you t~~ where you leave off. Do you know him, ~~Wegg~~?"

"The book's name Sir?" enquired Silas. [illegible deletion]

"~~His name is~~ I thought you might have know'd him without it," said Mr Boffin [illegible deletion] slightly disappointed. "His name is Decline-And-Fall-Off-The Rooshan-Empire." (Mr Boffin went over these stones ~~very~~ slowly, and with much caution) ...

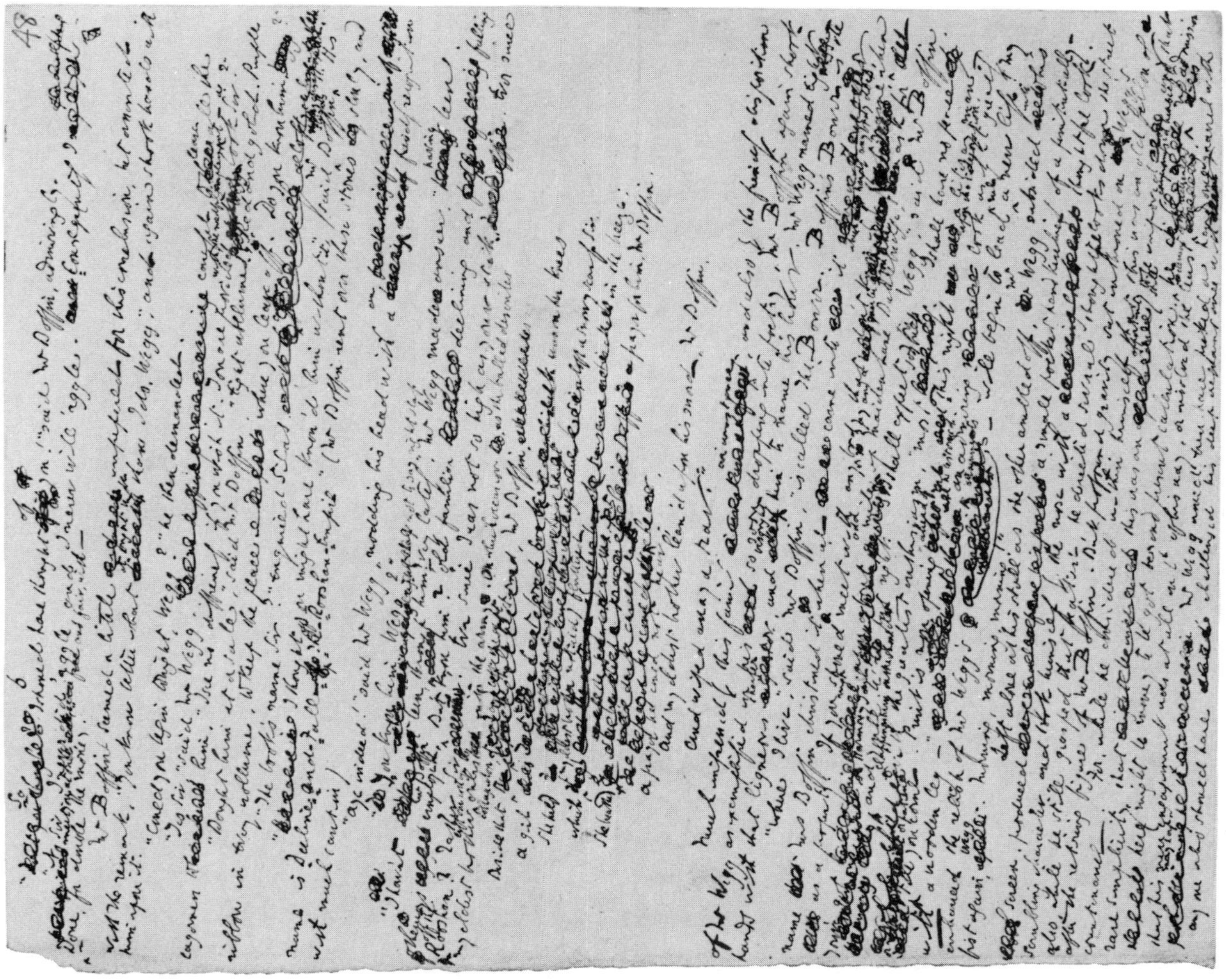

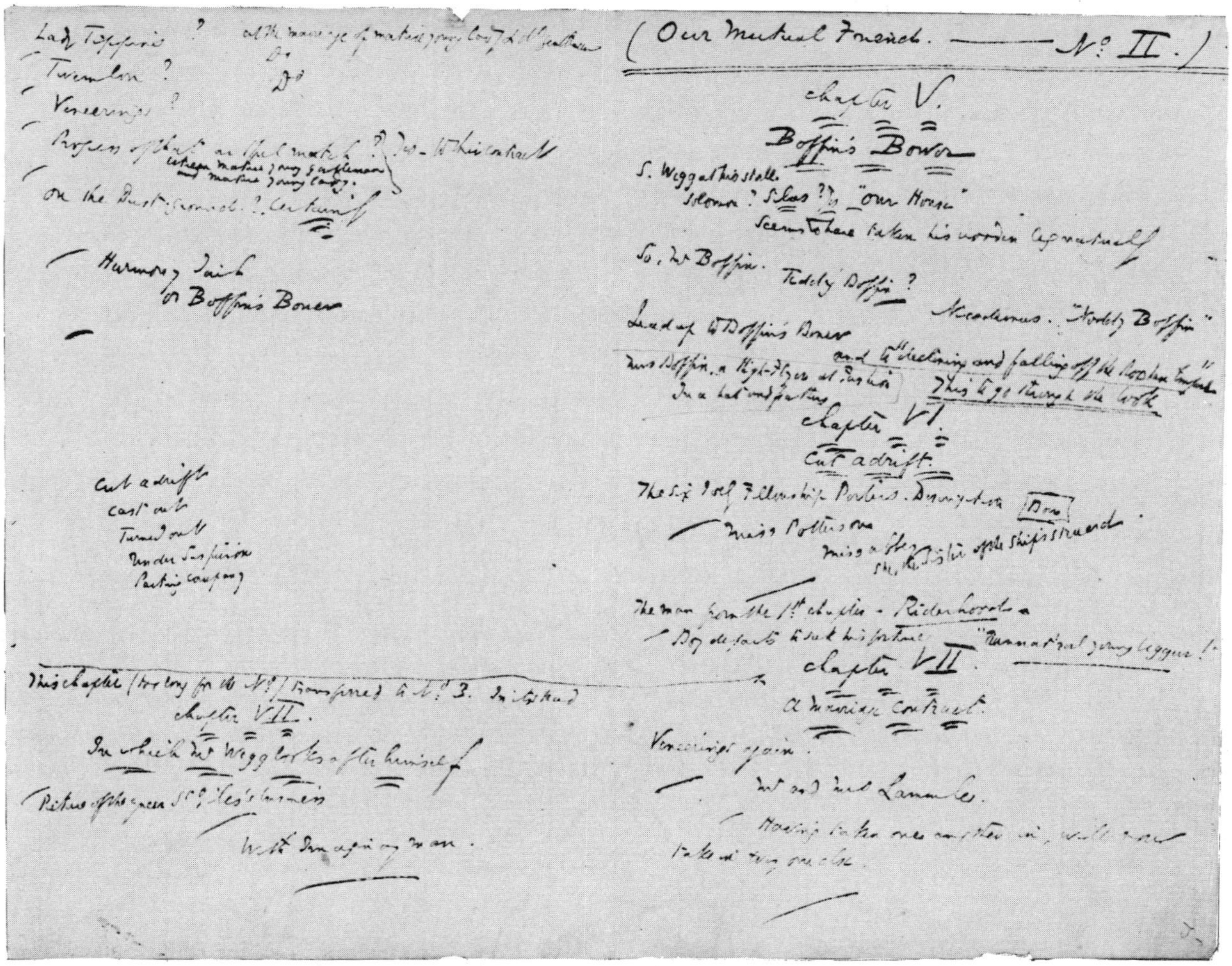

Lady Tippins ? — at the marriage of mature young lady and d° gentleman

Twemlow ? — D°

Veneerings ? — D°

Podsnap ... a match ? — mature young gentleman and mature young lady.

On the Dust Mounds ? Certainly

Harmony Jail

or Boffin's Bower

Cut adrift

Cast out

Turned out

Under Suspicion

Parting company

This chapter (too long for the N°.) transferred to N°. 3. Instead

chapter VII.

In which Mr Wegg looks after himself

Picture of the queer ... business

With ... man.

(Our Mutual Friend. —— N°. II.)

chapter V.

Boffin's Bower

S. Wegg at his stall.

Solomon? Silas? "Our House"

Seems to have taken his wooden leg naturally

So, Mr Boffin. Noddy Boffin?

Miscellaneous. "Noddy Boffin"

Lead up to Boffin's Bower

and the "declining and falling off the Rooshan Empire"

Mrs Boffin, a High-Flyer at Fashion

In a hat and feathers

This to go through the book

chapter VI.

Cut adrift.

The Six Jolly Fellowship Porters. Dry ... Bar

Miss Potterson

... of the ship's steward.

The man from the 1st chapter – Riderhood ...

Boy ... to seek his fortune. "Unnat'ral young beggar!"

chapter VII

A Marriage Contract.

Veneerings again.

Mr and Mrs Lammle.

Having taken one another in, will ... take in ... one else.

Charles Reade
1814–1884

Autograph manuscript of "Hard Cash," dated June 1862 to March 1863. 823 leaves. 427 x 257 mm. MA 357–9.

Charles Reade had little ability to create vivid characters, but he was a master of situations, or what might better be called predicaments. Something about the tangle of litigation intrigued him endlessly, particularly if litigation did not lead to justice. A brief chronology of his life resembles a crowded court calendar, and he prepared his novels as if they were complex legal briefs, apt to be scrutinized in detail (as they sometimes were) for factual accuracy. Newspaper clippings, transcripts of conversations, drafts of notes, and cards all accumulated until Reade was forced by the burden of evidence (or the pleadings of an editor) to stop research and start writing. His novels are in no sense dry, however. The subtitle of *Hard Cash*, "A Matter-of-Fact Romance," conveys a basic paradox about Reade's works: he strings proven facts, usually relating to some form of social or institutional abuse, along a thread of coincidences that would do justice to a brazen writer of romance. In *Hard Cash*, Reade attacks English lunatic asylums, which were often only brutal, hideously maladministered prisons. Though his plot is less ingenious than Wilkie Collins' in *The Woman in White* (both involve false imprisonment in an asylum), it is a true measure of his polemical skill that he provokes a greater sense of outrage and frustration in the reader than Collins does, while he employs far more conventional means.

The passage reproduced here marks the resolution of the plot in the third volume, when the missing piece of evidence (there is of course a trial going on) is recovered in the hands of one of the novel's chief villains. By a remarkable coincidence, the voice that utters the words "No; it is mine" belongs to the heroine's father, who until this moment was thought to be insane and was presumed lost at sea after his escape from an asylum. Typically, *Hard Cash* closes not only with a wedding, but also with an appendix that contains Reade's explicit defense of his novel in a public exchange of letters with a reader, a form of diversion that followed the publication of almost all his novels.

The Parrish Collection in the Princeton University Library owns a major collection of Reade manuscripts and drafts; the manuscript of his masterpiece of historical fiction, *The Cloister and the Hearth*, is in the Huntington Library, San Marino, California.

[Starting line 7:] ~~At last Fullalove applied the same tool took the dead~~ Then Fullalove came beside the arm chair and said I'm a man from foreign parts. I have no interest here but justice: and justice I'll do. He took the dead arm, and the ~~joint~~ joint creaked: he applied the same tool to the bone and parchmt hand he had to the door: it creaked too but more faintly and opened & let out this.

Here the block. Receipt shaded to imitate discoloration and with a bold thumb mark white . . . of which please send copy to author as soon as poss:

A stately foot came up the stair but no one heard it. All were absorbed in the strange weird sight and this great stroke of fate or Providence. This is yours I suppose, said Fullalove and handed it to Edward. No! no cried Compton. ~~He has left~~ See: Ive just found a will, bequeathing all he has in the world with his blessing to Miss Julia Dodd. . . .

Then, ~~there was a deadlock~~ [as a trifle hurt the sealing / the hesitation in terms / hesitation]: and Fullalove ~~undertook the task, and took the same little tool~~. all but Julia stood, and [instinctively] the ~~dead~~ [body that held] ~~[illegible]~~ the out the ~~[illegible]~~ [precious] [Soul of the lost] Each yet ~~holding it~~ still, as in life, ~~unwilling to part / [illegible] to [illegible]~~ ~~loth it~~ [seemed] loth to part with it. [29] [30] [292]

~~At last~~ ~~Fullalove applied the same tool~~ Then Fullalove came beside the arm chair, and said I'm a man for foreign parts. I have no interest here but justice: and justice I'll do. He took the dead ~~took the dead~~ arm. and the ~~[illegible]~~ [joint] creaked: he applied the same tool to the bone and parchment hand he had to the arm: it creaked [but more faintly] and opened & let out this.

here

Here the block

Receipt shaded to imitate discoloration and with a bold thumb mark

White .. of which please send copy to author as soon as poss.

A stately foot came up the stair but no one heard it. All were absorbed in the strange [weird sight, and] {this great stroke of fate or Providence}

This is yours, [I suppose] said Fullalove and handed it to Edward. No! no cried Compton. ~~He has~~ See: He ~~left~~ [just found] a will. bequeathing all he has in the world with his blessing to Miss Julia Dodd. These sovereigns are yours then. But about all the paper: as ~~Possession is nine points~~ ~~I take it Miss Dodd said he. it is yours in~~ ~~Law~~ [your legal advisers] { ~~All these sovereigns on the floor are yours~~ too. I insist on your taking it immediately. Possession is nine points. however it is actually yours in virtue of this bequest.

A solemn passionless voice ~~fell [illegible]~~ [seemed] to fall on them from the Clouds.

~~The voice said~~

small caps. No; it is mine.

End of 30 .

65

ROBERT BROWNING
1812–1889

Autograph manuscript of "Dramatis Personae," signed and dated 20 June 1864. 211 pp. 225 x 170 mm. MA 33.

Browning's notoriously eccentric style gave Victorian readers a rather difficult time, so much so that Carlyle—by no means renowned for perspicuity himself—was obliged to ask again and again about *Fifine at the Fair*, "What the *Devil* do you mean?" Even those who were disposed to praise Browning often found it difficult to do so in terms that were unequivocally positive; in what might be considered a consensus of those in Browning's favor, George Eliot remarked, "I do not find him unintelligible, but only peculiar and original." What was peculiar about Browning, at a time of slackening verse, was the density with which he packed ideas and perceptions into poems that seemed to find new uses and new idioms for the English language. Browning's adoption of dramatic masks, the *personae* in *Dramatis Personae*, freed him from the conventional limitations of Victorian poetic diction—nowhere more so than in "Caliban upon Setebos; or, Natural Theology in the Island," the manuscript of which is shown here—and allowed him to portray the psychological characteristics of a multitude of historical personages, a feat in which he was rivaled only by his neighbor in Florence, Walter Savage Landor. "Caliban upon Setebos" goes beyond even the norms of Browning's practice, for it is a dramatic monologue in which Shakespeare's Caliban, who in *The Tempest* had language only "to curse," lets "the rank tongue blossom into speech" and transcends his baseness in order to speculate on the possibility of God and the source of existence.

This manuscript was presented in June 1864 to Frederic Chapman, Browning's publisher, with whom he eventually quarreled and parted in 1868. Though many manuscripts of Browning's verse exist in libraries too numerous to list, there is no Browning poetical manuscript quite like this, for it contains all the poems that appeared in *Dramatis Personae*, one of Browning's most important collections of verse. No manuscript of *Men and Women* is known to survive. The Morgan Library also owns the manuscripts of *Asolando*, "Hervé Riel," "Home Thoughts from Abroad," "How They Brought the Good News from Ghent to Aix" and "A Last Word, To E. B. B."

'Thinketh, He made thereat the sun, this Isle,/ Trees and the fowls here, beast and creeping thing;/ Yon otter, sleek-wet, black, lithe as a leech—/ Yon auk, one fire-eye in a ball of foam;/ That floats and feeds—a certain badger brown/ He hath watched hunt with that slant white-wedge eye/ By moonlight—and the pie with the long tongue/ That pricks deep into oakwarts for a worm/ And says a plain word when he finds his prize/ But will not eat the ants—the ants themselves/ That build a wall of seeds and settled stalks/ About their hole—He made all these and more,/ Made all we see, and us—in spite: how else?/ He could not, Himself, make a second self/ To be His mate; as well have made Himself:/ He would not make what He mislikes or slights,/ An eyesore to Him, or not worth His pains,/ But did, in envy, listlessness and sport,/ Make what Himself would fain, in a manner, be—/ Weaker in most points, stronger in a few,/ Worthy, and yet mere playthings all the while,/ He could admire and mock too,—that is it: . . .

'Thinketh, He made thereat the sun, this Isle,
Trees and the fowls here, beast and creeping thing;
Yon otter, sleek-wet, black, lithe as a leech –
Yon auk, one fire-eye in a ball of foam,
That floats and feeds – a certain badger brown
He hath watched hunt with that slant white-wedge eye
By moonlight – and the pie with the long tongue
That pricks ~~deep~~ into oakwarts for a worm
And says a plain word when he finds his prize
But will not eat the ants – the ants themselves
That build a wall of seeds and settled stalks
About their hole – He made all these and more,
Made all we see, and us – in spite: how else?
He could not, Himself, make a second self
To be His mate; as well have made Himself:
He would not make what He mislikes or slights,
An eyesore to Him, or not worth His pains,
But did, in envy, listlessness and sport,
Make what Himself would fain, in a manner, be –
Weaker in most points, stronger in a few,
Worthy, and yet mere playthings all the while,
He could admire and mock too, – that is it:
Because, so brave, so better though they be,

Robert Browning

Autograph letter signed, dated 2 May 1882, to George Moulton-Barrett. 8 pp. 182 x 113 mm. MA 2148.

When Elizabeth Barrett Browning died in 1861, two tasks fell upon her husband: the education of their son Pen (who was twelve when his mother died), and the safeguarding of her literary reputation. Neither of these tasks proved to be as easy as Browning had anticipated. During the subsequent decade, he tried to place Pen in a respectable track at Oxford, even contemplated the possibility of his becoming a barrister, but Pen seemed destined to wander out of such conventional courses. Most of Browning's plans for his son's career ended with the words "Pen has failed again," that is, until Pen came under the influence of John Everett Millais and was encouraged to develop his evident, if not very extensive, artistic talents. As for Mrs. Browning's literary reputation, it was never higher than at her death, which seemed to critics and the public a tragic abbreviation of a life that still promised much poetry. While Browning was determined to keep interest in her poetry fresh, he was equally intent upon respecting her often-expressed desire for privacy, as the letter shown here makes evident. As his own social eminence increased, the annoyance of prospective biographers who needed information and a glimpse at her correspondence also increased, to the point where ludicrous yet irritating threats were made on Browning. As he tells his brother-in-law, George Moulton-Barrett, one writer had warned him that "unless I furnished these details for a memoir . . . the writer's *friend* would certainly print,—for instance,—that my wife had been a governess. . . ." But most applications to Browning were for "a publication of the Letters," which Browning vetoed with a single exception: his wife's correspondence with Richard Hengist Horne, with whom she had collaborated on *A New Spirit of the Age* (1844). Browning's reasons for this exception were largely charitable: "poor, old and pitiable, [Horne] saw a golden resource in the publication of the correspondence which began and, in the main, ended before I knew the writer."

The Morgan Library owns most of Mrs. Browning's correspondence with R. H. Horne, fifty-eight letters to her brother George, and one hundred and fourteen letters by her husband, including forty-seven to Chapman and Hall and thirty-four to George Barrett.

Your remarks refer to the inaccuracies in an article published by a magazine. As they are merely inaccuracies and no worse, I leave them unnoticed as on other similar occasions, from a determination not to be drawn into furnishing any biographical details on any pretence whatever. What a pressure has been put upon me to break my determination you do not imagine, I am sure: even threats *have been tried (years ago, I was informed that unless I furnished these details for a memoir in the* Revue des Deux Mondes, *the writer's* friend *would certainly print,—for instance,— that my wife had been a governess—"in vain, I tell my friend it is untrue; I cannot remove the conviction, unless &c." all which I stopped by myself appealing to the Editor. The applications have generally been for a publication of the Letters I may possess or have a control over—or at least for leave to inspect them for the sake of what biographical information they might contain. I have once,—by declaring I would prosecute by law,—hindered a man's proceedings who* had obtained all the letters to Mr Boyd, *and was soliciting, on the strength of that acquisition, letters in all the quarters he guessed likely. . . .*

is now before me, and which gives me the opportunity of saying what has long been much on my mind.

Your remarks refer to the inaccuracies in an article published by a magazine. As they are merely inaccuracies and no worse, I leave them un=noticed as on other similar occasions, from a deter=mination not to be drawn into furnishing any biographical details on any pretence whatever. What a pressure has been put upon me to break my determination you do not imagine, I am sure: even threats have been tried (years ago, I was in=formed that unless I furnished these details for a memoir in the _Revue des Deux Mondes_, the writer's friend would certainly print, for instance that my wife had been a governess—"in vain do I tell my friend it is untrue, I cannot remove the conviction, unless &c." all which I stopped by myself appealing to the Editor. The applications have generally been for a publication of the Letters I may possess or have a control over—or at least for leave to inspect them for the sake of what biographical information they might contain. I have once, by declaring I would prosecute by law, hindered a man's proceedings who had obtained all the letters to Mr Boyd, and was soliciting, on the strength of that acquisition, letters in all the quarters he guessed likely. The only instance in which I departed from my rule was that of Horne—who, poor, old and pitiable, saw a golden resource in the publication of the corres=pondence which began and, in the main, ended before I knew the writer. I found he would not take money for giving up these, and, on the whole, in my confidence that nothing but literature would have been discussed in them, I acted as I conceive her generous spirit would desire. It would be a long affair if I troubled you with my troubles of this nature during the last twenty years: I shall just enclose, as a sample, a letter I received a few weeks ago—the proposal mentioned in it, and my refusal to accede to it, having

Anthony Trollope
1815–1882

Autograph manuscript of "The Way We Live Now," unsigned and undated but written in 1873. 1,212 pp. 257 x 203 mm. MA 3206. Purchased as the gift of the Fellows, with the special assistance of individual Fellows.

One of Trollope's most devoted readers was Edward FitzGerald, translator of the *Rubáiyát*, who, while sorting out literary preferences with Thackeray's daughter, remarked, "I sincerely think I must be wrong in being utterly unable to relish G. Eliot. Now Trollope I can read forever—though I generally forget what I read: but I do think he is much profounder in Character than that dreadful Evans, only he goes along so easily that People think him shallow." Were the words "much profounder" modified somewhat, FitzGerald's statement is one to which most Trollopians would assent. Trollope's shallowness and the effect of his facility in composition have long been subjects of debate, but there is no question that he manages to evoke a world all his own, of perpetual interest, especially in the Barsetshire novels where he rivals George Eliot on her own clerical ground. *The Way We Live Now*, shown here in manuscript, is the product of a later period and a more specific satiric purpose, which may be described as a single-handed attempt to reverse, in the commercial world, the trend described by Carlyle and summarized by Trollope: "we are all going straight away to darkness and the dogs." *The Way We Live Now* was meant, among other things, to puncture the illusion of commercial empires financed by fragile credit, to show the moral hollowness behind the puffery of Augustus Melmotte, financier and swindler extraordinaire. The novel goes beyond a denunciation of Melmotte, however, and takes in the corruption of the current periodical press as well; above all, it depicts the willingness of the British to allow themselves to be duped by foreigners and their own cupidity.

The passage shown here recounts the rather legendary qualifications Melmotte brings to British society: "It was said that he had made a railway across Russia, that he provisioned the Southern Army in the American civil war... and had at one time bought up all the iron in England."

The Morgan Library also owns the manuscript of *He Knew He Was Right* and twenty-six letters by Trollope. The best collections of Trollope manuscripts are those owned by Yale University and Robert H. Taylor of Princeton, New Jersey.

[Starting line 9:] It was at any rate an established fact that Mr Melmotte had made his [illegible deletion] wealth in France. He ~~had~~ no doubt had had enormous dealings in other countries as to which stories were told which must surely have been exaggerated. It was said that he had made a railway across Russia, that he provisioned the Southern Army in the American civil war, that he had supplied Austria with arms, and had at one time bought up all the iron in England. He could make or mar any Company by buying or selling stock, and could make money dear or cheap as he pleased. All this was said of him in his praise,—but it was also said that he was regarded in Paris as the most gigantic swindler that had ever lived, that he had made that city to hot to hold him, that he had endeavoured to establish himself in Vienna but had been warned away by the police, and that he had at length found that British freedom would alone allow him to enjoy without persecution the fruits of his industry. ...

wife was a foreigner,—an admission that was necessary
No 1 as she spoke very little English. Melmotte himself spoke his
chap 4 "native" language fluently, but with an accent which betrayed
39 at least a long expatriation. Miss Melmotte,—who a very short time since
had been known as Mademoiselle Marie,—spoke English well, but as
a foreigner. In regard to her it was acknowledged that she had
been born out of England,—some said in New York, but Madame Melmotte, who must
have known, had declared that the great event had taken place in Paris.

N Williams It was at any rate an established fact that Mr
Melmotte had made his wealth in France. He had no doubt had
had enormous dealings in other countries as to which stories were told
which must surely have been exaggerated. It was said that he had
made a railway across Russia, that he provisioned the Southern army
in the American civil war, that he had supplied Austria with
arms, and had at one time bought up all the iron in England. He
could make or mar any Company by buying or selling stock, and
could make money dear or cheap as he pleased. All this was said
of him in his praise,—but it was also said that he was regarded
in Paris as the most gigantic swindler that had ever
lived, that he had made that city too hot to hold him, that
he had endeavoured to establish himself in Vienna and had
been warned away by the police, and that he had at length
found that British freedom would alone allow him to enjoy without
persecution the fruits of his industry. He was now established, privately
in Grosvenor Square, and officially in Abchurch Lane, and it was
known to all the world that a Royal Prince, a Cabinet Minister, and

CHARLOTTE BRONTË
1816–1855

Autograph manuscript of "The Professor," signed "Currer Bell," and dated 27 June 1846. 339 leaves. 230 x 185 mm. MA 31.

In Chapter Five of *Villette* the Aurora Borealis speaks to Lucy Snowe, saying in Biblical ones: "Leave this wilderness and go out hence." "Hence," for Charlotte Brontë and her sister Emily, meant Belgium; in February 1842 they left Haworth for that country in order to attend and teach in a Belgian school. Their further goal was to found a school of their own (with their sister Anne) after returning to England. "The Misses Brontë's Establishment for the Board and Education of a limited number of Young Ladies" never came into existence, but Charlotte's two years in Brussels (the second without Emily) were fruitful in other ways. Her experiences at the Pensionnat Heger and the conflict of her feelings for its proprietors, Zoë and Constantin Heger, provided an autobiographical mold into which she could pour the relatively unshaped intensity of her romantic adolescent writings. *The Professor*, Charlotte's first novel, and *Villette*, her last, are both set in Belgium (or Labassecour as it is called in *Villette*) and draw heavily on the trials of her life in the Pensionnat. Though all of Charlotte's novels retain something of the communal Angrian epic devised by the Brontës as children, *The Professor* reveals quite clearly the transition from heroic dreams to realistic fiction. The Angrian theme of hatred between brothers begins the novel, but soon falls away, leaving the more engaging and, to Charlotte, more heartfelt theme of the growth of love between William Crimsworth, the narrator, and his student, Frances Evans. In this novel Charlotte tried to leave behind the Byronic exoticism of Angria and to adopt a hero who "should share Adam's doom, and drain throughout life a mixed and moderate cup of enjoyment." But the publishers to whom she submitted the manuscript had, as she remarked, "a passionate preference for the wild, wonderful, and thrilling," and *The Professor* was not published until after her death. Shown here is the passage from Chapter 19 in which Crimsworth finds Frances Evans at the grave of her aunt and finally realizes how much he loves her.

[Starting line 6:] I loved the movement with which she confided her hand to my hand; I loved her, as she stood there, pennyless and parentless, for a sensualist—charmless, for me a treasure, my best object of sympathy on earth, thinking such thoughts as I thought, feeling such feelings as I felt; my ideal of the shrine in which to seal my stores of love; personification of discretion and forethought, of diligence and perseverance, of self-denial and self-control—those guardians, those trusty keepers of the gift I longed to confer on her—the gift of all my affections; Model of truth and honour, of independence and conscientiousness, those refiners and sustainers of an honest life; silent possessor of a well of tenderness, of a flame as genial as still, as pure as quenchless, of natural feeling, natural passion, those sources of refreshment and comfort to the sanctuary of home. I knew how quietly and how deeply the well bubbled in her heart; I knew how the more dangerous flame burned safely under the eye of reason; I had seen when the fire shot up a moment high and vivid, when the accelerated heat troubled life's current in its channels, I had seen reason reduce the rebel and humble its blaze to embers. I had confidence in Frances Evans . . . .

brow and insensate nerves, but I love the courage of the strong heart, the fervour of the generous blood; I loved with passion the light of Frances Evans' clear hazel eye when it did not fear to look straight into mine; I loved the tones with which she uttered the words:

"Mon maître! Mon maître!"

I loved the movement with which she confided her hand to my hand; I loved her, as she stood there, pennyless and parentless, for a sensualist - charmless, for me a treasure, my best object of sympathy on earth, thinking such thoughts as I thought, feeling such feelings as I felt; my ideal of the shrine in which to seal my stores of love; personification of discretion and forethought, of diligence and perseverance, of self-denial and self-control - those guardians, those trusty keepers of the gift I longed to confer on her - the gift of all my affections; Model of truth and honour, of independence and conscientiousness, those refiners and sustainers of an honest life; silent possessor of a well of tenderness, of a flame as genial as still, as pure as quenchless, of natural feeling, natural passion, those sources of refreshment and comfort to the sanctuary of home. I knew how quietly and how deeply the well bubbled in her heart; I knew how the more dangerous flame burned safely under the eye of reason; I had seen when the fire shot up a moment high and vivid, when the accelerated heat troubled life's current in its channels, I had seen Reason reduce the rebel and humble its blaze to embers. I had confidence in Frances Evans,

69

EMILY BRONTË AND ANNE BRONTË
1818–1848 1820–1849

Autograph manuscript signed of "The night of storms has past," dated 10 June 1837. 1 p. 123 x 75 mm. Bequest of Mrs. Henry Houston Bonnell. Autograph manuscript signed of "To Cowper," dated 10 November 1842. 3 pp. 180 x 113 mm. MA 28.

The appeal that the Brontë family makes to the imagination is crystallized in Emily Brontë, who, of all the children of Haworth Parsonage, possessed most intensely and most privately the visionary genius that united them all. Yet of all the Brontës, Emily is also the one who remains the least imaginable, precisely because of her ability to dwell in an inner world of her own creation. "So hopeless is the world without,/ The world within I doubly prize," she wrote in "To Imagination," and barring a handful of letters and the few recollections of those who knew her, only the records of her world within survive. The memoir prepared by Charlotte Brontë for the 1850 edition of *Wuthering Heights* contains only one salient fact about Emily, a fact that Charlotte clearly thought was the key to her character: "My sister Emily loved the moors. . . . She found in the bleak solitude many and dear delights; and not the least and best loved was—liberty." If Emily's poems—those published in 1846 under the pseudonym of Ellis Bell and those not published during her lifetime—do not tell us much about her relations to the external world, they nonetheless perfectly portray her sustaining faith in her inner visions, which seem to have fled in the year before her death. The poem shown here, written in Emily's miniature hand, recounts a troubling dream about "the sea of deep eternity/ The gulph o'er which mortality/ Has never never been."

The evangelical religion in which the Brontë children were raised seems to have taken deepest root in Anne, the author of *Agnes Grey* and *The Tenant of Wildfell Hall.* Frail from the first, Anne made her poems the expression of an abiding faith which was tried by an inwardly passionate nature. The poem shown here, one of her most famous, is addressed to the poet William Cowper, whose own faith endured the conviction that he had been irrevocably damned. Perhaps the most interesting feature of this manuscript is the deletions, which alter the meter of the second and fourth lines in each stanza and radically improve the poem.

The Morgan Library's collection of manuscripts by the Brontës was substantially increased in 1969 with the bequest of Mrs. Henry Houston Bonnell, whose husband had formed a superb gathering of Brontëana, part of which is now in the Brontë Parsonage Museum at Haworth.

June 10th 1837/ E. J. Brontë

The night of storms has past/ The sunshine bright and clear/ Gives glory to the verdant waste/ And warms the breezy air

And I would leave my bed/ Its cheering smile to see/ To chase the visions from my head/ Whose forms have troubled me

Of things that God alone could teach?/ And whence that ~~Angel~~ purity;/ That hatred of all sinful ways/ That ~~kind and~~ gentle charity?

Are these the symtoms of a heart/ Of ~~every~~ Heavenly grace bereft/ For ever banished from its God/ To Satans ~~wildest~~ fury left? . . .

June 10th 1837
E J Brontë

The night of storms has past
The sunshine bright and clear
Gives glory to the verdant waste
And warms the breezy air

And I would leave my bed
Its cheering smile to see
To chase the visions from my head
Whose forms have troubled me

In all the hours of gloom
My soul was wrapt away
I dreamt I stood by a marble tomb
Where royal corpses lay

It was just the time of eve
When parted ghosts might come
Above their prisoned dust to grieve
And wail their woeful doom

And truly at my side
I saw a shadowy thing
Most dim and yet its presence there
Curdled my blood with ghastly fear
And ghastlier wondering

My breath I could not draw
The air seemed ranny
But still my eye with maddening gaze
Were fixed upon its fearful face
And its were fixed on me

I fell down on the stone
But could not turn away
My words died in a voiceless moan
When I began to pray

And still it bent above
Its features full in view
It seemed close by and yet more far
Than this world from the farthest star
That tracks the boundless blue

Indeed twas not the space
Of earth or time between
But the sea of deep eternity
The gulph o'er which mortality
Has never never been

O bring not back again
The horror of that hour
When its lips opened and a sound
Awoke the stillness reigning round
Faint as a dream but the earth shrank
And heavens lights shivered neath its power

Woe for the day Regina's pride
Regina's hope is in the grave
And who shall rule my land beside
And who shall save

Woe for the day with gory tears
My country's sons this day shall rue
Woe for the day a thousand years
Can not repair what one shall do

Woe for the day mixt with the wind
That sad lament was ringing
It almost broke my heart to hear
Such dreary dreary singing

3

To holy things and holy men
And how ~~couldst thou~~ so sweetly
sing —

Of things that God alone could [teach?]
And whence that ~~Angel~~ purity;
That hatred of all sinful ways
That ~~kind~~ ~~and~~ gentle charity?

Are these the symptoms of a heart
Of ~~every~~ Heavenly grace bereft
For ever banished from its God
To Satans ~~wildest~~ fury left?

Yet should thy ~~blackest~~ [darkest] fears be true
If Heaven ~~decrees~~ be so severe
That such a soul as thine is lost
O! how ~~my God~~ shall I appear?

Anne Brontë
Nov — 10th. 1842

(1846.92)

ARTHUR HUGH CLOUGH
1819–1861

Autograph manuscript of "Mari Magno" ("Where lies the land to which the ship would go?"), unsigned and undated, but written ca. 1852–3. 2 pp. 114 x 181 mm. MA 925.

In the bustling exchange of literary cultures that took place between England and America in the 1850s, Arthur Hugh Clough played a modest, though engaging part. Unlike Thackeray, with whom he sailed to America in 1852, Clough did not take the new world by storm; his reputation as the author of *The Bothie of Tober-na-fuosich* (1848) was, of course, a smaller one than Thackeray's, but his relations with American society in Boston, Cambridge and Concord were more intimate than that permitted to awesome literary lions. In England Clough had resigned his fellowship at Oriel because of doubts about subscription to the thirty-nine articles; in the United States, whose religion he called "rococo," he explored the possibility of taking pupils and bringing his fiancée (whom he had left in England) "to a wooden Yankee-Doric Anglo-savage wigwam. . . ." Clough was as enthusiastic about "Yankeeland" as it was about him, and he made a rapid entrance into the finest society that Massachusetts had to offer; at the Emersons' he found "tea and Mr. Thoreau"; he dined regularly with the "Extremely-respectables" (the Ticknors and their circle) and became a particular intimate of the Nortons and Longfellows. But in June 1853 Clough suddenly sailed for England and an examinership in the Council Office on Downing Street, a decision prompted by eagerness to wed and unresolved diffidence about "pupillizing," the value of which he could not, in his own mind, adequately assess. As a friend remarked, Clough had a way (admirable, if not quite practical) of "putting a fine point on things": "I fear me much that you would turn aside to discuss in yourself whether you were 'doing any good'. . . ." In a letter to Emerson of 1854, Clough explained why he had felt at home in the United States, and his explanation (not as true as it once was) turns upon a recurring theme in his poetry: "I think you are better and more happily off in America, where the vastness of the machinery does not destroy the sense of an individual moral purpose. . . ."

Clough's travels, particularly during his final attempt to repair his broken health, enter largely into his poetry. The poem shown here, "Mari Magno," is one of a group of poems that was probably begun on his voyage out to America. It was also intended to serve as the envoi to the poem on which Clough was working at the time of his death, also called "Mari Magno," but with the added subtitle, "Tales on Board." This was to be a gathering of shipboard tales, linked together in the manner of *The Canterbury Tales* and calling to mind, for modern readers, Conrad's Marlowe stories.

The largest group of manuscripts and letters by Clough is in the Bodleian Library.

Mari Magno/ Where lies the land to which the ship wo^{d} go?/ Far, far, before, is all her seamen know,/ And where the land she cometh from? Away,/ Far, far, behind, is all that they can say.

On summer eves upon the deck's ~~broad~~ smooth face,/ Friend joined with friend, how pleasant here to pace,/ Or o'er the stern reclining, watch below/ The wide white wake still lengthening as we go. . . .

Mari Magno

Where lies the land to which the ship wd go?
Far, far, before, is all her seamen know;
And where the land she cometh from? Away
Far, far, behind, is all that they can say.

On summer eves upon the deck: ~~two~~ [smooth] space
Friend joined with friend, how pleasant 'tis to pace
Or o'er the stern reclining, watch below
The wide white wake still lengthening as we go.

On stormy nights when wild north westers rave
How proud a thing to fight with wind & wave;
The dripping sailor on the reeling mast
Exults to bear, & ~~and~~ nor deigns to wish 'twere past.

Where lies the land to which the ship wod go?
Far, far, behind : is all her seamen know
And where the land she cometh from? Away;
Far, far, behind, is all that they can say.

let this come the last
of all. —

?: Miftonst Natura
Naturians be as well left
out —

71

Charles Kingsley
1819–1875

Autograph letter signed, dated 29 December 1853, to Philip Gosse. 12 pp. 189 x 115 mm. MA 1960. Purchased as the gift of Mr. De Coursey Fales.

Kingsley's name is associated with numerous causes—Chartism, Christian Socialism, sanitary reform, "muscular Christianity" and any number of lesser movements—but today he is most often remembered as the author of *The Water-Babies* (1863), itself instrumental in ending the use of young children as chimney sweeps, and as the irritant that provoked John Henry Newman's pearl, *Apologia Pro Vita Sua* (1864). The range of Kingsley's reforming interests and the extent of his social elevation (from a country curacy to preaching before the Queen at Windsor Castle) betray a flexibility of mind which in other men would be called inconsistency. Not surprisingly, his career as a novelist presents a notable case of literature in the service of ideological ends, often to the detriment of literature. At least two constants prevailed throughout Kingsley's life, however: a love of nature, which began in his boyhood in the west of England, and an unconventionally overt passion for his wife Fanny. While his affection for the outdoors usually took the form of riding, otter hunting, and fishing, he was also a devoted amateur naturalist, as the letter shown here reveals. In 1853, Kingsley had been suspended from his clerical tasks by the Bishop of Exeter, who had taken a strong dislike to *Alton Locke* (1850), *Yeast* (1851) and *Hypatia* (1853). Though he considered himself only a "zoosciolist" (that is, a mere dabbler in zoology), he exuberantly offered to collect marine specimens in his spare time for the evangelical scientist Philip Gosse, the father of Edmund Gosse.

The Morgan Library also owns a group of Kingsley's letters to Fanny, written during a tour of Europe, a lecture given at the Chapel Royal in 1871, and a remarkable series of unpublished letters written to Kingsley (but not sent) from Germany by Fanny during their courtship.

The major collections of Kingsley manuscripts are at Princeton University and Cambridge University.

[But if I can really advance] science by acting as jackal, or sea-gamekeeper, to such a man as you, I am ready & delighted to take any trouble, well compensated by fresh air, sea-breezes, & the perpetual atmosphered wholesome wonder & reverence, in wh. these pursuits keep me, & my dear wife & children, whom I am trying to train to observe & to worship.

I have spoken with a shrewd fellow, who has a hooker & dredge, & is [in] the habit of dredging with Dr. Sutherland & Dr. Battersby (perhaps you can tell me whether the Dr. Sutherland who lives here is the Sanitary Reformer—if so, I must try to know him).

This man, Standyford, offers to dredge at 3s/6d a day, or a guinea a week; & says, that if he were employed at a guinea a week off & on, he wd. bring the haul to me every night, help me to pack, & take them up to the station....

science yachting as jackal, or sea-gamekeeper, to such a man as you, I am ready & delighted to take any trouble, well compensated by fresh air, sea-breezes, & the perpetual atmosphere of wholesome wonder & reverence, in w. these pursuits keep me, & my dear wife & children, whom I am trying to train to observe & to worship.

I have spoken with a shrewd fellow, who has a hooker & dredge, & is the habit of dredging with

Dr. Sutherland & Dr. Battersby (perhaps you can tell me whether the Dr. Sutherland who lives here is the Sanitary Reformer – if so, I must try to know him).

This man, Staddyford, offers to dredge at 3/6d a day, or a guinea a week; & says, that if he were employed at a guinea a week off & on, he w. bring the haul home every night, help me to pack, & take them up to the station (3/4 of a mile) him-

George Eliot (Marian Evans)
1819–1880

Autograph manuscript of "Scenes of Clerical Life," undated but written in 1856 and 1857. 552 pp. 275 x 215 mm. MA 722.

George Eliot once remarked, in a jesting metaphor truly of her time, that "the author's capital is his brain-power." As an editor of *Westminster Review*, a translator and a critic, Marian Evans Lewes had invested her "brain capital" quite successfully in what is misleadingly called "intellectual prose." Just what it was that impelled her to begin writing fiction in September 1856 remains uncertain. But in turning from one form of intellectual prose to another, she did not abandon her remarkable analytical powers of mind, she merely reconciled them with an interest in realistic fiction that had been increasing for some time, particularly during May and June 1856, when she and George Henry Lewes took a working holiday at Ilfracombe in Devon. On the shores of the Bristol Channel, they made detailed scientific observations and notes for Lewes's *Sea-Side Studies*, while she also worked on an explicit defense of realism in an article called "The Natural History of German Life." By November Lewes was writing to John Blackwood, editor of *Blackwood's Magazine*, to remind him of a proposed article on sea anemones and to offer the manuscript of "'Sketches of Clerical Life' which was submitted to me by a friend who desired my good offices with you." Blackwood accepted the first of the scenes, "Amos Barton," immediately; several years later he wrote to George Eliot remarking that "it is one of the strongest practical marks of my admiration for the Scenes that from the first I had ordered the M.S. to be set aside for me."

In spite of the climate of realism in which *Scenes of Clerical Life* developed, it partakes of many other elements as well: nostalgia, an occasional romantic tint and some fine satirical humor in the vein of Jane Austen, whose works Marian and Lewes had reread together before Marian began writing "Janet's Repentance." The passage shown here portrays Mrs. Linnet, one of the Tryanites and an amusingly shallow reader of religious books.

Most of George Eliot's major manuscripts are in the British Library, but the largest collection of her letters is housed in the Beinecke Library at Yale University.

Mrs Linnet had become a ~~great~~ reader of religious books, since Mr Tryan's advent, & as she was in the habit of confining her perusal to the purely secular portions, which have a very small proportion to the whole, she could make rapid progress through a large number of volumes. On taking up the biography of a celebrated preacher, she immediately turned to the end to see what disease he died of, & if his legs swelled, as her own occasionally did, she felt a stronger interest in ascertaining any earlier facts in the history of the dropsical divine—Whether he had ever fallen off a stage coach, whether he had married more than one wife, &, in general, any adventures or repartees recorded of him previous to the epoch of his conversion. She then ~~leaved~~ glanced over the letters & diary & wherever there was a predominance of Zion, the River of Life, & notes of Exclamation she turned over to the next page, but any passage in which she saw such promising nouns as "small-pox," "pony" or "boots & shoes" at once arrested her."...

Mrs Linnet had become a ~~great~~ reader of religious books, since Mr Tryan's advent, & as she was in the habit of confining her perusal to the purely secular portions, which
15 bore a very small proportion to the whole, she could make rapid progress through a large number of volumes. On taking up the biography of a celebrated preacher, she immediately turned to the end to see what disease he died of, & if his legs swelled, as her own occasionally did, she felt a stronger interest in ascertaining any earlier facts in the history of the dropsical divine – whether he had ever fallen off a stage coach, whether he had married more than one wife, & in general, any adventures or repartees recorded of him previous to the epoch of his conversion. She then ~~turned~~ glanced over the letters & diary, & wherever there was a predominance of Zion, the River of Life, & notes of exclamation she turned over to the next page, but any passage in which she saw such promising nouns as "small-pox," "pony" or "boots & shoes" at once arrested her.

"It is half past six now," said Mrs. Linnet, looking at her watch as the servant appeared with the tea tray, "I suppose the delegates are come back by this time. If Mr Tryan had not so kindly promised to call & let us know, I should hardly rest without walking to Milby myself to know what answer they have brought back. It is a great privilege for us – Mr. Tryan's living at Mrs Wagstaff's, for he is often able to take us on his way backwards & forwards into the town."

73

John Ruskin
1819–1900

Autograph manuscript of "Torcello," the second chapter of "The Stones of Venice," Volume Two, unsigned and undated, but written 1851–2. 16 leaves. 393 x 205 mm. MA 399.

After Prometheus gave the arts to mankind, Ruskin gave Art to the British. The nineteenth century was rich in presiding intellects—one thinks of Mill, Carlyle, Newman and the ghosts of Coleridge and Bentham—but after the publication of the first volume of *Modern Painters* in 1843, it had only one nervous system, and that was Ruskin's. It was a system that had a tendency to break down after great emotional stress or protracted labor (what labor of Ruskin's was not protracted?), but it was also uniquely susceptible to the exaltations of the sublime. Such an exaltation came in September 1845 when Ruskin and his drawing master, J. D. Harding, made a last-minute stop at the Scuola di San Rocco to view some paintings by Tintoretto. On the twenty-fourth of September, Ruskin wrote to his father: "I never was so utterly crushed to the earth before any human intellect as I was today, before Tintoret. . . . He took it so entirely out of me today that I could do nothing at last but lie on a bench & laugh. . . . As for *painting*, I think I didn't know what it meant till today. . . ." Not only did Ruskin recognize in Tintoretto a supreme intellect, he also recognized that such a display as he saw before him marked the end of his own attempts to become a painter of consequence. More important, in Tintoretto he also discovered "the schools of painting which crowned the power and perished in the fall of Venice," and in the decline of Venice he found "the laws of national strength and virtue." For him, the history of Venice, the island-city, was an eloquent commentary on the fate of England, the island-state.

As befitting Venice, *The Stones of Venice* is one of Ruskin's most romantic and lushly descriptive works. Ruskin intended to make this book the application of the principles set forth in *The Seven Lamps of Architecture* (1849), principles which are inherently moral. The decline of the city was apparent everywhere around him in 1851 and 1852 when he was at work on *The Stones of Venice*, and that fact lent additional poignancy to his writing. The passage shown here, from the chapter called "Torcello," is one of the most beautiful descriptions of the city that Ruskin ever wrote, for he describes Venice as it appeared then, in its "widowhood," and as it appeared before its birth.

The Morgan Library owns a superb collection of Ruskin manuscripts, including the complete manuscripts of both *The Stones of Venice* and *Modern Painters* and the collection of Ruskin materials formed by F. J. Sharp and Helen Gill Viljoen. There are also important collections of Ruskin manuscripts in the British Library and at Yale University.

[Starting with 2nd paragraph:] Then look far~~ther~~ to the south: ~~and~~ Beyond the widening branches of the lagoon—and ~~floating—as it seems on~~ rising out of the bright lake into which they gather, ~~behold, a dark cluster of goodly domes and pointed giddy towers: and the crowded darkness of a great city~~ there are a multitude of towers, ~~mas~~ dark, and scattered among square set shapes of ~~crowded~~ clustered ~~bui~~ palaces; a long & irregular line fretting the southern sky. . . .

Part I.

~~[illegible]~~ Chap 2 Torcello. 2.

the fourth a considerable church with nave and aisle but of which - in like manner - we can see little but the long ridge and lateral slopes of roof - which the sunlight separates in one glowing mass from the green field beneath - & grey moor beyond. There are no living creatures near these buildings - nor any vestige of village or city round about them. They lie like a little company of ships becalmed on a far away sea.

Then look further to the south: ~~and~~ Beyond the widening branches of the lagoon - and ~~floating - as it seems on~~ rising out of the bright lake into which they gather. ~~behold~~ ~~a dark cluster of ghostly domes and [illegible] towers: and the crowded darkness of a great city~~ there are a multitude of towers, dark, and scattered among square set shapes of ~~[illegible]~~ clustered palaces; a long & irregular line fretting the southern sky.

Mother and Daughter: you behold them, both in their widowhood. Torcello, & Venice.

Thirteen ~~[illegible]~~ hundred years ago, the ~~[illegible]~~ grey moorland looked ~~[illegible]~~ as it does this day: & the purple mountains stood as radiantly in the deep distances of evening: but from the ~~[illegible]~~ line of the Horizon there were strange fires mixed with the light of sunset: and ~~[illegible]~~ the lament of many human voices mixed with the ~~fret of the [illegible]~~ fretting of the waves on their ridges of sand: The flames rose from the ruins of Altinum - the lament from the multitude of its people, seeking, like Israel of old, a refuge from the Sword in the Paths of the Sea.

The ~~[illegible]~~ cattle are feeding and resting upon the site of the city that they left - ~~and~~ the mowers scythe swept, this day - at dawn - over the chief street of that city that they built: ~~and the swathes~~ of its soft grass are, now, sending up their scent into the night air: the only incense that fills the temple of their ancient worship. ~~But that temple is still unfallen - still beautiful - and through the doors of it we may go~~ Let us go down into that little space of meadowland.

§ 2 The ~~[illegible]~~ inlet which runs nearest to the base of the Campanile is not that by which Torcello is commonly approached. Another, somewhat broader, and overhung by ~~hedges of alder,~~ alder copse, ~~[illegible]~~ winds out of the main channel of the lagoon up to the very edge of the little meadow which was once the piazza of ~~Torcello~~ the city. and ~~forms its boundary on one side~~: there stayed by a few grey stones which present some semblance of a quay - forms its boundary at one extremity ~~[illegible]~~

John Ruskin

Autograph manuscript of "Peace," the final chapter of "Modern Painters," Volume Five, unsigned and undated, but written in the spring of 1860. 15 leaves. 321 x 200 mm. MA 397.

By a process as gradual as the sloping of foothills into the Alps, Ruskin moved from writing about the ethical implications of art to writing about the ethical and economic needs of man in society. The unity of these two subjects in Ruskin's mind is best exemplified by the fact that his principles of political economy were, as he writes in *Unto This Last* (1862), "all summed in a single sentence in the last volume of *Modern Painters* [1860]—'Government and co-operation are in all things the Laws of Life; Anarchy and competition the Laws of Death.'" Such a sentence alone illustrates how far Ruskin had traveled in the seventeen years since he had begun *Modern Painters* as an explicit defense of William Turner. In the intervening period he had published *The Seven Lamps of Architecture* (1849), *The Stones of Venice* (1851–3), numerous articles and essays and, most important for his thinking about society, *The Political Economy of Art* (1857), which rendered in plain words and with plain application to contemporary British life the arguments implicit in certain chapters of *The Stones of Venice*. Ruskin resumed the subject of Turner in the final volume of *Modern Painters*, but not before discussing the analogy between ideas of spatial relation in a painting and ideas of economic relation in society. And when he came to draw a moral from Turner's life, a moral about the struggle between God and the Devil, he asked: "Do you think I am irreverently comparing great and small things? The system of the world is entirely one; small things and great are alike part of one mighty whole."

Ruskin's task as an aesthetician and a political economist was to urge men and women to perceive the significance of this "whole," and to show how alien to its spirit the economic system that existed in England was. It is not a message that has ceased to have meaning. Turner no longer requires defense, but the principles for which Ruskin wrote most vehemently still do. Rightly, Ruskin was not optimistic about the success of his message, and he reveals his "dark-veiled" hope in the passage shown here, the revised and printed version of which reads: "I do not know what my England desires, or how long she will choose to do as she is doing now;—with her right hand casting away the souls of men, and with her left the gifts of God."

But I am not hopeless—though my hope may not be the recognizable—but Veronese's the dark-veiled ~~one. Since I began this book many changes have happened not likely to make its tone of conclusion triumphant Turner~~ [illegible deletion] ~~is dead—. and dead without seeing any issue from my labours for him: those of his works which used to give me chief delight are perished—the rest~~

Veiled—not because sorrowful—but because blind. I do not know what my England desires—or what will be the chosen course of her future labour. I cannot hope for her, because I ~~have~~ see she has yet no distinct hope for herself. ~~She has not determined what to be; but~~

In the ~~liturgy~~ prayer which she dictates to her children, she tells them to Fight against the world, the Flesh and the Devil. Some day perhaps it may also seem to be as desirable to tell her children also what she means by this.

What is this World, which they are to "fight with.' ~~It seems to me, she pays respect enough to the its opinion opinion of the world, and recommends to them the gathering of its treasures.~~ . . .

[illegible] — and that what I have written would do greater good if it encouraged more [illegible] — and blamed less.

But I am not hopeless — though my hope may not be the recognizable — [illegible] Venetian's [illegible].

Since I began this book many changes have happened — not likely to make its tone of conclusion triumphant. Turner is dead — and dead without seeing any issue from my labours for him: his works which used to give me chief delight are perished — this past.

Veiled — not because sorrowful — but because blind. I do not know what my England desires — or what will be the chosen course of her future labour. I cannot hope for her, because I [illegible] till she has yet no distinct hope for herself. [illegible]

In the prayers which she dictates to her children — she tells them to fight against the world, the Flesh and the Devil. Some day perhaps it may also seem to her as desirable to tell her children also what she means by this.

What is this World, which they are to "fight with"? [illegible] and how does it differ from the world in which they are to "get on in"? [illegible] for both her and them. [illegible]

John 12.25 [illegible] Ephes. [illegible]

The explanation seems to me the more needful because I do not in the book we profess to live by find anything very distinct about fighting with the world. I find something about fighting with the Rulers of its darkness, but it does not follow that this conquest is to be by hostility, since evil may be overcome with good; and something also about overcoming it; [illegible]. Nevertheless I find it on the other side written that God loved it. [illegible] What I understand by the passage [illegible] the world, and that Christ is the light of it.

What the much used words mean therefore I cannot tell. But this I believe they should mean. That there is indeed a world which is full of care and covetous desire [illegible] and hatred; a world of war; of which Christ is not the Light; which indeed is without light and has never heard the great "let there be." Which is therefore in truth as yet no world: but chaos: — on the face of which, moving, the Spirit of God yet causes men to hope that a World will come. The better one they call it; perhaps they might more wisely call it the Real one. Also I hear them speak continually of going to it; rather than of its coming to them — which again is strange, for in that prayer which they had straight from the lips of the Light of the World, and which He apparently thought sufficient prayer for them, there is not anything about going to another world; only something of another Government; coming into this; [illegible] or rather not another, but the only Government — that Government which will constitute it a world indeed

75

SIR RICHARD FRANCIS BURTON
1821–1890

Autograph letter signed, dated 14 Montagu Place, Bryanston Square, London, 21 December 1864 to an unidentified correspondent. 4 pp. 138 x 188 mm. From the Collection of Mr. Gordon N. Ray.

In *Poems and Ballads, Third Series*, Swinburne described Richard Burton as one who "hears/ Bright music from the world where shadows are." There were times in Burton's life when the bright music that led him into a world of shadows seems to have been nothing more than the imagined sound of his name on the lips of an applauding nation. But for someone with an eye out for the main chance, Burton's luck was atrocious. Headed for unexplored territory in East Africa and, he hoped, the source of the Nile, Burton left Zanzibar in 1857, accompanied by his subordinate partner, John Hanning Speke. After a nearly calamitous trek, the two men discovered Lake Tanganyika, which Burton believed to be the Nile's source. On the return trip he sent Speke northwards to investigate rumors of another large lake, and Speke stumbled upon Lake Victoria, which he immediately claimed as his candidate for the headwaters of the Nile. Unfortunately for Burton, Speke was right. Their difference swelled to outright feuding when Speke, back in England alone and having promised to await Burton's return before doing so, promptly announced his discoveries and took credit for having organized the entire expedition. Burton made no secret of his feelings about this treachery, and when Speke died of a gunshot wound near Bath in September 1864, he remarked in the letter shown here, "Nothing will ever be known of Speke's death. I saw him at 1.30 P.M. & at 4 P.M. he was dead. The charitable say that he shot himself the uncharitable that I shot him."

Burton saw more of the "uncivilized" globe than almost any man of his time, and not a day passed, not a journey was completed without significant additions to his written corpus. In his works he wandered almost as far afield as he did on the Indian subcontinent, in Africa or in South America. Today, however, he is remembered primarily for his translation of *The Arabian Nights*, completed late in life, and for the account he wrote of his disguised visit to Mecca, one of his earliest and most renowned expeditions, *Personal Narrative of a Pilgrimage to El-Medinah and Meccah* (1855).

Many of Burton's manuscripts, including his diaries, were burned by his energetic widow, but a substantial group of letters and the manuscript of a translation, *Uruguay*, are preserved in the Huntington Library, San Marino, California.

I hope that you have duly rec[d] your copy of Dahome. Can you get back Renan for me? Dahome has sold well & will do better after Xmas.

Weather awful, snow, thaw, frost & rain. Daylight between 11.30 & 2.30. It will they say be a severe winter. Hitherto it has treated me kindly. I am not quite sorry to change from Africa for a time. *And my next long tour shall certainly be given to the Niger. By that time I suppose the whole mountain side will be cleared of trees.*

Nothing will ever be known of Speke's death. I saw him at 1.30 P.M. & at 4 P.M. he was dead. The charitable say that he shot himself the uncharitable that I shot him. . . .

all his are at Whydah — from his greediness.

I hope that you have duly sent your copy of Dahome. Can you get back Renan for me? Dahome by itself will do better after Xmas.

Weather awful, snow, thaw, frost & rain. Daylight between 11.30 & 2.30. It will they say be a severe winter. Nevertheless it has treated me kindly. I am not quite sorry to change from Africa for a time. But my next long leave shall certainly be given to the Niger.

By that time I suppose the whole mountain side will be cleared of tree.

Nothing will ever be known of Speke's death. I saw him at 1.30 P.M. & at 4 P.M. he lay dead. The charitable say that he shot himself the uncharitable that I shot him.

Whenever you choose to write (Care of Hart, Ld) I will make a point of answering by mail after receipt. You must tell me something about the new man (C. Livingstone) who

Matthew Arnold
1822–1888

Autograph letter signed with initials, dated 28 December [1857] to Thomas Arnold. 4 pp. 181 x 114 mm.

At the end of "The Function of Criticism at the Present Time" (1864), Arnold pointed to "the epochs of Aeschylus and Shakespeare" and exclaimed: "there is the promised land, toward which criticism can only beckon. That promised land it will not be ours to enter, and we shall die in the wilderness. . . ." If the Elizabethan period was the promised land, then the Victorian age, Arnold implies, is Moab, a land of gesticulation and commentary, but not of supreme poetry. The notion of a liberating or imprisoning zeitgeist permeates Arnold's lectures on poetry, and in his own mind it accounted for his small popular success as a poet. A year after the letter shown here was written, Arnold explained to his sister the hindrances imposed upon him by the era into which he was born: "It is only in the best poetical epochs (such as the Elizabethan) that you can descend into yourself and produce the best of your thought and feeling naturally, and without an overwhelming and in some degree morbid effort. . . ." In this letter to his brother Thomas, written just after Arnold had begun his first series of lectures as Professor of Poetry at Oxford, he elaborates on the problems that develop when the synchronism of poetry and its epoch gets out of order: "Pope's poetry was *adequate* . . . to Pope's age—that is, it reflected completely the best general culture and intelligence of that age. . . ." For Arnold, Pope's liability is that he was a first-class poet in an inferior age, while the lamentable fate of poetry—as he saw it—in the Victorian age is due to the fact that "our *time* is a first class one—an infinitely fuller richer age than Pope's: but our poetry is not *adequate* to it. . . ."

This letter also explains the scarcity of Arnold manuscripts. Thomas Arnold had apparently asked to see the manuscript of the first of Arnold's Oxford lectures, but his brother responded by remarking, "I have a vow against sending MSS to anyone: the disadvantage to a work in being read in MSS is so incredibly great. . . ." This letter was given to the Morgan Library by Mrs. Humphry Ward, Thomas Arnold's daughter.

[Starting halfway down verso:] A great transformation in the intellectual nature of the English, and, consequently, in their Estimate of their own writers, is, I have long felt, inevitable. When this transformation comes the popularity of Wordsworth, Shelley, Coleridge, and others, remarkable men as they were, will not be the better for it. I am very much interested in what you say about Pope. I will read the Essay on Criticism again—certainly poetry was a power in England in his time, which it is not now—now it is almost exclusively "virginibus puerisque" and not for the sanest and most promising of those—then it was for men *at large. You ask why is this—I think it is because Pope's poetry was* adequate, *(to use a term I am always using), to Pope's age—that is, it reflected completely the best general culture and intelligence of that age: therefore the cultivated and intelligent men of that time all found something of themselves in it. But it was a poor time, after all—so the poetry is not and cannot be a first-class one. On the other hand our* time *is a first class one—an infinitely fuller richer age than Pope's: [but our poetry is not* adequate *to it. . . .]*

cultivated English are generally so ignorant. You do not now mention Alfieri, whose Merope is more famous than either of the other two, and is well worth reading — though I think Maffei's practically the best tragedy of the three, as you will see by my Preface, which I think you will find interesting.

A great transformation in the intellectual nature of the English, and, consequently, in their estimate of their own writers, is, I have long felt, inevitable. When this transformation comes the popularity of Wordsworth, Shelley, Coleridge, and others, remarkable men as they were, will not be the better for it.

I am very much interested in what you say about Pope. I will read the Essay on Criticism again — certainly

poetry was a power in England in his time which it is not now — [illegible] is almost exclusively "virginibus puerisque" and not for the sanest and most promising of these — then it was for men at large. You ask why is this. I think it is because Pope's poetry was adequate, (to use a term I am always using), to Pope's age — that is, it reflected completely the best general culture and intelligence of that age: therefore the cultivated and intelligent men of that time all found something of themselves in it. But it was a poor time, after all — so the poetry is not and cannot be a first-class one. On the other hand our time is a first class one — an infinitely fuller richer age than Pope's;

my justification in having recourse to French to say an uncivil

thing, and with our united love and good wishes for Xmas and the new year to you all, believe me always, your most affectionate — M.A.

Coventry Patmore
1823–1896

Autograph additions to Volume One of "The Angel in the House" (London: Parker & Son, 1854) in a copy inscribed to Sir John Simeon and dated 16 July 1856. From the Collection of Mr. Gordon N. Ray.

In the Victorian period, as in most others, the subject of marriage fell mainly to the novelists and the satirists, leaving those who sought an ennobling poetic rendering of the everyday joys of domesticity with little to choose from. If the Brownings' marriage seemed too romantic to prosper anywhere but in Italy and Meredith's *Modern Love* (1862) too tragic to be brought into the home, there was at least Coventry Patmore's *The Angel in the House*, a poem whose "scope should be the heart's events" within the confines of courtship and marriage. *The Angel in the House* is not merely a panegyric of ideal wedded love, for it is based on Patmore's own very real happiness in marriage. He lost two wives and a third survived him, and each of these women appears to have been "his Mistress, Wife, and Muse." Patmore's role as apologist for the wedded state is less important than his role as a poetic eminence behind the Pre-Raphaelite Brotherhood, a role he turned to good account when he persuaded Ruskin to defend in print the aesthetic aims of the P.R.B. His words abound in W. M. Rossetti's P.R.B. journal, written during the years he was at work on *The Angel in the House*, but there seems to have been some disagreement among the Brotherhood as to Patmore's abilities. Millais, for one, felt that "if he had seen Patmore's hand alone cut off, he could have sworn to it as that of a man of genius." D. G. Rossetti, who was better able to judge, came to a different conclusion, particularly after reading *The Angel in the House;* he called Patmore a "resolute poet" and then delivered a verdict which has proved to be that of posterity: "Of course it is very good indeed, yet will one ever want to read it again?"

The passage shown here was added by Patmore to Section IX ("The Railway") of "The Betrothal." The lover, whose beloved (Honoria) has just departed by train, seeks solace by walking past "the home of my regret" and into the church where Honoria regularly worshipped. The "Dean" is Honoria's father, the Dean of Salisbury, whom Meredith called "one of the superior police of the English middle class, for whom attendant seraphs in a visible far distance hold the ladder, not undeserved, when a cheerful digestion shall have ceased."

I pass'd the home of my regret:/ The clock was chiming in the hall,/ And one sad window open yet,/ Although the dews began to fall./ Her distance shew'd her worth's true scope!/ How airy of heart and innocent/ That loveliness which sicken'd hope,/ And wore the world for ornament!/ O, no one loved her half enough,/ Not ev'n her sisters and the Dean./ All tenderness save mine seem'd rough,/ Officious, ignorant, and mean./ I wonder'd, would her bird be fed,/ Her rose-plots water'd, she not by?/ Loading my breast with angry dread/ Of light, unlikely injury./ So, fill'd with love and fond remorse,/ I paced this Goshen, every part/ Endow'd with reliquary force/ To heal and raise from death my heart. . . .

~~5.~~

~~I found the Book she had used, and stay'd~~

~~For Evening Prayers; in grief's despite~~

~~Felt grief assuaged, then homeward~~ stray'd,

~~Weary beforehand of the night.~~

~~The blackbird, in the shadowy wood,~~

~~Talk'd to himself; and eastward grew~~

~~In heaven the symbol of my mood,~~

~~Where one bright star engross'd the blue~~.

5.

I pass'd the home of my regret:
The clock was chiming in the hall,
And one sad window open yet,
Although the dews began to fall.
Her distance shew'd her worth's true scope!
How airy of heart and innocent
That loveliness which sicken'd hope,
And wore the world for ornament!
O, no one loved her half enough,
Not ev'n her sisters and the Dean.
All tenderness save mine seem'd rough,
Officious, ignorant, and mean.
I wonder'd, would her bird be fed,
Her rose-plots water'd, she not by?
Loading my breast with angry dread
Of light, unlikely injury.
So, fill'd with love and fond remorse,
I paced this Goshen, every part

Endow'd with reliquary force
To heal and raise from death my heart.
How tranquil and unsecular
The precinct! Once, through yonder gate,
I saw her go, and knew from far
Her noble form and gentle state;
Her dress had touch'd this door-post; here
She turn'd her face and laugh'd, with looks
Like moonbeams on a wavering mere;
This was her stall; these were her books;
Here had she knelt; here, now, I stay'd
For Evening Prayers: in grief's despite
Felt grief assuaged; then homeward stray'd,
Weary beforehand of the night.
The blackbird in the shadowy wood
Talk'd to himself; and eastward grew
In heaven the symbol of my mood,
Where one bright star engross'd the blue.

=

Wilkie Collins
1824–1889

Autograph manuscript signed of "The Woman in White," dated 15 August 1859 to 26 July 1860. 492 pp. 288 x 220 mm. MA 79.

How a genius for the creation of suspense develops is no small mystery in itself; but in the case of Wilkie Collins some reasonable guesses may be made. The son of a successful, though pious painter, Wilkie grew up in an artistic household that unfortunately lacked the most attractive vices belonging to his father's profession. There has perhaps never been a less bohemian painter than William Collins, R.A., whose works include "The Sale of the Pet Lamb" and "The Stray Kitten." Collins intended his son to pursue a commercial or legal career and, as his letters to his wife (most of them now in the Morgan Library) show, he kept Wilkie and his younger brother Charles on a short tether. When Collins died in 1847, Wilkie defused the memory of his father by compiling an austere two-volume memoir, then promptly turned to novel writing and a manner of life that would have been his father's abhorrence. His familial conflicts engendered a deeply grained iconoclasm, as well as a love of domestic comfort. Throughout his life, Wilkie was a "social" novelist; that is he concerned himself with those awkward disjunctions between justice and convention that permeate society. The conditions that generate suspense in a novel—mystery, illusion, the threat of unsuspected evil—also served Wilkie as a means of lifting the masks of society and its ordained hypocrisies, the very hypocrisies that had lain about him as a youth.

There is no denying, however, that Wilkie also made his greatest suspense novels extremely saleable. When *A Tale of Two Cities* closed and *The Woman in White* opened in the November 1859 issue of *All the Year Round*, London was seized with the same thrill of horror that comes over Walter Hartwright when, in the passage shown here, he meets Anne Catherick, the woman in white, on a lonely crossroads above London late one night.

The Morgan Library has one of the greatest collections of Wilkie Collins manuscripts in the world. Besides *The Woman in White*, it preserves the manuscript of his other great novel, *The Moonstone*, the manuscripts of *Hide and Seek* and *The Frozen Deep*, and over two hundred and fifty of his letters, including his entire correspondence with his mother.

I had now arrived at that particular point of my walk where four roads met—the road to Hampstead, along which I had returned; the road to Finchley and Barnet; the road to Hendon; and the road back to London. I had mechanically turned in this latter direction, and was strolling along the lonely high-road—idly wondering, I remember, what the Cumberland young ladies would look like—when every drop of blood in my body was brought to a stop, in one moment, by the touch of a hand laid lightly and suddenly on my shoulder from behind me.

I turned on the instant, with my fingers tightening round the handle of my stick.

There, in the middle of the broad, bright high road—there, as if it had that moment sprung out of the earth or dropped from the heaven—stood the figure of a solitary woman, dressed from head to foot in white garments; her face bent in grave inquiry on mine, her hand pointing to the dark cloud over London, as I faced her.

I was far too much startled by the suddenness with which this extraordinary apparition stood before me, in the dead of night and in that lonely place, to ask what she wanted. The strange woman spoke first.

"Is that the road ~~which leads~~ to London?" she said. . . .

the time I had arrived at the end of the road, I had become completely absorbed in my own fanciful visions of Limmeridge House, of Mr Fairlie, and of the two ladies – whose practice in the art of sketching I was so soon to superintend.

I had now arrived at that particular point of my walk where four roads met – the road to Hampstead, along which I had returned; the road to Finchley and Barnet; the road to Hendon; and the road back to London. I had mechanically turned in this latter direction, and was strolling along the lonely high-road – idly wondering, I remember, what the Cumberland young ladies would look like – when every drop of blood in my body was brought to a stop, in one moment, by the touch of a hand laid lightly and suddenly on my shoulder from behind me.

I turned on the instant, with my fingers tightening round the handle of my stick.

There, in the middle of the broad, bright high-road – there, as if it had that moment sprung out of the earth or dropped from the heaven – stood the figure of a solitary woman, dressed from head to foot in white garments; her face bent in grave inquiry on mine, her hand pointing to the dark cloud over London, as I faced her.

I was far too much startled by the suddenness with which this extraordinary apparition stood before me, in the dead of night and in that lonely place, to ask what she wanted. The strange woman spoke first.

"Is that the road to London?" she said.

I looked attentively at her, as she put that singular question to me. It was then nearly one o'clock; and the moon was on the wane. All I could discern distinctly by the wan uncertain light, was a colourless, youthful face, meagre and sharp to look at, about the cheeks and chin; large, grave, wistfully-attentive eyes; and light hair of a dull, whitish-yellow hue. There was nothing wild, nothing immodest, in her manner: it was quiet and self-controlled, a little melancholy, and a little touched by suspicion: not exactly the manner of a lady, and, at the same time, not the manner of a woman in the humblest rank of life. The voice, little as I had yet heard of it, had something curiously still and mechanical in its tones, and the utterance was remarkably rapid. She held a small bag in her hand; and her dress – bonnet, shawl, and gown all of white – was, so far as I could guess, certainly not composed of very delicate or very expensive materials. Her figure was slight, and rather above the average height – her gait and actions free from the slightest approach to extravagance. This was all that I could observe of her, in the dim light and under the perplexingly strange circumstances of our meeting. What sort of woman she was, and how she came to be out alone in the high-road, an hour after midnight, I altogether failed to guess. The one thing of which I felt certain was, that the grossest of mankind could not have misconstrued her motive in speaking, even at that suspiciously late hour and in that

THOMAS HENRY HUXLEY
1825–1895

Autograph letter signed, dated Keswick, 22 August 1863, to Miss Edith Trench. 4 pp. 180 x 114 mm. From the Collection of Mr. Gordon N. Ray.

As he aged, perhaps the only thing that regularly astounded Huxley—a man by choice most willing to be astounded—was finding himself not merely tolerated but honored by a national orthodoxy which he had persistently offended. To Sir John Donnelly three years before his death he wrote, "To think of a Conservative Government—pride of the Church—going out of its way to honour one not only of the wicked, but of the notoriousest and plain-spoken wickedness." Huxley was a man of practical ideas and realistic expectations of his fellow men; his surprise is that of a reformer surrounded by the effects of his proposed reforms, a dreamer in a world suddenly peopled with the stuff of his dreams. After his triumphant championing of Darwin's cause, Huxley naturally moved on to urge in lectures and in print the virtues of a technical, scientific education; in the debate concerning the relative importance of scientific training and religion (or literary culture) in education—a debate which had begun with John Henry Newman opposing Sir Robert Peel and continued into Huxley's own day with Matthew Arnold as his chief adversary—he came to be the main spokesman for the priority of scientific studies. Recognizing Huxley's trenchant wit and superlative logic, Arnold dubbed him the "prince of debaters." The characteristic of Huxley that seems most evident today is his phenomenal energy, the adjunct of unceasing curiosity. Four years before his death, he could still say to a friend, "the cosmos remains always beautiful and profoundly interesting in every corner—and if I had as many lives as a cat I would leave no corner unexplored."

The letter shown here is all Huxley, witty, entertaining and illustrated. It was written in the year that Huxley published his most important individual work, *Evidence as to Man's Place in Nature*. The letter is addressed to Miss Edith Trench, daughter of Richard Chenevix Trench, who appears as figure E; three months after this letter was written, Trench became Archbishop of Dublin.

[I subjoin the explanation of the Plate & with many apologies for the somewhat Chinese character of my perspective which is wholly due to the] untreated character of the canvas of my picture I am yours very quickly T. H. Huxley Miss Edith Trench

A. B. the heroines of the pass/ C. A distinguished Alpine Acrobat/ D. Humble follower of ditto./ E. The Dean who has just led the way./ F. The oldest inhabitant of the Dales who has never seen anything so daring./ G. Goat who dares to emulate & fails miserably.

unrivalled character of the canvass of my picture

Ever

Yours very truly

T. H. Huxley

Miss Edith French

A. }
B. } the heroines of the pass

C. A distinguished alpine acrobat

D. Humble follower of ditto.

E. The Dean who has just led the way.

F. The oldest inhabitant of the Dales who has never seen anything so daring.

G. Goat who dares to emulate & fails miserably.

Richard Doddridge Blackmore
1825–1900

Autograph letter signed, dated 9 October 1889, probably to Edward Marston. 2 pp. 137 x 88 mm. MA 2806. Gift of Mr. Robert S. Pirie.

In the nineteenth century, when practically every familiar detail of life began to betray a sign of alteration, the surest tie to the past was the earth itself. Historical events are inextricably linked with the landscapes in which they occurred, and evocation of place was one of the historical novelist's primary techniques for conferring an illusion of immediacy upon incidents that took place long ago. Though Sir Walter Scott is, of course, the master of this genre, perhaps the finest example of the interweaving of topography and history is Richard Doddridge Blackmore's *Lorna Doone*, subtitled *A Romance of Exmoor*. As in the case of Arnold Bennett and the Potteries, Blackmore's imaginative landscape in *Lorna Doone* had a lingering effect on how the countryside he described, the border region of Somerset and Devon, was perceived. After the novel's great success, visitors to the Doone or Blackmore country found the landscape charming, but somewhat less magnificent than they had expected. Certainly, no farm was ever as snug as Plover Barrow Farm, no valley as precipitous and fortified by nature as the valley of the Doones. Though Blackmore generally described actual places (much as he borrowed the Doones and his narrator, John Ridd, from local legend), his coloring of them was heightened by pure affection and the conventions of romance.

In the letter shown here, written twenty years after the publication of *Lorna Doone*, Blackmore prematurely claims that there will be "No more novel-writing for me." After this date, however, he published three more novels, a tale in verse and a collection of stories. In a lifetime of writing (and market gardening), Blackmore produced one indubitable classic and a host of other works that deserve to be oftener read than they are.

The manuscript of *Lorna Doone* is in the Huntington Library, San Marino, California.

Teddn. October 9th 1889. Dear Mr. Marston No more novel-writing for me, for a long time, if at all in this world. Poets poetise in Elysium; but whether novelists novelise, we know not, & hope for the best about it.

If I attempt any prose-tale now, it will be about 1 Vol. regulation; & I shall offer it to Messrs. Harper, first for Mag. about 3 Nos., & then for my sandwich, wh. will do better in the new world than the old; at least I hope it may be so.

Several editors of Magazines have asked me, within the last few days, for a short tale; but I have declined, & think it wise to do so. Also a young man wants to come & have lessons in gardening gratis, promising to "devote all his energies to it," & being "of a robust disposition," & conscientiously Vegetarian. If he can eat all the pears blown down on Monday, he will be able to make fruit-growing pay, for a pig alone can do so, & get pork out of it. More heavy storms about; but the winds may crack their cheeks now.— In haste, Very truly yours R. D. Blackmore

Tedd: October 9th 1889.

Dear Mr. Marston

No more novel-writing for me, for a long time, if at all in this world. Poets poetise in Elysium; but whether novelists novelise, we know not, & hope for the best about it.
If I attempt any prose-tale now, it will be about 1 vol. regulation; & I shall offer it to Messrs. Harper, first for Mag. & then (about 3 mos.) for my Sandwich, wh. will do better in the new ~~world~~ than the old; at least I hope it may be so.

Several editors of Magazines have asked me, within the last few days, for a short tale; but I have declined, & think it is wise to do so. Also a young man wants to come & have lessons in gardening gratis, promising to "devote all his energies to it", & being "of a robust disposition, & conscientiously vegetarian." If he can eat all the pears blown down on Monday, he will be able to make fruit-growing pay, for no pig alone can do so, & get pork out of it. More heavy storms about; but the winds may crack their cheeks now.— In haste,

Very truly yours
R. D. Blackmore

81

Dante Gabriel Rossetti
1828–1882

Autograph manuscript of "The Blessed Damsel," signed with initials, dated 1847. 1 p. 326 x 202 mm. MA 1051.

In March 1847 Gabriel Rossetti sketched a small self-portrait which now hangs in the National Portrait Gallery, London. About his slightly turned head there is a quality somehow assertive and yet retiring, quite different from the later full-face portraits of the man. The ambiguity of this image is appropriate to the date of its creation, for Rossetti, then a student in the conservative Antique School of the Royal Academy, still awaited confirmation of his unconventional artistic gifts. Impatient with the stultifying routine of the Academy and as eager to find expression in verse as on canvas, he was fortunate to obtain in April 1847 the notebook of William Blake, which he purchased for ten shillings and cherished for his entire life. To discover in youth a figure of Blake's magnitude—brilliant, rebellious and at the time little known—promised great things for an artist as sympathetic to Blake's vision as Rossetti. But the true promise of spring 1847 was fulfilled when he completed "The Blessed Damozel"—one of his finest and most popular poems—before his nineteenth birthday in May of that year. While the Royal Academy struggled to impress basic techniques upon the young painter, his poetry flourished and bloomed without instruction.

This is the only known manuscript of "The Blessed Damozel." Rossetti wrote the poem for his family's manuscript magazine *Hodge-Podge;* in an extended version it was first published in 1850 in the Pre-Raphaelite journal *The Germ*. Though dated 1847, this manuscript was almost certainly transcribed at a much later date, possibly as late as 1873 when Rossetti began the painting of the same title. The handwriting belongs to a more mature period than the date would indicate, and the form of the poet's name represented by the initials—Dante Gabriel Rossetti—was not used until well after 1847.

The blessed damsel leaned against/ The silver bar of Heaven./ Her eyes knew more of rest and shade/ Than a deep water, even./ She had three lilies in her hand/ And the stars in her hair were seven.

Her robe, ungirt from clasp to hem,/ No wrought flowers did adorn,/ But a white robe of Mary's gift/ For service meetly worn;/ And her hair lying down her back/ Was yellow like ripe corn.

Herseemed she scarce had been a day/ One of God's choristers;/ The wonder was not yet quite gone/ From that still look of hers;/ Albeit to them she left, her day/ Had counted as ten years.

(To one it is ten years of years./ . . . . . Yet now, and in this place,/ Surely she leaned o'er me,—her hair/ Fell all about my face./ Nothing: the autumn fall of leaves:/ The whole year sets apace.)

It was the rampart of God's house/ That she was standing on;/ By God built over that sheer depth/ The which is Space begun;/ So high, that looking downward thence,/ She scarce could see the sun. . . .

The Blessed Damsel.

The blessed damsel leaned against
  the silver bar of Heaven.
Her eyes knew more of rest and shade
  Than a deep water, even.
She had three lilies in her hand
  And the stars in her hair were seven.

Her robe, ungirt from clasp to hem,
  No wrought flowers did adorn,
But a white robe of Mary's gift
  For service meetly worn;
And her hair lying down her back
  Was yellow like ripe corn.

Herseemed she scarce had been a day
  One of God's choristers;
The wonder was not yet quite gone
  From that still look of hers;
Albeit to them she left, her day
  Had counted as ten years.

(To one it is ten years of years.
  . . . . Yet now, and in this place,
Surely she leaned o'er me, — her hair
  Fell all about my face. . . .
Nothing: the autumn fall of leaves.
  The whole year sets apace.)

It was the rampart of God's house
  That she was standing on;
By God built over the sheer depth
  The which is Space begun;
So high, that looking downward thence
  She scarce could see the sun.

Heard hardly, some of her new friends,
  Playing at holy games,
Spake gentle-mouthed among themselves
  Their virginal chaste names;
And the souls mounting up to God
  Went by her like thin flames.

And still she bowed herself & stooped
  Into the vast waste calm,
Till her bosom's pressure must have made
  The bar she leaned on warm,
And the lilies lay as if asleep
  Along her bended arm.

From the fixt lull of Heaven, she saw
  Time like a pulse shake fierce
Through all the worlds. Her gaze still strove,
  Within that gulf to pierce
The swarm; and then she spake, as when
  The stars sang in their spheres.

"I wish that he were come to me,
  For he will come," she said.
"Have I not prayed in Heaven? — on earth,
  Lord, Lord, has he not prayed?
Are not two prayers a perfect strength?
  And shall I feel afraid?

"When round his head the aureole clings,
  And he is clothed in white,
I'll take his hand and go with him
  To the deep wells of light,
And we will step down as to a stream
  And bathe there in God's sight.

"We two will stand beside that shrine,
  Occult, withheld, untrod,
Whose lamps are stirred continually
  With prayers sent up to God;
And see our own prayers, granted, melt
  Each like a little cloud.

"We two will lie i' the shadow of
  That living mystic tree
Within whose secret growth the Dove
  Is sometimes felt to be,
While every leaf that His plumes touch
  Saith His name audibly.

"And I myself will teach to him —
  I myself, lying so, —
The songs I sing here; which his voice
  Shall pause in, hushed & slow,
And find some knowledge at each pause
  Or some new thing to know."

(Alas! just now, in that bird's song,
  Strove not her accents there
Fain to be hearkened? When those bells
  Possessed the midday air,
Was she not stepping to my side
  Upon a silver stair?)

"We two", she said, "will seek the groves
  Where the lady Mary is,
With her five handmaidens whose names
  Are five sweet symphonies; —
Cecily, Gertrude, Magdalen,
  Margaret and Rosalys.

"They sit in circle, with bound locks
  And brows engarlanded;
Into the fine cloth white like flame
  Weaving the golden thread
To fashion the birth-robes for them
  Who are just born, being dead.

"Herself shall bring us hand in hand
  To Him round whom all souls
Kneel, the unnumbered ransomed heads
  Bowed with their aureoles;
And Angels meeting us shall sing
  To their citherns and citoles.

"There will I ask of Christ the Lord
  Thus much for him and me: —
Only to live as once on earth
  At peace — only to be
As then awhile, for ever now
  Together, I and he."

She gazed and listened, and then said
  Less sad of speech than mild:
"All this is when he comes." She ceased;
  The light thrilled past her, filled
With Angels in strong level lapse.
  Her eyes prayed, and she smiled.

(I saw her smile.) But soon their flight
  Was vague in distant spheres.
And then she laid her arms along
  The shining barriers,
And laid her face between her hands,
  And wept. (I heard her tears.)

— D.G.R. - 1847

George Meredith
1828–1909

Autograph manuscript of "Diana of the Crossways," unsigned and undated, but written ca. 1883–4. 987 leaves. 228 x 180 mm. MA 781.

To Meredith, the rewards of a life in writing came late and were conveyed largely by the members of a younger generation, who found in him a devotion to the novelist's craft similar to their own and literary experience that far exceeded theirs. Few novelists in the nineteenth century wrote as much from themselves as Meredith did or refused as persistently as he to make concessions to the reading public. Understandably, this did him no good when it came to year-end accounting of sales. The difficulties some readers encountered in his novels were also faced by his friends in conversation over dinner at Box Hill, Meredith's home; as Sidney Colvin reported, "When in real life he would sometimes try to lift the talk of a commonplace company to his own plane, the result was apt to be that he would be left discoursing alone to auditors silent and gaping, disconcerted or perhaps even annoyed." Translated into literary terms, this lofty expectation became Meredith's besetting flaw, at least in the eyes of commonplace readers. Even so erudite a reader as William Butler Yeats felt that "He makes the mistake of making the reader think too much. One is continually laying the book down to think. He is so suggestive, one's mind wanders." Yeats's comment preserves a fundamental truth about Meredith's fiction; it is deeply philosophical and intended to be speculative. As Meredith observed in the introductory chapter of *Diana of the Crossways*, "To demand of us truth to nature, excluding philosophy, is really to bid a pumpkin caper. As much as legs are wanted for the dance, philosophy is required to make our human nature credible and acceptable."

Making human nature credible and acceptable is a large part of Meredith's purpose in *Diana of the Crossways*, one of his finest novels and one of the best studies written during the nineteenth century of a woman struggling to maintain what was then an awkward freedom. The passage shown here is the letter that Diana—of impulsive Celtic blood—sent to her friend Lady Dunstane announcing her marriage, the initial error that plagues her throughout a course of successive errors. Redworth, whom Meredith portrayed in a calculating, almost comic pose in the second chapter, is the man who by his modesty has apparently lost Diana Merion to a far lesser man.

The Morgan Library has a superb collection of Meredith's novels in manuscript, including *The Amazing Marriage* and *Lord Ormont and his Aminta*.

[Beginning with marginal insertion:] He was not a weaver of phrases in distress. His blank reserve was eloquent of it to her, & she liked him the better; could have thanked him, too, for leaving her promptly.

When she was alone she took in the contents of the letter at a [illegible deletion] hasty glimpse. It was of one paragraph, & fired its shot like a cannon with the muzzle at her breast:—

"My own Emmy, I have been asked in marriage by M.r Warwick, & have accepted him. Signify your approval, for I have decided that it is the wisest thing a waif can do. We are to live at the Crossways for four months of the year; so I shall have Dada in his best days & all my youngest dreams, my sunrise & morning dew, surrounding me; my old home for my new one. I write in haste, to you first, burning to hear from you. Send your blessing to Yours in life & death, through all transformations, "Tony." ...

backward at the letter on her desk. She had to answer the strangest of letters that had ever come to her, & it was from her dear Tony, the baldest intimation of the weightiest piece of intelligence which a woman can communicate to her heart's friend. The task of answering it was now doubled. "I fear so. I fancy so," she said, & she longed to cast eye over the letter again, to see if there might possibly be a loophole behind the lines.

"Then I must make my mind up to it," said Redworth. "I think I'll take a walk."

She smiled kindly. "It will be our secret."

"I thank you with all my heart, Lady Dunstane."

He was not a weaver of phrases in distress. His blunt reserve was eloquent of it to her, & she liked him the better; could have thanked him, too, for leaving her promptly.

When she was alone she took in the contents of the letter at a hasty glimpse. It was of one paragraph, & fired its shot

like a cannon with the muzzle at her breast: –

"My own Emmy, I have been asked in marriage by Mr. Warwick, & have accepted him. Signify your approval, for I have decided that it is the wisest thing a waif can do. We are to live at the Crossways for four months of the year; so I shall have Dada in his best days & all my youngest dreams, my sunrise & morning dew, surrounding me; my old home for my new one. I write in haste, to you first, burning to hear from you. Send your blessing to Yours in life & death, through all transformations,

"Tony."

That was all. Not a word of the lover about to be decorated with the title of husband. No confession of love. Not a single supplicating word to her friend, in excuse for the abrupt decision to so grave a step. Her previous description of him, as

83

George Meredith

Autograph manuscript signed of "The Main Regret," undated but written in 1901. 1 p. 188 x 237 mm. MA 749.

Meredith's poems were neither as perfect nor as abundant as he wished them to be. Writing to Augustus Jessop in November 1861, he explained: "It is true that I have fallen from what I once hoped to do. The fault is hardly mine. Do you know Vexation, the slayer?" While financial vexation might spur the writing of novels, spiritual vexation could, at least temporarily, be death to poetry, as Meredith knew all too well. In the autumn of 1861 his estranged wife, who had fled to Capri with an artist named Henry Wallis in 1858, became seriously ill; Meredith refused to see her, and in October she died. She had been, as Meredith recalled, a volatile woman, one who "dallied with responsibility, played with passions; rose suddenly to a height of exultation, sank to a terrible level. And was very clever." Under the blow of her death and the "melancholy recollections" it caused, Meredith's nerves collapsed. But with his recovery in November came a burst of poetic creativity that culminated in his masterpiece, *Modern Love*, "a dissection of the sentimental passion of these days," particularly the sentimental Victorian perception of marriage. The reaction to the fifty sonnets grouped under the title was just what might have been expected from a public that was used to having its sentimentality pandered to rather than dissected. In defense of Meredith, Swinburne—not, perhaps, the most useful of allies in a debate on such a subject— informed the editor of the *Spectator*, where the most virulent attack on Meredith had appeared, that "Mr. Meredith is one of the three or four poets now alive whose work, perfect or imperfect, is always as noble in design as it is often faultless in result."

The poem shown here, "The Main Regret," is a meditation on "sins of omission" as seen by the poet in his "autumn days." Meredith's handwriting provides clear evidence of the locomotor ataxia which gradually deprived the poet of some of his favorite activities: long, bounding walks over the region near Box Hill and animated, often hectic conversations over dinner. This poem was first published in *The May Book* (London: Macmillan, 1901), a work printed to aid Charing Cross Hospital.

The best collections of Meredith manuscripts and letters are those in the Beinecke Library, Yale University, and at the University of Texas, Austin.

The Main Regret./ Seen, too clear & historic within us! our sins of omission/ Frown when the autumn days strip us so ruthlessly bare./ They of our mortal diseases find never healing physician;/ Errors charged on the soul, past all hope to repair. Sunshine might we have been unto seed in the earth, or have scattered/ Seed to ascendant suns brighter than any that shone./ Even the lowly of men some lowlier creature had flattered/ Back to acceptance of life cheered by the mere human tone./ George M.

The Main Regret.

Seen, too clear & historic within us! our sins of omission
Frown when the autumn days strip us so ruthlessly bare.
They of our mortal diseases find never healing physician;
Errors charged on the soul, past all hope to repair.

Sunshine might we have been unto seed in the earth, or have scattered
Seed to ascendant suns brighter than any that shone.
Even the lowly of men some lowlier creature had flattered
Back to acceptance of life cheered by the mere human tone.

George M.

Christina Georgina Rossetti
1830–1894

Autograph manuscript of "Song" ("When I am dead, my dearest"), unsigned, dated 12 December 1848. 1 p. 161 x 99 mm. MA 1879. Purchased as the gift of Dr. Leroy E. Kimball.

In a famous painting by Gabriel Rossetti (done about the time this poem was written) and an equally famous photograph by Charles Dodgson, Christina Rossetti appears as the young Virgin Mary and as a rather dour maiden surrounded by her family at the back of Gabriel's house on Cheyne Walk in London. For many persons, these two portraits have summed up the character of the second most brilliant Rossetti, a woman who by the inclination of her whole being was given to piety and was bound by love as well as health to the Rossetti clan. In this, she resembles one of the Brontë sisters, but the talents and personalities of the Rossettis diverged much more than those of the Brontë children. Strangely, the two families are perhaps closest in their extremes; the contrast between Anne and Branwell Brontë is suggestive in some ways (if not flatteringly so) of the contrast between Christina and Gabriel Rossetti. Christina's genius clearly belonged to a different province from Gabriel's; her poetry—the great bulk of it religious—marks out a realm almost purely of the spirit, while Gabriel's often describes a region of sensation tinged, in Pater's words, with "mystic isolation." If Christina's poetic ability flagged (or evened out) in tone before Gabriel's, her precocity had certainly once been the equal of his. Her best and most acclaimed long poem, *Goblin Market* (1862), was also one of her earliest published; recalling his fondness for the poem in 1893, after the death of the laureate, Charles Dodgson declared it "a work of real *genius*. If only the Queen would consult *me* as to whom to make Poet-Laureate! I would say 'for once, Madam, take a *lady!*'"

The poem shown here, "When I am dead, my dearest," is one of Christina Rossetti's most famous lyrics. Twenty-two years after it was written, her brother William Michael Rossetti wrote in his diary the following entry: "Dined at Brown's—partly in order to hear [Franz] Hüffer's music, which I like much, to Christina's song, 'When I am dead, my dearest'." This poem was also set to music by Ralph Vaughan Williams and John Ireland.

Song./ When I am dead, my dearest,/ Sing no sad songs for me:/ Plant thou no roses at my head,/ Nor shady cypress tree:/ Be the green grass above me/ With showers and dew drops wet:/ And if thou wilt, remember,/ And if thou wilt, forget./ I shall not see the shadows:/ I shall not feel the rain:/ I shall not hear the nightingale/ Sing on as if in pain:/ And dreaming through the twilight/ That doth nor rise nor set,/ Haply, I may remember,/ And haply, may forget./ —12th December 1848.

28

×

Song.

When I am dead, my dearest,
  Sing no sad songs for me:
Plant thou no roses at my head,
  Nor shady cypress tree:
Be the green grass above me
  With showers and dewdrops wet:
And if thou wilt, remember,
  And if thou wilt, forget.
I shall not see the shadows:
  I shall not feel the rain:
I shall not hear the nightingale
  Sing on as if in pain:
And dreaming through the twilight
  That doth nor rise nor set,
Haply I may remember,
  And haply may forget.

—12th December 1848.

85

CHARLES LUTWIDGE DODGSON ("LEWIS CARROLL") 1832–1898

Autograph manuscript of "Double Acrostic" ("Two little maids were heard to say"), signed and undated. 1 p. 328 x 208 mm. From the Collection of Mr. Arthur A. Houghton, Jr.

No books are treasured more than those we loved as children and are able to love still as adults, for they provide a unique measure of stability and access to a refuge that is otherwise hard to find. No writer of children's books for grown-ups has ever been so nobly equipped with a gift for hiding sophistication beneath apparent simplicity (not to mention apparent nonsense) as Lewis Carroll. His own visage presents a puzzle of the first order; at a glance, his dreamy, almost mooning expression could hardly be suspected of concealing the acuity of mind required for his position as mathematical lecturer at Christ Church, Oxford, nor does it begin to reveal any glimmering of imaginative brilliance, especially of the kind capable of entertaining children endlessly. Yet behind eyes that seem always to be staring off into a mist was an intellect equally adept at the intricacies of formal logic and the fantasies of life in Wonderland. The starting point for Alice's adventures is boredom, the ennui of life without pictures or conversations; the starting point for Carroll's exorbitantly witty tales, poems and riddles was a life of studious reserve and carefully guarded privacy. Indeed, Carroll's satisfaction with *Alice's Adventures in Wonderland* was lessened only by the notoriety its success immediately conferred upon him. Responding to one of many persons who claimed to be "honoured" by his correspondence, he wrote, "please will you try and feel that it's rather a disgrace than otherwise to have a letter from me, and that *I'm* the kind of cat that *scratches* when you stroke it?"

Carroll's favorite correspondents (and favorite persons) were the young daughters of his friends, for whom he wrote his books and created his games and puzzles. Though only one, Alice Liddell, could inspire the Alice books, many of these girls inspired anagrams, acrostics and charades. The manuscript shown here contains, besides the "Double Acrostic" illustrated, two more double acrostics (which provide the names of two young friends each) and a charade.

The autograph manuscript of *Alice's Adventures in Wonderland* is now in the British Library.

Double Acrostic. [Addressed to two children, whose names form the two "upright" words, which are supposed to be described in the first stanza.]

Two little maids were heard to say,/ (They dwelt in London-city),/ "This summer-day's too hot to play,/ And picture-books are pretty."

So, curling up like little mice,/ And clasping hand in hand,/ They read (& whispered "Aint it nice!")/ The tale of Wonderland.

Bright streamed the sunlight on the floor,/ To tempt them out to run;/ But they (like mice, I've said before)/ Loved shadow more than sun. . . .

Double Acrostic.

[Addressed to two children, whose names form the two "upright" words, which are supposed to be described in the first stanza.]

Two little maids were heard to say,
(They dwelt in London-city),
"This summer-day's too hot to play,
And picture-books are pretty."

So, curling up like little mice,
And clasping hand in hand,
They read (& whispered "Ain't it nice!")
The tale of Wonderland.

Bright streamed the sunlight on the floor,
To tempt them out to run;
But they (like mice, I've said before)
Loved shadow more than sun.

And one cried "Sister, let's invent
A dream — and plan to go
Where Mr. Carroll says he went —
That Russian Fair, you know!"

The other said "It's nearly three:
Papa will call us soon.
His picture's on the stand, and we
Must sit this afternoon."

"And if we sit extremely good,"
The younger cried in haste,
"He'll give us wine — he said he would —
A little tiny taste!"

[In explanation of the last two verses, it should be added that they are an Artist's children.]

Sir Leslie Stephen
1832–1904

Autograph manuscript of "The History of English Thought in the Eighteenth Century," unsigned and undated, but written ca. 1875–6. 1,164 pp. 203 x 160 mm. MA 3393. Purchased as the gift of the Fellows, with the special assistance of individual Fellows.

As twentieth-century sons and daughters have tended to be hard on their fathers, so did their nineteenth-century fathers (on a somewhat broader philosophical, if nonetheless emotional, basis) tend to reject the century that preceded them. To a great extent, Leslie Stephen is an exception to this axiom, for he was more sparing of easy contempt, less hasty in rejection than almost any of his contemporaries when it came to evaluating the achievements of the eighteenth century. In a period that had the nerve—not to say the blindness to its own leading traits—to call the eighteenth century an "age of prose," Stephen defended the century of Pope and Johnson in such a way as to betray his sympathy with that era and his occasional irritation with his own. Reading Pope, for example, in a nineteenth-century edition, he felt "something like a boy at a pantomime with a schoolmaster by his side. The boy laughs at the clown, and the schoolmaster immediately nudges him and explains at length that it is very wrong to sit down upon babies, or brand the rear of policemen with red-hot pokers." Aside from such spirited popular defense of Pope and his peers, Stephen made a more important contribution to a correct estimate of the eighteenth century by writing his *English Thought in the Eighteenth Century*, the most comprehensive Victorian analysis of one of England's greatest philosophical eras and the natural offshoot of a subject, philosophy, which Stephen considered his true vocation.

For an opinion on no person can one more justly turn to the *Dictionary of National Biography* than for Stephen, who edited the venture for eight years and twenty-six volumes (from Abbadie to Hindley). It comments: "Stephen's work, alike in literary criticism and philosophy, was characterised by a frank sincerity which is vivified by a humorous irony. . . . At the same time . . . there was an equability of temper which preserved him from excesses of condemnation or eulogy." This fine critical balance is nowhere better shown in *English Thought* than in the passage shown here (the opening paragraph of Section III of Chapter I) in which Stephen assesses the philosophical characteristics of the English mind.

---

34. The critical movement initiated by Locke & culminating with Hume ~~seems to~~ reflects the national character. The strong point of the English mind is it's vigorous grasp of facts; it's weakness is it's comparative indifference to logical symmetry. English poetry is admirable because poetry thrives upon a love of concrete imagery; whilst Englishmen have always despised too indiscriminately the dreams of a mystical philosophy wh. seems to be entirely divorced from a solid ~~groundwork~~ basis of fact. In metaphysical speculation their flights have been short & near the ground. They have knocked pretentious systems to pieces with admirable vigour; they have been slow to construct or to accept systems, however elaborately organized, wh. cannot be constantly interpreted into definite statements & checked by comparison with facts. As one consequence we perhaps underrate our own philosophical merits. Comparing Locke or his successors with the great German writers, we are struck by the ~~want of~~ apparently narrow, fragmentary & inconsistent views of our ~~own~~ countrymen. . . .

III

34. The critical movement initiated by Locke & culminating with Hume ~~seems to~~ reflects the national character. The strong points of the English mind is its rigorous grasp of facts: its weakness is its comparative indifference to logical symmetry. English poetry is admirable because poetry thrives upon a love of concrete imagery: whilst Englishmen have always despised too indiscriminately the dreams of a mystical philosophy, wh. seems to be entirely divorced from the solid ~~groundwork~~ basis of fact. In metaphysical speculation their flights have been short & near the ground. They have knocked pretentious systems to pieces with admirable rigour; they have been slow to construct or to accept systems, however elaborately organized, wh. cannot be constantly interpreted into definite statements & checked by comparison with facts. As one consequence we perhaps underrate our own philosophical merits. Comparing Locke & his successors with the great German writers, we are struck by the ~~want of~~ apparently narrow, fragmentary & inconsistent views of our ~~own~~ countrymen. If the merit of a philosopher were ~~[illegible]~~ to be exhaustively measured ~~by~~ not by the number of fruitful ~~suggestions~~ principles but by the variety & order of his applications of his principles, Locke & his successors would occupy a low position. If the courage wh. passes over a difficulty in order to frame a system be more admirable than the prudence wh. refuses to proceed beyond the clearly established principles, they must be content with a secondary rank. Nor is it doubtful that our dislike to pretentious

James Thomson ("Bysshe Vanolis") 1834–1882

Autograph manuscript of "The City of Dreadful Night," dated 16 January 1870 to 29 October 1873. 63 pp. (in two notebooks). 154 x 93 mm. MA 676.

Ten years before Oscar Wilde reached the West, James Thomson, the poet of urban despair, turned up in Colorado in the service of the Champion Gold and Silver Mines Company. At the time, 1872, he was between drafts of *The City of Dreadful Night*, which he had begun in 1870 and laid aside upon leaving London. Central City, Colorado, did not meet all his expectations: he had been persuaded to buy a gun, but found that one "might as well carry a revolver between Euston Square and Somerset House as here." Still, the rough mining life west of Denver allowed Thomson to escape temporarily from his miseries in London. It would perhaps have been well had he remained in the United States or continued the sort of journalism that took him to Spain in the spring and summer of 1873. In London he was the prisoner of an execrable pattern of dipsomaniacal melancholy, aggravated by poverty which his work for the *National Reformer* could not relieve. To hear Thomson rhapsodize to W. M. Rossetti about the Rocky Mountains ("vast billowy land seas, with dense woods and deep ravines and exquisite emerald dells") is to encounter one of the more miserable ironies in English literature. Thomson returned finally to England in the summer of 1873 and there completed his masterpiece.

The City of Dreadful Night is a poem of blank despair, of alarming passivity in the midst of a terrifying landscape. The narrator wanders through a city that is confining, almost subterranean, in its deathlike closeness, though it is pervaded by voices, each a testimony to the loss of faith and hope that frees the wanderer from fear: "no hope could have no fear." The passage shown here is an allegorical presentation of the collapse of God and man before the silent and insoluble mystery of the universe, represented by a "couchant Sphinx." *The City of Dreadful Night* concludes with an evocation of Dürer's "Melancholia," the muse of this high-Victorian wasteland.

The major collection of Thomson manuscripts, gathered by Bertram Dobell, is in the Bodleian Library, Oxford.

XX. I sat me weary on a pillar's base/ And leaned against the shaft; for broad moonlight/ O'erflowed the peacefulness of cloistered space,/ A shore of shadow slanting from the right:/ The great cathedral's western front stood there,/ A waveworn rock in that calm sea of air.

2. Before it, opposite my place of rest,/ Two figures faced each other, large, austere;/ A couchant Sphinx in shadows from to the breast,/ An angel standing in the moonlight clear;/ So mighty by magnificence of form,/ They were not dwarfed beneath that mass enorm.

3. Upon the crosshilt of a naked sword/ The angel's hands as prompt to smite were held;/ His vigilant intense regard was poured/ Upon the ~~*monster*~~ creature *placidly unquelled,/ Whose front was set at level gaze which took/ No heed of aught, a solemn trancelike look./ Sunday 12.6.70.*

4. And as I pondered these opposèd shapes/ My eyelids sank in stupor, that dull swoon/ Which drugs and with a leaden mantle drapes/ The outworn to worse weariness. But soon/ A sharp and clashing noise the stillness broke/ And from the evil lethargy I woke. . . .

XX.

I sat me weary on a pillar's base
And leaned against the shaft; for broad moonlight
O'erflowed the peacefulness of cloistered space,
A shore of shadow slanting from the right:
The great cathedral's western front stood there,
A wave-worn rock in that calm sea of air.

2.

Before it, opposite my place of rest,
Two figures faced each other, large, austere;
A couchant Sphinx in shadows ~~to~~ from the breast,
An angel standing in the moonlight clear;
So mighty by magnificence of form,
They were not dwarfed beneath that mass enorm.

3.

Upon the cross-hilt of a naked sword
The angel's hands as prompt to smite were held;
His vigilant intense regard was poured
Upon the creature (monster) placidly unquelled,
Whose front was set at level gaze which took
No heed of aught, a solemn trancelike look.

Sunday
12.6.70.

4.

And as I pondered these opposed shapes
My eyelids sank in stupor, that dull swoon
Which drugs and with a leaden mantle drapes
The outworn to worse weariness. But soon
A sharp and clashing noise the ~~the~~ stillness broke
And from the evil lethargy I woke.

5.

The angel's wings had fallen stone on stone
And lay there shattered, hence the sudden sound;
A warrior leaning on his sword alone
Now watched the Sphinx with that regard profound;
The Sphinx unchanged ~~gazed~~ looked forthright as aware
Of nothing in the vast abyss of air.

Thursday
7.7.70.

6.

Again I sank in that repose unsweet,
Again a clashing noise my slumber rent;
The warrior's sword lay broken at his feet;
An unarmed man with raised hands impotent
Now stood before the Sphinx, which ever kept
Such wise mien as if with open eyes it slept.

88

William Morris
1834–1896

Autograph letter signed, dated 24 January 1885, to Thomas James Cobden-Sanderson. 4 pp. 203 x 125 mm. MA 1753.

Sooner or later, most artists come to contemplate the analogy between the order of art and the order of society and wonder what lessons are to be drawn from it. William Morris did not fully appreciate the analogy until he was in his forties, when increasing disillusionment with the Liberal Party under Gladstone led him to it. In a sense, Morris' political conclusions were always implicit in his aesthetic theory; just as he believed in the basic unity of all the arts—and that such arts should permeate life—he also came to believe in the potential unity of all men, and finally in the identity of artistic and political action. Partly, this last ideal stemmed from the nature of Morris' personality, for he threw himself into political planning and editorial work with the same energy and intellectual commitment he gave to the arts of painting, poetry, wallpaper and textile design, printing and stained glass. By 1885 he had come so far as to lead the Socialist League, which would later have important ties to the early Labour Party, and to disagree with his fellow printer and bookbinder Cobden-Sanderson on the relations between one's political commitment and one's artistic labor. In the letter shown here he explains to Cobden-Sanderson what he feels to be the primary function of a socialist: "To keep ourselves alive for revolution, and to gather what influence we can for that purpose are the only aims I can recognize in the daily work of those who consider themselves Socialists."

Among Morris manuscripts in the Morgan Library are *Beowulf*, *The House of the Wolfings*, *The Well at the World's End* and his private ledger of the Kelmscott Press. Significant collections of Morris manuscripts and letters are to be found in the British Library, the Morris Museum, Walthamstow, and the Huntington Library.

---

cannot release myself from that work on the one hand, and on the other it amuses me vastly: but if I could live and have money for the propaganda without working at it I would not do another stroke at it, but would give myself up wholly to the propaganda. That is I regard my work as far as it pretends to produce any thing as absolutely worthless; and what I say of my own work I feel of everybody else's that has in it any pretence to art or sentiment ~~in it~~. Society is to my mind wholly corrupt, & I can take no deep seated pleasure in anything it turns out, except the materials for its own distraction in the shape of discontent and aspirations for better things. To keep ourselves alive for revolution, and to gather what influence we can for that purpose are the only aims I can recognize in the daily work of those who consider themselves Socialists. At the same time I quite admit the necessity of amusing ourselves with work if we have the chance; ~~and~~ because (and here I imagine I touch your point of view somewhat) if we dont, we are like to become too bitter to be of any use, or at least to be of as much use as we other wise should be. Also I admit that a man may be of some use without actively working in the cause; nor am I sure that his little bit of work is of much more use than his existence in company with his passive conviction: I don't feel responsible for more than a very small, almost infinitesimal, portion of work: but that portion you see I am impelled to give, whether [I like it or not.]

cannot release myself from that work on the one hand, and on the other it amuses me vastly: but if I could live and have money for the propaganda without working at it I would not do another stroke at it, but would give myself up wholly to the propaganda. That is I regard my work as far as it pretends to produce anything as absolutely worthless; and what I say of my own work I feel of everybody elses' that has in it any pretence to art or sentiment ~~in it~~. Society is to my mind wholly corrupt, & I can take no deep seated pleasure in anything it turns out, except the materials for its own distruction in the shape of discontent and aspirations for better things. To keep ourselves alive for revolution, and to gather what influence we can for that purpose are the only aims I can recognize in the daily work of those who consider themselves Socialists. At the same time I quite admit the necessity of amusing ourselves with work if we have the chance; ~~and~~ because (and here I imagine I touch your point of view somewhat) if we dont, we are like to become too bitter to be of any use, or at least to be of as much use as we otherwise should be. Also I admit that a man may be of some use without actively working in the Cause; nor am I sure that his little bit of work is of much more use than his existence in company with his passive conviction: I dont feel responsible for more than a very small, almost infinitesimal, portion ~~of work~~: but that portion you see I am impelled to give, whether

GEORGE DU MAURIER
1834–1896

Autograph manuscript of "Peter Ibbetson," Volume I, undated but written ca. 1889–90. 154 leaves. 196 x 155 mm. MA 115.

Autobiography often carries with it a redemptive quality, redeeming the graceless present by bestowing grace upon the past. Few works of the nineteenth century indulge this romantic inclination more strongly than *Peter Ibbetson*, in which autobiography becomes reverie. George du Maurier, of French ancestry and upbringing, was a small, tense man who reached the top of his profession as an illustrator at a time when Victorian book illustration was attaining the status of a true art. His work as a social cartoonist for *Punch*, where he succeeded John Leech in 1864, reveals du Maurier's thorough Britishness, yet he remained, in imagination at least, a permanent expatriate. This is nowhere clearer than in *Peter Ibbetson*, which was begun one evening in March 1889 after a long walk in Bayswater with another expatriate, Henry James. *Peter Ibbetson* opens with an extended recollection of du Maurier's childhood in Passy, near the Bois de Boulogne. Even in this blissful setting, there is a suggestion of comic exile as Gogo Pasquier (du Maurier) and Mimsey Seraskier develop, in the passage shown here, a dual nonsense language, Frankingle and Inglefrank, which they alone understand. After years of separation, Gogo, who has been raised as an Englishman named Peter Ibbetson and detained in a prison for the criminally insane, and Mimsey, now the Duchess of Towers, meet at night by "dreaming true," for they possess the power to move back through time together, always remaining young and beautiful. This is the literature of escape at its most romantic.

Though *Peter Ibbetson* was du Maurier's favorite work, it was not his most popular. Published in 1894, *Trilby* became a best-seller almost overnight. It too is largely autobiographical, dealing with du Maurier's days as an art student in Paris, and like *Peter Ibbetson* it moves quickly into the realm of the fantastic, when Svengali gives Trilby the gift, or the curse, of musical perfection through hypnotic means. The Morgan Library houses the complete manuscripts of *Peter Ibbetson* and *Trilby*, as well as du Maurier's illustrations for them.

In time we made a kind of ingenious compromise—for Mimsey, who was full of resource, invented a new language, or rather, two—which we called Frankingle & Inglefrank respectively. They consisted in Anglicising French *nouns & verbs & then conjugating & pronouncing them* Englishly, *or* ~~*just the reverse*~~ vice versâ.

For instance it was very cold & the schoolroom window was open—So she would say, in Frankingle:—"dispeach yourself to ferm the feneeter, Gogo—It geals to pier-fend! we shall be inrhumed!" *or else, if I failed to immediately understand:* —"Gogo, il frise à splitter les stounes—maque aste et chute le vindeau. ~~nous taquerons coldel~~" mais chute-le donc vite—je sniffle déjà.'" *which was Inglefrank.*

With this contrivance we managed to puzzle & mystify the uninitiated, English or French alike. The intelligent reader, who sees it all in print, will not be so easily taken in.

32 A

In time we made a kind of ingenious compromise — for Mimsey, who was full of resource, invented a new language, or rather, two — which we called Frankingle & Inglefrank respectively. They consisted in Anglicising French nouns & verbs & then conjugating & pronouncing them Englishly, or vice versâ ~~just the reverse~~.

For instance it was very cold & the schoolroom window was open — so she would say, in Frankingle:

— "dispeach yourself to ferm the fenester, Gogo — It geals to pier-fend! we shall be enrhumed!"

or else, if I failed to immediately understand:

— "Gogo, il frise à splitter les stounes — maque aste et chute le vindeau ~~vous taquerons colde!~~" mais chute-le donc vite — je sniffle déjà!" which was Inglefrank.

With this contrivance we managed to puzzle & mystify the uninitiated, English or French, alike. The intelligent reader, who sees it all in print, will not be so easily taken in.

Samuel Butler
1835–1902

Autograph manuscript signed of "A lecture on the genesis of feeling delivered at the City of London College," dated 13 December 1887, delivered on 15 December 1887. 38 pp. 270 x 206 mm. MA 3166. Purchased as the gift of Mr. Claus von Bulow.

Somewhat less than a year before this lecture was delivered, Samuel Butler's father died, and every reader of his autobiographical novel *The Way of All Flesh* (1903) may readily guess what an epoch that formed in his life. Insofar as the transition from one generation to the next is the most basic link in the process of evolution, Butler seemed determined to make the transition in which he participated as advanced and meaningful as possible. Finding a settled world around him, Butler began to unsettle it, and in doing so moved from simple boyhood rebellion against an autocratic father to a more articulate and reasoned attack on the conventions of Victorian England. "All our lives long," he wrote in *The Way of All Flesh*, "every day and every hour, we are engaged in the process of accommodating our changed and unchanged selves to changed and unchanged surroundings. . . ." In a quarrel with Darwinists who argued that accommodation (i.e., evolution) was governed by chance, Butler proposed an alternative model, one based upon memory; this theory forms the basis for the work shown here, "A lecture on the genesis of feeling." Quite simply, Butler contends that each feeling registered by the nervous system is a remembrance of other feelings, which all originated in "a single, simple, and highly unspecialised form of feeling, namely a sense of shock. . . ." The passage shown here develops the analogy between the origin of language in the attribution of meaning to a single symbolic object and the origin of feelings in a simple, remembered feeling. The application of this theory is to be found in Butler's notion of feeling rightly and distinctly, that is, knowing when one feels strongly about a subject and when one doesn't. In a statement full of characteristic unconventionality, Butler concludes: "It is an exceedingly rare thing to find any one who has the courage of his want of opinions so firmly fixed as that it shall never fail him. . . ."

The best group of Butler manuscripts and letters is that in the Chapin Library of Williams College, Williamstown, Massachusetts.

The essence of language consisting in the closeness of association rather than in the symbol chosen.

It does not matter whether the symbol chosen be made with voice or gesture, or written character.

The essence is that any symbol shd be unvaryingly connected however arbitrarily, with the same idea.

If the symbols are few &c. the language is elementary

If the symbols are many &c. we have a highly developed language.

It is not easy to see how a rude language can be denied to the lower animals

And all things that live must be allowed to have ideas about their own business. . . .

The essence of language consisting in the closeness of association rather than in the symbol chosen.

It does not matter whether the symbol chosen be made with voice or gesture, or written character.

The essence is that any symbol shd be unvaryingly connected however arbitrarily with the same idea.

If the symbols are few &c. the language is elementary

If the symbols are many &c. we have a highly developed language.

It is not easy to see how a rude language can be denied to the lower animals

And all things that live must be allowed to have ideas about their own business.

We have only few & vague ideas about things that do not concern us.

shape? We have seen that the essence of language consists not in the choice of the symbol but in the sticking to it when it has been chosen; and ~~attaching this symbol or that to an idea and associating them till they cohare habitually in our minds, but in the attaching~~ any symbol ~~the virtue lying not in the symbol but in the coherence~~; it requires but little reflection to see that if this is so, the question whether the symbol shall be made with the tongue and vocal organs, or ~~whe- it shall be made~~ with the hand, as by a railway guard or the captain of a river steamer, or by ourselves when we write a letter, is a question of detail; the essential features of language are presented whenever any unvarying symbol is adopted for the purpose of conveyan idea. If the symbols are few, simple, but little specialised and admit but little formulation & coordination, the language is of the elementary ~~imper-~~ unspecialised character which alone exists among the lower animals; when they are many, highly specialised, and coordinated so as to admit of infinite complexity of arrangement and development, we have a language such as prevails among ourselves, but it is not easy to see how the possession of the germs of a rude elementary language can be denied to the lower animals, and as for the ideas that underly language, each living form that lives, moves, and has a business of any sort to attend to, must be allowed to have ideas no less definite about all that concerns the successful carrying on of that business, than we have about the management of our own affairs. We ~~have~~ ourselves have only few and ill defined ideas, if indeed we have any at all, about things that do not concern us and form no part of our daily life and interests; nor is there any reason to suppose

Sir William Schwenck Gilbert
1836–1911

Autograph manuscript signed of the libretto for Act I of "The Pirates of Penzance," undated but written in November 1879. 31 pp. 267 x 218 mm. Gift of Mr. Reginald Allen.

Lugubrious as the popular notion of Queen Victoria's reign is, the nineteenth century is nonetheless the era in which fun truly came of age. It is the century in which the word "fun" (a monosyllable whose red-faced linguistic forebears hide in the mists of time) matured, and it is certainly the only century that could have produced, in all adult seriousness, a periodical called *Fun*. Richard Barham, Thomas Hood, Winthrop Praed, the poets of *Punch*, Lewis Carroll and W. S. Gilbert together form a remarkable poetic tradition, one that is too little known; and if all but the last two provide fun nowadays for only the cultural historian, that is merely an indication of how much our twentieth-century fun differs from the Victorians'. As Gilbert demonstrates again and again in *The "Bab" Ballads* (1869, 1873, 1877), in his own plays and in his operas set to music by Sullivan, comic verse is more than funny ideas in short lines; rhyme and rhythm—the triumph of poetic form over seemingly insuperable obstacles created by the subject—are everything, and there can be no sacrilege in saying that as a poet, in matters of technique, Gilbert ranks with the best poets of the Victorian period. Fun for the Victorians was also "poking fun," the softer side of satire; Gilbert's poetry and lyrics create an image of Victorian society as reflected in a funhouse mirror, a society in which, for the first time, an audience had emerged which was capable of laughing across class borders, both upwards and downwards, within limits set by the Lord Chamberlain, and capable especially of laughing at itself.

The portion of the libretto for Act I of *The Pirates of Penzance* shown here needs no introduction, for it is the famous song in which Major General Stanley introduces himself to the pirate crew as "the very model of a modern Major General." Aside from the exuberance of Gilbert's wit, it also demonstrates the sudden release of energy—the triumph of form—that follows Major General Stanley's successful search for a rhyme to fit "About binomial Theorem I'm teeming with a lot o' news . . . ." This manuscript was probably written in New York after the discovery that Sullivan had left his copy of Act I of *The Pirates of Penzance* in England. It bears the *dramatis personae* of the cast which opened the play at the Fifth Avenue Theatre on New Year's Eve, 1879.

The most important collections of Gilbert and Sullivan manuscripts are the one formed by Reginald Allen, in the Pierpont Morgan Library, and the one in the British Library.

---

*Song, Major General./ I am the very pattern of a modern Major General./ I've information vegetable animal & mineral./ I know the Kings of England & I quote the fights historical/ From Marathon to Waterloo in order categorical./ I'm very well acquainted, too, with matters mathematical/ I understand equations—both the simple & quadratical/ About binomial Theorem I'm teeming with a lot o' news—(*bothered for next rhyme*)—lot o' news—lot o' news—(*struck with an idea*)/ With many cheerful facts about the square of the hypotenuse!/ (*joyously*) With many cheerful facts about the square of the hypotenuse!/ . . .*

Song. Major General.

I am the very pattern of a modern Major General.
I've information vegetable animal & mineral.
I know the Kings of England & I quote the fights historical
From Marathon to Waterloo in order categorical.
I'm very well acquainted, too, with matters mathematical
I understand equations — both the simple & quadratical
About binomial Theorem I'm teeming with a lot o' news —
(bothered for next rhyme) — lot o' news — lot o' news — (struck with an idea)
With many cheerful facts about the Square of the hypotenuse!
(joyously) With many cheerful facts about the square of the hypotenuse!
All — With many ~~cheerful facts~~ cheerful facts about the square of the hypotenuse!
Gen. — I'm very good at integral & differential calculus —
I know the scientific names of beings animalculous —
In short, in matters vegetable animal or mineral.
I am the very model of a modern Major General!
All — In short in matters vegetable, animal or mineral
He is the very model of a modern Major General!

Gen. — I know our mythic history — King Arthur's & Sir Caradoc's —
I answer hard acrostics — I've a pretty taste for paradox —
I quote in elegiacs all the crimes of Heliogabalus —
In conics I can floor peculiarities parabolous.
I can tell undoubted Raphaels from Gerard Dows & Zoffanies —
I know the croaking chorus from the Frogs of Aristophanes —
Then I can hum a fugue of which I've heard the music's din afore —
(bothered for next rhyme) din afore — din afore — din afore! (struck with an idea)
And whistle all the airs from that infernal nonsense — "Pinafore"!
joyously — And whistle all the airs from that infernal nonsense "Pinafore"!
All. — And whistle all the airs from that infernal nonsense "Pinafore"!

Gen — Then I can write a washing bill in Babylonic cuneiform —
And tell you every detail of Caractacus's uniform —
In short in matters vegetable, animal & mineral,
I am the very pattern of a modern Major General!
All. — In short in matters vegetable animal & mineral,
He is the very pattern of a modern Major General!

Gen. — In fact, when I know what is meant by mamelon & ravelin —
When I can tell at sight a Chassepôt rifle from a javelin —
When such affairs as sorties & surprises I'm more wary at —
And when I know precisely what is meant by Commissariat —
When I have learnt what progress has been made in modern gunnery —
When I know more of tactics than a novice in a nunnery —
In short when I've a smattering of elemental strategy —
(bothered for the rhyme) ~~[illegible]~~ strategy — strategy — (struck with an idea)
You'll say "A better Major General has never sat a gee"!
joyously — You'll say a better Major General has never sat a gee!
All — We'll say a better Major General has never sat a gee!
Gen. — For my military knowledge though I'm plucky & adventury
Has only been brought down to the beginning of the century —
But still, in learning vegetable animal & mineral,
I am the very model of a modern Major General!
All — But still in learning vegetable, animal & mineral
He is the very model of a modern Major General!

~~Samuel.~~ — ~~And now that you know who I am, may I ask what you are doing with my daughters? My dears, what are these gentlemen doing to you?~~
~~Edith~~ — ~~Father, they are going to marry us against our will!~~

Algernon Charles Swinburne
1837–1909

Autograph manuscript of "At Eleusis," undated but written ca. 1864–5. 10 pp. 240 x 180 mm. MA 2358.

In 1865 *Atalanta in Calydon* was published and Swinburne's "sinister career," hitherto championed by only a small coterie, was thrust upon the attention of a stiff but applauding public. Swinburne did not enjoy unblemished fame for long. *Poems and Ballads* (First Series) appeared in July 1866, and with an almost unanimous voice of alarm the reviewers condemned it, calling for the prosecution of its author for obscenity. The brilliance of the verse was all but forgotten in the enumeration of Swinburne's sins. As he later remarked in his own defense, he had deliberately affronted "these Tennysonian times": "We have idyls good and bad, ugly and pretty . . . idyls of the dining-room and the deanery; idyls of the gutter and the gibbet." The contents of *Poems and Ballads* could never be called idyllic; he best characterized his more outrageous poetic effects when he described the progress of the volume's most infamous poem, "Dolores," to his friend Charles Augustus Howell: "I have added yet four more jets of boiling and gushing infamy to the perennial and poisonous fountain of Dolores." But *Poems and Ballads* does not merely boil and gush. "At Eleusis," shown here in manuscript, represents a more sober and classical side of Swinburne, who was, in Ruskin's words, "simply one of the mightiest scholars of the age in Europe . . . ." This poem recounts, in Demeter's words, the rape of her daughter Persephone—that myth so vital to the Pre-Raphaelites and their followers—and her efforts to deify Triptolemus, who later established the Eleusinian mysteries in honor of the goddess. It is at once a poem of loss and regeneration, for though Demeter fails to make Triptolemus a god, she does teach him the arts of agriculture, thus restoring the earth, rendered sterile by her wrath at Hades' rape of Persephone, to fruitfulness.

Important collections of Swinburne manuscripts may be found in the libraries of the University of Texas, Austin, and Yale University and in the British Library.

[Beginning line 3:] For Hades & the sidelong will of Zeus/ And that lame wisdom that has ~~crooked~~ writhen feet,/ Cunning, begotten in the bed of Shame,/ These three took evil will at rue, & made/ Such counsel that when time got wing to fly/ This Hades out of summer & low fields/ Forced the bright body of Perspehone:/ Out of ~~warm~~ pure grass, where she lying down, red flowers/ Made their sharp little shadows on her sides,/ [illegible deletion] Pale heat, pale colour on pale maiden flesh—/ And chill water ~~caressed deepened her (white rose) feet.~~ slid over her reddening feet,/ Killing the throbs in their soft blood; . . .

> Out of fine grass, where she lying down, red flowers
Made their sharp little shadows on her sides,
Pale heat, pale colour on pale maiden flesh—
And chill water slid over her reddening feet,
Killing the heats in their soft blood; & birds,
Perched next her elbow & pecking at her hair,
Stretched their necks more to see her than even to sing;

With weeping wrinkles, & both lids
Sodden with salt continuance of tears.
For Hades & the sidelong will of Zeus
And that same wisdom that has winged feet,
Cunning, begotten in the bed of Shame,
These three took evil will at me, & made
Such counsel that when time got wing to fly
This Hades out of summer & low fields
Forced the bright body of Persephone:
A sharp thing is it I have need to say;
For Hades holding both white wrists of hers
Unloosed the girdle & with knot by knot
Bound her between his wheels upon the seat,
Bound her pure body, holiest yet & dear
To me & God as always, clothed about
With blossoms loosened as her knees went down,
Let fall as she let go of this & this
By tens & twenties, tumbled to her feet,
White waifs on purple of the pasturage.
Therefore with only going up & down
My feet were wasted, & the gracious air,
To me discomfortable & dim, became
As weak smoke blowing in the under world
And finding in the process of ill days

Walter Pater
1839–1894

Autograph manuscript signed of "Dante Gabriel Rossetti," undated but written in 1883. 18 pp. 209 x 167 mm. From the Collection of Mr. Gordon N. Ray.

Reputations have indeed been based on fewer works than Pater published in his lifetime, but not reputations greater than Pater's. Being considered a threat to the morals of the established order will always stand a book in good stead, and, as Mrs. Humphry Ward reported, there were cries of "neopaganism" and threats of persecution in the air at Oxford (where Pater was a fellow at Brasenose) when *Studies in the History of the Renaissance* was published in 1873. Because the intense devotion to beauty in this work was so controversial, Pater's writings became something of a dividing line between generations. As a consequence, he was undervalued by the old and overvalued by the young. George Eliot (in whom the puritan had not yet quite subsided) agreed with Mrs. Oliphant in condemning *The Renaissance* as "quite poisonous in its false principles of criticism and false conceptions of life." John Addington Symonds, almost exactly Pater's contemporary, outraged Roger Fry by saying, "Of course we are all very thankful to Botticelli for having inspired those pages of Walter Pater." But for the members of a still later generation, like Dowson's, the "very blankest Pessimism" of Pater's epicureanism ("For there is a certain grief in things as they are") was one of the qualities that made him, with Newman, one of the two greatest men of the century. Mrs. Ward observed that in the midst of all this praise and denigration "the author of the book was quite unmoved."

The manuscript shown here is an essay on Dante Gabriel Rossetti which Pater wrote for an anthology of English poetry edited by Mrs. Ward's husband, Thomas Humphry Ward; it was later reprinted in *Appreciations* (1889). The Pre-Raphaelites were among Pater's most important influences, and in describing Rossetti's style, he is, to a degree, describing his own: he had a "gift of transparency in language,—the control of a style which did but obediently shift and shape itself to the mental motion. . . ." In the passage shown here, Pater concludes his estimate of Rossetti by observing that Rossetti's contribution to English poetry was "the creation of a new ideal."

Perhaps, if one had to name a single ~~poem~~ composition of his to a reader who desired to make acquaintance with him for the first time, ~~one would choose~~ it is The King's Tragedy *one would ~~choose~~ select—that poem so moving, so popularly dramatic and life-like. Notwithstanding this, his work, it must be conceded, certainly through no narrowness or egotism, but in the faithfulness of a true workman to a vocation so emphatic, was [illegible deletion] mainly of the esoteric order. But poetry, at all times, exercises two distinct functions: it may reveal, it may unveil, to every age, the ideal aspects of common things, after Gray's way, (though Gray too, it is well to remember, seemed in his own day, seemed even to Johnson, ~~an~~ obscure;) ~~writer~~ or it may actually add to the number of motives, poetic and uncommon in themselves, by the imaginative creation of things, ideal from their very birth. Rossetti did something, something excellent, of the former kind; but his characteristic, his really revealing work, ~~was~~ lay in ~~wh~~ the adding to poetry of fresh poetic material, in a new order of phenomena, ~~a~~ the creation of a new ~~object~~ ideal. Walter H. Pater.*

filment of a task, plainly "given him to do". Perhaps, if one had to name a single ~~poem~~ composition of his to a reader who desired to make acquaintance with him for the first time, ~~one would choose~~ it is The King's Tragedy one would select ~~choose~~ — that poem, so moving, so popularly dramatic and life-like. Notwithstanding this, his work, it must be conceded, certainly through no narrowness or egotism, but in the faithfulness of a true workman to a vocation so emphatic, was ~~of~~ mainly of the esoteric order. But poetry, at all times, exercises two distinct functions: it may reveal, it may unveil to every eye, the ideal aspects of common things, after Gray's way, (though Gray too, it is well to remember, seemed in his own day, seemed even to Johnson, ~~ob~~ obscure) ~~poetry~~ or it may actually add to the number of motives, poetic and uncommon in themselves, by the imaginative creation of things, ideal from their very birth. Rossetti did something, something excellent, of the former kind; but his characteristic, his really revealing work, ~~was~~ lay in ~~the~~ the adding to poetry of fresh poetic material, in a new order of phenomena, the creation of a new ~~object~~ ideal.

Walter H. Pater.

LOUISE DE LA RAMÉE ("OUIDA") 1839–1908

Autograph manuscript of "The Child of Urbino," unsigned and undated, but written ca. 1882. 77 pp. 223 x 270 mm. MA 764.

Ouida, as her pseudonym and outsize handwriting attest, is perhaps the greatest over-writer in the English language. For her, descriptive detail is the soul of romance and no effort is too great to lavish on the creation of ambiance. In her finest novel, *Under Two Flags* (1867), for example, she creates an iridescent surface virtually unrippled by plot. In this, her novels mirror, though somewhat naïvely, the world they depict, a world of military and social fashion where apparently mindless languor is not inconsistent with the most intense feelings of honor and attraction. Ouida's novels and her particular form of rebellion belong very much to the 1870s and '80s; by the '90s her habit of being "fast and extravagant, running up great accounts at hotels etc., and leaving them unpaid" had left her in Italy, impoverished, surrounded by dogs, and replaced in English literary society by a younger and more brilliant generation of rebels. At Lucca and Viareggio she continued to express in her acerbic manner the cynical opinions that had given her notoriety. During the Boer War she wrote to Sydney Cockerell complaining that she was "ashamed of what the English nation has become;—suckled not on a creed outworn but on the vitriol and blood of your friend Kipling's doggerel." She pretty well summed up her cynical view of life in a criticism of Tolstoy also sent to Cockerell: "Tolstoy does not realise that man is a very rudimentary imperfect creature occupying a very small place in an immense and unknown universe."

But to Ouida one must offer the final apology available to all cynics: she was kind to dogs and children, her preference being greatly in favor of the former. (When pressed by Cockerell to return to England, her main excuse for staying in Italy was that "the dogs are very happy here.") Scattered among her numerous novels for adults are two collections of stories for children. The manuscript shown here, "The Child of Urbino," appeared in a volume called *Bimbi: Stories for Children* (1882). The child of Urbino is Raphael, who assists a much older friend in a competition to create a beautiful piece of pottery; this passage is a description of the winning "oval dish and the great jar" painted by Raphael.

What Luca saw were the great oval dish and the great jar or vase standing with the sunbeams full upon them and the brushes and the tools and the colours all strewn around And they shone with lustrous opaline hues and wondrous flame like ~~heat~~ glories and gleaming irridescence like melted jewels, and there were all manner of graceful symbols and classic designs wrought upon them, and their borders were garlanded with cherubs and flowers bearing the arms of the Montefeltro and the landscapes were the tender [illegible deletion] homely landscapes round about Urbino and the Mountains had the solemn radiance [that the Appennine's have at evening time . . . .]

What Lucca saw were the great oval dish
and the great jar or vase standing with
the sunbeams fell upon them and the flashes
and the lights and the colours all streaming around
And they shone with lustrous splendid hues
and wondrous flame like glorious ~~[illegible]~~ and gleaming
iridescence like melted jewels, and there
were all manner of graceful symbols and
classic designs wrought upon them, and
their borders were garlanded with cherubs
and flowers bearing the arms of the Montefeltro
and the landscapes were the tender Romagna ~~[illegible]~~
landscapes round about Urbino and the
mountains had the solemn radiance

95

Thomas Hardy
1840–1928

Autograph manuscript signed of "The Romantic Adventures of a Milkmaid," undated but written in the winter of 1882–3. 115 leaves. 201 x 165 mm. MA 820.

George Meredith, who, as reader for the firm of Chapman and Hall, had given Hardy discriminating advice about his (unpublished) first novel, once remarked in a letter that "there is no irony in Nature." To such an opinion, Hardy might have retorted in words like these, taken from a journal entry written in November 1883, roughly nine months after the manuscript shown here was completed: "We [human beings] have reached a degree of intelligence which Nature never contemplated when framing her laws, and for which she consequently has provided no adequate satisfactions." The ironic discrepancy between man's intelligence and Nature's laws is one of Hardy's most important and characteristic themes, one that captures the modern world's unfortunate sensation of having outgrown both its habitation and its history. Such a theme can, of course, be rendered as tragedy or comedy. In *Tess of the D'Urbervilles* (1891) and *Jude the Obscure* (1895) it is oppressively tragic; in "The Romantic Adventures of a Milkmaid," which bears some similarities to *Tess*, it is comic. Set in the 1840s, "The Romantic Adventures of a Milkmaid" is the story of the providential meeting between a young milkmaid—a true child of nature—and the sophisticated, Wertherian Baron von Xanten; Margery accidentally prevents the Baron from committing suicide, and he rewards her by granting her a wish. Her wish is to be taken to a ball, and in the passage shown here, the Baron has instructed her to enter the hollow trunk of an ancient tree, where she finds a rather ethereal gown and a selection of shoes. The flirtation thus begun is happily resolved, after a series of mischances, when Margery is reconciled to her rightful fiancé, a young lime burner. As W. H. Hudson said when he read this short novel in its reprinted form in 1913, "it is Hardy in his most fanciful mood, the Hardy of the *Return of the Native* with a fantastic fairy-land element mixed with it." "The Romantic Adventures of a Milkmaid" was first published in the summer 1883 number of the *Graphic* and was reprinted in a collection called *A Changed Man* (1913).

The Morgan Library owns the manuscript of another Hardy tale called "Emmeline, or Passion versus Principle," as well as one of several known typescripts of Hardy's dramatization of *Tess of the D'Urbervilles* with the author's corrections.

Have you told your father?" ["I have not yet told him sir." ["That's ~~too~~ very bad of you, Margery! How have you arranged it then?" ["She briefly related her plan, on which he made no comment, but taking her by the hand as if she were a little child he led her through the undergrowth to a spot where the trees were older, & standing at wider distances. Among them was the tree he had spoken of, an elm, huge, hollow, distorted & headless, ~~&~~ with a rift in its side. ["Now go inside," he said, before it gets any darker. You will find there everything you want. At any rate if you do not you must do without it. I'll keep watch, & don't be longer than you can help to be." ["What am I to do, sir?" ~~she~~ asked the puzzled maiden. ["Go inside, & you will see. When you are ready wave your handkerchief at that hole. [She stooped into the opening. The cavity within the tree formed a lofty circular apartment four or five feet in diameter, to which daylight entered at the top, & also through a round hole about six feet from the ground, ~~mat~~ marking the spot at which a limb had been amputated in the tree's prime. . . .

this would be useful for our purpose. Have you told your father?" ["I have not yet told him sir." ["That's ~~too~~ very bad of you, Margery! How have you arranged it then?" [She briefly related her plan, on which he made no comment, but taking her by the hand as if she were a little child he led her through the undergrowth to a spot where the trees were older, & standing at wider distances. Among them was the tree he had spoken of, an elm, huge, hollow, distorted & headless, # with a rift in its side. ["Now go inside," he said, before it gets any darker. You will find there everything you want. At any rate if you do not you must do without it. I'll keep watch, & don't be longer than you can help to be." ["What am I to do, sir?" ~~she~~ asked the puzzled maiden. ["Go inside, & you will see. When you are ready wave your handkerchief at that hole. [She stooped into the opening. The cavity within the tree formed a lofty circular apartment four or five feet in diameter, to which daylight entered at the top, & also through a round hole about six feet from the ground, ~~that~~ marking the spot at which a limb had been amputated in the tree's prime. The decayed wood of cinnamon-brown, forming the inner surface of the tree, & the warm evening glow reflected in at the top, suffused the cavity with a faint mellow radiance. [But Margery had hardly given herself time to heed these things. Her eye had been caught by ~~something~~ ~~contents~~ objects of quite another ~~nature~~ ~~sort~~ quality. A large white oblong

THOMAS HARDY

Autograph manuscript signed of "The Abbey Mason. Inventor of the 'Perpendicular' Style of Gothic Architecture," dated December 1911. 13 pp. 251 x 196 mm. MA 821.

Every now and then, a dated word sticks up in Hardy's later poems like a tombstone or a ruin on an otherwise level plain, reminding us of voices more ancient than Hardy's. Partly, this is due to the fact that he matured during the Victorian period and first mastered a poetic style which, to ears after 1914, sounded conspicuously out of date. But Hardy's occasional echoes of a previous era—whether they are allusive or nostalgic—also reflect his own extreme sensitivity to voices of the dead that speak only through artifacts of stone. Like Thomas Gray, Hardy knew that "Ev'n from the tomb the voice of nature cries. . . ." His alertness to these voices (for the most part interrogative—they ask "What of the world now?") was compounded when the tomb happened to be not merely a graveyard marker but a church or cathedral. His architectural training as a youth had taught him to read columns of stone like columns of verse, a skill which is nowhere more evident than in the poem "The Abbey Mason," the manuscript of which is shown here. "The Abbey Mason," which might be called a narrative meditation, was written just after Hardy had visited Gloucester Cathedral in December 1911. The poem describes the discovery of the perpendicular style in ecclesiastical architecture: an unknown mason, concerned because "This long-vogued style is quite outworn," traces a few lines of a new design, which is then completed when raindrops cause the chalk to run, thus adding their own delicate tracery. Hardy concludes that the abbey mason "did but what all artists do,/ Wait upon nature for his cue." This poem was first published in *Harper's Monthly Magazine* in December 1912. Like the manuscript of "The Romantic Adventures of a Milkmaid," it was purchased by Mr. Morgan from Hardy himself.

Hardy's manuscripts are distributed among many public institutions, notably the British Library, and many are preserved in the Dorset County Museum, as well as at the University of Texas, Austin, Yale University, the Berg Collection of the New York Public Library, and Princeton University.

. . . And, gazing at the forms there flung—/ Charmed from the rock by one unsung—

The ogee-arches, hansom-topped,/ The tracery stalks by spandrels stopped,

Petrified lacework, lightly lined/ On ancient massiveness behind—

Muse that some minds so modest be/ As to renounce fame's fairest fee

(Like him who crystallized on this spot/ His visionings, but he's forgot,

And many a mediæval one/ Whose symmetries salute the sun)

While others blow a baseless claim,/ And upon nothing rear a name./ December: 1911–

From Solway Frith to Dover strand
Its fascinations starred the land,

Not only on cathedral walls
But upon courts and castle-halls,

Till every edifice in the isle
Was patterned ~~to~~ no other style,

And till, long having played its part,
The curtain fell on Gothic art....

— Well: when in Wessex on your rounds
Take a brief step beyond its bounds,

And enter Gloucester: seek the quoin
Where choir and transept interjoin,

And, gazing at the forms there flung —
Charmed from the rock by one unsung —

The ogee-arches, transom-topped,
The tracery stalks by spandrels stopped,

Petrified lacework, lightly lined
On ancient massiveness behind —

Muse that some minds so modest be
As to renounce fame's fairest fee

(Like him who crystallized on this spot
His visionings, but lies forgot,

And many a mediaeval one
Whose symmetries salute the sun)

While others blow a baseless claim,
And upon nothing rear a name.

December: 1911 —

97

William Henry Hudson
1841–1922

Autograph manuscript signed of "Birding in the Marshes," Chapter XX of "Far Away and Long Ago," undated, but written in 1917. 14 leaves. 251 x 197 mm. From the Collection of Mr. H. Bradley Martin.

There is really only one way to become an exceptional naturalist—long hours of observation—but there are many ways to increase one's ability to observe. One of them is described in the manuscript shown here; it is a game called "hunting the ostrich," and by playing it again and again, W. H. Hudson learned in detail the habits and mannerisms of at least one bird, an ostrich (actually a rhea, a South American bird similar in appearance to the African ostrich) being madly pursued by young boys with wooden bolas. Hudson played the ostrich near his home on the pampas of Argentina until he caught rheumatic fever at the age of fifteen during a visit to what he describes as "pestilential" Buenos Aires. Hudson is a simple writer, but his portrayal of his illness and of the series of events (including the loss of his mother) that followed his recovery are exceptionally moving. He is able to convey the oppression of his melancholy as forcefully as he imparts the joy of being a naturalist. This period of illness became for Hudson an extended literary exploration in search of a feeling he knew inside himself but could not express or find echoed in works of pure natural history; he found it described, instead, in books on philosophy and the arts: "They did not tell me in so many words that it was the mystical faculty in me which produced those strange rushes or bursts of feeling and lifted me out of myself at moments; but what I found in their words was sufficient to show me that the feeling of delight in Nature was an enduring one, that others had known it, and that it had been a secret source of happiness throughout their lives." During several miserable years in London, while still searching for the proper outlet for his talent, Hudson confirmed the existence and the satisfactions of his "secret source," and learned to put it in plain words, where an increasing number of readers have found it, too.

The greatest collection of Hudson's manuscripts is that in the Royal Society for the Protection of Birds; other manuscripts and letters may be found in the Library of the University of Texas, Austin, and in the Dartmouth College Library, Hanover, New Hampshire.

[Starting at bottom of p. 12:] One of our favorite games at this period—the only game on foot we ever played with the gaucho boys—was hunting the ostrich. To play this game we had bolas, *only the balls at the ends of the thong were not made of lead like those with w^{h} the grown-up gaucho ~~hunted~~ hunter ~~captured~~ captures the real ostrich, or rhea. We used light wood to make balls so as not to injure each other. The fastest boy was chosen to play the ostrich & w^{d} be sent off to roam ostrich-fashion on the plain, pretending to pick clover from the ground as he walked in a stooping attitude, or making little runs & waving his arms about like wings, then standing erect & ~~still~~ mimicking the hollow booming sound the cock bird emits when calling the flock together.*

The hunters w^{d} then come on the scene & the chase begin, the ostrich putting forth all his speed, doubling to this side & that & occasionally thinking to escape by hiding dropping upon the ground in the shelter of a cardoon-thistle, only to jump up again when the shouts of the hunters drew near & rush on as before. At intervals the bolas would come whirling through the air & he wd ~~try to dog~~ dodge or avoid them by a quick turn, but eventually he w^{d} be hit & the thong w^{d} wind itself about his legs & down he w^{d} come. . . .

would it have been better, when I went out to him with the bamboo cane & he asked me a little apprehensive of what I was going to do with it, if I had gone up to him & shown him my face with that broad ~~black~~ band across it from the chin to the temple, where the skin had come off & a black crust had formed, & had said to him: This is the mark of the blow you gave me ~~on the right side of my face~~ day before yesterday, when you knocked me off my horse: you see it is on the right side of my face & head; now take this cane & give me another blow on the left side? Tolstoy (my favourite author by the way) wd have answered; Yes, certainly it wd have been better for you — better for your soul. Nevertheless, I still ask myself: Would it? & if this incident should come before me half a second before my final disappearance from earth I should still be in doubt.

One of our favourite games at this period — the only game on foot we ever played with the gaucho boys — was hunting the ostrich. To play this game we had bolas, only the balls at the ends of the thongs were not made of lead like those with wh the grown-up gaucho ~~hunter~~ hunter ~~captures~~ captures the real ostrich, or rhea. We used light wood

to make balls so as not to injure each other. The fastest boy was chosen to play the ostrich & wd be sent off to roam ostrich-fashion on the plain, pretending to pick clover from the ground as he walked in a stooping attitude, or making little runs & waving his arms about like wings, then standing erect & ~~still~~ mimicking the hollow booming sound the cock bird emits when calling the flock together.

The hunters wd then come on the scene & the chase begin, the ostrich putting forth all his speed, doubling to this side & that & occasionally thinking to escape by hiding dropping upon the ground in the shelter of a cardoon-thistle, only to jump up again when the shouts of the hunters drew near & rush on as before. At intervals the bolas would come whirling through the air & he wd ~~try to~~ dodge or avoid them by a quick turn, but eventually he wd be hit & the thong wd wind itself about his legs & down he wd come. Then the hunters wd gather round him & pulling out their knives begin operations by cutting off his head, then the body wd be cut up, the wings & breast removed, ~~this~~ these being the best parts for eating, & there wd be much talk about the condition &

Gerard Manley Hopkins
1844–1889

Autograph letter signed, dated 16 January 1867, to Edward William Urquhart. 4 pp. 180 x 113 mm. Anonymous loan.

Near the end of his remarkable correspondence with Robert Bridges, Hopkins says "that a kind of touchstone of the highest or most living art is seriousness; not gravity but the being in earnest with your subject—reality." However one defines what reality might have been for Hopkins, he was, without disfiguring gravity, earnest about it. Thus it happened that Hopkins, with an audience numbering no more than seven or eight, produced the most technically innovative body of poetry written in the nineteenth century, all the while serving the Society of Jesus with devotion and self-abnegation. But Hopkins' verse survives for more than reasons of technical ingenuity; in a century so thoroughly given to nature as subject and inspiration, his verse adds a tone of ecstasy (largely absent since Keats) which comes from the "swing" of his lines and from the spiritual manner in which he habitually perceives the world:

> And though the last lights off the black West went
> Oh, morning, at the brown brink eastward, springs—
> Because the Holy Ghost over the bent
> World broods with warm breast and with ah! bright wings.

Poetry like this does not require an audience to satisfy its composer, and it did not receive an audience much beyond Hopkins' small group of friends until nearly thirty years after the poet's death, when Bridges concluded that the world was ready for Hopkins.

Bridges' hesitation in arranging for the publication of Hopkins' poems was by no means misjudged, for Hopkins had met only with resistance when he had tried to have the more technically radical of his poems, such as "The Wreck of the Deutschland," published in Catholic journals. The letter shown here, to E. W. Urquhart, a friend from Balliol College, concerns Hopkins' technical freedom; he had been accused of taking too many "licences for a beginner." "I think," he writes, "you wd. find in the history of art that licences and eccentricities are to [be] found fully as often in beginners as in those who have established themselves and can afford them. . . ." He also mentions an impending visit to the Oratory at Edgbaston (near Birmingham), where John Henry Newman resided, and corrections in an early poem entitled "Barnfloor and Winepress," the title of which is taken from 2 Kings 6:27 and which was published in *The Union Review* in 1865.

Hopkins manuscripts may be found in Campion Hall, Oxford, and the Bodleian Library. Others remain in private possession.

I think you wd. find in the history of art that licences and eccentricities are to [be] found fully as often in beginners as in those who have established themselves and can [illegible deletion] afford them; those in Milton, Turner, and Beethoven are at the end, those in Shakspere, Keats, Millais, and Tennyson at the beginning. I did send this piece first to Macmillan's *wh. is always having things of Miss Rossetti. Part of it was written two years and a half ago and though that does not sound much one changes very fast at my age and I shd. write better now, I hope.*

Believe me yr. affectionate friend, Gerard M. Hopkins. . . .

XIII

Dear Urquhart, — My books were not sent me, so I went up to Oxford this day week ~~before yesterday~~ to fetch them. Among them I found The last glories of ~~the~~ Holy See greater than the first and I send it by this post. When you have done with it will you send it to Addis at 1 Alma Road, Junction Road, Highgate, N. or, if you keep it till term-time, to Smith's. Ann refused my cousins offer by letter: since term ended Mrs. Smith has been ill and Ann has had a great deal of work and wished to leave, but Smith raised her wages,

I think you wd. find in the history of art that weaknesses and eccentricities are to found fully as often in beginners as in those who have established themselves and can ~~**~~ afford them; those in Milton, Turner, and Beethoven are at the end, those in Shakspere, Keats, Millais, and Tennyson at the beginning. I did send this piece first to Macmillan's wh. is always having things of Miss Rossetti. Part of it was written two years and a half ago and though that does not sound much one changes very fast at my age and I shd. write better now, I hope.

Believe me yr. affectionate friend,

Gerard M. Hopkins.

I am going to Birmingham to the Oratory tomorrow for the last week.

Jan. 16, 1867. — Oak Hill, Hampstead.

I want to make some slight corrections in Barnfloor and Winepress wh. I have not time to do now, and I want you to get the book

at once, so I will send a copy shortly.

Robert Bridges
1844–1930

Autograph letter signed, dated 24 February 1891, to Alfred Miles. 4 pp. 177 x 113 mm. From the Collection of Mr. Gordon N. Ray.

The poet laureate in England has almost always been encumbered by the history of his position, conferred more often upon men with leaden than men with golden tongues, and by the awareness that he has been appointed the official organ of poetic perception, the regal instrument of celebration. Innumerable birthday and new-year's odes, anthems and elegies are his legacy; and his portion is to be linked, according to his skills, with the Drydens, Wordsworths and Tennysons—or the Eusdens, Cibbers and Southeys—who have preceded him. England has had no better laureate—as laureate—than Robert Bridges, who, like Yeats taking a Civil List Pension with the stipulation that he remain politically unconstrained, accepted his role with the understanding that *poetry* is far more necessary than poems, and that silence, in the world that followed his appointment in 1913, may be the most eloquent comment of all. More important than Bridges' poems after 1913 (with the exception of *The Testament of Beauty* [1929]) are his services to poetry as a sponsoring editor of Gerard Manley Hopkins' poems (1918), a spokesman for the necessity of poetry and pure English, and a personage in whom slightly archaic poetic virtues remained current. Bridges' life as a poet recalls his poem "Indolence": in a boat on a summer's day (like the critics in Dryden's "Of Dramatick Poesy"), the poet and a friend pass from a "landscape wide" down to the lower stream, which is clotted with "deserted wharfs and vacant sheds." "Then I who rowed leant on my oar, whose drip/ Fell without sparkle, and I rowed no more/ . . . And our trim boat let her swift motion die,/ Between the dim reflections floating by."

The letter to Alfred Miles, shown here, presents Bridges in a most typical attitude, arranging contributions to an anthology called *The Poets and Poetry of the Century* . . . (1892–7), which was edited by Miles. The placing of just a few of Hopkins' poems in this anthology was one of Bridges' first steps in the slow creation of an audience for Hopkins' work, a process that culminated in his edition of 1918. Also shown is a poem which Bridges describes as "one of the most beautiful hymns I know," by an author whose name Bridges could not discover.

Many of Bridges' letters, especially those to Hopkins' family, are in the Bodleian Library.

Yattendon Newbury. Feb 24. 91 Dear Mr Miles I have got permission from Mr Hopkins' family to send you a few of his poems with short acct of him. I shall write not more than one page about him & send some 4 or 5 short poems. Will that do?

It will be a question whether you do not put him among your religious poets.

I send you one of the most beautiful hymns I know. I have never been able to discover the author. but it first (as far as I know) appeared in the 2nd Ed. of "Hymns & Poems for the Sick & Suffering" edited by Thos Vincent Fosbery Rivington London 1850." . . .

Yattendon Newbury.
Feb 24. 91

Dear Mr Miles

I have got permission from Mr Hopkins' family to send you a few of his poems with short acc of him. I shall write not more than one page about him & send some 4 or 5 short poems. Will that do?

It will be a question whether you do not put him among your religious poets.

I send you one of the most beautiful hymns I know. I have never been able to discover the author. but it first (as far as I know) appeared in the 2nd Ed. of "Hymns & Poems for the Sick & Suffering" edited by Tho Vincent Fosbery Rivingtons London 1850." ; the 1st

AN EASTER HYMN.

Awake, thou wintry earth,
  Fling off thy sadness;
Fair vernal flowers, laugh forth
  Your ancient gladness: Christ is risen,

Wave, woods, your blossoms all,
  Grim death is dead:
Ye weeping funeral trees
  Lift up your head; Christ is risen.

—

Come, see the graves are green:
  It is light; let's go
Where our loved ones rest
  In hope below: Christ is risen

—

All is fresh and new,
  Full of spring and light:
Wintry heart, why ~~[illegible]~~ wearest the hue
  Of sleep and night? Christ is risen

—

T O

William Ernest Henley
1849–1903

Autograph manuscripts of "Night-Sketch" and "Ennui," unsigned and undated but written between 1873 and 1875. 2 pp. 238 x 190 mm. MA 1617. Gift of Edwin J. Beinecke.

W. E. Henley's first claim to notice was as the recipient of unusual treatment for tubercular arthritis. Having lost one foot to the disease in 1868, he traveled to the Royal Infirmary at Edinburgh in order to save the other by placing himself under the care of Joseph Lister, the man who developed antiseptic surgery. And as so often happens, the white rectangle of a hospital bed proved to be a land of intensive mental exploration; in Henley's case, hospital also became the rather odd nexus for the most important relationships of his future life. There he met his wife Anna, the sister of a bedside neighbor, and in January 1875 he was visited by Leslie Stephen, then editor of the *Cornhill Magazine*. Stephen soon returned bringing with him Robert Louis Stevenson, who visited again and again. One of the projects Henley had begun at the Royal Infirmary was a series of hospital poems, many of them innovative in technique, and nearly all realistic in content. For the *Cornhill*, Stephen had accepted a group of these poems, which was published in July 1875 under the title of *Hospital Outlines*. These verses, among the best Henley ever wrote, underwent considerable revision before they appeared in their final form as "In Hospital: Rhymes and Rhythms" in *A Book of Verses* (1888). One stage of revision included commentary by Stevenson; the pencil markings on the two poems shown here are in his hand, and the brusqueness of his comments give a clear indication of how far these two men, so different by nature, had progressed in their friendship.

George Meredith praised the poems of "In Hospital" for their "rude realism," and many writers who had dealings with Henley later might have adapted that phrase to suit their impression of the man himself. As a critic and editor of the *Scots Observer* and the *New Review*, he displayed a quality that is perhaps best described by Francis Thompson: "there is some secret, inexplicable provocation in Henley's language, which would make a snail butt its horns at him."

The Morgan Library owns a superb collection of manuscripts and letters by Henley and letters addressed to Henley by some of the most famous authors of his day. Among his poetical manuscripts are several versions of "In Hospital," including an early draft of what became "Invictus," and numerous other poems, some published in *A Book of Verses*, many still unpublished.

Night-~~Thoughts~~ Sketch/ At midnight when all things are hushed & still,/ Save for a resolute sonorous snore,/ Or cries of feline luxury that thrill/ The anguished echoes of the corridor;

When the wee point of gas implacable/ Burns sunlike in my fascinated eyes;/ When the clock striking seems to toll a knell/ And hot hard bumps along the mattress rise;

I lie & listen for ~~the nurse without~~ life that hums,/ Heard only in my dreams,—a cinder falls,/ The firelight flickers like a hushed regret,/ . . .

– XI =

Sketch

= Night ~~Thoughts~~ =

=

At midnight when all things are hushed & still,
  Save for a resolute sonorous snore,
  Or cries of feline luxury that thrill
The anguished echoes of the corridor;

When the wee point of gas implacable
  Burns sunlike in my fascinated eyes;
When the clock striking seems to toll a knell
  And hot hard lumps along the mattress rise;

I lie & listen for ~~[illegible]~~ life that hums,
  Heard only in my dreams, — a cinder falls,
    The firelight flickers like a hushed regret,
My neighbour groans & turns, then someone calls
  The snore ~~[illegible]~~ reverberates, the night-nurse comes,
    Noiseless & strange: — "Are ye no sleepin' yet?"

=

O AO good! | Good man!
That's what I do call realism, and yet like

– XII =

= Ennui =

=

Faith is impossible, for Hope is dying
  And Love is dead as her dark sister Lust;
For Youth's rich roses, all disleaved, are lying,
  Unheeded, in obscene & squalid dust;

For even the thought that life & time are flying
  ~~To~~ From me, corroded with disease's rust,
Not to return, impels not any sighing
  Nor curse on circumstance as too unjust.

Weary of heart, inert of brain & hand,
  Motionless I lie, exampling decay,
    Forgetfulness, insensibility:
Like an old battered sphinx chin-deep in sand,
  Alone, indifferent to dark & day,
    With desolation & despondency.

=

I don't say the sphinx isn't right; but the rest is rayther rubbish, isn't it?

101

Robert Louis Stevenson
1850–1894

Autograph manuscript of Chapters IV through IX of "Weir of Hermiston," undated but written probably in 1892–3. 44 leaves. 320 x 199 mm. MA 993 and MA 1582. MA 1582 is the gift of Edwin J. Beinecke.

Most readers of Stevenson know that when he died in that strange, fractious household of Vailima on the island of Upolu he left behind him an incomplete dictated draft of *Weir of Hermiston*, the novel he felt would be his masterpiece. That Stevenson in Samoa should have begun a tale that was, as he said, "pretty Scotch," is not surprising, at least not more surprising than the presence of his elderly mother in her widow's weeds and crinoline among the native retainers at Vailima. Travel writing satisfied much of Stevenson's strong autobiographical tendency, but when he paused between voyages and the spirit of the vagabond weakened somewhat, as it had begun to after the Stevensons settled on Upolu, he found a more precise use for his autobiographical inclinations. If he could not always portray himself as an amateur emigrant, he could certainly turn back for fictional matter to the days of his childhood and youth in Edinburgh. So, settled in uneasy domesticity in the tropics, Stevenson began *Weir of Hermiston*, a story, in part, about the natural struggle between father and son. The father, Adam Weir, was based on the eighteenth-century "hanging judge" Robert Macqueen, Lord Braxfield, but his pious youthful son, Archie Weir, carries about him more than a faint reflection of the author himself.

The first edition of *Weir of Hermiston* was published in 1896 and was based on the draft which Stevenson dictated to his stepdaughter Belle Strong, and which is now in the superb Stevenson collection at the Beinecke Library. But comprehensive earlier drafts written in Stevenson's hand, probably in 1892 and 1893, are preserved in the Morgan Library, and these contain material that was not used in the printed version. The Morgan Library manuscripts extend beyond the last words printed in 1896, adding about one and a half pages to what is generally known. Shown here is the penultimate page of *Weir of Hermiston*, in which Archie's interview with Kirstie continues past the "convulsion of brute nature" into a proposal of marriage which Kirstie refuses to understand. The Morgan Library also houses the opening chapters of this version of *Weir of Hermiston* under a separate accession number, as well as the manuscript of *Dr. Jekyll and Mr. Hyde.*

[Beginning line 4:] Archie ran to her and took the poor child in his arms, and she nestled to his breast as to ~~a~~ her mother's, and clasped him in hands that were strong like vices, and he felt her shaken by ~~those~~ the convulsions of distress, and had a pity ~~for~~ upon her beyond ~~words~~ speech. ~~A Pity and a fear! Looking back upon the interview, he saw not how he had offended.~~ Pity, and at the same time a ~~terrific~~ bewildered fear of this pretty explosive engine in his arms, whose works he did not understand and yet had been tampering with—, ~~and~~ There rose from before him the curtain of boyhood, and he saw for the first time the ambiguous face of woman as she is, [illegible deletion] ~~by potential explosions~~ In vain he ~~reviewed~~ looked back on the interview; he saw not where he had offended. It seemed unprovoked, a convulsion of brute nature. . . .

done that you should lightly me? What have I done? What have I done? O, what have I done?" she screamed at the third repetition. "I thought — I thought — I thought I was sae happy!" and then the first sob broke from her like the pang of some mortal sickness.

Archie ran to her and took the poor child in his arms, and she nestled to his breast as to her mother's, and clasped him in hands that were strong like vices, and he felt her shaken by the convulsions of distress, and had pity upon her beyond speech. Pity, and at the same time a terrified bewildered fear of this pretty explosive engine in his arms — whose works he did not understand and yet had been tampering with — and there rose from before him the curtains of boyhood, and he saw for the first time the ambiguous face of woman as she is. In vain he looked back on the interview; he saw not where he had offended. It seemed unprovoked, a convulsion of brute nature. It is a gate through which all boys must pass, and they carry the marks of that Jack-in-the-box surprise until the day of their death. Perhaps the girls have a similar unforgettable discipline the first time their feet thus strike on the iron breast and flint lugs of the schoolmaster aforesaid! It is to be said to Archie's credit that not even then his dire astonishment at Kirstie's behaviour deserted him on the path of duty. As soon as she was so far recomforted of caresses, of finding herself again in the arms of a lover, he returned to the charge.

"Kirstie," he said, "God knows, I didn't mean to wound you, and I must say this that I have come to say. Will you listen, my darling? will you let me say it to an end, and not set the angry again with your poor lover?"

"Yes, Mr Archie," she murmured, still gasping with her sobs.

"Archie!" cried he.

And she submissively assented, "Archie."

"Dear," said he.

And she echoed "Dear!"

They exchanged kisses, weakness came over him. "Kirstie," he began, and paused to kiss her again, so irresistible she looked in her unfinished grief, and she drew and held him down to her glittering, recovering herself, giving to herself that the terrible schoolmaster was gone, that her own Archie was come back again, and smiling on her.

The schoolmaster was there still, if she had any kent it, a good deal dishevelled and perturbed, his head half turned, but yet repeating to himself where lies his duty? But he made a confession, which, if he had made it at the first, would have strangely simplified his task. He drew her to the gravestone, set her down close to him, put his arm about her, and proceeded to follow the advice of that great artist, who was a representative of the visceral schoolmaster himself

Mary Augusta (Mrs. Humphry) Ward
1851–1920

Autograph manuscript of the final chapter of "Robert Elsmere," dated the spring of 1887. 45 pp. 202 x 125 mm. MA 1380. Gift of Mr. William H. McCarthy.

So many strands of theological and historical thought unite in *Robert Elsmere*, and its subject at first seems so austere, that one is hardly prepared to find in it such emotional richness as one does. Curates, rectors, parsons and vicars abound in nineteenth-century novels, but with only a few exceptions they serve more as emissaries from the world of learning (and candidates for marriage) than as spiritual men devoted to Christianity. Above all, Robert Elsmere is a servant of God; Mrs. Ward's novel describes the manner in which he ceases to be a servant of the Anglican Church. Mrs. Ward understood Elsmere's dilemma from her own experience. She was the daughter of Matthew Arnold's brother Thomas, a man who twice left the church, and she lived in Oxford when it was divided among those who had been touched by Newman's advocacy of Catholicism, those who favored the new Biblical criticism and those who defended the church in all its old vestments. But Mrs. Ward's portrayal of Elsmere's crisis is not primarily intellectual, though she grounds it firmly in the problem of valid Biblical "testimony" and what one of her correspondents called "the education of the historic sense." Her great achievement lies in the sympathetic rendering of Elsmere's emotional progress from an old faith to a new, more humanized faith. This quality brought *Robert Elsmere* a huge popular success, in spite of critical attacks by the conservative clergy.

Robert Elsmere struggles not only with his own faith, but also with that of his wife Catherine, a woman raised in the strong, old beliefs. The compromise she effects between religion and human love is described in the passage shown here, which briefly recounts her manner of life following her husband's death. The chapter of which this page is part comes from the first draft of the novel, completed in early March 1887 when Mrs. Ward was living on Russell Street in London. After considerable revisions, *Robert Elsmere* was published in February 1888. The manuscript of the novel is widely distributed; other chapters can be found in the major depositories of Mrs. Ward's manuscripts: Pusey House, Oxford; The Honnold Library, Claremont Colleges; and the Berg Collection in the New York Public Library.

(Break of three lines)

Five days later, Flaxman and Rose brought Catharine home. It was supposed that she would return to her mother at Burwood. Instead she settled down again in London, and not one of those whom Robert Elsmere had loved was forgotten by his ~~wife~~ widow. Every Sunday morning, with her child beside her, she worshipped in the old ways; every Sunday afternoon saw her black veiled figure sitting motionless in a corner of the Elgood St Hall. In the week she gave all her time & money to the various works of charity which he had started. But she held her peace. Many were grateful to her; some loved her; none understood her. She lived for one hope only; and the years pass all too slowly.

(Break of three lines)

Five days later, Flaxman and Rose brought Catharine home. It was supposed that she would return to her mother at Burwood. Instead she settled down again in London, and not one of those whom Robert Elsmere had loved was forgotten by his widow. Every Sunday morning, with her child beside her, she worshipped in the old ways; every Sunday afternoon saw her black veiled figure sitting motionless in a corner of the Elgood St Hall. In the week she gave all her time & money to the various works of charity which he had started. But she held her peace. Many were grateful to her; some loved her; none understood her. She lived for one hope only; and the years pass all too slowly.

103

GEORGE MOORE
1852–1933

Autograph draft of additional materials for "Spring in London," the first chapter of "Memoirs of My Dead Life," unsigned and undated, but written ca. 1905–6. 49 pp. 190 x 125 mm. MA 3421.

Yeats once wrote that George Moore had "sacrificed all that seemed to other men good breeding, honour, friendship, in pursuit of what he considered to be the root facts of life." In literature, stark presentation of the "root facts of life" constitutes realism, a mode which Moore imbibed to the full in France and with which his name is now customarily linked. How Moore, "a man carved out of a turnip," landed among the most advanced aesthetic circles of Paris is best explained by the long tradition of exile among literary Irishmen, a tradition that culminated in Joyce. The result of Moore's years abroad (1873–80) was a set of influences on his prose style that are hardly to be reconciled; in the painterly prose of his various autobiographical works, one finds daubs that recall Baudelaire, Rimbaud and Balzac, not to mention a more elusive influence that comes from the Impressionist painters. One thing that shines through all such make-up in *Confessions of a Young Man* (1888) and *Memoirs of My Dead Life* (1906) is the brazen countenance of Moore himself. These autobiographical works differ as much from the precision and control of a novel like *Esther Waters* (1894) as the style of Ernest Hemingway differs from that of Henry James. A formula used by Moore in *Confessions* to describe his Parisian years will suffice to describe *Memoirs of My Dead Life:* "one part art, two parts dissipation."

The history of the manuscript shown here is a rather strange one. It was intended to form a portion of "Spring in London," the opening section of *Memoirs of My Dead Life*, but was stolen, Moore claimed, "by one of my secretaries and sold, I think in America. . . ." The entire manuscript is an account of an amorous episode stretching over several years of Moore's life, "the story," as he describes it here, "of two intellectual sensualists meeting both incapable of tenderness and passion. . . ." On the whole this omitted section recalls Max Beerbohm's caricature of Moore, which bears the poetic inscription: "That she adored me as the most/ Adorable of males/ I think I may securely boast./ Dead women tell no tales."

Important collections of Moore manuscripts are to be found in the National Library, Dublin, the Berg Collection of the New York Public Library and the Library of the University of Texas, Austin.

[While walking in the woods one day, she would say: "Let us sit here," and after looking steadily at one for a few seconds,] her pale marmoreal eyes glowing she would say You can make love to me now if you like. There is a story I shall never write—the story of two intellectual sensualists meeting both incapable of tenderness and passion and the very absence of these qualities developing all there was of it in the other. ~~Here will~~ You see that I avoid the word create for we create nothing [we] develope. We used to meet in different parts of Europe—it is to her that I owe any knowledge I have of foreign cities and it was exciting to undertake a journey of a thousand miles for the [pleasure of meeting one's beloved for a few hours at midnight in a bedroom.]

her pale marmoreal eyes
glowing she would say
You can make love loved
now if you like - There is
a story I shall never write
- the story of two intellectual
sensualists meeting both
capable of tenderness
and passion and the
very absence of these qualities
developing all there was
of it in the other - You see
I avoid the word
create for we create nothing
develop - We used to meet
in different parts of Europe
- it is to her that I owe any
knowledge I have of foreign
cities and it was nothing
to me to take a journey of
a thousand miles for the

SIR ARTHUR WING PINERO
1855–1934

Autograph letter signed, dated 23 April 1889, to Sir Arthur Sullivan. 2 pp. 205 x 127 mm. From the Collection of Mr. Reginald Allen.

In his review of *Iris* (1901) Max Beerbohm denied the charge of being an "anti-Pineroite" and added an explanation of his own failure to praise Pinero to the skies: "Possibly my reluctance to hail Mr. Pinero as a genius may be due to a laudably nice sense of words—a sense which is not to be deflected by the electric atmosphere of a successful first-night. If Mr. Pinero is a genius, what are we to call Ibsen, for example?" Though brilliant in its own way, Pinero's reputation has always been overshadowed by questions like this. When he began his career as a playwright, he had the boards to himself; his light drama was superior to most that had been produced in the preceding half-century, and he was among the first dramatists in England to introduce more serious social themes to the theater in his superbly crafted plays, which clearly reveal the influence of Ibsen's genius. Just as he reached the peak of his reputation at the turn of the century, however, he became outmoded. Barrie was lighter and more elegant. Shaw's problem-plays were more fiercely problematic and, compared to Shaw's dialogue, the language Pinero's characters spoke seemed overtly "literary" and overwrought, so that when Beerbohm wished to accuse W. S. Gilbert of using in his prose "as many long words and as many formal constructions as possible," he had only to suggest how much he resembled Pinero. Yet even Beerbohm could admit that Pinero, whose plays were, after all, outstandingly successful, was endowed with dramatic riches of a unique kind; this, in fact, was his problem: "If Mr. Pinero were less brilliant in his specific way, there would be more room in him for ideas."

The letter shown here was written to Sir Arthur Sullivan, in order to thank him for contributing a song to Pinero's first serious play, *The Profligate*. (This letter also bears out some of Beerbohm's remarks about Pinero's literary style.) In its original format, *The Profligate* ended, as *The Second Mrs. Tanqueray* (produced in 1893) does, with a suicide; the disapproval of the public was so strong, however, that Pinero was prevailed upon to add a happy ending, much against his will. Pinero sent this letter to Sullivan the day before *The Profligate* opened at the Garrick Theatre; he also mentions Sir John Hare, the actor and theatrical producer.

Dear Sir Arthur Sullivan, Hare will have told you, I know, how charmingly the song comes out in "The Profligate" and what a great service it renders to the play. I feel very proud when I remember that my piece is to be adorned and brightened by some music from your hand. In the barest words but with all sincerity pray let me tender you my thanks for your kindness. Believe me, dear Sir Arthur Sullivan, to be most faithfully yours, Arthur W. Pinero. Sir Arthur Sullivan &c

Ans/

London, 23rd April 1889.
64, St. John's Wood Road,
N.W.

Dear Sir Arthur Sullivan.

Hare will have told you, I know, how charmingly the song comes out in "The Profligate" and what a great service it renders to the play. I feel very proud when I remember that my piece is to be adorned and brightened by some music from your hand. In the barest words

but with all sincerity pray let me tender you my thanks for your kindness. Believe me, dear Sir Arthur Sullivan, to be

Most faithfully yours,
Arthur W. Pinero.

Sir Arthur Sullivan &c

105

Oscar Wilde
1854–1900

Autograph manuscript signed of "The Picture of Dorian Gray," undated but written in early 1890. 328 x 200 mm. 264 pp. MA 883.

To a large degree, an aesthete's pose must be maintained by spectators; even a narcissist requires an audience of one. Early in his career, Oscar Wilde needed no alerting to the value of public attention: he sought it assiduously through curiously double-sided means. The indifference with which he taunted his observers and the calmness with which he accepted their praises and caricatures as "the tribute which mediocrity pays to genius" belie the careful planning that went into the shaping of his public persona, particularly during his American tour of 1882. Wilde might have mocked the notion of sincerity, but behind his many personae lay the common paradox of an earnest sinner. *The Picture of Dorian Gray* captures at least two sides of Wilde's complex character in Lord Henry Wotton and Dorian Gray. (Four years after the novel first appeared Wilde remarked, "Basil Hallward is what I think I am: Lord Henry what the world thinks me: Dorian what I would like to be. . . .") Lord Henry is the aphoristic Wilde, outrageous, but one whose danger lies primarily in words. In Dorian Gray there are shades of a less deliberate, but more dangerous outrageousness, what Wilde called a "soul hungry for rebellion," even against its own instincts of self-preservation. Wilde plays the desperate seriousness of Dorian against Lord Henry's wit, and it is Lord Henry's disengaged form of rebellion that survives. Virtually the only earnestness that Lord Henry displays occurs in the passage shown here, where he first confronts Dorian Gray and rhapsodizes about the meaning of youth and beauty.

The Picture of Dorian Gray was published in two versions: the first version, of which this is the manuscript, was published in *Lippincott's Monthly Magazine* in 1890; for the second version, published a year later, Wilde made substantial revisions and added six more chapters.

The finest collections of Oscar Wilde manuscripts are to be found in the William Andrews Clark Library, Los Angeles, and the Hyde Collection, Somerville, New Jersey.

---

the common, and the vulgar, which are the aims of the false ideal of our days. Live! Live the wonderful life that is in you! Let nothing be lost upon you. Be always searching for new sensations. Be afraid of nothing."

"A new Hedonism! That is what our age wants. You might be its visible symbol. With your personality there is nothing you could not do. The world belongs to you for a season." ["The moment I met you, I saw that you were quite unconscious of what you really are, and might be. There was so much about you that charmed me that I felt I must tell you something about yourself. I thought how tragic it would be if you were wasted. For, there is such a little time that your youth will last, such a little time."

"The common hillflowers wither, but they blossom again. The laburnum will be as golden next ~~year~~ June, as it is now. In a month there will be purple stars on the clematis, and year after year the green night of its leaves will have its purple stars. But we never get back our youth. The pulse of joy that beats in us at twenty, becomes sluggish. We degenerate into hideous puppets haunted by the memory of the passions of which we were afraid, and the exquisite temptations that we did not dare to yield to. Youth! Youth! There is absolutely nothing in the world but youth!"

the common, and the vulgar, which are the aims of the false ideal of our days. Live! Live the wonderful life that is in you! Let nothing be lost upon you. Be always searching for new sensations. Be afraid of nothing."

"A new Hedonism! That is what our age wants. You might be its visible symbol. With your personality there is nothing you could not do. The world belongs to you for a season."

["The moment I met you, I saw that you were quite unconscious of what you really are, and might be. There was so much about you that charmed me that I felt I must tell you something about yourself. I thought how tragic it would be if you were wasted. For, there is such a little time that your youth will last, such a little time."

"The common hillflowers wither, but they blossom again. The laburnum will be as golden next June, as it is now. In a month there will be purple stars on the clematis, and year after year the green night of its leaves will have its purple stars. But we never get back our youth. The pulse of joy that beats in us at twenty, becomes sluggish. We degenerate into hideous puppets, haunted by the memory of the passions of which we were afraid, and the exquisite temptations that we did not dare to yield to. Youth! Youth! There is absolutely nothing in the world but youth!"

George Bernard Shaw
1856–1950

Autograph manuscript and typescript signed of "Dramatists Self-Revealed," undated but written in 1925. 34 pp. 280 x 216 mm. MA 3435. Gift of Mr. and Mrs. Hans P. Kraus.

William Rothenstein once said that the secret of Shaw's "health at his age must be that he has been able to extract ultra-violet rays from lime-light." On the sources and use of his fame, Shaw was himself sufficiently ironic, calling it a trick of conspicuous self-promotion. In the preface to *Major Barbara* (1907), he chastised the English public for its failure to realize the difference between true moral and intellectual greatness (in Samuel Butler, one of his most important influences) and inferior goods (himself). "Really," he wrote, "the English do not deserve to have great men. They allowed Butler to die practically unknown, whilst I, a comparatively insignificant Irish journalist, was leading them by the nose into an advertisement of me which has made my own life a burden." Yet it was precisely Shaw's ability to launch himself that enabled him to transcend by so much the limited effect Butler's somewhat sullen intellect had on the world. Out of his fame, Shaw made a prodigious soapbox from which he might draw the attention of the English people to the inconsistencies in their society and the fallacies in their jumbled minds. Such work, of course, lends itself to paradox and the calculated inversion of treasured moral saws, a technique which is one of Butler's many legacies to Shaw. Shaw's plays often take the form of an elaborately exploded epigram, in which the audience is led to deceive itself into the truth; and his pugnacious manner of applying this method to any and all, inside the theater or out, led Wilde—another master of the inverted epigram—to provide his own interpretation of Shaw's fame: "Mr. Bernard Shaw has no enemies but is intensely disliked by all his friends."

The manuscript shown here is one of the most interesting of Shaw's critical documents, being a written interview between himself and his authorized biographer, Archibald Henderson. The first version consists largely of typed questions and penciled answers; the second version adds a stage setting, which includes a description of Shaw, written, no doubt, by Shaw himself: "the ruddy face, with its argentole of beard and hair, and blue-grey eyes, is that of a philosopher, genial and contemplative." Shaw's answer to the question proposed on the page shown here concerns the notion of beginning a play with an inverted apothegm: "The first fragment of Man & Superman that came into my head was the repartee: 'I am a brigand: I live by robbing the rich.' 'I am a gentleman: I live by robbing the poor.'" This interview was published in *The Fortnightly Review* in 1926.

Major collections of Shaw manuscripts can be found in the British Library and the National Library, Dublin.

---

2. In writing a play, do you start from one central or dominant or controlling idea?

In writing a play you ~~may~~ start anyhow you can. You may even have a plot, dangerous as that is. At the other extreme you may not see a sentence ahead of you from the rise of the curtain to its fall. You ~~often~~ mostly start with ~~a situation~~ what is called a situation, and write your play by leading up to it and taking its consequences. . . .

2. In writing a play, do you start from one central or dominant or controlling idea?

In writing a play you may start anyhow you can. You may even have a plot, dangerous as that is. At the other extreme, you may not see a sentence ahead of you from the rise of the curtain to its fall. You mostly start with what is called a situation, and write your play by leading up to it and taking its consequences. The situation may be a mere incident, or it may imply a character or a conflict of characters. That is, it may be schoolbogishly simple or sagely complex. Even a repartee may be the seedling of a play. Then there is the chronicle play, in which you just arrange history for the stage. Akin to this is the play founded on fact, when you arrange some incident in real life for the stage; but this involves a fictitious introduction and a fictitious finish; so that your slice of life is treated as a situation. Examples from my own plays are Heartbreak House, which began with an atmosphere and does not contain a word that was foreseen before it was written. Arms and the Man, The Devil's Disciple, and John Bull's Other Island grew round situations. The first fragment of Man & Superman that came into my head was the repartee: "I am a brigand: I live by robbing the rich." "I am a gentleman: I live by robbing the poor," though it afterwards developed into a thesis play, which is always a Confession of Faith, or a Confession of Doubt, on the author's part. The Philanderer began with a slice of life. Back to Methuselah is prophecy, in the scriptural, not the race tipster's sense. Sometimes the grand scene of the play is left out when you come to it. That happened in Pygmalion: the only person who spotted it was Barrie. Caesar & Cleopatra and St Joan are, of course, chronicles. The only play which I planned and plotted was Captain Brassbound's Conversion, which was neither the better nor the worse for that ceremony. The only rule I can give is that it matters very little what starts the play: what is important is to let it take you where it wants to without the least regard to any plans you may have formed. The more unforeseen the development the better. Nobody knows or cares about your plans and plots; and if you try to force your play to conform to them you will distort your characters, make the action unnatural, and bore and frustrate the audience. Trust your inspiration. If you have none, sweep a crossing. No one is compelled to write plays.

107

George Gissing
1857–1903

Autograph postal card signed, dated 27 November 1897, to Arthur Henry Bullen. 1 p. 140 x 90 mm. MA 3009.

Gissing's two spiritual habitations were poles apart with no apparent passage between: one was the Mediterranean, a bright land of classical ghosts, the other was Grub Street, a district of mind (once of fact) where very real and wretched authors dwell and literature shades off into bad dreams and used-up words. In *New Grub Street* (1891), his finest novel, Gissing portrays a minor author struggling not for success but for self-respect and mere financial subsistence. As an account of economic man caught in the trap of performing an antiquated task, *New Grub Street* is unsurpassed, for it provides an alarmingly frank display of Edward Reardon's (and what Gissing feared was his own) fate, the worst one that can befall a writer: "To have had even a small reputation, and to have outlived it. . . ." Like Reardon, Gissing was occasionally able to slip off into the first of his habitations, where "the water was as deep a blue as the sky, and sparkled with reflected brilliance." But while Reardon could do this only by drifting into unconsciousness, Gissing actually managed to visit Italy twice, once in 1890, and again in 1897 with H. G. Wells. The latter visit was the occasion of this postcard to the literary scholar A. H. Bullen, and the basis for Gissing's book *By the Ionian Sea: Notes of a Ramble in Southern Italy* (1901). Gissing seems to have carried with him a preternatural sensitivity to the foul conditions of Grub Street, for his delight in the classical remains of ancient Italy and his disgust with the sanitation of contemporary Italy raised for him a question about the relationship between the ideal creations of the antique mind and the actual setting in which ancient authors lived: "are we to suppose that the old Greeks & Romans lived with the stench of ordure perpetually in their nostrils? Not impossible, I fear."

The finest collections of Gissing manuscripts are in the Huntington Library, San Marino, California, and the Berg Collection of the New York Public Library, where the manuscript of *New Grub Street* is housed.

I think you will be glad to receive a card from Crotôn. *Not a stone of the old city remained, but the present town occupies the ~~sight~~ site of the Acropolis. Running into the sea, to the south, is the long Lacinian Promontory, at the end of which stands one last column of the great Temple of Hera—a column which was seen by Pythagoras. In the last century, blackguards built a sea-wall here out of the ruins of the Temple; & 300 years ago an ecclesiastical ruffian demolished the glorious structure itself to make his disgusting Palazzo.*

I was delighted to get your letter at Naples. Since then I have been to Cosenza (the grave of Alaric)—to Taranto—to Metaponto—& thence here. In a day or two I proceed to Catanzaro, where I hope letters will await me. After that to Squillace, & to Reggio.

The hotels are tolerable—if you are prepared for them. My worst experience was at Cosenza—an awful hole! Elsewhere, nothing worse than foul odours. By the bye, are we to suppose that the old Greeks & Romans lived with the stench of ordure perpetually in their nostrils? Not impossible, I fear. . . .

I think you will be glad to receive a card from <u>Croton</u>. Not a stone of the old city remains, but the present town occupies the site of the Acropolis. Running into the sea, to the south, is the long Lacinian Promontory, at the end of which stands one last column of the great Temple of Hera — a column which was seen by Pythagoras. In the last century, blackguards built a sea-wall here out of the ruins of the Temple; & 300 years ago an ecclesiastical ruffian demolished the glorious structure itself to make his disgusting Palazzo.

I was delighted to get your letter at Naples. Since then I have been to Cosenza (the grave of Alaric) — to Taranto — to Metaponto — & thence here. In a day or two I proceed to Catanzaro, where I hope letters will await me. After that to Squillace, & to Reggio.

The hotels are tolerable — if you are prepared for them. My worst experience was at Cosenza — an awful hole! Elsewhere, nothing worse than foul odours. By the bye, are we to suppose that the old Greeks & Romans lived with the stench of ordure perpetually in their nostrils? Not impossible, I fear. That is the present state of things here — & it affects one's appetite.

I am well, & in good spirits. Hope you & Lawrence are the same.

Yours always,

George Gissing.

Cotrone.
Nov 27. 97.

John Davidson
1857–1909

Autograph manuscript of "Ballads and Songs," unsigned and undated, but written ca. 1894. 143 leaves. 256 x 201 mm. MA 3395. Bequest of Miss Tessie Jones.

Davidson's predilection for suicide—which was satisfied in 1909 when he disappeared into the sea off Penzance—illuminates the nature of his visionary life. Unlike Blake, whose visions were coextensive with earthly reality, Davidson was painfully conscious of isolation from the normal course of life and dimly aware of what he called (in *The Testament of John Davidson* [1908]) "a door that opened into space." That door was poetry. In an essay published in *Holiday and Other Poems* (1906) Davidson observed that "nothing is easier than to recognise great poetry: simply, it makes men desire the fullness of time." Unfortunately, Davidson measured *himself* against the fullness of time. Long before he had made a mark in London with the publication of *Fleet Street Eclogues* (1893), Davidson wrote to Swinburne, whom he idolized, about his plans to become an actor: "If the theatre doors remain barred, the gate of heaven is open; and by means of a pistol or laudanum I will regain that inheritance which you and I and all poets have lost." The loss of this immortal inheritance ("the full material power of crystal vision and audience infinite") was compounded in Davidson's own life by a minute audience and constant, bitter poverty, the fatal irony of which is expressed in the very unvisionary poem shown here, "Thirty Bob a Week." As Shaw said of Davidson, "in short, he died of poverty."

The Morgan Library owns the complete manuscript of *Ballads and Songs* (1894), with the exception of its most famous poem, "A Ballad of a Nun," which appears in the form of corrected proofs. The manuscript of *The Testament of John Davidson* is in the Princeton University Library, the home of a superb collection of Davidson manuscripts and correspondence.

But you never hear her do a growl or whine,/ For she's made of flint and roses, very odd;/ And I've got to cut my meaning rather fine,/ Or I'd blubber, for I'm made of greens and sod:/ So p'raps we are in Hell for all that I can tell,/ And lost and damn'd and served up hot to God.

I ain't blaspheming, Mr. Silvertongue;/ I'm saying things a bit beyond your art;/ Of all the rummy starts you ever sprung,/ Thirty bob a week's the rummiest start!/ With your science and your books and your the'ries about spooks,/ Did you ever hear of looking in your heart?

I didn't mean your pocket, Mr.; no:/ I mean that having children and a wife/ With thirty bob on which to come and go,/ Isn't dancing to the tabor and the fife:/ When it doesn't make you drink, by Heaven it makes you think,/ And notice curious items about life. . . .

But you never hear her do a growl or whine,
For she's made of flint and roses, very odd;
And I've got to cut my meaning rather fine,
Or I'd blubber, for I'm made of greens and sod:
So p'raps we are in Hell for all that I can tell,
And lost and damn'd and served up hot to God.

I ain't blaspheming, Mr. Silvertongue;
I'm saying things a bit beyond your art:
Of all the rummy starts you ever sprung,
Thirty bob a week's the rummiest start!
With your science and your books and your the'ries about spooks,
Did you ever hear of looking in your heart?

I didn't mean your pocket, Mr.; no:
I mean that having children and a wife
With thirty bob on which to come and go,
Is n't dancing to the tabor and the fife:

When it doesn't make you drink, by Heaven it makes you think,
And notice curious items about life.

I step into my heart and there I meet
A god-almighty devil singing small,
Who would like to shout and whistle in the street,
And squelch the passers flat against the wall;
If the whole world was a cake he had the power to take,
He would take it, ask for more, and eat it all.

And I meet a sort of simpleton beside,
The kind that life is always giving beans;
With thirty ~~bob~~ a week to keep a bride
He fell in love and married in his teens:
At thirty bob he stuck; but he knows it isn't luck:
He knows the seas are deeper than tureens.

109

Joseph Conrad
1857–1924

Autograph letter signed, dated 18 October 1924, to W. E. Henley. 12 pp. 180 x 112 mm. MA 1617. Gift of Edwin J. Beinecke.

The literary partnership of Ford Madox Hueffer (later Ford Madox Ford) and Joseph Conrad began in 1898, shortly after the two first met, and lasted for roughly four years. Collaboration offered each man the peculiar virtues of the other: to Conrad it gave in Hueffer, the younger man, the freedom and colloquial virtuosity of a native speaker of English, while Hueffer benefited from Conrad's stringent discipline in matters of form and pace. Both writers frankly hoped that their mutual work, pitched toward the level of a popular audience, would be, if not the making of them, at least the saving of them financially. Hueffer had on hand a manuscript entitled "Seraphina" and it was to this that the two men, separated by only a few miles in Kent, applied their initial labors. Work proceeded fitfully, "Seraphina" was abandoned, and it was not until their second collaborative effort, *The Inheritors*, was published that Conrad and Hueffer turned back to see what could be made of the wreck they had left behind. By the summer of 1902, "Seraphina" had become *Romance*, an adventure tale set in the West Indies during the early part of the nineteenth century, and as *Romance* it was published in 1903. Pleased though they were at the publication of *The Inheritors*, *Romance* and a slight third work, *The Nature of a Crime*, the collaborators were disappointed by their reception.

Partisans of both men have made excessive claims for what Conrad and Hueffer derived from their association; Hueffer began the process by remarking somewhat absurdly that he had learned all he knew of literature from Conrad. There is evidence to suggest that Conrad perceived his role in their partnership with a certain irony, but this in no way prevented him from expending extraordinary amounts of energy on works that, in fact, amounted to very little, financially and artistically. His efforts are the more remarkable when one realizes that he was at the time also embroiled in the writing of "Heart of Darkness" and *Lord Jim*. This letter to Henley, who may have suggested the collaboration with Hueffer, bears witness to Conrad's desire to assist Hueffer without overwhelming him.

The largest concentrations of Conrad manuscripts are in the A. S. W. Rosenbach Foundation in Philadelphia, at Yale University, in the British Library and in private hands.

These considerations encouraged me in my idea. It never entered my head I could be dangerous to Hueffer in the way you point out. The affair had a material rather than an artistic aspect for me. It would give—I reflected—more time to Hueffer for tinkering at his verses; for digging hammering, chiselling or whatever process by which that mysterious thing—a poem—is shaped out of ~~inspi~~ that barren thing—inspiration. As for myself I meant to keep the right to descend into my own private little hell—whenever the spirit moved me to do that foolish thing—and produce alone from time to time—verbiage no doubt—my own— therefore very dear.

This is the truth—the whole truth. Now of course all this looks otherwise. Were I a Dumas I would eat up Hueffer without compunction. Was it you who called the old man "a natural force"? He was *that;* and *a natural force need not be scrupulous. . . .*

a man capable of the higher form could not care much for the lower. These considerations encouraged me in my idea. It never entered my head I could be dangerous to Hueffer in the way you point out. The affair had a material rather than an artistic aspect for me. It would give — I reflected — more time to Hueffer for tinkering at his verses; for digging hammering, chiselling or whatever process by which that mysterious thing — a poem — is shaped out of ~~inspi~~ that barren thing — inspiration. As for myself I meant to keep the ~~right~~ to descend into my own private little hell — whenever the spirit moved me to do that — foolish thing — and produce alone from time to time — verbiage no doubt — my own — therefore very dear.

II

This is the truth — the whole truth. Now of course all this looks otherwise. Were I a Dumas I would eat up Hueffer without compunction. Was it you who called the old man "a natural force"? He was that; and a natural force need not be scrupulous. Not being that I must navigate cautiously at this juncture lest my battered, ill-ballasted craft should run down a boat with youth at the helm and Hope at the prow — pursuing shapes — shapes. I know a man who at the end of a long talk was moved to tell me — "You don't seem to have a conception of what Sin is." Perhaps not! but it seems to me it would be sinful to sink Hueffer's boat which for all I know may be loaded with splendid gems or delicate roses — and all for my private ends.

Francis Thompson
1859–1907

Autograph letter signed, dated Pantasaph, Wales [20 March 1895] to Wilfrid Meynell. 6 pp. 152 x 99 mm. MA 3430. Purchased as the gift of Mr. Frederick Melhado.

Writing in "low spirits" to his future biographer, Everard Meynell, Francis Thompson observed, "the most terrible romances of to-day (indeed, of any day) are inward, & the intolerableness of them is that they pass in silence." Had it not been for the kindness and encouragement of Everard Meynell's parents, Wilfrid and Alice Meynell (herself an acclaimed poet), the terrible romance of Thompson's life might have passed in silence, too. At the time that Meynell, then the editor of a periodical called *Merry England*, received Thompson's first letter (1887), the poet was desolate on the streets of London much in the manner of De Quincey (who was his "pole-star" in prose) some eighty-five years before. To many persons, Thompson appeared enigmatic, for as Sir Sydney Cockerell remarked, "it seemed utterly impossible that so feeble a manikin could produce titanic poetry like *The Hound of Heaven*." The enigma was also spiritual and aesthetic. In the midst of his opium-shrouded life Thompson continually sought the formal manifestation of truth: in the Catholic Church (where Christ is the formal expression of theological truth) and in poetry, which gives shape to philosophical truth. "Of such immutable importance is form," wrote Thompson in an essay called "Form and Formalism," "that without this effigy and witness of spirit, spirit walks invisible among men."

The letter shown here concerns proof corrections to a volume of poetry called *Amphicypellon*, which was eventually published in 1895 as *Sister Songs: An Offering to Two Sisters*. As Thompson explained to Meynell, the earlier title "refers to the *amphicypellon* which Hephaestus, in Homer, bears round to the gods . . . ." The amphicypellon was a double cup, from which two persons could drink at once, and the title thus carries an allusion to the persons for whom the poem (largely written in 1890) was composed, Monica and Madeline, two of Wilfrid Meynell's daughters. The corrections that Thompson asks Meynell to make in proof were intended to increase the "directness and Spenserian clarity" of the poem.

The Morgan Library owns three Thompson letters (all apparently unpublished) and a poetical fragment. The best collection of Thompson manuscripts is at Boston College, Massachusetts.

But three corrections I can dictate from memory; and will you—to save time at this present pressing stage—make them for me, so that ȳ whole poem can go to Lane without further delay?

1º In ȳ lines:—"As form is laired in sound, as tinct may be/ A filmèd tone, as hoarded in ȳ vine &c," My recollection is that I found it possible to delete ȳ first line and a half, and leave ȳ remainder as a single short line, thus:—"As hoarded in the vine/ Hang the gold Skins &c." Any way, will you do this for me, and if ȳ result prove unsatisfying, I can amend it in proof.

2º In ȳ last stanza of ȳ poem to Monica; for—"Its stalactites of flame, its icicles of fire,"—Substitute—"Its honey of wild flame, its jocund spilth of fire." . . .

go unrevised, apart from
such slight alteration as will
admit of being made in proof.
But three corrections I can
dictate from memory; and
will you — to save time at
this present pressing stage —
make them for me, so that
ȳ whole poem can go to
Lane without further de-
lay?

1º In ȳ lines: —

"As form is laired in sound, as
tinct may be
A filmèd tone, as hoarded in ȳ vine &c".

My recollection is that I found
it possible to delete ȳ first line
and a half, and leave ȳ remainder as a single short line, thus: —

"As hoarded in the vine
Hang the gold skins &c."

Anyway, will you do this for me,
and if ȳ result prove unsatisfying,
I can amend it in proof.

2º In ȳ last stanza of ȳ poem
to Monica; for —

"Its stalactites of flame, its icicles of fire," —

Substitute —

"Its honey of wild flame, its jocund
spilth of fire."

And let ȳ stanza end on this line,
deleting ȳ remaining five lines, which

111

Sir Arthur Conan Doyle
1859–1930

Autograph manuscript signed of "Sir Nigel," dated 1905. 388 leaves. 329 x 190 mm. MA 3217.

The attempt to draw lines of connection between Doyle, the creator of Sherlock Holmes, and Doyle, the author of medieval romances like *Sir Nigel* (1906), may seem futile at first. Yet what is Holmes but a white knight warped by the mutations of history between 1300 and 1900?—brute strength has become acute intellect, a casque become cocaine, and a maiden in distress become any criminological problem that seems insoluble to Scotland Yard. Certainly, Holmes seized the interest of readers in a way that the fair Sir Nigel, in spite of the romance of his adventures, could not. And as Holmes triumphed over Sir Nigel in a literary way, he also seems to have triumphed over Doyle in a biographical way, as Doyle himself knew and resented. As the years have passed, Sir Arthur Conan Doyle, spokesman for British imperialism, spiritualist, and author of a widely disseminated pamphlet on the Boer War (*The War in South Africa: Its Cause and Conduct* [1902]), has come to appear increasingly remote, increasingly a man of his time. In fact, Doyle was himself as much a crusader as Sir Nigel, and the moral element so evident in his character appears more vividly in works like his historical novels and factual books than it does in *The Adventures of Sherlock Holmes* (1892), in which the intellect of Holmes is closer to the criminal mind than it is to Dr. Watson's. The conclusion of *Sir Nigel* provides a perfect example of Doyle speaking in his own voice about the moral relation between fiction and life: "Our own work lies ready to our hands; and yet our strength may be the greater and our faith the firmer if we spare an hour from present toils to look back upon the women who were gentle and strong, or the men who loved honour more than life on this green stage of England where for a few short years we play our little part." The passage shown here recounts Nigel's first trial of arms, in which, as a boy, he wears a man's suit of armor with an eyehole in the mail corslet that would cover a man's chest.

"Nay, not too fast, father Bishop" said one of the knights "when I made a campaign in South Germany I have seen at Nuremburg a cunning figure devised by an armourer which could both ride and wield a sword. If this be such a one—"

"I thank you all for your very gentle courtesy" said a booming voice from the figure upon the ground.

At the words even the valiant Manny sprang into his saddle. Some rode madly away from the horrid trunk. A few of the boldest lingered.

"Most of all" said the voice "would I thank the most noble knight, Sir Walter Manny, that he should lay aside his greatness and condescend to do a deed of arms upon so humble a Squire"

"Fore God" said Manny "if this be the devil then the devil hath a very courtly tongue. I will have him out of his armour if he blast me"

So saying he sprang once more from his horse, and plunging his hand down the open gorget he ~~closed~~ closed it tightly upon a fistful of Nigel's yellow curls. The groan that came forth was enough to convince him that it was indeed a man who lurked within. At the same time~~s~~ his eyes fell upon the slit in the mail corslet which had served the squire as a visor, and he burst into deep-chested mirth. ~~At the same moment~~ The King, the Prince and Chandos who had watched the scene, too much amused by it to explain or interfere, rode up weary with laughter now that all was discovered. ...

his hand on it. "There is no one in it. With what have I fought, father Bishop? Is it of this world or of the next?"

The Bishop had ~~mounted~~ clambered into his horse the better to consider the point.

"If the foul fiend is abroad" said he "my place is over yonder by the King's side. Certes, that sulphur-coloured horse hath a very devilish look and is fit to bear a suit of armour which rides and fights and yet hath no man within it."

"Nay, not too fast, father Bishop" said one of the Knights "when I made a campaign in South Germany I have seen at Nuremburg a cunning figure, devised by an armourer which could both ride and wield a sword. If this be such a one —"

"I thank you all for your very gentle courtesy" said a booming voice from the figure upon the ground.

At the words even the valiant Manny sprang into his saddle. Some rode madly away from the horrid trunk. A few of the boldest lingered.

"Most of all" said the voice "would I thank the most noble knight, Sir Walter Manny, that he should lay aside his greatness and condescend to do a deed of arms upon so humble a Squire"

"Fore God" said Manny "if this be the devil then the devil hath a very courtly tongue. I will have him out of his armour if he blast me"

So saying he sprang once more from his horse, and plunging his hand down the open gorget he ~~closed~~ closed it tightly upon a fistful of Nigel's yellow curls. The groan that came forth was enough to convince him that it was indeed a man who lurked within. At the same time his eyes fell upon the slit in the mail corslet which had served the squire as a visor, and he burst into deep-chested mirth. ~~At the same moment~~ The King, the Prince and Chandos who had watched the scene, too much amused by it to explain or interfere, rode up weary with laughter now that all was discovered.

"Let him out!" said the King, with

Alfred Edward Housman
1859–1936

Autograph letter signed, dated 24 July 1923, to Grant Richards. 5 pp. 177 x 115 mm. From the Collection of Mr. Gordon N. Ray.

Whatever flamboyance there was in the Housman family was settled upon the fourth son, Laurence, leaving the eldest, Alfred Edward, in possession of quiet rooms in Trinity College, Cambridge, high esteem as a classicist ("minute and pedantic studies in which I am fitted to excel"), and an enormous reputation as the author of *A Shropshire Lad* (1896) and *Last Poems* (1922). Housman made exceedingly few claims for himself as poet; he attributed his poetic inspiration to his solar plexus and "a relaxed sore throat," and when he did choose to think of himself in the great tradition of English poetry, he thought he might be placed above the author of "Elegy Written in a Country Churchyard": "In barrenness, at any rate, I hold a high place among English poets, exceeding even Gray." Popular response to the terse elegance of the lyrics in *A Shropshire Lad*, "moping melancholy mad" in a beloved rural landscape, became in itself enough of a reward for Housman. He accepted no payment for his poems: "so long," he told his publisher, Grant Richards, "as young men write to me from America saying that they would rather part with their hair than with their copy of my book, I do not feel the need of food and drink." When asked to be included in anthologies of "nineties" poetry and verse of the "new era," represented by *Georgian Poetry*, he declined, for though he admitted the influence of Shakespeare's songs and Heine's poetry, the attractions of his verse are almost *sui generis*. It was among the young men who wrote Georgian poetry and went to war that *A Shropshire Lad* acquired its first significant fame, and they took the book with them to the trenches, making Housman's favorite wish for his verse seem quite possible: "a soldier is to receive a bullet in the breast, and it is to be turned aside from his heart by a copy of *A Shropshire Lad* which he is carrying there. Hitherto it is only the Bible that has performed this trick."

This letter to Richards concerns, as so many of his letters do, unauthorized reprinting of his poetry and plans for one of his annual visits to France. From 1920 on, Housman flew across the channel; after his first trip in that manner he told his sister, "Well, I flew there, and am never going by another route in the future." He also mentions an impending visit from Robert Bridges, the poet laureate, whose early work he loved. On Bridges' death in 1930, he wrote to the laureate's widow, saying, "For myself, I do not suppose that there is anything which I have read oftener than the first four books of *Shorter Poems*."

Housman's manuscripts are located primarily in the Library of Congress, the library of Trinity College, the Fitzwilliam Museum and the Lilly Collection of Indiana University.

I shall come to Paris on the 31st by the Handley Page from Croydon at 4.30. I shall stay at the Continental for about 3 days, and then, I think, go by train to Le Mans and engage a car there, which will be cheaper than in Paris. My idea is to follow the south coast and come back by the north. Thanks for all your maps, books and other aids.

If we are in Paris together, I probably should not be free in the evenings but should be during the day. . . .

confined to the other book. But I am told by those who read the paper that the translations have never appeared; so I suppose you have terrorized it somehow.

I shall cross to Paris on the 31st by the Handley Page from Croydon at 4.30. I shall stay at the Continental for about 3 days, and then, I think, go by train to Le Mans and engage a car there, which will be cheaper than in Paris. My idea is to follow the south coast and come back by the north. Thanks for all your maps, books and other aids.

If we are in Paris together, I probably shall not be free in the evenings but should be during the day. I am afraid I cannot come up to town this week. The Poet Laureate is paying me a visit on Thursday.

113

Sir James Matthew Barrie
1860–1937

Autograph manuscript signed "X.Y.Z. A Comedy" ["The Admirable Crichton"], undated but written probably in the summer of 1902. 88 leaves. 205 x 185 mm. MA 1444. Purchased as the gift of Mr. C. Waller Barrett.

The notion of Max Beerbohm reviewing plays by J. M. Barrie is a happy one, for it presents to the mind the picture of two smallish, sentimental wasps buzzing on opposite sides of the proscenium arch, Barrie from the stage, Beerbohm from the stalls. Reviewing *Peter Pan* for *The Saturday Review* in January 1905, Beerbohm caught the essential fantasy of the playwright: "To remain, like Mr. Kipling, a boy, is not at all uncommon. But I know not any one who remains, like Mr. Barrie, a child." This characterization of Barrie as an aging child (reinforced by Beerbohm's caricature of Barrie in a nursery) has become standard. One rarely thinks of him as a breaker of new ground in the theater, yet it was precisely on this basis that Beerbohm praised *The Admirable Crichton*, perhaps Barrie's finest play, which opened on 4 November 1902 at the Duke of York's Theatre. "Mr. Barrie," he wrote, "has always been able to amuse us. But this is the first occasion on which he has succeeded in making us think." The admirable Crichton is, of course, the butler in the Loam family (in the version of the play shown here, the family of the Earl of Ambleside) to whom Barrie gives the name and epithet of the sixteenth-century Scottish scholar and swordsman. The play concerns the revolution in the social order that takes place when the Loams and two of their servants, Crichton and Tweeny (that is, the betweenmaid), are shipwrecked on an island. Nature soon prevails; in the passage shown here, Crichton proposes the "no work—no dinner" rule, for which he will take no credit: "I didn't invent it, my lady, I seemed to see it growing on the island." When all are rescued, the old order is reestablished in Mayfair—that is, until Crichton announces his desire to leave service and establish a public house "in the Harrow Road—the more fashionable end." The pub is to be called what Barrie originally called this play: "The Case is Altered."

The Morgan Library also owns an annotated prompt copy of *The Admirable Crichton*, the manuscript of *Shall We Join the Ladies?* and nearly forty letters from Barrie to W. E. Henley.

[Starting line 10:] Lady M *(in anguish) But it is all so awful. Crichton, is there any hope of a ship coming?*

Crichton *(brightly) Of course there is my lady—and until it comes, why surely three men can take care of three ladies and a woman. (resumes work)*

Lady M *Mr Ernest does ~~nothing~~ no work.*

Crichton *(cheerily) He will, my lady.*

Lady M *I doubt it.*

Crichton *No work—no dinner will make a great change in Mr Ernest.*

Lady M *No work—no dinner! when did you invent that rule, Crichton?*

Crichton *(still cheery) I didn't invent it, my lady, I seemed to see it growing on the island. ~~(He works~~*

Lady M *(uneasily) Crichton, your manner strikes me as curious.*

Crichton *(disturbed) I hope not, your ladyship.*

Lady M *You are not implying anything so monstrous, I presume, as that if I and sisters dont work there will be no dinner for* us?

Crichton *If it is monstrous, my lady, that is the end of it. (removes grass—end of cutting)...*

6.

to anguish, sobbing—he comes to her kindly) ~~Cheer up, my lady—you are the bravest of them all.~~ Don't give way—things might be worse.

Lady M (in real anguish) My poor father!

Crichton If I could have given my life for his—

Lady M You did all a man could do. Indeed I thank you, Crichton (with

Crichton ~~'Thank you, my lady, for your kind words.~~ some real admiration) You are a man.

Crichton 'Thank you, my lady. ~~for your kind words~~ (cuts twice)

Lady M (in anguish) But it is all so awful. Crichton, is there any hope of a ship coming?

Crichton (brightly) Of course there is, my lady—and until it comes, why surely three men can take care of three ladies and a woman. (resumes work)

Lady M Mr Ernest does ~~nothing~~ no work.

Crichton (cheerily) He will, my lady.

Lady M I doubt it.

Crichton No work—no dinner will make a great change in Mr Ernest.

Lady M No work—no dinner! When did you invent that rule, Crichton?

Crichton (still cheerily) I didn't invent it, my lady. I seemed to see it growing on the island. ~~(He walks~~

Lady M (uneasily) Crichton, your manner strikes me as curious.

Crichton (distressed) I hope not, your ladyship.

Lady M You are not implying anything so monstrous, I presume, as that if I and sisters don't work there will be no dinner for us? (resumes grass-end of cutting)

Crichton If it is monstrous, my lady, that is the end of it. ~~It would be most distressing to me to see your ladyship working—but I was afraid it might be the natural thing on an island—and we can't go against nature.~~

Lady M ~~If. It would be most unnatural to me. (sharply) So if you are anxious about that, Crichton, don't distress yourself. I shall certainly do nothing.~~

Crichton ~~You lift a great weight off my mind, my lady. And yet—perhaps it's only your brave way of talking. (By this time he has cut and carried to side or has pruned down so much of the undergrowth that the full view of the scene is at last got:~~ The hut is seen R,

7.

half built—a battered board stands to supposed on posts away used for sleeping under—the sea is seen at back with wild rocks &c—Lady M has been startled of his last remark—she goes to him haughtily)

Lady M Now, Crichton, I had suspected—now I understand. The perpetual-communal-at-home holds that we are all equal now. I see!

Crichton (hurt) My lady! Can you think me so inconsistent ~~—as that as my views of a lifetime are to be shattered by the accident of a wreck!~~

Lady M 'That is it!

Crichton My lady, I disbelieved in equality-at-home because it was against nature, and for that same reason I as utterly disbelieve in it on an island.

Lady M You truly mean that?

Crichton On my honour, your ladyship.

Lady M 'Then I suppose I have misunderstood you, Crichton. (nicely) I'm sorry—and very relieved.

see struggle – M

Crichton ~~It must have been my fault, my lady. All I meant to say was that natural changes are bound to come about in our life owing to circumstances altering cases. But equality will never come about. There must always be some to command and others to obey.~~

Lady M Quite true and admirably expressed. (she has suddenly the startling idea that perhaps he thinks he is now the one to command) Crichton! (she is very excited—she gazes fixedly and looks into his face)

Crichton What is it, my lady? Exit Lady M R

He puts a twig

(In great perturbation she backs from him and exit L. He looks after her puzzled, scratches head, then proceeds to dig a hole with a shell in middle of stage bringing up sand which he piles round the hole—while he is thus engaged enter Tweeny up stage carrying cocoanuts in her apron—she is dressed as a maid)

~~Tweeny Can you making a fire, sir?~~

~~Crichton Yes, Tweeny. (continues making hole)~~

Tweeny Look what I found!

Crichton Cocoa nuts! Bravo.

Tweeny They grows on trees!

Crichton Where did you think they grew?

RUDYARD KIPLING
1865–1936

Autograph manuscript of "Harvey Cheyne—Banker" ["Captains Courageous"], unsigned and undated, but written in 1896. 74 pp. 282 x 210 mm. MA 982.

America presented a provincial spectacle to Kipling which he, a scion of empire, enjoyed only with skepticism. Writing to W. E. Henley in the winter of 1893 from Brattleboro, Vermont, Kipling described the United States as "barbarism—barbarism plus telephone, electric light, rail and suffrage, but all the more terrible for that very reason. I like it." His perception of the ethical vacancy in American "lawlessness" led him to fall back more forcibly (though at times ironically) on the authority of British civilization, which had spread at least its law across the world. America, he told Henley, had taught him to "believe in Mudie, in the British Nation, in Mrs Grundy, in the Young Person, and in everything else that sits on the head of talent without form or rule." The Yankee "Young Person," freed from the restraints of Podsnappery, wild as a "colt training without bit," provided Kipling with the central figure of *Captains Courageous*, Harvey Cheyne, a mama's boy redeemed in the codfisheries of the Grand Banks off Newfoundland. Under the guise of a mere "boy's story of some 50,000 words," *Captains Courageous* conceals a blunt criticism of the sources of American hollowness: an economic "oligarchy" inattentive to the future (when the Western farms will be "as much mortgaged as the New England ones") and a pretense of culture without discipline (intent on "creating The Great American Literature"). Harvey Cheyne is the son of parents who embody (at least in part) these attitudes, but he is saved by being swept off an ocean liner and taken up on the fishing boat of Disko Troop, who—with the assistance of his cosmopolitan crew—teaches Harvey that he has been "wasting his power because he doesn't know how to carry himself."

This manuscript was presented by Kipling to Dr. James Conland, an American friend whose experiences as a boy at sea had led to the composition of *Captains Courageous*. The Morgan Library also owns several other Kipling manuscripts, including the manuscript of "The Brushwood Boy" and eighteen letters to Henley. Although many of Kipling's manuscripts remain in private hands, there is a fine collection in the Houghton Library of Harvard University.

After violent emotion most people and all boys demand food. They feasted the returned prodigal behind drawn curtains cut off in their great happiness while the trains roared in and out around them. Harvey ~~a~~ eat drank and enlarged on his adventures all in one breath and when he had a hand free his mother fondled it. His voice was thickened with living in the open, salt air; his ~~hands were~~ palms were rough and hard, his wrists dotted with gurry-sores and a fine full flavour of fish hung round rubber boots and blue jersey. The father well used to judging men looked at him keenly. He did not know what enduring harm the boy might have taken. Indeed, he caught himself thinking that he knew very little ~~of his son at all~~ whatever of his son but he distinctly remembered a dissatisfied, dough-complexioned youth who took delight in "calling down the old man" and reducing his mother to tears—such a person as adds to the gaiety of ~~hotel corridors and sun piazzas~~ public rooms and hotel piazzas where the ingenuous, ~~wealth~~ young & the wealthy play with or revile the bell-boys. But this well-set up fisherboy who did not wriggle, looked at him with eyes steady, ~~brigh~~ clear and unflinching and spoke in a tone distinctly, even startlingly respectful. . . .

After violent emotion most people and all boys demand food. They feasted the returned prodigal behind drawn curtains cut off in their great happiness while the trains roared in and out around them. Harvey ate and drank and enlarged on his adventures all in one breath ~~and when he had a hand free~~ his mother fondled it. His voice was thickened with living in the open, salt air; his [illegible] palms were rough and hard, his wrists dotted with gurry-sores and a fine full flavour of fish hung round rubber boots and blue jersey. The father well used to judging men looked at him keenly. He did not know what endurance harm the boy might have taken. Indeed, he caught himself thinking that he knew very little ~~[illegible]~~ whatever of his son but he distinctly remembered a dissatisfied, dough-complexioned youth who took delight in "calling down the old man" and reducing his mother to tears — such a person as adds to the gaiety of ~~hotel corridors and [illegible] piazzas~~ public rooms and hotel piazzas where the ingenuous, ~~[illegible]~~ young of the wealthy play with or revile the bell-boys. But this well-set up fisherboy who did not wriggle, looked at him with eyes steady, ~~[illegible]~~ clear and unflinching and spoke in a tone distinctly, even startlingly respectful. There was that in his voice which seemed to promise that the change might be permanent.

"Some one's been licking him into shape" thought Harvey. "Now Constance would never have allowed that. Don't see that Europe could have done it any better.

"But why didn't you tell this man Troop", the mother repeated.

"Disko Troop, dear. The best man that ever walked a deck. I don't care who the next may be."

"Why didn't you tell him to put you ashore. You know father would have made it up to him ten times over."

"I did but he thought I was crazy. I'm afraid I called him a thief because I couldn't find the bills in my pocket."

"The Quartermaster found them by the flagstaff" sobbed Mrs Cheyne.

"That's all right then. I don't blame Troop any. I just said I wouldn't work and he dropped me and — oh! — I bled like a pig.

"My poor darling. They must have abused you horribly."

"Dunno quite. Well, after that, I saw a light."

Cheyne slapped his leg and chuckled. This was going to be a boy after his own heart. He had never seen precisely that twinkle ~~[illegible]~~ in Harvey's eye, before.

"And the old man gave me ten and a half a month; and I took ~~[illegible]~~ hold with Dan and pitched in. I can't do ~~[illegible]~~ a full man's work yet. But I can handle a dory; and I don't get rattled in a fog: and I can take my trick in light winds — that's steering, dear, — and I can bait up a trawl and I know my ropes of course; and I can pitch fish till the cows come home: ~~and I'll show you how I can make coffee with a [illegible] of fish-skin. I'll have another cup please~~. I've been pitching out since sun-up: and I'll show you how I can make coffee with a piece of fish skin and I think I'll have another cup please. Say you've no notion what a heap of work there is in ~~twenty dollars~~ ten dollars a month. ~~a~~ I began with eight and half, my son" said Harvey.

"What so? You never told me!"

"You never asked Harve? I'll tell you about it some day if you care to listen. Have another stuffed olive

"Troop says the most interesting thing ~~[illegible]~~ in the world is to find out how the next man gets his vittles. ~~He sucked the olive~~. Oh Bully! It's great to get a trimmed up meal again, we were well fed though. Best grub on the Banks. Disko ~~[illegible]~~ fed us first class. He's a splendid man. And Dan that's his son; Dan's my ~~[illegible]~~ partner. And then there's Uncle Salters and his manures. He's sure I'm crazy yet. And there's poor little Penn; and he is crazy. You mustn't talk to him about Johnstown. And oh you must know Tom Platt and Long Jack and Manuel. Manuel saved my life ~~but~~ I'm sorry he's a Portugee. He can't talk much but he's an everlasting musician. He found me struck loose adrift and drifting ~~[illegible]~~ like a cut buoy.

"I wonder your nervous system isn't completely wrecked" said Mrs Cheyne.

What for, mother? I worked like a horse and I ate like a hog and I slept like a dead man.

That was too much for Mrs Cheyne who began to think of ~~what might have happened~~ her visions of ~~a [illegible]~~ a corpse rocking on the salty seas. She went to her stateroom and ~~[illegible]~~ Harvey curled up beside his father chattering nineteen to the dozen.

"You can depend upon me to do everything I can for the whole crowd of them, Harve. They seem to be good men on your showing.

"Best in the fleet, sir. Ask all Gloucester" said Harvey. "But Disko ~~[illegible]~~ believes still he's cured me of being crazy. Dan's the only one I've let on to about our private cars and all the rest of it. and I'm not sure Dan believes. ~~Can't~~ I want to paralyze 'em tomorrow. Can't ~~[illegible]~~ run the contraption over to Gloucester? Mother doesn't look fit to be moved out of the car, anyway. and ~~I've got to finish~~ ~~cleaning~~ we're bound to finish cleaning out the schooner by tomorrow. ~~[illegible]~~ Wouverman takes our fish. You see we're first off the banks this season and it's four twenty five a kintal. They want it quick."

"You mean you'll have to work tomorrow."

I told Troop I would. They want me to tally out: ~~and~~ I've got the tallies with me. ~~[illegible]~~ He looked at a greasy note book with an air of importance that ~~[illegible]~~ made his father gulp and choke. "There won't be three seventy — no — two hundred four or five kintal more by my reckoning.

115

William Butler Yeats
1865–1939

Autograph manuscript signed of "Aodh to Dectora," undated, but written ca. 1898. 3 pp. 220 x 179 mm. MA 3246.

Less than a year before his death, Yeats wrote to Dorothy Wellesley to tell her of an article about his work that had been written by Archibald MacLeish: "It commends me above other modern poets because my language is 'public.' That word, which I had not thought of myself, is a word I want." What is not public in Yeats's poetry is not necessarily private. Already in 1888, when he was only twenty-three, he could tell Katharine Tynan that "my life is altogether ink and paper." Over the course of his life this would come to mean that private and public experience meet on a common plane, eventually deflect the gaze of the reader with a common mask and, above all, take refuge in shared symbolism, which Yeats was usually at pains to explain. Yeats's poetic career was an increasingly successful series of attempts to blend the occult symbol and the public word into a single expression with a twofold valence. What is not public in Yeats's early poetry is largely esoteric. When *The Wind Among the Reeds* was published in 1899, Yeats included explanatory notes at the end of the volume intended to open the meaning of some of the personages and symbols. Even these notes, however, did not clarify everything. In his note on the figure "Aedh" (who appears in the manuscript shown here as "Aodh"), Yeats remarks: "It is probable that only students of the magical tradition will understand me when I say . . . that Aedh, whose name is not merely the Irish form of Hugh, but the Irish for fire, is fire burning by itself." Explained in another way, "Aedh is the myrrh and frankincense that the imagination offers continually before all that it loves." George Russell (AE), who thought Yeats's symbols "detestable," praised *The Wind Among the Reeds* for its lack of "semi-political aims" and called it "the most complete escape from the tyranny of the ephemeral passions of the hour into the world of pure art, idealism, and beauty," a compliment which indicates how far Yeats would progress by "Easter 1916."

The poems shown here were originally published in *The Dome* in May 1898 and were reprinted, with alterations, in *The Wind Among the Reeds* as "Aedh hears the cry of the Sedge" and "Aedh thinks of those who have spoken Evil of his Beloved." Many of Yeats's manuscripts and letters are in private collections, but significant groups may be found in the National Library, Dublin, the Berg Collection of the New York Public Library and the Library of the University of Texas, Austin.

Aodh to Dectora. I. I wander by the edge/ Of this desolate lake/ Where wind cries in the sedge,/ Until the axle break/ That keeps the stars in their round/ ~~*The banners of east and west/*~~ And hands hurl in the deep/ The banner of east & west/ And the girdle of light is unbound/ Your breast will not lie on the breast/ Of your beloved in sleep

III. Half close your eye lids, loosen your hair/ And dream about the great & their ~~pri~~ pride,/ They have spoken against you every where/ But weigh this song with the great & their pride:/ I made it out of a mouthful of air/ Their childrens children shall say they have lied./ W B Yeats

Aodh to Dectora.

1.

I wander by the edge
Of this desolate lake
Where wind cries in the sedge,
Until the axle break
That keeps the stars in their round
~~The banners of east and west~~
And hands hurl in the deep
The banners of east & west
And the girdle of light is unbound
Your breast will not lie on the breast
Of your beloved in sleep

III.

Half close your eye lids, loosen your hair
And dream about the great & their ~~pride~~ pride,
They have spoken against you everywhere
But weigh this song with the great & their pride:
I made it out of a mouthful of air
Their children's children shall say they have lied.

W B Yeats

HERBERT GEORGE WELLS
1866–1946

Autograph letter signed, dated Arnold House, Sandgate, 4 February 1900, to W. E. Henley. 1 p. 264 x 210 mm. MA 1617. Gift of Edwin J. Beinecke.

Some dream about the future hoping that its promise or threat will soon be fulfilled, others because it maintains a constant distance and remains the exclusive preserve of the imagination. Wells belonged to the latter class of dreamers, for whom the past offers no refuge and the present is only a subtle form of imprisonment. The pattern of Wells's life was one of flight, establishment and subsequent flight, and this pattern is reflected in his writings. As a novelist, he proposed many futures, simply because one alone would have grown stale; in later life, he was ineffective as an agent of social reform for a similar reason: had he ever succeeded in constructing his model society he would have wrecked it for the diversion of building another. In 1981 nothing appears quainter than the visions of the future—all sinuous lines and miraculous sources of power—engendered by our great-grandparents; but this is not entirely true of Wells's work. His "tales of invention" are not prophecies of technological salvation, but moral and mythological essays about man's natural limitations, revealed by science. Wells remains interesting today because he consistently reminds his readers how seldom and how unsystematically we think about the future.

By the date of this letter, 1900, Wells had achieved nationwide fame as the author of *The Time Machine* and *The War of the Worlds*, and had earned true respect as a literary craftsman from some of the finest writers then living, many of whom were his near neighbors on the southern coast of England. Within the next five years there would pass through the Wells household and its domestic frenzy such men as Henry James, Joseph Conrad, Ford Madox Hueffer, Stephen Crane, George Bernard Shaw and George Gissing. In this year he also published *Love and Mr. Lewisham*, one of his many nonscientific novels, a genre which culminated in *Tono-Bungay* (1909), perhaps the finest of all his works. Wells wrote this letter to Henley in his customarily peppery style; comments like "Blethers being tuneful are still Blethers to me" are altogether typical. "R.A.M.S." is Robert Alan Mowbray Stevenson, Robert Louis Stevenson's cousin.

The Wells Archive at the University of Illinois, Urbana-Champaign, is the best in the world.

My dear Henley. The Lord God bless & keep you & make you forgive me for not writing before. Excuse I have none. My head is mud & my bowels muddle. Why should I go about pretending to be a Decent Person? I have no excuse whatever. I didn't write V'la tout. And R.A.M.S. He's not a Decent Person either. He goes & has things that are strokes & ought to be treated as such. Only in some subtle way they are not They are something wrong with his veins that is practically the same thing. He lies in bed & he cannot talk & I'm damned if I see how it is going to go on. The thing has no point at all. It is one of those disastrous muddy affairs that you cannot take hold of anywhere. It makes me think there is something confoundedly George Gissingish about Almighty God. It's grey & eternal & that's all the point it has. There's nothing to be done. It all rests with R.A.M. The doctors say he has his prospect of getting in a sort of way better. He will not be able to work much again or be very lively. . . .

Arnold House. Sandgate

Feb 4th already 1900.

My dear Henley.

The Lord God bless & keep you & make you forgive me for not writing before. Excuses I have none. My head is mud & my bowels muddle. Why should I go about pretending to be a Decent Person? I have no excuse whatever. I don't write [illegible]. And R.A.M.S. He's not a Decent Person either. He goes & has things that are strokes & ought to be treated as such. Only in some subtle way they are not. They are something wrong with his veins that is practically the same thing. He lies in bed. He cannot talk & I'm damned if I see how it is going to go on. The thing has no point at all. It is one of those ~~[illegible]~~ disastrous muddy affairs that you cannot take hold of anywhere. It makes me think there is something confoundedly George Gissingish about Almighty God. It's grey & dismal & that's all the point it has. There's nothing to be done. It all rests with R.A.M.S. The doctors say he has his prospect of getting in a sort of grey better. He will not be able to work much again in his[illegible] living. The best chance for him is to get out to Capri and settle down in a way of life there. . . . It's the worst thing I've seen for some time as one sees it now. I don't see where the daughter & the small boy are going to be in fifteen years time. [illegible] all that Stevens memories, but this beats me altogether.

Schillings got the N.A.R. for November a few days ago. I like that year all round & some of it is altogether gaudy. ~~[illegible]~~. You say things I feel & understand and you say them better than I would imagine them said. There's IV, V. IX X XIV XIX XXI XXIII & XXIV, all to my sense simply & entirely beautiful. There's just a few other spots do that, living or dead. Come to think of it — dead all of them. But then I have deficiencies of appreciation. I understand there are points in this game of poetry, I haven't mastered. Blather being beautiful are still Blather to me. Most poetry strikes me as unnecessary blathering. (I class it with lace at its best — the common poetry.) You are in some way out of that trade. This of yours is organic. It is life, singing.

Why don't you do some impressions of the war?

Our love to you both.

Yours ever

H. G. Wells

117

Ernest Christopher Dowson
1867–1900

Autograph manuscript of "Non sum qualis eram bonae sub regno Cynarae" in the "Flower Notebook," unsigned but dated 7 February 1891. 83 leaves. 179 x 112 mm. MA 1480. Gift of Mr. C. Waller Barrett.

The poetry of the '90s in England seems at times to be a falling away from the brilliant polychromes of the Pre-Raphaelites, at best a "hectic flush" before the onset of the monochromatic twentieth century. Certainly, Dowson's verse evokes a world of only half-remembered colors and half-recalled emotions. Oscar Wilde, whom Dowson knew in France after Wilde's release from prison, described the poet (in a letter in the Morgan Library) as a "poor wounded wonderful fellow . . . a tragic reproduction of all tragic poetry. . . ." Wounded (by tuberculosis) though Dowson was, he chose to mollify in lyrical form the tragedy of his consumptive fate and his hopeless love for a young girl named Adelaide Foltinowicz. His bitterest reflections about life are reserved for his correspondence and a single poem, "To Nature," which bears the epigraph "Morituri te salutant"—"those who are about to die salute you." For the rest, Dowson's poems are cast in a mood of languishing, despairing desire, the mood (for him) of nightfall or sunrise: "But I was desolate and sick of an old passion,/ When I awoke and found the dawn was gray. . . ." The poem shown here is Dowson's most famous work, considered by many to be the supreme expression of the lyricism of the '90s. Though Dowson was writing in a meter in which he felt "my Muse is not quite at her ease," "Non sum qualis eram bonae sub regno Cynarae" has proved to be the poem by which he is most frequently remembered.

The notebook in which this poem (and sixty-six other poems) was written is called the "Flower Notebook" after its previous owner, Sir Newman Flower. It was kept by Dowson between 1886 and 1892 and it has been suggested that he copied poems from this notebook into another, which was presumably lost in Brittany. The "Flower Notebook" provides the unique source for forty of Dowson's poems. Besides the "Flower Notebook," the Morgan Library also owns one hundred and seventy-three letters from Dowson to Arthur Moore, many of which also contain poems.

Last night, ah, yesternight, betwixt her lips and mine,/ There fell thy shadow, Cynara! thy breath was shed/ Upon my soul, between the ~~roses~~ kisses and the wine,/ And I was desolate and sick of an old passion,/ Yea, I ~~grew~~ was desolate and bowed my head:/ I have been faithful to thee, Cynara, ~~after~~ in my fashion.

All night upon my breast I felt her warm heart beat,/ Night long within mine arms in love and sleep she lay;/ Surely the kisses of her bright, red mouth were sweet?/ But I was desolate and sick of an old passion,/ When I awoke, and found the dawn was gray:/ I have been faithful to thee, Cynara, in my fashion!

I have forgot much, Cynara, gone with the wind,/ Flung roses, roses riotously with the throng,/ Dancing to put thy pale, lost lilies out of mind/ But I was desolate and sick of an old passion/ Yea desolate because the dance was long:/ I have been faithful to thee, Cynara, in my fashion! . . .

70

Non sum qualis eram bonae
Sub regno Cynarae!

Last night, ah, yesternight, betwixt her lips and mine,
There fell thy shadow, Cynara! thy ~~breath~~ was shed
Upon my soul, between the ~~roses~~ kisses and the wine,
And I was desolate and sick of an old passion,
Yea, I ~~[illegible]~~ was desolate and bowed my head:
I have been faithful to thee, Cynara, ~~after~~ in my fashion.

—

All night upon my heart I felt her warm heart beat,
Night long within mine arms in love and sleep she lay;
Surely the kisses of her bought, red mouth were sweet?
But I was desolate and sick of an old passion,
When I awoke, and found the dawn was gray:
I have been faithful to thee, Cynara, in my fashion!

—

I have forgot much, Cynara, gone with the wind,
Flung roses, roses riotously with the throng,
Dancing to put thy pale, lost lilies out of mind
But I was desolate and sick of an old passion
Yea desolate because the dance was long:
I have been faithful to thee, Cynara, in my fashion!

71

I cried for madder music and for stronger wine,
But when the ~~cups are empty~~ feast is finished and the lamps expire,
There falls thy shadow, Cynara: the night is thine!
And I am desolate and sick of an ~~[illegible]~~ old passion,
Yea hungry for the lips of my desire.
I have been faithful to thee, Cynara, in my fashion.

—

Feb 7th 1891.

Arnold Bennett
1867–1931

Autograph manuscript of "Clayhanger," Volume I, signed with initials and dated Brighton, 5 January to 7 February 1910. 217 pp. 197 x 170 mm. From the Collection of Mr. Gordon N. Ray.

Naturally enough, Arnold Bennett enjoyed watching his career take shape as the years went by. After all, his was a pleasant career to behold: as Bennett's reputation and earnings grew by regular increments, he recorded with diminishing surprise the incidents and publishers' contracts that transformed the son of a provincial solicitor into the most renowned literary man of his day. Bennett's journal, the admiration of anyone who has tried to keep a journal with consistency, is a monument of dutiful, if occasionally limited self-awareness. *Clayhanger* is an obverse expression of his autobiographical leanings, a sympathetic rendering of a failure of self-awareness. The first part of *Clayhanger*, called "His Vocation," concerns Edwin Clayhanger's dawning consciousness of greater intellectual possibilities than those that lie before him in his father's printing shop. The tragedy of *Clayhanger* arises not only from Darius Clayhanger's refusal to apprentice his son to an architect, but also from the insensibility, the lapse of high intentions, that steal over Edwin as years pass and routine afflicts him. The failure, perhaps the inadequacy, of Edwin's desire to escape the printing shop offers a poignant comment on the intensity of Bennett's yearning to ascend in the world and to remain conscious of his ascent through the rigorous self-discussion of his journal.

The passage shown here, from Chapter XVII, Section v of "His Vocation," is the beginning of Edwin's final argument with his father about architecture. It is worth noting that the forty thousand words of the first book of one of Bennett's greatest novels were written in just over a month. The most important collection of Arnold Bennett manuscripts, including his journal from 1896 to 1928, is in the Berg Collection of the New York Public Library.

In spite of his advanced age Edwin began to cry. Yes, the tears came out of his eyes.

"And now you begin blubbing!" said his father.

"You say naught for six months—and ~~they~~ then you start writing letters!" said his father.

"And what's made ye settle on architecting, I'd like to be knowing?" Darius went on.

Edwin ~~could not~~ was not able to answer this question. He had never put it to himself. ~~And~~ Assuredly he could not, at ~~an insta~~ the pistol's point, explain why *he wanted to be an architect. He did not know. He announced this truth ingenuously:*

"I don't know—I—

"I sh'd think not!" said his father. "D'ye think architecting'll be any better than this?" 'This' meant printing.

"I don't know—"

"Ye don't know! Ye don't know!" Darius repeated testily. His testiness was only like ~~the~~ foam on ~~a~~ the great wave of his resentment

"Mr. Orgreave—" Edwin began. It was unfortunate because Darius had had a difficulty with Mr. Orgreave, who was notoriously somewhat exacting in the matter of prices.

"Don't talk to me about Mester Orgreave!" Darius almost shouted.

In spite of his advanced age Edwin began to cry. Yes, the tears came out of his eyes.

"And now you begin blubbing!" said his father.

"You say naught for six months—and ~~they~~ then you start ~~xx~~ writing letters!" said his father.

"And what's made ye settle on architecting, I'd like to be knowing?" Darius went on.

Edwin ~~could not~~ was not able to answer this question. He had never put it to himself. ~~And~~ Assuredly he could not, at ~~answer~~ the pistol's point, explain *why* he wanted to be an architect. He did not know. He announced this truth ingenuously:

"I don't know—I—"

"I sh'd think not!" said his father. "D'ye think architecting 'll be any better than this?" 'This' meant printing.

"I don't know—"

"Ye don't know! Ye don't know!" Darius repeated testily. His testiness was only like the foam on ~~a~~ the great wave of his resentment.

"Mr. Orgreave—" Edwin began. It was unfortunate, because Darius had had a difficulty with Mr. Orgreave, who was notoriously somewhat exacting in the matter of prices.

"Don't talk to me about Mester Orgreave!" Darius almost shouted.

119

John Galsworthy
1867–1933

Autograph manuscript of "The Pagan," unsigned and undated, but written ca. 1901. 479 leaves. 200 x 165 mm. MA 1413. Gift of Mr. H. Bradley Martin.

In 1904 Galsworthy dropped his pseudonym of "Sinjohn" and appeared under his own name as the author of *The Island Pharisees*, a rather testy work that elaborates on a theme which Galsworthy restated in his Nobel Prize acceptance speech in 1932: "Verily I say unto you it is harder for one of the black-coated fraternity to enter the world of the disinherited than for a camel to pass through the eye of a needle." *The Island Pharisees* cost Galsworthy nearly four years of labor; it was begun in 1901 as a novel called *The Pagan*, the manuscript of which is shown here, and was rewritten twice before publication in 1904 and revised again for a new edition in 1908. *The Pagan* and *The Island Pharisees* are essentially opposite sides of the same coin. Each version reveals the shallowness and pharisaical hypocrisy of upper middle-class British society; each concerns itself with the perceptions required to drive a man out of the ordinary path pursued by most unthinking members of society. *The Pagan* is told from outside that society, in the first person, by a character named Ferrand, who already dwells in "the world of the disinherited," while *The Island Pharisees*, though written in the third person, is largely seen through the eyes of a young man named Shelton. On the verge of marrying into the settled way of life, he meets Ferrand and is gradually led to reject the complacent "world of safety and tradition" represented by his fiancée and her family.

The Morgan Library's collection of Galsworthy manuscripts includes those of *Beyond* and *The Saint's Progress* and the corrected typescripts of numerous short stories. Other important groups of Galsworthy manuscripts are to be found in the British Library and the University of Birmingham Library.

~~Being a fool~~ I came from Ostend that morning in the forepeak of the early boat among ~~the~~ other penniless animals. ~~without money.~~ The fever was ~~in~~ pushing me ~~to get~~ to London, the city of fortunes where all ~~we~~ of us vagabonds come sooner or later full of the hope of better things. [illegible deletion] ~~I would not even give~~ I gave myself no time to walk, & got into the ~~slow~~ train though not in the habit of travelling that way. ~~An~~ There followed a costly incident ~~followed which costing me money I could not afford, but which I~~ which I do not regret since it gave me a good little picture of Society. ~~for each group of where you get have six or seven individuals represents there you get have more or less Society, at large.~~

Following my habits I was studying ~~my fellow~~ the other passengers, ~~as is my habit,~~ when ~~at the last minute~~ a girl entered, & sat down opposite ~~to me~~. We started. . . .

I
First of April

I came from Ostend that morning in the first boat among the other penniless animals. The fever was pushing me to London, the city of fortunes, where all of us vagabonds come sooner or later full of the hope of better things. I gave myself no time to walk, & got into the train, though not in the habit of travelling that way. There followed a costly incident which I do not regret since it gave me a first little picture of Society, where you have — there you have 'Society'.

Following my habits I was studying the other passengers, when a girl entered, & sat down opposite to me. We started.

She was a little bourgeoise, burgheress with a pale face, pale hair, and large brown eyes — a rare enough type; She held a brown bag, bit her lips and seemed on the point of tears. When we had gone some distance leaning forward, she touched me timidly on the arm. "Monsieur," she said, "do you speak French?" "I do." "Then perhaps you can tell me where they collect tickets?" "I am a stranger." "Forgive me. I don't know what to do: I must have advice; I am very miserable — perhaps you can help me." "I will do my best." "I must get to London", she said; "I have a friend in London who might help me, but I had no money for the ticket; I am here without a ticket & I don't know what to do." There was boldness in this situation. "It is a thing," I said, "that might happen to anybody, we must see what can be done." "I haven't a sou in the world,"

George William Russell ("AE") 1867–1935

Autograph letter signed "A.E." dated 24 May 1921, to Mr. William Hard. 2 pp. 260 x 205 mm. MA 2999. Gift of Mr. Gerard Kirsopp Lake.

Writing to Lady Gregory about George Russell in 1900, Yeats recalled, with some impatience, that Russell had "bemoralized" him as long as he could remember, and then concluded that "the attitude of bemoralization is not the attitude of understanding." On behalf of AE (as he later preferred to be called), one must add that his kind of bemoralizing was at least the attitude of enthusiasm, an attitude he was continually striking. AE quite earnestly divided his energies between this world and the next; besides being a mystic, he was also a painter, poet, political and economic organizer and an editor of the *Irish Homestead* and the *Irish Statesman*. Each of these activities called forth the same exuberant AE. Strange as the conjunction of an expert on "rural reconstruction" (about which he lectured in America during the Depression) and a "mystical poet" may seem, AE managed to make his two halves work together. Far from detracting from his practical abilities as a bank organizer for the Irish Agricultural Organisation Society, his occasional otherworldliness may have made him a better negotiator; as Yeats recalled, "he had, and has, the capacity, beyond that of any man I have known, to put with entire justice not only the thoughts, but the emotions of the most opposite parties and personalities, as it were dissolving some public or private uproar into drama by Corneille or by Racine. . . ." Even the mystical world, however, could get to be too much for AE at times; when he first began organizing banks in the west of Ireland in 1897, he discovered that "around Mt. Nephin the atmosphere is so thick with faerys that you draw them in with every breath."

The letter shown here was occasioned by reports from America that a bad portrait of AE had recently been published. AE responds with enthusiastic forgiveness and includes two sketches, one illustrating a portrait in which he was made to look like a German statesman, the other intended to resemble the new portrait: "I suppose the new portrait is something like this, supplied by some enemy of Ireland to show what ruffians Irish poets are."

Manuscripts by AE are primarily in the National Library, Dublin, the Lilly Library of Indiana University, Colby College, Maine, and Yale University.

---

84 Merion Sq Dublin. 24 May 21 Dear Hard. I know you have been writing articles on Ireland but I have not seen the Metropolitan only short extracts. I am not concerned about the appearance of the portrait for which you express "profound regret." I do not mind, and I can say this sincerely because I have not seen it. But I remember once before a portrait of myself which appeared I think in the New York Sun was really a portrait of Prince Buelow or some German statesman. It had seven chins with no beard, a moustache turned up like the Kaisers, a pair of goggle eyes and brushed up hair something like this. I made no protest. I felt the Lord in His own good time would compensate by the shortening of Purgatory or whatever other retribution for bad conduct is exacted from us on the other shore. I gather from the "profound regret" "most unfortunate picture" that this time the Lord will have to let me off Purgatory altogether if my wounded feelings are to be appeased & justice done. I suppose the new portrait is something like this, supplied by some enemy of Ireland to show what ruffians Irish poets are. Never mind I forgive you & the Metropolitan. . . .

84 Merrion Sq
Dublin.
24 May 21

Dear Hand. I know you have been writing articles on Ireland but I have not seen the Metropolitan only short extracts. I am not concerned about the appearance of the portrait printed. You express "profound regret". I do not mind, and I can say this sincerely because I have not seen it. But I remember once before a portrait of myself which appeared I think in the New York Sun was really a portrait of Prince Buelow a noble German statesman. It had seven chins with no beard, a moustache turned up like the Kaiser's, a pair of goggle eyes and brushed up hair something like this. I made no protest. I felt the Lord in

this one Good time would compensate by the shortening of Purgatory or whatever other retribution for bad conduct is expected from us on the other shore. I gather from the "profound regret" "most unfortunate picture" that this time the Lord will have to let me off Purgatory altogether if my wounded feelings are to be appeased & justice done. I suppose the new portrait was

something like this. supplied by some enemy of Ireland to show what ruffians Irish poets are. Never mind I forgive you & the Metropolitan. But I would really prefer to be let off Purgatory and

121

Hilaire Belloc
1870–1953

Autograph manuscript signed of "John Vavassour, who lost a fortune by throwing stones," undated, printed in "New Cautionary Tales" (1930). 3 pp. 253 x 202 mm. MA 3317. Purchased as a gift in memory of Benjamin Sonnenberg.

Anthony Trollope, whose writing habits are legendary, compared himself in his *Autobiography* to a shoemaker, but Belloc goes him one better: "The whole art is to write and write and write and then offer it for sale, just like butter. The more one writes, the more one gets known. The more enormous one's output the more the publishers get to regard you as a reliable milch cow." There will always be those who condemn such an opinion, but for a mind as restless and as vigorous as Belloc's was, "to write and write and write" was the only possible manner of being an author. The early twentieth century was particularly well populated by authors whose books were as diverse as they were numerous—Wells, Shaw and Chesterton, for example—but no one exceeds Belloc as "a reliable milch cow." Before 1918, in what is generally considered the more brilliant half of his career, he had written, edited or translated nearly seventy books and pamphlets; after 1918 he added over eighty more. This was not merely facility on Belloc's part; it was, as Chesterton said in his review of *The Path to Rome* (1902), the ability to write recklessly. If, as Belloc asserted, being a man of letters was a trade, like being a shoemaker, then it only made sense to have stock on hand; the more aesthetic forms of the art simply would not pay their way, for he learned early what Sarah Byng, who could not read and was tossed into a thorny hedge by a Bull, learned with great pain: "Moreover she has wisely grown/ Confirmed in her instinctive guess/ That literature breeds distress."

Like A. E. Housman, whose literary output was just as slender as Belloc's was enormous, Belloc had a wonderfully spontaneous gift for comic and satiric verses. Among the best of these poems are those he wrote for children, *Cautionary Tales* (1907) and *New Cautionary Tales* (1930), which capture so well the fascination children so often find in the grotesque, particularly the humorous grotesque. John Vavassour is one of many children who come to horrible ends in these poems, all to point a simple moral, and who differ so much from the one good boy in *Cautionary Tales*, Charles Augustus Fortescue: "In eating Bread he made no Crumbs,/ He was extremely fond of sums,/ To which, however, he preferred/ The Parsing of a Latin Word . . . ."

John Vavassour de Quentin Jones de Quentin/ Was very fond of throwing stones./ At Horses, People, Passing Trains,/ But 'specially at Window Panes./ Like many of the Upper Class/ He liked the sound of Broken Glass;[1]/ It bucked him up and made him gay;/ It was his favourite form of play./ But this amusement cost him dear,/ My Children, as you now shall hear.

John Vavassour ~~an Uncle had~~ de Quentin had/ An Uncle who adored the Lad/ And often chuckled: "Wait until/ You see what's left you in my Will!"/ Nor were the words without import,/ Because this Uncle did a sort/ Of something in the City, which/ Had made him fabulously rich,/ (Although his brother, John's Papa/ Was poor, as many ~~Fathers are~~ Fathers are).

[1] I stole this line with subtle daring/ From Wing-Commander Maurice Baring.

In typescript please keep the Capitals as in the M.S.S.

Cautionary Tale.

John Vavassour, who lost a fortune by throwing stones.

de Quentin

John Vavassour de Quentin Jones
Was very fond of throwing stones.
At Horses, People, Passing Trains,
But 'specially at Window Panes.
Like many of the Upper Class
He liked the sound of Broken Glass; (1)
It bucked him up and made him gay:
It was his favourite form of play.
But this amusement cost him dear,
My Children, as you now shall hear.

John Vavassour ~~[illegible]~~ de Quentin had
An Uncle who adored the Lad
And often chuckled: "Wait until
You see what's left you in my Will!"
Nor were the words without import,
Because this Uncle did a sort
Of something in the City, which
Had made him fabulously rich,
(Although his brother, John's Papa
Was poor, as many ~~Fathers are~~ Fathers are).

---

(1) I stole this line with subtle daring
From Wing-Commander Maurice Baring.

John Millington Synge
1871–1909

Autograph letter signed, dated 17 December 1903, to John Masefield. 4 pp. 253 x 203 mm. Anonymous loan.

John Synge's gift to the Irish theater was the language of the Irish people, which becomes in his plays what Edward Thomas, in a review of *The Playboy of the Western World* (1907), called "a poetry that has nothing to do with invention but falls naturally out of the life of the speakers, as apples fall in a still night." In his notebooks, Synge distinguished between "the poetry of real life . . . and the poetry of a land of the fancy"; he attempted to give Ireland a dramatic perception of itself untainted by visions of "the fancy land only," whether those visions were conventional, like the image of stock nineteenth-century stage Irishmen, or political, a kind of sentimental fancy about Ireland that particularly seemed to afflict Synge's enemies. In his preface to *The Playboy of the Western World*, which caused such a riotous protest when first acted in Dublin, Synge claimed: "On the stage one must have reality, and one must have joy; and that is why the intellectual modern drama has failed, and people have grown sick of the false joy of the musical comedy . . . ." Acting on the suggestion of Yeats, Synge found his reality and joy amidst the folk of the Aran Islands, off the west of Ireland, and he called his art "collaboration": "I am glad to acknowledge how much I owe to the folk-imagination of these fine people." Though Yeats credited Synge with little political interest (because there is so little explicit in his plays), the attack made on *The Playboy of the Western World* clearly wounded him, and his response, though not partisan, was deeply political: "A hundred years ago Irishmen could face a dark existence in Kilmainham Jail, or lurch on the halter before a grinning mob, but now they fear any gleam of truth. How are the mighty fallen!"

Yeats called Synge "a sick man picturing energy, a doomed man picturing gaiety," alluding to the fact that Synge died slowly of Hodgkin's disease. He completed only six plays during his lifetime, mainly for the reason he gives Masefield in the letter shown here: "I have other plays on hand but Heaven knows when they will be finished, as I have been off work for the last month with influenza and a sick lung." In this letter Synge also discusses his revision of *The Tinker's Wedding* and, in a section not shown here, plans for publication of his prose account of his life in the west of Ireland called *The Aran Islands*, which appeared in 1907 with illustrations by Jack Yeats.

Most of Synge's manuscripts are still privately held; others may be found in the Berg Collection of the New York Public Library.

You increase my debt of gratitude by proposing to persuade Matthews to bring out my plays in the spring. I would be delighted to have them out in book-form if he can be induced to take them up. How would it be to add the tinker-play—you remember the one you heard with an abortive wedding and a priest in it—so as to have three peasant plays? What is this shilling series? The tinkers have been re-written since you heard them and are now twice as long (in two acts) and I think many times stronger and wickeder. I have other plays on hand but Heaven knows when they will be finished, as I have been off work for the last month with influenza and a sick lung.

I suppose it is too late to felicitate you on your marriage, I heard of it long ago—in the summer I think— . . .

Part IV was tacked on the rest rather hastily and I have always suspected that there was (too much) folklore and ill-digested doggerel running through it, though I had not ~~the~~ the courage to cut out the erring parts with decision. I hope to go over to London in a month or two, and then we can talk it over, if you have ever a moment to spare, and I will do any pruning that is needed.

You increase my debt of gratitude by proposing to persuade Matthews to bring out my plays in the spring. I would be delighted to have them out in book-form if he can be induced to take them up. How would it be to add the Tinker play—you remember the one you heard with an abortive wedding and a priest in it—so as to have three peasant plays? What is his shilling series? The Tinkers have been re-written since you heard them and are now twice as long (in two acts) and I think many times stronger and wickeder. I have other plays on hand but Heaven knows when they will be finished, as I have been off work for the last month with influenza and a sick lung.

I suppose it is too late to felicitate you on your marriage, I heard of it long ago—in the summer I think—from W.B.Y. but I did not then know where you were. I am glad to see in

123

Max Beerbohm
1872–1956

Autograph manuscript of "The Golden Drugget," undated but written in 1918. 5 pp. 328 x 213 mm. MA 3319. Purchased as a gift in memory of Benjamin Sonnenberg.

Caricatures can exert a strange authority: if they are incisive enough, they invade the memory and drive out its rightful inhabitants, like squatters in mansions of the dead. Max Beerbohm's caricatures and literary parodies have precisely this effect. It is easy to think of Kipling, Aubrey Beardsley or Yeats (introducing George Moore to the Queen of the Fairies) solely in terms of Beerbohm's witty sketches, simply because they visibly embody more of the spirit of these men than any photograph ever could. This is true, too, of Beerbohm himself, for he often appears in the midst of that vast literary evening of the 1890s evoked in his cartoons, always casting a somewhat listless eye on the imposing figures grouped around him. His curious ability to detach himself from society—enabling him to satirize it all the more effectively—culminated in 1910, when he and his bride left London and settled in Rapallo, Italy, later the home of another, rather different expatriate, Ezra Pound. Living serenely in a sort of comic isolation at Villino Chiaro, Beerbohm finished his only novel, *Zuleika Dobson*, and his volume of uncanny literary parodies, *A Christmas Garland*, before the outbreak of the First World War caused him to return to England for its duration. Those years were a sort of exile from self-exile and, in spite of the social crush in which he was soon involved, they were also years of remarkable writing.

Among the essays in *And Even Now* (written during the war years and published in 1920) is "The Golden Drugget," the most reflective and measured of Beerbohm's many wonderful essays. The Morgan Library owns the manuscript of this work, and its final page is reproduced here. What begins as praise for the "primitive and essential things" of life diverges momentarily to satirize the school of art that produces works like a "picture of a young mother seconding a resolution at a meeting of a Board of Guardians." But the heart of this conservative essay is Beerbohm's description of a "lonely wayside inn" between Rapallo and Zoagli, an inn that even in wartime, he supposes, casts across the road at night a drugget of light "that is as the span of our human life, granted between one great darkness and another."

The major depository of Beerbohm caricatures and manuscripts is the Humanities Research Center Library of the University of Texas in Austin.

There it is, familiar, serene, festal. That the pilgrim knew he would see it in due time does not diminish for him the queer joy of seeing it; nay, this emotion would be far less without that foreknowledge. Some things are best at first sight. Others—and here is one of them—do ever improve by recognition. I remember that when first I beheld this steady strip of light, shed forth over a threshold level with the road, it seemed to me conceivably sinister. It brought Stevenson to my mind: the chink of doubloons and the clash of cutlasses; and I think I quickened my pace as I passed it. But now!—now it inspires in me a sense of deep trust and gratitude; and such awe as I have for it is altogether a loving awe, as for holy ground that should be trod lightly. A drugget of crimson cloth across a London pavement is rather resented by the casual passer-by, as saying to him "Step across me, stranger, but not along me, not in!" and for answer he ~~cursorily grinds~~ spurns it with his heel. . . .

supernatural allies working with her — witches on broomsticks circling closely round him, demons in pursuit of him or waiting to leap out on him. And how about mere robbers and cut-throats? Suppose — but look! that streak, yonder, look! — the Golden Drugget.

= There it is, familiar, serene, festal. That [redacted] the pilgrim knew he would see it in due time does not diminish for him the queer joy of seeing it; nay, this emotion would be far less without that foreknowledge. Some things are best at first sight. Others [redacted] — and here is one of them — do ever improve by recognition. I remember that when first I beheld this steady strip [redacted] of light, shed forth over a threshold level with the road, it seemed to me conceivably sinister. It brought Stevenson to my mind: the chink of doubloons and the clash of cutlasses; and I think I quickened pace as I passed it. But now! — now it inspires in me a sense of deep trust and gratitude; and such awe as I [redacted] have for it is altogether a loving awe, as for holy ground that [redacted] should [redacted] be trod lightly. A drugget of crimson cloth across a London pavement is rather resented by the casual passer-by, as saying to him "Step across me, stranger, but not along me, [redacted] not in!" and for answer he ~~casually spurns~~ spurns it with his heel. ~~with~~ "Stranger, come in!" is the clear message of the Golden Drugget. "This is but a humble and earthly hostel, yet you will find [redacted] here [redacted] a radiant company of angels and archangels." And always I cherish the belief that if I obeyed the summons I should receive [redacted] fulfilment of the promise. Well, the beliefs that [redacted] one most cherishes one is least willing to test. I do not go in at that open door. But lingering, but [redacted] reluctant, is my tread as I pass by it; and [redacted] I pause to bathe in the light that is as the span of our human life, granted between [redacted] one great darkness and another.

Ford Madox Ford
1873–1939

Original typescript of "Galsworthy," an article published in "The American Mercury" in April 1936. 24 pp. 270 x 207 mm. MA 1417. Gift of Mr. H. Bradley Martin.

Memory was in some ways a burdensome thing for Ford Madox Ford. He could look back to being a child among the greatest of the Pre-Raphaelite figures and could remember Turgenev, if only as a smile, but his memory also brought back to him the oppressive assumption on the part of his elders that he, too, would be a genius. Speaking of Carlyle, Ruskin, Holman Hunt and Browning in the dedication to his *Ancient Lights and Certain New Reflections* (1911), Ford recalled that "these people were perpetually held up to me as standing upon unattainable heights, and at the same time I was perpetually being told that if I could not attain to these heights I might just as well not cumber the earth. What then was left for me? Nothing. Simply nothing." Memories like this carry with them a special kind of pain and emptiness, and they explain why Ford, though sad to see the "lights of individualities" fading as the world grew older around him, was also glad that those who lived in the shadow of those great lights no longer suffered from the contrast quite as much. In the modern (post-Boer War) world, even Ford could be "told sometimes that I am the finest—or let us say the most precious—stylist now employing the English language." Ford's reminiscences are often impressionistic, to use his word for them; that is, he remembered not so much for content as for style, for atmosphere of feeling. Obviously, such a means of remembrance has a certain defensive value, which became essential when he wreathed his memoirs around the living.

The article shown here in typescript, "Galsworthy," appeared first in *The American Mercury* in 1936 and was then included in Ford's compilation of such articles, *Portraits from Life* (1937). As a portrait, this article too is impressionistic. The passage shown here, which concerns an anecdote of Turgenev (whom Ford considered a dangerous influence on Galsworthy), is a perfect example of Ford's method. Rather than present Galsworthy in an objective manner, Ford hovers over his own impressions, creating more a picture of himself perceiving Galsworthy than of Galsworthy himself.

Though many of Ford's manuscripts are in private collections, others may be found in the libraries of Princeton University, Yale University and the University of Virginia.

known him to show.

The anecdote was this: Turgenev had a peasant girl for mistress. One day he was going to St. Petersburg and he asked the girl what he should bring her back from town. She begged him to bring her back some cakes of scented soap. He asked her why she wanted scented soap and she answered: "So that it may be proper for you to kiss my hand as you do those of the great ladies, your friends."

Start

I never liked the anecdote much, myself. But Galsworthy, telling it in the sunlit breakfast room of my cottage at Winchelsea, found it so touching that he appeared to be illuminated, and really had tears in his eyes. I daresay the reflection of the sunlight from the table-cloth may have had something to do with the effect of illumination, but it comes back to me as if, still, I saw him in a sort of aura that emanated from his features. And from that day he was never quite the same.... The morning is also made memorable for me by the ghost of the odour of a very strong embrocation that hung about us both. He was, at the moment, suffering from severe sciatica and I had spent the last half-hour of the night before and the first half-hour of that morning in rubbing him in his bed with that fluid which consisted of turpentine, mustard, and white of egg. And suddenly I had of him a conception of a sort of frailty, as if he needed protection from the hard truths of the world. It was a conception that remained to me till the very end... till the last time but one when I came upon him accidentally watching one of his own plays in New York, all alone and, seemingly, very perturbed. I don't know by what .

125

Gilbert Keith Chesterton
1874–1936

Autograph manuscript signed of "Open Letter: On the Collapse of the Cosmopolitan Club," undated, but written probably in the winter of 1912–3. 5 pp. 250 x 202 mm. MA 3394. Purchased as the gift of Mr. Frederick Melhado.

"Man is an exception, whatever he is. If he is not the image of God, then he is a disease of the dust." It is difficult to ignore words as trenchant as these, and the fact that they appear in an essay about drinking ("Wine When It Is Red" in *All Things Considered* [1908]) does not diminish their trenchancy; it merely makes one wonder about the author who can apply such a lofty argument to such an earthly question as whether or not it is healthy to drink. The end sought and the means employed are both typical of G. K. Chesterton, who can be called typical only in reference to himself. The quality of innocence so often attributed to Chesterton can be at least partly explained by his remarkable ability to move through life without taking its taint; as he remarks in the manuscript shown here, "I am a journalist and never believe the newspapers," yet no one would disbelieve him. Precisely because he kept his eyes on the stars and his feet on the ground, Chesterton was able to be so clearheaded about the many excruciating moral questions that beset the English during the early decades of this century. (He also got lost a lot.) Not only did this make Chesterton one of the great essayists and journalists of the early century, it also made him a superb, if today unfashionable, critic of literature. In his *Appreciations and Criticisms of the Works of Dickens* (1911), he explained the immediacy of Dickens' humor in *The Pickwick Papers:* "A good joke is the one ultimate and sacred thing which cannot be criticized. Our relations with a good joke are direct and even divine relations." Though to Chesterton the world was far from being a joke, it was at least a novelty, of the very best kind: "To me, like sudden laughter,/ The stars are fresh and gay;/ The world is a daring fancy,/ And finished yesterday."

This manuscript, almost half of which is written in his wife's hand, concerns the failure of the English to consider current political facts (the election of Wilson and Poincaré and the victory in the Balkans) as realities "on the spot." The Cosmopolitan Club, which was breaking up because of the election of men unknown to England, consisted of international figures and international concepts, such as the British Empire "on which the sun never sets—a horribly unpoetical state of things. Think of having a nature without any sunsets!"

Many of Chesterton's manuscripts are still in private hands, but an important group is located at John Carroll University, Cleveland, Ohio.

[Starting at foot of p. 4:] Theis ~~Cosmopolitan~~ International Club is breaking up. Men are more & more trusting men they know to have been honest in a small way; men faithful in one city to rule over many cities. ~~In America~~ Imperialists like Roosevelt & Rhodes stood for unrealities—please observe that I do not for one moment say insincerities. Tolstoy was splendidly sincere; but the cult of him was an unreality to this extent, that it left large masses in America & England with a general idea that he was the only Christian in the east of Europe. Since then we have seen Christianity on the march as it was in the Middle Ages; a thing of thousands, ready for pilgrimage,~~—&~~ and crusade. . . .

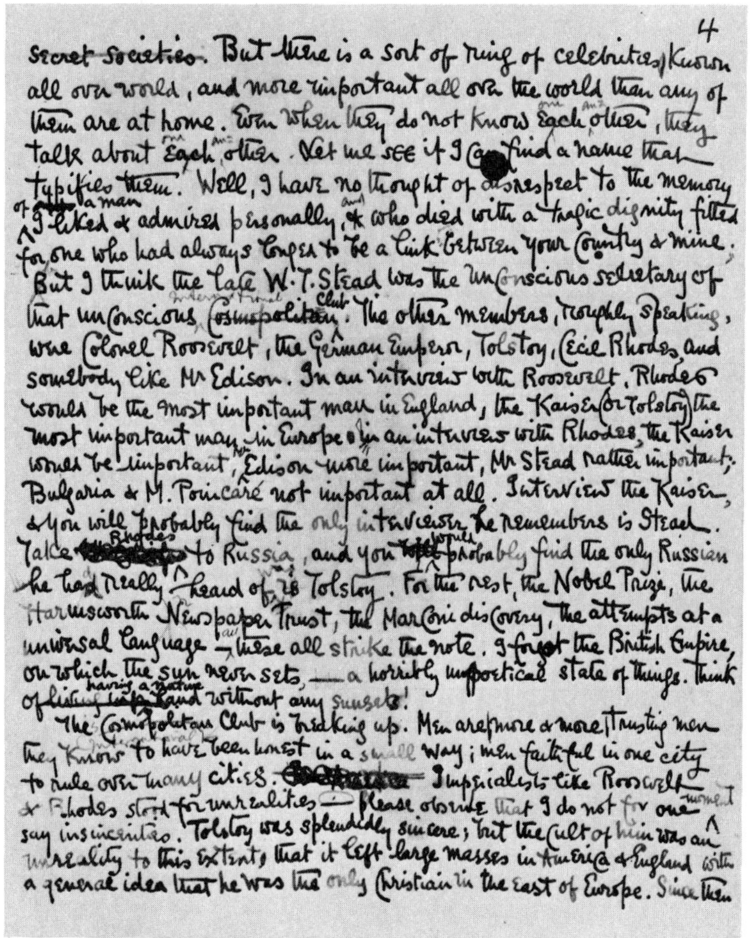

4

Secret societies. But there is a sort of ring of celebrities, known all over world, and more important all over the world than any of them are at home. Even when they do not know one another, they talk about one another. Let me see if I can find a name that typifies them. Well, I have no thought of disrespect to the memory of a man I liked & admired personally, and who died with a tragic dignity fitted for one who had always longed to be a link between your country & mine. But I think the late W. T. Stead was the unconscious secretary of that unconscious International Club. The other members, roughly speaking, were Colonel Roosevelt, the German Emperor, Tolstoy, Cecil Rhodes, and somebody like Mr Edison. In an interview with Roosevelt, Rhodes would be the most important man in England, the Kaiser (or Tolstoy) the most important man in Europe; in an interview with Rhodes, the Kaiser would be important, Mr Edison more important, Mr Stead rather important; Bulgaria & M. Poincaré not important at all. Interview the Kaiser, & you will probably find the only interviewer he remembers is Stead. Take Rhodes to Russia, and you would probably find the only Russian he had really heard of was Tolstoy. For the rest, the Nobel Prize, the Harmsworth Newspaper Trust, the Marconi discovery, the attempts at a universal language — these all strike the note. I forgot the British Empire, on which the sun never sets, — a horribly unpoetical state of things. Think of having a native land without any sunsets!

The Cosmopolitan Club is breaking up. Men are more & more trusting men they know to have been honest in a small way; men faithful in one city to rule over many cities. Imperialists like Roosevelt & Rhodes stood for unrealities — please observe that I do not for one moment say insincerities. Tolstoy was splendidly sincere; but the cult of him was an unreality to this extent, that it left large masses in America & England with a general idea that he was the only Christian in the east of Europe. Since then

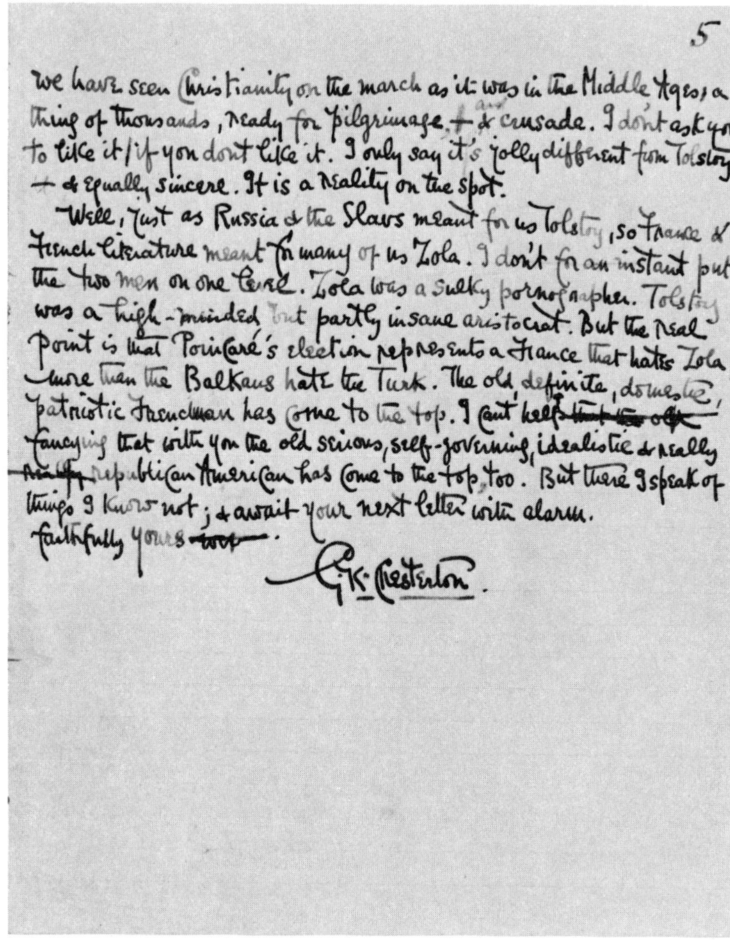

5

we have seen Christianity on the march as it was in the Middle Ages, a thing of thousands, ready for pilgrimage and crusade. I don't ask you to like it / if you don't like it. I only say it's jolly different from Tolstoy, & equally sincere. It is a reality on the spot.

Well, just as Russia & the Slavs meant for us Tolstoy, so France & French literature meant for many of us Zola. I don't for an instant put the two men on one level. Zola was a sulky pornographer. Tolstoy was a high-minded but partly insane aristocrat. But the real point is that Poincaré's election represents a France that hates Zola; more than the Balkans hate the Turk. The old, definite, domestic, patriotic Frenchman has come to the top. I can't help fancying that with you the old serious, self-governing, idealistic & really republican American has come to the top, too. But there I speak of things I know not; & await your next letter with alarm.

Faithfully yours.

G. K. Chesterton.

EDWARD THOMAS
1878–1917

Autograph letter signed, dated 27 November 1914, to C. F. Cazenove.
1 p. 259 x 202 mm. From the Collection of Mr. Gordon N. Ray.

In his longest flight, Edward Thomas carried to the war eyes open to its hideous reality, but still fixed internally on the countryside of England. This is what he saw, just weeks before he was killed by enemy artillery on 9 April 1917: on 16 February, "Four or five planes hovering and wheeling as kestrels used to over Mutton and Ludscombe," and on 20 March, "Huns shelled chiefly over our heads into Beaurains all night—like starlings returning 20 or 30 a minute." For Thomas, the war was not the leap into cleanness it was for Rupert Brooke; instead, it offered the obliteration of person, refuge in the dark: "I have come to the borders of sleep,/ The unfathomable deep/ Forest, where all must lose/ Their way . . . ." Even at the edge of the unknown, however, Thomas could still discover a moment that "unveiled something unwilling to die/ And I had what most I desired, without search or desert or cost." What Thomas most desired had been a matter of painful conjecture before the end of 1914; he had written or edited some thirty-five books, none particularly successful, published no poetry, and considered himself a failure. For a long time, he had been "travelling/ In search of something chance would never bring"; chance, however, brought about his friendship with Robert Frost, in whom Thomas discovered the clue to his own literary desires. With Frost's encouragement, Thomas began to write poetry in December 1914 and leaped almost immediately into strong verse full of his love of English earth, as in "Haymaking," written just before he enlisted in the Artists' Rifles:

> The men, the beasts, the trees, the implements,
> Uttered ever what they will in times far hence—
> All of us gone out of the reach of change—
> Immortal in a picture of an old grange.

This letter to C. F. Cazenove, Thomas' literary agent, was written from Little Iddens, Robert Frost's cottage near Dymock, where W. W. Gibson, a friend of Thomas, Frost and Rupert Brooke, lived. This was one of several visits Thomas paid to Frost, the manuscript of whose poem "To E. T." is now in the Morgan Library. During this visit, Thomas was, as he says here, "bothered whether I ought to enlist yet"; he was also gathering material for an article on reactions to the war, called "It's a Long, Long Way," which was published in the *English Review* in December 1914.

The most important groups of Thomas manuscripts are in the Lockwood Memorial Library, Buffalo, the Berg Collection of the New York Public Library, the British Library and the Bodleian Library.

---

c/o Robert Frost Ryton Dymock Gloucester 27 XI 14 Dear Cazenove, Thanks for Secker's account. But what about the English Review? Aren't they paying? I haven't got that article clearer yet, being bothered whether I ought to enlist yet. yours sincerely E Thomas

C/o Robert Frost
Ryton
Dymock
Gloucester

27 xi 14

Dear Cazenove,

Thanks for Secker's account. But what about the English Review? Aren't they paying? I haven't got that article cleared yet, being bothered whether I ought to enlist yet.

Yours sincerely

E Thomas

127

Edward Morgan Forster
1879–1970

Original typescript with autograph corrections and additions of "Art for Art's Sake," unsigned and undated, but written in 1949. 10 pp. 259 x 201 mm. MA 1248. Gift of Mr. Russell Lynes.

In his introductory remarks to *Aspects of the Novel* (1927), surely the most engaging piece of criticism ever written, E. M. Forster prescribed an ahistorical method: "We are to visualize the English novelists not as floating down that stream which bears all its sons away unless they are careful, but as seated together in a room, a circular room, a sort of British Museum reading-room—all writing their novels simultaneously." Forster mentioned no seating arrangement for this assembly, but one would like to imagine that he would be placed between "Miss Austen" and "Mr. James," always admitting the possibility that he might look over their shoulders and perhaps introduce them to each other. Like James and Austen, Forster gingerly measures and explains the eruptions that take place within what is, in works like *The Longest Journey* (1907) and *Howard's End* (1910), an established suburban order. The people of his novels, barring the morally and imaginatively exceptional ones, are the people one finds in a late poem by Lawrence: "The English are so nice/ so awfully nice/ They are the nicest people in the world." Of course, they are neither so nice nor so orderly when Forster presents them from a moral perspective which, though humane, can hardly be described as suburban.

The typescript shown here was prepared for an address given before the American Academy of Arts and Letters in May 1949 (it incorporates part of an article called "The New Disorder") and, though late in his career, it extends Forster's thoughts on the same problems of order and disorder that appear in his novels. In this lecture, however, he discusses these problems as they apply to the artist's role in society. Society creates disorder, Forster argues, and it is the artist's role to create the only self-defining and self-supporting order in existence. Because of the conflict of disorder and order, the artist must remain detached from society, living for art's sake alone: "Estimable is mateyness, and the man who achieves it gives many a pleasant little drink to himself and to others. . . . The artist who is seduced by mateyness may stop himself from doing the one thing which he, and he alone, can do—the making of something . . . which has internal harmony and presents order to a permanently disarranged planet." This talk was published as an article in *Harper's Magazine* in August 1949.

Forster's manuscripts are primarily in the library of King's College, Cambridge.

Art for art's sake does not mean that only art matters, and I would also like to rule out such phrases as, "The life of Art," "Living for Art," and even, "Art's High Mission." They confuse and mislead. . . .

A work of art—whatever else it may be—is a self-contained entity, with a life of its own imposed on it by its creator. It has internal order. It may have external form. That is how we recognise it. . . .

it, I want to keep them in proportion. No one can spend his or her life entirely in the creation or the appreciation of masterpieces. Man lives, and ought to live, in a complex world, full of conflicting claims, and if we simplified them down into the aesthetic he would be sterilized. Art for art's sake does not mean that only art matters, and I would also like to rule out such phrases as "The Life of Art," "Living for Art," and even "Art's High Mission." They confuse and mislead.

(Space)

What does the phrase mean? Instead of generalising let us take a specific instance - Shakespeare's Macbeth, for example, and pronounce the words "Macbeth for Macbeth's sake." What does that mean? Well, the play has several aspects – it is educational, it teaches us something about legendary Scotland, something about Jacobean England, and a good deal about human nature and its perils. We can study its origins, and study and enjoy its dramatic technique and the music of its diction, as Edith Sitwell has. ~~That is all~~ All that is true. But Macbeth is furthermore a world of its own, created by Shakespeare and existing in virtue of its own poetry. It is in this aspect Macbeth for Macbeth's sake, and that is what I ~~mean~~ intend by the phrase "Art for Art's sake." A work of art – whatever else it may be – is a self-contained entity, with a life of its own imposed on it by its creator. (It has internal order. It may have external form. That is how we recognise it.)

¶ Take for another ~~instance~~ example: that picture of Seurat's which I saw two years ago, in ~~at~~ Chicago – La Grande Jatte ~~Les Grandes Jattes~~. Here again there is much to study and to enjoy: the pointillisme, ~~the rendering of sunlight~~, the charming face of the seated girl, ~~the composition~~ (the nineteenth-century Parisian Sunday sunlight), the sense of motion in immobility. But here again there is something more; ~~the picture~~ La Grande Jatte forms a world of its own,

James Joyce
1882–1941

Autograph manuscript of "Chamber Music," unsigned and undated, but written ca. 1903–4. 33 leaves. Anonymous loan.

In 1905, AE, an arbiter of literary influence in Dublin, warned a friend: "We have a young scamp named Joyce here who writes with a more perfect art than anyone except Yeats who is I believe going to publish a book of lyrics. . . . I have not heard anything more of it as the poet has decamped to the continent with a barmaid. It will be a good book when it appears." That book, Joyce's first, was *Chamber Music* (1907), a collection, in AE's words, of "art poems as delicate and dainty as Watteau pictures . . . ." They are indeed a far cry from the realistic *copia* of *Ulysses* (1922) and *Finnegans Wake* (1939), so far from the kind of artistic honesty Joyce sought that he nearly prevented Elkin Mathews from printing them and later spoke of them as "meagre verses." Still, the songs in *Chamber Music* are as close to the gritty life Joyce led at the time as anything he ever wrote. His presence in these poems is not to be found in their content or their romanticism (though that was surely a noticeable strain in the artist as a youth) but in their formal perfection and their pure melodies. Verse may have been a room too narrow for Joyce to work in, but he filled these poems with as much in the way of artistic stillness as they could hold. Instead of seeming limited by the magnitude of his later accomplishments in prose, they somehow seem more luminous, misplaced in the maze of Joyce's subsequent reputation. Joyce published one more, equally slim volume of poetry, *Pomes Penyeach*, in 1927, somewhat belying his remark of 1909 that "There is no likelihood of my writing any more verse unless something unforeseen happens to my brain."

The manuscript shown here is the earliest of three manuscripts of *Chamber Music* (the other two are located at Cornell University and Yale University). The illustration is somewhat misleading as to size, for Joyce wrote the poems in a small hand in the center of very large sheets of paper. The two poems shown here are numbers four and thirty-one in the manuscript sequence, numbers four and twenty-six in the printed edition.

Major Joyce manuscripts are to be found at Yale University, the British Library, the Rosenbach Foundation, Philadelphia, the Library of the State University of New York, Buffalo, and the National Library, Dublin.

When the shy star goes forth in heaven,/ All maidenly, disconsolate,/ Hear you amid the drowsy even/ One who is singing by your gate./ His song is softer than the dew/ And he is come to visit you.

O bend no more in revery/ When he at eventide is calling/ Nor muse, who may this singer be/ Whose song about my heart is falling?/ Know you by this, the lover's chant,/ 'Tis I that am your visitant.

Thou leanest to the shell of night,/ Dear lady, a divining ear./ In that soft choiring of delight/ What sound hath made thy heart to fear?/ Seemed it of rivers rushing forth/ From the grey deserts of the North?

That mood of thine, O timorous,/ Is his if thou but scan it well/ Who a mad tale bequeaths to us/ At ghosting hour conjurable—/ And all for some strange name he read/ In Purchas or in Holinshed.

When the shy star goes forth in heaven,
All maidenly, disconsolate,
Hear you amid the drowsy even
One who is singing by your gate.
His song is softer than the dew
And he is come to visit you.

O bend no more in revery
When he at eventide is calling
Nor muse, who may this singer be
Whose song about my heart is falling?
Know you by this, the lover's chant,
'Tis I that am your visitant

Thou leanest to the shell of night,
Dear lady, a divining ear.
In that soft choiring of delight
What sound hath made thy heart to fear?
Seemed it of rivers rushing forth
From the grey deserts of the North?

That mood of thine, O timorous,
Is his if thou but scan it well
Who a mad tale bequeaths to us
At ghosting hour conjurable—
And all for some strange name he read
In Purchas or in Holinshed.

129

DAVID HERBERT LAWRENCE
1885–1930

Autograph manuscript signed of "Eloi, Eloi, lama sabachthani?," undated but written probably in the winter of 1914–5. 4 pp. 252 x 203 mm. MA 1892. Gift of Mr. James P. Magill.

On 2 March 1930, D. H. Lawrence died of tuberculosis, thus becoming the last great British poet to be killed by the disease (once called consumption) that was so ravenous of young writers during the preceding centuries. For Lawrence, it was the end of years of health that was bad "enough to depress the Archangel Michael himself." Lawrence did not make of death a prison house, from which his self-conscious soul might sing of its freedom; that formula was reversed, and death became a means by which "the body, the pristine consciousness, the great sympathetic life-flow, the steady flame of the old Adam," was enabled to escape modern man's destructive, conscious soul, grown too strong, and arise in resurrection. As he wrote in one of his last poems, "The Ship of Death," "The flood subsides, and the body, like a worn seashell/ emerges strange and lovely./ And the little ship wings home, faltering and lapsing/ on the pink flood,/ and the frail soul steps out, into the house again/ filling the heart with peace." In 1915, during the second winter of the war with Germany, Lawrence was not as confident about death and resurrection as he would become when his end came closer. The war was too bleak, the power of death too strong, and in the midst of his fears, Lawrence wrote to Lady Asquith: "The fact of resurrection is everything now: whether we dead can rise from the dead and love, and live, in a new life, here," then added, "I tremble very much in front of this."

The poem shown here, "Eloi, Eloi, lama sabachthani?," directly concerns the war and the problem of resurrection. The title is taken from Matthew 27:46, in which Christ on the cross "cried with a loud voice, saying, Eli, Eli, lama sabachthani? that is to say, My God, my God, why hast thou forsaken me?" It is a bitter denunciation of the war, which converted the "body glad as the bell of a flower" into an object of hatred because it has been forced to destroy "that shadow's shadow of me,/ The enemy!" This poem was published in *The Egoist* for May 1915.

The largest collections of Lawrence manuscripts are those in the Library of the University of Texas, Austin, and the University of California, Berkeley.

How I hate myself, this body which is me;/ How it ~~galls~~ dogs me, what a galling shadow!/ How I would like to cut off my hands,/ And take out my intestines to torture them!

But I can't, for it is written against me I must not,/ I must preserve my life from hurt.

But then, that shadow's shadow of me,/ The enemy!/ God, how glad I am to hear the shells/ Droning over, threatening me!/ It is their threat, their loud, jeering threat,/ Like screaming birds of Fate/ Wheeling to lacerate and rip up this my body,/ It is the loud cries of these ~~evil~~ birds of ~~death~~ pain/ That gives me peace.

For I hate this ~~my~~ body, which is so dear to me:/ My legs, my breast, my belly:/ My God, what agony they are to me;/ For I dote on them with tenderness, and I hate them,/ I hate them bitterly.

My God, that they should always be ~~before~~ with me!/ ~~Thank God at last~~ Nay, now at last thank God for the jeopardy,/ For the shells, that the question is ~~no~~ now no more before me.

(Title to be in ordinary capitals not Black lettering) 1. Send proof to me R.A.

[illegible]

Eloi, Eloi, lama sabachthani?

How I hate myself, this body which is me;
How it ~~[illegible]~~ dogs me, what a galling shadow!
How I would like to cut off my hands,
And take out my intestines to torture them!

But I can't, for it is written against me I must not,
I must preserve my life from hurt.

But then, that shadow's shadow of me,
The enemy!

God, how glad I am to hear the shells
Droning over, threatening me!
It is their threat, their loud, jeering threat,
Like screaming birds of Fate
Wheeling to lacerate and rip up this my body,
It is the loud cries of these ~~[illegible]~~ birds of ~~death~~ pain
That gives me peace.

For I hate this ~~my~~ body, which is so dear to me:
My legs, my breast, my belly:
My God, what agony they are to me;
For I dote on them with tenderness, and I hate them,
I hate them bitterly.

My God, that they should always be ~~before~~ with me!
~~Thanks God at last~~ Nay, now at last thank God for the jeopardy,
For the shells, that the question is ~~no~~ now no more before me.

—

RUPERT BROOKE
1887–1915

Autograph manuscript signed of "Sonnet" ("Oh! Death will find me"), dated 25 June 1914. 1 p. 229 x 178 mm. MA 3110. Purchased as the gift of Miss Julia P. Wightman.

In a review of the first volume of *Georgian Poetry* (1912) published in the March 1913 issue of *Rhythm*, D. H. Lawrence asked: "What are the Georgian poets, nearly all, but just bursting into a thick blaze of being?" Such a question as this would become painfully ironic on 4 August 1914, when England entered the war against Germany, but it adequately describes the poetic life of Rupert Brooke—consummate Georgian and "rich-hair'd Youth of Morn"—which ended in April 1915, when Brooke died of septicemia in a French hospital ship off the Greek island of Skyros. Like the generation to which he belonged, Brooke's poetry hesitates while looking forward and backward simultaneously, creating the illusion of an impossibly aged youth, in whom fullness of memory contends for expression with empty eagerness of anticipation. The poem shown here, one of Brooke's most famous sonnets, was composed in 1909, and was inscribed in the notebook of his friend and heir, W. W. Gibson, when Brooke visited him in June 1914, some months before he composed the five great sonnets of 1914. In tone "Oh! Death will find me" is more elegiac than the war sonnets; it anticipates the possibility of looking back from "the last land" and awaiting the approach of one who will come "Amusedly, among the ancient Dead." Like Shelley in "Stanzas Written in Dejection, Near Naples," Brooke was more immediately prophetic than he knew. And yet the expectation of death by a young poet is, as Lawrence remarked after learning of Brooke's death, "all in the saga," a saga about the destruction of youth and poetry. Lawrence told Lady Ottoline Morell that Brooke "was slain by bright Phoebus' shaft," but he was wrong, for Brooke and the generation whose "Greek god" he became perished under the dark shadow of Mars, like any number of generations before and since.

The notebook in which this poem was inscribed also contains poems by Robert Frost, Lascelles Abercrombie and Robert Fitzgerald, among others. The largest collections of Brooke manuscripts are those in the Temple Library of Rugby School and in the Library of King's College, Cambridge.

Sonnet./ Oh! Death will find me, long before I tire/ Of watching you; and swing me suddenly/ Into the shade and loneliness and mire/ Of the last land! There, waiting patiently,

One day, I think, I'll feel a cool wind blowing,/ See a slow light across the Stygian tide,/ And hear the Dead about me stir, unknowing,/ And tremble. And I shall know that you have died,

And watch you, a broadbrowed and smiling dream,/ Pass, light as ever, through the lightless host,/ Quietly ponder, start, and sway, and gleam—/ Most individual and bewildering ghost!—

And turn, and toss your brown delightful head,/ Amusedly, among the ancient Dead./ June 25th 1914 Rupert Brooke

Sonnet.

Oh! Death will find me, long before I tire
Of watching you; and swing me suddenly
Into the shade and loneliness and mire
Of the last land! There, waiting patiently,

One day, I think, I'll feel a cool wind blowing,
See a slow light across the Stygian tide,
And hear the Dead about me stir, unknowing,
And tremble. And *I* shall know that you have died,

And watch you, a broad-browed and smiling dream,
Pass, light as ever, through the lightless host,
Quietly ponder, start, and sway, and gleam,—
Most individual and bewildering ghost!—

And turn, and toss your brown delightful head,
Amusedly, among the ancient Dead.

June 25th 1914. Rupert Brooke

Complete Checklist of

British Literary Manuscripts and Autographs in The Pierpont Morgan Library

by Herbert Cahoon, Curator of Autograph Manuscripts

This Checklist includes not only autographs of literary figures but also those of men and women in many related fields who are not primarily thought of as authors but whose manuscripts and letters may have literary interest. Actors and actresses, architects, artists, bibliographers, booksellers, calligraphers, churchmen, collectors, engravers, explorers, librarians, patrons, physicians, publishers, scientists and sculptors are also listed here with a brief description of how they are represented in the Morgan Library's collections. Letters and manuscripts of predominantly military or political leaders have not been included, and those of composers and musicians may be found in *The Mary Flagler Cary Music Collection*, published by the Library in 1970. Manuscripts of the earliest English authors such as Bede, Chaucer and Langland, and which are not autograph, may be found listed in the *Census of Medieval and Renaissance Manuscripts in the United States and Canada*, edited by Seymour de Ricci and W. J. Wilson (New York, 1940) and in its *Supplement*, edited by W. H. Bond (New York, 1962).

In general, The *National Union Catalog* has been followed for forms of name entry and dates. Nobility are entered under their titles and not under family names. Additional information may be found on many of these manuscripts and letters in the various publications of the Library, especially in exhibition catalogues and in the *Reports to the Fellows*, which began in 1950.

Among the names which appear frequently in this Checklist as recipients of letters are those of William Angus Knight (1836–1916), Professor of Moral Philosophy at the University of St. Andrews, and Sir John Everett Millais, Baronet (1829–1896), the painter. Large groups of letters addressed to them acquired by the Library have been catalogued by writers.

The following bibliographical abbreviations have been used in this Checklist: Acs (autograph card signed), Ad (autograph document), Ads (autograph document signed), Al (autograph letter), Als (autograph letter signed), Ams (autograph manuscript), Aps (autograph postal card, or postcard, signed), Ds (document signed), Ls (letter signed), n.d. (no date), Tls (typed letter signed). The numbers in parentheses refer to the total number of items immediately preceding; these numbers are followed by the range of dates of the items and frequently, when known, the name or names of recipients.

I wish to thank my predecessor in this Curatorship, Dr. George K. Boyce, for descriptions he prepared for many of our letters and manuscripts; Dr. Charles A. Ryskamp, Director; Mr. Verlyn Klinkenborg, my associate in this compilation; Mr. J. Rigbie Turner, Assistant Curator of Autograph and Music Manuscripts; Mrs. Sara Feldman Guérin; and the many students and scholars of England and America who have assisted over the years in helping to assign a date, decipher a difficult text or name, and who have shared generously knowledge of their special fields.

ABBOT, GEORGE, 1562–1633. Ds (4) 1612–25.

ABBOTT, EVELYN, 1843–1901. Als (5) 1895–1900 to W. A. Knight.

À BECKETT, ARTHUR WILLIAM, 1844–1909. Als 9 August 1878 to George Grossmith.

À BECKETT, GILBERT ABBOTT, 1811–1856. "Dawn," 1 p. Als (2) 1850, 1855 to Charles Dickens and Horace Mayhew.

À BECKETT, GILBERT ARTHUR, 1837–1891. Als (3) 1866–78.

ABERCROMBIE, LASCELLES, 1881–1938. "The Sale of St. Thomas," 2 pp.

ABERDEEN AND TEMAIR, JOHN CAMPBELL GORDON, 1st Marquis of, 1847–1934. Als, tls (7) 1885–1898 to W. A. Knight.

ABINGTON, FRANCES (BARTON), 1737–1815. Als n.d. to Mr. Webster.

ACLAND, SIR HENRY WENTWORTH DYKE, 1st Bart., 1815–1900. Als (6) 1862–96.

ACLAND, SIR THOMAS DYKE, 1787–1871. Als 30 April 1835 to Bishop McIlvaine.

ACTON, SIR HAROLD, 1904–   . Als 18 June 1961 to Herbert Cahoon.

ACTON, JOHN EMERICH EDWARD DALBERG ACTON, 1st Baron, 1834–1902. Als March 1862 to J. S. Northcote.

ADAIR, SIR ROBERT, 1763–1855. Als 24 May 1844 to Henry Wheaton.

ADAM, ROBERT, 1728–1792. Als (8) 1757–79.

ADAM, WILLIAM, 1751–1839. Als (3) 1784–89.

ADAMS, SARAH FULLER (FLOWER), 1805–1848. "Nearer, my God, to Thee," 2 pp.; sonnet to W. J. Fox, 1 p.

ADDINGTON, ANTHONY, 1713–1790. Als 11 May 1778 to the Marquis of Granby.

ADDISON, JOSEPH, 1672–1719. *Remarks on Several Parts of Italy in 1701* (not autograph), 172 pp.; als, ls (3) 1694/5–1717; ds 31 August 1717. *See also* TICKELL, THOMAS.

"AE": *see* RUSSELL, GEORGE WILLIAM.

AICKIN, JAMES, ca. 1735–1803. Als n.d.

AÏDÉ, CHARLES HAMILTON, 1826–1906. Als (4) 1883–91 and n.d.

AILESBURY, THOMAS BRUCE, 2nd Earl of, 1656–1741. Ds 29 September 1683.

AINGER, ALFRED, 1837–1904. Als (12) 1883–1900 to W. A. Knight.

AINSWORTH, ROBERT, 1660–1743. Als 9 February 1730.

AINSWORTH, WILLIAM HARRISON, 1805–1882. "Ket's Rebellion" [*The Fall of Somerset*] and portions of *Chetwynd Calverley*, *Preston Fight*, *Manchester Rebels* and a novel dealing with Prince Rupert, 558 pp.; als (20) 1839–70; publication agreements (8) 1861–9.

AIRD, THOMAS, 1802–1876. Als (2) 1853, 1858 to Mr. Ebsworth.

AIRY, SIR GEORGE BIDDELL, 1801–1892. Als 15 August 1857 to J. P. Nichol.

ALBEMARLE, GEORGE MONCK, 1st Duke of, 1608–1670. Als (2) 1666 to Lord Berkeley; ls (6) 1655–66; ds (11) 1652–8.

ALBERT, consort of Queen Victoria, 1819–1861. Memorandum regarding Sir James Graham, 1 p.; als and ls (16) 1838–60.

ALBERT VICTOR, Duke of Clarence and Avondale, 1864–1892. Notebooks (3) 1877–80; als 28 January 1885 to Mrs. Hampden.

ALBERY, JAMES, 1838–1889. Als 13 November 1883 to George Grossmith.

ALDIN, CECIL CHARLES WINDSOR, 1870–1935. Als 16 September 1917 to Mrs. H. J. Byron.

ALDINGTON, RICHARD, 1892–1962. Als, tls (5) 1931–2 to Carlo Linati.

ALEXANDER, MARGARET. Calligraphic manuscript of "Why dost thou shade thy lovely face," by Francis Quarles, 1950, 4 *ll.*

ALFRED, Duke of Saxe-Coburg-Gotha, 1844–1900. Als (31) 1863–99 including 22 to Sir Arthur Sullivan; ds n.d.

ALICE, consort of Louis IV, Grand Duke of Hesse-Darmstadt, 1843–1878. Als (2) 1855, 1858.

ALISON, SIR ARCHIBALD, Bart., 1792–1867. Als 9 June 1852 to Mr. Maitland.

ALLAN, SIR WILLIAM, 1782–1850. Als 7 March 1842 to David Scott.

ALLEN, GEORGE, 1832–1907. Als, tls (11) 1885–1902; ads 1907.

ALLEN, WILLIAM, Cardinal, 1532–1594. Als 15 April 1581.

ALLINGHAM, HELEN (PATERSON), 1848–1926. Als 27 February 1876 to Joan Severn.

ALLINGHAM, WILLIAM, 1824–1889. "The Touchstone," 1 p.; als (2) 1857, 1862 to Mary Howitt.

ALLON, HENRY, 1818–1892. Als (4) 1871–9 to W.A. Knight.

ALMA-TADEMA, LAURENCE, d. 1940. "An undivined tragedy" (page 1 only of the dialogue).

ALMA-TADEMA, SIR LAWRENCE, 1836–1912. Als (7) 1878–99 to Sir John Millais and Mary Millais.

ALMON, JOHN, 1737–1805. Inscriptions in books (3) presented to George Washington.

AMHERST, JEFFREY AMHERST, 1st Baron, 1717–1797. Als, ls (10) 1760–94; ds (2) 1773, 1794.

ANDERSON, JOHN REDWOOD, 1883– "The Queue," 4 pp.

ANDERSON, ROBERT , 1750–1830. Als 13 June 1805 to Thomas Percy, Bishop of Dromore.

ANDRÉ, JOHN, 1751–1780. "Prologue on opening the Theatre at New York, January 9, 1779" (not autograph), 2 pp.; als 7 September 1780 to Colonel Sheldon.

ANDREWES, LANCELOT, 1555–1626. Ds (2) n.d.

ANGELO, DOMENICO, 1716–1802. Als 3 August 1796.

ANGELO, HENRY, 1756–1835. Als (2) 1832, 1834.

ANGLESEY, ARTHUR ANNESLEY, 1st Earl of, 1614–1686. Ds (2) 1660, 1680.

ANSTEY, CHRISTOPHER, 1724–1805. Als 9 January 1784 to Richard Jackson.

"ANSTEY, F.": *see* GUTHRIE.

ANSTIS, JOHN, 1669–1744. Ds n.d.

ANSTRUTHER, SIR JOHN, 1753–1811. Als (2) n.d. to Sir Peter Burrell.

APPERLEY, CHARLES JAMES, 1778–1843. Poems (2), 3 pp.; als n.d. to Henry Colburn.

ARBLAY, FRANCES BURNEY D', 1752–1840. 2 pp. of *Evelina;* "First Edition of Cecilia/Advertisement," 1 p.; als (51) 1787–1831 mainly to members of her family, including 41 to her brother James; with letters (11) addressed to her; and letters and papers of other members of her family including 4 of her father, 50 of her brother James and 4 of her brother Charles.

ARBUTHNOT, GEORGE, 1846–1922. Als 15 August 1883 to W. W. Baldwin.

ARCHER, WILLIAM, 1856–1924. Als (8) 1882–94, of which 6 are to W. E. Henley, 1 to W. M. Thomas and 1 to Robert Browning.

ARCHER, WILLIAM GEORGE, 1907–1979. Als 30 June 1931 to E. McKnight Kauffer.

ARGYLL, GEORGE DOUGLAS CAMPBELL, 8th Duke of, 1823–1900. Als (12) 1881–97 to W. A. Knight and Sir John Millais.

ARGYLL, JOHN GEORGE EDWARD HENRY DOUGLAS SUTHERLAND CAMPBELL, 9th Duke of, 1845–1914. Poem, 1 p.; tribute to the memory of J. C. Shairp, 3 pp.; als (16) 1869–1904 including 10 to W. A. Knight; ds (2) 1868, 1869.

ARLINGTON, HENRY BENNET, 1st Earl of, 1618–1685. Als, ls (4) 1668–81; ds (12) 1665–81.

ARMFIELD, ANNE CONSTANCE (SMEDLEY), 1881–1941. "Notes on Prospice," with autograph notes by Robert Browning, 4 pp.

ARMSTRONG, CECIL FERARD. Als 19 December 1908 to G. F. Byron.

ARMSTRONG, JOHN, 1709–1779. Als (2) 1762 and n.d.

ARMSTRONG, TERENCE IAN FYTTON ("JOHN GAWSWORTH"), 1912–1970. "Twilights (for W. W. G.)," 1 p.

ARNE, THOMAS AUGUSTINE, 1710–1778. Als 1770 to David Garrick.

ARNOLD, SIR EDWIN, 1832–1904. "The Gita Govinda, or Indian Song of Songs," 86 pp.; "The Punjab Wife," 10 pp.; als (5) 1890 and n.d.

ARNOLD, MATTHEW, 1822–1888. Als (26) 1858–88 including 16 to W. A. Knight and 5 to Sir John Millais.

ARNOLD, SAMUEL JAMES, 1774–1852. Als 22 November 1815.

ARNOLD, THOMAS, 1795–1842. Als (2) 1841 and n.d.

ARNOLD, THOMAS, 1823–1900. Als 5 September 1887 to W. A. Knight.

ARUNDEL AND SURREY, THOMAS HOWARD, 2nd Earl of, 1586–1646. Als 23 June 1636 to Charles I.

ASCHAM, ROGER, 1515?–1568. Presentation inscription in Xenophon, *Cyri Paediae* (Paris, 1538–9).

ASHBEE, CHARLES ROBERT, 1863–1942. Als 21 July 1899 to Colonel Prideaux.

ASHBY-STERRY, JOSEPH, d. 1917. Als 11 September 1878 to George Grossmith.

ASHE, ST. GEORGE, 1658?–1718. Als 23 February 1707/8 to Jonathan Swift and Sir Andrew Fountaine.

ASHPITEL, ARTHUR, 1807–1869. Als (2) 1858 and n.d. to S. L. Sotheby.

ASHTON, WINIFRED ("CLEMENCE DANE"), d. 1965. "How clear she shines!" [*Wild Decembers*], 126 *ll.* (corrected typescript); als n.d. to Belle da Costa Greene.

ASQUITH: *see* OXFORD AND ASQUITH.

ASTLE, THOMAS, 1735–1803. Als (4) 1768–91 and n.d.

ASTLEY, SIR JOHN DUGDALE, 3rd Bart., 1828–1894. Als (2) January 1880 to J. E. Millais.

ATTERBURY, FRANCIS, 1662–1732. Als (2) 1713 and n.d.

AUDEN, WYSTAN HUGH, 1907–1973. Review of Hindemith's *A Composer's World*, 5 pp.; illustrations and calligraphic manuscripts, by Robert Andrew Parker, for *The Dog Beneath the Skin* and *The Ascent of F.6*, by Auden and Christopher Isherwood, 12 pp. and 13 pp.; als (2) 1943, tls 1964 to Herbert Cahoon.

AUGUSTUS FREDERICK, Duke of Sussex, 1773–1843. Extracts from the Bible, 246 pp.; als (44) 1792–1841 including 26 to Sir William Hamilton.

AUSTEN, JANE, 1775–1817. *Lady Susan*, 158 pp.; *Northanger Abbey* (title only), 1 p.; "Plan of a Novel according to Hints from Various Quarters," 4 pp.; *The Watsons*, the first 6 *ll.*; miscellaneous fragments (4) including memoranda on the dates of writing several novels and her profits, and of personal accounts December 1807; als (51) 1796–1816 including 41 to her sister Cassandra. With als (2) 1817 of Cassandra Elizabeth Austen and her list of the novels of Jane Austen with dates of their composition, 2 pp.

AUSTEN-LEIGH, AUGUSTUS, 1840–1905. Als 3 December 1889 to O. F. Adams.

AUSTIN, ALFRED, 1835–1913. Als (8) 1888–96 including 5 to Sir John Millais.

AUSTIN, JOHN, 1790–1859. Als 28 October 1819.

AVEBURY, JOHN LUBBOCK, Baron, 1834–1913. Als, tls (23) 1883–1907 to W. A. Knight and Sir John Millais.

AYLMER, JOHN, 1521–1594. Ds n.d.

AYSCOUGH, SAMUEL, 1745–1804. Als 18 August 1800 to Henry Ellis.

AYTOUN, WILLIAM EDMONSTOUNE, 1813–1865. Als n.d. to Mr. Bell.

BABBAGE, CHARLES, 1792–1871. Als (2) 1849, 1864 to Mrs. Crosse.

BABINGTON, GERVAISE, 1550–1610. Ds 23 May 1596.

BACON, ANN (COOKE), Lady, 1528–1610. Ds (2) 14 May 1565 and n.d.

BACON, FRANCIS, Viscount St. Albans, 1561–1626. Autograph opinion signed ca. 1595–6, 1 p.; transcript of his submission to the House of Lords 22 April 1621 with autograph corrections, 4 pp. "Admonition to Sir Edward Coke" (attributed to Bacon), 20 pp. "The Charge of Sir Francis Bacon . . . touching Duells uppon an Information in the Starr-chamber against Preiste and Wright" [with 12 other Charges and Speeches], 98 pp.; "An Essay or Character of a King," 5 pp. (All contemporary copies.) Als (2) 1604, 1616 to Sir Nicholas Bacon and Sir Thomas Monson; ds (3) 1597, 1615, 1616.

BACON, JOHN, 1740–1799. Autograph verse unsigned, 1 p.; als (3) 1792, 1797.

BACON, JOHN, 1777–1859. Als (2) 3 March 1813 to Richard Cosway and n.d.

BACON, SIR NATHANIEL, Bart., 1547–1622. Ds 28 February 1598.

BACON, SIR NICHOLAS, 1509–1579. Als 14 April 1576 to his son Nathaniel; ls 7 October 1563; ds (7) 1560–79 and n.d.

BACON, SIR NICHOLAS, 1st Bart., d. 1624. Als 6 February 1591 to his brother Nathaniel; ds (2) 1565, 1579/80.

BADEN-POWELL, AGNES SMYTH, 1858–1945. Acs n.d. to W. A. Knight.

BAGOT, WALTER, 1731–1806. Als (9) 1785–94 to William Cowper.

BAILEY, BENJAMIN, 1791–1853. An account of his interview with [John Gibson] Lockhart in July 1818, 7 pp.; als (13) 1818–21 to John Taylor.

BAILLIE, JOANNA, 1762–1851. Als (6) 1820–7 and n.d.

BAILY, EDWARD HODGES, 1788–1867. Als (2) 1852 and n.d.

BAIN, ALEXANDER, 1818–1903. Als (8) 1869–96 and n.d. to W. A. Knight; ds n.d.

BAIN, FRANCIS WILLIAM, 1863–1940. Als (2) 1911, 1926 to S. C. Cockerell.

BAIRDSMITH, FLORENCE (DE QUINCEY). Als (9) 1887–1901 to W. A. Knight.

BAKER, HENRY, 1698–1774. Als 10 June 1758.

BAKER, SIR HENRY WILLIAMS, Bart., 1821–1877. Als 7 November 1871 to W. A. Knight.

BALDWIN, STANLEY BALDWIN, 1st Earl, 1867–1947. Als, tls (6) 1923–40.

BALFOUR, ARTHUR JAMES BALFOUR, 1st Earl of, 1848–1930. Als, tls, ls (50) 1874–1907, including 43 to W. A. Knight and 4 to W. E. Henley.

BALLANTYNE, JAMES, 1772–1833. Als (3) 1801–25; ads (2) 1821, 1822; ds 14 November 1823.

BALLANTYNE, JOHN, 1774–1821. Diary, 18 February 1819–15 June 1821, containing copies of letters and accounts bearing on the printing of Scott's works, 110 pp.; als 1816? to C. K. Sharpe.

BALLANTYNE, THOMAS, 1806–1871. Als 18 August 1841.

BALMANNO, ROBERT, 1780–1861. Als 25 October 1852 to G. P. Putnam.

BANCROFT, MARIE EFFIE (WILTON), Lady, 1839–1921. Als (4) n.d.

BANCROFT, RICHARD, 1544–1610. Als 1609; ds 13 November 1605.

BANCROFT, SIR SQUIRE BANCROFT, 1841–1926. Als (14) 1878–1926.

BANDINEL, BULKELEY, 1781–1861. Als (16) 1851–60 to S. L. Sotheby.

BANIM, JOHN, 1798–1842. Als 30 December 1830 to A. F. R. Lesser.

BANIM, MICHAEL, 1796–1874. Als 2 November 1863 to Chapman & Hall.

BANKS, ISABELLA VARLEY, 1821–1897. Als 23 May 1870 to Benjamin Webster.

BANKS, SIR JOSEPH, 1743–1820. Als (11) 1786–1819.

BANNISTER, JOHN, 1760–1836. Als (6) 1803–33; ds November 1804.

BARBAULD, ANNA LETITIA (AIKIN), 1743–1825. Als (7) 1782–1813 and n.d.

BARETTI, GIUSEPPE MARCO ANTONIO, 1719–1789. Als 2 September 1768 to Captain Faulkner.

BARHAM, RICHARD HARRIS, 1788–1845. "The Jackdaw of Rheims," 8 pp.; als (4) 1825–44 and n.d.

BARING, MAURICE, 1874–1945. Als 7 February 1900 to H. B. Forman.

BARING-GOULD, SABINE, 1834–1924. "Onward, Christian Soldiers," 1 p.; als (2) 1864 and n.d.

BARKER, THOMAS, 1769–1847. Als ca. 1805 to Mr. Pratt.

BARLOW, THOMAS, 1607–1691. Als 23 January 1672 to Charles Spilman.

BARNADO, THOMAS JOHN, 1845–1905. Als 25 November 1875 to Mrs. Salton.

BARNARD, CHARLOTTE ALINGTON, 1830–1869. "There's sun beyond the rainfall," 1 p.

BARRET, GEORGE, ca. 1732–1784. Als n.d.

BARRET, GEORGE, d. 1842. Ads 22 January 1827.

BARRETT, WILSON, 1846–1904. Als 5 November 1884 to Joan Severn.

BARRIE, SIR JAMES MATTHEW, Bart., 1860–1937. *XYZ. A Comedy [The Admirable Crichton]*, ams, 88 *ll.*, annotated typewritten prompt copy, 4 vols.; *Shall We Join the Ladies?* with explanatory note by the author, 20 pp.; als (45) 1891–1928 including 42 to W. E. Henley and his family.

BARRINGTON, DAINES, 1727–1800. Als (3) 1769–75.

BARRINGTON, RUTLAND, 1853–1922. Als (10) 1885–1900.

BARRINGTON, SHUTE, 1734–1826. Als (3) 1788–1816.

BARRON, WILLIAM, d. 1803. Als 3 January 1780.

BARROW, SIR JOHN, 1764–1848. Als 22 May 1845 to Henry Paterson, Jr.

BARRY, SIR CHARLES, 1795–1860. Als (5) 1836–53.

BARRY, JAMES, 1741–1806. Als (3) 1786, 1801 and n.d.

BARRY, SPRANGER, 1717?–1777. Als 31 January 1769 to David Garrick.

BARTLEY, GEORGE, 1782?–1858. Als (3) 1813, 1852 and n.d.

BARTON, BERNARD, 1784–1849. Als (4) 1814–46.

BARTON, THOMAS, d. 1683. Als 13 November 1661 to the Earl of Clarendon.

BATES, HERBERT ERNEST, 1905–1974. "In view of the Fact That . . . ," 12 *ll.*

BATHURST, ALLEN BATHURST, 1st Earl, 1684–1775. "On the death of Mr. Southern," 1 p.; ads (2) 1763, 1768.

BATHURST, HENRY BATHURST, 2nd Earl, 1714–1794. Als (3) 1733–90; ds 18 November 1790.

BAX, SIR ARNOLD EDWARD TREVOR, 1883–1953. Als (3) n.d.

BAXTER, CHARLES, 1848–1919. Als 21 January 1903 to W. E. Henley.

BAXTER, RICHARD, 1615–1691. "Address to the Reader," ams, n.d.; "A Preface opening the true state of the controversie between the Papists & the Protestants . . . ," 5 April 1664, 6 pp.

BAYLISS, SIR WYKE, 1835–1906. Als 24 February 1888 to Sir John Millais.

BAYLY, THOMAS HAYNES, 1797–1839. "My married Daughter could you see!," 2 pp.

BAYNES, ARTHUR HAMILTON, 1854–1942. Als 8 November 1888 to W. A. Knight.

BEACONSFIELD: *see* DISRAELI, BENJAMIN.

BEALE, DOROTHEA, 1831–1906. Als (2) 1894, 1901.

BEATTIE, JAMES, 1735–1803. Als (2) 1771, 1779.

BEAUMONT, SIR GEORGE HOWLAND, 7th Bart., 1753–1827. Als (11) 1803–26 including 3 to W. L. Bowles and 3 to S. T. Coleridge.

BECKFORD, WILLIAM, 1760–1844. Als (2) 1788 and n.d.

BEDFORD, JOHN RUSSELL, 9th Duke of, 1766–1839. Als 12 February 1828 to William Nicol.

BEECHEY, SIR WILLIAM, 1753–1839. Als (3) n.d.

BEERBOHM, SIR MAX, 1872–1956. "The Golden Drugget," 5 pp.; als (6) 1905–29 and n.d.

BEITH, SIR JOHN HAY ("IAN HAY"), 1876–1952. Als, tls (3) 1917–38.

BELL, VANESSA (STEPHEN), 1879–1961. Als (83), aps (6), ca. 1907–36 to J. M. Keynes.

BELL, WILLIAM, 1626–1683. Als 15 January 1682/3 to Dudley North.

BELLEW, JOHN CHIPPENDALL MONTESQUIEU, 1823–1874. Als (2) 1871.

BELLOC, ANNE LOUISE (SWANTON), 1796–1881. Als (2) 1847 and n.d.

BELLOC, HILAIRE, 1870–1953. "Ballade of Hell & of Mrs. Roebeck," 1 p.; "Cautionary Tale, John Vavassour, who lost a fortune by throwing stones," 3 pp.

BENGER, ELIZABETH OGILBY, 1778–1827. Als (2) 1822 and n.d.

BENLOWES, EDWARD, 1602–1676. Inscription and notes in his *Theophila* (1652).

BENN, ALFRED WILLIAM, 1843–1915. Als 9 March 1898 to W. A. Knight.

BENNETT, ARNOLD, 1867–1931. "Books & Persons [mainly about Dickens and Sterne]," 2 pp.; als, tls (25) including 21 to E. McKnight Kauffer.

BENNETT, JOSEPH, 1831–1911. Als 14 May 1884 to Sir Arthur Sullivan.

BENSON, ARTHUR CHRISTOPHER, 1862–1925. "The Book of Job, the Song of Songs, Lamentations, Prophets, etc.," corrected typescript, 71 pp.; als (6) 1907–11 including 5 to Joan Severn.

BENSON, EDWARD FREDERIC, 1867–1940. Als 2 July 1925 to S. C. Cockerell.

BENSON, EDWARD WHITE, 1829–1896. Als (4) 1886–9.

BENSON, SIR FRANK ROBERT, 1858–1939. Ls (2) 20 and 21 May 1904 to W. A. Knight.

BENTHAM, EDWARD, 1707–1776. Als 4 October 1735 to Robert Hoblyn.

BENTHAM, JEREMY, 1748–1832. "Indications respecting Lord Eldon," 3 pp.; als 12 February 1831 to Dr. Southwood Smith; ads 3 July 1811.

BENTLEY, GEORGE, 1828–1895. Als (2) 1877 to Joseph Bennett.

BENTLEY, RICHARD, 1662–1742. Ads 23 May 1732.

BERENGER, RICHARD, d. 1782. Als (3) 1772 and n.d.

BERESFORD, CHARLES WILLIAM DE LA POER BERESFORD, 1st Baron, 1846–1919. "The Powers and China," 20 pp.; als 3 February 1888 to Sir John Millais.

BERKELEY, GEORGE, 1685–1753. Als 5 September 1728 to the Bishop of London.

BERKELEY, JOHN BERKELEY, 1st Baron, d. 1678. Als, ls (4) 1676–7; ds (3) 1643–63.

BERNAL, RALPH, d. 1854. Als 15 October 1851.

BERRY, MARY, 1763–1852. Als (10) 1783–1830 including 7 to Horace Walpole. Written with her sister Agnes Berry, 1764–1852.

BERWICK, JAMES FITZ-JAMES, 1st Duke of, 1670–1734. Als, ls (5) 1710–32; ds 6 and 7 November 1701.

BESANT, ANNIE (WOOD), 1847–1933. Als 10 July 1889 to T. J. Cobden-Sanderson.

BEVERIDGE, WILLIAM, 1637–1708. Als 7 November 1688.

BEWICK, THOMAS, 1753–1828. Als 4 August 1826.

BICKERSTAFFE, ISAAC, 1735?–1812? Als 26 January 1768 to George Colman; ads n.d.

BICKERSTETH, EDWARD, 1786–1850. Sermon notes, 8 pp.; ls 4 March 1846 to Bishop McIlvaine.

BICKERSTETH, ROBERT, 1816–1884. Als 6 December 1858 to Baroness Burdett-Coutts.

BINDLEY, JAMES, 1737–1818. Als n.d. to John Scott.

BINNS, HENRY BRYAN, b. 1873. Als 27 November 1905 to Laurens Maynard.

BIRD, EDWARD, 1772–1819. Als 12 June 1817 to F. L. Chantrey.

BIRDWOOD, WILLIAM BIRDWOOD, 1st Baron, 1865–1951. Als 5 January 1934 to Sir Sydney Cockerell.

BIRLEY, SIR ROBERT, 1903– . "Eton College Library," an address at the Morgan Library 4 May 1977, 16 *ll.*

BIRRELL, AUGUSTINE, 1850–1933. Als 8 September 1922 to Mrs. Cobden-Sanderson.

BLACK, WILLIAM, 1841–1898. *Judith Shakespeare* (1 p. only); als (10) 1876–90 and n.d.

BLACKBURN, VERNON, d. 1907. Als 4 November 1890 to W. E. Henley.

BLACKIE, JOHN STUART, 1809–1895. Als (8) 1834–95 including 5 to W. A. Knight.

BLACKMORE, RICHARD DODDRIDGE, 1825–1900. Als 9 October 1889 to Edward Marston.

BLACKSTONE, SIR WILLIAM, 1723–1780. Als 18 June 1779 to Charles Eyles.

BLACKWOOD, ALGERNON, 1869–1951. Als 29 January 1932 to Nicholas Carroll.

BLADES, WILLIAM, 1824–1890. Als 12 October 1859 to S. L. Sotheby.

BLAGDEN, SIR CHARLES, 1748–1820. Als (3) 1784, 1814 to Sir Joseph Banks and Sir Philip Francis.

BLAGDEN, ISABELLA, 1816?–1873. Als 13 July 1861 to Sophia Eckley.

BLAIKIE, WALTER BIGGAR, 1847–1928. Als 25 January 1903 to W. E. Henley.

BLAIR, HUGH, 1718–1800. Als (8) 1782–96.

BLAKE, WILLIAM, 1757–1827. Illustrations (12) to Milton's "L'Allegro" and "Il Penseroso," with notes and transcription of the lines of the poems which his designs illustrate, 12 pp.; the Pickering Manuscript, ca. 1807, 22 pp.; "To my dear Friend Mrs. Anna Flaxman" (in the autograph of Mrs. Blake), 2 pp.; als (7) 1800–26 to John Flaxman, William Hayley and John Linnell; ads 14 July 1826. Among the drawings by Blake in the Library are watercolor illustrations (21) to the *Book of Job*, drawings (3) for woodcuts in *The Pastorals of Virgil* (1821), a drawing and a sketch for Dante's *Inferno* and a design for an engraving in Hayley's *Ballads* (1802 or 1805).

BLANCHARD, EDWARD LITT LAMAN, 1820–1889. Als 19 January 1854 to E. T. Smith.

BLANCHARD, SAMUEL LAMAN, 1804–1845. Als (2) 1840 and n.d.

BLESSINGTON, MARGUERITE (POWER) FARMER GARDINER, Countess of, 1789–1849. "To Sir William Massey Stanley, bart.," 1 p.; "The Lilly [*sic*]," 1 p.; als (4) 1833–46.

BLEWITT, OCTAVIAN, 1810–1884. Als 8 May 1858 to S. L. Sotheby.

BLIGH, WILLIAM, 1754–1817. Ds 18 August 1801.

BLIND, KARL, 1826–1907. "The Transvaal War," 81 pp.

BLOMFIELD, CHARLES JAMES, 1786–1857. Als (5) 1844–52.

BLOMFIELD, SIR REGINALD THEODORE, 1856–1942. Als 23 March 1921 to T. J. Cobden-Sanderson.

BLUMENFELD, RALPH DAVID, 1864–1948. Als, tls, 1927, 1929.

BLUNDEN, EDMUND CHARLES, 1896–1974. "Art thou gone in haste?," "Elegy," "Masks of Time," "The Masquerade" and "Warning to Troops," 5 pp.

BLUNT, WILFRID SCAWEN, 1840–1922. Sonnets (2), 2 pp.; als (4) 1889–1906.

BOADEN, JAMES, 1762–1839. Als (2) 1825 and n.d. to John Taylor.

BODLEY, SIR THOMAS, 1545–1613. Als 27 May ca. 1589–98 to Christiaan Huygens.

BOEHM, SIR JOSEPH EDGAR, 1st Bart., 1834–1890. Als (7) 1879–89 to Sir John Millais and John Ruskin.

BOHN, HENRY GEORGE, 1796–1884. Als 22 September 1859 to S. L. Sotheby.

BOHN, JAMES STUART BURGES, 1803–1880. Als (2) 1855 to S. L. Sotheby.

BOLINGBROKE, HENRY ST. JOHN, 1st Viscount, 1678–1751. Als (11) 1712–40 including 5 to Charles Ford; ds (8) 1707–13.

BOLTON, GAMBLER, 1854–1928. Als 20 February 1892 to Frederick Keppel.

BOLTON, GUY, 1884–1979. Als, tls, acs (20) ca. 1960–78 to Mrs. Edward Hillman.

BOLTON, SIR RICHARD, 1570?–1648. Ds 24 March 1636.

BOND, SIR EDWARD AUGUSTUS, 1815–1898. Als (2) 1858 to S. L. Sotheby.

BONE, HENRY, 1755–1834. Als 26 May 1817.

BONE, HENRY PIERCE, 1779–1855. Ads 9 April 1839.

BONE, SIR MUIRHEAD, 1875–1953. Als (2) 1921, 1942 to Sir Sydney Cockerell.

BONNEY, THOMAS GEORGE, 1833–1923. Acs (2) 1898 to W. A. Knight.

BOONE, THOMAS. Als (10) 1855 and n.d. to S. L. Sotheby.

BOOTH, BALLINGTON, 1859–1940. Tls 4 September 1887 to *Harper's Weekly.*

BOOTH, BARTON, 1681–1733. Ds 20 March 1713/4.

BOSCAWEN, EDWARD, 1711–1761. Ds 1 October 1747.

BOSWELL, SIR ALEXANDER, 1775–1822. Als (2) 1792, 1821.

BOSWELL, EUPHEMIA, 1774–1834. Als 10 August 1807.

BOSWELL, JAMES, 1740–1795. Als (97) 1758–95 to the Rev. William Temple; als (3) 1765–8 to Sir Alexander Dick; with letters (17) written by or to members of the Boswell family or to Temple.

BOSWELL, JAMES, 1778–1822. Als (4) 1795 to the Rev. William Temple.

BOSWELL, MARGARET (MONTGOMERIE), d. 1790. Als 29 August 1787 to her daughter Euphemia.

BOSWORTH, JOSEPH, 1789–1876. Als 14 July 1825 to J. H. Wiffen.

BOTFIELD, BERIAH, 1807–1863. Als (3) 1854–5 to S. L. Sotheby.

BOTTOMLEY, GORDON, 1874–1948. "The Ploughman," 1 p.; "To May Morris in Kelmscott," 1 p.; als 26 November 1939 to Sir Sydney Cockerell.

BOUCICAULT, DION, 1822?–1890. Als (6) 1854–90.

BOUGHTON, GEORGE HENRY, 1833–1905. Als 22 June 1883 to George Grossmith.

BOUQUET, HENRY, 1719–1765. Als (2) 1763.

BOURGEOIS, SIR PETER FRANCIS, 1756–1811. Als (2) 1810 and n.d.

BOURNE, HENRY RICHARD FOX, 1837–1909. Als 2 June 1898 to W. A. Knight.

BOWEN, CHARLES SYNGE CHRISTOPHER BOWEN, Baron, 1835–1894. Als (2) n.d.

BOWRING, SIR JOHN, 1792–1872. Als (5) 1828–41 including 4 to Henry Wheaton.

BOWYER, ROBERT, 1758–1834. Als 2 November 1824.

BOWYER, WILLIAM, 1699–1777. Extract from an essay on the Roman Senate, 1 p.; als 29 January 1759.

BOYD, ANDREW KENNEDY HUTCHINSON, 1825–1899. Als 22 December 1867.

BOYDELL, JOHN, 1719–1804. Als 24 May 1791 to Sir Peter Burrell.

BOYDELL, JOSIAH, 1752–1817. Als (3) 1792, 1812 and n.d.

BOYLE, GEORGE DAVID, 1828–1901. Als (24) 1881–1901 to W. A. Knight.

BOYSE, SAMUEL, 1708–1749. Als 7 May 1744 to Daniel McKercher.

BRABOURNE, EDWARD HUGESSEN KNATCHBULL-HUGESSEN, 1st Baron, 1829–1893. Als 16 January 1891.

BRADBURY, WILLIAM, 1800–1869. Als n.d. to Robert Balmanno.

BRADDON, MARY ELIZABETH: *see* MAXWELL, MARY ELIZABETH (BRADDON).

BRADFORD, MARY FRANCES, 1839–1913. Als 30 June 1863 to M. A. Bell.

BRADLEY, ANDREW CECIL, 1851–1935. Als (7) 1896–1914 including 6 to W. A. Knight.

BRADLEY, EDWARD, 1827–1889. *Adventures of Mr Verdant Green*, Part I, Chap. VI, to Part II, Chap. X, 74 pp.; original drawings, cartoons and illustrations (150) for contributions to *Punch* and other periodicals, some of them dated 1848–57; als (2) 1877 to J. E. Millais.

BRADLEY, GEORGE GRANVILLE, 1821–1903. Als (11) 1883–93 to W. A. Knight.

BRADLEY, KATHERINE HARRIS: *see* "FIELD, MICHAEL."

BRADSTREET, JOHN, 1711–1774. Als 3 June 1759 to Abraham Mortier.

BRASSEY, THOMAS BRASSEY, 1st Earl, 1836–1918. Als (2) 1894, 1896 to Sir John Millais and Mary Millais.

BRAY, ANNA ELIZA (KEMPE) STOTHARD, 1790–1883. Als (2) 1826, 1849.

BREADALBANE, ALMA IMOGEN LEONORA CHARLOTTA (GRAHAM) CAMPBELL, Marchioness of, 1854–1932. Als (39) 1892–5 to W. A. Knight.

BRETT, JOHN, 1831–1902. Als 24 February 1881 to M.B. Huish.

BREWSTER, SIR DAVID, 1781–1868. Als 14 April 1830 to J. G. Lockhart.

BRIDGES, ROBERT SEYMOUR, 1844–1930. Als 11 January 1926 to S. C. Cockerell.

BRIGHT, HENRY ARTHUR, 1830–1884. Als (6) 1860–5 to Mrs. Nathaniel Hawthorne.

BRIGHT, JOHN, 1811–1889. Als (27) 1844–88.

BRIGHT, RICHARD, 1789–1858. Als 5 May 1858.

BRISTOL, GEORGE DIGBY, 2nd Earl of, 1612–1677. Speech in the House of Commons, 1663, 5 pp. (contemporary copy); ds n.d.

BRITTON, JOHN, 1771–1857. Als 17 February 1825 to J. H. Wiffen.

BROADLEY, ALEXANDER MEYRICK, 1847–1916. Als (2) 7–8 May 1911 to J. Pierpont Morgan..

BROCKEDON, WILLIAM, 1787–1854. Als (3) 1819 and n.d.

BRODERIP, WILLIAM JOHN, 1789–1859. Als (2) 1824, 1850.

BRODIE, SIR BENJAMIN COLLINS, 1783–1862. Als 3 January 1855.

BRONTË, ANNE, 1820–1849. "To Cowper," 3 pp.; "To —" ("I will not mourn thee, lovely one"), 3 pp.; "A Hymn" ("Eternal powers of earth and air!"), 4 pp.; "The Captive Dove," 3 pp.; "The Consolation," 4 pp.; "Tis strange to think," 3 pp.; "A Word to the Calvinists," 4 pp.; "Night," 2 pp.; "My soul is awakened, my spirit is soaring," 2 pp.; "The North Wind," 3 pp.; "The Captive's dream," 2 pp.; "The parting," 4 pp.; "The lady of Abyerno's hall," 4 pp.; "Verses to a Child," 3 pp.; "The Bluebell," 4 pp.; "An Orphans Lament," 4 pp.; "Lines written at Thorp Green," 2 pp.; "Maiden, thou were thoughtless once [Self Congratulations]," 4 pp.; "Tell him that earth is not our rest," 2 pp.

BRONTË, CHARLOTTE, 1816–1855. "Arthuriana, or Odds and Ends . . . by Lord Charles A. F. Wellesley," 24 pp.; "Passing Events," 36 pp.; *The Professor*, 339 *ll.* Poems and prose: "The Churchyard, a Poem," "Written on the Summit of a High Mountain in the North of England," "Description of the Duke of Wellington's small palace," "True Pleasure breathes not city air," "Now rolls the sounding ocean," "The Vision," "Now sweetly shines the golden sun," 12 pp. Poems and prose in microscopic handwriting: "Miss Hume's Dream," 2 pp., "The Bridal," 14 pp.; "Two gentlemen in earnest conversation," "Well here I am at Roe-Head," "Now as I have a little bit of time," 4 pp.; "The day is closed, that spectral sun," 3 pp.; prose fragments of a story: "Alexander Percy was a man much known about the country," 1 p., "Leeds and the clotheries of Bradford," 4 pp., "Miss Percy and Miss Thornton being both now settled in Yorkshire," 12 pp., "Hand over the heart," 1 p., "Miss Percy was a pupil in Mrs. Turner's Seminary at Kensington," 1 p.; poems copied and revised from earlier manuscripts: "We take from life one little share," "The Town Besieged," "Presentiment," "Remembrance," "Lament," "Apostacy," "Passion," "Parting," "Life, believe, is not a dream," "If thou be in a lonely place," 22 pp.; exercise book of French translations and exercises, 26 pp.; "The Poetaster. A Drama in two volumes vol II by Lord Charles Wellesley," 16 pp. (microscopic hand); "Catalogue of My Books, with the Periods of their completion up to August 3, 1830," 2 pp.; "Last Will and Testament of Florence Marian Wellesley, Marchioness of Douro," 2 pp. (microscopic hand); als (26) 1834–54 including 10 to Ellen Nussey, 6 to W. S. William, 2 to her father, 1 to Mrs. Gaskell and a draft of a letter to William Wordsworth.

BRONTË, EMILY JANE, 1818–1848. Poems in microscopic handwriting: "And now the house dog stretched once more," 1 p., "Cold in the earth and the deep snow piled above thee," 2 pp., "Companions all day long we've stood," 1 p., "I saw the child one summers day," 1 p., "The night of storms has past," 1 p. "No Coward Soul is Mine" (copy in the hand of Charlotte Brontë), 1 p.

BRONTË, PATRICK, 1777–1861. Sermon, 24 pp.; als (2) 1858 including 1 to Sir Joseph Paxton.

BRONTË, PATRICK BRANWELL, 1817–1848. Prose in microscopic handwriting: "Five years have now elapsed since the close of the Angrian war . . . ," "My Lord, Circumstances which have occurred," "To legion in the received manner," "Matilda, said I to the Countess in the evening," "Upon one of the small plantations," 22 pp.; manuscript relating to the battle of Loango and the political upheavals following it, 20 pp. Poems in microscopic handwriting: "Wide I hear the wild winds sighing," "Still and bright in twilight shining," 12 pp.; "Hours and days my Heart has lain," 1 p.; "Oh all the cares those Noontide airs," 1 p.; "Land of the West! Thy glorious skies," 1 p.; "Upon her dying bed," 1 p.; "As such a hush was like to do?" [prose fragment], 1 p.

BROOKE, FULKE GREVILLE, 1st Baron, 1554–1628. Ls 7 May 1621; ds (4) 1601/2–20.

BROOKE, GUSTAVUS VAUGHAN, 1818–1866. Als 21 October 1853 to E. T. Smith.

BROOKE, SIR JAMES, Rajah of Sarawak, 1803–1868. Als 10 February 1852 to Edward Magrath.

BROOKE, RALPH, 1553–1625. Ds 1614.

BROOKE, RUPERT, 1887–1915. "Sonnet. Oh! Death will find me, long before I tire," 1 p.

BROOKE, STOPFORD AUGUSTUS, 1832–1916. "On the poetry of Wordsworth," 10 pp.; als (61) 1878–1914 including 58 to W. A. Knight.

BROOKFIELD, JANE OCTAVIA (ELTON), 1821–1896. Als (9) 1887 and n.d. including 6 to W. M. Thackeray.

BROOKS, SHIRLEY, 1816–1874. Als (3) 1863, 1873 and n.d.

BROUGH, LIONEL, 1836–1909. Als (2) 1879 and n.d.

BROUGH, ROBERT BARNABAS, 1828–1860. Als (2) 1852, 1858.

BROUGHAM AND VAUX, HENRY PETER BROUGHAM, 1st Baron, 1778–1868. Als (8) 1828–47 and n.d.

BROUGHTON, JOHN CAM HOBHOUSE, Baron: *see* HOBHOUSE.

BROUGHTON, RHODA, 1840–1920. Als (49) 1883–1913 to Sir John Millais and his family and to Joan Severn.

BROUNCKER, WILLIAM BROUNCKER, 2nd Viscount, 1620/1–1684. Ls 2 June 1670, ds 22 June 1672.

BROWN, ALEXANDER CRUM, 1838–1922. Als 6 August 1902 to W. A. Knight.

BROWN, CHARLES ARMITAGE, 1787–1842. "List of Mr. John Keats' Books," 3 pp.; "On some skulls in Beauley Abbey, near Inverness [poem by Keats and Brown]," 4 pp.; als (5) 1820–1 to John Taylor and J. A. Hessey.

BROWN, FORD MADOX, 1821–1893. Diary, January 1856–January 1868, 86 pp.; als 9 June 1854 to Thomas Seddon.

BROWN, JOHN, 1810–1882. Als (5) 1862–81.

BROWN, JOHN TAYLOR, 1811–1901. Als (2) 1887, 1888 to W. A. Knight.

BROWN, LANCELOT, 1715–1783. Als 16 December 1779; ds 2 November 1775.

BROWN, RAWDON LUBBOCK, 1803–1883. Als (18) 1869–81 including 7 to John Ruskin and Joan Severn.

BROWN, SAMUEL, 1817–1856. Als (2) 1847 to J. P. Nichol.

BROWNE, EDWARD GRANVILLE, 1862–1926. Als 30 April 1911 to S. C. Cockerell.

BROWNE, HABLOT KNIGHT ("PHIZ"), 1815–1882. Als (3) 1851 and n.d. to F. E. Smedley; original drawings (65) for the works of Charles Dickens and Charles Lever.

BROWNE, ISAAC HAWKINS, 1745–1818. Als 8 August 1793 to George Romney.

BROWNE, SIR JAMES CRICHTON: *see* CRICHTON-BROWNE.

BROWNE, MARY ANNE, 1812–1844. "Thoughts on a distant-burial place," 3 pp.; als (2) 1840 and n.d.

BROWNE, WILLIAM GEORGE, 1768–1813. Als n.d. to J. Pinkerton.

BROWNING, ELIZABETH BARRETT, 1806–1861. *Aurora Leigh* (corrections for the printer), 12 pp.; "Caterine to Camoens," 3 pp.; "Grateful keep returning spring . . . ," 1 p.; *Last Poems*, 68 pp.; "Plea for the Ragged Schools of London," 4 pp.; "The Sleep," 2 pp.; *Sonnets from the Portuguese*, 27 pp.; als (123) 1810–61 including 58 to George Barrett and 14 to other members of her family with her occasional poems and family letters to her, 46 to R. H. Horne.

BROWNING, ROBERT, 1812–1889. *Asolando*, 100 pp. and corrected proof copy; *Dramatis Personae*, 211 pp.; "Hervé Riel," 5 pp.; "Home Thoughts from Abroad," 1 p.; "How They Brought the Good News," 2 pp.; "A Last Word, To E. B. B.," 6 pp.; "Prospice" (comments on an essay entitled "Notes on Prospice," written by a schoolgirl, Constance Smedley), 2 pp.; notes for his *The Ring and the Book*, 2 pp.; "She was fifteen—had great eyes," 1 p.; "The Twins," 1 p.; Latin tour de force, "Plane te valvam fas est pressisse salutis," 1 p.; als (114) 1840–89 including 47 to Chapman & Hall, 34 to George Barrett, 15 to W. A. Knight, 8 to W. W. Story and his wife. With als (9) 1897–1906 from his son Robert W. Barrett Browning (of which 3 are written by the latter's wife) to W. A. Knight.

BRUMMELL, GEORGE BRYAN ("BEAU"), 1778–1840. Als 11 February 1827 to M. Biré.

BRYANT, JACOB, 1715–1804. Als 18 November 1788.

BRYCE, JAMES BRYCE, Viscount, 1838–1922. "Some thoughts on Commercial Education," 23 pp.; "Stray Thoughts on American Literature," 7 pp.; als (21) 1889–99 to W. A. Knight.

BRYDGES, SIR SAMUEL EGERTON, 1762–1837. "Contrast between Byron and Scott," 3 pp.; articles (3) each headed "Sir Walter Scott," 21 pp.; "Life of Milton" (incomplete), 32 pp.

BUCHAN, JOHN: *see* TWEEDSMUIR.

BUCHANAN, GEORGE, 1506–1582. "Detection of the doeings of Marie Queen of Scottes touching the murther of her Husband," 176 pp.; "De Maria Scotorum Regina . . . ," 45 pp.; "Detectio Mariae, sive, de Maria Scotorum Regina . . . ," 156 pp.; "Epithalamium upon the marriage of Mariae Queene of Scots to the Dauphin of France," 15 pp. (All contemporary copies.)

BUCKINGHAM, GEORGE VILLIERS, 1st Duke of, 1592–1628. Als, ls (3) including 2 to Frederick V, King of Bohemia; ds [after 1617].

BUCKINGHAM, GEORGE VILLIERS, 2nd Duke of, 1628–1687. Als, ls (2) 1670 and n.d.; last will and testament, dated 4 September 1674, 2 pp.

BUCKINGHAM, JAMES SILK, 1786–1855. Als 14 January 1829.

BUCKINGHAM AND NORMANBY, JOHN SHEFFIELD, Duke of, 1648–1721. Als 1717? to Alexander Pope; ds 7 October 1685.

BUCKINGHAMSHIRE, JOHN HOBART, 2nd Earl of, 1723–1793. Als (3) 1765, 1786 and n.d.

BUCKLAND, FRANCIS TREVELYAN, 1826–1880. Als 29 November 1866 to Mrs. Cross.

BUCKLAND, WILLIAM, 1784–1856. Als 9 April 1846 to W. H. Brookfield.

BUCKSTONE, JOHN BALDWIN, 1802–1879. Als (3) 1870 and n.d.

BULLEN, ARTHUR HENRY, 1857–1920. Als 23 May 1903 to S. C. Cockerell.

BULLEN, FRANK THOMAS, 1857–1915. Preface to an unidentified pamphlet, 1 p.; als 5 October 1897 to Sir James T. Knowles.

BULLOCH, JAMES MALCOLM, 1867–1938. Tls, 7 January 1918, to Percy Home.

BULMER, WILLIAM, 1757–1830. Als n.d.

BULWER, SIR HENRY LYTTON: *see* DALLING AND BULWER.

BULWER-LYTTON: *see* Lytton.

BUNBURY, SIR HENRY EDWARD, 1778–1860. Als (3) 1804–29.

BUNYAN, JOHN, 1628–1688. Warrant, 4 March 1674/5, addressed to the constables of Bedford, under which Bunyan was apprehended and imprisoned; the name "John Bunyan" written on the title page of *The Whole Book of Psalmes* (Cambridge, 1637).

BURDER, GEORGE, 1752–1832. "Comparison between Wordsworth and Byron," 39 pp.

BURDETT, SIR FRANCIS, Bart., 1770–1844. Als (3) 1821–39.

BURDETT-COUTTS, ANGELA GEORGINA, Baroness, 1814–1906. Als, ls (6) 1842–71. *See also* DICKENS.

BURGES, SIR JAMES BLAND, Bart., 1752–1824. Als 29 February 1788.

BURGESS, THOMAS, 1756–1837. Als 20 March 1804.

BURGHLEY, WILLIAM CECIL, Baron: *see* CECIL.

BURGOYNE, JOHN, 1722–1792. "Articles of Convention between Lt. General Burgoyne and Major General Gates at Saratoga, 16 October 1777," signed, 2 pp.; als (5) 1764–82; ds 30 September 1777.

BURKE, EDMUND, 1729–1797. Last will and testament, dated 30 January 1797; als, al (30) 1757–96; ads 10 February 1788; with family letters and letters from other persons to or concerning Burke.

BURNAND, SIR FRANCIS COWLEY, 1836–1917. Als (19) 1869–98. *See also:* GILBERT, SIR WILLIAM SCHWENCK.

BURNE-JONES, SIR EDWARD COLEY, Bart., 1833–1898. Als (47) 1871–97 including 38 to John Ruskin and 5 to Sir John Millais and Mary Millais. With als (2) 1883, 1917 of his wife, Georgiana (Macdonald) Burne-Jones and als 1897 of his son, Sir Philip Burne-Jones, 2nd Bart.

BURNES, SIR ALEXANDER, 1805–1841. Als 25 April 1841.

BURNET, GILBERT, 1643–1715. Als 20 September 1707; ds (3) 1689–1707.

BURNEY,CHARLES, 1726–1814. Als (4) 1796–1808 and n.d.

BURNEY, CHARLES, 1757–1817. Als (4) 1800–9 and n.d.

BURNEY, FRANCES: *see* ARBLAY, D'.

BURNEY, JAMES, 1750–1821. Als, al, copies of letters (50) 1762–1821.

BURNEY, SARAH HARRIET, 1772–1844. Als n.d.

BURNEY, SOPHIA ELIZABETH, 1777–1856. Stories (8) for Miss Cecilia Charlotte Esther Burney, aged five years, 50 pp.

BURNEY, WILLIAM, 1762–1832. Als 7 May 1812 to Cadell & Davies.

BURNS, JOHN, 1858–1943. Als (5) 1905–7 to T. J. Cobden-Sanderson and S. C. Cockerell.

BURNS, ROBERT, 1759–1796. "Address of the Scots Distillers, a Petition to William Pitt," 3 pp.; "The Cotter's Saturday Night," 7 pp.; "Twa Herds," 4 pp.; copy in Burns's hand of Clarinda's "When first you saw Clarinda's charms," 2 pp.; als (118) 1786–96 including 44 to Mrs. Frances Dunlop (containing 45 poems), 57 to George Thomson (containing 92 poems) and 10 to Peter Hill; with letters (102) 1786–95 from Mrs. Dunlop to Burns. With an als from his brother Gilbert Burns 2 April 1797 to Mrs. Dunlop.

BURTON, DECIMUS, 1800–1881. Als 7 August 1848 to Samuel Prout.

BURTON, SIR FREDERIC WILLIAM, 1816–1900. Als (3) 1882–8 to Sir John Millais.

BURTON, SIR RICHARD FRANCIS, 1821–1890. "Appendix No. 9 Visit to Hauran [Syria]," 5 pp.; als 2 April 1874. With als 1872 of Lady Burton.

BURY, LADY CHARLOTTE SUSAN MARIA, 1775–1861. Al 21 May 1833 to Mr. Moyse.

BUTCHER, SAMUEL HENRY, 1850–1910. Als (37) 1886–1904 to W. A. Knight.

BUTLER, CHARLES, 1750–1832. Als (3) 1818.

BUTLER, HENRY MONTAGUE, 1833–1918. Als (2) 1895 to W. A. Knight.

BUTLER, JOSEPHINE ELIZABETH GREY, 1828–1906. Als (2) n.d. to W. A. Knight.

BUTLER, SAMUEL, 1774–1839. Als 10 December 1835.

BUTLER, SAMUEL, 1835–1902. "A lecture on the genesis of feeling," 38 pp. (corrected typescript); als 11 June 1873 to O. M. Brown.

BUXTON, SYDNEY CHARLES BUXTON, 1st Earl, 1853–1934. Als n.d.

BYRON, GEORGE GORDON NOEL BYRON, 6th Baron, 1788–1824. *Beppo*, 51 pp.; *The Corsair*, 94 pp.; *Don Juan*, Cantos I–V, XIII, 329 pp.; *Manfred*, 106 pp.; *Marino Faliero*, 166 pp.; *Mazeppa*, 41 pp.; "Morgante Maggiore," 26 pp.; *The Prophecy of Dante*, 33 pp.; *Werner*, 167 pp. Shorter poems: "Ashtaroth's Song" (*Manfred*, Act III, Sc. i), 2 pp.; "Castled Crag of Drachenfels" (*Childe Harold*, Canto III), 3 pp.; "Could love forever," 4 pp.; "Edinburgh Ladies Petition" and "Reply to the . . . Petition," 3 and 17 pp.; "Farewell, If Ever Fondest Prayer," 1 p.; "Francesca da Rimini": Canto V [of Dante's *Inferno*], 7 pp.; "Give me thy kisses" (trans. of Martial VI.34), 1 p.; "Hints from Horace" (annotated proofsheets with autograph "Note to a part of the 'Hints . . .'"), 6 and 2 pp.; "Ode [on Venice]," 8 pp.; "Oh! my lonely—lonely—lonely pillow," 3 pp.; stanza 72 of "Oscar of Alva," beginning "Ambition nerved young Allan's hand," 1 p.; "Stanzas to the Po," 5 pp.

Als (69) 1805–24, including 19 to his mother, 2 to his sister Augusta, 1 to Shelley, 1 to the *Quarterly Review* and 12 to Alexander Scott. Letters or MSS (75) 1788–1852 written by members of Byron's family or friends, including 5 of his mother, 9 of his wife, 8 of his sister Augusta, 19 of his daughter Ada, 1 of his daughter Allegra, 10 of Teresa Guiccioli—all bearing on Byron's life, death or works. Letters or MSS (28) 1843–70 concerning the Medora Leigh controversy, including 5 letters from Medora Leigh and her autobiography, 17 pp.; and other letters written by or to Thomas Smith, Charles Mackay or George Stephen.

BYRON, GEORGE GORDON DE LUNA, forger, ca. 1810–1882. Als (8) 1847 to Mr. Bohn and George Loddy. Examples of his Byron and Shelley forgeries.

BYRON, HENRY JAMES, 1834–1884. Als (6) 1877–80.

BYRON, MAY CLARISSA (GILLINGTON), d. 1936. Als 12 March 1909 to S. Baring-Gould.

BYWATER, INGRAM, 1840–1914. Als 27 January 1885 to Mr. Butler.

CADELL, ROBERT, 1788–1849. Als (3) 1823–33.

CADELL, THOMAS, 1742–1802. Als (2) 1769, 1793.

CAESAR, SIR JULIUS, 1558–1636. Ls 29 March 1608 to Sir Vincent Skinner; ds (17) 1597–1623.

CAINE, SIR HALL, 1853–1931. Als (5) 1881–1919.

CAIRD, EDWARD, 1835–1908. Als (54) 1875–1904 and n.d. to W. A. Knight.

CAIRD, JOHN, 1820–1898. Als (38) 1872–87 including 35 to W. A. Knight.

CAIRNS, HUGH MCCALMONT CAIRNS, 1st Earl, 1819–1885. Als 1862.

CALDECOTT, ALFRED, 1850–1936. Als (2) 1891 to W. A. Knight.

CALDECOTT, RANDOLPH, 1846–1886. Als 15 May 1885 to Mr. Gatty.

CALDERWOOD, DAVID, 1575–1650. *History of the Kirk of Scotland, 1555–1638* (Manuscript copy with autograph notes and corrections), 607 pp.

CALDERWOOD, HENRY, 1830–1897. Als (5) 1893–7 to W. A. Knight.

CALLCOTT, MARIA (DUNDAS) GRAHAM, Lady, 1785–1842. Als (2) 1828 to Lady Caledon.

CALVERT, CHARLES ALEXANDER, 1828–1879. Als n.d. to Lewis Wingfield.

CAMBRIDGE, RICHARD OWEN, 1717–1802. Als 1792 to Edmond Malone.

CAMDEN, CHARLES PRATT, 1st Earl, 1714–1794. Als (2) 1775, 1788; ds 1766.

CAMDEN, WILLIAM, 1551–1623. Als (3) 1577–1606.

CAMPBELL, BEATRICE STELLA (MRS. PATRICK), 1865–1940. Als n.d. to Joan Severn.

CAMPBELL, JAMES DYKES, 1838–1895. Als (86) 1884–95, of which 85 are to W. A. Knight and 1 to T. J. Wise.

CAMPBELL, JOHN, 1708–1775. Als (2) 1771, 1773 to Sir Philip Francis.

CAMPBELL, JOHN CAMPBELL, 1st Baron, 1779–1861. Als (2) 1859 and n.d.; ds 9 December 1840.

CAMPBELL, LEWIS, 1830–1908. Als (2) 1876, 1894.

CAMPBELL, ROY, 1901–1957. Als ca. 1953 to Graham Greene.

CAMPBELL, THOMAS, 1777–1844. "Adelgitha," 1 p.; from "Theodoric," 1 p.; "Hohenlinden," 2 pp.; "Lines Spoken at the Opening of the Drury Lane Theatre," 4 pp.; "Lochiel's Warning," 3 pp.; "Ode, On Leaving a Scene in Bavaria," 2 pp.; lines beginning "Snatch'd from an Indian Ocean's roar," 1 p.; "Stanzas on the Battle of Navarino," 4 pp.; "Medea, A Tragedy from the Greek [of Euripides] by a Non Togatus Student," 216 pp.; *Life of Mrs. Siddons*, 196 pp.; als (15) 1809–33.

CAMPION, THOMAS, 1567–1620. "What if a daie . . . ," 1 p. (Contemporary manuscript.)

CANNING, GEORGE, 1770–1827. Als, ls (191) 1798–1826 mainly to Richard, Marquis Wellesley; with letters (60) 1809–23 from Wellesley and others to Canning.

CANT, ANDREW, 1590?–1663. Poem, 1 p.; als 29 August 1662.

CAREY, WILLIAM PAULET, 1759–1839. Als 15 February 1826.

CARLISLE, GEORGE WILLIAM FREDERICK HOWARD, 7th Earl of, 1802–1864. Als n.d. to J. H. Jesse.

CARLYLE, THOMAS, 1795–1881. "Excursion (Futile Enough) to Paris, Autumn 1851," 32 pp.; "Leave it alone; time will mend it," 6 pp.; *Wotton Reinfred*, 51 pp.; als (64) 1825–70 including 20 to W. D. Christie, 16 to printers, principally Chapman & Hall (with 9 signed bills or receipts), 6 to John Taylor and 16 to his wife, brother or friends; with als (42) 1816–51, addressed to Carlyle, including 30 from his wife and members of the immediate family.

CARPENTER, EDWARD, 1844–1929. Als 26 October 1893 to Mrs. Cobden-Sanderson.

CARPENTER, JOSEPH ESTLIN, 1844–1927. Als (49) 1872–1903 to W. A. Knight.

CARPENTER, WILLIAM BENJAMIN, 1813–1885. Als (8) 1873–82 to W. A. Knight.

CARPENTER, WILLIAM BOYD, 1841–1918. "In Memoriam J. Pierpont Morgan—The Commodore is come to port," 1 p.; als (4) 1911–2 to J. Pierpont Morgan.

CARPENTER, WILLIAM HOOKHAM, 1792–1866. Als (10) 1837–59 including 6 to S. L. Sotheby.

CARROLL, LEWIS: *see* DODGSON, CHARLES LUTWIDGE.

CARTE, RICHARD D'OYLY, 1844–1901. Als, tls, ls (18) 1878–1900; ds 10 March 1898. With als (12) from his wife, Helen (Lenoir) Carte.

CARTE, RUPERT D'OYLY, 1876–1948. Als 20 November 1914 to Louie René.

CARTE, SAMUEL, 1653–1740. Als 29 September 1721 to John Bridges.

CARTE, THOMAS, 1686–1754. Als 31 July 1736 to William Cooke, bookbinder.

CARTER, ELIZABETH, 1717–1806. Copy of a poem dedicated to Miss Sutton, 1 p.; als (4) 1779–84.

CARTER, JOHN, 1748–1817. Als 10 December 1791 to Thomas Barrett of Lee.

CARTWRIGHT, JOHN, 1740–1824. Als (2) 1802, 1807.

CASSON, SIR HUGH MAXWELL, 1910– . Als n.d. to Charles Ryskamp.

CASTLEREAGH, LORD: *see* LONDONDERRY, R. S.

CATESBY, MARK, 1682–1749. *The Natural History of Carolina*, 1743, 11 pp. only.

CATON-THOMPSON, GERTRUDE, 1888– . Als (2) 1937, 1939 to Sir Sydney Cockerell.

CATTERMOLE, GEORGE, 1800–1868. Als (5) 1845–66 and n.d.

CAVENDISH: *see* DEVONSHIRE.

CECIL, WILLIAM, Baron Burghley, 1520–1598. Als (5) 1562–84; ds (20) 1552–97.

CHALKHILL, JOHN, 1595?–1642. "The Sheepheards Elegie," "A Melancholy Fitt," "A Propper New Ballet Called the Coy Virgin . . . ," "Theare is a servant which I knowe," "There is a useful little creatre," "Goe happy verse for thou art free"; als March 1638 to his cousin Katherine Packerre; mock love letter n.d. to Josias Clarke, 16 pp.

CHALMERS, GEORGE, 1742–1825. Als 10 February 1819 to James Perry; ls 23 January 1781 to Sir William Pulteney.

CHAMBERLAIN, SIR AUSTEN, 1863–1917. Tls 5 April 1928 to Sir George Grahame.

CHAMBERLAIN, JOSEPH, 1836–1914. Als (7) 1890–1904 to W. A. Knight and Sir John Millais.

CHAMBERLAIN, NEVILLE, 1869–1940. Als 10 October 1938 to J. P. Morgan.

CHAMBERS, ROBERT, 1802–1871. Als (3) 1833–63.

CHAMBERS, SIR WILLIAM, 1726–1796. Als (2) 1790–1.

CHANTREY, SIR FRANCIS LEGATT, 1781–1841. Als (4) 1821–8.

CHAPPELL, WILLIAM, 1809–1888. Als (3) 1875–6 to Joseph Bennett.

CHARLES I, King of Great Britain, 1600–1649. "On a quiet conscience by K. Cha. I" (eighteenth-century copy), 1 p.; als, ls (10) 1627–44 including 5 to Frederick V of Bohemia and 2 to his nephew, Prince Rupert; ds (25) 1619–47.

CHARLES II, King of Great Britain, 1630–1685. "The Phoenix" (eighteenth-century copy), 1 p.; als, ls (17) 1651–85 including 7 to Louis XIV; ads (2) 3 March 1679 and n.d.; ds

(50) 1648–84.

CHATFIELD, EDWARD, 1800–1839. Als n.d.

CHATHAM, WILLIAM PITT, 1st Earl of, 1708–1788. Als, al, ls (19) 1753–70; ds (2) 1750, 1761.

CHATTERTON, THOMAS, 1752–1770. "Eldred," Act I (not in his hand and probably not of his authorship), 15 pp.

CHENERY, THOMAS, 1826–1884. Als 17 March 1883 to J. E. Millais.

CHENEY, ROBERT HENRY, d. 1866. Als (12) 1837–49 to Thomas Cromek.

CHERRY-GARRARD, APSLEY, 1889–1959. Als 22 August 1931 to S. C. Cockerell.

CHESTERFIELD, PHILIP DORMER STANHOPE, 4th Earl of, 1694–1773. Als, al, ls (5) 1730–62.

CHESTERFIELD, PHILIP STANHOPE, 2nd Earl of, 1633–1713. Als (3) 1679–87.

CHESTERTON, GILBERT KEITH, 1874–1936. "Open Letter: On the Collapse of the Cosmo[poli]tan Club," 5 pp.; "Sonnets In Summer Heat," 3 pp.

CHEYNE, ELIZABETH (GIBSON), 1869–1931. "A Rover," 1 p.

CHEYNE, GEORGE, 1671–1743. Als 1740 to Sir Alexander Dick.

CHIPPENDALE, WILLIAM HENRY, 1801–1888. Als n.d. to Lewis Wingfield.

CHRISTIE, JAMES, 1773–1831. Als (2) 1825, 1826.

CHRISTMAS, HENRY, 1811–1868. Als (2) 1858, 1859 to S. L. Sotheby.

CHURCH, RICHARD WILLIAM, 1815–1890. Als 2 June 1890 to W. A. Knight.

CHURCHILL, CHARLES, 1731–1764. Als n.d. to Dr. Cook.

CHURCHILL, SIR WINSTON LEONARD SPENCER, 1874–1965. Tls 1 June 1939 to Sir Edward Marsh.

CIBBER, COLLEY, 1671–1757. "Bill for ye Stage," 1716, 1 p. Als (2) 1713/4 and n.d.

CLARE, JOHN, 1793–1864. "Autumn," 1 p.; "Village Scenes and Subjects on rural Occupations," 116 pp.

CLAREMONT ,WILLIAM, d. 1832. Als 22 February 1825 to Mr. Cribbs.

CLARENDON, EDWARD HYDE, 1st Earl of, 1609–1674. Als (4) ca. 1649–52; ads, ds (11) 1645–67; annotations in his *The History of the Rebellion* (1702–4).

CLARK, KENNETH MACKENZIE CLARK, Baron, 1903– . Als, tls (6) 1929–73.

CLARKE, CHARLES COWDEN, 1787–1877. Als 29 December 1823 to Richard Woodhouse.

CLARKE, EDWARD DANIEL, 1769–1822. Notes, 2 pp.

CLARKE, JAMES STANIER, 1765–1823. Als (5) 1800–15 including 2 to Jane Austen.

CLARKE, JOHN, d. 1879. Als (2) 1863, 1864.

CLARKE, MARY COWDEN-, 1809–1898. "Sonnet on receiving a copy of 'A Treasury of English Sonnets,'" 1 p.; als (2) 1857, 1885.

CLARKE, SAMUEL, 1675–1729. Als 18 April 1722 to Philip Doddridge; ds 4 April 1711.

CLIFFORD, MARTIN, d. 1677. Als 10 August 1675 to Sir Henry Thompson.

CLOUGH, ANNE JEMINA, 1820–1892. Als 28 December 1891 to W. A. Knight.

CLOUGH, ARTHUR HUGH, 1819–1861. "Mari Magno," 2 pp.; als 1 November 1857 to Alfred Tennyson.

CLUTTERBUCK, ROBERT, 1772–1831. Als 12 December 1823 to J. B. Nichols.

COBB, JAMES, 1756–1818. Als 5 October 1795.

COBBAN, JAMES MACLAREN, 1849–1903. Als 27 November 1891 to W. E. Henley.

COBBE, FRANCES POWER, 1822–1904. Als n.d. to W. A. Knight.

COBBETT, WILLIAM, 1762–1835. "Epitaph to George IV," 1 p.; als, ls (6) 1792–1832.

COBBOLD, RICHARD, 1797–1877. "Valentine Verses, or Lines of Truth & Virtue," 223 *ll.*

COBDEN, RICHARD, 1804–1865. Als (11) 1850–64.

COBDEN-SANDERSON, THOMAS JAMES, 1840–1922. Als 15 May 1906 to F. L. Poynder.

COCHRAN-PATRICK, ROBERT WILLIAM, 1842–1897. Als (11) 1887–96 to W. A. Knight.

COCKERELL, CHARLES ROBERT, 1788–1863. Als (2) 1824, 1842.

COCKERELL, SIR SYDNEY CARLYLE, 1867–1962. Als (53) 1891–1954.

COKE, SIR EDWARD, 1552–1634. Ds 25 November 1601.

COLE, SIR HENRY, 1808–1882. Als (4) 1844–77.

COLENSO, FRANCES ELLEN, 1849–1887. Als 13 March 1880 to John Ruskin.

COLENSO, JOHN WILLIAM, 1814–1883. Als 30 April 1862.

COLERAINE, GEORGE HANGER, 4th Baron, 1751–1824. Als (3) 1793–1812.

COLERIDGE, ERNEST HARTLEY, 1846–1920. Als (20) 1885–1904 to W. A. Knight.

COLERIDGE, HARTLEY, 1796–1849. "On reading the memoirs of Lady Grizzle Baillie," 1 p.; sonnets (4), 3 pp.; als 2 May 1829? to his mother.

COLERIDGE, SIR JOHN DUKE, 1st Baron, 1820–1894. Als (64) 1880–93 including 59 to W. A. Knight.

COLERIDGE, MARY ELIZABETH, 1861–1907. Als 14 July 1895 to Mary Millais.

COLERIDGE, SAMUEL TAYLOR, 1772–1834. "Confession of Belief with respect to the true grounds of Christian morality," 4 pp.; an essay on the death of Queen Charlotte (incomplete), 3 pp.; "Fears in Solitude, Written April 1798, during the Alarm of the Invasion," 11 pp.; "On an infant that died unbaptised," 1 p.; "Romance," 1 p.; manuscript sequence of poems July 1794 in the hand of Anne Evans, the second poem revised by Coleridge, 4 pp.; autograph manuscript copybook, 28 pp.; autograph manuscript notes on various subjects, 23 pp.; marginalia in his *Aids to Reflection* (1825), *Fears in Solitude* (1798) and *The Friend* (1818), 3 vols.; also in Richard Byfield *The Doctrine of the Sabbath Vindicated* (1631), Jeremy Collier's translation of Marcus Aurelius Antoninus (1701) and *The Works of the Holy Mother St. Teresa of Jesus* (1675); *The Rime of the Ancient Mariner*, calligraphic manuscript by David Soshensky, 1948–9, 162 *ll.* Als (388) including 47 to his wife, 24 to Sir George and Lady Beaumont, 48 to J. H. Green, 40 to Mr. and Mrs. J. J. Morgan, 92 to Robert Southey, 41 to William Godwin, 5 to James Gillman, 16 to John Thelwall and 16 to his nephew the Rev. Edward Taylor. With an als of his brother George 10 November 1814 and an als of his wife 25 August 1803, both to Robert Southey.

COLLES, WILLIAM MORRIS, 1855–1926. Als 18 February 1892 to May Gillington.

COLLETTE, CHARLES, 1842–1924. Als (2) 1908 to G. F. Byron.

COLLIER, JOHN PAYNE, 1789–1883. Als (7) 1836–80 including 2 to S. L. Sotheby.

COLLINGWOOD, WILLIAM GERSHOM, 1854–1932. Als (5) 1888–1902.

COLLINS, CHARLES ALLSTON, 1828–1873. Als (57) 1858–65 including 52 to his mother and 3 to his brother Wilkie.

COLLINS, WILLIAM, 1788–1847. Als (81) 1822–44 including 80 to his wife.

COLLINS, WILLIAM WILKIE, 1824–1889. *The Frozen Deep*, 3 drafts, the final manuscript and a prompt copy partly in the hand of Charles Dickens, 6, 42, 55, 112, 74 pp.; *Hide and Seek*, 203 pp.; *The Moonstone*, 413 pp.; *No Thoroughfare* (a portion of Collins' contribution to this collaboration with Dickens), 60 pp.; *The Woman in White*, 492 pp.; als (270) 1838–79 including 118 to his mother, 86 to Charles Ward, 25 to Harper & Bros. and 5 to his brother Charles.

COLMAN, GEORGE, 1732–1794. Als (11) 1779–87, including 9 to Sir William (Johnstone) Pulteney.

COLMAN, GEORGE, 1762–1836. "An address . . . for the Widow and Children of the late John Emery," 2 pp.; als (10) 1800–33.

COLSON, JOHN, 1680–1760. Ads 2 April 1754.

COLUM, PADRAIC, 1881–1972. "[Collected] Poems," 1931, 133 *ll.* (typescript with autograph additions); "Cradle Song," 1 p.

COLVIN, SIR SIDNEY, 1845–1927. Als (18) 1894–1914 and n.d. including 15 to W. W. Baldwin.

COMBE, GEORGE, 1788–1858. Als (2) 1836, 1838.

COMBE, WILLIAM, 1741–1823. Als 12 November 1798 to George Romney; ads 2 April 1798.

COMPTON, HENRY, 1632–1713. Als (4) ca. 1682–99.

CONGLETON, HENRY BROOKE PARNELL, Baron, 1776–1842. Als 13 August 1806 to Mr. Budd.

CONGREVE, RICHARD, 1818–1899. Als (5) 1885–6 to W. A. Knight.

CONGREVE, WILLIAM, 1670–1729. Als (2) 1702, 1710 to Joseph Keally.

CONRAD, JOSEPH, 1857–1924. "Legends," 12 pp.; als (8) 1897–1924.

CONSTABLE, ARCHIBALD, 1774–1827. Als 9 December 1808 to Cadell & Davies.

CONSTABLE, JOHN, 1776–1837. Als (19) 1820–36 and n.d.; ds 1829.

CONWAY, HENRY SEYMOUR, 1721–1795. Als (5) 1780–90; ds 25 February 1766.

CONWAY, WILLIAM MARTIN CONWAY, Baron, 1856–1937. Als (2) 1890 and n.d. to W. A. Knight.

COOK, SIR EDWARD TYAS, 1857–1919. Als 16 January 1888 to John Ruskin.

COOK, ELIZA, 1818–1889. Als 26 March 1846.

COOK, JAMES, 1728–1799. Als ca. 1775 to Dr. Charles Burney; ds 18 November 1772.

COOKE, GEORGE FREDERICK, 1756–1811. Als 5 March 1811 to J. H. Payne.

COOKE, WILLIAM BERNARD, 1778–1855. Ds 12 December 1799.

COOPER, ABRAHAM, 1787–1868. Als (3) 1823 and n.d.

COOPER, SIR ALFRED, 1838–1908. Als (2) 1881, 1883 to Sir Arthur Sullivan.

COOPER, SIR ASTLEY PASTON, 1768–1841. Als 7 September 1837 to Lady Bell.

COOPER, CHARLES ALFRED, 1829–1916. Als (3) 1892–8 to W. A. Knight.

COOPER, EDITH EMMA, 1862–1913: *see* "FIELD, MICHAEL."

COOPER, JOHN GILBERT, 1723–1769. Als 28 February 1765 to Mr. Dodsley.

COOPER, THOMAS SIDNEY, 1803–1902. Als (2) 1896 to Sir John and Lady Millais.

COPLEY, EDWARD, 1776–1849. Als 25 March 1827 to the Duke of Buckingham and Chandos.

COPPARD, ALFRED EDGAR, 1878–1957. Short stories (4): "Juan Cotton," "The Hasty Man," "Vassals *or* Braddle," "Able Staple Disapproves," 52 pp.

CORBET, RICHARD, 1582–1635. Als 27 April 1628 to the Chancellor of Oxford University.

CORBOULD, EDWARD HENRY, 1815–1905. Als 12 February 1857 to W. E. Dalton.

CORELLI, MARIE, 1855–1924. *Thelma*, manuscript in a scribal hand with autograph additions, 1,598 *ll.*; "Utterances of the Master," 5 *ll.*; als (7) 1895–1906.

CORK AND ORRERY, JOHN BOYLE, 5th Earl of, 1707–1762. Ads 16 May 1751.

CORNEY, BOLTON, 1784–1870. Ls 19 July 1858.

CORNFORD, FRANCES (DARWIN), 1886–1960. Als 14 October 1925 to S. C. Cockerell.

COSTELLO, DUDLEY, 1803–1865. Als 19 January 1856 to T. K. Hervey.

COSWAY, MARIA LOUISA CATHERINE CECILIA (HADFIELD), 1759–1838. Als (3) 1806 and n.d.

COURTHOPE, WILLIAM JOHN, 1842–1917. Als 16 June 1883 to Joseph Bennett.

COURTNEY, WILLIAM LEONARD, 1850–1928. Als (5) 1886–9 to W. A. Knight.

COWARD, SIR NOËL PIERCE, 1899–1973. Als 28 May 1946 to Mrs. Belousoff.

COWLEY, ABRAHAM, 1618–1667. Als 1 January 1650; ds 1660.

COWPER, WILLIAM, 1731–1800. Translation of Horace *Odes* II.16, 3 pp.; translations from Vol. 3 of the poems of Mme de la Mothe Guion, 18 pp.; contemporary copies of 16 poems, 24 pp.; marginalia on Bks. I–III of *Paradise Lost* in a copy of the 9th ed. (London, 1790); commonplace book, signed and dated 12 February 1757, containing extracts and opinions on legal matters (not autograph, but having notations in Cowper's hand), 400 pp.; "The Nightingale and the Glow Worm," 2 pp.; "The Rose," 2 pp.; "Song on Peace written at the request of Lady Austen," 2 pp.; "To George Romney Esqr.," 1 p.; als (59) 1749–93 including 42 to Walter Bagot.

COWPER, WILLIAM COWPER, 1st Earl, ca. 1665–1723. Als January 1714 to Paul Jodrel; ds 14 March 1716.

COXE, HENRY OCTAVIUS, 1811–1881. Als (2) 1858 to S. L. Sotheby.

COXE, PETER, d. 1844. Als 10 July 1838 to William Jerdan.

COXE, WILLIAM, 1747–1828. Als 11 December 1803 to Cadell & Davies.

CRABBE, GEORGE, 1754–1832. "Verses written on revisiting a Place . . . ," 1 p.; als (3) 1791–1831.

CRADOCK, JOSEPH, 1742–1826. Als n.d.

CRAIG, JAMES THOMSON GIBSON, 1799–1886. Als 19 November 1857 to S. L. Sotheby.

CRAIG, WILLIAM MARSHALL, fl. 1788–1828. Als (3) 1809 and n.d.

CRAIGIE, PEARL MARY TERESA (RICHARDS) ("JOHN OLIVER HOBBES"), 1867–1906. Als (2) 1892, 1895.

CRAIK, DINAH MARIA (MULOCK), 1826–1887. "Could you come back to me, Douglas," 1 p.; *Miss Tommy*, 2 pp.; als (31) 1849–77 including 28 to Frederic Chapman.

CRAIK, GEORGE LILLIE, 1798–1866. Als n.d. to Thomas Carlyle.

CRAIK, SIR HENRY, 1846–1927. Als (4) 1885–97 to W. A. Knight.

CRANE, WALTER, 1845–1915. Als (2) 1890, 1905.

CRANMER, THOMAS, 1489–1556. Als (2) 1539 and n.d.; ds 12 June 1530.

CRASHAW, RICHARD, 1612?–1649. "Hymn to St. Teresa" (contemporary manuscript with autograph title page and corrections), 12 pp.

CRAUFORD, QUINTIN, 1743–1819. Als (2) 1794, 1803.

CRAWFORD, JAMES LUDOVIC LINDSAY, 26th Earl of, 1847–1913. Als (3) 1884–98, of which 2 are to W. E. Henley and 1 to Bernard Quaritch.

CREASY, SIR EDWARD SHEPHERD, 1812–1878. Als 13 March 1866 to Captain Baldwin Hall.

CREIGHTON, MANDELL, 1843–1901. Als 20 July 1900.

CRICHTON, HALDANE, 1853–1938. Als (9) 1882–3 to W. E. Henley and R. L. Stevenson.

CRICHTON-BROWNE, SIR JAMES, 1840–1938. Als 7 October 1899 to W. A. Knight.

CRISTALL, JOSHUA, 1767–1847. Als (3) 1836, 1837 and n.d.

CROCKETT, SAMUEL RUTHERFORD, 1860–1914. Als (9) 1894–9 to Joan Severn.

CROKER, JOHN WILSON, 1780–1857. Als (4) 1823–52; with als (103) 1815–29 written to Croker by Sir Thomas Lawrence.

CROME, JOHN BERNAY, 1794–1842. Als 8 April 1839.

CROMEK, ROBERT HARTLEY, 1770–1812. Als 18 December 1810.

CROMER, EVELYN BARING, 1st Earl of, 1841–1917. Als 1882 to George Grossmith.

CROUCH, FREDERICK NICHOLLS, 1808–1896. "Kathleen Mavourneen," 10 pp.

CRUIKSHANK, GEORGE, 1792–1878. Als (21) 1831–72.

CUDLIP, ANNIE HALL (THOMAS), 1838–1913. Als (4) 1869–74.

CULLUM, SIR JOHN, 6th Bart., 1733–1785. Als 16 February 1776.

CUMBERLAND, RICHARD, 1732–1811. Als (8) 1775–1808.

CUNNINGHAM, ALLAN, 1784–1842. "The Mariner," 1 p.; "Song of Richard Faulder," 1 p.; als (7) 1822–34.

CUNNINGHAM, PETER, 1816–1869. Als (4) 1851–67.

CUNNINGHAME GRAHAM, ROBERT BONTINE, 1852–1936. Als (2) 1930 and n.d.

CURTIS, WILLIAM, 1746–1799. Als 2 June 1799 to Dr. John Sims.

CURWEN, JOHN CHRISTIAN, 1756–1828. Als (2) 1803 and n.d.

CURZON, ROBERT: *see* ZOUCHE.

CUST, SIR LIONEL HENRY, 1859–1929. Als (2) 1896, 1917.

DADD, RICHARD, 1819–1887. Als 7 February 1863.

DAHL, MICHAEL, 1656–1743. Ds 5 April 1741.

DALBY, SIR WILLIAM BARTLETT, 1840–1918. Als 21 November 1892 to Sir John Millais.

DALLING AND BULWER, WILLIAM HENRY LYTTON EARLE BULWER, Baron, 1801–1872. Als (3) 1837, 1840 and n.d.

DALLINGER, WILLIAM HENRY, 1842–1909. Als 24 May 1886 to John Ruskin.

DALRYMPLE, ALEXANDER, 1737–1808. Als (3) 1781, 1782 and n.d. including 1 to James Burney.

DALRYMPLE, SIR JOHN, Bart., 1726–1810. Als (2) 1787 to Thomas Cadell.

DALTON, JOHN, 1766–1844. Als 20 February 1834 to Michael Faraday.

DALZIEL, EDWARD, 1817–1905. Als (3) 1879 and n.d.

DAMER, ANNE SEYMOUR (CONWAY), 1749–1828. Als (2) 1811, 1817.

DANBY, FRANCIS, 1793–1861. Als (2) 1848, 1860.

DANCE, GEORGE, 1741–1825. Als (2) ca. 1795, 1808 to Samuel Lysons and John Flaxman.

"DANE, CLEMENCE": *see* ASHTON.

DANIEL, CHARLES HENRY OLIVE, 1836–1919. Als (2) ca. 1896–7 to Michael Field.

DANIEL, GEORGE, 1789–1864. Autograph notes in *An Elizabethan Garland* (1856); als 24 August 1858 to S. L. Sotheby.

DANIELL, JOHN FREDERIC, 1790–1845. Als 28 July 1824 to Parker Cleaveland.

DANIELL, THOMAS, 1749–1840. Als 1 May 1825 to Robert Balmanno.

DANIELL, WILLIAM, 1769–1837. Als n.d. to W. J. Huggins.

DARK, SIDNEY, 1874–1947. Ls 4 July 1923 to Nancy McIntosh.

DARWIN, BERNARD RICHARD MEIRION, 1876–1961. Als 8 January 1945 to Sir Sydney Cockerell.

DARWIN, CHARLES ROBERT, 1809–1882. Als (4) 1839–82 and n.d. including 1 to John Henslow; ls 7 June 1877; autograph quotation signed from his *Fertilisation of Orchids* [*sic*], 1869, 1 p.

DARWIN, ERASMUS, 1731–1802. Als 25 September 1800.

DARWIN, SIR FRANCIS, 1848–1925. Als 28 August 1913 to S. C. Cockerell.

DAVEY, HORACE DAVEY, Lord, 1833–1907. Als (5) 1881–92 to W. A. Knight.

DAVIDS, CAROLINE AUGUSTA (FOLEY) RHYS, d. 1942. Als (10) 1892–9 to W. A. Knight.

DAVIDS, THOMAS WILLIAM RHYS, 1843–1922. Als (4) n.d. to W. A. Knight.

DAVIDSON, JOHN, 1857–1909. *Ballads and Songs*, 143 *ll.*; "Song" in *La Reine Fiammete*, 1 p.; als 4 March 1896 to A. W. Pinero.

DAVIDSON, RANDALL THOMAS, 1848–1930. Sermon preached at Marlborough House, 29 June 1902, 10 pp.; als (4) 1901–11 including 3 to W. A. Knight and 1 to J. Pierpont Morgan.

DAVIES, JOHN, OF HEREFORD, 1565?–1618. Autograph verse and notes signed in *Coryat's Crudities* (1611).

DAVIES, THOMAS, 1712?–1785. Als (2) 1770, 1772 to James Granger.

DAVIES, WILLIAM, 1751–1809. Als ca. January 1772 to David Garrick.

DAVIES, WILLIAM, 1830–1896. Als (21) 1862–95 to W. A. Knight.

DAVIES, WILLIAM HENRY, 1871–1940. "Thunderstorms," 1 p.

DAVIS, HENRY WILLIAM BANKS, 1833–1914. Als (2) 1881, 1895 to Sir John Millais.

DAVISON, JAMES WILLIAM, 1813–1885. Als (8) n.d. to Joseph Bennett.

DAVY, SIR HUMPHREY, 1778–1829. Als (4) 1800–20 and n.d. including 2 to Sir George Beaumont and 1 to S. T. Coleridge.

DAVY, WILLIAM, 1743–1826. Als 2 November 1825 to Mr. Nichols.

DAWES, SIR WILLIAM, 3rd Bart., 1671–1724. Als 28 July 1722; ds 25 August 1714.

DAY, THOMAS, 1748–1789. Als 1789 to John Stockdale.

DAY-LEWIS, CECIL, 1904–1972. "Beauty's end," 1 p.

DEARMAN, JOHN, d. 1856 or 1857. Als 24 July 1848.

DEE, JOHN, 1527–1608. Ls 16 January 1577 to Abraham Ortelius.

DEFOE, DANIEL, 1660–1731. Als 11 October 1704 to Samuel Elisha.

DEIGHTON, J., bookseller, Cambridge. Als (3) 1853 to S. L. Sotheby.

DE LA MARE, WALTER JOHN, 1873–1956. *Flora* (corrected typescript), 25 *ll.*; "The Listeners," 2 pp.; "Mirage," 1 p.; "Ruth V. V. MDCCCXV," 1 p.; als, tls (84), of which 82 are to Tom Turner and 1 each to Sir Sydney Cockerell and Harper & Bros.

DELANE, JOHN THADEUS, 1817–1879. Als 14 July 1871 to Sir Augustus Clifford.

DELAP, JOHN, 1725–1812. Als 7 September 1794 to James Heath.

DE LA RAMÉE, LOUISE ("OUIDA"), 1840–1908. "The Child of Urbino", 77 pp.; "The Nürnberg Stove," 66 pp.; "Matthew Arnold, April 1888," 3 pp.; *A Rainy June*, 167 pp.; als (9) 1887–1904 and n.d.

DE LOLME, JOHN LOUIS, 1740–1807. Als ca. 1776 to Sir William (Johnstone) Pulteney; ads 15 May 1778.

DE MORGAN, WILLIAM FREND, 1839–1917. Als (2) 1907, 1909.

DEMPSTER, GEORGE, 1732–1818. Als (5) 1772–1813.

DENHAM, JOHN CHARLES, fl. 1796–1858. Als 6 September 1836.

DENMAN, THOMAS DENMAN, Baron, 1779–1854. Als (2) 15 April 1844 to Charles Dickens and n.d.

DENNE, SAMUEL, 1730–1799. Ads 27 September 1766.

DENT, EDWARD JOSEPH, 1876–1957. Als 18 April 1915 to Ronald Firbank.

DE QUINCEY, THOMAS, 1785–1859. "On the London Magazine," 15 pp.; incomplete portions of essays and notes, 23 pp.; als (6) 1821–39 and n.d. *See also*: BAIRDSMITH.

DERBY, EDWARD GEORGE GEOFFREY SMITH STANLEY, 14th Earl of, 1799–1869. Als (3) 1833–58.

DERBY, ELIZABETH FARREN, Countess of: *see* FARREN.

DERING, SIR EDWARD, 1598–1644. Als 15 December 1642 to George Brydges.

DERMODY, THOMAS, 1775–1802. Als (2) 1800, 1801.

DERRICK, SAMUEL, 1724–1769. Als 5 January 1766.

DESPARD, CHARLOTTE (FRENCH), 1844–1939. Als 25 June 1910 to Mrs. T. J. Cobden-Sanderson.

DE TABLEY, JOHN FLEMING LEICESTER, 1st Baron, 1762–1827. Als (2) 1796, 1802.

DETHICK, SIR WILLIAM, 1543–1612. Ds 30 May 1605.

DE VERE, AUBREY THOMAS, 1814–1902. Als (44) 1880–95, of which 40 are to W. A. Knight and 4 to Joan Severn.

DEVONSHIRE, ELIZABETH (HERVEY) CAVENDISH, Duchess of, 1758–1824. Als (63) 1790–1820 to Harriet, Lady Duncannon, and the Duchess of Bessborough.

DEVONSHIRE, GEORGIANA (SPENCER) CAVENDISH, Duchess of, 1757–1806. Als (4) ca. 1795 and n.d.

DEVONSHIRE, SPENCER COMPTON CAVENDISH, 8th Duke of, 1833–1908. Als (5) 1852–87 including 4 to Sir John Millais.

DIBDIN, CHARLES, 1745–1814. "Verse addressed to J. R. Honeyman," 1 p.; als (2) n.d. including 1 to David Garrick.

DIBDIN, THOMAS FROGNALL, 1776–1847. Als (6) 1806–26.

DIBDIN, THOMAS JOHN, 1771–1841. Als (2) 1818 and n.d.

DICEY, ALBERT VENN, 1835–1922. Ls (4) 1894–6 to W. A. Knight.

DICK, SIR ALEXANDER, Bart., 1703–1785. "A Journal to Italy by Doctor Cuninghame 1736 now Sir Alexander Dick 1780," 197 pp. (manuscript in the hand of William Crawfurd).

DICKENS, CHARLES, 1812–1870. *The Battle of Life*, 50 pp.; *The Chimes* (title page only), 1 p.; *A Christmas Carol*, 68 *ll.*; *The Cricket on the Hearth*, 74 pp.; *Holiday Romance*, 30 pp.; *Hunted Down*, 15 pp.; 1 p. of *Nicholas Nickleby* (corresponding to p. 539 of the first edition); "Opinion," 8 March 1859, signed "J. Buzfuz," 2 pp.; "O'Thello," 2 pp.; *Our Mutual Friend*, dated 2 September 1865 and 4 January 1866, with 19 pp. of Dickens' preliminary notes for the development of the novel, 2 vols.; 1 p. of *The Posthumous Papers of the Pickwick Club* (corresponding to the first page of Chap. XXXVII in the first edition); "Prologue" to J. W. Marston's *The Patrician's Daughter*, 2 versions, 4 pp.; "Reflections of a Lord Mayor," 7 pp.; *Sketches of Young Gentlemen*, 113 pp.; "That Other Public," 11 pp.

Original drawings for illustrations to the novels: for *Pickwick*, 26 by H. K. Browne, 10 by R. W. Buss, 1 by John Leech; for *Oliver Twist*, 28 (24 watercolor replicas, title page and 3 pencil sketches) by George Cruikshank; for *A Christmas Carol*, 1 (watercolor) by H. K. Browne.

Miscellaneous manuscripts and letters (10) on private theatricals; publication agreements (3) with Chapman & Hall for *Pickwick* (1837), with Chapman & Hall and Ticknor & Fields for American publication rights (1867), and to edit *Bentley's Miscellany* (a draft), n.d.; checks (200) on Coutts and Company, December 1868–March 1870; catalogue of the library at Gad's Hill (not autograph), 100 pp.; 4 pp. from his Visitors Book (not autograph); Brass seal and "Traveling Inkwell" presented to Dickens by John Forster in 1833 and 1837; engraved silver bookmark and engraved silver matchbox presented to Dickens by Georgina Hogarth in 1868 and 1869.

Als (1,392) 1832–70 including 77 to his sister Letitia, 4 to his sister-in-law Georgina Hogarth, 136 to Henry Austin, 32 to Mary Boyle, 609 to Baroness Burdett-Coutts or her companion Mrs. Brown, with 70 letters addressed to the Baroness or to Dickens as her representative, 24 to Edward Chapman, Frederic Chapman or the firm Chapman & Hall, 145 to Wilkie Collins, 194 to W. C. Macready or members of his family, 37 to J. Macrone with 11 others relating to Dickens' dispute with him, 25 to Marcus Stone. With als (25) written by members of the Dickens family and als (60) addressed to Dickens.

See also: COLLINS, WILLIAM WILKIE.

DICKSEE, SIR FRANCIS BERNARD, 1853–1928. Als (2) 1883 and n.d.

DIGBY, SIR KENELM, 1603–1665. Ds 15 December 1660.

DILKE, CHARLES WENTWORTH, 1789–1864. Als (3) 1854, 1859 and n.d.

DILKE, SIR CHARLES WENTWORTH, 2nd Bart., 1843–1911. "The New Administration in England," 9 pp.; als (7) 1878–88 and n.d.

DIMOND, WILLIAM, ca. 1780–ca. 1836. Als 12 May 1820 to R. W. Elliston; ads 30 May 1824.

DISRAELI, BENJAMIN, 1st Earl of Beaconsfield, 1804–1881. *The Voyage of Captain Popanilla*, 222 pp.; als (9) 1845–81.

D'ISRAELI, ISAAC, 1766–1848. Als (3) 1819, 1835 and n.d.

DIXON, WILLIAM HEPWORTH, 1821–1879. Als 30 August 1859 to S. L. Sotheby.

DOBSON, AUSTIN, 1840–1921. "Angel-court," 1 p.; als (12) 1878–1908 and n.d. including 5 to W. E. Henley and 1 to Andrew Lang.

DODD, CHARLES TATTERSHALL, 1815–1878. Ads 1843.

DODDRIDGE, PHILIP, 1702–1751. Shorthand notebooks of Academical Lectures (2), 309 pp.; als (2) 1742.

DODGSON, CAMPBELL, 1867–1948. Als 9 July 1909 to C. F. Murray.

DODGSON, CHARLES LUTWIDGE ("LEWIS CARROLL"), 1832–1898. "Knot II" from *A Tangled Tale*, 3 pp.; als (79) 1877–93 including 70 to Harry Furniss with drawings (25) by Furniss for *Sylvie and Bruno*. The Lewis Carroll Collection of Mr. Arthur A. Houghton, Jr. is on deposit in the Morgan Library.

DODINGTON, GEORGE BUBB: *see* MELCOMBE.

DODSLEY, JAMES, 1724–1797. Als 30 November 1793 to Thomas Webster; ds 6 May 1783.

DOGGETT, THOMAS, ca. 1670–1721. Als 17 April 1714 to Sir Thomas Coke.

DONALDSON, THOMAS LEVERTON, 1795–1885. Als 15 May 1843.

DONKIN, SIR HORATIO BRYAN, 1845–1927. Als (2) 1901, 1903 to W. E. Henley.

DONNE, JOHN, 1572–1631. Signature and motto in Campion's *Poemata* (1595).

DORSET, THOMAS SACKVILLE, 1st Earl of, 1536–1608. Als 8 June 1602 to Sir Vincent Skinner; ls 6 August 1605 to Sir Richard Verney; ds (16) 1598–1608.

DOUCE, FRANCIS, 1757–1834. Als (3) 1822 and n.d., of which 2 are to S. L. Sotheby and 1 to Isaac D'Israeli.

DOUGHTY, CHARLES MONTAGU, 1843–1926. Als 17 August 1922 to S. C. Cockerell.

DOUGLAS, LORD ALFRED BRUCE, 1870–1945. Als (3) 1899 to Leonard Smithers.

DOUGLAS, JOHN, 1721–1807. Als 17 November 1803.

DOUGLAS, NORMAN, 1868–1952. Als (2) 1929, 1934.

DOWNTON, WILLIAM, 1764–1851. "The Invitation," 1 p.; ads 30 May 1820.

DOWSON, ERNEST CHRISTOPHER, 1867–1900. "A Case of Conscience," 15 pp.; "Colloque Sentimental," 1 p.; "Fleur de la lune," 1 p.; the "Flower Notebook," 83 *ll.*; "O Mors, quam amara est memoria tua . . . ," 1 p.; "Sea-dreams for Mademoiselle Elizabeth de Krouglicoff," 1 p.; als (177) 1888–99 including 173 to A. C. Moore.

DOYLE, SIR ARTHUR CONAN, 1859–1930. *The Refugees*, 1 p. only; *Sir Nigel*, 388 *ll.*; "The Voyage of the 'Flowery Land,'" 13 *ll.*; als 15 February 1906 to Sir Arthur Pinero.

DOYLE, CHARLES ALTAMONT, 1832–1893. Als (3) n.d. to John Doyle.

DOYLE, SIR FRANCIS HASTINGS CHARLES, 1810–1888. Als n.d. to W. A. Knight.

DOYLE, HENRY EDWARD, 1827–1892. Als (25) 1840–5 to John Doyle.

DOYLE, RICHARD, 1824–1883. "Beauty and the Beast a Fairy Tale," 36 *ll.* translated by Adelaide Doyle and illustrated by Dick Doyle; als (56) 1842–65 and n.d. including 51 to John Doyle.

D'OYLY CARTE: *see* CARTE, RICHARD D'OYLY *and* CARTE, RUPERT D'OYLY.

DRESSLER, CONRAD, 1856–1940. Autograph account of experiences while making a bust of Ruskin in 1884, 7 pp.; als 18 June 1890 to M. H. Spielmann.

DREW, SAMUEL, 1765–1833. Als 16 April 1807 to Davies Giddy [Gilbert].

DRINKWATER, JOHN, 1882–1937. "A Town Window," 1 p.

DRUMMOND, ROBERT HAY, 1711–1776. Als 15 December 1763 to John Symonds; ls 17 December 1762.

DRUMMOND, SAMUEL, 1765–1844. Als (2) n.d.

DRUMMOND (OF HAWTHORNDEN), WILLIAM, 1585–1649. Signature in Juan Huarte, *Examen de Ingenios para las Sciencias . . .* (1591).

DRYDEN, JOHN, 1631–1700. "Commonplace Book" (not autograph), containing translations from Vergil and Juvenal, 152 pp.; "Eleonora" (not autograph), 6 *ll.*; als (17) 1690–1700, of which 9 are to Mrs. Steward, 4 to Jacob Tonson and 4 to William Walsh. With an undated letter from his son, Charles Dryden.

DUDLEY, SIR HENRY BATE, 1st Bart., 1745–1824. Als ca. 1778 to David Garrick.

DUDLEY, SIR ROBERT, 1574–1649. Als (7) 1628–39 including 6 to Balli Cioli, secretary of state to the grand duke of Tuscany.

DUFF, EDWARD GORDON, 1863–1924. Als 25 May 1897 to Richard Bennett.

DUFF, SIR MOUNTSTUART ELPHINSTONE GRANT: *see* GRANT DUFF.

DUFFERIN AND AVA, FREDERICK TEMPLE HAMILTON-TEMPLE BLACKWOOD, 1st Marquess of, 1826–1902. Als (7) 1884–99.

DUGDALE, JOHN, 1628–1700. Als 10 September 1698.

DUGDALE, SIR WILLIAM, 1605–1686. Als (3) 1652–77.

DU MAURIER, DAME DAPHNE, 1907– . "A Wish," 1 p.

DU MAURIER, GEORGE LOUIS PALMELLA BUSSON, 1834–1896. *Peter Ibbetson*, 345 pp.; with drawings (85) and a notebook with drafts for the novel, 33 pp.; *Trilby*, 740 pp., with drawings (120) and a corrected typescript of the novel, 406 pp.; *Trilby*, uncorrected typescript of the dramatization by Paul M. Potter, 102 pp.; als, ls, ds (49) 1860–96 including 22 to Sir John Millais and Mary Millais and 5 to his wife; correspondence relating to the suit brought by J. A. M. Whistler against Harper & Bros. for an alleged libel against him in *Trilby*, 1894–5, 65 pp.; correspondence relating to motion-picture and other rights to *Trilby* in the U.S. and Canada, 1893–1922, 222 pieces; als (26) to du Maurier from various correspondents mainly concerning *Trilby*.

[DUNBAR, WILLIAM, 1460?–1513?] "London thow arte the flowre of cytes all," 3 pp.

DUNCOMBE, JOHN, 1729–1786. Als n.d.

DUNCOMBE, SUSANNA (HIGHMORE), 1730?–1812. Als 15 May 1779 to Mrs. Brooke.

DUNCOMBE, WILLIAM, 1690–1769. Als 3 February 1748.

DUNLOP, FRANCES ANNE (WALLACE), 1730–1815. Als (102) 1786–95 to Robert Burns.

DUREL, JOHN, 1624–1683. Als 21 May 1654 to William Edgeman.

DYCE, ALEXANDER, 1798–1869. Als (3) n.d.

DYCE, WILLIAM, 1806–1864. Als (2) 1852, 1859.

DYER, SIR EDWARD, d. 1607. Als 24 August 1597 to the Governors of the Free School of St. Mary Overey; ds 10 May 1575.

EARLOM, RICHARD, 1743–1822. Als 7 March 1811 to Josiah Boydell.

EASTLAKE, SIR CHARLES LOCK, 1793–1865. Als (11) 1834–57 including 5 to C. R. Leslie.

EASTLAKE, ELIZABETH (RIGBY), Lady, 1809–1893. Als (21) 1850–82 including 18 to Mrs. John Ruskin.

EDGEWORTH, MARIA, 1767–1849. "Beaujolin's Travels

of two Frenchmen," 2 pp.; 1 p. of her novel *Helen* (1834); "The Miner" ["Lame Jervas"], 45 pp.; "The Union," 1 p.; notes for plays and stories, 10 pp.; als (13) 1813–49 and n.d. including 1 to D. F. J. Arago, 1 to Wilkie Collins and 6 to Thomas Spring-Rice.

EDGEWORTH, RICHARD LOVELL, 1744–1817. Als 2 July 1807 to Mr. Elliott.

EDMONDS, JOHN MAXWELL. Als 18 July 1929 to S. C. Cockerell.

EDWARDS, GEORGE, 1694–1773. Als 5 December 1761 to Thomas Pennant.

EGAN, PIERCE, 1772–1849. "Ad Valorem," in the form of a letter, 18 January 1838, to W. J. Simpson, 4 pp.

EGG, AUGUSTUS LEOPOLD, 1816–1863. Als (3) 1852 and n.d.

EGREMONT, GEORGE O'BRIEN WYNDHAM, 3rd Earl of, 1751–1837. Als (2) 1795 and n.d. to George Romney.

EHRET, GEORGE DIONYSIUS, 1710–1770. Als 26 December 1754.

ELGIN, THOMAS BRUCE, 7th Earl of, 1766–1841. Als (3) 1798, 1809.

ELIBANK, PATRICK MURRAY, 6th Baron, 1719–1794. Als 24 March 1765 to his brother.

ELIOT, GEORGE, 1819–1880. *Scenes of Clerical Life*, 552 pp.; als (4) 1865–79.

ELIOT, THOMAS STEARNS, 1888–1965. "Defence of the Islands," 1 p.; als, tls (23) 1928–50 including 21 to E. McKnight Kauffer.

ELIZABETH I, Queen of England, 1533–1603. Als (2) 1548, 1589; ls (2) 1564, 1589; ds (18) 1561–1602.

ELLERTON, JOHN LODGE, 1801–1873. Als 6 March 1869 to his publisher.

ELLESMERE, FRANCIS EGERTON, 1st Earl of, 1800–1857. Ds 4 May 1836.

ELLIOTSON, JOHN, 1791–1868. Als (7) 1854 and n.d. including 4 to Charles Dickens.

ELLIOTT, EBENEZER, 1781–1849. Als 10 January 1836 to the Rev. William J. Fox.

ELLIOTT, SIR WALTER, 1803–1887. Als 12 August 1845 to Henry Wheaton.

ELLIS, FREDERICK STARTRIDGE, 1830–1901. Als (8) 1865–97 including 5 to C. F. Murray.

ELLIS, SIR HENRY, 1777–1869. Als (8) 1827–58.

ELLIS, HENRY HAVELOCK, 1859–1939. Als 3 November 1922 to R. Cobden-Sanderson.

ELLISTON, ROBERT WILLIAM, 1774–1831. Copy of verse, intended to be spoken by Mr. Elliston for the Benefit Night for the British prisoners in France, 3 pp.; als (37) 1793–1827 including 23 to his uncle, William Elliston; ads 11 November 1809; ds 23 March 1813.

ELLISTON, WILLIAM, 1732–1807. Als (12) 1796–1804 to his nephew, R. W. Elliston.

ELMORE, ALFRED, 1815–1881. Ads n.d.

ELWIN, WHITWELL, 1816–1900. Als (7) 1894–6.

EMIN, EMIN JOSEPH, 1726–1809. Als 30 October 1762 to Dr. Mounsey.

EMPSON, SIR WILLIAM, 1906– . Als, tls (22) 1944–6 to John Davenport.

ENGLEFIELD, SIR HENRY CHARLES, 1752–1822. Als (3) 1800–8, of which 2 are to Sir George Beaumont and 1 to J. S. Cotman.

EPSTEIN, SIR JACOB, 1880–1959. Als 15 August 1935 to E. A. Lowe.

ERSKINE, DAVID STEUART BUCHAN, 11th Earl of, 1742–1829. Journal, 2 and 4 April 1802, 8 pp.; original sketches and notes, 1 p.; als, ls (8) 1802–18 including 7 to Lady Anne Hamilton and 1 to Mrs. Damer; ads (2) 22 March 1802 and n.d.

ERSKINE, HENRY, 1746–1817. Ds n.d.

ERSKINE, THOMAS, 1788–1870. Als n.d. to W. A. Knight.

ERSKINE, THOMAS ERSKINE, 1st Baron, 1750–1823. Als (3) 1795–1814.

ESCOTT, THOMAS HAY SWEET, 1844–1924. Als (2) 1875, 1883.

ESSEX, ROBERT DEVEREUX, 2nd Earl of, 1566–1601. "An apologie of the Earl of Essex" (contemporary manuscript inscribed to Mr. Anthonie Bacon); als, ls (4) ca. 1592–8.

ETTY, WILLIAM, 1787–1849. Als (7) 1825–46 and n.d.

EVANS, RICHARD, 1784–1871. Als 23 May 1830.

EVANS, SEBASTIAN, 1830–1909. Als 6 July 1894 to Joseph Hatton.

EVELYN, JOHN, 1620–1706. "Of statues" (by Leon Battista Alberti, translated from the Italian of Cosimo Bartoli by J. Evelyn, contemporary copy); autograph inscription to Sir Thomas Browne, als, ls (3) 1674–80 including 1 to Samuel Pepys and 1 to Thomas Tenison; ds 24 September 1647. With a letter from his wife 22 March 1668 to Ralph Bohun.

EWING, JULIANA HORATIA (GATTY), 1841–1885. Als (2) 1879 to John Ruskin and to Joan Severn.

EYTON, JOSEPH WALTER KING. Als (3) 1858–9 to S. L. Sotheby.

FAIRBANK, ALFRED JOHN, 1895– . Calligraphic copybook made for Vera Law, 1926, 7 pp.; draft of instructions for manipulating the pen, ca. 1926–7, 3 pp.; draft of a "Woodside Writing Card," ca. 1932, 2 pp.; draft of an illustration for *A Handwriting Manual* (1932), 2 pp.; als 8 March 1958 to John Carter.

FAIRHOLT, FREDERICK WILLIAM, 1814–1866. Als (5) 1845–60; ds 14 August 1860.

FAITHFULL, EMILY, 1835–1895. Als (4) 1868, 1877 including 2 to Harper & Bros.

FALCONER, WILLIAM, 1732–1769. Ds 1768?

FANSHAWE, SIR RICHARD, 1608–1666. Presentation inscription to Mr. Cotton in his translation of Camões' *The Lusiad* (1655).

FARADAY, MICHAEL, 1791–1867. Als (4) 1829–56.

FARINGTON, JOSEPH, 1747–1821. Als (6) 1793–1821, including 2 to Sir George Beaumont.

FARJEON, BENJAMIN LEOPOLD, 1838–1903. Als 29 April 1878 to Harper & Bros.

FARMER, JOHN STEPHEN, 1845–1915? Als (2) 1900, 1901 to W. E. Henley.

FARRAR, FREDERIC WILLIAM, 1831–1903. "Lord Shaftesbury," 18 pp.; "The Salvation Army," 2 pp.; als (4) 1872 and n.d.

FARREN, ELIZABETH, Countess of Derby, 1762–1829. Als (2) 19 May 1794 to Mrs. Piozzi and n.d.

FAUCIT, HELENA: *see* Martin, Helena.

FAULKNER, THOMAS, 1777–1855. "Lord Byron criticizing Thomas Campbell for his championship of Lady Byron," 1 p.

FAWCETT, JOHN, 1768–1837. Als 21 March 1810 to the Duke of Clarence.

FEARON, WILLIAM ANDREWES, 1841–1924. Als n.d. to W. A. Knight.

FEATHERSTONHAUGH, GEORGE WILLIAM, 1780–1866. Als (2) 1819, 1820 to F. R. Hassler and André Thoüin.

FECHTER, CHARLES ALBERT, 1824–1879. Als 7 June 1865.

FEILDEN, HENRY WEMYSS, 1838–1921. Als 3 January 1913 to W. H. Mullens.

FELL, JOHN, 1625–1686. Als (2) 1685 and n.d.

FELLOWES, EDMUND HORACE, 1870–1951. Als 4 January 1944 to Sir Sydney Cockerell.

FENN, GEORGE MANVILLE, 1831–1909. Als (3) 1883–1904 including 1 to George Grossmith.

FENTON, SIR GEOFFREY, 1539?–1608. Ds (2) 1583, 1589.

FENWICK, THOMAS FITZROY PHILLIPPS, 1856–1938. Als 16 April 1904 to Sotheby, Wilkinson & Hodge.

FERGUSON, ADAM, 1723–1816. Als (14) 1769–94 including 7 to Sir William (Johnstone) Pulteney.

FERRIER, SIR DAVID, 1843–1928. Als 8 January 1904 to W. A. Knight.

FERRIER, JAMES WALTER, d. 1883. Als (7) 1878–80 including 6 to W. E. Henley.

"FIELD, MICHAEL." Pseudonym of Katherine Harris Bradley (1846–1914) and Edith Emma Cooper (1862–1913). Sonnets: "Brown Willy," "Constancy," "Old Ivories," 5 pp. Als (10) including 6 from Miss Bradley to Miss Cooper and 1 to Mary Berenson.

FIELDING, HENRY, 1707–1754. Ads 11 June 1748 to Andrew Millar; ds 25 March 1749.

FIELDING, SIR JOHN, d. 1780. Ls 22 February 1776 to David Garrick; ds (2) 1769, 1771.

FILDES, SIR SAMUEL LUKE, 1844–1927. Als (5) 1882–1914.

FINDEN, WILLIAM, 1787–1852. Als 23 March 1843 to Henry Graves & Co.

FINDLAY, JOHN RITCHIE, 1824–1898. Als 25 August 1890 to W. A. Knight.

FINLAYSON, JAMES, 1840–1906. Als 6 July 1893 to W. A. Knight.

FISHER, HERBERT ALBERT LAURENS, 1865–1940. Als 20 January 1906 to T. J. Cobden-Sanderson.

FISHER, JOHN, 1459?–1535. Ds 8 March 1511.

FITCH, SIR JOSHUA GIRLING, 1824–1903. Als (2) 1891, 1894 to W. A. Knight.

FITZGERALD, EDWARD, 1809–1883. Als (30) 1862–82 including 22 to Horace Basham; wash drawing of "Goldington Hall, Bedford."

FITZGERALD, PERCY HETHERINGTON, 1834–1925. "Amuse the crowds," 6 pp.; als (3) n.d.

FITZHERBERT, MARIA ANNE (SMYTHE), 1756–1837. Als (188) 1802–35 and undated, to her ward Minney Seymour Damer.

FITZMAURICE-KELLY, JAMES, 1857–1923. Als (2) 1903 to W. E. Henley.

FITZPATRICK, RICHARD, 1747–1813. Als n.d. to Sir Peter Burrell; ls (2) 1806 to Sir James Murray-Pulteney.

FITZWILLIAM, CHARLES WILLIAM WENTWORTH, 3rd Earl, 1786–1857. Als 13 December 1855.

FLAMSTEED, JOHN, 1646–1719. Ads 30 June 1715; ds 20 June 1693.

FLAXMAN, JOHN, 1755–1826. "The Tinder Box, a Probationary Ode," 10 *ll.*; als (14) 1783–1819 including 9 to William Hayley. With an als from Mrs. Flaxman 23 May 1796? to William Hayley.

FLETCHER, MARIA JANE (JEWSBURY): *see* JEWSBURY, MARIA JANE.

FLETCHER, WILLIAM. "An Inventory of Sundry Effects the Property of the late Rt. Honourable Lord Byron Taken July 31st 1824," 10 pp.; portion of a diary, written after Byron's death disproving and contradicting statements in Medwin's book on the poet, 2pp.

FLEXMORE, RICHARD, 1824–1860. Als (2) 1856 and n.d.

FLINT, ROBERT, 1838–1910. Als (28) 1879–1906 to W. A. Knight.

FLOOD, HENRY, 1732–1791. Als 17 November 1783 to Edmond Malone.

FLOWER, ROBIN ERNEST WILLIAM, 1881–1946. "Tomás," 2pp.

FOLKARD, HENRY TENNYSON, 1850–1916. *The Dyke House, a Drama*, 40 pp. (not autograph).

FOOTE, SAMUEL, 1720–1777. Als May 1768 to David Garrick.

FORBES, ALEXANDER PENROSE, 1817–1875. Als (2) 1875 to W. A. Knight.

FORBES, ARCHIBALD, 1838–1900. "Outlook for war in Europe," 20 pp.; als n.d. to Mr. & Mrs. Millais.

FORBES, DUNCAN, 1685–1747. Ds 9 January 1741.

FORBES, SIR WILLIAM, Bart., 1739–1806. Als (2) n.d.

FORBES-ROBERTSON, SIR JOHNSTON, 1853–1937. Als (6) 1891–1913.

FORD, FORD MADOX, 1873–1939. "Galsworthy," 24 pp. (corrected typescript).

FORDYCE, GEORGE, 1736–1802. Als n.d.

FORDYCE, JAMES, 1720–1796. Als (2) 1783 and n.d.

FORREST, THOMAS, 1729?–1802? Als (2) 1774, 1779 to Sir William (Johnstone) Pulteney.

FORSTER, EDWARD MORGAN, 1879–1970. "Art for Art's Sake," 10 pp. (corrected typescript); als (4) 1925–50.

FORSTER, JOHN, 1812–1876. Untitled poem 23 December 1847, 1 p.; als (16) 1841–73 and n.d.

FORSTER, THOMAS IGNATIUS MARIA, 1789–1860. Als 12 September 1849 to H. B. H. Beaufoy.

FOSS, HENRY, bookseller. Als (2) 1855, 1857 to S. L. Sotheby.

FOSTER, SIR MICHAEL, 1836–1907. Als n.d. to W. A. Knight.

FOSTER, MYLES BIRKET, 1851–1922. Als 28 July 1885 to Miss Gillington.

FOTHERGILL, JOHN ROWLAND, 1876–1957. Als 16 November 1929 to R. Cobden-Sanderson.

FOULIS, ANDREW & ROBERT, publishers. Als (2) 1773, 1775.

FOX, CHARLES JAMES, 1749–1806. Als, ls (10) 1772–1806; ds (2) 1773, 1782.

FOX, GEORGE, 1624–1691. Als 8 August 1673 to William Penn.

FOX, ROBERT WERE, 1789–1877. Als 29 November 1838 to John Griscom.

FOXE, JOHN, 1516–1587. Autograph inscription to Mathew Parker, Archbishop of Canterbury, in *Gospels of the fower Evangelistes* (1571).

FOXWELL, HERBERT SOMERTON, 1849–1936. Als (3) 1896–7 to W. A. Knight.

FRAMPTON, SIR GEORGE JAMES, 1860–1928. Als (2) 1912 to Joan Severn.

FRANCIS, SIR PHILIP, 1740–1818. "A memorial of several noblemen & gentlemen of the first rank & fortunes," 4 pp.; als (63) 1765–1809 including 12 to Philip Baggs and 41 to Alexander Mackrabie. With several letters from members of the Francis family.

FRANCKLIN, THOMAS, 1721–1784. Als 5 November 1778 to the Dean of Carlisle; ds 14 January 1775.

FRANKLIN, COLIN. "The Bookseller and the Librarian,"

ams of an address given in 1975, 17 pp.

FRANKLIN, SIR JOHN, 1786–1847. Als 10 November 1830.

FRASER, ALEXANDER CAMPBELL, 1819–1914. Als (30) 1879–1904 to W. A. Knight.

FRAZER, SIR JAMES GEORGE, 1854–1941. Als (2) 1925, 1928.

FREEMAN, JOHN, 1880–1929. "The Pigeons," 4 pp.

FRERE, JOHN HOOKHAM, 1769–1846. Als (2) 1819 and n.d.

FRITH, WILLIAM POWELL, 1819–1909. Als (16) 1845–1905 including 12 to Sir John Millais and Mary Millais.

FROST, WILLIAM EDWARD, 1810–1877. Als 9 November 1847 to Alexander Johnston.

FROUDE, JAMES ANTHONY, 1818–1894. Als (97) 1862–93 including 38 to John Ruskin and 27 to Joan Severn.

FRY, ELIZABETH (GURNEY), 1780–1845. Als 13 July 1844?

FRY, FRANCIS, 1803–1886. Als 3 May 1858 to S. L. Sotheby.

FRY, ROGER ELIOT, 1866–1934. "Mr. McKnight Kauffer's Posters," 4 pp.; untitled manuscript on the work of Kauffer. With "Notes taken at Roger Fry's lecture on 'Commerce and Art'" taken down and transcribed by Kauffer, 7 pp; aps 21 October 1933 to Julian Bell.

FULLER, HESTER THACKERAY (RITCHIE), 1878–1960. Als 19 August 1907 to S. C. Cockerell.

FULLER-MAITLAND, JOHN ALEXANDER, 1856–1936. Als (2) to Joan Severn.

FURNIVALL, FREDERICK JAMES, 1825–1910. Als 3 July 1908 to T. J. Cobden-Sanderson.

FURSE, CHARLES WELLINGTON, 1868–1904. Als (2) n.d. to W. E. Henley.

FUSELI, HENRY, 1741–1825. Als (10) 1798–1823; ads n.d.; ds (2) 1813, 1820.

GADBURY, JOHN, 1627–1704. Als 6 June 1679 to Edward Lloyd.

GAINSBOROUGH, THOMAS, 1727–1788. Als (3) ca. 1770, 1772?, 1782 including 1 to Sir Joshua Reynolds; ads 5 August 1769.

GAIRDNER, SIR WILLIAM TENNANT, 1824–1907. Als 6 January 1896 to W. A. Knight.

GALE, ROGER, 1672–1744. Als 27 January 1743/4.

GALSWORTHY, JOHN, 1867–1933. *Beyond*, 896 *ll.*; "Defeat," 41 pp.; "The First and the Last," 152 pp. and corrected typescript, 108 pp.; Preface to *Fraternity*, 5 pp. (corrected typescript); "The Hondekoeter," 16 pp. (corrected typescript); *The Pagan* (an early version of *The Island Pharisees*), 479 *ll.*, with explanatory notes by the author, 1 p.; *Punch and Go, a Comedy*, 31 pp.; *The Saint's Progress* (first draft), 580 pp.; "The Tragedy of St. Valentine," 15 pp.; translation (with Ada Galsworthy) of the Meilhac and Halévy libretto for Bizet's *Carmen*, 48 *ll.* (corrected typescript); corrections and stage directions in his *Full Moon* (1915), *Justice* (1910) and *Skin Game* (1920); extensive corrections and additions in the English typescript draft ca. 1929 of *John Galsworthy*, by Leon Schalit, 436 pp.; note concerning the Forsyth character, 1 p.; quotation from *The Pigeon* (1912), 1 p.; als (20) 1908–31 including 7 to Lillah McCarthy, 1 to John Martin-Harvey and 3 to Frank Vernon. With als (6) 1908–33 of his wife, Ada Galsworthy, to Lillah McCarthy.

GALT, JOHN, 1779–1839. Als 25 January 1836 to Richard Bentley.

GANCIA, G., bookseller, Brighton. Als (3) 1855–6 to S. L. Sotheby.

GARDINER, SIR ROBERT WILLIAM, 1781–1864. Als (2) 1821 to Sir George Nayler.

GARDINER, STEPHEN, 1483?–1555. Ds (3) 1554, 1555.

GARDINER, WILLIAM, 1770–1853. Als (2) 1826, 1842.

GARDNER, DAME HELEN LOUISE, 1908– . "Four Quartets," 13 pp. (typescript); als 30 March 1978 to Charles Ryskamp.

GARNETT, DAVID, 1892–1981. Als ca. March 1918 to J. M. Keynes.

GARNETT, RICHARD, 1835–1906. Als (12) 1889–1905 including 11 to W. A. Knight.

GARRICK, DAVID, 1717–1779. "The Old Painter's Soliloquy," 1 p.; "Wilmot & Garrick," 3 pp.; als (19) 1758–75 and n.d.; with 7 letters written by others to or about Garrick; and 5 letters 1734 and n.d. written by Garrick's father, mother or wife.

GASELEE, SIR STEPHEN, 1882–1943. Als 26 February 1911 to Messrs. J. & J. Leighton.

GASKELL, ELIZABETH CLEGHORN (STEVENSON), 1810–1865. Als, ads (22) 1841–59, of which 18 are to Chapman & Hall, 2 to Charles Dickens, 1 to the Rev. John Pierpont and 1 to John Ruskin; also including an agreement, 23 August 1852, for the purchase of the copyright to her *Ruth* by Chapman. With agreements and receipts (6) 1848–56 of her husband William Gaskell, concerning the publication of her works by Chapman & Hall.

GATTIE, HENRY, 1774–1844. Als (2) 1836 and n.d.

GATTY, SIR ALFRED SCOTT: *see* SCOTT-GATTY.

"GAWSWORTH, JOHN": *see* ARMSTRONG, TERENCE IAN FYTTON.

GAY, JOHN, 1685–1732. "Receipt to Make a Soupe, By Mr Pope to Dean Swift" (poem attributed to Gay, written in an unidentified hand), 1 p.; als (2) 1713–4 to William Fortescue and Charles Ford.

GAY, JOHN, 1813–1885. Als 3 September 1878 to J. E. Millais.

GELL, SIR WILLIAM, 1777–1836. Als (12) 1798–1834 and n.d

GERHARDIE, WILLIAM ALEXANDER, 1895–1977. Tls 15 September 1931 to K. L. Dickman.

GERMAIN, LADY ELIZABETH, 1680–1769. Als n.d. to Mrs. Knight.

GIBBON, BENJAMIN PHELPS, 1802–1851. Als 13 August 1842.

GIBBON, EDWARD, 1737–1794. Diary with brief entries February–November 1776; notebook containing historical notes, 13 *ll.*; corrected proofsheets from the Preface to the *Decline and Fall*, Vol. IV, 4 pp.; notes on his own *Essai sur l'étude de la littérature* written in a copy of that work (1761); "Catalogue des livres de la bibliothèque de Monsieur Gibbon," Lausanne, 1785 (not autograph), 150 pp.; receipts acknowledging payments made by Gibbon, March 1773–August 1783, 2 vols.; cash book of receipts and disbursements, August 1783–June 1786; miscellaneous bonds, notes, receipted bills, etc. (22) 1766–89; als (4) 1758–75 and n.d. including 1 to Suzanne Curchod.

GIBBONS, GRINLING, 1648–1720. Ds 10 October 1713.

GIBBS, SIR PHILIP HAMILTON, 1877–1962. Als (2) 1935 and n.d.

GIBSON, EDMUND, 1669–1748. Manuscript in Latin concerning the early church in Britain, 4 pp.; "Memorial concerning sending of bishops to the English plantations abroad," 22 pp.; als (3) 1691, 1698 and 1747.

GIBSON, JOHN, 1790–1866. Als (3) 1860, 1863 and n.d.

including 1 to Lady Bunbury and 1 to Harriet Hosmer.

GIBSON, WILFRID WILSON, 1878–1962. "So long had I travelled the lonely road," 1 p. Notebook containing autograph poems written out and signed by 28 English, American and European poets, 1914–37, 46 pp.; poems by English poets are listed separately in this checklist.

GIFFORD, WILLIAM, 1756–1826. Als (3) 1815 and n.d.

GILBERT, ANN (TAYLOR), 1782–1866. "Israelites," 2 pp.

GILBERT, DAVIES, 1767–1839. Als 19 November 1831.

GILBERT, SIR JOHN, 1817–1897. Als (2) 1872 and n.d. to J. E. Millais.

GILBERT, SIR WILLIAM SCHWENCK, 1836–1911. *The "Bab" Ballads:* "Babette's Love," Damon vs. Pythias" (both incomplete), "A Drop of Pantomime Water," "The Yarn of the Nancy Bell" (not autograph), 8 pp.; *Fifty "Bab" Ballads:* "Preface," 1 p.; "A Colossal Idea" (partly autograph), 38 pp.; *Eyes and No Eyes* (not autograph), 53 pp.; *Fair Rosamond* (not autograph), 8 pp.; *Foggerty's Fairy* (corrected proof copy), 72 pp.; "Great Expectations," 75 pp.; *The Happy Land. Burlesque. Part II*, 20 pp.; *Iolanthe* (notebook containing a draft of the plot and notes for *Utopia Limited* and *The Grand Duke*), 229 pp.; "The King and The Stroller. A Comparison," 2 pp.; "The Lady in the Plaid Shawl," 7 pp.; "My Maiden Brief," 15 pp.; *The Pirates of Penzance* (Act I only of the libretto), 28 pp.; *The Pretty Druidess*, 38 pp.; *Utopia Limited* (draft of the story with notes), 111 pp.; verses for *Fallen Fairies, The Gondoliers* (2), *The Mikado* (3), *The Yeoman of the Guard* (2) and limericks (2); als, ls (ca. 900). With Sir Arthur Sullivan: "Little Maid of Arcadee" (from *Thespis*), 3 pp.; *The Pirates of Penzance*, 2 vols.; *Trial by Jury*, 169 pp.; also *Cox and Box*, by Sullivan and F. C. Burnand, 220 pp.; als, ls, from Sullivan (ca. 1,450).

GILCHRIST, ALEXANDER, 1828–1861. Poems: "A Dirge," "Sonnet—A Portrait: Miss E——," "To a Gentle Spirit of My Youth," "Sonnet—To W. H.," "Sonnet—Of My Love," 4 pp.; als 16 January 1856 to Mr. White.

GILCHRIST, JOHN BORTHWICK, 1759–1841. Als 30 June 1801 to James Currie.

GILFILLAN, GEORGE, 1813–1878. Verses, 2 pp.; als (4) 1871–2 to W. A. Knight.

GILL, ERIC, 1882–1940. Als 15 March 1914 to T. J. Cobden-Sanderson. With an als 8 December 1942 from Mrs. Gill to Edward Johnston.

GILPIN, WILLIAM, 1724–1804. Als (11) 1801–2 to Sir George Beaumont.

GISSING, GEORGE ROBERT, 1857–1903, Als 10 December 1902 to F. G. Kitton; aps 27 November 1897 to A. H. Bullen.

GLADSTONE, HUGH STEUART, 1877–1949. Tls 14 January 1913 to W. H. Mullens.

GLADSTONE, WILLIAM EWART, 1809–1898. "Impregnable Rock of Holy Scripture" (revised proofsheets, 2 sets, 126 and 129 pp.); "Mr. Gladstone on Russians, Turks, and Bulgarians," corrections and additions, dated December 1877, to printed version published in the *Times*, 24 November 1877, 11 pp.; "On the Condition of Man in a Future State," 50 pp.; "Personal Recollections of Arthur Henry Hallam," 18 pp. (corrected typescript); als (115) 1837–96 including 20 to A. W. Haddon, 10 to Sir John Millais and 2 to Sir Arthur Sullivan.

GLENESK, ALGERNON BORTHWICK, Baron, 1830–1908. Als 11 July 1878 to George Grossmith.

GLOVER, JOHN, 1767–1849. Als 20 September 1818 to John Lord.

GLOVER, JOHN HULBERT. Als (5) 1856, 1858 to S. L. Sotheby.

GLOVER, JULIA (BETTERTON), 1779–1850. Als (2) n.d.

GLYN, ISABELLA DALLAS, 1823–1889. Als n.d. to E. T. Smith.

GODWIN, WILLIAM, 1756–1836. Als (3) 1800 and n.d. including 1 to S. T. Coleridge. *See also:* LAMB, CHARLES.

GOLDING, LOUIS, 1895–1958. Als 11 May 1921 to an editor.

GOLDSMITH, OLIVER, 1730?–1774. *The Captivity: An Oratorio*, 18 pp.; als December 1773 to Catherine Bunbury.

GOLLANCZ, SIR ISRAEL, 1864–1930. Als 2 June 1923 to J. P. Morgan.

GOODALL, FREDERICK, 1822–1904. Als (2) 1852, 1888.

GOODRICH, THOMAS, d. 1564. Als 15 June 1552/3 to Thomas Smyth, Mayor of Chester.

GORDON, SIR HENRY WILLIAM, 1818–1887. Als 7 July 1864 to Julius Reuter.

GORDON, SIR JOHN WATSON-, 1788–1864. Ads 24 July 1848.

GORELL, RONALD GORELL BARNES, 3rd Baron, 1884–1963. "The Spirit of Happiness," 152 pp.

GOSCHEN, GEORGE JOACHIM GOSCHEN, 1st Viscount, 1831–1907. Als (3) n.d. to W. A. Knight.

GOSSE, SIR EDMUND WILLIAM, 1849–1928. Sonnet on the death of Robert Browning, entitled "R. B.," 1 p.; "Letter [in verse] to Dr. Oliver Wendell Holmes on his 75th birthday," 2 pp.; als (8) 1878–1915 including 5 to W. E. Henley.

GOUGH, RICHARD, 1735–1809. Als (2) 1783 and n.d.

GOULBURN, EDWARD MEYRICK, 1818–1897. Als (4) 1887 to W. A. Knight.

GOUPY, JOSEPH, d. 1763. Ads 18 April 1721.

GRAFTON, AUGUSTUS HENRY FITZROY, 3rd Duke of, 1735–1811. Als (4) 1776–82.

GRAHAM, AARON, 1753–1818. Als (2) 1799 and n.d.

GRAHAM, ROBERT BONTINE CUNNINGHAME: *see* CUNNINGHAME GRAHAM.

GRAHAME, KENNETH, 1859–1932. Als 24 February 1913 to John Lane.

GRAIN, RICHARD CORNEY, 1844–1895. Als (2) 1876 and n.d.

GRAINGER, JAMES, 1721?–1766. Als 5 June 1762 to the Earl of Sussex.

GRANGER, FRANK STEPHEN, 1864–1936. Als 19 March 1908 to W. A. Knight.

GRANT, DUNCAN JAMES CORROWR, 1885–1978. Als 15 January 1926 to E. McKnight Kauffer; aps (3) 3 April 1916 and ca. February 1920 to J. M. Keynes.

GRANT, SIR FRANCIS, 1803–1878. Als (4) n.d. including 3 to J. E. Millais.

GRANT, JAMES, 1822–1887. Als (2) 1859, 1877.

GRANT DUFF, SIR MOUNTSTUART ELPHINSTONE, 1829–1906. Als 6 April 1900 to W. A. Knight.

GRATTAN, THOMAS COLLEY, 1792–1864. Als (2) n.d.

GRAVES, CHARLES LARCOM, 1856–1944. Als 14 April 1910 to Mrs. Byron.

GRAVES, RICHARD, 1715–1804. Als 27 May 1772 to Robert Barton.

GRAVES, ROBERT, 1895– . "Augeias and I," autograph versions (9) and final typescript, 10 pp.; *Goodbye to all that* (1957; corrected page proofs), 314 pp.; "Why I live in Majorca" (corrected typescript), 16 pp.; als (3) 1971–2 to Brendan Gill.

GRAY, SIR ALBERT, 1850–1928. Als n.d. to his sister,

Lady Millais.

GRAY, JOHN, 1866–1934. Letters (2) n.d. to Michael Field (copies by Katherine Bradley); telegrams (2) 1907 to Michael Field; als (3) 1907 from his housekeeper, Florence Gribbell, to Michael Field.

GRAY, THOMAS, 1716–1771. "The Fatal Sisters," 3 pp.; "On the Death of a favourite Cat," 2 pp.; epitaph beginning "Here free'd from pain, secure from misery, lies," 1 p.; lines beginning "Thyrsis, when we parted, swore," 1 p.; notebooks (9) containing the catalogue of his library (alphabetical and subject arrangements), and notes on the works of eight Greek authors and on the contents of the *Journal des Sçavans* and other serial publications; copy (not autograph) of his will, dated 2 July 1770, 21 pp.; marginalia in copies of his *Odes* (1757), Boccaccio's *Decamerone* (1725), Paulus Jovius' *De Romanis Piscibus Libellus* (1524) and Matthew Paris' *Historia Major* (1640); als (2) 1753, 1757 to the Rev. James Brown.

GREEN, THOMAS HILL, 1836–1882. Als n.d. to J. P. Nichol.

GREEN, VALENTINE, 1739–1813. Als 7 July 1803.

GREENAWAY, KATE, 1846–1901. Als (3) 1883, 1884, 1887 to Frederick Locker, John Ruskin and Joan Severn.

GREENE, GRAHAM, 1904– . Als, tls (62) 1945–55 and n.d. to his brother Herbert.

GREENE, HARRY PLUNKET, 1865–1936. Als n.d. to Alfred Mapleson.

GREENHAUGH, THOMAS. Cookery and medical recipes, 1699, 23 *ll.*

GREENWELL, DORA, 1821–1882. Als (17) 1864–6 to W. A. Knight.

GREGG, AMY. *A Choice Collection of Experemental Receipts for Pickling, Cookery &c.*, 1784, 80 *ll.*

GREGORY, ISABELLA AUGUSTA (PERSSE), Lady, 1852–1932. Als 15 November 1922 to Mrs. T. J. Cobden-Sanderson.

GREGORY, OLINTHUS GILBERT, 1774–1841. Als 27 December 1819 to Henry Andrews.

GRENVILLE, GEORGE, 1712–1770. Als (3) 1731–69; ds (4) 1751–63.

GRENVILLE, THOMAS, 1755–1846. Als (4) 1813–44.

GRENVILLE, WILLIAM WYNDHAM GRENVILLE, Baron, 1759–1834. Als, ls (17) 1793–1806; ads 9 November 1793.

GRESHAM, SIR THOMAS, 1519–1579. Als, ls (8) 1553–79; ds (2) 1547, 1577.

GREVILLE, FULKE, 1st Baron Brooke: *see* BROOKE, FULKE GREVILLE.

GREVILLE, H. F., fl. 1771–1811? Als n.d. to Mr. Phipps.

GREVILLE, ROBERT FULKE, 1751–1824. Als (2) 1 May 1819 to the Duke of York and n.d.; ads March 1795.

GREY, EDWARD GREY, 1st Viscount, 1862–1933. Als 9 August 1932 to J. P. Morgan.

GREY, HENRY GEORGE GREY, 3rd Earl, 1802–1894. Ds 16 June 1851.

GRIEVE, THOMAS, 1799–1882. Als n.d.

GRIFFITHS, JOHN, 1806–1885. Als 30 September 1852 to S. L. Sotheby.

GRIGNION, CHARLES, 1754–1804. Als 3 September 1783 to Sir William Chambers.

GRINDAL, EDMUND, 1519–1583. Als (2) 1569 to the Vidame of Chartres.

GROSE, FRANCIS, 1731?–1791. Als 16 January 1791.

GROSSMITH, GEORGE, 1847–1912. Als (15) 1872–96 and n.d.

GROTE, GEORGE, 1794–1871. Als 11 April 1835 to W. W. Hickson.

GROVE, SIR GEORGE, 1820–1900. Als (56) 1858–96 and n.d. including 22 to Joseph Bennett and 6 to W. A. Knight.

GRUNDY, SYDNEY, 1848–1914. Als (2) 1892, 1893.

GUEST, EMILY, 1837–1919. Als, ls (34) 1890–1919 to S. C. Cockerell.

GULL, SIR WILLIAM WITHEY, 1st Bart., 1816–1890. Als (2) 1885, 1886 to Joan Severn.

GUTCH, JOHN, 1745–1831. Als 23 March 1792 to John Nichols.

GUTCH, JOHN MATTHEW, 1777–1858. Als (24) 1843–56 to F. W. Fairholt.

GUTHRIE, THOMAS ANSTEY ("F. ANSTEY"), 1856–1934. Als 29 June 1884 to George du Maurier.

GWILT, GEORGE, 1775–1856. Als 9 July 1847 to J. P. Bowerbank.

GWYN, ELEANOR ("NELL"), 1650–1687. Ds (7) 1677–85.

GWYN, FRANCIS, 1648?–1734. Als (2) 1687 including 1 to Lord Bulstrode.

HADDEN, JAMES MURRAY, d. 1817. Letter (secretarial copy) 28 July 1793 to Evan Nepean.

HADEN, SIR FRANCIS SEYMOUR, 1818–1910. Ls 19 October 1874 to Philippe Burty.

HAGGARD, SIR HENRY RIDER, 1856–1925. Als (2) 8 June 1888 to W. E. Henley and n.d.

HAGHE, LOUIS, 1806–1885. Als (2) 1848, 1852 to Mr. and Mrs. Elhanan Bicknell.

HAILES, SIR DAVID DALRYMPLE, Lord, 1726–1792. Als (5) 1765–90 including 4 to Thomas Percy; ads 18 April 1783.

HAKE, GORDON, 1809–1895. "The Poet's Feast. To W. E. H.," 1 p.; als (7) 1887–9 to W. E. Henley.

HALE, SIR MATTHEW, 1609–1676. Answers to legal questions, 29 January 1658, 2 pp.; ds (2) 1668, 1673.

HALE, WILLIAM HALE, 1795–1870. Als 13 May 1843 to James Cottle.

HALES, STEPHEN, 1677–1761. Als 4 January 1760.

HALFORD, SIR HENRY, 1st Bart., 1766–1844. Als (2) 1830.

HALIFAX, GEORGE SAVILE, 1st Marquis of, 1633–1695. Ds (4) 1668–89 and n.d.

HALL, ANNA MARIA (FIELDING), 1800–1881. Als (5) 1828–79.

HALL, BASIL, 1788–1844. Memorandum concerning Sir Walter Scott, 1 p.; als (53) 1828–42 including 37 to Edward Moxon.

HALL, CHRISTOPHER NEWMAN, 1816–1902. Als 19 February 1868 to F. H. Morse.

HALL, JOSEPH, 1574–1656. Als 21 December 1649 to James Calthrop.

HALL, ROBERT, 1764–1831. Als 4 November 1800 to John Barnard.

HALL, SAMUEL CARTER, 1800–1889. Als (5) 1864–81 including 2 to John Ruskin; ds 20 September 1874.

HALL-STEVENSON, JOHN, 1718–1785. Letter 13 July 1766 to Laurence Sterne (copy by Sterne).

HALLAM, ARTHUR HENRY, 1811–1833. Als (5) 1831–2 to W. H. Brookfield.

HALLAM, HENRY, 1777–1859. Als (5) 1829–46 and n.d.

HALLAM, HENRY FITZMAURICE, 1824–1850. Als n.d. to W. H. Brookfield.

HALLÉ, SIR CHARLES, 1819–1895. Als (6) 1878–86, including 3 to Sir John Millais.

HALLIDAY, ANDREW, 1830–1877. Als (3) 1859, 1874 and n.d.

HALLIWELL-PHILLIPPS, JAMES ORCHARD, 1820–1889. Als 24 July 1868 to J. Harrison.

HALPINE, CHARLES GRAHAM ("MILES O'REILLY"), 1829–1868. Als (4) 1852–68 and n.d.

HAMILTON, ALEXANDER, 1762–1824. Als 11 February 1804.

HAMILTON, EMMA (LYON), Lady, 1761?–1815. Als (5) 1806–9 and n.d.

HAMILTON, JAMES, 1769–1829. Als n.d. to the French Ministry of War.

HAMILTON, LILLIAS. Als (2) 1899, 1903 to W. A. Knight.

HAMILTON, SIR WILLIAM, 1730–1803. Als (4) 1767–1802; ads 17 October 1798.

HAMILTON, WILLIAM GERARD, 1729–1796. Als 1 October 1793 to Mr. Leader.

HAMLEY, SIR EDWARD BRUCE, 1824–1893. Als 19 March 1888 to Sir John Millais.

HANMER, SIR THOMAS, 4th Bart., 1677–1746. Als (2) 4 December 1712 to the Duke of Shrewsbury, 20 March 1713 to Sir Richard Steele.

HANNA, WILLIAM, 1808–1882. Als (2) 1867, 1869 to W. A. Knight.

HANNAY, DAVID, 1853–1934. Als 3 November 1890 to W. E. Henley.

HANNAY, JAMES OWEN, 1865–1950. Als 2 January 1915 to S. C. Cockerell.

HANWAY, JONAS, 1712–1786. Ds (2) 1762, 1782.

HARCOURT, SIR WILLIAM GEORGE GRANVILLE VENABLES VERNON, 1827–1904. Als (6) 1874–90 and n.d. to Sir John Millais.

HARDIE, JAMES KERR, 1856–1915. Als 26 December 1909 to T. J. Cobden-Sanderson.

HARDING, JAMES DUFFIELD, 1798–1863. Als (2) 1852, 1860 to Elhanan Bicknell.

HARDWICK, PHILIP, 1792–1870. Als 25 April 1852 to Mr. and Mrs. Elhanan Bicknell.

HARDWICKE, PHILIP YORKE, 1st Earl of, 1690–1764. Als 8 August 1752.

HARDY, THOMAS, 1752–1832. Als n.d. to Mr. Walker.

HARDY, THOMAS, 1840–1928. "The Abbey Mason," 13 pp.; "Emmeline, or Passion versus Principle," 25 pp.; "The Romantic Adventures of a Milkmaid," 115 *ll.*; *Tess of the D'Urbervilles, a tragedy in five acts. In the old English manner* (corrected typescript), 93 pp.; *Tess of the D'Urbervilles,* dramatization in four acts by Lorimer Stoddard (typescript), 2 vols.; als, ls (11) 1889–1912; ds (2) 1895, 1897.

HARE, AUGUSTUS JOHN CUTHBERT, 1834–1903. Als 26 November 1889 to Joan Severn.

HARE, SIR JOHN (FAIRS), 1844–1921. Als (20) 1878–1908 including 16 to Sir John Millais and Mary Millais and 2 to Sir Arthur Sullivan.

HARINGTON, SIR JOHN, 1561–1612. Ds 30 September 1588.

HARLEY, JOHN PRITT, 1786–1858. Als (3) 1823–51.

HARLOWE, SARAH WALDRON, 1765–1852. Als n.d. to Mr. Durrant; ds 10 July 1820.

HARNESS, WILLIAM, 1790–1869. Als (2) 25 February 1846 to W. M. Thackeray and n.d.

HARRADEN, BEATRICE, 1864–1936. Als n.d. to Joan Severn.

HARRINGTON, JAMES, 1611–1677. Ls 23 September 1652.

HARRIS, AUGUSTUS GLOSSOP, 1825–1873. Als 8 July 1871 to Joseph Bennett.

HARRIS, SIR AUGUSTUS HENRY GLOSSOP, 1852–1896. Als (7) 1888–92 to Joseph Bennett.

HARRIS, JAMES, 1709–1780. Als (4) 1753–77.

HARRIS, THOMAS, d. 1820. Als 17 April 1783 to John Webster.

HARRIS, THOMAS LAKE, 1823–1906. Als (2) 24 June 1867 and n.d. to Mr. and Mrs. William Cowper.

HARRISON, FREDERIC, 1831–1923. Als (11) 1868–1902 including 2 to John Ruskin and 5 to Joan Severn.

HARRISON, MARY ST. LEGER (KINGSLEY), 1852–1931. Als (2) 1899 to Mary Millais.

HARRISON, WILLIAM, 1802–1884. Als 30 June 1858 to S. L. Sotheby.

HARRISON, WILLIAM HENRY, d. 1874. Autograph poems signed (26) 1842–51; toasts (2) 1861, 1864; als (4) 1842, 1856 and n.d. including 1 to John Ruskin and 1 to John James Ruskin.

HARSNETT, SAMUEL, 1561–1631. Ds 6 November 1619.

HART, SIR ROBERT, 1st Bart., 1835–1911. "China and her foreign trade," 20 pp.

HART, SOLOMON ALEXANDER, 1806–1881. Als 3 January 1861 to David Roberts.

HARTLEY, MARY. Memorandum of David Hartley (1732–1813) by his sister, 9 pp.

HARTSHORNE, CHARLES HENRY, 1802–1865. Als (8) 1851–8 to S. L. Sotheby.

HARVEY, GABRIEL, 1550?–1631. Signature and annotations in Sir Thomas Littleton's *Tenures* (1581).

HARVEY, WILLIAM, 1578–1657. Als 20 March 1637 to Basil Feilding.

HARVEY, WILLIAM, 1796–1866. Als 17 December 1823 to William Mayor.

HARVIE-BROWN, JOHN ALEXANDER, 1844–1916. Als 6 January 1913 to W. H. Mullens.

HARWOOD, EDWARD, 1729–1794. Als n.d.

HASTED, EDWARD, 1732–1812. Als 13 February 1765 to A. C. Ducarel.

HASTIE, WILLIAM, 1842–1903. Als (8) 1893–6 to W. A. Knight.

HATSELL, JOHN, 1742–1820. Als n.d.

HATTON, ANNA JULIA (KEMBLE), 1764–1838. Als (4) 1811 to Miss Smith in Dublin.

HATTON, SIR CHRISTOPHER, 1540–1591. Als (2) 1573 and n.d. to Queen Elizabeth I; ds (2) 1583, 1587.

HATTON, JOSEPH, 1841–1907. Als (3) 1895 and n.d.

HAWEIS, HUGH REGINALD, 1838–1901. Als 25 May 1892 to Mary Millais.

HAWILL, MARY. Als 1846 to Bayard Taylor.

HAWKESWORTH, JOHN, 1715?–1773. Als 5 May 1773 to Joseph Cradock.

HAWKINS, SIR ANTHONY HOPE, 1863–1933. Als (28) 1890–1926.

HAWKINS, EDWARD, 1780–1867. Als 5 October 1859 to S. L. Sotheby.

HAWKINS, EDWARD, 1789–1882. Als 4 August 1858 to S. L. Sotheby.

HAWKINS, SIR JOHN, 1719–1789. Als 26 February 1785 to Thomas Cadell.

HAY, MARY CECIL, 1840?–1886. Als (2) 1878 to Harper & Bros.

HAYDON, BENJAMIN ROBERT, 1786–1846. "Sonnets addressed to & MS Written by B. R. Haydon From 1817 to 1841. Twenty Four Years. Copied for Fun. 1844," 11 pp.; als (5) 1816–46; ads n.d.

HAYLEY, WILLIAM, 1745–1820. "The departed Dutchess

to her preeminent Bard," 1 p.; "Shall Walter wish for Geoffrey's Lyre?" 1 p.; "Sonnet" ("Departed Spirit of my social Friend!"), 1 p.; "Sonnet to Mr. John Flaxman Sculptor with a little copy of Milton Sept 1784," 1 p.; "To Mrs. Flaxman," 3 pp.; als, ls (34) 1794–1819 including 13 to Sir Walter Scott and 2 to William Wilberforce.

HAYTER, SIR GEORGE, 1792–1871. Als 12 February 1835.

HAYTER, JOHN, 1800–1891. Als 17 May 1844 to Mrs. Sartoris.

HAYWARD, ABRAHAM, 1801–1884. Als 9 February 1880 to J. E. Millais.

HAYWARD, SIR JOHN, 1564?–1627. Ds 7 January 1625.

HAZLITT, WILLIAM, 1778–1830. "The Fight" (incomplete), 35 pp.; als 16 April 1822 to Messrs. Taylor & Hessey.

HEAD, SIR FRANCIS BOND, 1793–1875. Als 26 September 1834 to W. Chisholm.

HEARNE, THOMAS, 1678–1735. Ads 25 February 1722.

HEARNE, THOMAS, 1744–1817. Als 1814, 1815 to Sir George Beaumont and Peter Coxe.

HEATH, CHARLES, 1785–1848. Als (3) 1815, 1836 and n.d.

HEATON, ELLEN. Als 11 March 1878 to W. A. Knight.

HEBER, REGINALD, 1783–1826. "Brightest and best of the sons of the morning," 1 p.; "Palestine," 18 *ll.*; als (7) 1811–27. With an als 16 January 1829 from Mrs. Heber to Robert Southey.

HEBERDEN, WILLIAM, 1767–1845. Als n.d. to Edward Sally.

HELMORE, THOMAS, 1811–1890. Als (25) 1854–62 mainly to the parents of Sir Arthur Sullivan.

HELPS, SIR ARTHUR, 1813–1875. *The Conquerors of the New World* (Vol. 2 only, partly autograph); *The Spanish Conquest in America* (manuscript of Bks. 9–16 with autograph corrections and insertions), 3 vols.; als, ls (7) 1845–74 including 3 to John Ruskin.

HEMANS, FELICIA DOROTHEA (BROWNE), 1793–1835. Poems: "And for all this heart's wealth wasted," 1 p.; "The Antique Sepulchre," 3 pp.; "The Chamois Hunter's Love," 3 pp.; "The Coronation of Inez de Castro," 5 pp.; "The Deserted House," 4 pp.; "The Dying Improvisatore," 3 pp.; "The Graves of a Household," 2 pp.; "An Hour of Romance," 3 pp.; "The Invocation," 2 pp.; "The Subterranean Stream," 3 pp.; "The Sound of the Sea," 2 pp.; "The Things that Change," 2 pp.; "The Vaudois Valley," 2 pp.; als (3) n.d. including 1 to A. A. Watts.

HENDERSON, JOHN, 1747–1785. Als 9 August 1782 to Isaac Reed.

HENLEY, ANTHONY, d. 1711. Als n.d. to Charles Ford.

HENLEY, WILLIAM ERNEST, 1849–1903. "Bibliographical Notes and Commentary on Byron's Poems," 106 pp.; "Essay on Henry Fielding," 72 pp.; "Essay on Victor Hugo," 15 pp.; "Essay on J. F. Millet," 76 pp.; "Father and Son, A Drama," 213 pp.; "Hospital Outlines," 10 pp. (with 3 series of corrected proofs); "In Hospital," 28 pp. (with annotations by R. L. Stevenson); "Invictus," 1 p.; "The Legend of Juan Soldado," 16 pp.; "Men and Women," 57 pp.; "The Romance of the Elephant," 4 pp.; "Sileniad," 1 p.; "A Thanksgiving," 1 p. (early draft of "Invictus"); poems (68), some published in *A Book of Verses* (1888) and others unpublished; drafts of book reviews, 9 pp.; correspondence cards (48) with quotations furnished for *Slang and its Analogues* (by J. S. Farmer and Henley); miscellany of poetry and prose fragments, proofs, clippings, prospectuses and photographs by or relating to Henley; als (210) 1870–1903 including 9 to William Archer, 93 to J. S. Farmer, 25 to his wife and 49 to Lord Windsor.

HENNIKER, FLORENCE ELLEN HUNGERFORD (MILNES), d. 1923. Als (2) 1891 to W. A. Knight.

HENNING, JOHN, 1771–1851. Als 6 May 1850.

HENRY, MATTHEW, 1662–1714. Notes for sermons and Biblical exposition, 4 pp.; als 30 September 1696 to Francis Tallents.

HENRY, PHILIP, 1631–1696. Sermon notes, 8 pp.; als (3) 1657/8–93 including 2 to Francis Tallents.

HENRY, ROBERT, 1718–1790. Als (2) 1782, 1783 to Thomas Cadell.

HENSON, HERBERT HENSLEY, 1863–1947. Als 26 March 1920 to T. J. Cobden-Sanderson.

HENTY, GEORGE ALFRED, 1832–1902. Als n.d. to H. F. Levy.

HERBERT, SIR ALAN PATRICK, 1890–1971. *The Secret Battle*, 163 pp.

HERBERT, JOHN ALEXANDER, 1862–1948. Als (2) 1919 to Belle da Costa Greene.

HERBERT OF CHERBURY, EDWARD HERBERT, 1st Baron, 1583–1648. Ds 11 March 1645/6.

HERBERT OF LEA, SIDNEY HERBERT, 1st Baron, 1810–1861. Als (2) 1859 to S. L. Sotheby.

HERING, GEORGE EDWARD, 1805–1879. Als n.d. to Elhanan Bicknell.

HERKOMER, SIR HUBERT VON, 1849–1914. Als (109) 1877–1910 and n.d. including 39 to W. W. Baldwin, 51 to Joseph Bennett and 9 to Sir John and Lady Millais.

HERRICK, ROBERT, 1591–1674. Als ca. 1615–6 to his uncle, Sir William Hearick.

HERRING, THOMAS, 1693–1757. Als (3) 1733–54; ds (2) 1752.

HERSCHEL, SIR JOHN FREDERICK WILLIAM, 1st Bart., 1792–1871. Verses, 10 April 1857, 1 p.; als (4) 1841–7 and n.d.

HERSCHEL, SIR WILLIAM, 1738–1822. Als 21 April 1789 to J. Baker.

HERVEY, JAMES, 1714–1758. Als (2) 24 January 1746/7 to Samuel Richardson and n.d. to his sister.

HESKETH, HARRIOT (COWPER), Lady, 1733–1807. Als (4) 1802 and n.d. including 2 to Walter Bagot.

HESSEY, JAMES AUGUSTUS, 1785–1870. Als 6 March 1818 to John Taylor.

HEWITT, GRAILY, 1864–1952. Calligraphic manuscripts: "The Epistle of John," 11 pp.; "Friend! When thou layest down thy head . . . ," 1 p.; "The Gospel According to St. Mark," 50 *ll.*; drawing in ink on vellum for the title page of *The Oxford Copy-Books*, Bk. II, 1 p.; Walter Pater, *The Child in the House*, 44 pp.; "Prayer for King George VI," 1 p.; als (5) 1910–24.

HEWLETT, MAURICE HENRY, 1861–1923. Als (3) 1910 to Joan Severn.

HEYDON, SIR CHRISTOPHER, d. 1623. Ds 28 February 1598/9.

HICHENS, ROBERT SMYTHE, 1864–1950. Als 15 January 1896 to Mary Millais.

HICKEY, EMILY HENRIETTA, 1845–1924. Als 18 February 1897 to W. A. Knight.

HILL, AARON, 1685–1750. Als 20 January 1743/4 to Samuel Richardson.

HILL, ALEX, 1856–1929. Als (2) 1900 to W. A. Knight.

HILL, DAVID OCTAVIUS, 1802–1870. Als 15 October 1857 to Elhanan Bicknell.

HILL, JAMES, d. 1817? Als 14 March 1758 to David Garrick.

HILL, JOSEPH, 1625–1707. Als 2 November 1704.

HILL, JOSEPH, 1733–1811. Als 16 August 1808 to William Hayley.

HILL, OCTAVIA, 1838–1912. Als 12 February 1892 to S. C. Cockerell.

HIND, ARTHUR MAYGER, 1880–1957. Als 21 February 1955 to F. B. Adams.

HOARE, CHARLES JAMES, 1781–1865. Als 31 May 1835 to Bishop McIlvaine.

HOARE, PRINCE, 1755–1834. Als (3) 1825 and n.d.

HOARE, SIR RICHARD COLT, 1758–1838. Als (2) n.d.

"HOBBES, JOHN OLIVER": *see* CRAIGIE.

HOBBS, JOHN THOMAS, ca. 1825–1892. Travel diary with the Ruskins in France, Switzerland and Italy during the periods April–October 1846, July–October 1848 and April–August 1849, 245 pp.

HOBHOUSE, JOHN CAM, Baron Broughton, 1786–1869. Als (8) 1808–44.

HODGKIN, JOHN EVAN, 1831–1895. Als (2) 1886 and n.d. to Sir John Millais.

HODGSON, SHADWORTH HOLLWAY, 1832–1912. Als (9) 1887–98 to W. A. Knight.

HOFLAND, BARBARA, 1770–1844. Als (3) 1841 and n.d.

HOGARTH, GEORGE, 1783–1870. Als (2) 1829, 1860.

HOGARTH, GEORGINA, 1827–1917. Als (11) 1863–99; ads n.d.

HOGARTH, WILLIAM, 1697–1764. Als 30 April 1761 to Lord Charlemont; ds 10 March 1761.

HOGG, JAMES, 1770–1835. *Familiar Anecdotes of Sir Walter Scott*, 14 pp.; "Song," 1 p.; als 1 March 1816 to a publisher.

HOLCROFT, THOMAS, 1745–1809. "Lie still, be still my pretty Babe," 2 pp.; als (2) 1826 to Mr. Elliston; ds 8 May 1787.

HOLE, SAMUEL REYNOLDS, 1819–1904. Acs 13 May 1880.

HOLFORD, ROBERT STAYNER, 1808–1892. Als (3) 1851–4 to S. L. Sotheby.

HOLGATE, WILLIAM, ca. 1590–1634. *Common-place book of Mr. W. H.*, 331 pp.

HOLIDAY, HENRY, 1839–1927. Als 27 March 1889 to W. A. Knight.

HOLL, FRANCIS MONTAGUE, 1845–1888. Als (5) 1878–87 including 3 to Sir John Millais.

HOLLAND, ELIZABETH (VASSALL) FOX, Lady, 1770–1845. Als ca. 1799 to John Romney.

HOLLAND, HENRY, 1746?–1806. Als ca. 1790–1 to R. B. Sheridan.

HOLLAND, SIR HENRY, 1st Bart., 1788–1873. Als n.d.

HOLLAND, HENRY FOX, 1st Baron, 1705–1774. Als (2) 1752, 1753; ds (3) 1754–6.

HOLLAND, HENRY RICHARD VASSALL FOX, 3rd Baron, 1773–1840. als, ls (11) 1812 and n.d.

HOLLAND, JAMES, 1800–1870. Als 9 March 1848 to S. C. Hall.

HOLLINGSHEAD, JOHN, 1827–1904. Als (10) 1869–79.

HOLLINS, PETER, 1800–1886. Als (2) 1828, 1829 to N. G. Philips.

HOLLOWAY, THOMAS, 1748–1827. Ads 14 April 1787.

HOLMES, SIR RICHARD RIVINGTON, 1835–1911. Als (54) 1892–1900 to Messrs. Pearson.

HOLROYD, SIR CHARLES, 1861–1917. Als 4 December 1905 to Anna Thackeray Ritchie.

HOLT-WHITE, RASHLEIGH. Als (2) 1913 to W. H. Mullens.

HOLYOAKE, GEORGE JACOB, 1817–1906. Als (2) 1874, 1878.

HOME, JOHN, 1722–1808. Als (7) 1783–1800 and n.d.

HONE, WILLIAM, 1780–1842. Als (4) 1824–32.

HOOD, THOMAS, 1799–1845. Contributions (22) in prose and verse to *The Comic Annual*, 71 pp.: "Ali Ben Nous," "The Assistant Drapers' Petition," "Black, White, and Brown," "Carnaby Correspondence," "Clubs," "Fatal Bath," "Intercepted Dispatch," "Letter from an Absentee," "Lord Durham's Return," "Love and Lunacy," "The Ocean," "Poetry, Prose, and Worse," "Preface—Being an Inaugural Discourse on . . . Practical Philosophy," "Protocol," "Review, *The Rambling Piscator*," "Right and Wrong," "Rural Felicity," "Serio-Comic Reminiscence," "Sketches on the Road—The Morning Call," "Railway," "Spanish Pride," "Yeomanry"; als (6) 1825–40.

HOOD, THOMAS, 1835–1874. Ads 6 August 1868.

HOOK, JAMES CLARKE, 1819–1907. Als (4) 1878–82 to J. E. Millais.

HOOK, THEODORE EDWARD, 1788–1841. Als (4) 1828–31 and n.d.

HOOK, WALTER FARQUHAR, 1798–1875. "Sermon . . . June 29, 1859," 56 pp.

HOOKE, ROBERT, 1635–1703. Als (draft) 25 May 1678 to Sir Isaac Newton.

HOOLE, JOHN, 1727–1803. "The argument of the Orlando Inamorato prepared for translation . . . ," 58 pp.

HOPE, ANTHONY: *see* HAWKINS, SIR ANTHONY HOPE.

HOPKINS, GERARD MANLEY, 1844–1889. "Musical exercises in counterpoint," 2 pp.; als 25 December 1881 to R. W. Dixon.

HOPLEY, EDWARD WILLIAM JOHN, 1816–1869. Als (3) n.d. to Henry Mogford.

HOPPNER, JOHN, 1758–1810. Als (3) 1801–9 including 2 to Sir George Beaumont.

HOPPNER, RICHARD BELGRAVE, 1786–1872. Als 9 July 1819 to Lord Byron.

HORNBY, CHARLES HARRY ST. JOHN, 1867–1946. Als (9) 1901–46 including 8 to Sir Sydney Cockerell.

HORNE, HERBERT PERCY, 1864–1916. Als 6 December 1893 to T. J. Cobden-Sanderson.

HORNE, RICHARD HENRY, 1803–1884. Als (70) 1843–80 including 66 to E. B. Browning.

HORNE, THOMAS HARTWELL, 1780–1862. Als 5 May 1835.

HORSLEY, JOHN CALLCOTT, 1817–1903. Als (2) 1882, 1896 to Mary Millais.

HOTTEN, JOHN CAMDEN, 1832–1873. Als (3) 1868–70.

HOUGHTON, RICHARD MONCKTON MILNES, 1st Baron, 1809–1885. "To Oliver Wendell Holmes," 1 p.; "To Fanny Ellsler [*sic*] leaving England for the United States," 3 pp.; als (18) 1841–85 and n.d.

HOUSMAN, ALFRED EDWARD, 1859–1936. "Morns abed and daylight slumber . . . ," 1 p.; "Over the hill the highway marches . . . ," 1 p.; als 18 May 1920 to Martin Secker.

HOWARD, HENRY, 1769–1847. Als 17 February 1813 to Sir William Beechey.

HOWARD, JOHN, 1726?–1790. Als (3) 1784–5.

HOWARD, SIR ROBERT, 1626–1698. Als 15 August 1675; ads 27 January 1695; ds 29 September 1683.

HOWE, HENRY, 1812–1896. Als (2) 1866 and n.d.

HOWITT, MARY (BOTHAM), 1799–1888. Als (3) n.d.

HOWITT, WILLIAM, 1792–1879. Als 22 May 1846.

HUDDESFORD, WILLIAM, 1732–1772. Als (2) 1769, 1770.

HUEFFER, FRANCIS, 1845–1889. Als 22 September 1883 to Sir Arthur Sullivan.

HUGGINS, SIR WILLIAM, 1824–1910. Als 6 July 1897 to Sir Alexander Mackenzie; tls 12 July 1897.

HUGHES, ARTHUR, 1832–1915. Als 9 August 1907 to S. C. Cockerell.

HUGHES, EDWARD, 1832–1908. Als 3 September 1878 to J. E. Millais.

HUGHES, EDWARD ROBERT, 1851–1914. Als (4) 1913 to C. F. Murray.

HUGHES, RICHARD ARTHUR WARREN, 1900–1976. *The Human Predicament*, 124 pp. (carbon typescript of 17 chapters in early versions); als, tls (33) 1925–69 and n.d. to J. H. Brewer.

HUGHES, THOMAS, 1822–1896. Als (4) 1859–72.

HUISH, MARCUS BOURNE, 1845–1921. Als 28 April 1879 to John Ruskin.

HULL, THOMAS, 1728–1808. Als (2) 1781 and n.d.

HULLAH, JOHN PYKE, 1812–1884. Als (4) 1873–6 and n.d.

HULME, FREDERICK WILLIAM, 1816–1884. Als (5) 1853–5 and n.d. to Henry Mogford.

HUME, DAVID, 1560?–1630? Notes, possibly for his "History of the House of Wedderburn," 4 pp.

HUME, DAVID, 1711–1776. Journal, May–June 1746, 3 pp.; als, al (12) 1746–67.

HUMPHREYS, W. Als 17 April 1826 to Charles Ollier.

HUMPHRY, OZIAS, 1742–1810. Als (4) 1801, 1804 and n.d.; ads 21 July 1808.

HUNT, ALFRED WILLIAM, 1830–1896. Als (5) 1872–3, of which 4 are to W. A. Knight and 1 to John Ruskin.

HUNT, LEIGH, 1784–1859. "Abou Ben Adhem," 1 p.; "Love-Letters Made of Flowers," 4 pp.; "On Hearing a Little Musical Box," 3 pp.; "The Palfrey," 47 pp.; als (19) 1812–56.

HUNT, MARGARET (RAINE), 1831–1912. "My lady's garden full of roses," 1 p.; "She left her place within the door," 2 pp.; als (10) n.d. to W. A. Knight.

HUNT, THORNTON LEIGH, 1810–1873. Als 4 June 1862 to Octavian Blewitt.

HUNT, VIOLET, d. 1942. Als (2) n.d. to Lady Millais and Mary Millais.

HUNT, WILLIAM HOLMAN, 1827–1910. Als (32) 1863–96 including 27 to Sir John Millais, his wife and daughter.

HUNTER, JOHN, 1728–1793. Als 20 November 1786 to William Eden.

HUNTER, JOHN, 1745–1837. Als 30 September 1800 to Charles Hunter.

HUNTER, JOSEPH, 1783–1861. Als (2) 1836, 1847.

HUNTER, WILLIAM, 1718–1783. Als 15 June 1781 to Mr. Baker.

HUNTINGTON, SELINA (SHIRLEY) HASTINGS, Countess of, 1707–1791. Als (2) 26 April 1785 to Mr. Carpenter and n.d. to John Wesley.

HUNTLY, CHARLES GORDON, 11th Marquis of, 1847–1937. Als 12 January 1894 to W. A. Knight.

HURD, RICHARD, 1720–1808. "Be still, my fears, suggest no false alarms," 2 pp.; als (6) 1791–1804 and n.d.

HUTTON, RICHARD HOLT, 1826–1897. Als (45) 1871–96 including 42 to W. A. Knight.

HUXLEY, ALDOUS LEONARD, 1894–1963. *Eyeless in Gaza*, 2 pp. (typewritten synopsis); als, tls (9) 1931–63.

HUXLEY, LEONARD, 1860–1933. Als (2) 1892, 1900 to W. A. Knight.

HUXLEY, SIR JULIAN SORELL, 1887–1975. Tls 17 February 1928 to Dannie Heineman.

HUXLEY, THOMAS HENRY, 1825–1895. Als 6 December 1886 to W. A. Knight.

HYDE, EDWARD: *see* CLARENDON.

IDDLESLEIGH, STAFFORD HENRY NORTHCOTE, 1st Earl of, 1818–1887. Als (5) 1882–6 including 4 to J. E. Millais.

IMAGE, SELWYN, 1849–1930. "The Landscapes of Thomas Bewick," 3 pp.; als (6) 1897–1915.

INCHBALD, ELIZABETH (SIMPSON), 1753–1821. "Dictionary," 9 pp.; "Father Paul to Mrs. Inchbald," 1 p.; als (3) 1792–1803.

INGE, WILLIAM RALPH, 1860–1954. Als 10 March 1951.

INGELOW, JEAN, 1820–1897. Als (14) 1867–85 and n.d. including 7 to John Ruskin, 4 to Joan Severn and 1 to A. S. Sullivan.

INGLIS, ESTHER, 1571–1624. Calligraphic manuscript executed for Master Thomas Puckering, 1607, 33 *ll.*

INGLIS, JOHN BELLINGHAM, 1780–1870. "Introduction to the *Speculum Humanae Salvationis*," 22 pp.; als (7) 1846–54 to S. L. Sotheby.

INGRAM, ARTHUR FOLEY WINNINGTON: *see* WINNINGTON-INGRAM.

INNES, ALEXANDER TAYLOR, 1833–1912. Als (5) 1871–97 to W. A. Knight.

INWOOD, WILLIAM, ca. 1771–1843. Als 22 April 1824 to Robert Abraham.

IRELAND, ALEXANDER, 1810–1894. Als (2) 1886.

IRELAND, JOHN, d. 1808. Als n.d. to Mr. Harrison.

IRELAND, WILLIAM HENRY, 1777–1835. Als 28 July 1825 to Mrs. Colepeper; forgery of a receipt signed by William Shakespeare; forgery of a letter written by Oliver Cromwell.

IRVING, DAVID, 1778–1860. Als 7 December 1805 to Thomas Park.

IRVING, EDWARD, 1792–1834. Als 26 February 1824 to Lady Beaumont.

IRVING, SIR HENRY, 1838–1905. Als (14) 1878–1905 including 7 to W. A. Knight; ds 22 June 1889.

ISHERWOOD, CHRISTOPHER, 1904– . Als 26 June 1933 to Mrs. Kurath. *See also:* AUDEN.

JACKS, LAWRENCE PEARSALL, 1860–1956. Als 24 September 1917 to T. J. Cobden-Sanderson.

JACKSON, HOLBROOK, 1874–1948. Als 18 October 1904 to T. J. Cobden-Sanderson.

JACKSON, JOHN. Als 5 June 1700 to his uncle, Samuel Pepys.

JACKSON, JOHN, 1778–1831. Als (5) 1804–26 and n.d.

JACKSON, JOHN, 1811–1885. Als (2) 1870.

JACKSON, SIR THOMAS GRAHAM, 1835–1924. Als (2) 1894 to W. A. Knight.

JACOBS, WILLIAM WYMARK, 1863–1943. Statement on the conflicts between the works of artists and authors, 3 pp.

JAMES I, King of Great Britain, 1566–1625. Inscription to his son Henry in his *Basilikon Doron* (1603); als (2) 1621 to Frederick V, King of Bohemia; ls (17) 1580–1623; ds (7) 1589–1625.

JAMES, EDWIN JOHN, 1812–1882. Als, ls (19) 1867–8 to Harper & Bros.

JAMES, GEORGE PAYNE RAINSFORD, 1799–1860. *Blanche of Navarre*, 99 pp.; als (5) 1828–55.

JAMES, MONTAGUE RHODES, 1862–1936. "A Warning to the Curious," 22 pp.; als (8) 1917–34.

JAMES, SIR WILLIAM MILBOURNE, 1807–1881. Als 16 May 1881 to J. E. Millais.

JAMESON, ANNA BROWNELL (MURPHY), 1794–1860.

Als (12) 1830–46 and n.d. including 5 to Lady Noël Byron.

JAMESON, ROBERT, 1774–1854. Als 26 October 1830 to Mr. Aiken.

JAMIESON, JOHN, 1759–1838. Als 10 June 1837 to W. S. Maclean.

JAY, HARRIETT, 1863–1932. Als n.d. to Stephen Massett.

JEBB, JOHN, 1775–1833. Als 17 May 1819 to John Nichols.

JEBB, SIR RICHARD CLAVERHOUSE, 1841–1905. Als (18) 1884–1903 to W. A. Knight.

JEFFREY, FRANCIS JEFFREY, Lord, 1773–1850. Als (7) 1831–43 and n.d.; ads 1816.

JENINGS, EDMUND, 1731–1819. Als 21 July 1766.

JENKIN, HENRY CHARLES FLEEMING, 1833–1885. Als (49) 1880–3 to W. E. Henley. With als (28) ca. 1878–83 from Mrs. Jenkin to W. E. Henley.

JENNER, EDWARD, 1749–1823. Als (2) 1804, 1817.

JERDAN, WILLIAM, 1782–1869. Als n.d.

JERROLD, DOUGLAS WILLIAM, 1803–1857. "Shakespeare's Crab Tree," 1 p.; *Time Works Wonders* (rough draft and final manuscript), 227 pp.; als (31) 1845–8 and n.d.

JESSE, JOHN HENEAGE, 1815–1874. Als 3 April 1844.

JEWSBURY, GERALDINE ENDSOR, 1812–1880. Als (9) 1844–74.

JEWSBURY, MARIA JANE, 1800–1833. Als 1 July 1830 to S. C. Hall.

JOACHIM, HAROLD HENRY, 1868–1938. Als (4) 1892 and n.d. to W. A. Knight.

JOHN, AUGUSTUS EDWIN, 1878–1961. Als December 1903 to D. S. Robertson.

JOHNES, THOMAS, 1748–1816. Als 18 March 1816 to Messrs. Dulau & Co.

JOHNSON, JOHN, 1769–1833. Als (6) 1806 to Walter Bagot.

JOHNSON, JOSEPH, 1738–1809. Als 18 February 1782 to William Cowper.

JOHNSON, LIONEL PIGOT, 1867–1902. Als 8 April 1895.

JOHNSON, MANUEL JOHN, 1805–1859. Als (2) 1858 to S. L. Sotheby.

JOHNSON, SAMUEL, 1709–1784. *Life of Pope* (partly autograph, partly in the hand of Mrs. Piozzi), 184 pp.; "Prayer," dated 1 January 1784; als (22) 1746–84; quotation in Latin, 1 p.; ds (2) 1749, 1752.

JOHNSON, SIR WILLIAM, 1715–1774. Als 9 April 1769; ds 25 December 1764.

JOHNSTON, EDWARD, 1872–1944. "Calligraphy and illumination," 8 *ll.*; "Decoration and its uses," 56 *ll.*; *Writing & Illuminating* (corrections for later printings), 20 pp.; large collection of calligraphic manuscripts, drafts and experiments; als (6) 1902–34.

JOHNSTONE, JOHN HENRY, 1749–1828. Als (2) n.d. to Mr. Winston.

JONES, GEORGE, 1786–1869. Als (5) 1830–68 and n.d. to James and Harriet Moore.

JONES, HENRY ARTHUR, 1851–1929. Als 28 October 1924 to Mr. Shelley.

JONES, INIGO, 1573–1652. Ds n.d.

JONES, JOHN WINTER, 1805–1881. Als (20) 1846–58 to S. L. Sotheby; ds 10 June 1858.

JONES, SIR WILLIAM, 1746–1794. Als (2) 1775, 1787.

JONSON, BEN, 1573?–1637. Signature and inscription (2).

JOPLING, JOSEPH MIDDLETON, 1831–1884. Als (2) 1878, 1881 to J. E. Millais.

JORDAN, DOROTHEA, 1762–1816. Als (3) 1799, 1815 and n.d.

JOWETT, BENJAMIN, 1817–1893. Als (13) 1866–93.

JOYCE, JAMES, 1882–1941. One leaf of *Ulysses* (draft of passage pp. 631–632 of 1st edition) and on the reverse, corrected typescript (pp. 629–630); typewritten copies (3) of a French translation of the concluding paragraphs of *Finnegans Wake* (*FW* 215–216) with corrections and additions in various hands, incuding those of Philippe Soupault and Paul L. Léon.

JUNIUS, *pseud.* Als September 1769.

KAMES, HENRY HOME, Lord, 1696–1782. Als n.d. to John Home.

KAUFFMANN, MARIA ANNA ANGELICA CATHARINA, 1741–1807. Als 20 November 1784 to John Thane.

KAY-SHUTTLEWORTH, SIR JAMES PHILLIPS, 1st Bart., 1804–1877. Als 29 December 1849 to W. H. Brookfield.

KAYE, SIR JOHN WILLIAM, 1814–1876. Als (2) 1870–2 to Sir Henry Rawlinson.

KEAN, CHARLES JOHN, 1811?–1868. Als (6) 1850–60 and n.d.

KEAN, EDMUND, 1787–1833. Als 19 April 1826 to John Cooper; ds 3 December 1819.

KEAN, ELLEN (TREE), 1805–1880. Als (5) 1876 and n.d.

KEATS, JOHN, 1795–1821. "The Cap and Bells," stanzas 1–8, 17–44, 52–81, 45 pp.; *Endymion*, 184 *ll.*, with separate title page, dedication and preface, 6 pp.; "The Eve of St. Mark," fragment containing vv. 99–130, 2 pp., and version in letter of 17–27 September 1819 to George Keats; *Hyperion*, fragment containing II, 116–127, with note of Leigh Hunt explaining that it was clipped from the original manuscript, 1 p.; "I stood tip-toe upon a little hill," 2 fragments (14 vv.) beginning "I was light-hearted" and "So do they feel who pull the boughs aside"; sonnets: "The day is gone and all its sweets are gone," "On First Looking into Chapman's Homer," "On leaving some Friends at an early Hour," "To a Friend who sent me some Roses" and "Spenser! a jealous honourer of thine"; other short poems: "God of the golden bow," 2 pp.; "Ode to Psyche," 3 pp.; "Think not of it, sweet one, so," 1 p.; "Unfelt, unheard, unseen," 1 p. Als (9) 1818–20, of which 1 (17–27 September 1819) is to his brother George, containing drafts of 5 poems, 1 (2, 3, 5 July 1818) to his sister Fanny, containing drafts of 2 poems, 6 to John Taylor and 1 to Benjamin Haydon. Signed agreement, 16 September 1820, assigning copyright in *Poems* (1817) and *Lamia, Isabella*, etc. (1820) to Taylor and Hessey, 3 pp.

Woodhouse volume of Keatsiana, including copies of 40 poems and other writings of Keats, the majority of them in the autograph of Richard Woodhouse; 25 letters and manuscripts of Woodhouse concerning Keats; letters and manuscripts of others of the Keats circle, including 6 of John Taylor or J. A. Hessey, 13 of Benjamin Bailey and 9 of Charles A. Brown. Wash drawing of Keats on his deathbed, by Joseph Severn.

KEBLE, JOHN, 1792–1866. *The Psalter, or Psalms of David in English Verse*, first draft and corrected version (the latter partly autograph), in notebooks (10), with 25 pp. of corrected proof; notebooks (3) containing theological notes of his student days, and receipts and expenditures, 1852–9 and n.d., 30, 35 and 75 pp.; marginalia in a proof copy of *Hymns Ancient and Modern* (1859); als (9) 1832–64 and n.d.

KEELEY, MARY ANN (GOWARD), 1805?–1899. Als (9) 1862–82 and n.d.

KEELEY, ROBERT, 1793–1869. Als (2) 1843? and 1858.

KEENE, CHARLES SAMUEL, 1823–1891. Als (5) n.d. to

Sir John Millais.

KELLY, FRANCES MARIA, 1790–1882. Als n.d. to Mr. Mitchell.

KELLY, JOHN, 1680?–1751. Als n.d.

KELLY, MICHAEL, 1764?–1826. Als 22 January 1793 to D. E. McDonnell.

KELVIN, WILLIAM THOMSON, 1st Baron, 1824–1907. Als (3) 1890, 1896 to W. A. Knight.

KEMBLE, ADELAIDE: *see* SARTORIS.

KEMBLE, CHARLES, 1775–1854. Als (4) 1827–54 and n.d.

KEMBLE, FRANCES ANNE, 1809–1893. "To Miss xx" ("By the pure spring"), 2 pp.; als (5) 1865 and n.d.

KEMBLE, HENRY, 1848–1907. Als 25 May 1896 to Sir John Millais.

KEMBLE, JOHN MITCHELL, 1807–1857. Diary, October 1830–21 May 1831, 88 *ll.*; als (2) 1842 and n.d. to W. H. Brookfield.

KEMBLE, JOHN PHILIP, 1757–1823. Als (8) 1780–1810 and n.d. including 2 to Mrs. Inchbald.

KEMBLE, PRISCILLA (HOPKINS) BRERETON, 1756–1845. Als 18 January 1782 to R. B. Sheridan.

KEMBLE, STEPHEN, 1758–1822. Als (2) 1808 and n.d.

KENDAL, DAME MADGE, 1849–1935. Als (3) 1873 and n.d.

KENDAL, WILLIAM HUNTER GRIMSTON, 1843–1917. Als 28 March to J. E. Millais.

KENNICOTT, BENJAMIN, 1718–1783. Als 30 May 1781 to Bishop Lowth.

KENT, WILLIAM CHARLES MARK, 1823–1902. Als (2) 1884 and n.d.

KENYON, SIR FREDERIC GEORGE, 1863–1952. Als 11 December 1912 to T. J. Cobden-Sanderson.

KEPPEL, SIR HENRY, 1809–1904. Als (2) 4 June 1830 to Mr. Woodhead, 13 April 1895 to Sir Arthur Sullivan.

KER, DAVID, 1842–1914. "A Snake in the Nursery: A True Story," 2 pp.

KER, WILLIAM PATON, 1855–1923. Als (3) 1894–1902 to W. A. Knight.

KERNAHAN, MARY JEAN HICKLING (GWYNNE), 1857–1941. Als 20 February 1907 to W. A. Knight.

KIDD, BENJAMIN, 1858–1916. Als 23 March 1895 to Mrs. Cobden-Sanderson.

KIDD, WILLIAM, 1790?–1863. Ads 2 May 1848.

KILLIGREW, THOMAS, 1612–1683. Als (3) 1637–50; ls 25 July 1672.

KILLIGREW, SIR WILLIAM, 1606–1695. Ds (2) 1665, 1676.

KING, BASIL, 1859–1928. Als, tls (6) 1909–10 to Harper & Bros.

KING, EDWARD, 1735?–1807. Als 3 January 1805 to Samuel Lysons.

KING, JOHN, 1559?–1621. Als 11 October 1615.

KING, THOMAS, 1730–1805. Als (5) ca. 1768–1800 including 1 to Charles Dibdin and 1 to David Garrick.

KING, WILLIAM, 1650–1729. Als (2) 1721 to Mr. Southwell.

KING, WILLIAM, 1685–1763. Als 3 June 1748.

KINGLAKE, ALEXANDER WILLIAM, 1809–1891. Als (4) 1884 and n.d.

KINGSLEY, CHARLES, 1819–1875. "A.D. 1100" ("Evil sped the battle play"), 3 pp.; "The Sands of Dee," 1 p.; "The Three Fishers," 1 p.; sermon preached at the Chapel Royal, March 1871, 40 pp.; als (12) 1853–70.

KINGSLEY, FRANCES ELIZA (GRENFELL), d. 1891. Als in the form of a diary 1841–2 to Charles Kingsley, her future husband, 116 pp.; als 24 February 1859 to Thomas Longstaff. *See also:* POPE-HENNESSY.

KINNAIRD, DOUGLAS JAMES WILLIAM, 1788–1830. Als 16 November 1819 to Lord Byron; copies of letters to John Howard Payne 1815–6 in Payne's autograph.

KIPLING, JOHN LOCKWOOD, 1837–1911. Als (2) 1886, 1898.

KIPLING, RUDYARD, 1865–1936. "The Brushwood Boy," fragments of an early draft, 6 pp., and corrected typescript, 63 pp.; *Captains Courageous*, manuscript entitled "Harvey Cheyne—Banker," 74 pp.; poems (6) from *Departmental Ditties:* "Arithmetic on the Frontier," "Ballade of Burial," "Ballade of Jakko Hill," "L'envoi," "Lucifer," "The Overland Mail," together 8 pp.; "The English Metres" (version of a poem by Alice Meynell), 2 pp.; "In Memoriam—August 1883," 4 pp.; drafts of poems (2) from *Naulahka:* "The Nursing Sister" and "The Sack of the Gods," 1 p.; "On Fort Duty," 1 p.; "Recessional," 1 p.; "Saint Valentine His Day," 4 pp.; 11 of 12 rhymes written to accompany *Almanac of the Twelve Sports*, by William Nicholson; pencil drawings, with legends, of fellow travelers, done on stationery of the R. M. S. *Cuzco*, 9 pp.; als, tls (38) 1883–1932 including 18 to W. E. Henley and 2 to Sir Arthur Sullivan.

KIPPIS, ANDREW, 1725–1795. Als (2) 1780 and n.d.

KITCHINER, WILLIAM, 1775?–1827. Als 26 December 1823 to Charles Mathews.

KITTON, FREDERIC GEORGE, 1856–1904. Als (2) 1898 to Egan Mew.

KNELLER, SIR GODFREY, 1st Bart., 1646–1723. Als (2) n.d. including 1 to Jacob Tonson; ds (4) 1701–14/5. With letters and manuscripts (7) 1816–21 relating to the sale of paintings at Donhead Hall, by Godfrey John Kneller.

KNIGHT, CHARLES, 1791–1873. Als (2) 1848, 1860.

KNIGHT, EDWARD, 1774–1826. Ds 1820.

KNIGHT, HENRY GALLY, 1786–1846. "On the Apollo of Belvidere," 1 p.; als (2) 1812, 1818.

KNIGHT, JOHN PRESCOTT, 1803–1881. Als (2) 1841, 1842.

KNIGHT, RICHARD PAYNE, 1750–1824. Als 10 February 1818 to Sir George Beaumont.

KNIGHT, THOMAS ANDREW, 1759–1838. Als (2) 1812 and n.d.

KNIGHT, WILLIAM ANGUS, 1836–1916. Als 7 January 1886 to W. W. Tulloch.

KNOLLYS, FRANCIS KNOLLYS, 1st Viscount, 1837–1924. Als (12) 1880–91 to Sir Arthur Sullivan.

KNOWLES, JAMES SHERIDAN, 1784–1862. Als (12) 1830–47 including 7 to Edward Moxon.

KNOWLES, SIR JAMES THOMAS, 1831–1908. Als (13) 1873–1901 to W. A. Knight.

KYNASTON, EDWARD, 1640–1706. Als 28 February 1676 to Edward Lloyd of Llanvorda.

LABOUCHÈRE, HENRY DU PRÉ, 1831–1912. Als (3) 1880 and n.d. including 2 to A. S. Sullivan.

LACAITA, SIR JAMES PHILIP, 1813–1895. Als 26 September 1883 to Gibson Craig.

LACY, THOMAS HAILES, 1809–1873. Als (3) n.d.

LACY, WALTER, 1809–1898. Als n.d. to Lewis Wingfield.

LACY, WILLOUGHBY, 1749–1831. Als 27 June 1776 to David Garrick.

LAMB, LADY CAROLINE (PONSONBY), 1785–1828. Als (2) 1823 and n.d.

LAMB, CHARLES, 1775–1834. "A Dissertation upon Roast Pig," 5 pp.; "Hercules Pacificatus," 6 pp.; "Lazy-bones, lazy-bones," 1 p.; annotations and revisions in Godwin's *Antonio* (1800); als (20) 1798–1833 and n.d. "Dream Children," calligraphic manuscript by Madelyn Walker, 1924, 9 *ll.* With als (8) 1803–9 and n.d. of his sister Mary and a sonnet of hers, "To Emma," written in the autograph of Charles Lamb.

LAMB, GEORGE, 1784–1834. Als n.d.

LANCE, GEORGE, 1802–1864. Als (2) 1848, 1863.

LANDON, LETITIA ELIZABETH: *see* MACLEAN, LETITIA ELIZABETH (LANDON).

LANDOR, WALTER SAVAGE, 1775–1864. "Kisses in former times . . . ," 1 p.; compositions (5) written out for Edith Story: "Imaginary Conversations, Garibaldi and Bosco," and poems (4), 3 of them in Latin, "To the Princess Belgioioso," "Ad Garibaldum," "Epitaphium," "Palinodia," 5 pp.; als (55) 1841–64 including 48 to Mrs. Lynn Linton.

LANDSEER, CHARLES, 1799–1879. Als (2) 1865 and n.d.

LANDSEER, SIR EDWIN HENRY, 1802–1873. Als (8) 1838–67 and n.d.

LANDSEER, JOHN, 1769–1852. Als 12 September 1847 to Dawson Turner.

LANDSEER, THOMAS, 1795–1880. Als (3) 1856, 1877 and n.d.

LANE, JOHN, 1854–1925. Als (2) 1899 and n.d. to Mary Millais.

LANE, RICHARD JAMES, 1800–1872. Als (2) 1850, 1852.

LANG, ANDREW, 1844–1912. "Enchanted Cigarettes," 15 pp.; "Ode to Golf," 2 pp.; "A Toast," 1 p.; "Unekal to the Occasion," 1 p.; als (98) ca. 1876–95 and n.d. including 26 to W. E. Henley, 69 to W. A. Knight and 2 to Sir Arthur Sullivan.

LANG, COSMO GORDON LANG, Baron, 1864–1945. Als (8) 1918–41 to J. P. Morgan.

LANG, JOHN MARSHALL, 1834–1909. Als 28 August 1907 to W. A. Knight.

LANG, LEONORA BLANCHE (ALLEYNE), fl. 1875–1912. Als (2) n.d. to W. A. Knight.

LANGBAINE, GERARD, 1656–1692. Presentation inscription in his *An account of the English dramatick poets* (1691).

LANGTRY, LILLIE, 1852–1929. Als (4) n.d.

LANKESTER, SIR EDWIN RAY, 1847–1929. Als 13 February 1884 to George Grossmith.

LANDSDOWNE, WILLIAM PETTY, 1st Marquis of, 1737–1805. Als (3) n.d.

LARDNER, DIONYSIUS, 1793–1859. Manuscript fragment, possibly for his *Cyclopaedia*, 1 p.; als 8 January 1843 to F. W. Bartow.

LARKIN, HENRY, 1820–1899. Als 3 June 1892.

LASKI, HAROLD JOSEPH, 1893–1950. Additions and corrections to Bonar's *A Catalogue of the Library of Adam Smith* (1894), 11 *ll.*

LATEY, JOHN, 1842–1902. Als n.d.

LATHBURY, THOMAS, 1798–1865. Als n.d. to S. L. Sotheby.

LATIMER, HUGH, 1485?–1555. Signature cut from a document, n.d.

LA TOUCHE, MARIA (PRICE), d. 1904. Als (78) 1858–1900 including 6 to John Ruskin and 63 to Joan Severn.

LA TOUCHE, ROBERT, d. 1844. Description of the character, last illness and death of Anne La Touche, 1835, 12 pp.

LA TOUCHE, ROSE, 1849–1875. Journal of 1861, autobiography of 1867, 33 pp., typescript made from the originals in 1929 before they were destroyed; als 1868 to Mrs. Cowper.

LATROBE, BENJAMIN, 1728–1786. Als 12 July 1777.

LATROBE, CHRISTIAN IGNATIUS, 1758–1836. Als 27 September 1821 to Peter Latrobe.

LAUD, WILLIAM, 1573–1645. "On Church Government" (contemporary copy), 84 pp.; ls (2) 1638, 1640; ds (6) 1616–39.

LAUDER, ROBERT SCOTT, 1803–1869. Als n.d. to Alexander Johnston.

LAUDERDALE, JAMES MAITLAND, 8th Earl of, 1759–1839. Als (2) 1788 and n.d. to Sir Peter Burrell.

LAURIE, HENRY. Als (36) 1860–1903 to W. A. Knight.

LAVER, JAMES, 1899–1975. Als 1 March 1961 to Mr. Byron.

LAWLER, DENNIS. Ds 11 November 1809.

LAWLEY, FRANCIS CHARLES, 1825–1901. Als 2 June 1880 to James Toovey.

LAWRENCE, DAVID HERBERT, 1885–1930. "Eloi, Eloi lama sabachthani?," 4 pp.; *Studies in Classic American Literature* (portion of the chapter on Whitman), 7 pp.

LAWRENCE, GEORGE ALFRED, 1827–1876. Als (5) ca. 1860–8 to Tinsley Brothers.

LAWRENCE, HENRY, 1600–1664. Ls 22 April 1659 to Col. Francis Underwood.

LAWRENCE, SIR THOMAS, 1769–1830. Als (147) 1794–1829 and n.d. including 19 to J. J. Angerstein and his son and 103 to J. W. Croker.

LAWRENCE, THOMAS EDWARD, 1888–1935. Als (7) 1919–35.

LAYARD, SIR AUSTEN HENRY, 1817–1894. Als (5) 1855–91.

LEAN, FLORENCE (MARRYAT) CHURCH, 1837–1899. Als (2) 1877, 1878.

LEAR, EDWARD, 1812–1888. "The Duck and the Kangaroo" (two versions), 2 pp.; "The Owl and the Pussey cat" (two versions), 2 pp.; a nonsense alphabet, 26 pp.; als (10) 1831–86 and n.d.

LECKY, WILLIAM EDWARD HARTPOLE, 1838–1903. *Democracy and Liberty*, 2 vols.; *History of . . . Rationalism in Europe*, 2 vols.; als (5) 1886–1901 to W. A. Knight. With als (2) 1890 from Mrs. Lecky to W. A. Knight.

LEE, FREDERICK GEORGE, 1832–1902. Als 5 June 1888 to James Toovey.

LEE, SIR SIDNEY, 1859–1926. Als (9) 1891–1911 including 6 to W. A. Knight.

LEECH, JOHN, 1817–1864. Als 23 October 1852 to John Scott.

LEEDS, FRANCIS GODOLPHIN OSBORNE, 5th Duke of, 1751–1799. Als (2) 1787, 1798.

LE FANU, JOSEPH SHERIDAN, 1814–1873. Als 4 May 1869 to J. F. Clarke.

LE GALLIENNE, RICHARD, 1866–1947. "Orestes—Act 2," 6 pp.; "Three American poets," 19 pp.; als (5) 1895–1909.

LEHMANN, RUDOLF, 1819–1905. Als 20 February 1881 to J. E. Millais.

LEICESTER, ROBERT SIDNEY, 1st Earl of, 1563–1626. Ads 19 October 1624.

LEICESTER'S COMMONWEALTH. Contemporary copy, 25 *ll.*

LEIGH, AUGUSTA BYRON, 1783–1851. Als (7) 1829–31 including 6 to Col. Wildman.

LEIGH, ELIZABETH MEDORA, 1814–1849. Portion of her autobiography, 17 pp.; als (4) 1843 to her mother.

LEIGH, PERCIVAL, 1813–1889. "The Request of the Red-Cross Knight," 1 p.

LEIGHTON, FREDERIC LEIGHTON, Baron, 1830–1896.

Als (27) 1877–95 and n.d. including 4 to George du Maurier and 16 to Sir John Millais.

LEITCH, WILLIAM LEIGHTON, 1804–1883. Als 1 April 1864 to George Cattermole.

LEMON, MARK, 1809–1870. "To Henry Riley Bradbury with a pair of Razors," 1 p.; als (15) 1851–63 and n.d. including 5 to John Forster.

LEMON, ROBERT. Als 27 August 1858 to S. L. Sotheby.

LEMPRIÈRE, JOHN, 1765?–1824. Als 14 July 1816 to Cadell & Davies.

LE NEVE, JOHN, 1679–1741. Als 16 September 1715 to Peter Le Neve.

LE NEVE, PETER, 1661–1729. Als (3) 1702–29.

LENNOX, CHARLOTTE (RAMSAY), 1720–1804. Als 1751 to Samuel Richardson.

LE NOIR, ELIZABETH ANN (SMART), ca. 1755–1841. Als 23 December 1809 to George Dyer.

LENTON, FRANCIS, fl. 1625–1650. *The Muses Oblation on Hymens Altar . . . on the Happy Espousalls of . . . James, Lord Compton, Earle of Northampton . . . and Isabella Sackville . . . Apr. 1647*, 9 *ll.*

LESLIE, CHARLES ROBERT, 1794–1859. Als (8) 1823–58 and n.d.

LESLIE, GEORGE DUNLOP, 1835–1921. Als 1 February 1896 to Sir John Millais.

LESLIE, JOHN, 1527–1596. Als, ls (4) 1573–7 to La Mothe Fénelon.

LESLIE, SIR SHANE, Bart., 1885–1971. Als 22 March 1929 to Mr. and Mrs. Cobden-Sanderson.

LETHABY, WILLIAM RICHARD, 1857–1931. Als 20 July 1901 to S. C. Cockerell.

LEVER, CHARLES JAMES, 1806–1872. Notebook with entries, 1843–57, concerning his writings and payments for them, expenditures and travel notes, 140 pp.; als (126) 1829–71 including letters to Chapman & Hall, Charles Dickens and Alexander Spencer; drawings by H. K. Browne for illustrations to his novels *Charles O'Malley* (43) and *Harry Lorrequer* (20).

LEVESON-GOWER, SIR GEORGE GRANVILLE, 1858–1951. Als 6 January 1938 to R. Cobden-Sanderson.

LEWES, GEORGE HENRY, 1817–1878. Als (5) 1863–71 and n.d.

LEWIS, CECIL DAY-: *see* DAY-LEWIS, CECIL.

LEWIS, ERASMUS, 1670–1754. Als 26 August 1739 to Jonathan Swift.

LEWIS, JOHN, 1675–1747. Als 29 March 1729 to Peter Le Neve.

LEWIS, KATE (TERRY), 1844–1924. Als (6) 1868, 1878 and n.d.

LEWIS, MATTHEW GREGORY, 1775–1818. "Albion," 1 p.; "Lines—on receiving an Inkstand . . . ," 1 p.; "Lines Written on returning from The Funeral Of the Rt. Honble. C. J. Fox," 8 pp. (not autograph); "On the failure of her Royal Highness's efforts to reclaim a worthless Object of her bounty," 1 p.; als (2) 1798 and n.d.

LEWIS, WILLIAM THOMAS, 1749–1811. Als 10 June 1775 to R. B. Sheridan.

LEWIS, WYNDHAM, 1882–1957. "Foreword" describing an association of artists known as X group, 5 *ll.* (corrected typescript); als (12) 1919–25 and n.d. to E. McKnight Kauffer.

LEYBURN, JOHN, 1620–1702. Als 18 August 1689.

LIDDELL, HENRY GEORGE, 1811–1898. Als 15 October 1885 to Sir John Millais.

LIGHTFOOT, JOSEPH BARBER, 1828–1889. Als 12 July 1886 to W. A. Knight.

LINDSAY, CAROLINE BLANCHE ELIZABETH (FITZROY), Lady, 1844–1912. Als (7) 1899–1900 and n.d. to W. A. Knight.

LINDSAY, WALLACE MARTIN, 1858–1937. Als (2) 1903–4 to W. A. Knight.

LINGARD, JOHN, 1771–1851. Als (2) 1845, 1848.

LINLEY, THOMAS, 1732–1795. Als 12 October 1772 to David Garrick.

LINLEY, THOMAS, 1766–1835. "Glees, elegies, madrigals and epigrams" (manuscript in the hand of R. H. Billings), 321 pp.; "O Virgin Pale," 11 pp.; als 31 October 1812.

LINNELL, JOHN, 1792–1882. Als (6) 1817–63.

LINTON, ELIZABETH (LYNN), 1822–1898. Als (6) 1894–6 to W. A. Knight.

LINTON, SIR JAMES DROMGOLE, 1840–1916. Als 2 February 1888 to Sir John Millais.

LINTON, WILLIAM JAMES, 1812–1897. Als (2) 1846, 1881.

LISTER, JOSEPH LISTER, 1st Baron, 1827–1912. Als (3) 1875–88 including 2 to W. E. Henley.

LISTON, JOHN, 1776–1846. Als 9 May 1832.

LISTON, ROBERT, 1794–1847. Als 16 August 1816 to Alexander Nasmyth.

LITTLETON, HENRY, 1823–1888. Als 6 November 1877 to Joseph Bennett.

LIVERPOOL, CHARLES JENKINSON, 1st Earl of, 1729–1808. Als (2) 1776 and n.d.

LIVERSEEGE, HENRY, 1803–1832. Als n.d. to W. F. Ayrton.

LIVINGSTONE, DAVID, 1813–1873. Als 26 September 1856 to L. W. Peyton.

LLOYD, CHARLES, 1775–1839. Als 4 April 1797 to Robert Southey.

LLOYD, EDWARD, 1815–1890. Als (4) 1875, 1885 and n.d. to Joseph Bennett.

LLOYD, ROBERT, 1733–1764. Als n.d.

LOCH, CHARLES STEWART, 1849–1923. Als 4 October 1896 to S. C. Cockerell.

LOCKE, JOHN, 1632–1704. *An Essay concerning Humane Understanding, in fower books*, Bks. I–II, 383 pp.; notes and expenditures written in a copy of P. Nierop, *Nieuw . . . Almanach* (1684); translation of three of P. Nicole's *Essais de morale*, with preface, 477 pp.; als (24) 1678–1703 including 21 to Cornelius Lyde.

LOCKE, WILLIAM JOHN, 1863–1930. Als 30 October 1918 to Sir Charles C. McLeod.

LOCKER, ARTHUR, 1828–1893. Als (2) 1873 and n.d.

LOCKER LAMPSON, FREDERICK, 1821–1895. "The Rose and the Ring—Christmas 1854 and Christmas 1863," 2 pp.; "To J. R. Lowell," 2 pp.; als (13) 1861–88.

LOCKHART, JOHN GIBSON, 1794–1854. Als (33) 1820–49; ds (2) 1820, 1847.

LOCKWOOD, SIR FRANK, 1846–1897. Als 30 March 1893 to A. W. Pinero.

LOCKYER, SIR JOSEPH NORMAN, 1836–1920. Als n.d.

LOFFT, CAPELL, 1751–1824. Als 21 September 1785 to Samuel Adams.

LOFTUS, DUDLEY, 1619–1695. "Queries presented to the Duke of Ormond . . . ," 2 pp.

LONDONDERRY, CHARLES WILLIAM STEWART VANE, 3rd Marquis of, 1778–1854. Ls (2) 1809 to Sir James Murray-Pulteney.

LONDONDERRY, ROBERT STEWART, 2nd Marquis of, 1769–1822. Als n.d. to Sir James Murray-Pulteney; ls 24 July 1816 to William Hill.

LONG, EDWIN LONGSDEN, 1829–1891. Als 2 February 1876.

LONGLEY, CHARLES THOMAS, 1794–1868. Als (4) 1861–4 and n.d.

LONGMAN, WILLIAM, 1813–1877. Als (2) 1859 to S. L. Sotheby.

LONGMANS, GREEN & CO., firm, publishers. Als (4) 1881 to Otto Goldschmidt.

LORT, MICHAEL, 1725–1790. Als 26 November 1771 to the Rev. Mr. Grainger.

LOSCOMBE, CLIFFORD WINTRINGHAM, b. 1784. Als (3) 1852 to S. L. Sotheby.

LOUTHERBOURG, PHILIP JAMES DE, 1740–1812. Als 24 January 1804 to J. Jamet.

LOVELACE, RALPH GORDON NOËL MILBANKE, 2nd Earl of, 1839–1906. Als (4) 1885, 1902 and n.d.

LOVELACE, WILLIAM KING-NOËL, 1st Earl of, 1805–1893. Als (4) 1841–3.

LOVER, SAMUEL, 1797–1868. "Why sought you not the silent hour," 2 pp.; als (4) 1859–67 and n.d.

LOW, SAMPSON, 1797–1886. Ds 9 July 1847.

LOWTH, ROBERT, 1710–1787. Als (5) 1768–77.

LUBBOCK, PERCY, 1879–1965. Als (6) 1920–43 to L. P. Smith.

LUCAS, EDWARD VERRALL, 1868–1938. Als (18) 1903–35 including 13 to E. F. Saxton.

LUCAS, JOHN SEYMOUR, 1849–1923. Als (2) 1888–9 to Sir John Millais.

LUDLOW, JOHN MALCOLM FORBES, 1821–1911. Als 18 June 1888 to John Ruskin.

LUMISDEN, ANDREW, 1720–1801. Ds (2) 1745 and n.d.

LUMLEY, BENJAMIN, 1811–1875. Als (2) 1873 and n.d.

LUPTON, THOMAS GOFF, 1791–1873. Als n.d. to Mr. Gosden.

LUSHINGTON, CECILIA, 1846–1921. Als (2) 1894 to W. A. Knight.

LUSHINGTON, EDMUND LAW, 1811–1893. Als (5) 1876–92.

LUSTED, CHARLES T. Als 9 April 1896 to Sir John Millais.

LUXBOROUGH, HENRIETTA (ST. JOHN) KNIGHT, Lady, 1699–1756. Als 19 March 1755 to William Shenstone.

LYALL, SIR ALFRED COMYN, 1835–1911. Als (19) 1890–5 and n.d. to W. A. Knight.

LYELL, SIR CHARLES, Bart., 1797–1875. Als 19 July 1849 to George Sumner.

LYND, ROBERT WILSON, 1879–1949. Als 16 May 1922 to R. Cobden-Sanderson.

LYTTELTON, CHARLES, 1714–1768. Als 22 May 1767 to Sir William Hamilton.

LYTTELTON, GEORGE LYTTELTON, 1st Baron, 1709–1773. Als (3) 1741–70.

LYTTELTON, GEORGE WILLIAM LYTTELTON, 4th Baron, 1817–1876. Als (2) to W. H. Brookfield, with 7 stanzas of verse.

LYTTELTON, SARAH (SPENCER) LYTTELTON, Baroness, 1787–1870. Als 9 February 1846 to W. H. Brookfield.

LYTTELTON, WILLIAM HENRY LYTTELTON, 1st Baron, 1724–1808. Als (2) 1771 and n.d.

LYTTON, EDITH (VILLIERS) BULWER-LYTTON, Countess of, 1841–1936. Als (4) 1894–5 to W. A. Knight.

LYTTON, EDWARD GEORGE EARLE LYTTON BULWER-LYTTON, 1st Baron, 1803–1873. *Alice*, 3 vols.; "The death of Sir Walter Scott," 8 pp.; *Ernest Maltravers*, 3 vols.; *Harold*, 3 vols.; *The Last Days of Pompeii* (incomplete), 2 vols.; *Zanoni*, 2 vols.; als (159) 1827–73 and n.d. including 40 to Chapman & Hall and 108 to W. C. Macready; ds (2) 1833, 1847.

LYTTON, EDWARD ROBERT BULWER-LYTTON, 1st Earl of, 1831–1891. Als (2) 1875, 1882.

LYTTON, ROSINA DOYLE (WHEELER) BULWER-LYTTON, Baroness, 1802–1882. Als (3) 1841–72.

LYTTON, VICTOR ALEXANDER GEORGE ROBERT BULWER-LYTTON, 2nd Earl of, 1876–1947. Als (7) 1906–7 to W. A. Knight.

MACARTNEY, GEORGE MACARTNEY, Earl, 1737–1806. Als, al (4) 1780, 1800 and n.d.

MACAULAY, CATHARINE (SAWBRIDGE), 1731–1791. Als 20 September 1774 to the Earl of Buchan.

MACAULAY, THOMAS BABINGTON MACAULAY, 1st Baron, 1800–1859. *History of England*, Vol. V, 357 *ll.*; "The Late Lord Holland," 35 pp.; notebooks (12) containing historical notes and memoranda; review of Ranke's *History of the Papacy*, 90 pp.; als (53) 1830–59 and n.d. including 43 to his sisters; with als (24) 1892–3 written by or to Lady Margaret Knutsford concerning the unauthorized use of Macaulay's letters.

MACCARTHY, SIR DESMOND, 1878–1952. Als 9 November 1920 to T. J. Cobden-Sanderson.

MCCARTHY, JUSTIN, 1830–1912. Als (2) 1889 and n.d.

MCCARTHY, JUSTIN HUNTLY, 1861–1936. Als 31 December 1900 to Harper & Bros.

MACCOLL, MALCOLM, 1831–1907. Als (36) 1897–1903 including 35 to W. A. Knight.

MACCORMAC, SIR WILLIAM, Bart., 1836–1901. Als n.d. to Sir John Millais.

MCCULLOCH, JOHN RAMSAY, 1789–1864. Als 13 September 1833.

MACCUNN, JOHN, 1846–1929. Als n.d. to W. A. Knight.

MACDONALD, JAMES RAMSAY, 1866–1937. Tls (2) 1923, 1929 to Mrs. T. J. Cobden-Sanderson.

MACDONELL, JAMES, 1842–1879. Als (3) 1872–7 to W. A. Knight.

MACDOUGALL, PATRICK CAMPBELL, 1806–1867. Als n.d. to W. A. Knight.

MACDOWELL, PATRICK, 1799–1870. Als February 1833 to Elhanan Bicknell.

MACFARREN, GEORGE, 1788–1843. Als 13 May 1820 to Mr. Glossop.

MACFARREN, SIR GEORGE ALEXANDER, 1813–1887. Als, ls (18) 1873–85 including 15 to Joseph Bennett.

MACGREGOR, JOHN, 1825–1892. Als 27 August 1877 to J. E. Millais.

MACKAIL, JOHN WILLIAM, 1859–1945. Als (2) 1921, 1940.

MACKAY, AENEAS JAMES GEORGE, 1839–1911. Als (26) 1883–96 and n.d. to W. A. Knight.

MACKAY, CHARLES, 1787–1857. Als 20 October 1849.

MACKAY, CHARLES, 1814–1889. "The Primrose," 2 pp.; als (3) 1840–70 including 2 to Horace Greeley.

M'KENDRICK, JOHN GRAY, 1841–1926. Als 30 October 1888 to W. A. Knight.

MCKENNA, REGINALD, 1863–1943. Tls 15 March 1923 to C. F. Adams.

MACKENZIE, HENRY, 1745–1831. Als (2) 1788, 1802.

MACKENZIE, SIR MORELL, 1837–1892. Als (2) 1888, 1891.

MACKENZIE, ROBERT SHELTON, 1809–1880. Als 1 October 1836 to W. D. Gallagher.

MACKGILL, JAMES, d. 1579. Ds 7 July 1548.

MACKINTISH, JAMES, 1858–1944. Als 1 December 1893

to W. A. Knight.

MACKINTOSH, SIR JAMES, 1765–1832. Als (3) 1797–1827.

MACKLIN, CHARLES, 1697?–1797. Als (3) 1774, 1775 and n.d.

MACLAGAN, WILLIAM DALRYMPLE, 1826–1910. Als (2) 1889, 1891.

MACLEAN, LETITIA ELIZABETH (LANDON), 1802–1838. Als (4) 1832–7 and n.d.

MACLEAN, THOMAS NELSON, 1845–1894. Als 1878 to J. E. Millais.

MACLEHOSE, AGNES (CRAIG), 1759–1841. "When first you saw Clarinda's charms" (copy in the hand of Robert Burns), 2 pp.; als 1786 to Robert Burns.

MACLEOD, DONALD, 1831–1916. Als n.d. to W. A. Knight.

MACLEOD, FIONA: *see* SHARP, WILLIAM, 1855–1905.

MACLISE, DANIEL, 1806–1870. Als (11) 1842–67 and n.d.

MACMILLAN AND CO., firm, publishers, London. Ls 19 October 1868 to Harper & Bros.

MCNABB, VINCENT JOSEPH, 1868–1943. Als (7) 1909–10 to Michael Field.

MACNEE, SIR DANIEL, 1806–1882. Als 3 September 1878 to J. E. Millais.

MACPHERSON, FRANCIS, publisher, London. Als 3 September 1836 to Lancelot Holland.

MACPHERSON, JAMES, 1736–1796. Als 19 February 1791 to Paul Benfield.

MACQUOID, PERCY, d. 1925. Als n.d. to Mary Millais.

MACREADY, WILLIAM CHARLES, 1793–1873. Als (15) 1821–66.

MACRONE, JOHN, 1809–1837. Als (6) 1833–7.

MACSWINNY, OWEN: *see* SWINNY.

MACVICAR, JOHN GIBSON, 1800–1884. Als 11 September 1879 to W. A. Knight.

MACWHIRTER, JOHN, 1839–1911. Als (9) n.d., of which 5 are to W. A. Knight and 4 to Sir John Millais.

MADAN, MARTIN, 1726–1790. Legal opinions and memoranda in William Cowper Commonplace Book, 400 pp.

MADDEN, SIR FREDERIC, 1801–1873. Als (11) 1829–58 including 7 to S. L. Sotheby.

MAGEE, WILLIAM CONNOR, 1821–1891. Als n.d.

MAGINN, WILLIAM, 1793–1842. "That dreadful time may come . . . ," 5 pp.

MAGNUS, LAURIE, 1872–1933. Als 4 August 1896 to W. A. Knight.

MAHAFFY, SIR JOHN PENTLAND, 1839–1919. Als (18) 1879–81 to W. A. Knight.

MAHONEY, DOROTHY LOUISE, 1902– . "Some English Garden Flowers" (calligraphic manuscript), 32 pp.

MAITLAND, JOHN, Baron of Thirlestane, 1543–1595. Ds (2) 1586 and n.d.

MAJOR, RICHARD HENRY, 1818–1891. Als 18 May 1859 to S. L. Sotheby.

MALET, SIR EDWARD BALDWIN, 4th Bart., 1837–1908. Als 23 September 1891 to Sir Arthur Sullivan.

MALLET, DAVID, 1705?–1765. Als (2) 1747, 1762; ds 1764.

MALLOCK, WILLIAM HURRELL, 1849–1923. Als (4) 1908–9 and n.d.

MALMESBURY, JAMES HARRIS, 1st Earl of, 1746–1820. Als (3) 1770–1812.

MALMESBURY, JAMES EDWARD HARRIS, 2nd Earl of, 1778–1841. Als 29 November 1832 to Mr. Murchison.

MALONE, EDMOND, 1741–1812. Als (3) 1802, 1809 and n.d.

MALTBY, EDWARD, 1770–1859. Als 27 April 1836 to the Earl of Lichfield.

MANCHESTER, HENRY MONTAGU, 1st Earl of, ca. 1563–1642. Ds (2) 1623, 1625.

MANGLES, JAMES, 1786–1867. Als 26 December 1828 to John Booth.

MANN, SIR HORACE, 1701–1786. Als (6) 1780–1 and n.d.; ads (2) 1752, 1755; ds 1784.

MANNERS, GEORGE, 1778–1853. Als n.d.

MANNING, HENRY EDWARD, Cardinal, 1808–1892. Als (2) 1848, 1888.

MANNING, THOMAS, 1772–1840. Als (2) 1834, 1835 to Mrs. John Payne.

MANNING-SANDERS, RUTH, 1895– "Horses to Market," 2 pp.

MAPLESON, JAMES HENRY, 1830–1901. Als, ls (7) 1870, 1891 and n.d. including 6 to Joseph Bennett.

MAPLETOFT, JOHN, 1631–1721. Ds 14 November 1684.

MARA, GERTRUDE ELISABETH, 1749–1833. Als 28 December 1790 to Mr. Weeks.

MARCHMONT, HUGH HUME, 3rd Earl of, 1708–1794. Als 18 October 1763.

MARKLAND, JEREMIAH, 1693–1776. Als 8 March 1768 to Mr. Bowyer.

MARKS, DAVID WOOLF, 1811–1909. Als 18 September 1871 to W. A. Knight.

MARKS, HENRY STACY, 1829–1898. Als (4) 1891–8 including 3 to Sir John Millais.

MARLBOROUGH, JAMES LEY, 1st Earl of, 1550–1629. Ds ca. 1628.

MARLBOROUGH, JOHN CHURCHILL, 1st Duke of, 1650–1722. Als, ls (14) 1684–1712; ds (5) 1707–18.

MARLBOROUGH, SARAH (JENNINGS) CHURCHILL, Duchess of, 1660–1744. Als, ls (16) 1721–41; ds (6) 1717–38.

MARLOWE, CHRISTOPHER, 1564–1593. "The passionate Sheepheard to his love" (contemporary copy), 1 p.

MAROCHETTI, CARLO, Baron, 1805–1868. Als (3) 1830–63.

MARRIOTT, ELIZABETH. Als 16 September 1899 to W. J. Rolfe.

MARRYAT, FLORENCE: *see* LEAN.

MARRYAT, FREDERICK, 1792–1848. *Masterman Ready* (incomplete), 194 pp.; *Mr. Midshipman Easy*, Chap. VI to the end, 292 pp.; *Percival Keene* manuscript entitled "Percival Sharp" (incomplete), 190 pp.; als (18) 1829–44 and n.d.

MARSH-CALDWELL, ANNE (CALDWELL), 1797–1874. Als (2) 1844, 1845 to Chapman & Hall.

MARSHALL, ALFRED, 1842–1924. Als 4 January 1887 to W. A. Knight.

MARSHALL, BENJAMIN, ca. 1767–1835. Als n.d .to Mr. White.

MARSHALL, JULIAN, 1836–1903. Als (2) 1875, 1876 to Joseph Bennett.

MARSHALL, WILLIAM CALDER, 1813–1894. Als 31 October 1853 to Elhanan Bicknell.

MARSTON, EDWARD, 1825–1914. Als 9 April 1880 to Harper & Bros.

MARSTON, JOHN WESTLAND, 1819–1890. Als (5) 1842, 1861 including 4 to W. C. Macready.

MARTEN, HENRY, 1602–1680. Als ca. 11 July 1654 to Mary Ward.

MARTIN, HELENA SAVILLE (FAUCIT), Lady, 1817–1898. Als (2) 1871, 1882.

MARTIN, SIR THEODORE, 1816–1909. "The Queen at St. Pauls's, June 22, 1897," 1 p.; "The Queen at Kensington,

June 28, 1897," 1 p.; als (10) 1866–1904 including 9 to W. A. Knight.

MARTINEAU, GERTRUDE. Als (2) 1892, 1903 to W. A. Knight.

MARTINEAU, HARRIET, 1802–1876. *Society in America*, 745 pp.; als (5) 1844–55 and n.d.

MARTINEAU, JAMES, 1805–1900. Als 18 July 1897 to W. A. Knight.

MARTYN, THOMAS, 1735–1825. Als (3) 1796–1807 to R. W. Elliston.

MARVELL, ANDREW, 1621–1678. Als (2) 1660, 1673/4.

MARY I, Queen of England, 1516–1558. Als 14 August 1557 to Emperor Charles V; ls (2) 1555, 1556; ds (3) 1553–5.

MARY STUART, Queen of Scots, 1542–1587. Als (3) 1562–71; ls (5) 1565–72; ds 1559; with contemporary copies of her letters (12) and of documents relating to her life and trial.

MASEFIELD, JOHN, 1878–1967. "Lemmings," 1 p.; "The Wanderer," 13 pp.; "The Widow in the Bye Street" (extract), 1 p.; als, tls (4) 1915–62 and n.d.

MASKELL, WILLIAM, 1814?–1890. Als 3 June 1880 to James Toovey.

MASKELYNE, NEVIL, 1732–1811. Als 2 October 1796 to D. C. Lysons.

MASON, ALFRED EDWARD WOODLEY, 1865–1948. "A verified Conjecture," 11 pp.

MASON, WILLIAM, 1724–1797. "The Rise of Fashion," 8 pp.; "Sonnet" ("To snatch tho late from dark oblivions shade"), 1 p.; als (4) 1774–95 including 2 to Dr. Charles Burney.

MASSEY, GERALD, 1828–1907. "Song," 1 p.

MASSON, DAVID, 1822–1907. Als (3) 1889–1900 to W. A. Knight.

MATHERS, HELEN BUCKINGHAM: *see* REEVES, HELEN BUCKINGHAM (MATHERS).

MATHEW, GEORGE FELTON, b. 1795. "Oh—, thou bright bearer of joy," "To a poetical friend" (addressed to John Keats), "To a young lady," poems in the autograph of Richard Woodhouse with his notes on them.

MATHEWS, CHARLES, 1776–1835. Biographical sketch of Joe Hayns [Haines], an actor, 1 p.; als (6) 1806, 1830 and n.d.

MATHEWS, CHARLES EDWARD, 1834–1905. Als 22 March 1903 to W. A. Knight.

MATHEWS, CHARLES JAMES, 1803–1878. Als (6) 1854, 1877 and n.d.

MATHEWS, LUCIA ELIZABETH ("MADAME VESTRIS"), 1797–1856. Als (2) n.d.

MATURIN, CHARLES ROBERT, 1780–1824. Als (3) 1801 and n.d.

MAUDUIT, JASPER, fl. 1760–1765. Als 25 April 1764.

MAUGHAM, WILLIAM SOMERSET, 1874–1965. *Ah King, Six Stories of Malaya*, 409 pp.; als (2) 1940 and n.d.

MAURICE, JOHN FREDERICK DENISON, 1805–1872. Als (4) 1854.

MAURICE, THOMAS, 1754–1824. Als (2) 1817, 1818 to Sir Philip Francis.

MAX MÜLLER: *see* MÜLLER, FRIEDRICH MAX.

MAXWELL, SIR HERBERT EUSTACE, Bart., 1845–1937. Als 15 December 1896 to W. A. Knight.

MAXWELL, SIR JOHN MAXWELL STIRLING-, Bart., 1866–1956. Als (3) 1894 to W. A. Knight.

MAXWELL, MARY ELIZABETH (BRADDON), 1837–1915. Als (3) 1881, 1889 and n.d.

MAYHEW, HORACE, 1816–1872. Als n.d. to Henry Bradbury.

MEAD, JOSEPH, 1586–1638. Als n.d. to Lady Bell.

MEADOWS, JOSEPH KENNY, 1790–1874. Als n.d. to Alexander Johnston.

MEDWIN, THOMAS, 1788–1869. Notes for a new edition of his *Life of Shelley*, in an interleaved copy of the work (London, 1847); als (2) 1835 and n.d.

MELBOURNE, WILLIAM LAMB, 2nd Viscount, 1779–1848. Als, ls (5) 1830–46.

MELCOMBE, GEORGE BUBB DODINGTON, Baron, 1691–1762. Ds 7 May 1730.

MELLON, SARAH JANE (WOOLGAR), 1824–1909. Als (7) n.d. including 6 to Lewis Wingfield.

MELMOTH, WILLIAM, 1710–1799. Als (2) 1759, 1770.

MELVILLE, HENRY DUNDAS, 1st Viscount, 1742–1811. Als, ls (109) 1770–1806 and n.d. including 92 to Sir James Murray-Pulteney.

MENNES, SIR JOHN, 1599–1671. Ds (73) 1662–7 (signed with Samuel Pepys).

MEREDITH, GEORGE, 1828–1909. *The Amazing Marriage* (lacks Chaps. I–VIII), 468 pp.; *Diana of the Crossways*, 987 *ll.*, with contract for its publication by Chapman & Hall, 21 July 1884; *Lord Ormont and his Aminta*, 465 pp.; poems: "Il y a cent ans," 6 pp., with corrected proofsheets, and "The Main Regret," 1 p.; als (4) 1892–8.

MEREDITH, SIR WILLIAM, 3rd Bart., d. 1790. Als 4 December 1780 to Sir James Lowther.

MERIVALE, HERMAN CHARLES, 1839–1906. Als (3) 1870–89.

MEYERSTEIN, EDWARD HARRY WILLIAM, 1889–1952. "England," 1 p.

MEYNELL, ALICE CHRISTIANA (THOMPSON), 1847–1922. "The English Metres," 2 pp.; als (2) n.d.

MEYNELL, SIR FRANCIS, 1891–1975. Als, tls (68) 1923–33 to E. McKnight Kauffer.

MEYNELL, GERARD TUKE, b. 1877. Als 2 March 1943 to Edward Johnston.

MICKLE, WILLIAM JULIUS, 1735–1788. Als 17 June 1785 to Mr. Butler.

MIDDLETON, THOMAS FANSHAW, 1769–1822. Als 1 June 1807 to Cadell & Davies.

MILDMAY, SIR WALTER, ca. 1520–1589. "The chardges of the dyette provided for certayne of the queenes majesties honourable Counsell . . . at Westminster," signed manuscript, 1567, 5 pp.; ds (4) 1565–86.

MILL, JOHN STUART, 1806–1873. *Principles of Political Economy*, 3 vols.; *A System of Logic*, 300 pp.; "Traité de Logique redigé d'après le cours de Philosophie de M. Gergonne . . . ," 90 pp.; als (14) 1835–70 and n.d.

MILLAIS, SIR JOHN EVERETT, Bart., 1829–1896. Collection of drafts or transcripts of his writings in prose or verse, including notes for speeches, drafts of letters, writings on art, etc., ca. 110 pieces; als (ca. 500) 1854–95 including ca. 400 to his wife and to members of his family; with 804 letters written by other persons to Millais or his family.

MILLAR, ERIC GEORGE, 1887–1966. Als 2 March 1946 to Charles Sessler.

MILLINGEN, ALEXANDER VON, 1840–1915. Tls 26 October 1904 to W. A. Knight.

MILMAN, ARTHUR, b. 1829. Als n.d. to W. A. Knight.

MILMAN, HENRY HART, 1791–1868. Als (3) 1824 and n.d.

MILNE, ALAN ALEXANDER, 1882–1956. "Notes on the Way," 5 pp.; als 4 December 1935.

MILNER, ALFRED MILNER, 1st Viscount, 1854–1925. Als (2) 1896, 1901.

MILTON, SIR CHRISTOPHER, 1615–1693. Ds (2) 1674, 1684.

MILTON, JOHN, 1608–1674. *Paradise Lost*, Bk. I, manuscript written from his dictation, 33 pp.; with letter of Jacob Tonson, ca. 1732, concerning the manuscript; ds 27 November 1623.

MINTO, WILLIAM, 1845–1893. Als (24) 1889–92 to W. A. Knight.

MITCHEL, JOHN, 1815–1875. Als (2) 1857, 1866.

MITCHELL, ROBERT, ca. 1795–1836. Als 22 October 1816 to Thomas Carlyle.

MITFORD, MARY RUSSELL, 1786–1855. *Belford Regis* (incomplete manuscript of the book with some corrected proofs); "To G. L. Wardle. Esqr M.P.: on the death of his child," 2 pp.; als (3) 1836 and n.d.

MITFORD, WILLIAM, 1744–1827. Als 13 November 1819 to Cadell & Davies.

MOFFAT, ROBERT, 1795–1883. Als n.d. to Mr. Vavasseur.

MOIR, DAVID MACBETH ("Δ"), 1798–1851. "Casa's Dirge," 4 pp.

MOLLOY, JAMES LYNAM, 1837–1909. Als (2) ca. 1876, 1890.

MONBODDO, JAMES BURNETT, Lord, 1714–1799. Als 21 March 1782 to Mr. Cadell.

MONCK, GEORGE: *see* ALBEMARLE.

MONCKTON, LIONEL, 1861–1924. Als n.d. to Joseph Bennett.

MONCRIEFF, WILLIAM THOMAS, 1794–1857. Als 12 September 1835 to Mr. Mitchell.

MONEY, JOHN, 1752–1817. Als 17 April 1809 to Sir James Murray-Pulteney.

MONKHOUSE, WILLIAM COSMO, 1840–1901. Als (2) 1896, 1898.

MONKSWELL, ROBERT PORRETT COLLIER, 1st Baron, 1817–1886. Als (2) 1874, 1881 to J. E. Millais.

MONMOUTH, ROBERT CAREY, 1st Earl of, 1560–1639. Ds (10) 1618–22.

MONRO, DAVID BINNING, 1836–1905. Als 28 March 1888 to W. A. Knight.

MONRO, HAROLD EDWARD, 1879–1932. "Memory opens," 1 p.

MONSELL, JOHN SAMUEL BEWLEY, 1811–1875. Als 20 August 1872 to A. S. Sullivan.

MONTAGU, ELIZABETH (ROBINSON), 1720–1800. Als n.d. to John Stoole.

MONTAGU, GEORGE, 1751–1815. Als (2) 1789 to Gilbert White.

MONTAGU, LADY MARY (PIERREPONT) WORTLEY, 1689–1762. Poems: "born to be slaves . . . ," "While fruitfull Nile . . . ," 3pp.; copies of poems in Lady Mary's hand: "On Lady Mary Wortley Montagu's Portrait" [Pope] and "Venus to ye courts above" [unidentified], 3pp.; als (2) n.d.

MONTAGUE, HENRY JAMES, 1843?–1878. Als (2) n.d.

MONTALBA, CLARA, 1842–1929. Als (5) 1893–6 and n.d. to W. W. Baldwin.

MONTEFIORE, CLAUDE JOSEPH GOLDSMID-, 1858–1938. Als n.d. to W. A. Knight.

MONTGOMERY, JAMES, 1771–1854. "For an American Visitor," 1 p.; als 8 May 1828 to Rudolph Ackermann.

MONTGOMERY, ROBERT, 1807–1855. Als n.d.

MONTGOMERY, WALTER, 1827–1871. Als (2) 1857, 1865.

MOODY, JOHN, 1727?–1812. Als 16 August 1775 to David Garrick.

MOORE, CHRISTOPHER, 1790–1863. Als 10 May 1849 to Alexander Johnston.

MOORE, GEORGE, 1852–1933. *Memoirs of My Dead Life* (draft of additional material for "Spring in London"), 49 pp. (corrected proofsheets), 336 pp.; als 26 July 1923 to Miss Liveright.

MOORE, HENRY, 1831–1896. Als 26 March 1888 to Sir John Millais.

MOORE, JOHN, 1646–1714. Als 2 June 1690.

MOORE, JOHN, 1729–1802. Als (2) 8 November 1787 to Robert Burns, 16 November 1797 to Cadell & Davies.

MOORE, SIR JOHN, 1761–1809. Als (6) 1802–4 and n.d. including 5 to Sir James Murray-Pulteney; ds 22 March 1780.

MOORE, THOMAS, 1779–1852. *Lalla Rookh*, 3 manuscript versions (1st draft of "Paradise and the Peri" and introductory pages of "The Fire-Worshippers," 200 pp.; 2nd draft, complete except for "The Light of the Haram," 187 *ll.*; final manuscript, 140 pp.) and corrected proofsheets, 405 pp.; "Memorial of Chaste and Pious Women," 26 pp.; commonplace book containing draft material for "Alciphron," and notes on theology, philosophy and the classics, 140 pp.; shorter poems: "Alone by the Schuylkill," 2 pp.; "Dear Harp of My Country," 1 p.; words and music to: "The earth is the planet," "The Girl I Left Behind Me," "Sweet Star of Eve," "They May Rail at This Life," "Venetian Air," "When First That Smile" and "When Thou Art Nigh," together 12 pp.; collection of juvenile poems, 20 pp.; als (20) 1802–43 and n.d.; ds n.d.

MOORE, THOMAS STURGE, 1870–1944. "The Dying Swan," 1 p.; als 5 June 1914 to S. C. Cockerell.

MORANT, PHILIP, 1700–1770. Als 12 December 1752.

MORE, HANNAH, 1745–1833. "The Bazaar," 4 pp.; "The Negro Boy's Petition" (partly autograph), 3 pp.; als (7) 1798–1827 and n.d.

MORE, SIR THOMAS, Saint, 1477/8–1535. Ds 1 June 1523.

MORGAN, CHARLES, 1894–1958. Als 17 December 1919 to George Cookson.

MORISON, STANLEY, 1889–1967. "The Anatomy of fair writing. An Anthology of divers hands" (calligraphic notebook by Edward Johnston); als 7 January 1923 to Holbrook Jackson.

MORLAND, GEORGE, 1763–1804. Als (2) 1785 to Philip Dawe; ads 11 May 1795; ds 19 April 1802.

MORLEY, GEORGE, 1597–1684. Als 2 November 1660 to King Charles II.

MORLEY, HENRY, 1822–1894. Als 17 May 1889 to W. A. Knight.

MORLEY, JOHN MORLEY, Viscount, 1838–1923. Als (12) 1876–1906 including 7 to W. A. Knight.

MORRELL, OTTOLINE (BENTINCK), Lady, 1873–1938. Als 16 August 1922 to T. J. Cobden-Sanderson.

MORRIS, THOMAS, fl. 1750–1800. Als n.d. to Mr. Scott.

MORRIS, WILLIAM, 1834–1896. *Beowulf* (two versions), 72 and 105 pp.; "Frithiof the Bold," 4 pp.; "Gossip about an Old House," 8 *ll.*; *The House of the Wolfings*, 168 pp.; *Kormák's Saga* (translation written out in a calligraphic hand), 42 pp.; "Notes on Lord Rosebery's Ministry," 2 pp.; sonnet: "Rhyme Slayeth Shame," 1 p.; "The Story of Halfdan the Black. The Story of King Harald," 24 *ll.*; *The Well at the World's End*, 629 pp.; unidentified verse, 2 pp.; trial calligraphic scripts, 1 *l.*; private ledger and costs ledger of the Kelmscott Press, Hammersmith, 1893–8, 250 pp.; als (22) 1868–95 and n.d. With als (5) 1897–1929 from Morris' wife and daughters.

Morrison, Arthur, 1863–1945. Als 21 February 1902 to W. E. Henley.

Morrison, George Herbert, 1866–1928. Als 19 June 1902 to W. A. Knight.

Morrison, Robert, 1782–1834. Als 31 January 1825 to Francis Arundell.

Mortimer, John Hamilton, 1741–1779. Als 16 May 1776 to David Garrick.

Morton, Andrew, 1802–1845. Als 6 September 1836 to William Collins.

Morton, John Maddison, 1811–1891. Als (4) 1870 and n.d.

Moser, Mary, d. 1819. Als 20 October 1768.

Moss, William Edward. Tls 1 June 1946 to Martin Breslauer.

Motherwell, William, 1797–1835. "Of birds that sing . . . ," 2 pp.

Mottram, Ralph Hale, 1883–1971. Als 13 November 1928 to R. Cobden-Sanderson.

Motte, Benjamin, d. 1738. Als (2) 1726, 1727/8 including 1 to Jonathan Swift; ds (2) 1727, 1729.

Mountain, Rosoman (Wilkinson), 1768?–1841. Als 3 June 1840.

Moxon, Edward, 1801–1858. Als (2) 1834, 1852.

Muir, William, fl. 1880–1902. Als 19 May 1902.

Mulgrave, Constantine John Phipps, 2nd Baron, 1744–1792. Als (3) 1775, 1777 and n.d.

Mulgrave, Henry Phipps, 1st Earl of, 1755–1831. Als, ls (10) 1805–9 including 9 to Sir James Murray-Pulteney.

Müller, Friedrich Max, 1823–1900. *The Science of Thought* (preface and pages 1–8 only), 11 pp.; als (17) 1886–98 to W. A. Knight.

Mulock, Dinah Maria: *see* Craik, Dinah Maria (Mulock).

Mulready, William, 1786–1863. Als n.d.

Munby, Alan Noel Latimer, 1913–1974. "Robert Curzon" (corrected typescript), 30 pp.

Munden, Joseph. Ds 3 December 1819.

Munnings, Sir Alfred James, 1878–1959. Als 10 July 1947 to Sir Sydney Cockerell.

Munster, George Augustus Frederick Fitz-Clarence, 1st Earl of, 1794–1842. Als (56) 1813–41 mainly to Minney Seymour Damer.

Murphy, Arthur, 1727–1805. Autobiographical notes, 4 pp.; als 2 December 1778 to Dr. Shepheard.

Murray, Alexander Henry Hallam, 1854–1934. Als 15 June 1903 to W. A. Knight.

Murray, Charles Fairfax, 1849–1919. Als (41) 1889–1916 including 35 to J. & J. Leighton, booksellers, and 4 to Harry Quilter.

Murray, David Christie, 1847–1907. Als 7 May 1889.

Murray, Gilbert, 1866–1957. Als (3) 1901–7.

Murray, John, 1778–1843. Als (9) 1808–36 and n.d.; ads 1809.

Murray, John, 1808–1892. Als (2) 1873 and n.d.

Murray, Sir John, 1851–1928. Tls 26 October 1911 to Joan Severn.

Murray, John, firm, publishers, London. Als (7) 1843–78 including 3 to Harper & Bros.

Murray, John Clark, 1836–1917. Als (26) 1856–1900 to W. A. Knight.

Murray, Lindley, 1745–1826. Als (3) 1805–7.

Murry, John Middleton, 1889–1957. Als 25 February 1920 to R. Cobden-Sanderson.

Muspratt, James Sheridan, 1821–1871. Als 5 February 1852 to Charles Dickens.

Musters, John, 1777–1849. Als (2) 1845, 1847 to B. Campbell.

Musters, Mary Anne (Chaworth), d. 1843. Als n.d. to John Wadsworth.

Myers, Ernest James, 1844–1921. Als (2) 1880, 1904 to W. A. Knight.

Myers, Frederic William Henry, 1843–1901. "The Passing of Youth," 10 pp.; als 13 April 1878 to Mr. Cowper-Temple. With an als from Mrs. Myers 5 January 1904 to W. A. Knight.

Mylne, Robert, 1734–1811. Als (3) 1785, 1809 and n.d.

Naish, John George, 1824–1905. Als 31 March 1881 to J. E. Millais.

Napier, Sir Charles James, 1782–1853. Als (2) 1852, 1853.

Napier, Macvey, 1776–1847. Als 3 August 1831 to Mr. Black.

Napier, Sir William Francis Patrick, 1785–1860. Als (2) 1857 and n.d. to Lt.-Col. Rathbone.

Nares, Edward, 1762–1841. Als 30 March 1818 to Cadell & Davies.

Nares, Sir George Strong, 1831–1915. Als 15 May 1875 to J. E. Millais.

Nash, John, 1752–1835. Als n.d. to Charles Mathews the elder.

Nash, Paul, 1889–1946. Als (4) 1930–35 to E. McKnight Kauffer.

Nash, Treadway Russell, 1725–1811. Als (2) 1807 and n.d.

Naunton, Sir Robert, 1563–1635. *Fragmenta Regalia* (contemporary copy), 36 *ll.*

Neal, Nathaniel. Als 15 October 1743 to Philip Doddridge.

Neale, John Preston, 1780–1847. Ads n.d.

Nelson, Horatio Nelson, Viscount, 1758–1805. Last will and testament, dated 28 December 1802 and 10 March 1803, 18 pp.; bankbook, 1804–5; als (28) 1778–1805 including 4 to Lady Hamilton; ds (7) 1781–1805.

Nelson, Robert, 1656–1715. Als 4 December 1712 to Dr. Francis Lee.

Nethersole, Olga, 1870–1951. Als 25 June 1915 to Sir Johnston Forbes-Robertson.

Nettleship, Henry, 1839–1893. Als 5 January 1888 to Sir Henry Acland.

Neville, Henry, 1837–1910. Als (2) 1900 and n.d.

Neville, William Paine, 1830?–1905. Als (4) 1882–96 to W. A. Knight.

Nevinson, Christopher Richard Wynne, 1889–1946. Als n.d. to E. McKnight Kauffer.

Nevinson, Henry Woodd, 1856–1941. Als 14 January 1912 to T. J. Cobden-Sanderson.

Newbery, Francis, 1743–1818. Als 4 November 1791 to Sir Joseph Banks.

Newman, Ernest, 1868–1959. Als, tls (20) 1900–21 to Grant Richards.

Newman, Francis William, 1805–1897. Als (2) 1864, 1878.

Newman, John Henry, Cardinal, 1801–1890. Als (19) 1837–90 including 4 to A. W. Hutton and 10 to W. A. Knight.

Newton, Sir Charles Thomas, 1816–1894. Als 21 February 1887 to Mrs. W. W. Story.

Newton, Gilbert Stuart, 1794–1835. Als 21 March

1833 to John Martin.

NEWTON, SIR ISAAC, 1642–1727. Nine papers on counterfeiting, gold & silver coinage, paper credit, 25 *ll.*; notes on astronomical observations, including Halley's observation of a comet, 1 p.; notes on chronology, 2 pp.; pocket memorandum book, ca. 1659, 94 *ll.*; als 16 May 1678 to Robert Hooke; ds (3) 1704, 1718 and n.d.

NEWTON, JOHN, 1725–1807. Diary, September 1756–December 1772, 459 pp.; als (44) 1777–98 including 39 to Mrs. Gardiner and 4 to Hannah More.

NEWTON, SIR WILLIAM JOHN, 1785–1869. Als (12) 1829, 1849.

NICHOL, JOHN, 1833–1894. Als (26) 1873–94 to W. A. Knight.

NICHOLLS, ARTHUR BELL, 1817–1906. Ads 22 September 1856.

NICHOLLS, NORTON, 1742?–1809. Als 3 November 1779 to the Rev. W. J. Temple.

NICHOLS, JOHN, 1745–1826. Als (2) 1804, 1824.

NICHOLS, JOHN BOWYER, 1779–1863. Als 9 February 1808.

NICHOLS, JOHN GOUGH, 1806–1873. Als (2) 1859 to S. L. Sotheby.

NICHOLS, WILLIAM LUKE, 1802–1889. Als (2) 1880 to W. A. Knight.

NICHOLSON, BRINSLEY, 1824–1892. Als 5 March 1887 to J. W. Ebsworth.

NICHOLSON, SIR CHARLES, Bart., 1808–1903. Als 6 November 1889 to W. A. Knight.

NICHOLSON, HENRY ALLEYNE, 1844–1899. Als (3) 1875–8 to W. A. Knight.

NICHOLSON, JOSEPH SHIELD, 1850–1927. Als (3) 1890 to W. A. Knight.

NICHOLSON, PETER, 1765–1844. Als 7 December 1799 to Mr. Webster.

NICHOLSON, SIR WILLIAM, 1872–1949. Als 15 November 1934 to Sir Sydney Cockerell.

NICKLIN, JOHN ARNOLD, 1871–1917. "A Modern Novelist. To W. E. Henley," 2 pp.

NICOL, GEORGE, ca. 1741–1829. Als n.d.

NICOLL, SIR WILLIAM ROBERTSON, 1851–1923. Als (6) 1894–1900 to W. A. Knight.

NICOLSON, SIR HAROLD GEORGE, 1886–1968. Tls 1 September 1931 to E. McKnight Kauffer.

NICOLSON, WILLIAM, 1655–1727. Als 6 April 1719 to George Holmes.

NIECKS, FREDERICK, 1845–1924. Als (2) 1880, 1900.

NIGHTINGALE, FLORENCE, 1820–1910. Als (2) 1855, 1883.

NISBETT, LOUISA (CRANSTOUN), 1812?–1858. Als 6 January 1857 to E. T. Smith.

NOBLE, MARK, 1754–1827. Als 7 June 1819 to William Smith.

NOEL, RODEN BERKELEY WRIOTHESLEY, 1834–1894. Als (18) 1882–92 to W. A. Knight.

NOLLEKENS, JOSEPH, 1737–1823. Als (3) 1804–10; ads 25 September 1801.

NORDEN, JOHN, 1548–1625? Ds 23 April 1621.

NORMAN, MONTAGU COLLET NORMAN, 1st Baron, 1871–1950. Als, tls (10) 1924–42 to J. P. Morgan.

NORRIS, EDWIN, 1795–1872. Als (2) 1865–7 to Sir Henry Rawlinson.

NORRIS, WILLIAM EDWARD, 1847–1925. "A Partie Carrée" (first two pages of the story only).

NORTHAMPTON, HENRY HOWARD, Earl of, 1540–1614. Als (2) 1606 to the Mayor of Thetford; ds (3) 1604–8.

NORTHAMPTON, SPENCER JOSHUA ALWYNE COMPTON, 2nd Marquis of, 1790–1851. Als 19 March 1833.

NORTHCOTE, JAMES, 1746–1831. *Fables* (120) ca. 1823–8, with original designs and drawings; als (5) 1824–31. With als (2) 1822, 1825 from his sister Mary Northcote to Miss Moore.

NORTHUMBERLAND, SIR ROBERT DUDLEY, styled Duke of: *see* DUDLEY, SIR ROBERT.

NORTON, HON. MRS. CAROLINE (SHERIDAN), 1808–1877. Als (10) 1837–70 and n.d. including 3 to Mrs. Charles Dickens.

NOYES, ALFRED, 1880–1958. "Armistice," 2 pp.; als (9) 1928–30 to St. John Adcock.

O'CONNELL, DANIEL, 1775–1847. Als (2) 1829, 1831; ds 22 August 1831.

O'CONNOR, JOHN, 1830–1889. Als 2 September 1878 to J. E. Millais.

OGILBY, JOHN, 1600–1676. Als 6 August 1674 to Daniel Fleming.

OGLETHORPE, JAMES EDWARD, 1696–1785. Ads 20 April 1728.

OKEY, THOMAS, 1852–1935. Als 2 October 1930 to S. C. Cockerell.

OLIPHANT, LAURENCE, 1829–1888. Als (6) 1880–6 to Harper & Bros.

OLIPHANT, MARGARET OLIPHANT (WILSON), 1828–1897. Als (7) 1877–88 and n.d. including 5 to W. A. Knight.

O'MEARA, BARRY EDWARD, 1786–1836. Diary, 18 April 1816–8 February 1817, 19 vols.; notes on Napoleon, 29 pp.; als (2) 1816, 1817.

ONGLEY, ROBERT HENLEY-ONGLEY, 1st Baron, 1721?–1785. Als 2 October 1782 to Mr. Wingrave.

OPIE, AMELIA (ALDERSON), 1769–1853. Als (4) 1816–50.

OPIE, JOHN, 1761–1807. Als (3) 1788 and n.d.

"O'REILLY, MILES": *see* HALPINE.

ORFORD, HORACE WALPOLE, 4th Earl of: *see* WALPOLE, HORACE.

ORR, ALEXANDRA SUTHERLAND (LEIGHTON), 1828–1903. Als (13) 1890–1 to W. A. Knight.

ORRERY, ROGER BOYLE, 1st Earl of, 1621–1679. Als 3 October 1665 to the Duke of York (James II).

ORSAY, ALFRED GUILLAUME GABRIEL, Comte d', 1801–1852. Als (4) 1833–42 and n.d.

OSLER, SIR WILLIAM, Bart., 1849–1919. Als n.d. to W. W. Baldwin.

O'SULLIVAN, SAMUEL, 1790–1851. Als 10 April 1825.

"OUIDA": *see* DE LA RAMÉE.

OULESS, WALTER WILLIAM, 1848–1933. Als (2) 1882, 1888 to Sir John Millais.

OUSELEY, SIR GORE, 1770–1844. Als 7 June 1821 to Messrs. Nichols & Son.

OUSELEY, SIR WILLIAM, 1767–1842. Als 3 July 1788 to Richard Gough.

OUVRY, FREDERIC, 1814–1881. Als (2) 1856 to Mrs. Hannah Brown.

OVERALL, JOHN, 1560–1619. Notes and accounts, 3 April 1607, 2 pp.

OWEN, SIR FRANCIS PHILIP CUNLIFFE-, 1828–1894. Als (5) 1877, 1886 to Sir Arthur Sullivan.

OWEN, SIR RICHARD, 1804–1892. Als (10) 1860–89.

OWEN, ROBERT, 1771–1858. Als n.d.

OWEN, WILLIAM, 1769–1825. Als n.d. to James Heath.

OXENFORD, JOHN, 1812–1877. Als 9 December 1868 to

George Grossmith.

OXFORD, EDWARD HARLEY, 2nd Earl of, 1689–1741. Als (2) 1733, 1735; ads 1718.

OXFORD, ROBERT HARLEY, 1st Earl of, 1661–1724. Als (5) 1704–13; ds (4) 1710–1.

OXFORD AND ASQUITH, HERBERT HENRY ASQUITH, 1st Earl of, 1852–1928. Als 26 July 1901 to W. A. Knight.

OXFORD AND ASQUITH, MARGOT ASQUITH, Countess of, 1864–1945. Als 22 May 1896 to Sir John Millais.

PAGET, FRANCIS, 1851–1911. Als (3) 1893–1900 to Joan Severn.

PAGET, SIR JAMES, 1st Bart., 1814–99. Als (4) 1872–95.

PALGRAVE, FRANCIS TURNER, 1824–1897. Als (8) 1870–89, of which 6 are to W. A. Knight and 2 to A. S. Sullivan.

PALGRAVE, WILLIAM GIFFORD, 1826–1888. Als 30 June 1888 to John Ruskin.

PALMER, ARTHUR, 1841–1897. Als 18 March 1896 to W. A. Knight.

PALMER, JOHN, 1742?–1798. Als 18 July 1798 to a daughter.

PALMER, SAMUEL, 1805–1881. Als (149) 1827–81 to George Richmond and members of his family.

PALMERSTON, HENRY JOHN TEMPLE, 3rd Viscount, 1784–1865. Als, ls (7) 1821–62.

PANIZZI, SIR ANTHONY, 1797–1879. Als 5 February 1846 to D. Olivieri; ds (2) 1858.

PAOLI, PASQUALE DI, 1725–1807. Als, ls (4) 1769–92 and n.d.

PARK, THOMAS, 1759–1834. Als 20 December 1800 to William Hayley.

PARKER, CHARLES STEWART, 1829–1910. Als (2) 1892, 1907 to W. A. Knight.

PARKER, SIR GILBERT, Bart., 1862–1932. Als (7) 1891–1910 to W. E. Henley and his wife.

PARKER, MATTHEW, 1504–1575. Ls n.d.

PARKER, ROBERT ANDREW: *see* AUDEN.

PARNELL, THOMAS, 1679–1718. Als (2) 1714 and n.d.

PARR, SAMUEL, 1747–1825. Als, ls (4) 1784–1824.

PARRIS, EDMUND THOMAS, 1793–1873. Als 18 May 1852 to Elhanan Bicknell.

PARRY, SIR CHARLES HUBERT HASTINGS, Bart., 1848–1918. Als (9) 1889–1918 including 4 to Joseph Bennett.

PARRY, JOHN, 1776–1851. Als 26 March 1839 to Thomas Cazalet.

PARSONS, ALFRED WILLIAM, 1847–1920. Als (2) 1886, 1892 to Harper & Bros.

PARSONS, WILLIAM, 1736–1795. Als n.d. to Mr. Warren.

PASSFIELD, BEATRICE POTTER WEBB, Lady, 1858–1943. Als (2) 1932 and n.d.

PASSFIELD, SIDNEY JAMES WEBB, Baron, 1859–1947. Als 22 May 1929 to S. C. Cockerell.

PATMORE, COVENTRY KERSEY DIGHTON, 1823–1896. Als (3) 1877 and n.d.

PATON, SIR JOSEPH NOËL, 1821–1901. Als (2) 1878, 1886 to Sir John Millais.

PAUL, HOWARD, 1835–1905. Als 16 July 1877 to George Grossmith.

PAUL, ISABELLA HOWARD, 1833?–1879. Als October 1877 to George Grossmith.

PAXTON, SIR JOSEPH, 1801–1865. Als (3) 1851–62.

PAYN, JAMES, 1830–1898. "In Peril & Privation Among the Moors" (first page only of the story); als (30) 1878–98, of which 13 are to Mr. and Mrs. Grant Allen and 17 to W. E. Henley.

PAYNE, JOHN, d. 1787. Ds 27 June 1752.

PAYNE, ROGER, 1739–1797. Bookbinding memorandum, 1 p.; ads (35) 1786 and n.d.

PEACOCK, THOMAS LOVE, 1785–1866. *Crotchet Castle* and *Maid Marian*, 4 pp. (only); additions and corrections in a proof copy of *The Genius of the Thames* (1810).

PEARCE, HORACE, b. 1838. Als 1 June 1894 to W. A. Knight.

PEARCE, STEPHEN, 1819–1904. Als 28 March 1896 to Sir John Millais.

PEARCE, ZACHARY, 1690–1774. Als (2) 1749, 1756.

PECK, FRANCIS, 1692–1743. Als April 1740 to Thomas Martin.

PEEL, SIR ROBERT, 2nd Bart., 1788–1850. Als (18) 1812–47 and n.d.

PEEL, SIR ROBERT, 4th Bart., 1867–1925. Als (3) 1887–1902 to W. A. Knight.

PELHAM, HENRY FRANCIS, 1846–1907. Als n.d. to W. A. Knight.

PEMBER, EDWARD HENRY, 1833–1911. Als 4 November 1897 to W. A. Knight.

PEMBROKE, HENRY HERBERT, 9th Earl of, 1693–1751. Als 26 March 1739.

PEMBROKE, WILLIAM HERBERT, 3rd Earl of, 1580–1623. Ds 23 January 1623.

PENGELLY, WILLIAM, 1812–1894. Als 17 November 1869.

PENN, WILLIAM, 1644–1718. Last will and testament, dated 6 June 1684, 3 pp.; als (2) 9 July 1675 to George Fox, 6 June 1684 to his wife; ds (4) 1681–1703. With an als of his son, Thomas Penn, 8 November 1766 to Sir William Johnson.

PENNANT, THOMAS, 1726–1798. Als (16) 1758–98 including 12 to Sir Joseph Banks.

PENNY, ANN, d. 1782. "Elegy upon the death of Thomas Gray Esq.," 2 pp.

PEPYS, SAMUEL, 1633–1703. Memorandum on royal childbirths, 1 p.; shorthand notes, 3 pp.; als 13 June 1700 to his nephew, John Jackson; ls (6) 1670–89; ds (80) 1662–88.

PERCEVAL, SPENCER, 1762–1812. Als (3) 1807–12.

PERCY, THOMAS, 1729–1811. Als (2) 1788, 1802.

PERRINS, CHARLES WILLIAM DYSON, 1864–1958. Als 24 January 1908 to J. Pierpont Morgan; ls 1 March 1912 to Messrs. J. & J. Leighton.

PERRY, JAMES, 1756–1821. Als n.d.

PETERBOROUGH, CHARLES MORDAUNT, 3rd Earl of, 1658–1735. Als 3 March 1702 to Queen Anne.

PETERBOROUGH, HENRY MORDAUNT, 2nd Earl of, 1624?–1697. Als 17 December 1661.

PETERS, HUGH, 1598–1660. Ds ca. 1651.

PETERS, MATTHEW WILLIAM, 1742–1814. Als January 1775 to George Romney.

PETHICK-LAWRENCE, FREDERICK WILLIAM, 1871–1961. Als 15 September 1922 to Mrs. T. J. Cobden-Sanderson.

PETRIE, SIR WILLIAM MATTHEW FLINDERS, 1853–1942. Als (5) 1903–13.

PETTIE, JOHN, 1839–1893. Als (5) n.d. to Sir John Millais and Mary Millais.

PETTIGREW, THOMAS JOSEPH, 1791–1865. Als 16 February 1859 to S. L. Sotheby.

PETTY, SIR WILLIAM, 1623–1687. Al December 1687 to his son.

PHILLIP, JOHN, 1817–1867. Als 28 November 1857 to J. P. Knight.

PHILLIPPS, SIR THOMAS, Bart., 1792–1872. Als (3) 1856 to S. L. Sotheby.

PHILLIPS, HENRY, 1801–1876. Als (2) 1844 and n.d.

PHILLIPS, STEPHEN, 1868–1915. Poems: "The Blow," "Be Then Your Life" and "An Autumn Day," 2 pp.

PHILLIPS, THOMAS, 1770–1845. Als (2) 1827 and n.d.

PHILLPOTTS, EDEN, 1862–1960. Aps 2 July 1920 to R. Cobden-Sanderson.

PHIPPS, SIR CHARLES BEAUMONT, 1801–1866. Als (6) 1853–60 including 3 to Charles Dickens and 2 to Charles Kean.

"PHIZ": *see* BROWNE, HABLOT KNIGHT.

PICKERING, WILLIAM, 1796–1854. Als 13 September 1848 to R. S. Turner.

PICKERSGILL, FREDERICK RICHARD, 1820–1900. Als n.d. to Sir John Millais.

PICKERSGILL, HENRY WILLIAM, 1782–1875. Als (2) 1848, 1868 to Henry Vaughan.

PICTON, JAMES ALLANSON, 1832–1910. Als 20 March 1880 to W. A. Knight.

PIGOT, ELIZABETH BRIDGET, 1783–1866. Als (3) 1831–2; ads 1824.

PILSBURY, JOAN. Calligraphic manuscript of "Fidele" from Shakespeare's *Cymbeline*, 2 *ll.*

"PINDAR, PETER": *see* WOLCOT.

PINERO, SIR ARTHUR WING, 1855–1934. Als (2) 1882, 1895 to Percy Middlemist; tls (2) 1933; ads 23 April 1889.

PINKERTON, JOHN, 1758–1826. Als 4 April 1800.

PIOZZI, HESTER LYNCH (SALUSBURY) THRALE, 1741–1821. *Anecdotes of the Late Samuel Johnson*, 211 pp.; Last will and Testament, dated 19 April 1814, 2 pp.; als (18) 1789–1821 including 11 to W. A. Conway. *See also:* JOHNSON, SAMUEL.

PISTRUCCI, BENEDETTO, 1784–1855. Als (2) 1831, 1843.

PITT, WILLIAM, 1708–1788: *see* CHATHAM.

PITT, WILLIAM, 1759–1806. Als (57) 1781–1806 and n.d.; ads 4 July 1795; ds (10) 1784–1805.

PLANCHÉ, JAMES ROBINSON, 1796–1880. Als (2) 1875, 1877.

PLANTA, JOSEPH, 1744–1827. Als (2) 1814, 1819; ds 24 March 1800.

PLARR, VICTOR GUSTAVE, 1863–1929. *Ernest Dowson*, 152 *ll.*

PLAYFAIR, JAMES, 1738–1819. Als 3 June 1811.

PLAYFAIR, LYON PLAYFAIR, 1st Baron, 1818–1898. Als (7) 1865–98 including 6 to W. A. Knight.

PLAYFAIR, SIR ROBERT LAMBERT, 1828–1899. Als 8 June 1898 to W. A. Knight.

PLIMSOLL, SAMUEL, 1824–1898. Ls 6 August 1875.

PLUMPTREE, ANNABELLA, fl. 1795–1812. Als 6 September 1809 to Mr. Crosby.

PLYMOUTH, ROBERT GEORGE WINDSOR-CLIVE, 1st Earl of, 1857–1923. Als (3) 1898–1903 to W. E. Henley.

POLE, REGINALD, Cardinal, 1500–1558. Als 14 January 1555 to Cardinal Giovanni Morone; ds (2) 1550, 1557.

POLLARD, ALFRED WILLIAM, 1859–1944. Als (2) 1924 and n.d.

POLLOCK, SIR FREDERICK, 3rd Bart., 1845–1937. Als 17 September 1882 to W. A. Knight.

POLLOCK, SIR WILLIAM FREDERICK, 2nd Bart., 1815–1888. Als (4) 1868–83.

PONSONBY, SIR HENRY FREDERICK, 1825–1895. Als (22) 1880–93.

POOLE, JOHN, 1786?–1872. Als (2) 1822 to R. W. Elliston.

POPE, ALEXANDER, 1688–1744. *Epistle to Dr. Arbuthnot* (mostly autograph), 16 pp.; *An Essay on Man*, 40 pp.; *Of Taste*, 2 pp.; *Sapho to Phaon*, 7 pp.; "Satires on Horace Translated . . ." (title page and contents only), 4 pp. Shorter poems: "The Capon's Tale" ("In Yorkshire dwelt"), 2 pp.; "Sandys's Ghost" ("Ye Lords and Commons"), 5 pp.; "A Wish on Mrs. M. B.'s Birth-day" ("Oh be thou blest"), 2 pp.; poetical fragment ("What fair one, what brown one . . ."), 2 pp. Als (90) 1714–44 including 38 to the Earl of Orrery, 19 to Lady Mary Wortley Montagu, 18 to William Fortescue and 6 to Benjamin Motte (with agreement, 29 March 1727, for the publication by Motte of Pope's and Swift's *Miscellanies*); ads 13 January 1708/9; ds (2) 1729 and n.d.

POPE, ALEXANDER, 1763–1835. Als 11 July 1817 to Mr. Ward.

POPE, ELIZABETH (YOUNGE), 1744?–1797. Als January 1775 to David Garrick.

POPE-HENNESSY, DAME UNA (BIRCH), 1876–1949. "Unposted letters: the Journal of Frances Grenfell" (corrected typescript), 116 pp.

PORTER, ENDYMION, 1587–1649. Als ca. 1624 to his wife.

PORTER, JANE, 1776–1850. Als (2) 1811, 1827.

PORTEUS, BEILBY, 1731–1808. Als (3) 1783–1806.

PORTSMOUTH, LOUISE RENÉE DE PENANCOËT DE KÉROUALLE, Duchess of, 1649–1734. Ds (3) 1712–4.

POSTE, EDWARD, 1823–1902. Als 15 May 1888 to W. A. Knight.

POSTGATE, JOHN PERCIVAL, 1853–1926. Als (2) 1900 to W. A. Knight.

POTTER, BEATRIX, 1866–1943. Als (11) 1892–8 to Noël Moore.

POTTER, JOHN, 1674?–1747. Als 1745; ls 1737.

POTTER, ROBERT, 1721–1804. Als 17 December 1778.

POTTS, ALEXANDER WILLIAM, 1834–1889. Als (2) 1887 and n.d. to W. A. Knight.

POWER, MARGUERITE A., 1815?–1867. Als 6 October 1861 to Anna Maria Hall.

POWNALL, THOMAS, 1722–1805. Als (2) 1778 and n.d.; ds 28 May 1793.

POYNTER, SIR EDWARD JOHN, Bart., 1836–1919. Als (6) 1878–98.

PRAED, WINTHROP MACKWORTH, 1802–1839. "There hangs a portrait in an ancient hall," 1 p.; als (2) 1835, 1838.

PRICE, BONAMY, 1807–1888. Als (3) 1881–7 to W. A. Knight.

PRICE, RICHARD, 1790–1833. Als 31 December 1801 to Mr. Robins.

PRICE, SIR UVEDALE, Bart., 1747–1829. Als (108) 1794–1827 including 106 to Sir George and Lady Beaumont.

PRIESTLEY, JOSEPH, 1733–1804. "A chart of biography," 1 p.; als (2) 1774, 1802.

PRINGLE, SIR JOHN, Bart., 1707–1782. Als (4) 1770–8 and n.d.

PRINGLE-PATTISON, ANDREW SETH, 1856–1931. Als (2) 1902–3 to W. A. Knight.

PRINSEP, VALENTINE CAMERON, 1838–1904. Als (5) 1878 and n.d. to J. E. Millais and Mary Millais.

PRIOR, MATTHEW, 1664–1721. Als (14) 1704–16 and n.d. including 11 to Sir Thomas Hanmer.

PROCTER, ANNIE BENSON (SKEPPER), 1799–1888. Als (15) 1846–85 including 9 to R. M. Milnes, Lord Houghton, and 3 to W. A. Knight.

PROCTER, BRYAN WALLER, 1787–1874. "An Epitaph," 1 p.; "The Sea," 1 p.; als (7) 1825–68 and n.d.

PROTHERO, SIR GEORGE WALTER, 1848–1922. Als n.d.

to W. A. Knight.

PROUT, SAMUEL, 1783–1852. Als (10) 1825–35 and n.d.

PUGIN, AUGUSTUS CHARLES, 1762–1832. Als (3) 1819–31.

PUGIN, EDWARD WELBY, 1834–1875. Als 29 November 1855 to L. G. Lee.

PULTENEY, RICHARD, 1730–1801. Als (2) 1758, 1767 to Mr. Nourse.

PULTENEY, SIR WILLIAM (JOHNSTONE), 1729–1805. Als 15 January 1770 to Joshua Sharpe.

PURNELL, THOMAS, 1834–1889. Als n.d.

PUSEY, EDWARD BOUVERIE, 1800–1882. Als 13 October 1837 to G. Townsend.

PYE, CHARLES, 1777–1864. Als n.d.

PYE, HENRY JAMES, 1745–1813. Als 15 October 1803 to S. T. Pratt.

PYM, JOHN, 1584–1643. Als 12 July 1638 to his daughter Philipa.

PYM, SIR WILLIAM, 1772–1861. Als (2) 1809 to Sir James Murray-Pulteney.

PYNE, WILLIAM HENRY, 1769–1843. Als 28 June 1802 to Rudolph Ackermann.

QUARITCH, BERNARD, 1819–1899. Als (2) 1858 to S. L. Sotheby.

QUICK, ROBERT HERBERT, 1831–1891. Als (2) 1878 to Mr. Cowper-Temple.

QUILLER-COUCH, SIR ARTHUR THOMAS, 1863–1944. Als (3) 1888–1919.

QUILLINAN, EDWARD, 1791–1851. Als 30 March 1850.

RACKHAM, ARTHUR, 1867–1939. Als 28 September 1912 to Frank Crowninshield.

RADCLIFFE, JOHN, 1650–1714. Ds 27 October 1707.

RAEBURN, SIR HENRY, 1756–1823. Als (2) 22 August 1821 to David Wilkie and 3 May 1823 to Viscount Melville.

RAIMBACH, ABRAHAM, 1776–1843. Als (3) 1807–8 to William Hayley.

RALE(I)GH, SIR WALTER, 1552?–1618. Reply to Christopher Marlowe's "The passionate Sheepheard to his love," 1 p. (contemporary copy); als n.d. to his nephew, Sir John Gilbert; als 1610 to Sir Walter Cope; ls 1592. Contemporary accounts of Ralegh's speech upon the scaffold and execution on 29 October 1618, by Edmund Elms and Sergeant Fleetwood.

RALEIGH, SIR WALTER ALEXANDER, 1861–1922. Als (7) 1895–1907 including 6 to W. A. Knight.

RALSTON, WILLIAM RALSTON SHEDDEN-, 1828–1889. Als 6 March 1877 to Mr. Strahan.

RAMÉE, LOUISE DE LA: *see* DE LA RAMÉE.

RAMSAY, ALLAN, 1686–1758. "Henry to Emma," 2 pp.

RAMSAY, ALLAN, 1713–1784. Als 19 May 1761 to Sir William (Johnstone) Pulteney.

RAMSAY, ANDREW MICHAEL, 1686–1743. Al 6 August 1713 to Mr. Bayne; ads 1 October 1738.

RAMSAY, SIR WILLIAM, 1852–1916. Aps 6 July 1902 to W. A. Knight.

RANDOLPH, JOHN, 1749–1813. Als 12 March 1813; ds 27 April 1812.

RANSON, THOMAS FRAZER, 1784–1828. Als January 1818 to Mr. Gosden.

RATTIGAN, SIR TERENCE MERVYN, 1911–1977. *Separate Tables*, 90 pp.

RAWLINSON, SIR HENRY CRESWICKE, 1810–1895. "Vale, 18 April 1826," 2 pp.

RAWNSLEY, HARDWICKE DRUMMOND, 1851–1920. "In the Malvern," 1 p.; als (17) 1878–95 including 16 to W. A. Knight.

READ, SIR CHARLES HERCULES, 1857–1929. Als (3) including 2 to C. F. Murray.

READE, CHARLES, 1814–1884. *Hard Cash*, original manuscript, 823 *ll.*, fair copy made for the printer, 420 pp., and 11 pp. of passages not printed in the final version, with agreement, dated 31 January 1862 and signed by Charles Dickens and W. H. Wills, covering the writing of *Hard Cash* for *All the Year Round; Love Me Little, Love Me Long*, 619 pp.; als, ls (18) 1852–84 and n.d. including 9 to Harper & Bros.

REAY, DONALD JAMES MACKAY, 11th Baron, 1839–1911. Als (6) 1893–1906 to W. A. Knight.

REDESDALE, ALGERNON BERTRAM FREEMAN-MITFORD, 1st Baron, 1837–1916. Als 17 July 1889 to T. J. Cobden-Sanderson.

REDGRAVE, RICHARD, 1804–1888. Als 24 May 1845; ads 25 July 1848.

REECE, ROBERT, 1838–1891. Als 28 December 1877 to George Grossmith.

REED, EDWARD TENNYSON, 1860–1933. Als 26 December 1907 to Henry Sotheran & Co.

REED, ISAAC, 1742–1807. Als 8 July 1779 to Thomas Sherlock; ads n.d.

REED, PRISCILLA (HORTON), 1818–1895. Als 13 August 1875 to George Grossmith.

REED, THOMAS GERMAN, 1817–1888. Als (5) 1867–70 to A. S. Sullivan.

REEVE, HENRY, 1813–1895. Als 22 March 1845 to Henry Wheaton.

REEVE, LOVELL AUGUSTUS, 1814–1865. Als (3) 1852 to Sir Frederic Madden.

REEVES, HELEN BUCKINGHAM (MATHERS), 1853–1920. *Cherry Ripe!*, 2 vols.; *Comin' thro' the Rye*, ca. 235 pp.

REEVES, JOHN SIMS, 1818–1890. Als (17) 1858–97 including 8 (plus 4 telegrams) to Sir Arthur Sullivan. With als (3) n.d. from Mrs. Reeves to Sullivan.

REID, SIR GEORGE, 1841–1913. Als (3) 1901 to W. A. Knight.

REID, SIR GEORGE HOUSTOUN, 1845–1918. Als (4) 1885–6 to Sir John Millais or Mary Millais.

REID, MAYNE, 1818–1883. Als (8) 1874–82.

REID, SIR THOMAS WEMYSS, 1842–1905. Als 19 November 1897 to W. A. Knight.

REINAGLE, RAMSAY RICHARD, 1775–1862. Als (5) 1825–32 including 4 to Nathaniel Ogle.

RENDALL, GERALD HENRY, 1851–1945. Als 23 November 1902 to W. A. Knight.

RENNELL, JAMES, 1742–1830. Als (2) 1813, 1819.

RENNIE, JOHN, 1761–1821. Als 4 March 1807 to Messrs. Cuthell & Martin.

REPTON, HUMPHRY, 1752–1818. Als 31 January 1808 to Charles Smith.

REPTON, JOHN ADEY, 1775–1860. Als 12 June 1845.

REYNOLDS, CHARLOTTE, 1802–1884. Als (2) 1820, 1821 to Richard Woodhouse.

REYNOLDS, FREDERIC, 1764–1841. Als (3) n.d.

REYNOLDS, JOHN HAMILTON, 1796–1852. Als (4) 1819–20 to John Taylor.

REYNOLDS, SIR JOHN RUSSELL, 1828–1896. Als 8 April 1883 to J. E. Millais.

REYNOLDS, SIR JOSHUA, 1723–1792. "Felicity," 1 p.; manuscript concerning the training of an artist, 2 pp.; als (5) 1784–89 and n.d.; ds 8 March 1784.

REYNOLDS, SAMUEL WILLIAM, 1794–1872. Als 17 April 1834 to D. P. Colnaghi.

Rhys, Ernest, 1859–1946. Als (5) 1887–90 and n.d.

Rich, John, 1682?–1761. Als 11 December 1732 to Mr. Wood.

Richard, John Inigo, d. 1810. Ds 8 August 1809.

Richardson, Jonathan, 1665–1745. Als 6–7 May 1731 to Ralph Palmer.

Richardson, Joseph, 1755–1803. Als (3) n.d.

Richardson, Samuel, 1689–1761. *History of Mrs Beaumont*, in the form of a letter from Dr. Bartlett to Miss Byron, 19 pp.; als (12) 1747–58.

Richmond, George, 1809–1896. Als (10) 1828–90.

Richmond, Margaret (Beaufort) Tudor, Countess of, 1441–1509. Ds 10 April 1487?

Richmond, Legh, 1772–1827. Als (2) 1804, 1826.

Richmond, Sir William Blake, 1842–1921. Als (4) 1881, 1896 and n.d. including 3 to Sir John Millais.

Richmond and Lennox, Charles Lennox, 3rd Duke of, 1735–1806. Als, ls (16) 1763–1801; secretarial copies of letters and documents (12) 1793.

Ripon, Frederick John Robinson, 1st Earl of, 1782–1859. Als (3) 1842, 1854 including 2 to Thomas Carlyle.

Ritchie, Anne Isabella (Thackeray), Lady, 1837–1919. Notes concerning the manuscript of Thackeray's *The Rose and the Ring*, 2 pp.; als (72) 1877–1917 including 25 to W. A. Knight, 26 to Sir John Millais and his family and 4 to Joan Severn.

Ritchie, David George, 1853–1903. Als (2) 1895–6 to W. A. Knight.

Ritson, Joseph, 1752–1803. Als 1 December 1796 to Alexander Laing.

Rivers, George Pitt, Baron, 1722?–1803. Ds 25 February 1766.

Rivière, Briton, 1840–1920. Als (8) 1881–99, of which 4 are to W. A. Knight and 4 to Sir John Millais.

Rivington, Charles, 1754–1831. Als (3) 1801–26 to Walker King.

Roberts, Sir Charles George Douglas, 1860–1943. Als (4) 1893–8 including 3 to Small, Maynard & Co., publishers.

Roberts, David, 1796–1864. Als (5) 1848–57.

Roberts, Frederick Sleigh Roberts, 1st Earl, 1832–1914. Als (4) 1893–7 to W. E. Henley.

Roberts, William, 1862–1940. Als (16) 1913–30 to Belle da Costa Greene.

Robertson, Andrew, 1777–1845. Als 1 January 1830 to William Brockedon.

Robertson, George Croom, 1842–1892. Als (29) 1879–91 to W. A. Knight.

Robertson, Walford Graham, 1866–1948. Als n.d. to Mrs. Cobden-Sanderson.

Robertson, William, 1721–1793. Als (3) 1781–9.

Robertson, William, 1740–1803. Als (4) 1791–1802 to George Chalmers.

Robins, George Henry, 1778–1847. Als 23 October 1821 to Mr. Reese; ls 27 July 1831 to Mr. Winston; ds 2 June 1826.

Robinson, Frederick William, 1830–1901. Als (2) 1868 to Harper & Bros.

Robinson, Henry Crabb, 1775–1867. Als 6 November 1830 to Edward Foss, Jr.

Robinson, John, 1650–1723. Als 21 July 1712.

Robinson, Mary (Darby), 1758–1800. Als n.d. to Sir Peter Burrell.

Robinson, Peter Frederick, 1776–1858. Als 17 June 1806 to Lord Palmerston.

Rochester, Laurence Hyde, 1st Earl of, 1641–1711. Als 13 May 1701 to the Lord Justices of Ireland; ds 30 November 1686.

Rodker, John, 1894– . Als 25 September 1920, tls 3 August 1927 to Carlo Linati.

Rodney, George Brydges Rodney, 1st Baron, 1719–1792. Als (3) 1762–89.

Rogers, James Edwin Thorold, 1823–1890. Als n.d.

Rogers, Samuel, 1763–1855. Als (31) 1791–1853.

Roget, Peter Mark, 1779–1869. Als 19 December 1819 to Thomas Smith of Tetbury.

Rolfe, Frederick William ("Baron Corvo"), 1860–1913. Als (4) 1904 to J. B. Pinker.

Romanes, George John, 1848–1894. Als 14 March 1873 to W. A. Knight.

Romney, George, 1734–1802. Als (3) 1773–97 to his father and his son John.

Ros, Amanda (McKittrick), 1860–1939. Typewritten copy of a letter 5 March 1910 to Mr. Von Glehn.

Roscoe, Sir Henry Enfield, 1833–1915. Als, ls 1890 to W. A. Knight.

Roscoe, William, 1753–1831. "Stanzas," 2 pp.; als (3) 1801–22.

Roscoe, William Stanley, 1782–1843. Als 9 October 1820 to Robert Balmanno.

Rose, George, 1744–1818. Als (3) 1784, 1811, n.d.; ds 10 June 1788.

Rose, William Stewart, 1775–1843. Als n.d.

Rosebery, Archibald Philip Primrose, 5th Earl of, 1847–1929. Als, ls (24) 1884–1914 including 11 to W. A. Knight and 9 to Sir John Millais.

Ross, Sir John, 1777–1856. Als (2) 1850, n.d.

Ross, Robert Baldwin, 1869–1918. Tls (4) 1907 including 3 to C. G. Osborne.

Ross, Sir William Charles, 1794–1860. Als (3) 1849–53.

Rossetti, Christina Georgina, 1830–1894. "A Dirge," 1 p.; "Song" ("When I am dead, my dearest"), 1 p.; als (3) 1864–94.

Rossetti, Dante Gabriel, 1828–1882. "The Blessed Damozel," ams entitled "Blessed Damsel," dated "1847" but certainly later, 1 p.; description of his drawing "The Return of Tibullus to Delia," 2 pp.; manuscript written to help complete Alexander Gilchrist's *Life of William Blake*, 44 pp.; als (219) 1843–81 and n.d. including 64 to William Allingham, 34 to Edmund Bates, 36 to Mr. and Mrs. Cowper-Temple, 13 to B. R. Haydon and 62 to Alexander Gilchrist or his wife. Some of the Rossetti letters include poems.

Rossetti, William Michael, 1829–1919. Preface, dedication and list of contents to his edition of the poems of Walt Whitman, 50 pp., with corrected proofs of the volume; *Swinburne's Poems & Ballads*, 101 *ll.*; als (20) 1850–1907 and n.d.

Rossi, John Charles Felix, 1762–1839. Als 5 May 1823 to Edmund Balfour.

Rothenstein, Sir William, 1872–1945. Als (2) 1922, 1926.

Rothschild, Lionel Nathan, 1808–1879. Als 8 July 1873 to P. Crampton.

Rothschild, Nathan Meyer, 1777–1836. Als 25 July 1829 to William Cullen.

Rothwell, Richard, 1800–1868. Als n.d. to Henry Howard.

Rouw, Peter, II, 1771–1852. Als 6 February 1830 to

Thomas Robson.

ROWE, ELIZABETH (SINGER), 1674–1737. Als (2) n.d.

ROWSON, SUSANNA (HASWELL), 1762–1824. Als n.d. to Captain Hugh McCall.

ROXBURGHE, JOHN KER, 3rd Duke of, 1740–1804. Als 10 February 1789.

RUMFORD, SIR BENJAMIN THOMPSON, Count: *see* THOMPSON, SIR BENJAMIN.

RUPERT, Prince, Count Palatine, 1619–1682. "The particular arms of hostility mentioned in Dr. Watts' journal," 4 pp.; als, ls (4) 1644, 1645, n.d.; ads 11 February 1678; ds 17 November 1668.

RUSHWORTH, JOHN, 1612?–1690. Ls 26 June 1647 to Sir Thomas Fairfax.

RUSKIN, JOHN, 1819–1900. "Cent Ballades," translations of songs in *Livre des Cent Ballades* with notes on French words, 54 *ll.*; *The Brantwood Diary*, 1876–84, 244 pp., with diary entries for 1873, 5 pp., and diary abstracts for 1840, 3 pp.; [Essay on Literature] "Does the perusal of works of fiction act favourably, or unfavourably, on the moral character," 1836, 8 pp.; "The Exile of St. Helena," 14 pp.; "The Fairies," 2 pp.; *Fors Clavigera* (letter 88 only), 16 pp.; "Italian Sketchbook of 1872" (with Arthur Severn), 41 pp.; *The Laws of Fésole*, preface (incomplete) and portions of Chap. X, 24 pp.; *Modern Painters*, Vols. I–V and four volumes of loose sheets, also a revised version of Vol. II, 150 pp., the preface for the 1883 edition of Vol. II, 5 pp., and three passages not in Ruskin's autograph, 43 pp.; notebook with drafts for portions of *Fors Clavigera*, *Ariadne Florentina* and *Deucalion*, 195 *ll.*; "Pocketbook of 1848," with studies of architectural details for *The Seven Lamps of Architecture; The Poetry of Architecture* (incomplete), 2 vols.; *Praeterita*, Vol. III, Chap. IV, "Joanna's Care" (dictated to Joan Severn), 25 pp., including a first and unpublished version and with galley and page proofs, mainly corrected by Joan Severn and uncorrected, for the chapter; "The Puppet Show or Amusing Characters for Children with Coloured Plates," ca. 1829, 30 pp.; *The Queen of the Air. II. Athena Keramitis*, 53 *ll.*; sermons written as a child, 100 pp., with modern transcripts of four other sermons, 46 pp.; *The Stones of Venice*, 3 vols., with 50 original drawings; *The Storm-Cloud of the Nineteenth Century*, preface (incomplete), 3 pp.; "A Tour of the Lakes in Cumberland" (written in 1830 with his cousin, Mary Richardson), 64 pp.; "Verses composed . . . and given to Effie Gray on her birthday May 7th 1847," 2 pp. (not autograph); one or two pages each from the following works: *The Art of England*, *The Bible of Amiens*, "A Knight's Faith," *Lectures on Art*, "Liber Studiorum—Chord in D flat," "Notes on Prout and Hunt," *The Pleasures of England*, *Proserpina*, *The Three Colours of Pre-Raphaelitism*, *Usury: A Reply and a Rejoinder*, and various pages relating to St. George's Guild; marginalia in F. Howard's *The Sketcher's Manual* (1837) and in Vols. I–II of Bunsen's *Egypt's Place in Universal History* (1848–9); with examples of Ruskin's designs, sketches, checkbooks, canceled checks, financial statements, household accounts, chess games and minerals he collected; with photographs of Ruskin and his circle and of Brantwood, Coniston, and with clippings mainly concerning Ruskin.

Als (ca. 1,900) 1828–95 including 256 to Miss Bell and pupils of Winnington Hall School, 164 to Mr. and Mrs. William Cowper-Temple, 56 to F. C. D. Drewitt and his sister, Mrs. Tuck, 592 to Kate Greenaway, 99 to Mrs. Hewitt, 98 to C. F. Murray, 45 to Kathleen Olander (Mrs. Prynne), 47 to Thomas Richmond and his family and 66 to Sir John and Lady Simon; transcripts of letters (154); letters and documents (17) concerning the annulment of the marriage between Euphemia Chalmers Gray and John Ruskin; letters and documents (40) 1776–1838 concerning Ruskin's parents and grandparents, and letters of his father and mother, mainly to him or to members of the Gray family.

RUSSELL, BERTRAND RUSSELL, 3rd Earl, 1872–1970. Als 8 January 1913 to T. J. Cobden-Sanderson; tls 9 August 1962 to L. L. Leffler.

RUSSELL, CHARLES RUSSELL, Baron, 1832–1900. Als 14 January 1895 to Sir John Millais.

RUSSELL, GEORGE WILLIAM ("AE"), 1867–1935. Als 24 May 1921 to William Hard.

RUSSELL, JOHN RUSSELL, 1st Earl, 1792–1878. Memorandum respecting interposition in the American contest, 13 October 1862, 22 pp.; als, ls (9) 1836–62.

RUSSELL, MARY ANNETTE (BEAUCHAMP) RUSSELL, Countess, 1866–1941. Als 7 January 1920 to T. J. Cobden-Sanderson.

RUSSELL, SIR WILLIAM HOWARD, 1820–1907. Als (21) 1878–96 including 19 to Sir John Millais or members of his family.

RUTLAND, JOHN JAMES ROBERT MANNERS, 7th Duke of, 1818–1906. Als 2 August 1863.

RUTLAND, VIOLET (LINDSAY) MANNERS, Duchess of, 1856–1932. Als (3) 1901 and n.d. to W. E. Henley.

RYALL, HENRY THOMAS, 1811–1867. Als n.d. to Henry Graves.

SABATINI, RAFAEL, 1875–1950. *The Sea-Hawk* (corrected typescript), 412 *ll.*

SACKVILLE-WEST, HON. VICTORIA MARY, 1892–1962. Als (2) 1943, 1953 to Sir Sydney Cockerell.

SADDLER, JOHN, 1813–1892. Als 2 September 1878 to J. E. Millais.

SADLEIR, MICHAEL, 1888–1957. Als 5 August 1944 to Sir Sydney Cockerell.

SADLIER, ANNA THERESA, 1854–1932. Als (2) 1878 to J. Henry Harper.

SAINT ALBANS, HENRY JERMYN, 1st Earl of, d. 1684. Ds 15 December 1660.

ST. HELIER, SUSAN MARY ELIZABETH (STEWART-MACKENZIE) JEUNE, Baroness. Als 5 January 1910 to T. J. Cobden-Sanderson.

ST. JOHN, HENRY: *see* BOLINGBROKE.

SAINTSBURY, GEORGE EDWARD BATEMAN, 1845–1933. Als (10) 1926–32 including 9 to Major G. Dawson.

SALA, GEORGE AUGUSTUS HENRY, 1828–1895. Diary and commonplace book, 1862–94, including newspaper clippings, 400 pp.; als (5) 1875–86.

SALAMAN, CHARLES KENSINGTON, 1814–1901. Als (6) 1857–88.

SALISBURY, ROBERT ARTHUR TALBOT GASCOYNE-CECIL, 3rd Marquis of, 1830–1903. Als (4) 1882–96.

SALMON, FREDERICK, 1796–1868. Als 15 February 1822 to Richard Woodhouse.

SALT, HENRY STEPHENS, 1851–1939. Als (2) 1926, 1928.

SAMBOURNE, EDWARD LINLEY, 1844–1910. Als (6) 1880–93 including 5 to Sir John Millais.

SAMPSON, RICHARD, d. 1554. Als n.d.

SANCHO, IGNATIUS, 1729–1780. Als 21 July 1766 to Laurence Sterne (copy in Sterne's autograph).

SANCROFT, WILLIAM, 1617–1693. Ls 30 September 1682 to Samuel Warren; ds (3) 1677–82.

SANDBY, PAUL, 1725–1809. "Song for 1797," 4 pp.; als

29 December 1799 to Benjamin West.

SANDFORD, FRANCIS, 1630–1694. *Scuta Scutarum of the Geographie and armes of the empires... of Europe*, 1656, 89 pp.

SANT, JAMES, 1820–1916. Als (4) 1878 and n.d. to J. E. Millais and Mary Millais.

SARTORIS, ADELAIDE (KEMBLE), 1814?–1879. Als (3) 1829 and n.d.

SASSOON, SIEGFRIED LORRAINE, 1886–1967. "Five Serious Poems by SS," 7 pp.; als (2) 1942 and n.d.

SAVAGE-ARMSTRONG, GEORGE FRANCIS, 1849–1906. Als 19 November 1902 to W. A. Knight.

SAVILE, SIR HENRY, 1642–1687. Als 10 May 1679.

SAXTON, CHRISTOPHER, fl. 1570–1596. Ads July 1596.

SAXTON, ROBERT, fl. 1607. Ads 1607.

SCHARF, SIR GEORGE, 1820–1895. Als 1 June 1855 to S. L. Sotheby.

SCHETKY, JOHN CHRISTIAN, 1778–1874. Als 1 September 1848 to Henry Vaughan.

SCHIAVONETTI, LUIGI, 1765–1810. Als (2) 1806, 1808.

SCHWABE, RANDOLPH, 1885–1948. Als 4 December 1930 to Edward Johnston.

SCLATER, PHILIP LUTLEY, 1829–1913. Als 20 March 1893 to Mary Millais.

SCOTT, CLEMENT WILLIAM, 1841–1904. Als (2) 1879 and n.d.

SCOTT, DAVID, 1806–1849. Als n.d. to Alexander Hill.

SCOTT, HENRY YOUNG DARRACOTT, 1822–1883. Ls 16 May 1871 to A. S. Sullivan.

SCOTT, JOHN, 1774–1827. Als 31 July 1819 to W. Cribb.

SCOTT, THOMAS, 1780–1835. Als 23 March 1816.

SCOTT, SIR WALTER, Bart., 1771–1832. *Anne of Geierstein*, 3 vols.; *The Antiquary*, with a note of Scott's explaining his preference for this novel, 3 vols.; *The Black Dwarf*, 150 pp.; *Guy Mannering*, 3 vols.; *The House of Aspen. A Tragedy* (two manuscripts not autograph), 146 pp. and 150 pp.; *Ivanhoe* (incomplete), 115 pp.; *Letters on Demonology and Witchcraft* (6 pages only); *The Monastery*, 3 vols.; "The Mother & the Son, a Tragedy" (translation of *Die heilige Fehme*, by Veit Weber [pseud.] and later retitled *The House of Aspen*), 61 *ll.*; *Old Mortality*, 3 vols.; *Paul's Letters to his Kinsfolk*, 327 pp.; *Peveril of the Peak*, 4 vols.; *St. Ronan's Well*, 3 vols.; *A Third Letter... on the Proposed Change of Currency* (corrected galley proofs), 7 pp.; *Waverley* (scattered leaves from Vols. I–III), 15 pp.; *Woodstock*, 3 vols.

Poems: "Battle of Killiecrankie," 4 pp.; "Bonnets of Bonnie Dundee," 2 pp.; *The Bridal of Triermain* (incomplete), 55 pp.; "Carle, Now the King's Come," 3 pp.; "Jock o' Hazeldean," 3 pp.; *The Lady of the Lake*, 270 pp. and corrected proof copy; stanzas 10–12 of Canto IV of *The Lay of the Last Minstrel*, entitled "For the fifth edition—Verses for the Lay to be inserted after the [9th] stanza in Canto 3d [*sic*]"; *Marmion* (corrected proofsheets of the "Introduction to Canto I"), 16 pp.; "Poem on Lord Melville's Trial," 1 p.; *Rokeby*, 170 pp., with 18 letters or notes to James Ballantyne concerning the printing of the poem; transcript of "Bonny Laddie, Highland Laddie," 3 pp.

Historical and critical prose writings: abstract of *Guy of Warwick*, 12 pp.; abstract of J. Turpin's *History of Charlemagne*, 14 pp.; "Ex-King of France [Charles X]," 3 pp.; *History of Scotland*, approximately Chaps. II–VI, 40 pp.; "Selkirk, a royal burgh" and "Selkirk, a county" (corrected proofsheets of articles for *The Edinburgh Gazeteer*, 1822), 2 pp.; *Tales of a Grandfather*, Ser. III, Vols. I, II and part of III, 95 pp.; book reviews: *Histoire de la vie et des ouvrages de Molière*, par J. Taschereau, 33 pp.; *Mémoires du Comte de Modène sur la révolution de Naples* and *Le Duc de Guise à Naples*, 44 pp.; an unidentified discussion of the works of Henry Weber (partly autograph), 7 pp.; unidentified portion of the history of James VI of Scotland, 20 pp.

Journal, November 1825–April 1832, 2 vols.; als (438) 1797–1831 including 95 to the Marchioness of Abercorn, 60 to George Ellis, 53 to John Gibson, 7 to Joseph Train, and with 33 written by or to members of the Scott family.

Account books (2) kept by Scott's publisher, Cadell, 1827–46, containing details on the cost of publication of his works and of receipts from their sales. *See also:* BALLANTYNE, JOHN.

SCOTT, WILLIAM BELL, 1811–1890. "Anthony the Anchorite," 22 *ll.*; "An Ode to the Sphinx," 9 *ll.*; als 4 April 1878 to Miss Hunt.

SCOTT-GATTY, SIR ALFRED SCOTT, 1847–1918. Als (2) 1881, 1892.

SECKER, MARTIN, 1882– . Tls 3 June 1925 to H. Spurr.

SECKER, THOMAS, 1693–1768. Als (3) 1760–7.

SEDDON, JOHN POLLARD, 1827–1906. Als 12 March 1881.

SEELEY, SIR JOHN ROBERT, 1834–1895. Als (4) 1888–90 to W. A. Knight.

SELBOURNE, ROUNDELL PALMER, 1st Earl of, 1812–1895. Als (17) 1880–94 to W. A. Knight.

SELBY, CHARLES, 1802?–1863. Als 20 September 1853.

SELDEN, JOHN, 1584–1654. Ds 22 July 1650; presentation inscription in Eadmer's *Historiæ novorum* (1623).

SELKIRK, THOMAS DOUGLAS, 5th Earl of, 1771–1820. Als 25 December 1815 to Mr. Walker.

SELLAR, WILLIAM YOUNG, 1825–1890. Als (3) n.d. to W. A. Knight.

SEMON, SIR FELIX, 1849–1921. Als n.d. to Sir Arthur Sullivan.

SENIOR, NASSAU WILLIAM, 1790–1864. Als (2) n.d.

SERRES, OLIVIA (WILMOT), 1772–1834. Als (8) 1818–31.

SETH, ANDREW: *see* PRINGLE-PATTISON.

SETTLE, ELKANAH, 1648–1724. Als ca. 1701.

SEVERN, ARTHUR, 1842–1931. Als (3) 1915 and n.d.

SEVERN, JOAN RUSKIN (AGNEW), 1847–1924. European travel diary with John Ruskin, 1870, 155 pp.; als, ls (28), 1871–1923 and n.d. With about 1,000 letters of condolence written to her on the death of Ruskin in 1900.

SEVERN, JOSEPH, 1793–1879. Als (3) 1825, 1878 and n.d.

SEVERN, WALTER, 1830–1904. Als n.d. to Sir John Millais.

SEWARD, ANNA, 1747–1809. "To My Fellow Sponsor, Mrs. King," 1 p.; als (8) 1803–6 and n.d.

SEWARD, EDMUND, 1771–1795. Als 5 May 1793 to Robert Southey.

SEWARD, WILLIAM, 1747–1799. Als (2) n.d.

SEYMOUR, ROBERT, 1800?–1836. Als n.d.

SEYMOUR, WILLIAM KEAN, 1887–1975. "Caesar Remembers" and "Frost," 2 pp.

SHACKLETON, SIR ERNEST HENRY, 1874–1922. Als 25 July 1911 to J. Pierpont Morgan.

SHADWELL, THOMAS, 1641/2–1692. Ads 12 March 1676.

SHAFTESBURY, ANTHONY ASHLEY COOPER, 1st Earl of, 1621–1683. "The E. of Shaftesbury's recognition & submission att ye Barr of ye Lords House, Feb. 25th [16] 77/78." 2 pp.; ds (2) 1672 and n.d.

SHAFTESBURY, ANTHONY ASHLEY COOPER, 7th Earl

of, 1801–1885. Als (8) 1846–79.

Shairp, John Campbell, 1819–1885. Als (33) 1875–85 to W. A. Knight.

Sharp, Cecil James, 1859–1924. Als 12 October 1914 to S. C. Cockerell.

Sharp, Elizabeth Amelia (Sharp), 1856–1933. Journal, 25 March 1906–June 1909, 155 pp.; als 11 June 1912 to Mrs. Grant Allen.

Sharp, Granville, 1735–1813. Als 13 June 1804 to Mr. Phillips.

Sharp, John, 1645–1714. Als 18 October 1793.

Sharp, William, 1749–1824. Als n.d. to John Boydell; ds 10 April 1783.

Sharp, William, 1856–1905. "A Hazard of Love," 1 p.; "The Man and the Centaur," 2 pp.; "Remembrance," 1 p.; als (32) 1882–1903 and n.d. including 21 to Grant Allen and members of his family.

Sharpe, Charles Kirkpatrick, 1781?–1851. Als 29 March 1838.

Shaw, George Bernard, 1856–1950. "Dramatists Self-Revealed" (typescript with autograph additions), 34 pp.; als, tls (9) 1904–42. With a letter from Mrs. Shaw 30 May 1938 to Sir Sydney Cockerell.

Shaw, John, 1776–1832. Als 14 November 1829 to Col. Thomas Wildman.

Shaw, Richard Norman, 1831–1912. Als (2) 1898–9 to Mary Millais.

Shebbeare, John, 1709–1788. Als 5 October 1764.

Shee, Sir Martin Archer, 1769–1850. Als (10) 1800–34.

Sheepshanks, John, 1787–1863. Als (3) 1821–40.

Sheffield, John Baker-Holroyd, 1st Earl of, 1735–1821. Als 29 November 1803 to Sir James Murray-Pulteney.

Sheldon, Gilbert, 1598–1677. Als (2) 1653, 1662.

Shelley, Mary Wollstonecraft (Godwin), 1797–1851. *Valperga* (scattered leaves), 17 pp.; notes and corrections in her *Frankenstein* (1818); als (6) 1825–32.

Shelley, Percy Bysshe, 1792–1822. "The Aziola" (autograph of Mary Shelley), 2 pp.; "Indian Serenade" (autograph of Mary Shelley, and with a note authenticating the manuscript as found in the wreck of the *Don Juan*), 3 pp.; "Julian and Maddalo," 27 pp.; sonnet "Lift not the painted veil," 1 p.; "Stanzas, Written in Dejection, Near Naples," 3 pp.; three poems: "Goodnight," "The Question" and "Sonnet" ("Ye hasten to the grave"), 6 pp.; marginalia in a copy of his *Laon and Cythna* (1818); prose fragments: leaf from his "Essay on Christianity," headed "Chap. 2," 2 pp.; 20 pp. from a notebook containing an essay "On Life"; als (15) 1815–22 including 2 each to Claire Clairmont, T. L. Peacock and William Godwin; 1 each to Lord Byron, Leigh Hunt and Joseph Severn. Notes of Thomas Medwin for a new edition of his *Life of Shelley*, in an interleaved copy of the work (London, 1847).

Shenstone, William, 1714–1765. Als (5) 1751–9.

Shepherd, Richard Herne, 1842–1895. Ads n.d.

Sherbrooke, Robert Lowe, 1st Viscount, 1811–1892. Als 16 April 1864.

Sherburne, Sir Edward. Als 2 February 1675 to Sir Thomas Chicheley; ad 1675.

Sheridan, Elizabeth Ann (Linley), 1754–1792. Als n.d. to Sir Peter Burrell.

Sheridan, Richard Brinsley Butler, 1751–1816. Als (10) 1776–1816 and n.d.; ads 19 May 1796.

Sheridan, Thomas, 1719–1788. Als n.d. to Robert Dodsley.

Sheridan, Thomas, 1775–1817. Als n.d. to his godmother.

Sherlock, Martin, d. 1797. Als 26 May 1782 to Henry Beaufoy.

Sherlock, Thomas, 1678–1761. Als (3) 1726–34; ls 27 April 1749; ds 6 May 1720.

Sherlock, William, 1641?–1707. Als (2) 1691, 1698.

Sherwin, John Keyse, 1751?–1790. Ads 18 April 1787; ds 21 September 1785.

Shipley, Jonathan, 1714–1788. Als (3) 1769–85.

Shorter, Clement King, 1857–1926. Als (3) 1920 and n.d. to Percy Hume.

Shorthouse, Joseph Henry, 1834–1903. *John Inglesant*, 570 pp., and an earlier draft of Chap. XL, 19 pp.; als (28) 1880–93 including 27 to W. A. Knight.

Shrewsbury, Charles Talbot, Duke of, 1660–1718. Als 29 July 1701; ds (3) 1689, 1714.

Sibthorp, John, 1758–1796. Als 28 January 1784.

Sickert, Walter Richard, 1860–1942. Als (6) 1932 and n.d. including 4 to Sir Arthur Wing Pinero.

Siddons, Sarah (Kemble), 1755–1831. Als (8) 1781–1822 and n.d.

Sidgwick, Arthur, 1840–1920. Als 18 March 1903 to T. J. Cobden-Sanderson.

Sidgwick, Eleanor Mildred (Balfour), 1845–1936. Als 28 June 1902 to W. A. Knight.

Sidgwick, Henry, 1838–1900. Als n.d. to William Cowper-Temple.

Sidmouth, Henry Addington, 1st Viscount, 1757–1844. Als, ls (10) 1791–1831; ds 31 January 1820.

Sidney, Algernon, 1622–1683. Als 13 June 1650 to John Thane.

Sidney, Sir Philip, 1554–1586. *The Defence of the Earl of Leicester*, 14 pp.; als ca. 1586 to Christopher Plantin; ds 11 June 1575.

Siemens, Sir William, 1823–1883. Ls 17 November 1877.

Simeon, Charles, 1759–1836. "Advantages of the spiritual man," 18 pp.

Simon, Sir John, 1816–1904. Als 7 July 1884 to John Ruskin. With als (5) 1878 from Lady Simon to John Ruskin and Joan Severn.

Simonides, Konstantinos, 1824?–1880? Als 31 January 1861 to S. L. Sotheby.

Simpson, Sir James Young, Bart., 1811–1870. Ds 18 April 1862.

Simpson, John, 1782–1847. Ads n.d.

Simpson, John Palgrave, 1805–1887. Als (2) 1857, 1864.

Simson, Robert, 1687–1768. Als 15 May 1749 to Joshua Sharpe.

Sinclair, Sir John, Bart., 1754–1835. Als (4) 1782–91.

Singer, Samuel Weller, 1783–1858. Als (6) 1854–6 to S. L. Sotheby; annotations in Spenser's *Faerie Queene* (1590).

Singleton, Henry, 1766–1839. Ads n.d.

Sitwell, Dame Edith, 1887–1964. *Bucolic Comedies*, manuscripts of 20 poems for the book and with manuscripts of five other poems, 84 *ll.*; collection of fair copies of poems (29) ca. 1947–64 with an als 24 July 1947 sent to Lord and Lady Clark, 123 pp.; als (3) 1954 to David Pleydell-Bouverie.

Sitwell, Sir Osbert, 1892–1969. Als (2) 1923, 1951.

Sitwell, Sacheverell, 1897– . Als 8 June 1971 to Charles Ryskamp.

SKELTON, SIR JOHN, 1831–1897. Als (3) 1895–6 to W. A. Knight.

SLOANE, SIR HANS, Bart., 1660–1753. Als 6 November 1730 to Servington Savery of Shilston.

SMART, HAWLEY, 1833–1893. Als (2) n.d. to Sir John Millais.

SMART, WILLIAM, 1853–1915. Als, tls 1893, 1896 to W. A. Knight.

SMEDLEY, CONSTANCE: *see* ARMFIELD.

SMETHAM, JAMES, 1821–1889. Als (10) 1863–5 to W. A. Knight.

SMILES, SAMUEL, 1812–1904. Als (2) 1868 to Harper & Bros.

SMIRKE, SIR ROBERT, 1781–1867. Als (3) 1803, 1849 and n.d.; ds 14 February 1814.

SMIRKE, SYDNEY, 1798–1877. Als n.d.; ads n.d.

SMITH, ADAM, 1723–1790. Als (7) 1758–86.

SMITH, ALBERT RICHARD, 1816–1860. Als (2) 1848 and n.d.

SMITH, ALEXANDER, 1830–1867. "To —," 2 pp.

SMITH, ANKER, 1759–1819. Ds 4 September 1787.

SMITH, ANNIE S. (SWAN), 1859–1943. Als 26 November 1901 to W. E. Henley.

SMITH, CHARLOTTE (TURNER), 1749–1806. Als (2) 1796, 1798.

SMITH, GEORGE, 1824–1901. Als 17 April 1878 to John Simon.

SMITH, GEORGE, 1840–1876. Als (2) 1872, 1876 to Sir Henry Rawlinson.

SMITH, GOLDWIN, 1823–1910. "Berlin and Afghanistan," 75 pp.; als (2) n.d.

SMITH, HORATIO, 1779–1849. Als 18 April 1827.

SMITH, JAMES, 1775–1839. Als n.d. to Edward Du Bois.

SMITH, JOHN THOMAS, 1766–1833. Notes concerning Mr. Upcott, 1 p.; als May 1818 to Dawson Turner.

SMITH, LOGAN PEARSALL, 1865–1946. Als (2) 1943 to Belle da Costa Greene.

SMITH, SYDNEY, 1771–1845. Als (6) 1829–39 and n.d.

SMITH, SIR THOMAS, 1513–1577. "A communication or discourse of the Quenes highnes mariage," 66 pp. (contemporary copy).

SMITH, THOMAS. "The Byron Controversy, Dec. 1869," 18 pp. (annotations by Charles Mackay); "Conversations with Lord Byron in 1823," 12 pp.; "Mem. of Conversation with Dr. Lushington, 21 July 1843," 8 pp.; "Yet more of the Byron mystery. To The Editor of the Times, 24 Sep. 1869," 2 pp.; als (7) 1869 to Charles Mackay.

SMITH, WALTER CHALMERS, 1824–1908. Als (18) 1867–1900 and n.d. to W. A. Knight.

SMITH, WILLIAM, 1711–1787. "Farewell sermon preached at St. George's, Liverpool, 28 June 1767," 23 pp.

SMITH, WILLIAM, 1730–1819. Als (16) 1774–1819 including 13 to Sir George Beaumont.

SMITH, SIR WILLIAM, 1813–1893. Als 1 November 1867 to Sir Henry Rawlinson.

SMITH, WILLIAM HENRY, 1808–1872. Als (2) 1882 to J. E. Millais.

SMITHSON, HARRIET CONSTANCE (MME BERLIOZ), 1800–1854. Als 18 December 1834.

SMOLLETT, TOBIAS GEORGE, 1721–1771. Als (3) 1750–9 to William Strahan; ads (2) 1758, 1766.

SMYTH, DAME ETHEL MARY, 1858–1944. Als 10 May 1915 to R. H. Legge.

SNOWDEN, PHILIP SNOWDEN, Viscount, 1864–1937. Als 28 August 1931 to J. P. Morgan.

SOANE, SIR JOHN, 1753–1837. Als (4) 1814–1828; ds 2 November 1795.

SOLOMON, SIMEON, 1840–1905. Als n.d.

SOMERS, JOHN SOMERS, Baron, 1651–1716. Als 25 June 1697.

SOMERVILLE, JOHN SOUTHEY SOMERVILLE, 15th Baron, 1765–1819. Als 9 April 1808 to Sir James Murray-Pulteney.

SORLEY, WILLIAM RITCHIE, 1855–1935. Als 1 December 1902 to W. A. Knight.

SOSHENSKY, DAVID: *see* COLERIDGE, SAMUEL TAYLOR.

SOTHEBY, SAMUEL LEIGH, 1805–1861. Als (12) 1852–60.

SOTHEBY, WILLIAM, 1757–1833. "To Sir George Beaumont at Rome," 2 pp.; als (3) 1813, 1827 and n.d.

SOTHERN, EDWARD ASKEW, 1826–1881. Als, ls (7) n.d. to Hermann Vezin.

SOUTHEY, CHARLES CUTHBERT, 1819–1888. Als 20 February 1855 to W. A. Knight.

SOUTHEY, ROBERT, 1774–1843. *The Life of Bunyan*, dated 1830, 85 pp.; *The Life of Cowper*, dated 6 October 1835, 276 *ll.*; "Lines written in 1814 & intended to be prefixed to A Tale of Paraguay," 8 pp.; notes addressed to James Burney, concerning the loss of the *Wager*, 3 pp.; *Poems*, manuscript sent to Joseph Cottle for publication, with letter [1797] to Cottle concerning the printing, 170 pp.; *Thalaba the Destroyer* (fair copy, partly in the hand of Mrs. Southey), 230 pp.; "To Ignorance" (not autograph), 4 pp.; "To the Exiled Patriots [Muir and Palmer]," 3 pp.; list of books sent to the binder, December 1832, 4 pp.; marginalia in his copy of *Palmerin of England* (1664); als (35) 1795–1837 and n.d. including 16 to J. W. Croker.

SOUTHWELL, ROBERT, 1561–1595. "An humble peticion to her Majestie . . . ," 37 pp. (contemporary copy).

SOWERBY, JAMES, 1757–1822. Als 8 July 1799.

SPARK, FREDERICK ROBERT, 1831–1919. Als (2) 1894, 1899 to Sir Arthur Sullivan.

SPELMAN, SIR HENRY, 1564–1641. Ds 28 February 1598.

SPENCER, FREDERICK SPENCER, 4th Earl, 1798–1857. Als (3) 1857 to S. L. Sotheby.

SPENCER, GEORGE JOHN SPENCER, 2nd Earl, 1758–1834. Als (6) 1796–1824 and n.d.

SPENCER, HERBERT, 1820–1903. Ls (7) 1872–1900 to W. A. Knight.

SPENDER, STEPHEN, 1909–   . Tls 20 August 1949 to Jane Quinby.

SPIELMANN, MARION HARRY, 1858–1948. Als 29 July 1905 to Joan Severn.

SPOONER, WILLIAM ARCHIBALD, 1844–1930. Als (3) 1898–1917 including 2 to Joan Severn.

SPRIGGE, SIR SAMUEL SQUIRE, 1860–1937. Als (2) 1890 and n.d. to Miss Gillington.

SPRING-RICE, SIR CECIL ARTHUR, 1859–1918. Als (9) 1895–6 to Miss Helen Carroll and to Mrs. Robbins.

STANFIELD, CLARKSON, 1793–1867. Als (10) 1822–60 and n.d.

STANHOPE, CHARLES STANHOPE, 3rd Earl, 1753–1816. Als 26 March 1784 to Sir William (Johnstone) Pulteney.

STANHOPE, GEORGE, 1660–1728. Ds 12 September 1715.

STANHOPE, LADY HESTER LUCY, 1776–1839. Als (2) 1804, 1814.

STANHOPE, PHILIP DORMER: *see* CHESTERFIELD.

STANHOPE, PHILIP HENRY STANHOPE, 4th Earl, 1781–1855. Als (2) 1823, 1837.

STANHOPE, PHILIP HENRY STANHOPE, 5th Earl, 1805–1875. Als (7) 1836–65.

STANLEY, ARTHUR PENRHYN, 1815–1881. Als (8)

1851–80.

STANLEY, SIR HENRY MORTON, 1841–1904. Als 26 March 1880 to Robert Newton.

STANNARD, HENRIETTA ELIZA VAUGHAN (PALMER) ("JOHN STRANGE WINTER"), 1856–1911. Als (20) 1887–8 to John Ruskin and Joan Severn.

STARK, DAME FREYA MADELINE, 1893– . Als 23 February 1937 to Sir Sydney Cockerell.

STARK, JAMES, 1794–1859. Als 14 August 1848.

STAUNTON, SIR GEORGE THOMAS, 1781–1859. Als 11 March 1819.

STEEL, FLORA ANNIE (WEBSTER), 1847–1929. Als n.d.

STEELE, JOSHUA, 1700–1791. Als 24 June 1779.

STEELE, SIR RICHARD, 1672–1729. Als (3) 1713–4; ads 8 April 1720.

STEER, PHILIP WILSON, 1860–1942. Als 10 December 1928 to R. Cobden-Sanderson.

STEEVENS, GEORGE, 1736–1800. Als (4) 1773–83 and n.d. including 1 to David Garrick and 1 to Samuel Johnson.

STEPHANOFF, JAMES, 1788?–1874. Ads n.d.

STEPHEN, SIR GEORGE, 1794–1879. Als (2) 1843 to Thomas Smith.

STEPHEN, SIR LESLIE, 1832–1904. *English Thought in the Eighteenth Century*, 2 vols.; als (33) 1878–1900 including 30 to W. A. Knight and 2 to J. Pearson & Co.

STEPHENS, CATHERINE, 1794–1882. Als ca. 1822 to G. T. Smart.

STEPHENS, JAMES, 1882–1950. *Deirdre*, 220 pp. (corrected typescript); *The Insurrection in Dublin*, Chap. XI (1st draft, final manuscript and original notes), 21 pp.; als 31 December 1924 to Mrs. W. Murray Crane.

STEPHENSON, GEORGE, 1781–1848. Ads 26 February 1832.

STEPNIAK, SERGIUS, pseudonym, 1852–1895. Als 23 February 1892 to T. J. Cobden-Sanderson.

STERLING, JOHN, 1806–1844. Als 25 July 1837 to Thomas Carlyle.

STERN, GLADYS BRONWYN, 1890–1973. Als n.d. to George Oppenheimer.

STERNE, LAURENCE, 1713–1768. "A Fragment in the Manner of Rabelais," 23 pp.; *Sentimental Journey* (manuscript in two different hands), 358 pp.; sermon on "Penancies," delivered 8 April 1750, 29 pp.; "Memorandum left with Mrs. Montague in case I should die abroad, 28 December 1761," 4 pp.; als (38) 1758–67 and undated, originals and author's copies, including 12 to Catherine Fourmantel. *See also:* HALL-STEVENSON.

STERNE, RICHARD, 1596?–1683. Ads 8 January 1675.

STEUART, JOHN ALEXANDER, 1861–1932. Als (2) 1898 to W. E. Henley.

STEVENSON, JOHN HALL: *see* HALL-STEVENSON.

STEVENSON, ROBERT LOUIS, 1850–1894. "Feast of Famine," dated 5–16 October 1888, 13 pp.; "The School Boys Magazine. No. 1," 10 pp.; *Strange Case of Dr. Jekyll and Mr. Hyde* (incomplete), 33 *ll.*; "To a Warrior Dead," 1 p.; *Weir of Hermiston*, 104 pp.; als (7) 1875–88.

STEWART, DUGALD, 1753–1828. Als n.d.; ls 26 September 1824 to Thomas Jefferson.

STEWART, JOHN ALEXANDER, 1846–1933. Als 24 October 1894 to Joan Severn.

STILLINGFLEET, EDWARD, 1635–1699. Ds 15 January 1682/3.

STIRLING, JAMES HUTCHINSON, 1820–1909. Als (16) 1887–1900 to W. A. Knight.

STIRLING-MAXWELL, SIR WILLIAM, Bart., 1818–1878. Als (3) 1862 to Mr. and Mrs. W. W. Story.

STOCKDALE, PERCIVAL, 1736–1811. Als 4 December 1788 to Mr. Pearson.

STODDART, SIR JOHN, 1773–1856. Als (4) 1800–1 to S. T. Coleridge.

STOKER, BRAM, 1847–1912. Als (3) 1895–8 to W. A. Knight.

STONE, FRANK, 1800–1859. Als 11 April 1837 to Henry Howard.

STONE, MARCUS, 1840–1921. Als (5) 1865–98.

STOREY, GEORGE ADOLPHUS, 1834–1919. Als 3 January 1886 to Sir John Millais.

STORRS, SIR RONALD, 1881–1955. Tls 19 December 1953 to F. B. Adams.

STOTHARD, THOMAS, 1755–1834. Als (3) 1828 and n.d.

STRACHEY, GILES LYTTON, 1880–1932. Als 24 August 1921 to E. McKnight Kauffer.

STRACHEY, JOHN ST. LOE, 1860–1927. Als (4) 1897–1901 to W. A. Knight.

STRAHAN, ALEXANDER. Als (4) 1871–9 to W. A. Knight.

STRAHAN, ANDREW, 1749–1831. Als 24 April 1789.

STRAHAN, WILLIAM, 1715–1785. Als (2) 1778 and n.d. to Benjamin Franklin.

STRANGFORD, PERCY CLINTON SYDNEY SMYTHE, 6th Viscount, 1780–1855. Als 2 August 1805 to Lord Nelson.

STREET, GEORGE EDMUND, 1824–1881. Als 12 April 1878 to A. W. Hunt.

STRICKLAND, AGNES, 1796–1874. Als (3) 1859 and n.d.

STRONG, LEONARD ALFRED GEORGE, 1896–1958. Tls 15 May 1934 to Mrs. H. J. Byron.

STRONG, THOMAS BANKS, 1861–1944. Als (2) 1904, 1926 to T. J. Cobden-Sanderson.

STRYPE, JOHN, 1643–1737. Ads n.d.

STUART, DANIEL, 1766–1846. Als (2) 1802 to S. T. Coleridge.

STUART, GILBERT, 1742–1786. Als 21 February 1783.

STUKELEY, WILLIAM, 1687–1765. Untitled hymn (two different versions), 3 pp.; als 30 June 1737 to John Cawdron.

STURGIS, JULIAN RUSSELL, 1848–1904. Als (4) n.d. to Mrs. Bronson.

SUCKLING, SIR JOHN, 1609–1642. Ds n.d.

SULLIVAN, SIR ARTHUR SEYMOUR, 1842–1900: *see* GILBERT, SIR WILLIAM SCHWENCK.

SULLY, JAMES. 1842–1923. Als (4) 1880–1900 to W. A. Knight.

SUMNER, CHARLES RICHARD, 1790–1874. Als (3) 1842, 1867 and n.d.

SUMNER, JOHN BIRD, 1780–1862. Als (2) 1841 and n.d.

SUNDERLAND, CHARLES SPENCER, 3rd Earl, 1674–1722. Als (2) 1709; ds (3) 1708, 1717.

SUNDERLAND, DOROTHY SPENCER, Countess, 1617–1684. Als 20 February 1637 to her father.

SWANWICK, ANNA, 1813–1899. Als (14) 1889–93 and n.d. including 6 to Michael Field.

SWIFT, JONATHAN, 1667–1745. "Apollo to the Dean," 3 pp.; "Discovery," dated 1699, 3 pp.; "The History of Vanbrug's House," dated 1706, 3 pp., and "Vanbrug's House Built from the burnt Ruins of Whitehall," dated 1703, 5 pp.; "In pity to the empty'ing Town," 2 pp.; "Stella at Wood-Park," 2 pp., and a copy in the hand of Charles Ford, 3 pp.; "The Story of Baucis and Philemon," 8 pp.; "To Lady Carteret" (contemporary copy), 3 pp. For the poems formerly attributed to Swift which are contained in the "Fountaine Manuscripts," see Swift's *Poems*, ed. Sir

Harold Williams (Oxford, 1937), III, 1141–3. Prose works: "Dialogue in the Castilian Language," 3 pp.; "Draft of a Petition to the House of Lords," 3 pp.; "Memoirs . . . Written by the Dean of St. Patrick's" (not autograph), 26 pp.; "A Modest Defence of Punning," dated 15 November 1716, 3 pp.; "To My Lord High Admirall," 3 pp. See also Swift's *Prose Works*, ed. H. J. Davis (Oxford, 1939–68). Als and copies of letters (40) 1709–38 including 19 to the Earl of Orrery, 6 to Charles Ford and 6 to Benjamin Motte, 2 of the last being signed "Richard Sympson" and concerned with the sale of *Gulliver's Travels* (with als [2] from Motte to Swift); ds (3) 1732–42.

SWINBURNE, ALGERNON CHARLES, 1837–1909. "At Eleusis," 10 pp.; "A Channel Passage. 1855," 5 *ll.*; "Christmas to Fordy," 1 p.; "Daughter in spirit . . ." [dedication to Mrs. Lynn Linton of his *Studies in Song* (1880)], 1 p.; *Marino Faliero*, 167 pp.; "Où vont les vieilles lunes?," 1 p.; "Roundel," 1 p.; "Whitmania," 12 pp.; essay on Byron, 19 pp.; essay on Landor, 5 pp.; review of William Morris' *The Well at the World's End*, 3 pp.; als (57) 1866–97 including 12 to J. C. Collins, 15 to Mme Tola Dorian, 18 to Mrs. Lynn Linton and 5 to W. A. Knight. With an als from his sister Isabel 17 May 1911 to S. C. Cockerell.

SWINNERTON, FRANK ARTHUR, 1884– . Als, ls (62) 1938–49 to Tom Turner.

SWINNY, OWEN MAC, d. 1754. Als 29 July 1730 to Mons. Colman.

SYKES, MARK MASTERMAN, 1771–1823. Als 7 April 1801 to Mr. Molteno.

SYLVESTER, JOSUAH, 1563–1618. "To the worthilie Honored Sr. Edward Lewis, Knight," 1 p.

SYME, JOHN, 1755–1831. Als 31 July 1797 to George Thomson.

SYMES, JOHN ELLIOTSON, 1847–1921. Als 20 November 1902 to W. A. Knight.

SYMONDS, JOHN ADDINGTON, 1840–1893. Als (12) 1872–89 including 11 to Smith, Elder & Co.

SYMONS, ALBERT JAMES ALROY, 1900–1941. Als (3) 1934–9 to Blake Brown.

SYMONS, ARTHUR, 1865–1945. "The Poet Tramp: W. H. Davies," 28 pp.

TABOR, MARY C. Als (33) 1876–1903 to W. A. Knight.

TAIT, ARCHIBALD CAMPBELL, 1811–1882. Als (4) 1860–81; ds 24 February 1862.

TAIT, PETER GUTHRIE, 1831–1901. Als (4) 1880–95 to W. A. Knight.

TALBOT, WILLIAM, 1659?–1730. Ls 25 April 1721 to the Treasurer of the South Sea Company.

TALFOURD, SIR THOMAS NOON, 1795–1854. Als (5) 1845–53 and n.d.

TARLETON, SIR BANASTRE, Bart., 1754–1833. Als (3) 1782–1815; ds 3 December 1791.

TATE, SIR HENRY, Bart., 1819–1899. Als 27 April 1893 to Sir John Millais.

TAYLOR, ANN: *see* GILBERT, ANN (TAYLOR).

TAYLOR, HELEN, 1831–1907. Als (2) 1881, 1883 to W. A. Knight.

TAYLOR, SIR HENRY, 1800–1886. Als (2) 1880, 1885 to W. A. Knight.

TAYLOR, SIR HERBERT, 1775–1839. Als (42) 1794–1801 including 40 to Sir James Murray-Pulteney; ds 4 February 1801.

TAYLOR, ISAAC, 1787–1865. Als 16 January 1852 to Henry Bowie.

TAYLOR, JANE, 1783–1824. Als 12 February 1806 to Miss Conder.

TAYLOR, JEREMY, 1613–1667. Als 10 February 1659/60 to John Evelyn.

TAYLOR, JOHN, 1757–1832. Als 1 September 1826 to J. B. Nichols.

TAYLOR, JOHN, 1781–1864. Als (4) 1820–1 including 1 to John Keats.

TAYLOR, MEADOWS, 1808–1876. Als 16 November 1874 to A. S. Sullivan.

TAYLOR, SIR ROBERT, 1714–1788. Als 18 March 1761.

TAYLOR, TOM, 1817–1880. "The Burial of an Angle Chieftain [from Beowulf]," 1 p.; als (8) 1875–6 and n.d.

TEMPLE, FREDERICK, 1821–1902. Als (5) 1857–1900.

TEMPLE, SIR WILLIAM, 1555–1627. Ds (2) 1609–21.

TEMPLE, SIR WILLIAM, 1624–1699. Als (4) 1669–76. With a ds 7 September 1668 from his wife, Dorothy (Osborne), Lady Temple.

TEMPLE, WILLIAM, 1881–1944. Tls 20 March 1931 to J. P. Morgan.

TENISON, THOMAS, 1636–1715. "Recognitum S. Clementis ad Jacobum fratrem Domini libri decem" (autograph copy of the letter of Saint Clement to James—a portion of the false decretals of the Pseudo-Isidore), 200 pp.; als (3) 1699–1705; ds 20 February 1701.

TENNENT, SIR JAMES EMERSON, 1804–1869. Als (5) 1828–60 and n.d. including 2 to S. L. Sotheby.

TENNIEL, SIR JOHN, 1820–1914. Als (5) 1881–1901 and n.d. including 3 to Sir John Millais and Lady Millais.

TENNYSON, ALFRED TENNYSON, 1st Baron, 1809–1892. "Achilles Over the Trench," 2 pp., and other translations from the *Iliad* beginning "Nor lingered Paris" (VI.503 ff.) and "But when they came together to one place," together 5 pp.; "All in the Wild March Morning," 1 p.; "The Brook," 8 pp.; "No nobler men methinks are bred" (dedication of his *Poems* to Queen Victoria), 2 pp.; "Northern Farmer" (manuscript entitled "Property—N.F."), 4 pp.; "Wages" (in a letter to J. T. Fields), 2 pp.; two fragments beginning "Why how was this, Was not the wide earth free," 1 p., and "Whether his not unwillingness," 1 p.; ten lines in Hebrew; marginalia in a copy of his *Ode on the Death of the Duke of Wellington* (1852), with letter from Edward Moxon concerning its publication and note of Tennyson in reply; copies of various poems from the edition of 1833 made by J. R. Lowell, 12 pp.; als (27) ca. 1831–89 and n.d.

TENNYSON, CHARLES: *see* TURNER, CHARLES TENNYSON.

TENNYSON, HALLAM TENNYSON, 2nd Baron, 1852–1928. Als (23) 1862–97 including 15 to W. A. Knight and 4 to Sir Arthur Sullivan.

TERRICK, RICHARD, 1710–1777. Als (2) 1770, 1776.

TERRY, DANIEL, 1780?–1829. Als (3) 1814–24.

TERRY, EDWARD O'CONNOR, 1844–1912. Als 13 June 1882 to George Grossmith.

TERRY, DAME ELLEN, 1847–1928. Als (7) 1878–1911.

TERRY, KATE: *see* LEWIS, KATE (TERRY).

TERRY, MARION, 1852–1930. Als (3) 1891–1918 to Joan Severn.

THACKERAY, WILLIAM MAKEPEACE, 1811–1863. *Denis Duval*, Chaps. I–V (with a second version of Chap. I) and parts of VI–VII, 112 pp.; 1 p. of *Henry Esmond; Lovel the Widower*, 110 pp. and 4 drawings; *The Rose and the Ring* (text and drawings), 90 pp.; *Vanity Fair*, Chaps. I–VI (with a second version of Chap. VI), VIII–XIII, 112 *ll.*; *The Virginians* (mostly autograph), 4 vols. Other prose works: *The Four Georges:* "Lecture on George I" (mostly autograph), 40 pp., "Lecture on George III" (partly autograph), 67 pp.; "On a Medal of George IV" (*Roundabout Papers*), 1 p.; *Paris Sketch Book* (section on Parisian Caricatures, comprising pp. 151–168 of the *Westminster Review* for 1839), 25 pp.; *The Poor Poet, a Drama*... from the German of A. von Kotzebue, 19 pp.

Poems: "Horae Carthusianae," dated 4 December 1828, 7 pp.; *The Famous History of Lord Bateman* (7 drawings and 1 page of text); "Sonnet. Written in Solitude," 1 p.; "The Terrible Hayes Tragedy," 2 pp.; "Where Shannon's broad waters pour down," 2 pp.; "There were three sailors in Bristol City," 2 pp.; transcript of "Sonnet by Lord Moira" ("What splendid vision o'er my fancy flies"), with explanatory note, 1 p.

Writings of student days in Germany: transcript of an English version of C. Mannert's *Compendium of German History*, pp. 53–114, dated 1831, 75 pp.; commonplace book kept while a student at Weimar containing stories, poems, etc. in English or German, and numerous sketches, 85 pp.

Brief entries, September–December 1852 and first week of 1853, in *Punch's Pocket Book for 1852*, including lecture engagements in America; als (185) 1846–62 and n.d. including 110 to Mr. or Mrs. W. H. Brookfield (with 9 from Mrs. Brookfield to or about Thackeray), 13 to Chapman & Hall and 8 (four with drawings) to Comte d'Orsay.

Drawings (in addition to those mentioned above): 20 to illustrate *Pendennis*, *Vanity Fair*, the Christmas books and other works; 28 captioned watercolors of a humorous character including "Vingt Un" and "Pitch and Toss"; 35 early sketches done while a student at Cambridge.

THELWALL, JOHN, 1764–1834. Als (3) 1797–1830 including 2 to his wife.

THICKNESSE, PHILIP, 1719–1792. Als (2) 1777 and n.d.

THIRLESTANE, JOHN MAITLAND, Baron: *see* MAITLAND.

THOMAS, BERTRAM SIDNEY, 1892–1950. Als 1 June 1933 to Sir Sydney Cockerell.

THOMAS, DYLAN, 1914–1953. Drafts (4) of a poem beginning "Too proud to die," 2 pp.; als (2) 1952 to Ellen Kay.

THOMAS, HENRY, 1878–1952. Als (2) 1914 to C. F. Murray.

THOMAS, WILLIAM (ISLWYN), 1832–1878. Als (2) 1852 and n.d. to Sir Frederic Madden.

THOMAS, WILLIAM MOY, 1828–1910. Als (2) 1860, 1887.

THOMPSON, SIR BENJAMIN, Count Rumford, 1753–1814. Als 5 December 1778? to Thomas Davies.

THOMPSON, BENJAMIN, 1776?–1816. Als (2) 1800–1 to Thomas Hill.

THOMPSON, EDWARD JOHN, 1886–1946. "Royal Audience" and "The Sufi's Prayer," 2 pp.

THOMPSON, SIR EDWARD MAUNDE, 1840–1929. Als 28 September 1890 to Mrs. Palmer.

THOMPSON, FRANCIS, 1859–1907. Fragment of verses, 2 pp.; als (3) 1895–1905 including 2 to Wilfrid Meynell.

THOMPSON, SIR HENRY, 1820–1904. Als (5) 1881–92 including 4 to Sir John Millais.

THOMPSON, SIR HENRY FRANCIS HERBERT, 2nd Bart., 1859–1944. Als 27 January 1901 to T. J. Cobden-Sanderson.

THOMPSON, HENRY YATES, 1838–1928. Annotations to a printed list of Ashburnham, "Barrois" and "Appendix" manuscripts (1881).

THOMPSON, WILLIAM HEPWORTH, 1810–1886. Als 24 June 1883 to R. H. Groome.

THOMS, WILLIAM JOHN, 1803–1885. Als (2) 1852 and n.d. to Sir Frederic Madden.

THOMSON, ANTHONY TODD, 1778–1849. Als (5) 1833 to William Collins.

THOMSON, GEORGE, 1757–1851. Als 10 August 1839 to Mrs. Laing.

THOMSON, JAMES, 1700–1748. Note altering v. 120 of "Autumn," 1 p.; poems addressed to Elizabeth Young: "Come, dear Eliza, quit the Town," "Come gentle Power of soft desire," "Hail to the day!," "One day the God of fond desire,"; als (15) 1736–45 including 12 to Elizabeth Young.

THOMSON, JAMES ("BYSSHE VANOLIS"), 1834–1882. *The City of Dreadful Night*, 63 pp.

THOMSON, JOHN, 1778–1840. Als 23 May 1820 to Mr. Martin.

THOMSON, SIR JOHN ARTHUR, 1861–1933. Als 29 July 1892 to W. A. Knight.

THOMSON, SIR JOSEPH JOHN, 1856–1940. Als (2) 1922, 1927.

THOMSON, WILLIAM, 1819–1890. Als (2) 1863, 1875.

THORBURN, GRANT, 1773–1863. Als 22 September 1837 to L. J. Cist.

THORBURN, ROBERT, 1818–1885. Als 23 November 1849 to Alexander Christie.

THORNBURY, GEORGE WALTER, 1828–1876. Als (5) 1860, 1861 and n.d.

THORNE, THOMAS, 1841–1918. Als 26 February 1878 to George Grossmith.

THORNHILL, SIR JAMES, 1675–1734. Ds ca. 1713 with pen and ink sketch; ds 27 April 1720.

THORNTON, ROBERT JOHN, 1768?–1837. Als 15 July 1806 to Henry Wheaton.

THORPE, THOMAS, 1791–1851. Als n.d.

THROCKMORTON, JOB, 1545–1601. Speeches in Parliament (3) 1586–7 (contemporary copies), 51 pp.

THURLOE, JOHN, 1616–1668. Als (3) 1651–5 to Francis Underwood.

THURLOW, EDWARD THURLOW, 1st Baron, 1731–1806. Notes regarding the payment for the furnishings of Carleton House, 4 pp.; translations from Anacreon's odes, 1 p.; als (20) 1772–1802 including 16 to Thomas Tyrwhitt.

THURSFIELD, SIR JAMES RICHARD, 1840–1923. Als 9 February 1890 to the Dean of Salisbury.

TICKELL, RICHARD, 1751–1793. Als 1 February 1788.

TICKELL, THOMAS, 1686–1740. Draft of a proposed preface to the collected edition of Vol. VIII (second series) of the *Spectator*, 1 p.

TILLOCH, ALEXANDER, 1759–1825. Als 25 April 1816 to J. B. Nichols.

TILLOTSON, JOHN, 1630–1694. Notes, 1692, 1 p.

TITE, SIR WILLIAM, 1798–1873. Als 6 January 1855.

TODHUNTER, JOHN, 1839–1916. Als 27 May 1890 to W. A. Knight.

TOLLEMACHE, BEATRIX LUCIA CATHERINE (EGERTON), d. 1926. Als (5) 1882–1901 to W. A. Knight.

TOLLEMACHE, LIONEL ARTHUR, 1838–1919. Als, ls (5) 1886–8 to W. A. Knight.

TOMLINE, SIR GEORGE PRETYMAN, 1750–1827. Als (2) 1794 and n.d.

TOMLINSON, HENRY MAJOR, 1873–1958. Synopsis of his novel *Gallions Reach*, 2 pp.; als (2) 1928, 1936 to Harper & Bros.

TOMSON, CLIFTON, fl. 1830. Als 4 November 1811 to John Scott.

TONSON, JACOB, 1656?–1736. Als ca. 1732 to his nephew, Jacob.

TOOKE, JOHN HORNE, 1736–1812. Als n.d. to Sir Philip Francis; ads (2) 1782, 1798.

TOOKE, WILLIAM, 1777–1863. Als 10 January 1850 to John Britton.

TOOLE, JOHN LAWRENCE, 1830–1906. Als (12) 1856–1900.

TOOVEY, JAMES, 1814–1893. Notes in his *Catalogue of...productions of the Aldine press* (1880).

TOPHAM, EDWARD, 1751–1820. Als n.d.

TOPSELL, EDWARD, d. 1638? Ds 14 July 1615.

TOUP, JONATHAN, 1713–1785. Als 14 October 1770 to Richard Hole.

TOWNLEY, SIR CHARLES, 1713–1774. Als 21 December 1750.

TOWNSHEND, CHAUNCEY HARE, 1798–1868. Als (3) 1818–62.

TRATTLE, MARMADUKE, 1751–1831. Als 13 July 1822 to Mr. Young.

TREE, ELLEN: *see* KEAN, ELLEN (TREE).

TREE, SIR HERBERT BEERBOHM, 1853–1917. Als (7) 1890 to W. E. Henley.

TREHERNE, GEORGE GILBERT TREHERNE, 1837–1923. Als 7 November 1892 to Sir John Millais.

TRENCH, RICHARD CHENEVIX, 1807–1886. Als, ls (6) 1858–82 and n.d.

TRESHAM, HENRY, 1749?–1814. Presentation inscription to Mrs. Cosway, 1 p.; als (2) 1811 and n.d.

TREVELYAN, CHARLES PHILIPS, 1870–1958. Als 20 November 1940 to F. J. Sharp.

TREVELYAN, GEORGE MACAULAY, 1876–1962. Als 2 January 1934 to Sir Sydney Cockerell.

TREVELYAN, SIR GEORGE OTTO, 1838–1928. Als (3) 1880–1904.

TREVELYAN, JANET PENROSE (WARD), 1879–1956. Als 30 October 1932 to Sir Sydney Cockerell.

TREVELYAN, PAULINE JERMYN (JERMYN), Lady, 1816–1866. Als (8) 1848–62 to John Ruskin.

TREVELYAN, ROBERT CALVERLEY, 1872–1951. "Krishna," 1 p.

TREVELYAN, SIR WALTER CALVERLEY, 6th Bart., 1797–1879. Als 22 April 1878.

TREVELYAN-THOMSON, HILDA. Als 2 October 1936 to Julia N. Terry.

TREVES, SIR FREDERICK, 1853–1923. Als 2 January 1898 to Mary Millais.

TRIMMER, SARAH (KIRBY), 1741–1816. Als 8 June 1814.

TROLLOPE, ANTHONY, 1815–1882. *He Knew He Was Right*, 1,300 pp.; *The Way We Live Now*, 1,212 pp.; als (26) 1863–82 including 9 to Chapman & Hall, with agreements (13) 1858–64 between Trollope and Chapman & Hall, and receipts (5) for money received from the firm, and 14 to J. E. Millais and Effie Millais.

TROLLOPE, FRANCES ELEANOR (TERNAN), d. 1913. Als (2) 1868, 1893.

TROLLOPE, THOMAS ADOLPHUS, 1810–1892. Als 28 August 1889.

TRÜBNER, NIKOLAUS, 1817–1884. Als 1 March 1858 to S. L. Sotheby.

TUCKER, JOSIAH, 1712–1799. Als (2) 1776, 1781 to Thomas Cadell.

TULLOCH, JOHN, 1823–1886. Als, ls (29) 1870–85 including 26 to W. A. Knight.

TUNSTALL, CUTHBERT, 1474–1559. Ls (2) 1542, 1554; ds (2) 1554 and n.d.

TUPPER, MARTIN FARQUHAR, 1810–1889. "England to America in the prospect of invasion," 4 pp.; als (2) 1848, 1849.

TURNER, CHARLES, 1774–1857. Als n.d. to J. P. Knight.

TURNER, CHARLES TENNYSON, 1808–1879. Als (2) 1834–5 to E. B. Drury.

TURNER, DAWSON, 1775–1858. Als (2) 1841, 1847.

TURNER, JOSEPH MALLORD WILLIAM, 1775–1851. Tour in parts of Wales in 1792, 19 pp.; als (2) 1828 and n.d.

TURNER, SHARON, 1768–1847. Als 9 May 1810.

TUTTIETT, MARY GLEED, d. 1923. Als (2) 1892 and n.d.

TWEEDSMUIR, JOHN BUCHAN, Baron, 1875–1940. "Scott" (corrected typescript), 8 pp.; ls (2) 1932, 1933.

TWINING, THOMAS, 1735–1804. Als 5 October 1793 to Mme d'Arblay.

TWISS, HORACE, 1787–1849. Als 9 December 1838.

TYLOR, SIR EDWARD BURNETT, 1832–1917. Als (5) 1890–2 to W. A. Knight.

TYNDALL, JOHN, 1820–1893. Als (5) 1879 and n.d.

TYRRELL, GEORGE, 1861–1909. Als 27 April 1906 to T. J. Cobden-Sanderson.

UNDERHILL, EVELYN, 1875–1941. Als 17 June 1922 to T. J. Cobden-Sanderson.

UNWIN, MARY (CAWTHORNE), 1724–1796. Als n.d. to Walter Bagot.

UNWIN, THOMAS FISHER, 1848–1935. Als 26 April 1878 to A. W. Hunt.

UPCOTT, WILLIAM, 1779–1845. Als (2) 1828, 1844.

UPTON, CHARLES BARNES, 1831–1920. Als 12 November 1902 to W. A. Knight.

URE, ANDREW, 1778–1857. Als 14 January 1835 to James Bradshaw.

USSHER, JAMES, 1581–1656. Als 14 August 1639 to Sir Henry Spelman.

UWINS, THOMAS, 1782–1857. Als (11) 1836–50 and n.d. incuding 2 to William Collins and 6 to Miss Minshull; ads 1838.

VAILLANT, PAUL. Als 16 May 1751 to the Earl of Cork & Orrery.

VALLANCEY, CHARLES, 1721–1812. Als 27 October 1807 to Dr. James Lind.

VANBRUGH, SIR JOHN, 1664–1726. Memorandum concerning the salaries of actors, ca. 1708, 1 p.; ds 1710.

VANE, SIR HENRY, 1613–1662. Ds (3) 1644–53.

VANHOMRIGH, BARTHOLOMEW, d. 1714? Verse letter (not autograph) 28 August 1713 to Charles Ford.

VAN MILDERT, WILLIAM, 1765–1836. Als 29 July 1823.

VARLEY, JOHN, 1778–1842. Als n.d. to Allan Cunningham.

VAUGHAN, CHARLES JOHN, 1816–1897. Als 2 April 1866.

VAUGHAN, HENRY, 1809–1899. Als 25 April 1878 to William Cowper-Temple.

VAUGHAN, ROBERT, 1592–1667. Als 17 April 1641.

VAUX, THOMAS VAUX, 2nd Baron, 1510–1556. Ds 28 March 1553.

VAUX, WILLIAM SANDYS WRIGHT, 1818–1885. Als 11 May 1859 to S. L. Sotheby; ds n.d.

VEITCH, JOHN, 1829–1894. Als (7) 1882–93 to W. A. Knight.

VELEY, MARGARET, 1843–1887. Als 21 November 1886 to Miss Gillington.

VENN, JOHN, 1834–1923. Als 24 February 1895 to Mr. Ward.

VERNON, GEORGE JOHN WARREN, 5th Baron, 1803–1866. Als (3) 1861 and n.d. to Octavian Blewitt.

VERTUE, GEORGE, 1684–1756. Als, ls (3) 1749, 1750 and n.d.

VESTRIS, MADAME: *see* MATHEWS, LUCIA ELIZABETH.

VEZIN, HERMANN, 1829–1910. Als 18 July 1878 to George Grossmith.

VICTORIA, Queen of Great Britain, 1819–1901. Als (183) 1827–96; ds (16) 1838–61.

VILLIERS, GEORGE: *see* BUCKINGHAM.

VINCENT, WILLIAM, 1739–1815. "Bruce's system of the Monsoons for proving that Sofala is the Ophir of Solomon" and "System contrary to Bruce," 2 pp.; als (2) 1799 and n.d.

VIZETELLY, ERNEST ALFRED, 1853–1922. Als 9 October 1902 to John Lane.

WAGHORN, THOMAS, 1800–1850. Als 30 April 1834 to Mr. Bailey.

WAITE, ARTHUR EDWARD, 1857–1942. Als 7 June 1889 to Miss Gillington.

WAKE, WILLIAM, 1657–1737. Als n.d.

WAKEFIELD, GILBERT, 1756–1801. Als 1 November 1800 to William Shepherd.

WALDEGRAVE, FRANCES ELIZABETH ANNE (BRAHAM), Countess, 1821–1879. Als 25 March 1873 to J. E. Millais.

WALDRON, FRANCIS GODOLPHIN, 1744–1818. Als 15 June 1790.

WALEY, ARTHUR DAVID, 1889–1966. Als 4 March 1955 to Camille Honig.

WALKER, SIR EMERY, 1851–1933. Als (2) 1903, 1919 to S. C. Cockerell.

WALKER, FREDERICK, 1840–1875. Als 24 March 1874 to J. E. Millais.

WALKER, MADELYN. "Dream Children, by Charles Lamb," 1924, 9 *ll.*, "The word made flesh, indeed, Sophrosynê," 1 *l.* (calligraphic manuscripts).

WALLACE, ALFRED RUSSEL, 1823–1913. Als (5) 1871–91 and n.d. incuding 4 to W. A. Knight.

WALLACE, EDWIN, 1848–1884. Als 27 March 1884 to W. A. Knight.

WALLACE, EGLANTINE (MAXWELL), Lady, d. 1803. Als n.d. to Sir Peter Burrell.

WALLACE, ROBERT, 1831–1899. Als 24 March 1873 to W. A. Knight.

WALLACE, WILLIAM, 1844–1897. Als (7) 1881–92 to W. A. Knight.

WALLER, EDMUND, 1606–1687. Commonplace book containing philosophical notes (in Latin), 115 pp.; als ca. 1657 to William Cavendish.

WALMESLEY, GILBERT, 1680–1751. Als 3 November 1746 to David Garrick.

WALPOLE, GEORGE, 3rd Earl of Orford, 1730–1791. Als 12 October 1782 to G. B. Cipriani.

WALPOLE, HORACE, 4th Earl of Orford, 1717–1797. "A catalogue of The Right Honble. Sir Robert Walpole's collection of pictures. 1735," 36 pp.; *The Mysterious Mother*, 110 pp. (not autograph); *Reminiscences Written for the Amusement of Miss Mary and Miss Agnes Berry* (two drafts), 90 pp.; shorter prose pieces: "Life of René of Anjou King of Naples," 2 pp.; "Loose Thoughts [on Government]," 3 pp.; "Parody of Lord Chesterfield's Letters," 2 pp.; [Plan for encouraging Painting], 2 pp.; list of his own writings, 6 pp.; miscellaneous notes, on Chatterton, Lord Lyttelton, epic poetry, etc., 11 pp.; transcripts of verses of Dryden, Gray, Pope and Lord Bolingbroke, 4 pp.; marginalia in his copy of his *The Mysterious Mother* (1768) and in Edward Moore's *The World. By Adam Fitz-Adam* (1757). Als (210) 1735–96 including 173 to the Misses Berry (with 7 from the Misses Berry to him) and 11 to Benjamin Ibbott.

WALPOLE, SIR HUGH SEYMOUR, 1884–1941. "Sons and Lovers. A Preface," 11 pp.; als (3) 1922–30.

WALPOLE, SIR ROBERT, 1st Earl of Orford, 1676–1745. Als (3) 1723–7; ds (4) 1708–24.

WALPOLE, THOMAS, 1727–1803. Als 9 January 1773 to Sir Philip Francis.

WALSINGHAM, SIR FRANCIS, 1530?–1590. Ls 10 December 1586; ds (3) 1577/8–83.

WALSINGHAM, SIR THOMAS, 1568–1630. Ds 5 May 1575.

WALTON, IZAAK, 1593–1683. Presentation inscriptions in copies of his *The Life of Mr. Rich. Hooker* (1665), *The Lives of Dr. John Donne,...* (1675) and *The Universal Angler* (1676).

WARBURTON, BARTHOLOMEW ELIOT GEORGE, 1810–1852. Als n.d. to W. H. Brookfield.

WARBURTON, WILLIAM, 1698–1779. Als (7) 1739–68.

WARD, SIR ADOLPHUS WILLIAM, 1837–1924. Als (12) 1903 and n.d. to W. A. Knight.

WARD, MARY AUGUSTA (ARNOLD), 1851–1920. *Robert Elsmere*, final chapter, 45 pp.; als (10) 1888–1909 including 7 to W. A. Knight.

WARD EDWARD MATTHEW, 1816–1879. Als (2) 1852 and n.d.

WARD, EMILY MARIA (LA TOUCHE), d. 1868. Als (3) n.d. to John Ruskin.

WARD, JAMES, 1769–1859. Als 22 March 1824 to Michael Faraday.

WARD, JAMES, 1843–1925. Als (13) 1891–1904 to W. A. Knight.

WARD, THOMAS HUMPHRY, 1845–1926. Als (2) 1886, 1891.

WARD, WILFRID PHILIP, 1856–1916. Als (3) 1903–7 to W. A. Knight.

WARD, WILLIAM GEORGE, 1812–1882. Als (2) 1879–80 to W. A. Knight.

WARDE, BEATRICE LAMBERTON (BECKER), 1900–1969. Als 8 January 1969 to F. B. Adams.

WARDLE, SIR THOMAS, 1831–1909. Als 17 April 1878.

WARDROP, JAMES, 1905–1957. Calligraphic commonplace book, 6 *ll.*; als 28 July 1945 to Bridget Johnston.

WARNER, SIR GEORGE FREDERIC, 1845–1936. Als 17 January 1907 to C. F. Murray.

WARRE-CORNISH, FRANCIS, 1839–1916. Als (7) 1897–1900 to W. A. Knight.

WARREN, CHARLES TURNER, 1762–1823. Als (2) 1819 and n.d.

WARTON, JOSEPH, 1722–1800. Als (3) 1790–8 including 2 to Edmond Malone.

WARTON, THOMAS, 1728–1790. Als (5) 1785 including 4 to Benjamin Forster.

WARWICK, SIR PHILIP, 1609–1683. Als 11 April 1638 to Sir Robert Pye.

WATERTON, CHARLES, 1782–1865. Als 20 May 1835 to Neville Wood.

WATSON, SIR PATRICK HERON, 1832–1907. Als 23 January 1890 to W. A. Knight.

WATSON, RICHARD, 1737–1816. Als n.d.

WATSON, ROBERT, 1730?–1781. Als (2) 1776, 1777 to Sir William (Johnstone) Pulteney.

WATSON, ROBERT SPENCE, 1837–1911. Als (21) 1880–98 to W. A. Knight.

WATSON, SIR THOMAS, Bart., 1792–1882. Als 21 January 1867.

WATSON, SIR WILLIAM, 1858–1935. Als (9) 1896–1918 including 7 to W. A. Knight.

WATSON-TAYLOR, GEORGE, d. 1841. "The old Hag in a red Cloak," 4 pp.

WATT, JAMES, 1736–1819. Als (2) 1785, 1791.

WATTS, ALARIC ALEXANDER, 1797–1864. Als (2) 1828 and n.d.

WATTS, ANNA MARY (HOWITT), 1824–1884. "What a nightingale sings," 1 p.

WATTS, GEORGE FREDERICK, 1817–1904. Als (7) 1880–96 including 5 to Sir John Millais. With als (23) from Mrs. Watts 1894–1904 to W. A. Knight.

WATTS, ISAAC, 1674–1748. Translations from Horace and other ancient poets, 26 pp.; commonplace book containing literary notes and an abstract of Jeremy Collier's *Short View of the Immorality... of the English Stage*, 108 pp.; als (23) 1725–46 including 10 to Philip Doddridge, 4 to Bishop Edmund Gibson and 1 (8 February 1702) "To the Church of Christ in Mark Lane," setting forth his religious principles; with letters (7) 1700–48 addressed to or concerning Watts.

WATTS, THOMAS, 1811–1869. Als 3 May 1858 to S. L. Sotheby.

WATTS, WALTER HENRY, 1776–1842. Als 10 September 1811 to John Romney.

WATTS-DUNTON, WALTER THEODORE, 1832–1914. Als, ls (3) 1883–1909.

WAUGH, EVELYN ARTHUR ST. JOHN, 1903–1966. Als ca. 1930 to a publisher.

WAVELL, ARCHIBALD PERCIVAL WAVELL, 1st Earl, 1883–1950. Als 13 June 1935 to Sir Sydney Cockerell.

WEBB, SIR ASTON, 1849–1930. Als ca. 1918 to T. J. Cobden-Sanderson.

WEBB, BEATRICE: *see* PASSFIELD, BEATRICE POTTER WEBB.

WEBB, SIR JOHN, 1772–1852. Ads 28 August 1806.

WEBB, MARY GLADYS (MEREDITH), 1881–1927. Als 18 January 1925.

WEBB, PHILIP CARTERET, 1700–1770. Ds 11 October 1759.

WEBB, PHILIP GEORGE LANCELOT, 1856–1937. Als (2) 1886, 1902.

WEBB, SIDNEY JAMES: *see* PASSFIELD, SIDNEY JAMES WEBB.

WEBER, HENRY WILLIAM, 1783–1812. Notes in the manuscript of Scott's *The Lady of the Lake* (1804).

WEBSTER, BENJAMIN NOTTINGHAM, 1797–1882. Als 18 May 1869 to Arthur Collinge.

WEBSTER, JOHN, 1610–1682. Presentation inscription in his *The Displaying of supposed Witchcraft* (1677).

WEBSTER, MARGARET, 1905–1972. Als n.d. to Reginald Allen.

WEBSTER, THOMAS, 1800–1886. Als (2) 1845, 1859.

WEDDERBURN, ALEXANDER DUNDAS OGILVY, 1854–1931. Als, ls (3) 1902–23 including 2 to W. G. Collingwood.

WEDDERBURN, SIR WILLIAM, Bart., 1838–1918. Als 26 June 1917 to T. J. Cobden-Sanderson.

WEDGWOOD, JOSIAH, 1730–1795. Ls 3 December 1787 to Thomas Wedgwood. With an als of his son Josiah 19 April 1787 to William Leake.

WELLESLEY, HENRY, 1791–1866. Als (2) 1858 to S. L. Sotheby.

WELLINGTON, ARTHUR WELLESLEY, 1st Duke of, 1769–1852. Als (174) 1804–49 including 99 to Thomas Raikes, his agent in France, and 40 to Lord John Russell.

WELLS, HENRY TANWORTH, 1828–1903. Als (3) 1878–88 to Sir John Millais or Mary Millais.

WELLS, HERBERT GEORGE, 1866–1946. Als (6) 1900–1 including 4 to W. E. Henley.

WELLS, SIR THOMAS SPENCER, Bart., 1818–1897. Als 15 July 1885 to Sir John Millais.

WESLEY, JOHN, 1703–1791. Als (20) 1765–89, with als (14) of his brother Charles, other members of the family or persons associated with him.

WEST, BENJAMIN, 1738–1820. Als (10) 1806–18.

WEST, DAME REBECCA, 1892– , pseudonym. Als, tls (4) 1976 including 3 to Charles Ryskamp.

WESTALL, RICHARD, 1765–1836. Als (4) 1800–31.

WESTALL, WILLIAM, 1781–1850. Als 26 March 1811 to George Cooke.

WESTMACOTT, SIR RICHARD, 1775–1856. Als (2) n.d.

WESTMACOTT, RICHARD, 1799–1872. Als n.d.

WETHERELL, T. F. Als (4) 1870–1 to W. A. Knight.

WHATELY, THOMAS, d. 1772. Als n.d. to George Grenville.

WHEWELL, WILLIAM, 1794–1866. Als 20 July 1847.

WHIBLEY, CHARLES, 1859–1930. Als n.d. to W. E. Henley.

WHISTLER, REX, 1905–1944. Als 29 November 1933 to Mr. and Mrs. R. Cobden-Sanderson.

WHITBREAD, SAMUEL, 1764–1815. Als (4) 1800–14.

WHITE, GILBERT, 1720–1793. "The Naturalist's Journal" (transcript of British Library Add. MS. 31846–31851 made for W. H. Mullens in 1909), 6 vols.; als (10) 1773–80 and n.d. including 7 to his brother John White.

WHITE, GLEESON, 1851–1898. Als n.d. to W. A. Knight.

WHITE, HENRY, 1761–1836. Als (2) 1807, 1809 to Lucretia Sharp.

WHITE, HENRY, 1812–1880. Als 16 January 1868 to Harper & Bros.

WHITE, JAMES, 1803–1862. Als 17 January 1847 to W. H. Brookfield.

WHITE, JOHN, 1727–1780. Introduction to his "Fauna Calpensis" (incomplete), 24 pp., with four drawings of Gibraltar for the work; contemporary copies of an exchange of letters between White and Carolus Linnaeus, 1771–4, 34 pp.

WHITE, JOSEPH BLANCO, 1775–1841. Als 21 June 1826 to S. T. Coleridge.

WHITE, MAUDE VALÉRIE, 1855–1937. Als (3) 1887 and n.d. to Sir John Millais and Mary Millais.

WHITE, ROBERT, fl. 1617. *Cupids Banishment. A Maske Presented To Her Majesty By younge Gentlewomen of the Ladies Hall in Deptford at Greenwich the 4th of May 1617*, 44 pp. (contemporary copy on vellum, presented to Lucy, Countess of Bedford).

WHITE, TERENCE HANBURY, 1906–1964. Als 7 September 1945 to Sir Sydney Cockerell.

WHITE, WILLIAM, publisher, London. Als (6) 1850–2.

WHITE, WILLIAM HALE, 1831–1913. Als (7) 1869–1912 including 3 to W. A. Knight.

WHITEFIELD, GEORGE, 1714–1770. "General Account of the First Part of My Life Begun August 1739...," 129 pp.; als 12 February 1767 to Captain Scot.

WHITEHEAD, SIR CHARLES, 1834–1912. Als 28 September 1887 to Benjamin Webster.

WHITELOCK, ELIZABETH (KEMBLE), 1761–1836. Als (2) 1818 to Miss Smith in Dublin.

WHITELOCKE, BULSTRODE, 1605–1675. Als 17 June 1656, ls (3) 1656–9.

WHITGIFT, JOHN, 1530?–1604. Ds (6) 1587–1602.

WHITTINGHAM, CHARLES, 1767–1840. Ds 1827.

WHYTE-MELVILLE, GEORGE JOHN, 1821–1878. Als n.d. to Sir John Millais.

WIFFEN, JEREMIAH HOLMES, 1792–1836. Als n.d. to Charles Lewis, bookbinder.

WIGAN, ALFRED SYDNEY, 1814–1878. Als 13 July 1855.

WIGAN, HORACE, 1818?–1885. Als (2) 1846 and n.d. to Mr. Kinloch.

WIGAN, LEONORA (PINCOTT), 1805–1884. Als 24 November 1881 to George Grossmith.

WILBERFORCE, SAMUEL, 1805–1873. Als (2) 1843, 1846.

WILBERFORCE, WILLIAM, 1759–1833. Als, ls (6) 1809–19 and n.d.

WILDE, OSCAR, 1854–1900. "Latin unseen" (a school exercise), 14 pp.; *The Picture of Dorian Gray*, the original version in 13 chapters, 264 pp.; with the manuscript of Chap. IV [V] as printed on pp. 88–95 of the first edition of 1891, 10 *ll.*; als (15) 1881–1900 including 5 to W. E. Henley.

WILENSKI, REGINALD HOWARD, 1887–1975. Als 2 April 1933 To R. Cobden-Sanderson.

WILKES, JOHN, 1727–1797. Als (6) 1763–97; ds (5) 1770–5.

WILKIE, SIR DAVID, 1785–1841. Als (45) 1806–41 including 34 to Sir George and Lady Beaumont.

WILKINSON, GEORGE HOWARD, 1833–1907. Als (9) 1889–1900 including 8 to W. A. Knight.

WILKINSON, TATE, 1739–1803. Als n.d.

WILKS, ROBERT, 1665–1732. Ds (2) 20 March 1713/4 and n.d.

WILL, PETER, fl. 1795–1816. Als (2) 1806, 1808 to Cadell & Davies.

WILLIAMS, CHARLES, 1886–1945. "The Other Side of the Way," 2 pp.

WILLIAMS, ERNEST EDWIN, 1866–1935. Als 22 January 1903 to W. E. Henley.

WILLIAMS, HELEN MARIA, 1762–1827. Als 1 June 1824.

WILLIAMS, IOLO ANEURIN, 1890–1962. "When we are old, are old," 1 p.

WILLIAMS, JOHN, 1636?–1709. Als 19 April 1696 to John Evelyn.

WILLIS, BROWNE, 1682–1760. Als (2) 1723 and n.d.

WILLIS, FRANCIS, 1718–1807. Als 4 November 1791 to Frances Burney.

WILLS, WILLIAM HENRY, 1810–1880. Ds 1 January 1862.

WILSON, CHARLES HEATH, 1809–1882. Als 23 August 1880 to J. E. Millais.

WILSON, DANIEL, 1778–1858. Als ca. 10 May 1827 to Miss Nichols.

WILSON, HARRIETTE, 1786–1846. Als (2) 1824 and n.d.

WILSON, JAMES MAURICE, 1836–1931. Als (3) 1885–90 to W. A. Knight.

WILSON, JOHN, 1774–1855. Ads 25 July 1848.

WILSON, JOHN, 1785–1854. Als (3) 1816, 1842 and n.d.

WILSON, SIR ROBERT THOMAS, 1777–1849. Als 27 April 1818 to Dr. Walker.

WILTON, JOSEPH, 1722–1803. Als (2) 1774, 1784.

WINDHAM, WILLIAM, 1717–1761. Als 22 December 1745.

WINDHAM, WILLIAM, 1750–1810. Als (8) 1775–1807 and n.d. including 3 to Sir James Murray-Pulteney.

WINGFIELD, LEWIS STRANGE, 1842–1891. Als 15 April 1878 to George Grossmith.

WINNINGTON-INGRAM, ARTHUR FOLEY, 1858–1946. Sermon 2 October 1907, 25 pp.

WINSTON, JAMES, 1773–1843. Als 14 December 1832 to W. E. Benke.

"WINTER, JOHN STRANGE": *see* STANNARD.

WISE, THOMAS JAMES, 1859–1937. Als (10) 1893–1929, of which 2 are to J. D. Campbell, 7 to S. C. Chew and 1 to J. P. Morgan.

WISEMAN, NICHOLAS PATRICK STEPHEN, Cardinal, 1802–1865. Als 8 October 1858.

WISHART, WILLIAM, 1660–1729. Als 21 May 1717 to the Duke of Roxburghe.

WITHER, GEORGE, 1588–1667. *Justiciarius justificatus*, 1 p. (contemporary copy).

WITHERINGTON, WILLIAM FREDERICK, 1785–1865. Als 6 May 1852 to Mr. & Mrs. Elhanan Bicknell.

WIVELL, ABRAHAM, 1786–1849. Als n.d.

WODEHOUSE, SIR PELHAM GRENVILLE, 1881–1975. Tls 27 May 1959 to Mrs. di Benedetto.

WOFFINGTON, MARGARET ("PEG"), 1714?–1760. Als 18 December 1742 to Thomas Robinson.

WOLCOT, JOHN ("PETER PINDAR"), 1738–1819. "I who could by a single frown," 1 p.; als (3) 1790, 1800 and n.d.

WOLLASTON, ALEXANDER FREDERICK RICHMOND, 1875–1930. Als 19 March 1926 to S. C. Cockerell.

WOLSELEY, GARNET JOSEPH WOLSELEY, 1st Viscount, 1833–1913. Als (6) 1883–90 and n.d. to Sir John Millais and Lady Millais.

WOLSEY, THOMAS, Cardinal, 1475?–1530. Ls 3 June 1516 to Pope Leo X; ds (2) 6 July 1517 and n.d.

WOOD, ANTHONY À, 1632–1695. Als 22 July 1687 to Dr. William Lloyd.

WOODFALL, WILLIAM, 1746–1803. Als 29 August 1785.

WOODHOUSE, RICHARD, JR., 1788–1834. "To Apollo. Written after reading Keats's 'Sleep and poetry,'" 1 p.; lines from Shakespeare, Spenser, Keats and Home, 1 p.; als (14) 1818–20 and n.d. including 11 to John Taylor and 1 to John Keats; ads (9) 1818–23; copies of poems written by John Keats (30).

WOODHOUSELEE, ALEXANDER FRASER TYTLER, Lord, 1747–1813. Als 17 January 1784 to Thomas Cadell.

WOODS, HENRY GEORGE, 1842–1915. Als 8 January 1913 to W. H. Mullens.

WOOLF, VIRGINIA (STEPHEN), 1882–1941. *A Letter to a Young Poet*, 52 pp.; als, tls (3) 1931 and n.d. to E. McKnight Kauffer.

WOOLNER, THOMAS, 1825–1892. Als (4) 1882–9 and n.d.

WOOLTON, JOHN, 1535?–1594. Ds 9 October 1591.

WORDSWORTH, CHARLES, 1806–1892. Speech given at a tree planting in memory of William Wordsworth, 4 pp.; als (33) 1878–92 to W. A. Knight.

WORDSWORTH, CHRISTOPHER, 1807–1885. Als (6) 1850–84 including 3 to Sir George Beaumont, 9th Bart., and 2 to W. A. Knight.

WORDSWORTH, DOROTHY, 1771–1855. "Journal of a Mountainous Ramble, 7–13 November 1805," 16 pp. *See also:* WORDSWORTH, WILLIAM, 1770–1850.

WORDSWORTH, DAME ELIZABETH, 1840–1932. Als 6 April 1904 to W. A. Knight.

WORDSWORTH, GORDON GRAHAM. Als (8) 1885–95 and n.d. including 7 to W. A. Knight.

WORDSWORTH, WILLIAM, 1770–1850. "Description of a Beggar" ["The Old Cumberland Beggar"] ("He travels on a solitary man"), 1 p.; "Elegiac Stanzas suggested by a Picture of Peele Castle"—the last four lines, 1 p.; sonnets:

"Druidical Excommunication" [Ecclesiastical Sonnet IV] (early draft beginning "Yes! whether Earth receives"), 1 p.; "Long Meg and her Daughters" (early draft), 2 pp.; unidentified poems (3) beginning: "Gone—or a theme might else be found," 1 p., "Like the shy blackbird when his destined mate," 1 p., "Yet once again do I behold the forms," 1 p. Poems in the hand of his sister Dorothy Wordsworth: Ecclesiastical Sonnets (4) Nos. XX, XXIII–XXV, 4 pp., "Composed when a probability existed of our being obliged to quit Rydal Mount," 10 pp., "Incident at Bruges," 2 pp., "A Jewish Family," 2 pp., "The Poet and the caged Turtledove," 2 pp.; sonnets: "On the Sight of a Manse in the South of Scotland," "Lowther," 2 pp.; "There is an Eminence," 1 p. Contemporary copies of poems: "On a Flower Garden at Coleorton," 3 pp., "On Seeing a Needle case In the form of a Harp the work of Edith May Southey," 3 pp., "The Pass at Kirkstone," 3 pp.; manuscript book of contemporary poems, including some by Wordsworth, compiled for Sir George and Lady Beaumont. Als (65) 1804–49 and n.d. (many written with Dorothy Wordsworth) including 50 to Sir George and Lady Beaumont and to his cousin and successor Sir George Beaumont, 8th Bart., some of which contain poems, e.g., "George and Sarah Greene," "Pastor and Friend," "Star-Gazers," "To the Lady Fleming," "Upon the Sight of a Beautiful Picture," verses about the Beaumonts, Coleorton Hall, their country home in Leicestershire, and translations (2) of sonnets by Michelangelo.

WORDSWORTH, WILLIAM, 1810–1883. Als 26 November 1878 to W. A. Knight.

WORDSWORTH, WILLIAM, 1835–1917. Als (6) 1899–1901 to W. A. Knight.

WORSLEY, THOMAS, 1710–1778. Als 27 December 1768 to Sir William Hamilton.

WOTTON, SIR HENRY, 1568–1639. Als 5 June 1604; ads 1605.

WOTTON, WILLIAM, 1666–1727. Ads n.d.; ds 15 January 1682/3.

WRAXALL, SIR NATHANIEL WILLIAM, 1751–1831. Als (3) 1785–95.

WREN, SIR CHRISTOPHER, 1632–1723. Als (2) 1692, 1707; ads 9 October 1674; ds 3 August 1694.

WREY, SIR BOURCHIER, 1714–1784. Als 21 June 1763.

WRIGHT, JOSEPH, 1734–1797. "A List of the principal of Mr. Wrights Historical Pictures & Landscapes," 4 pp. (not autograph).

WRIGHT, RICHARD, 1730–1814. Als 4 May 1801.

WRIGHT, WILLIAM ALDIS, 1831–1914. Als (6) 1883 to George Crabbe.

WROUGHTON, RICHARD, 1748–1822. Als 13 January 1799 to James Aickin.

WYATT, JAMES, 1746–1813. Als 2 November 1808 to Charles James.

WYATT, SIR MATTHEW DIGBY, 1820–1877. Als (3) 1859–65 including 2 to S. L. Sotheby.

WYATVILLE, SIR JEFFRY, 1766–1840. Als 16 April 1804 to Charles James.

WYCHERLEY, WILLIAM, 1640?–1716. Presentation inscription in his *Miscellany Poems* (1704).

WYLLIE, WILLIAM LIONEL, 1851–1931. Als n.d. to J. M. Swan.

WYNDHAM, SIR CHARLES, 1837–1919. Als (2) 1882 and n.d.

WYON, BENJAMIN, 1802–1858. Ls December 1830 to M. S. Jones.

WYON, LEONARD CHARLES, 1826–1891. Als (6) 1889–90 to W. A. Knight.

WYON, WILLIAM, 1795–1851. Als 19 April 1848 to P. Melvill.

YATES, EDMUND HODGSON, 1831–1894. Als (6) 1856–86.

YATES, FREDERICK HENRY, 1797–1842. Als (2) n.d.

YATES, MARY ANN (GRAHAM), 1728–1787. Als n.d.

YEATMAN-BIGGS, HUYSHE WOLCOTT, 1845–1922. Als, ls (7) 1905–8 to W. A. Knight.

YEATS, WILLIAM BUTLER, 1865–1939. "Aodh to Dectora," 3 pp.; als, ls (3) 1902–22. "Where dips the rocky highland," calligraphic manuscript of the poem by Edward Johnston, 1899, 4 pp.

YONGE, CHARLOTTE MARY, 1823–1901. Als (2) 1874 and n.d.

YOUNG, ARTHUR, 1741–1820. Als, ls (4) 1780–1808.

YOUNG, CHARLES MAYNE, 1777–1856. Als (2) 1844, 1850.

YOUNG, EDWARD, 1683–1765. *Busiris*, 96 pp. (not autograph); als 10 April 1750 to Samuel Richardson.

YOUNG, JOHN, 1835–1902. Als (3) n.d. to W. A. Knight.

YULE, SIR HENRY, 1820–1889. Als (2) 1872, 1875 to Sir Henry and Lady Rawlinson.

ZANGWILL, ISRAEL, 1864–1926. Als (6) 1897–1900 including 5 to Laurens Maynard.

ZOUCHE, ROBERT CURZON, Baron, 1810–1873. Dialogue between Robert Curzon and the Earl of Arundel on Roman Catholicism, 1847, 33 *ll.*; als n.d. to Lady Rawlinson.